LOVE and CHRISTIAN ETHICS

Selected Titles from the Moral Traditions Series

David Cloutier, Kristin Heyer, Andrea Vicini, SJ, Series Editors
James F. Keenan, SJ, Founding Editor

LOVE and CHRISTIAN ETHICS

TRADITION, THEORY, and SOCIETY

Edited by Frederick V. Simmons
with Brian C. Sorrells

GEORGETOWN UNIVERSITY PRESS
Washington, DC

Library of Congress Cataloging-in-Publication Data

Names: Simmons, Frederick V., editor | Sorrells, Brian, editor
Title: Love and Christian ethics: tradition, theory, and society / edited by Frederick V. Simmons with Brian Sorrells.
Description: Georgetown University Press: Washington, DC, 2016. | Includes bibliographical references and index.
Identifiers: LCCN 2016004715 (print) | LCCN 2016006129 (ebook) | ISBN 9781626163669 (hc: alk. paper) | ISBN 9781626163676 (pb: alk. paper) | ISBN 9781626163683 (eb)
Subjects: LCSH: Love--Religious aspects--Christianity. | Christian ethics.
Classification: LCC BV4639 .L663 2016 (print) | LCC BV4639 (ebook) | DDC 241/.4—dc23
LC record available at http://lccn.loc.gov/2016004715

♾ This book is printed on acid-free paper meeting the requirements of the American National Standard for Permanence in Paper for Printed Library Materials.

17 16   9 8 7 6 5 4 3 2   First printing
Printed in the United States of America

Cover design by Martyn Schmoll. Cover image by iStockphoto.

Contents

Acknowledgments

I AM HONORED AND DELIGHTED to be able to thank the following people for their help in bringing this volume to fruition. An edited book obviously depends on the work of its contributors, several of whom offered much to the project beyond their own essays. I'm particularly indebted to Margaret Farley and John Hare for sage counsel as the book took shape and appreciative of the initial contributors' patience and encouragement while the book came to completion. Several other colleagues have also offered support and advocacy for me and this venture, and I'm profoundly grateful to them: Neil Arner, Jennifer Herdt, Willis Jenkins, David Kelsey, Gerald McKenny, John Pittard, Carolyn Sharp, Roberto Sirvent, Chloë Starr, Kathryn Tanner, Mary Evelyn Tucker, and Andrea Vicini. Within this latter group, David Bartlett deserves special mention since, as in multiple other contexts, here too I repeatedly relied on his wisdom and sense of decency at pivotal junctures.

A Morse Fellowship allowed me to advance this project significantly, and I thank Yale University and then–Yale Divinity School dean Harold Attridge for this research leave. The Houston Witherspoon Fellowship in Theology and the Natural Sciences enabled me to finish the book while I was a resident member of the Center of Theological Inquiry, and I thank its director, William Storrar, for a propitious scholarly environment and its Scheide Senior Fellow, Robin Lovin, for his gracious and insightful intellectual leadership. As director of Georgetown University Press and my editor, Richard Brown provided judicious guidance that strengthened the book, and his genial adaptability facilitated our thoroughly enjoyable collaboration.

I particularly thank Brian Sorrells for his manifold contributions to this project. From deliberations about the scope and structure of the collection to detailed discussions concerning the contours of the chapters to commission and the editorial suggestions that might best hone them, Brian shared his vast knowledge of Christian ethics, expertise in the Christian moral theology of love, intellectual creativity, and overall discernment. This was a cooperative endeavor, and I'm grateful for Brian's partnership in it.

Love and Christian Ethics was conceived to honor Gene Outka by stimulating and bringing together renewed scholarly reflection of the highest caliber on this topic to which he has contributed so much. Indeed, one facet of this contribution is that Gene has been a teacher, colleague, or friend of most of this volume's authors. He has been all of these to me, and thus it is a fitting pleasure to join with all of the others involved in this book in dedicating it to him.

Introduction

A Conjunctive Approach to Christian Love

FREDERICK V. SIMMONS

LOVE IS OFTEN EXTOLLED as the source, substance, standard, and goal of Christian ethics. Yet a perception that love has seldom been its subject is also prevalent. Anders Nygren began *Agape and Eros* by juxtaposing love's centrality and neglect within contemporary Christian ethics, and love's prominence in Christian moral and theological reflection since he made these claims in 1930 is one indication of his study's significance.[1] It is hardly the volume's only opposition. Indeed, although Nygren categorized his inquiry into love as "motif-research" and thus disclaimed any evaluative intent, his assurance that "Agape and Eros are contrasted with one another here, not as right and wrong, nor as higher and lower, but as Christian and non-Christian" seemed to many a normative thesis as much as a methodological statement.[2] Moreover, it compounded the controversy inherent to his summary interpretation of agape as "sacrificial giving" and eros as "the will to get and possess" since this categorical disjunction led him to reject these loves' combination in caritas, disregard their complement in philia, and consequently criticize much of the Christian tradition from the second century to the Reformation.[3]

Unsurprisingly, Nygren's provocative positions were widely disputed. John Burnaby and Martin D'Arcy were among the initial and most influential dissenters. Burnaby denounced Nygren's acknowledged inability to accommodate genuinely human love for God or neighbor as a refutation of his schema and considered Nygren's exclusion of philia "a fatal defect in his whole construction."[4] D'Arcy decried Nygren's antithetical construal of both grace and nature and agape and eros as effectively eliminating love, human response to God, and hence human participation in friendship with God.[5]

Not all reaction to Nygren was critical, however, nor was all scholarly Christian consideration of love around the middle of the twentieth century a reply to Nygren. In 1932 Emil Brunner's *The Divine Imperative* presented a relatively comprehensive theological ethic that featured an account of love with notable affinities to Nygren's views apparently independent of Nygren.[6] Similarly, in 1937 Fritz Tillmann's *The Master Calls* began a shift in contemporary Catholic moral theology toward conceiving love of God, self, and neighbors as the heart of the Christian moral life that was powerfully developed by Gérard Gilleman, Bernard Häring, and Robert Johann in the following two decades.[7] Among prominent Protestant ethicists at midcentury, Reinhold Niebuhr and Paul Ramsey offered extensive analyses of Christian love that enjoyed wide audiences.[8] Love was likewise a central topic in Christian theology of the period, with Howard Thurman, Paul Tillich, Karl Barth, C. S. Lewis, Hans Urs von Balthasar, and Karl Rahner according it extended attention.[9] In fact, Lewis and Denis de Rougemont published prodigious, synthetic interpretations of enduring Western understandings of love a generation earlier as literary and cultural critics.[10]

Yet although many have disagreed with Nygren's starkly dichotomous characterization of agape and eros and insistence that agape is the sole genuine Christian love, his contention that love had been largely overlooked by several prior generations of Christian writers has proved less controversial. Of course, given love's prominence in Christian scripture and tradition, Christian scholars in the nineteenth and early twentieth centuries did not wholly disregard it. For example, Søren Kierkegaard published *Works of Love* in his own name in 1847 and closely anticipated several of Nygren's claims about the nature of Christian love.[11] Likewise, while advancing a different taxonomy of love, Pierre Rousselot's study of medieval Christian conceptions of love presaged Nygren's attempt to interpret a vast sweep of Christian history with a love typology.[12] Indeed, just a year before the first volume of Nygren's tome appeared, Heinrich Scholz issued an account of Christian love animated by an invidious contrast with eros.[13] Nevertheless, love was scarcely the focus of most Christian theological and ethical attention in the era preceding Nygren.

Since the seventeenth century, Roman Catholic moral theology had been devoted to the moral manuals. Designed to help priests administer the sacrament of penance by specifying the severity of sins, the manuals sought to establish minimum moral standards and primarily cast the ethical life as a matter of avoiding evil rather than pursuing good. Commands and law generally superseded virtue, and love was largely eclipsed in these texts.[14] Different dynamics had a similar effect among American Protestants of the period. Initially concentrating on social problems, these Protestants frequently regarded love fundamental to Christians' proper response and began a movement that would later coalesce as the field of Christian ethics. Even so, in these early years, Christian ethicists often took the meaning of love for granted as they drew on the then-nascent social sciences to facilitate their promotion of social justice and foreground the importance of God's kingdom to Jesus's gospel.[15]

Thus, many Christians' sustained, explicit attention to love in the middle third of the twentieth century constituted a considerable shift from the preceding era. Nor has it abated. For example, in the years immediately following the period I have already sketched, Martin Luther King Jr., Joseph Fletcher, Jules Toner, Daniel Day Williams, Gustavo Gutierrez, Gene Outka, Josef Pieper, Judith Plaskow, Beverly Harrison, and Barbara Andolsen all made major contributions to the study of Christian love's ethical significance.[16] Indeed, Outka's *Agape* proved a landmark interpretation of Christian neighbor love that began his several decades of influential scholarship on the topic.[17] Like Nygren in avowedly seeking to specify previous Christian understandings of love rather than commend his own, yet commonly taken to offer a constructive account of Christian love, Outka's *Agape* stimulated renewed Christian reflection on love much as Nygren's treatise had two generations earlier.[18] Characterizing proper Christian love as equal regard "for every person qua human existent" that both is "committed to the other's well-being independently and unalterably" and "view[s] the other as irreducibly valuable," Outka's sophisticated examination of Christian love's moral meanings has facilitated further investigation of its ethical import from a variety of vantages and for an array of subjects, as the work of this volume's authors attests.[19]

Accordingly, it is notable that Garth Hallett, Edward Vacek, and Timothy Jackson each begin erudite contemporary monographs on love and Christian ethics by echoing Nygren's contention that Christian moral theologians and ethicists have overlooked love.[20] The persistence of this perception undoubtedly has many causes, and the differences in these scholars' claims indicate some of them. For example, Hallett calls his endeavor to delineate and assess various possible preference rules that might convey Christian love's ethical significance "A Neglected Question" and avers, "Strange as this assertion may sound after nearly two millennia of Christian emphasis on agape, the Christian norm of neighbor-love offers relatively virgin territory for inquiry."[21] Similarly, Vacek writes, "Any hesitation to explore the role of love in ethics would seem peculiar. It is, nevertheless, typical. Love has *not* been central in most Christian ethics and dogmatic theology [italics original]."[22] Vacek adduces a few explanations for this peculiarity—a prior emphasis on reason within Catholic theology coupled with a contemporary concentration on justice and hope; imprecision, confusion, and incoherence besetting many discussions of love—and the factors he cites are difficult to dispute. Indeed, Hallett's review of Christians' diverse and conflicting depictions of the proper relationship between others' interests and one's own thoroughly confirms Vacek's sense of cacophony. For his part, Hallett cites several other potential explanations for love's supposed neglect, among them the suspicion that thought impedes love, analysis of love courts legalism, love is too indeterminate to guide action, and Christians' common concentration on persons and attitudes instead of actions and norms.[23] Jackson, in turn, titles the first section of his volume "The Eclipse of Christian Charity" and attributes love's recent obscuring within Christian ethics primarily to "ill-considered defenses of three related virtues: prudence, freedom, and justice."[24]

Surely other concerns have been involved as well.[25] Yet rather than regard all these additional interests as leading to love's neglect, marginalization, or eclipse within contemporary Christian ethics, it may be fruitful to construe at least some of these alternative pursuits as aspects of a more comprehensive approach now crucial to advancing insight into Christian love's moral meanings. Commenting on Nygren's efforts to understand Christian love by distilling one form of love and excluding others, Burnaby tartly observed eighty years ago, "Against the 'Both-and' of the Catholic, Protestantism here as everywhere sets with obtuse insistence its 'Either-Or.'"[26] Given all that has transpired since in the field of Christian ethics, conjunctive ventures that explore the moral significance of love not simply by including its multiple forms, as Burnaby and others after him have so ably done, but by directly addressing other values, virtues, authorities, and traditions are opportune. Hoping to promote and harness such possibilities, *Love and Christian Ethics* offers a set of commissioned, complementary essays on many of the main historical figures, concepts, and cultural consequences integral to the Christian ethical exploration of love, and thus each of its chapters engages and develops principal aspects of Christian love's moral meanings in connection with another major topic.

Contents and Contributors

Part I: Tradition

The volume's inquiry is organized into three parts: influential sources and exponents of Western Christian thought about the ethical significance of love, perennial theoretical questions accompanying that consideration, and the implications of Christian love for salient social realities. The Bible is obviously fundamental to Christian tradition, and so the first part of the collection begins with Thomas Ogletree's examination of the different yet related interpretations of the love commands provided by the book of Deuteronomy and Jesus's Sermon on the Mount as recorded in the Gospel of Matthew. Ogletree argues that Deuteronomy specifies the obligations inherent to the duty to love God, self, and neighbors, first through the Decalogue and then with an extensive compilation of more specific laws and edicts, in order to apply the covenantal traditions rooted in such love to the pervasive social changes incurred by Israel's acceptance of a monarchical aristocratic class and status system. Jesus's Sermon on the Mount likewise expounds on the meaning of the duty to love God, self, and neighbors by elaborating on the Decalogue, among other resources. However, according to Ogletree, Jesus addresses an inclusive group of followers, fitting them for collaboration in a grassroots coalition that furthers God's final redemptive transformation, and therefore, Jesus concentrates on the law's potential to facilitate comprehensive human flourishing. Ogletree contends that these canonical examples remain relevant to contemporary interpretations of the love commands and thereby indicate that differences in social context decisively shape the ethical significance of these teachings.

Ancient Greek philosophy is of course another corpus with a formative influence on Christian tradition, and thus, in the second chapter of part 1, Terence Irwin compares Christian and ancient Greek understandings of love. Irwin concentrates on conflicting Christian evaluations of these Greek understandings, identifying a "moderate" tradition, which affirms basic continuities between Christian and Greek interpretations of love, and a "radical" tradition, which asserts fundamental discrepancies between them. Irwin then analyzes and attempts to adjudicate some of the philosophical disagreements that separate these traditions. Rather than attribute the differences between these Christian views of love exclusively to such philosophical disagreements, Irwin maintains that philosophical reflection can narrow and clarify the theological controversies underlying them. Specifically, he considers these traditions' opposing conceptions of love's relation to value, connection to one's own happiness, and inclusivity. After accounting for the potential appeal of the radical tradition, Irwin sides with the moderates and argues that whatever distinctive convictions Christians may have about love for God, love for other people, or love's concrete exigencies, these convictions do not substantially diverge from the Greek belief that love is oriented to value, oriented to self, and selective.

The remaining four chapters in this first part of the volume examine influential Christian authors' assessments of love's ethical significance. Oliver O'Donovan begins this sequence by explicating Augustine's interpretation of the connections between the biblical love commandments that Augustine embeds in his *Confessions*. O'Donovan maintains that Augustine deliberately planned the structure of Book 10 of *Confessions* to make a foundational point about the relationships among self-love, love for God, and neighbor love, and thus that the book displays a cardinal truth about Augustine's ethics of love as a whole. According to O'Donovan, Augustine depicts our understanding of true Christian love as developing in two stages. He suggests that Augustine uses the first section of Book 10 to elaborate the first stage, in which we learn that proper self-love takes the form of love for God. Having established this meaning of self-love, O'Donovan argues that Augustine then uses the second section of the book to present the second stage in our understanding of love, wherein self-love—construed as love for God—can now serve as a trustworthy model for neighbor love.

Jean Porter's essay on Thomas Aquinas both continues this sequence of chapters devoted to pivotal Christian authors and returns to Irwin's exploration of Christian love's proper relationship to one's own happiness. Porter explicates Aquinas's central and subsequently controversial claim that rational agents necessarily desire and pursue their own happiness and joins Irwin in advocating that position. However, rather than concentrate on the Bible and the

Greeks with Irwin, Porter primarily looks ahead to Kant. She argues that Aquinas's position is closer to a prevalent modern view linked to Kant and some magisterial reformers than is often recognized. Yet Porter also insists that Aquinas's position is ultimately preferable to this Kantian view because Aquinas provides a better explanation of the coherent functioning of practical reason. In particular, Aquinas's metaphysics of value posits a unity of the good whereby the perfection and therefore happiness of individual rational agents cannot conflict with more general goods. This is not simply convenient stipulation, for Aquinas understands an agent's perfection in terms of activities that place the agent in proper relation to these greater goods. Porter acknowledges that such metaphysics may seem susceptible to communitarian or authoritarian abuse. Nevertheless, because Aquinas also holds that these higher goods involve justice, she concludes that his overall position mitigates that danger.

John Hare follows Irwin and Porter in investigating the nature of the connection between genuine Christian love and one's own happiness. Hare also joins Porter in identifying and exploring affinities and divergences between Aquinas and Kant on these topics. However, unlike both Irwin and Porter, Hare endorses the Kantian claim that Christian love should not be primarily oriented to one's own happiness. Hare begins by analyzing Kant's conception of the relation of emotion and reason in practical love to explain what Kant means by doing our duty gladly. Hare suggests a series of five stages through which Kant envisions moral deliberation to pass that clarifies how emotion facilitates and detracts from this process. Hare then compares his interpretation of Kant's view of practical love with the position that Porter ascribes to Aquinas in her essay for this volume. Hare agrees with Porter that there are several fundamental commonalities between Thomist and Kantian ethics. For example, Hare observes that both Aquinas and Kant emphasize reason's place within practical love, and both also accord emotion an important role; both regard God essential to the moral life, and both accentuate duties in addition to virtues. Further, Hare claims that differences in these thinkers' vocabularies and use of key terms have frequently been mistaken for substantive disagreements. Even so, Hare contends that major discrepancies remain. Hare argues that Kant's insistence that neither the object nor end of practical love may have any indispensable self-reference is the most important of these divergences, and he defends the superiority of Kant's view.

In the final chapter of part 1, M. Jamie Ferreira extends the volume's comparative analysis of principal figures in the Christian tradition by examining Kant's and Kierkegaard's mature ethical understandings of the duty to love others. She compares and contrasts their interpretations of the biblical commandment to love the neighbor, highlighting the scope, stringency, and content they attribute to that obligation. Ferreira holds that Kant and Kierkegaard both interpret the obligation to love the neighbor as universal in scope and unconditional in stringency, but that only Kant at times appeals to the reciprocity that would follow from actualization of this scope and stringency to explain the obligation. Ferreira next explores Kant's and Kierkegaard's conception of the relation of duty to inclination and delineates the specific manner in which they believe that duty should be met. Ferreira argues that Kant first qualitatively distinguishes duties of love and duties of respect and then normatively unites them in a single fulfillment of both duties. She also maintains that this approximates Kierkegaard's account of the original normative unity of love and respect in love of neighbor. Ferreira concludes that Kant's comparatively complex conception illuminates Kierkegaard's exposition by distinguishing not simply duties of love from duties of respect but beneficence from sympathetic participation as well.

Part II: Theory

The second part of the volume addresses theoretical questions that consistently attend Christian interpretations of love's ethical significance. In its lead essay, Edward Vacek probes two of the most central of these queries, namely, whether Christians ought to love God, and if so, what such love would mean. Although the answer to at least the first of these questions may seem obvious, Vacek observes that contemporary Christian ethicists frequently disregard Jesus's first great commandment to love God with all of one's heart, soul, mind, and strength; substitute faith in or obedience to God for such love; or effectively reduce it to the second great commandment to love one's neighbor as oneself. Vacek counters that such treatments of love for God are profoundly mistaken, explains how several underdeveloped accounts of love skew interpretations of love for God, and shows how dominant motifs in Christian doctrines of God complicate Christians' formulation of a theology of love for God. Vacek then adumbrates such a theology by depicting love for God as affective participation in God and explicating three of its forms—eros, in which we love God for our own sake; agape, in which we express our love for God to God, for God's sake; and philia, in which we love and cooperate with God for the sake of the relationship we share with God.

In the second essay of part 2, John Reeder concentrates on Jesus's second great commandment to love the neighbor as oneself. Specifically, Reeder investigates attempts by Diana Cates, Edith Wyschogrod, and Søren Kierkegaard to elucidate and warrant compassion in terms of three different models of an identification of interests. According to Reeder, Cates argues that the interests of the other become included in one's self-love in the experience of friendship so that compassion stems from an expansion of self-love. Wyschogrod maintains that the nonconceptual demand of the Other enjoins substitution of the Other's interests for all of one's own and thus that compassion is an expression of other-regard wholly distinct from self-love. Kierkegaard proffers a middle view in which equal status before God norms neighbor love and proper self-love, such that compassion is a manifestation of equal love for all human beings. Having established these options, Reeder contends that empathy is necessary but insufficient for compassion because some identification of interests is also requisite to the latter. He then combines Cates's and Kierkegaard's understandings of how we are to identify interests in order to construct an account of morally appropriate compassion. Reeder suggests that the dissonance between interpretations of the commandment to love the neighbor as the self that emphasize self-sacrifice and those that concentrate on the self's own good may be attributed to prioritization of different dimensions of an understanding of love that includes both the self-giving of a parent or friend and that love's equal embrace of multiple siblings or friends. He concludes that this tension should be resolved by allowing God's equal love to set the standard for neighbor love as a moral obligation and acclaiming God's sacrificial love as a supererogatory ideal that may be particularly apposite in certain special relationships.

Margaret Farley continues Reeder's exploration of concepts integral to neighbor love by supplementing his consideration of compassion with her reflections on forgiveness. Appreciative of many religious traditions' long-standing emphasis on forgiveness, Farley notes that growing awareness of events and circumstances that test the limits of forgiveness and call for clarification of its nature have also prompted many contemporary, nonreligious thinkers to consider such questions. Farley reviews some of these tests, analyzes the experience of forgiveness, and identifies central connections among forgiveness, love, and other core Christian convictions. She conceives love as essential to the possibility, meaning, and dynamics of

Christian forgiveness, arguing both that Christian forgiveness requires love and that the duty to love at the heart of Christian discipleship involves a duty to forgive. Correlatively, Farley characterizes forgiveness as a form of love while also affirming a role for judgment and efforts to seek justice within forgiveness. Farley refers to such forgiveness of those whose injustice we must also resist as anticipatory forgiveness and acknowledges that it can constitute one of love's greatest challenges. Nevertheless, Farley holds that forgiveness can evoke a decentering of even aggrieved selves that makes an other-centered love possible as acceptance of God's reconciling love enables people to offer this love to one another.

Edmund Santurri extends the second part of the volume's examination of ever more demanding aspects of Christian neighbor love, moving from Reeder's concentration on compassion and Farley's investigation of forgiveness to a discussion of self-sacrifice. Santurri maintains that Christian neighbor love is essentially self-sacrificial, whatever other characteristics it may also necessarily have. According to Santurri, such love involves the lover's disposition to sacrifice the lover's own interests for the sake of the neighbor in morally, religiously, and spiritually suitable settings—where the criteria for such suitability are determined by this love itself. Further, Santurri holds that Christian love does not simply harbor a readiness for self-sacrifice in case it happens to be needed, as if this love might in principle have no occasion for self-sacrifice and yet remain itself. Santurri also denies that self-sacrifice is merely an extrinsic—however indispensable—means that Christian love must employ to realize its ends, even ends that are intrinsic to this love. Instead, Santurri insists that self-sacrifice is internal to Christian love, such that love that does not sacrifice itself for the sake of the neighbor is not Christian. Santurri concedes that many prevailing doctrines of Christian love flatly reject his position for multiple reasons. He identifies several of these criticisms and defends his view from three of the most trenchant, arguing that cruciform and kenotic norms of Christian love promulgated by Johannine and Pauline sources and buttressed by the New Testament as a whole affirm an indispensable link between this love and self-sacrifice.

In his essay Frederick Simmons considers Christian conceptions of the relationships between the interests of the lover and the beloved from another vantage, returning to the topic of eudaimonism broached by Irwin, Porter, and Hare in the first part of the volume. Addressing eudaimonism as a theory rather than primarily with reference to a particular figure, Simmons explores whether eudaimonism per se affords an adequate interpretation of Christian love. Given the diversity of meanings attributed to both eudaimonism and Christian love, Simmons observes that there is more than one answer to this question. Accordingly, he identifies common senses of each notion to assess their compatibility and indicate some of the reasons that eudaimonism has proved so controversial among Christians. Taking eudaimonism as the doctrine that the moral life aims at one's own eudaimonia and Christian love as potentially self-transcending affirmation of the beloved, he argues that Christian morality advances its adherents' eudaimonia more robustly if it does not appear wholly eudaimonist, may be basically eudaimonist even if not technically so, and can have a different relation to eudaimonism in different periods of salvation history. Specifically, because he treats blessedness—interpreted as joyful participation in a loving relationship with God and others with God—as an appropriate Christian conception of eudaimonia, he maintains that for Christians moral excellence only partially constitutes eudaimonia and thus does not necessarily conduce to it while God's salvation from sin remains incomplete. In light of these possibilities, Simmons concludes that even basically eudaimonist accounts of Christian love involve Christian faith and hope in addition to ethical analysis.

Further tempering the increasingly stringent depictions of proper Christian neighbor love advocated earlier in part 2, Stephen Pope broadens Simmons's contention that such love is often effectively eudaimonist by claiming that genuine Christian neighbor love flows from God's friendship love and thus invariably fulfills the lover. Drawing on a Thomistic conception of charity as grace-inspired friendship love, Pope argues that friendship love is the central Christian love. Pope then illustrates how a Thomistic theology of grace as restoring and fostering appropriate human love of God and neighbor can enable Christians to appreciate that charity, or agape, repairs and reorients rather than opposes other "kinds" of love, especially eros and philia. Combining these Thomistic premises, Pope asserts that charity is expressed in every virtue, including healed and rightly ordered eros and philia; is a choice to affirm the good of the friend for the sake of the friend rather than a feeling that may vacillate; realizes human communion with God and so is authentic self-love; and calls forth love for all people as fellow friends of God. Pope also holds that charity is not simply completed by but is in addition always already our participation in God's friendship with us, and hence that charity is finally living in joy as transformed by God's love. Pope therefore commends Aquinas's interpretation of friendship love as the wellspring, aim, and essence of Christian virtue and ethics generally, which begins with God's friendship love of us and culminates in our acceptance and extension of that love to others as likewise God's friends.

Timothy Jackson's chapter completes part 2 by rebutting a prominent contemporary challenge to the possibility of Christian love itself. Confronting the claim that evolutionary biology gainsays Christian agape because it excludes the emergence of beings open to self-sacrifice for the sake of strangers or even enemies, Jackson does not reject evolutionary biology but several sorts of reductive naturalism that their proponents frequently purport to adduce from it. In particular, Jackson avers that Stephen Jay Gould's interpretation of evolution is incompatible with Christian love but incorrect because it misconstrues the relationship between science and religion and neglects the import of evolutionary convergence. However, Jackson also dismisses attempts to reconcile evolution with Christian love that appeal to group selection or game theoretic explanations of cooperation's personal benefits because he contends that they wrongly reduce Christian love to enlightened self-interest. Instead, Jackson argues that Darwinian evolution and Christian love are compatible given a more adequate interpretation of each, and he identifies three elements that are integral to such an interpretation: appreciation for the role of self-conscious motives in the moral significance of human behavior, precluding a wholly mechanistic account of the world; recognition that natural selection is not the only process inducing evolution since, as even Gould acknowledges, it generates and preserves traits that confer no adaptive benefit; and realization that chance is not incompatible with progress or even purpose in the natural world. In fact, rather than simply dispel the challenge to Christian love that some seek to cull from biological evolution, Jackson concludes that Christian love constrains and channels such evolution.

Part III: Society

The third part of the volume concerns principal social dimensions of Christian love's moral meanings. The relationship between love and justice is a foundational subject of Christian social ethics, and M. Cathleen Kaveny addresses a largely neglected aspect of it by considering connections between theological ethics and the secular common law. In particular, Kaveny utilizes Gene Outka's analysis of Christian neighbor love to examine the well-known contracts case of *Watts v. Watts*, which attempted to divide the property of a separating couple who had lived together as man and wife without actually being married. She argues that Outka's work and the judicial opinion in *Watts* combine to offer insights on three questions relevant to both Christian ethics and the law: (1) When should preference be given to the unique attributes of persons, and when ought common human characteristics take precedence? (2) How should respect for general rules be balanced with sensitivity to special circumstances? (3) What sorts of responsibilities are neighbors unable to make one another fulfill? Kaveny emphasizes the common law tradition's development of general rules in deciding specific cases involving concrete individuals, and its remedial, pedagogical, and channeling functions, while she foregrounds Outka's exploration of both our relative obligations to near and distant neighbors and the differences between our obligations to others and ourselves. She concludes that legal studies and Christian ethical reflection on love may enrich one another in many respects, not least by together delineating the facets of neighbor love that the law ought to obligate and those it cannot.

Exploring the implications of Christian love for public health in the developing world, Lisa Cahill examines another aspect of the relationship between love and justice that merits further attention. She argues that twenty-first-century conditions of global poverty, including inequitable distribution of health care resources, summon Christian social ethics to show the difference that a personal and communal morality of love makes in the quest for more just global conditions of human existence amid cultural and religious pluralism. Cahill maintains that Christian love implies moral responsibility for social justice, and she marshals biblical and theological grounds for hope of ameliorating global inequalities in health care access and structural sin more broadly. In particular, Cahill contends that new interpretations of Augustine, as well as recent work on Luther by the "Finnish school," support the robust estimates of possibilities for personal sanctification and ecclesial and social regeneration often identified with Roman Catholicism and suggest a widening Christian conviction that the union of believers with Christ through the Spirit may enlarge and strengthen a Christian politics of social change. Cahill likewise commends growing Christian appreciation of the prospects for collaboration with other constructive groups facilitated by recent Christian emphasis on the goodness of creation, the inclusive significance of God's incarnation, the sacramental character of the world, and the importance of justice to many different cultures and religious traditions. She urges that fitting social expression of Christian love—both with respect to global health care and justice more generally—must foster the social and economic participation and agency of those it seeks to serve.

In addressing Christian sexual ethics, Mark Jordan hardly ponders a topic too often overlooked. On the contrary, Jordan concurs with many commentators in ruing Christians' frequent fixation on sex, alleging that it distorts the nature, importance, and specificity of appropriate Christian sexual ethics. Accordingly, Jordan departs from the preoccupations that have recently dominated much of this discourse and instead seeks to fashion a loving vocation for Christian sexual ethics in a contemporary milieu. He proceeds by considering what Christian ethics should study about sex; the knowledge of such sex that ethics should pursue; and what should distinguish a Christian sexual ethic. Jordan also explores how Christians ought to approach sex in the interim as Christian ethics discerns this vocation. Jordan answers each of these questions by suggesting that Christian ethics is presently called to compose genres for language suitable to a loving knowledge of sex that honors Jesus's refusal to prescribe a sexual code and to cultivate people able to speak it. Thus, Jordan recommends sexual moral teaching motivated by love that recognizes an array of fundamental interests, resists an exaggeration of sexual sins as the gravest affronts to God, and facilitates sex's fulfillment in the fuller love of the eschaton.

Emilie Townes joins Mark Jordan in forging a creative approach to a familiar topic in Christian ethics, examining the relationships between love and violence by emphasizing koinonia and through the prism of lament. She interprets koinonia as a communal manifestation of love that is implicit to justice, expressive of mutuality, and necessary for the realization of other forms of love. She perceives such koinonia in Toni Morrison's admonition that members of oppressed communities must love their "beat and beating heart" as they seek to resist pervasive violence.[27] Townes then appeals to the biblical practice of lament to cultivate koinonia and illustrates this possibility with a mournful dirge about the violent washing away of a culture in the wake of Hurricane Katrina. In particular, Townes advocates confession, which, as a constitutive element of lament, enables us to reckon with our complicity in the violence we would overcome and to extend koinonia to others without condescension. Insistent that love as koinonia links theological and social concerns—and thereby opposes the violence inherent in their separation—Townes concludes that a vital love ethic unites faith, hope, love, and justice; accepts the fullness of our humanity without denying its brokenness; and builds communities that help transform their members by facilitating these integrations.

While not a perennial focus of Christian ethical attention like justice, sex, or violence, moral concern for the environment has burgeoned among Christians and many others over the last several decades. Yet although love is now frequently exalted as fundamental to Christian ethics, the suitability of love as a central category in environmental ethics remains unclear. Holmes Rolston III addresses this subject by asking whether, in addition to loving God and neighbor, Christians ought to love a loveless nature as well. Rolston acknowledges that agape appears wholly absent from nature and that multiple virtues associated with love—like kindness, mercy, generosity, compassion, justice, patience, and forgiveness—do not seem germane to our interaction with wilderness either. Nevertheless, Rolston also observes that wilderness is amoral, and thus that its lack of agape reflects no deficiency in it. Similarly, Rolston contends that wild animals do not need human beneficence but simply respect for their wildness and sufficient habitat to be themselves. Accordingly, Rolston insists that we may still have moral obligations to the wild even if loving it would be inappropriate. Indeed, Rolston finds ample evidence of and support for environmental ethics within the Judeo-Christian tradition, noting that loving the land is a principal facet of Hebrew faith and that Jesus repeatedly discerned God's presence in the landscape around him. Beyond such rural settings, Rolston recalls that words translated as "wilderness" appear almost 300 times in the Bible as a whole, that the Gospels portray Jesus as regularly returning to places so named, and that throughout Christian scripture God is depicted as relishing biodiversity independent of human beings. Further, biblical wisdom literature persistently attests that God glories in such places and does not commission human beings to till and keep them all. Rolston therefore advises Christians to deny that wilderness has fallen into sin or requires redemption. Instead, Rolston maintains that wilderness has value, makes claims that warrant human care and protection, and as such invites a fullest form of altruism that brings a uniquely human self-actualization.

The third part of the volume concludes with three chapters comparing love's ethical significance across the three Abrahamic faiths. Eric Gregory's essay helps to frame this final section by examining the social and personal implications of religious pluralism for how Christians understand the relation between love of God and love of neighbor. Observing that recognition of diversity has heightened attention to both moral pluralism with respect to values and political pluralism as a social practice that addresses difference, Gregory concentrates on the ways that this recognition affects continuing controversy concerning the particularity of Christian ethics and the compatibility of Christianity with liberalism. Gregory identifies methodological affinities between comparisons of interpretations of love across Christian communities and between Christianity and other religious traditions, and he appeals to Outka's conception of the normative ties among love of God, neighbors, and oneself along with Outka's construal of Christian neighbor love as equal regard to guide Christian-interreligious encounter. Delineating symmetries and asymmetries between God's love and our own, Gregory asserts that appropriate Christian responses to religious pluralism must eschew fear, self-justification, and noetic or emotional closure. Thus insistent that exclusion cannot determine Christian identity, Gregory affirms that proper Christian love reflects a yearning for truth and relationship that approaches the world's religious variety with delight and curiosity. Moreover, Gregory emphasizes the importance of religious diversity for Christians' experience of God's presence and Christians' assessment of theological and ethical diversity within their own tradition.

Ronald Green's essay is the first of two that examine ethical analyses of love in two specific religious faiths. He explores the meanings of neighbor love in the Hebrew Bible and later rabbinic tradition and compares these interpretations and applications with those given in the New Testament. Green concludes that despite considerable differences between Jewish and Christian understandings of the biblical commandment to love one's neighbor as oneself, the disagreements within each tradition are greater than those between them. Perceiving broad continuity across scripture in the meaning of the love commanded for the neighbor, Green denies that any divergence in Jewish and Christian conceptions of the obligation to love others is due simply to discrepancies in their notions of love per se. He discerns less consensus about the proper scope of neighbor love yet finds the contours of the controversy to be similar within Judaism and Christianity. Green acknowledges that the Christian tradition sometimes understands neighbor love in self-sacrificial terms while the Jewish tradition generally emphasizes an ethical duty of self-preservation. Nevertheless, Green contends that both traditions connect the commandment to love God and neighbor to the unity of God and the kinship of all human beings, interpret the latter command to enjoin universal human respect and concern, and at times respond to severe persecution by restricting the range of full neighbor love to coreligionists. Consequently, Green commends recognition of a common Jewish and Christian love ethic based on these traditions' shared commitment to the commandment of neighbor love promulgated in Leviticus.

John Kelsay concludes part 3 by comparing Muslim and Christian understandings of the moral duty to love one's neighbors. He holds that dominant Muslim interpretations of mandatory neighbor love correspond to a scheme of ranked relationships that differentiate obligatory love for Muslims from obligatory love for non-Muslims. Kelsay associates this distinction with a Muslim assessment of an individual's proximity to God that is manifest in the alignment of the individual's loves and hates with God's loves and hates. According to this interpretation, appropriate Muslim neighbor love follows the prioritization established in God's differential love for human beings of different religious communities. Kelsay argues that this order of love reflects the type of social-political organization delineated in the discourse of *fiqh* or Shari'a reasoning developed during the Abbasid period. In particular, Kelsay claims that the principles regulating military force in this period illustrate the disparity that Muslims posit between proper love of Muslim and non-Muslim neighbors. Given the profound geopolitical and cultural transformations that have occurred in the intervening eight centuries, a number of contemporary Muslim scholars are calling for the retrieval of an Islamic humanism that could interpret the Qur'an and Muslim legal tradition more flexibly to accommodate the needs of new historical contexts. Specifically, such humanism could join a version of Sufism in construing Muslims as obligated to love all neighbors equally, whatever their religious identities. Kelsay describes a similar trajectory within Christianity and encourages this sort of approach as Muslims and others seek to formulate conceptions of justice and neighbor love suitable to the religious pluralism of a global nation-state system.

Afterword

William Werpehowski completes the volume by identifying and extending its exploration of three themes that recur in several of its chapters—assessment of eudaimonism's adequacy as a framework for interpreting the moral significance of Christian love, conceptual clarification of the ethical meaning of the command to love the neighbor as oneself, and examination of the social implications of Christian neighbor love in multiple domains. Concerning Christian evaluations of eudaimonism, Werpehowski endorses Irwin's contention that much depends on whether Christians posit a robust continuity or stark contrast between Greek and Christian conceptions of love. Nevertheless, he wonders how Irwin's alternatives categorize Christians, like Ramsey, who affirm and transform such Greek conceptions. Werpehowski then interprets Simmons's analysis of Christian love and eudaimonism as offering an intermediate position between Porter's eudaimonism and Hare's non-eudaimonism that implicitly builds on commonalities and convergences that Porter and Hare discern in Aquinas's and Kant's views. He urges Simmons to reckon with Barth's insistence that a sense of abandonment by God is crucial to our eudaimonia and the Roman Catholic Catechism's approbation of Thérèse of Lisieux's wish to live for God's love alone rather than any eschatological reward.

Werpehowski next draws connections between King's and Outka's understandings of the normative content of neighbor love. He notes their common advocacy of a universal, unilateral regard for the neighbor's good that proves a middle path between Santurri's claim that Christian neighbor love is essentially self-sacrificial and Pope's thesis that Christian neighbor love is always a kind of friendship. Werpehowski further wonders whether King's conception of the relation among neighbor love, sacrifice, and friendship brings him closer to both Santurri and Pope than Outka is to either one. He invites Santurri to construe Christian neighbor love as essentially self-giving rather than self-sacrificial and asks Pope to consider incorporating a disposition to self-sacrifice into the friendship of Christian neighbor love so long as sin persists.

Werpehowski turns at last to five of the volume's interpretations of Christian love's practical import in diverse social settings. He observes that Cahill's linking of Christian love with justice and hope allows her to foreground the perspective of the poor and amplify love's motivational force in the endeavor to improve global health care. Jordan's vocational image of Christian sexual ethics then stimulates Werpehowski to envision a similarly vocational treatment of politics and business that could help Christians fashion a loving knowledge of these fundamental social realities and thereby facilitate further ethical reflection on them. Werpehowski next couples Farley's attention to love's role in forgiveness with Townes's interest in love's contribution to cultural repair, underscoring their shared insistence on love's significance for justice and discernment in the wake of violence. Finally, Werpehowski commends Gregory's appeal to Christian ethical reflection on love for insights into interreligious dialogue as also affording advances in a theology of religions.

So much for this volume's contents. Yet a methodological misgiving may linger. If love is truly the source, substance, standard, and goal of Christian ethics, does this study's conjunctive approach to love distract from the Christian moral life and perhaps even distort it? If not, ought Christians instead abandon the "short and simple precept" Augustine thought given to us once and for all: "love, and do what you will"?[28] Advocating the latter course would be an unexpected outcome given Augustine's conviction that love is central to the Christian life and his consistently synthetic engagement with love and much else. Accepting the former option, however, would contravene a premise of the volume. Happily, here again it seems sensible to resist disjunction. Augustine's precept must surely be taken to mean "love rightly, and do what you will."[29] After all, Augustine acknowledged that love may be misguided and maintained that properly ordered love is morally obligatory, essential to human happiness, and constitutive of Christian identity.[30] Moreover, when interpreted this way, the precept finds support not only in the Johannine literature from which Augustine distilled this maxim but in the Synoptic Gospels, James, and even the great biblical champion of righteousness by faith, Paul.[31] Accordingly, since Augustine also affirmed that other values, virtues, and duties were necessary to love rightly, his concentration on love did not exclude additional moral considerations; it consistently invited and integrated them.[32] This volume shares that Augustinian commitment. Hence, it explores Christian love from multiple perspectives and in conjunction with many topics—not to supplant love but to understand its ethical significance more fully.

Notes

1. Nygren writes, "It might reasonably have been expected that theologians would have given special attention to [the meaning of the Christian idea of love], for it is plain that the idea of love occupies a—not to say the—central place in Christianity, both from a religious and an ethical point of view. Yet we have only to glance at the treatment the subject has received from theologians in recent times, to see that it is among the most neglected. . . . Nor is the position any different when we turn to the history of Christian ethics." Anders Nygren, *Agape and Eros*, trans. Philip Watson (London: Society for Promoting Christian Knowledge, 1953), 27; Swedish title, *Den kristna kärlekstanken genom tiderna. Eros och Agape* (Stockholm: Svenska Kyrkans Diakonistyrelses Bokförlag, 1930, 1936).

2. Ibid., 39.

3. Ibid., 210.

4. John Burnaby, *Amor Dei: A Study of the Religion of St. Augustine* (London: Hodder & Stoughton, 1938), 18–19.

5. Martin D'Arcy, *The Mind and Heart of Love, Lion and Unicorn: A Study in Eros and Agape* (London: Faber and Faber, 1945), 70–72, 76–78, 127.

6. Brunner made no mention of Nygren in *The Divine Imperative: A Study in Christian Ethics*, trans. Olive Wyon (Philadelphia: Westminster Press, 1947); German title, *Das Gebot und die Ordnungen: Entwurf einer protestantisch-theologischen Ethik* (Tübingen: Mohr Siebeck, 1932). Nevertheless, like Nygren, Brunner emphasized the distinction between agape and eros (55, 332, 517), attributed the former to God (301) and the latter to human beings apart from God's love (164–65), interpreted agape as self-sacrificial giving (327) and eros as self-interested acquisition (115, 330), and championed agape as the distinctive mark of genuine Christianity (328). By contrast, three decades later, in *Faith, Hope, and Love* (Philadelphia: Westminster Press, 1956), Brunner explicitly began his account of love with Nygren's *Agape and Eros*.

7. Fritz Tillmann, *Der Meister Ruft* (Düsseldorf: Patmos, 1937); English title, *The Master Calls: A Handbook of Christian Living*, trans. Gregory Roettger (Baltimore: Helicon Press, 1962). In particular, see Gérard Gilleman, *Le primat de la charité en théologie morale: essai méthodologique* (Louvain: E. Nauwelaerts, 1952); English title, *The Primacy of Charity in Moral Theology*, trans. William F. Ryan and André Vachon (Westminster, MD: Newman Press, 1959); Bernard Häring, *Das Gesetz Christi* (Freiburg: Verlag Wewel,

1954); English title, *The Law of Christ: Moral Theology for Priests and Laity*, trans. Edwin Kaiser, 3 vols. (Paramus, NJ: Newman Press, 1961); and Robert Johann, *The Meaning of Love: An Essay towards a Metaphysics of Intersubjectivity* (Westminster, MD: Newman Press, 1955).

    8. In particular, see Reinhold Niebuhr, *The Nature and Destiny of Man*, 2 vols. (New York: Charles Scribner's Sons, 1941, 1943); and Paul Ramsey, *Basic Christian Ethics* (New York: Scribner, 1950).

    9. In particular, see Howard Thurman, *Jesus and the Disinherited* (New York: Abingdon-Cokesbury Press, 1949); Paul Tillich, *Love, Power, and Justice: Ontological Analyses and Ethical Applications* (New York: Oxford University Press, 1954) and *Systematic Theology*, vol. 3 (Chicago: University of Chicago Press, 1963); Karl Barth, *Die Kirchliche Dogmatik IV: Die Lehre von der Versöhnung 2* (Zollikon-Zürich: Evangelischer Verlag A.G., 1955); English title, *Church Dogmatics* IV, 2, trans. G. W. Bromiley (Edinburgh: T&T Clark, 1958); C. S. Lewis, *The Four Loves* (New York: Harcourt, Brace, 1960); Hans Urs von Balthasar, *Glaubhaft ist nur Liebe* (Einsiedeln: Johannes Verlag, 1963); English title, *Love Alone Is Credible*, trans. D. C. Schindler (San Francisco: Ignatius Press, 2004); and Karl Rahner, *Schriften zur Theologie* (Einsiedeln: Benziger, 1965); English title, *Theological Investigations: Concerning Vatican Council II*, trans. Karl Kruger and Boniface Kruger, vol. 6 (Baltimore: Helicon, 1969).

    10. C. S. Lewis, *The Allegory of Love: A Study in Medieval Tradition* (London: Oxford University Press, 1936); and Denis de Rougemont, *L'Amour et L'Occident* (Paris: Plon, 1939); English title, *Love in the Western World*, trans. Montgomery Belgion (New York: Pantheon, 1956).

    11. Søren Kierkegaard, *Kjerlighedens Gjerninger* (Kjøbenhavn: C. A. Reitzel, 1847); English title, *Works of Love*, trans. Howard Hong and Edna Hong (Princeton: Princeton University Press, 1995).

    12. Pierre Rousselot, *Pour l'histoire du problem de l'amour au moyen âge* (Münster: Aschendorffsche Buchhandlung, 1908); English title, *The Problem of Love in the Middle Ages: A Historical Contribution*, trans. Alan Vincelette (Milwaukee: Marquette University Press, 2001).

    13. Heinrich Scholz, *Eros und Caritas: Die platonische Liebe und die Liebe im Sinne des Christentums* (Halle: Max Niemeyer Verlag, 1929).

    14. Cf., e.g., Gilleman, *Primacy of Charity in Moral Theology*, xxi, xxviii–xxix, 3; James Keenan, *A History of Catholic Moral Theology in the Twentieth Century: From Confessing Sins to Liberating Consciences* (London: Continuum, 2010), 1–34; and Stephen Pope, *The Evolution of Altruism and the Ordering of Love* (Washington, DC: Georgetown University Press, 1995), 19–49.

    15. Cf., e.g., Walter Rauschenbusch, *Christianizing the Social Order* (New York: MacMillan, 1914), 40–127, 262–71; Gary Dorrien, *Social Ethics in the Making: Interpreting an American Tradition* (Malden, MA: Wiley-Blackwell, 2011), 1–5.

    16. In particular, see Martin Luther King Jr., *Strength to Love* (New York: Harper & Row, 1963); Joseph Fletcher, *Situation Ethics: The New Morality* (Philadelphia: Westminster Press, 1966); Jules Toner, *The Experience of Love* (Washington, DC: Corpus Books, 1968); Daniel Day Williams, *The Spirit and Forms of Love* (New York: Harper & Row, 1968); Gustavo Gutierrez, *Teología de la liberación, Perspectivas* (Lima: Centro de Estudios y Publicaciones, 1971); English title, *A Theology of Liberation: History, Politics and Salvation*, trans. Caridad Inda and John Eagleson (Maryknoll, NY: Orbis Books, 1973); Gene Outka, *Agape: An Ethical Analysis* (New Haven, CT: Yale University Press, 1972); Josef Pieper, *Über die Liebe* (Munich: Kösel, 1972); English title, *About Love*, trans. Richard Winston and Clara Winston (Chicago: Franciscan Herald Press, 1974); Judith Plaskow, *Sex, Sin, and Grace: Women's Experience and the Theologies of Reinhold Niebuhr and Paul Tillich* (Washington, DC: University Press of America, 1980); Beverly Harrison, "The Power of Anger in the Work of Love," *Union Seminary Quarterly Review* 36, supplementary (1981): 41–57; Barbara Andolsen, "Agape in Feminist Ethics," *Journal of Religious Ethics* 9, no. 1 (Spring 1981): 69–83.

    17. Outka, *Agape*, 8. Among Outka's numerous publications, see "Following at a Distance: Ethics and the Identity of Jesus," in *Scriptural Authority and Narrative Interpretation*, ed. Garrett Green (Philadelphia: Fortress Press, 1987), 144–60; "Universal Love and Impartiality," in *The Love Commandments: Essays in Christian Ethics and Moral Philosophy*, ed. Edmund N. Santurri and William Werpehowski (Washington, DC: Georgetown University Press, 1992), 1–103; "Theocentric Agape and the Self: An Asymmetrical Affirmation in Response to Colin Grant's Either/Or," *Journal of Religious Ethics* 24, no. 1 (Spring 1996): 35–42; "Agapeistic Ethics," in *A Companion to Philosophy of Religion*, ed. Philip Quinn and Charles Taliaferro (Cambridge, MA: Blackwell, 1997), 481–88; "Theocentric Love and the Augustinian Legacy: Honoring Difference and Likenesses between God and Ourselves," *Journal of the Society of Christian Ethics* 22 (2002): 97–114; and

"Self and Other in a Theological Framework," in *A Just and True Love: Feminism and the Frontiers of Ethics: Essays in Honor of Margaret A. Farley*, ed. Maura Ryan and Brian Linnane (Notre Dame, IN: University of Notre Dame Press, 2007), 135–62.

18. Outka, *Agape*, 3–5.

19. Ibid., 9–10.

20. Garth Hallett, *Christian Neighbor-Love: An Assessment of Six Rival Versions* (Washington, DC: Georgetown University Press, 1989); Edward Vacek, *Love, Human and Divine: The Heart of Christian Ethics* (Washington, DC: Georgetown University Press, 1994); Timothy Jackson, *The Priority of Love: Christian Charity and Social Justice* (Princeton, NJ: Princeton University Press, 2003).

21. Hallett, *Christian Neighbor-Love*, vii, title of chap. 1.

22. Vacek, *Love, Human and Divine*, xiii.

23. Hallett, *Christian Neighbor-Love*, 15–31.

24. Jackson, *Priority of Love*, 1, 6. However, Jackson also notes that some Christians laud love's putative eclipse, and he discusses Hauerwas and Hays's misgivings about interpretations of Christian ethics that would make love central (15–27). David McCarthy likewise celebrates what he perceives as the infrequency of Christians' appeal to the concept of love within fundamental moral theology, although for different reasons. David McCarthy, "Love in Fundamental Moral Theology," in *Moral Theology: New Directions and Fundamental Issues*, ed. James Keating (Mahway, NJ: Paulist Press, 2004), 182.

25. For example, Christian ethicists often relegated love to prolegomenon or epilogue—if they explicitly invoked it at all—as they helped develop the professional ethics that began to burgeon over the last third of the twentieth century for pluralist, procedurally oriented public life; cf., e.g., Edward Long, "Ethics in Vocational and Policy-Making Settings," in *A Survey of Recent Christian Ethics* (Oxford: Oxford University Press, 1982).

26. Burnaby, *Amor Dei*, 4.

27. Toni Morrison, *Beloved* (New York: Alfred A. Knopf, 1987), 88.

28. Augustine, *Ten Homilies on the First Epistle General of St. John: Seventh Homily* (1 John 4:4–12) §8, in *The Library of Christian Classics*, vol. 8, *Augustine: Later Works*, trans. John Burnaby (Philadelphia: Westminster Press, 1955), 316.

29. Indeed, elsewhere Augustine states explicitly that "I mean by 'charity' the love of living virtuously, even if sometimes people talk of charity in the context of something bad." *Sermon 335c* (Sermo Lambot 2) §2, in *Augustine: Political Writings*, ed. E. M. Atkins and R. J. Dodaro (Cambridge: Cambridge University Press, 2001), 53.

30. Cf., e.g., Augustine's concise insistence that "two cities were created by two kinds of love: the earthly city was created by self-love reaching the point of contempt for God, the Heavenly City by the love of God carried as far as contempt of self." Augustine, *CD* 14.28, trans. Henry Bettenson (London: Penguin, 1984). Other important discussions include *On the Morals of the Catholic Church* 8.13–30.64, *On Christian Doctrine* 1.3.3–5.5 and 1.22.20–40.44, and *Sermon 368*.

31. Among multiple passages in each, cf., e.g., Matt. 7:12, Mark 2:23–28, Luke 10:25–28, James 2:8, Rom. 13:8–10, and Gal. 5:13–14.

32. Cf., e.g., Augustine's treatises *Enchiridion: On Faith, Hope, and Love* 1.1–2.8 and 31.117–32.121; *Against Lying*; and his *Letter 155 Augustine to Macedonius* (413/414), §13 and §15; see also William Frankena, *Ethics* (Englewood Cliffs, NJ: Prentice-Hall, 1963), 42–45.

Part I

TRADITION

1

Interpreting the Love Commands in Social Context

Deuteronomy and Jesus's Sermon on the Mount

THOMAS W. OGLETREE

BIBLICAL PORTRAYALS of the love commands are interwoven with presentations of more comprehensive bodies of commandments, laws, and ordinances that order human affairs in particular social settings. The love commands provide a substantive foundation for these more complex resources, undergirding their authority and informing efforts to observe them faithfully in ongoing life practices. This essay focuses on distinctive yet overlapping treatments of the love commands contained in the book of Deuteronomy and in Matthew's presentation of Jesus's Sermon on the Mount, with selective references to related materials in other biblical texts. Deuteronomy ventures a comprehensive yet realistic vision of a well-ordered society, one firmly grounded in repeated declarations of the Lord's steadfast love for the people of Israel with a corresponding summons to the people to love the Lord in return. It directly addresses the challenges of adapting Israel's covenant legacy to a social order structured by an aristocratic class and status system subject to the rule of kings, a form of social organization that typically routinizes the exploitation of vulnerable people. In this setting, implementations of the love commands included generous contributions by the privileged to support those in need. In contrast, Jesus's teachings in the Sermon on the Mount are directed toward a socially inclusive company of followers, equipping them for faithful participation in an emerging grassroots social movement, one informed by a life-transforming vision of God's redemptive purposes (Matt. 5–7; cf. Luke 6:17–49). These teachings are substantially illumined by Jesus's climactic claim that the enduring authority of the law and the prophets derives from the commands to love God with heart, soul, and mind and to love our neighbors as we love ourselves (Matt. 22:34–40). They direct attention to the underlying moral and spiritual substance of the law, including calls for justice and righteousness by Israel's prophets. Both of these classic models are pertinent for contemporary reflections on the love commands, underscoring the point that love has different implications within different social contexts.

The Love Commands in the Book of Deuteronomy

Deuteronomy opens with the narrative of the exodus of the people of Israel from Egypt, their wilderness wanderings, and their struggles to possess and defend the land that the Lord had promised them. This narrative is followed by the ten "words," *devarim*—a term usually translated as "commandments"—that the Lord delivered to the people on Mount Horeb (Deut. 5:1–21). These words set forth the basic requisites for covenant fidelity in the lives of the people.[1] Moses then declares the Lord's steadfast love for his people (cf. Deut. 5:10), and he summons the people to love the Lord their God in return with all their hearts, with all their souls, and with all their might (Deut. 6:4–9). The Hebrew word for "heart," *levaveka*, has cognitive and volitional connotations. Greek translations in New Testament texts capture this richness with two separate words: heart, or *kardia*, and mind, or *dianoia* (cf. Mark 12:30; Matt. 22:37; Luke 10:25–27). The Hebrew word for soul, *naphsheka*, suggests the depths of the self, and the word for might, *me'odeka*, calls for the full investment of one's strength and energy. Accordingly, the Lord's words are grounded in his love for his people, and they are delivered to the people for their well-being. The people are urged to "heed" the words of the Lord, to study them diligently, and to embrace them with their hearts and souls (Deut. 6:10–25, cf. 11:18–20), a message that pervades the book of Deuteronomy (cf. Deut. 5:10, 7:7–13, 10:15–22, 11:1–22, 13:3, 30:6).

Deuteronomy contains no explicit references to neighbor love or to love for self, though it does emphasize the Lord's impartiality in executing justice for orphans and widows, and it declares his love for strangers, when he provides them with food and clothing. Accordingly, the people are instructed to love strangers with the reminder that they were themselves strangers in the land of Egypt (Deut. 10:17–19). These references serve as tacit endorsements of self-love combined with equivalent love for neighbors and strangers, a message that is explicitly stated in Leviticus (19:18, 34). Deuteronomy's basic message is that the people must love neighbors and strangers living among them in accordance with the Lord's own steadfast love.

Along with declarations of the Lord's love and a corresponding summons to love the Lord in return, the book of Deuteronomy directs attention to the persistent stubbornness, hard-heartedness, and disobedience of the people of Israel. The underlying message is that the people have not demonstrated a readiness to love themselves or their neighbors in appropriate ways. They constantly allow their fears and uncertainties to dominate their lives, and they invest themselves too narrowly in the pursuit of their own self-interests. This message is vividly displayed in the story of Moses coming down from Mount Horeb with tablets of stone that recorded the words the Lord had spoken directly to the people. Moses discovered to his dismay that the people were constructing an image of a calf as a sacral object, a blatant example of idolatry. Confronting the wickedness of the people, Moses concluded that they were in no way disposed to fulfill their covenant commitments, and he cast to the ground the tablets of stone, shattering them into pieces (Deut. 9:6–21). The prophet Jeremiah expressed similar anguish as he struggled to make sense of the pervasive faithlessness and disobedience of the people of Judah. He became convinced that the Lord's words would never be effective if they were simply engraved on tablets of stone; they had to be engraved on human hearts (Jer. 31:33–34).[2] In a parallel manner, the prophet Ezekiel proclaimed the Lord's promise to give his people a new heart and a new spirit, replacing their hearts of stone with hearts of flesh more responsive to the Lord's instructions (Ezek. 36:26–27). Having pleaded with the Lord not to destroy his people despite their idolatrous behavior, Moses seized the calf, burned it with fire, and crushed it, reducing it to dust. The Lord then summoned Moses to bring to the mountain two more tablets of stone on which he would once again engrave his words. Returning from the mountain, Moses addressed the people, urging them to fear the Lord, to walk in his ways, to love him and serve him with heart and soul, love that would honor God's glory and enhance their own well-being (Deut. 10–11). Deuteronomy concludes with Moses's final instructions for the people, in which he extensively elaborates these basic themes (Deut. 29–31).

The persistent disobedience of the people is manifest in the predominately negative form of the words that the Lord spoke directly to the people: no other gods; no graven images; no wrongful uses of the Lord's name; no killing, adultery, or theft; no false witness against a neighbor; and no covetous dispositions of any kind, whether driven by greed, arrogance, or sexual lust (Deut. 5:6–21; cf. Exod. 20:1–17). The rigorous observance of these prohibitions would hardly amount to acts of love, whether for God, self, neighbors, or strangers. Instead, they underscore the urgency of constraining forms of human misconduct that render authentic expressions of love virtually impossible. Only two of the Lord's words convey positive obligations: keep the Sabbath and honor your father and mother. The Sabbath takes on special importance because it is not simply a day for worship, sacrificial offerings, and instruction. It is above all a time of rest because it exemplifies the seventh day following the Lord's completion of the original work of creation (Gen. 2:1–3). Indeed, the word "Sabbath" comes from the Hebrew word *shabat*, which means "to rest." Therefore, God blessed the Sabbath as a time of rest for all creatures, including sons and daughters, slaves, resident aliens, and even livestock. The inclusion of slaves is reinforced by the reminder that the people of Israel had themselves been slaves in Egypt (Deut. 5:12–15; cf. Exod. 20:8–11, 31:12–17).[3] Honor for parents undergirds family bonds that were central components of the distinctive identity of a covenant people.

The Ten Words are then elaborated in a more detailed set of statutes, laws, and ordinances that addressed virtually all aspects of life in the ancient kingdom of Judah (Deut. 12–26). With the exception of standards regulating dietary practices and purity codes (Deut. 14:3–22, 22:5, 9–12), most of these statutes are related, directly or indirectly, to one or more of the Ten Commandments. Taken as a whole, however, they should not be viewed as integral components of Israel's covenant traditions. Instead, they represented practical attempts to reconstruct those traditions in ways that could accommodate an aristocratic class and status system subject to the rule of kings, a system marked by wide social disparities in wealth, status, and honor.

Deuteronomy directly addresses the challenges of rendering monarchy compatible with Israel's covenant legacy. The central message is that monarchy will be viable for a covenant people only if kings are themselves committed to ruling in ways that are congruent with the law of the Lord. Kings must not seize power by force, accumulate great wealth, have multiple wives, or build large standing armies, and they must not afflict or oppress their people (Deut. 17:14–20). The books of Samuel and Kings indicate that Deuteronomy's vision of righteous kings was actually unrealistic. Apart from David's penitent responses to prophetic critics and Solomon's alleged wisdom, only two of Judah's kings are portrayed as righteous: Josiah and Hezekiah. Even Solomon violated some of the basic standards, accumulating great wealth, having multiple wives, and using forced labor for ambitious construction projects (1 Kings 5–11). Kings ruling in the northern kingdom of Israel are uniformly condemned as cruel, unjust, and disobedient. Deuteronomy bestows substantial responsibility on the Levites for instructing the people, especially their rulers, in the law of the Lord (Deut. 18:1–8). It also directs attention to the centrality of prophetic testimonies, with emphasis on the urgency of exposing the spurious claims of false prophets. Deuteronomy does not mention the roles prophets played in calling kings and priests to account for unjust and abusive practices. It focuses instead on prophetic responsibilities in advising kings, exemplified by the activities of Isaiah, Jeremiah, and Ezekiel (Deut. 18:15–22).

What is striking about the statutes in Deuteronomy is the prominence of the death penalty, especially for dealing with idolatrous acts, false prophecies, and spurious claims of divine authority (Deut. 13:1–11), and also for addressing virtually all forms of sexual misconduct, including adultery, rape, incest, sexual contacts between males and between humans and animals, and false claims to virginity by newly married women (Deut. 22:13–30). Given the patriarchal order, adultery, rape, and incest were portrayed as violations of male prerogatives, either the rights of a husband, a man engaged to be married, or a father.[4] Acts of this kind were considered a serious threat to stable kinship ties that were central to Israel's covenant legacy. Concepts of homosexuality or sexual orientation are not discussed in these statues, so sexual contacts between males were presumed to be manifestations of lust out of control. There are no such references to sexual contacts between females. The death penalty was applied as well for kidnapping a fellow Israelite and for unjustified killing, including physical assaults that resulted in death. Kidnapping was associated with efforts to secure slave labor or perhaps to sell a slave for financial gain (Deut. 24:7). Persons who unintentionally killed a neighbor were permitted to flee to a refuge city where they could live in peace, sheltered from possible assault by vengeful relatives (Deut. 4:41–49, 19:1–13). Finally, a father could have a son stoned to death should the son become a glutton and a drunkard (Deut. 21:18–21). Given the prominence of the death penalty, fear and terror rather than love were crucial incentives for upholding the law.

How do the love commands figure in these statutes, laws, and ordinances? The spirit of love becomes manifest in part when basic prohibitions are elaborated in a more positive form. The commandment against stealing finds expression in a summons to return a neighbor's lost goods, including straying animals and lost garments, and also to care for a neighbor's fallen donkey (Deut. 22:1–4). There is an important exception to these instructions: slaves who escaped from their masters should not be returned. They must be given freedom to reside where they please, and they must in no case be oppressed (Deut. 23:15–16). This mandate places in question the legitimacy of slavery, for it suggests that slaves cannot be viewed simply as property. Deuteronomy also stresses the urgency of honest weights and measures in commercial transactions, declaring that dishonesty is abhorrent. People who purchase goods in the market must have confidence that the size and weight of those goods have been correctly represented (Deut. 25:13–16). The commandment against killing includes a summons to manage one's property in ways that do not put others at risk, for example, building a parapet on the roof of a newly constructed house lest someone should fall from the roof and be seriously injured (Deut. 22:8). These examples illustrate positive initiatives to care for the well-being of neighbors and strangers.

The commandment against a false witness leads to the establishment of reliable judicial processes for dealing with criminal acts and serious human conflicts. Locally appointed judges bore almost total responsibility for these processes, questioning witnesses, evaluating relevant evidence, determining guilt or innocence, and ordering the proper penalty. Judges were charged with pursuing "justice and only justice": no partiality, no bribes, and diligent inquiry into alleged crimes, drawing on the testimonies of at least two witnesses and, if possible, three. Anyone who delivered a false witness faced a penalty equivalent to the one normally imposed for the crime at issue. When death by stoning was ordered, the lead witness was obliged to cast the first stone, thereby confirming the truth of his or her testimony (Deut. 16:18–17:13). Judges also played vital roles in resolving conflicts between individuals and families. Cases that could not be settled at local levels were assigned to a Temple priest acting with a judge in office.[5] Decisions at the highest level were final, and anyone who disobeyed priestly orders would die (Deut. 17:8–13). These examples move beyond simple prohibitions of wrongdoing, suggesting positive initiatives people should take to foster the well-being of neighbors and resident aliens.

The message of love becomes most explicit in expressions of concern for highly vulnerable people, especially widows, fatherless children, orphans, strangers living in the land, and more generally, people who were poor. Calls to address the needs of the vulnerable were essentially directed toward people of privilege who had substantial resources at their disposal. Household masters were obliged to pay the wages of hired servants at the end of each day (Deut. 24:14–15). In harvesting their crops, landowners were expected to leave remnants of the harvest behind for gathering by those who were poor (Deut. 24:14–15). The poor were permitted to enter fields and orchards to gather food provided they took only what they could immediately consume or grains gathered solely with their hands (Deut. 23:24–25). People with substantial resources were instructed to bring tithes to their towns every third year to provide support for Levites, who had no inheritance of their own, and also to aid resident aliens, widows, and orphans (Deut. 24:28–29). Widows along with their fatherless children would be especially vulnerable because a widow could not inherit her deceased husband's estate. She would have no resources to sustain herself and her children unless her deceased husband had a male relative who would take her as one of his own wives. Men were permitted to have multiple wives.

During the Sabbath year, which came every seventh year, the prosperous were obliged to remit all debts owed by their neighbors, though the same requirement did not hold for foreigners (Deut. 15:1–18, 24:10–13). Hebrew slaves were to be released after six years of service, and they could not be sent away empty-handed. Masters were reminded that their ancestors had been slaves in Egypt (Deut. 15:12–18). Foreigners captured in war were subject to lifelong servitude. Hebrew slaves who loved their masters could themselves choose to remain in slavery (Deut. 15:19), a commitment that could give them long-term security.

Deuteronomy's general message is that there must be no one in need among the people of Israel. Those with ample resources must not be hard-hearted toward their needy neighbors. They must open their hands and willingly give or lend to their neighbors what they required to meet basic needs. Even as the seventh year, when all debts must be forgiven, approached, they must not view their neighbors with hostility or give them nothing, for their neighbors could cry out to the Lord, thereby disclosing their guilt. These mandates conclude with the observation that there will never cease to be some people who are in need, so the prosperous must open their hands to the poor. Three major festivals of the calendar year served as times for generous giving to people in need: the Passover, the festival of weeks, and the festival of booths (Deut. 16:1–17).

Thus, love for God, for self, and for neighbors and strangers required actions that were compatible with an existing social order, even one marked by vast inequalities of wealth, status, and honor. Standards of justice and fairness played a role in these undertakings, yet there were no calls for reconstructing prevailing social arrangements. The primary strategy for loving care consisted of generous gifts by the prosperous for those in need.

Jesus's Teachings on the Love Commands in the Sermon on the Mount

In the Sermon on the Mount, Jesus offers an innovative reading of the enduring authority of the law and the prophets in the context of a radically reconstructed vision of God's redemptive purposes for the world (Matt. 5–7). In this new frame of reference, the law and the prophets are no longer linked closely to the requisites of a well-ordered society. Instead, they address the concrete practices and states of mind of those who would become active participants in Jesus's mission to the world, a mission that included transformative initiatives to foster justice and peace in a sinful and fallen world. Jesus's teachings are congruent with Deuteronomy's emphasis on heartfelt obedience to God's commands (cf. Deut. 6:6). They also embody the spirit of Jeremiah's projection of a "new covenant" graven on the hearts of the people (Jer. 31:33–34) and Ezekiel's call for a "new heart and a new spirit" (Ezek. 18:31). Of central importance is Jesus's claim that the whole of the law and the prophets *depends* on the two great commandments: the command to love God with heart, soul, and mind and the command to love our neighbors as we love ourselves (Matt. 22:37–40; cf. Mark 12:28–34).[6]

The Sermon on the Mount opens with "beatitudes," that is, words of assurance and encouragement that Jesus offered his followers (Matt. 5:1–12; cf. Luke 6:20–26). K. C. Hanson makes a compelling case that the Greek term for "blessed" (*macharioi*) and the contrasting term for "woe" (*ouai*) might better be translated as declarations of honor and shame, terms that display one's moral and spiritual standing.[7] Jesus directs attention to dispositions and states of mind that are requisite for embracing the authority of the law and the prophets. His words of shame are subsequently delivered to scribes and Pharisees in the Jerusalem Temple as he sought to expose their hypocritical practices (Matt. 23).[8] Jesus concludes with images of consequences that follow from faithful and unfaithful responses to his message (Matt. 7:13–27).

The Sermon on the Mount opens with declarations of honor for the "poor in spirit" and those who "hunger and thirst for righteousness" (Matt. 5:3, 6), people who are deeply conscious of their own limitations while earnestly striving to achieve righteousness. Jesus assured them that their longings would be realized (Matt. 5:3). The poor in spirit are not tempted to engage in public displays of piety or generosity, nor do they heap up empty phrases when they pray or disfigure their faces when they fast. Their prayers embody the spirit of the Lord's Prayer—reverent and humble in tone, focused on fundamentals, and oriented toward the realization of God's ultimate purposes (Matt. 6:1–18). Similarly, those who hunger and thirst for righteousness will not lay up for themselves treasures on earth, nor will they become anxious about their bodily needs. They will seek first the righteousness of God's kingdom and trust God to provide for their basic needs (Matt. 6:19–34). The merciful, the pure in heart, and peacemakers strive to heal broken relationships and resolve serious human conflicts, including relationships with enemies (Matt. 5:7–9). Jesus also honors those who are persecuted, reviled, and falsely accused of all sorts of evil, precisely on his account. He assures them that their reward will be great in heaven, for prophets who preceded them were persecuted as well (Matt. 5:10–12; cf. Luke 6:26).[9] He describes his true followers as the "salt of the earth," "light for the world," and a "city set upon a hill" that cannot be hidden. He calls them to serve as models for all who strive for righteousness (Matt. 5:13–15; cf. Luke 11:14, 14:34–35) and to become perfect as the Father in heaven is perfect (Matt. 5:48).

Jesus then elaborates his understanding of the law and the prophets. "Think not that I have come to abolish the law and the prophets," he declared. "I have not come to abolish them but to fulfill them. Till heaven and earth pass away, not an iota, *iota*, not a dot, *keraia*, will pass from the law until all is accomplished" (Matt. 5:17–18; cf. Luke 16:16–17; cf. also Matt. 24:35; Mark 13:31; Luke 21:33). The combination of law and prophets is highly significant. All three of the Synoptic Gospels direct attention to the prophetic substance of Jesus's mission, though they provide a more equivocal account of the status of the law. Indeed, Jesus repeatedly found himself in conflict with Pharisees, scribes, and Temple priests over legal matters such as Sabbath observances, ritual practices, food laws, and standards of purity (cf. Matt. 23:1–36). The terms *iota* and *keraia* refer to markers added to Hebrew texts to ensure correct and accurate readings of various laws and ordinances, especially where misunderstandings were likely.[10] By using these terms, Jesus initially appears to be directing attention to minute details of the law. As the Sermon on the Mount unfolds, however, it becomes apparent that he is by no means preoccupied with legalistic details, nor does he venture a comprehensive overview of the law. His purpose is to uncover the underlying meaning of the law as a vision for human wholeness and to integrate the binding authority of the law and the prophets with promises borne by the coming kingdom of heaven. He provides a model for critical reflection on life-transforming possibilities resident in the law, one that can inform contemporary deliberations as well.

Jesus begins his discussion of the law and the prophets with a focus on difficulties and strains in human relationships, embracing conflicts between brothers, the challenges of fidelity in marriage, standards of truthfulness and trustworthiness in mutual agreements between fellow human beings, and counsel on creative ways of coping with routinized patterns of social abuse. These teachings conclude with visions of love that embrace not simply neighbors and friends but enemies and persecutors as well, a message that exemplifies Jesus's mission to gather a new and more inclusive family of God (Matt. 5:43–48).

Glen Stassen has significantly enriched our reading of the Sermon on the Mount by emphasizing the "triadic" structure that orders Jesus's teachings on the law.[11] He observes that Jesus begins the discussion of each of his examples by citing "traditional righteousness," that is, what was said to "men of old." He then directs attention, at times only implicitly, to limitations inherent in traditional standards. These limitations disclose underlying problems that traditional teachings cannot effectively address. Speaking with authority, Jesus then calls on his followers to take "transformative initiatives" that could significantly reconfigure and ultimately overcome persisting difficulties resident in traditional understandings.

The first example Jesus examines builds on the command "You shall not kill." While traditional teaching was clearly binding, it still left substantial space for destructive human behavior. Jesus emphasized the harm that a man can inflict on a brother by intense expressions of anger or by deliberate insults, such as calling him a "fool." Jesus did not insist that his followers should never to be angry. Indeed, synoptic accounts of the Temple takeover display Jesus's own anger. Properly channeled, anger need not lead to violent or abusive actions; it may even empower courageous prophetic acts. At the same time, expressions of anger and demeaning insults can inflict severe emotional harm, and they often generate turmoil in the lives of those who are angry as well. Consequently, intense feelings of anger cannot be denied or ignored, not even when they do not impel violent acts. Jesus summoned his followers to take practical steps to address the underlying difficulties that provoked their anger in the first place. Thus, a man should deal with anger toward a brother by reaching out to that brother and seeking to resolve the issues that made him angry (Matt. 5:21–26). Jesus further insisted that no one should offer a gift at the altar of the Lord if a brother has something against him. He must first be reconciled to that brother and then offer his gift (Matt. 5:23–24). Constructively addressing our conflicts with others is a prerequisite for ritual observances that authentically express our faith commitments. Similarly, Jesus urged his followers to "make friends quickly with your accuser" while going with him to court, lest he should hand you over to the judge, and the judge should hand you over to the guard who would put you in prison and refuse to release you until you have paid the "very last copper" (Matt. 5:25–26). In this example, Jesus appears to offer prudent counsel on ways to protect one's own self-interests. At the same time, responsiveness to a fellow human being remains central. The summons is not simply to seek an out-of-court settlement for addressing the complaint; it is to *make friends with your accuser.*[12]

In the Sermon on the Mount, Jesus emphasized initiatives for resolving interpersonal conflicts. At the same time, both Matthew and Luke record Jesus's public acknowledgment that the prophetic substance of his mission was actually causing serious divisions in Galilean households and villages. He made clear, moreover, that he had not come to bring peace on earth but rather division, largely because of his commitment to form a more inclusive family of God (cf. Matt. 10:34–38; Luke 12:49–53). He was even more determined to disclose the hypocritical practices of Pharisees and Temple authorities, testimonies that provoked their relentless efforts to secure his death (cf. Matt. 23:23–39, 24:9–14; Luke 11:42–52, 20:41–48). Jesus eloquently described the prophetic calling. It is about disclosing unjust and deceitful practices that have been hidden or concealed (Matt. 10:26–28; Luke 12:2–3). Nonetheless, Jesus's ultimate goal was to secure peace, which requires persistent efforts to address a wide array of intense, divisive, and potentially violent human conflicts. His central message is that we must not ignore or deny the possibilities for serious harm that are generated by broken human relationships. When we fail to address such possibilities, we display indifference toward the command that prohibits killing. While positive outcomes cannot be guaranteed, becoming a new people of God entails persistent commitments to this vitally important task.

The next example Jesus discusses builds on the commandment "You shall not commit adultery." Jesus contended that traditional understandings of this commandment did not suffice because they limited its application to explicit acts of adultery. They did not take account of the fact that a man who looks on a woman as a potential source of sexual gratification has already committed adultery with her in his heart (Matt. 5:27–30). This passage does not offer a general characterization of sexual desire. It describes a particular way of looking at a woman. The key phrase in the passage, *pros to epithymesai*, designates a look specifically formed by sexual desire. When a man gazes on a woman lustfully, he is looking at her as a sexual object that essentially exists for his pleasure, thereby demeaning and trivializing her.[13] Such lust does not only give rise to marital infidelity; it can also lead to rape, to various forms of sexual abuse, and more generally, to inappropriate sexual advances. Moves of the latter sort can be especially harmful when they are initiated by persons in positions of power or authority toward those who are accountable to them, for example, managers toward employees, professionals toward clients, teachers toward students, or adults in general toward children and adolescent youth.

The seriousness of these issues is reflected in the jolting images that Jesus used in specifying transformative initiatives. A man who looks lustfully on a woman should pluck out the offending eye. If he improperly touches her body, he must cut off the offending hand (Matt. 5:29–30; cf. Mark 9:43–48). Given that the classic legal penalty for adultery and also for incest was death by stoning (Lev. 20:10–17), should we take Jesus's words literally? The larger context of the Sermon on the Mount rules out such a reading. Jesus was not proposing a new set of penal procedures. Using hyperbolic metaphors, he was suggesting forceful initiatives by individuals to take personal responsibility for their own impulses and dispositions. The challenge is to discern concretely what it might mean to pluck out an eye or to cut off a hand. The basic task is to remove conditions that make inappropriate acts possible in the first place. Any man who realizes that he is looking at a woman with lust must simply stop looking at her as though she were a potential sexual object. He must fundamentally change his typical ways of relating to her and treat her with respect, thereby restoring any future interactions to a proper frame of reference. Likewise, a man who touches a woman inappropriately must simply stop touching her. In general, he must consistently maintain a certain physical distance from her. His sexual desires may not wholly disappear as a result of these changes, but he can at least modify the circumstances and the patterns of relating that have improperly unleashed those desires in the first place. Transformative initiatives of this kind are relevant for all conscientious human attempts to constrain harmful expressions of sexual desire, especially those that are potentially abusive or exploitative in their impact. Contemporary policies aimed at reducing sexual misconduct, whether in the workplace or in contexts of pastoral ministry, focus precisely on eliminating inappropriate patterns of human interaction, especially between persons in positions of authority and those who are accountable to them. These strategies amount to "transformative initiatives" that can potentially enable us to embrace the law in our hearts, enhancing our commitments to fulfill the law and the prophets in our ongoing life practices.

Jesus does not offer any systematic overview of human sexuality or of sexual ethics. He says nothing, for example, about a woman who self-consciously strives to stimulate a man's sexual desires nor about adults who look lustfully on children or adolescents in their care. Likewise, he gives no attention to the positive role that sexual desires can play in fostering deep bonds between married couples, giving vitality to their enduring mutual commitments. When Jesus's disciples raised concerns about the prudence of marriage, his response suggested indirectly that marriage was an important means for restraining inappropriate sexual activity. He apparently expected his own disciples to uphold his commitment to a celibate life, yet he acknowledged that not all men would be capable of maintaining that standard (Matt. 19:10–12; cf. 1 Cor. 7:9). Even the procreative purpose of sexual activity received only indirect attention in Jesus's warm responses to children. Similarly, Jesus says nothing about sexual orientation, nor are there any indications that contemporary discussions of homosexuality played any role in the public discourses of the first-century Palestinian world. It is important to recognize, therefore, that issues specifically discussed by Jesus in biblical accounts of his teachings must not be taken as indications of the full scope of the law and the prophets in their bearing on faithful living. What Jesus offered was rather a model, a way of thinking about fundamental moral issues. He was inviting his followers to undertake innovative thinking of this kind in their own personal reflections on the enduring authority of the law and the prophets.

In Matthew's account of Jesus's discussion of adultery, Jesus did concede a man's right to give his wife a certificate of divorce on grounds of unchastity (Matt. 5:23, cf. 19:9; Deut. 24:1–4), a concession that is not recorded in Mark or Luke (Mark 10:1–12; Luke 16:18). There are no references to a woman's right to divorce her husband. In this respect, Jesus is portrayed as a vigorous defender of classic teachings on marriage and divorce. What is surprising is the absence of any references to efforts to resolve marital problems, efforts that might parallel his counsel on conflict resolution between estranged brothers. Likewise, Jesus's counsel about confronting a brother for harm he has caused would be applicable to the case of a woman who had been abused by her husband. If the husband was unwilling to change his behavior, might not the gathered community, whether a synagogue or a church, be justified in authorizing a divorce so that she could push the abusive husband aside? Here too Jesus's discussion remains focused on particular issues, though his larger model provides openings for further reflection on a broad array of moral concerns. Matters he did not specifically address are by no means off limits.

Jesus then discussed the prohibition of false swearing and the mandate to perform before the Lord what one has sworn to do (cf. Lev. 19:12; Num. 30:2; Deut. 23:21; cf. also Matt. 23:16–22). Traditional teaching was intended to restrain human temptations to deceit and falsehood by requiring individuals to take formal public oaths in which they swear to tell the truth or to fulfill a pledge. By swearing, they appealed to some ultimate source of meaning or value that undergirded their fundamental life commitments, and they made themselves accountable for maintaining those commitments. Jesus's message is that swearing does not in any way add to the credibility of our declarations, whether we swear by heaven, by earth, by Jerusalem, or by our own heads. If truthfulness is not integral to our own sense of who we are as human beings, then we cannot be trusted to tell the truth even when we formally take an oath of some kind. Indeed, Jesus suggested that by taking oaths we disclose our lack of truthfulness. To paraphrase Paul, the commandment that promises life proves to be death for us, for sin, "finding opportunity in the commandment," deceives us and destroys us (Rom. 7:10–11). Jesus did not call for the prohibition of all oaths and vows. His purpose was to stress the fundamental urgency of truthfulness. The transformative initiative to which Jesus calls us is that we should simply speak the truth, letting our yes be yes and our no be no. Anything more, Jesus adds, simply comes from evil (Matt. 5:33–37).

Jesus then addressed the long-standing principle of *lex talionis*, that is, the "law of retribution." In ancient Israel, the family head or the head of an extended family was normally obliged to retaliate against anyone who had injured or harmed a family member (Lev. 25:48–49). Those who inflicted harm were to be held accountable for their deeds, and the punishments imposed on them were to be proportionate to the wrong done. The standard of proportionate punishment was subsequently incorporated into penal codes that regulated judicial processes (Exod. 21:12–36; Lev. 24:13–23). The purpose of *lex talionis* was both to constrain criminal behavior and to ensure "just retribution" for crimes committed: "life for life, eye for eye, tooth for tooth, hand for hand, foot for foot, burn for burn, wound for wound, stripe for stripe" (Exod. 21:23). Apart from the death penalty, this standard normally did not require penalties that literally replicated the harm done. The challenge was to discern a penalty that was equivalent to such harm in its impact on the life of the person who had caused it.

The concrete import of the examples cited by Jesus are by no means self-evident: being struck on the right cheek, being sued for one's coat, being forced to go one mile, dealing with a beggar asking for aid or urgently seeking a loan (Matt. 5:38–42). None of these examples unequivocally qualifies as a criminal act. To strike someone on the right cheek could be an assault, yet the reference to the right cheek suggests a rebuke that someone in authority inflicts on a person who has behaved improperly. Thus, it might be an acceptable form of discipline for human misconduct. The person rebuked could, of course, experience the act as a form of "persecution" for conscientiously held beliefs or for practices that were maintained with integrity. Similarly, a lawsuit demanding a person's coat might be spurious, yet it could have legitimate moral and legal grounds. In the latter case, the proper response would essentially be the same as the one Jesus had already specified: "Make friends quickly with your accuser" (Matt. 5:25). Yet Jesus's reference to suing someone for a coat suggests legal action against a person with virtually no resources, someone who would be extremely vulnerable with the loss of a coat, especially during cold weather. Being forced to go one mile could refer to a demand imposed by a person in authority for the performance of some kind of public service, for example, carrying mail or transporting military supplies. For residents of a vassal state under imperial dominion, cooperation in cases of this kind would normally be recognized as both appropriate and prudent.[14] The final examples do not have any manifest relation to traditional teachings on retribution, though the reference to needy persons begging for donations does suggest desperate circumstances. In general, the examples cited by Jesus appear to reflect social and political arrangements that prevailed in the Palestinian region under Roman rule. In this respect, they involved practices that might have been personally demeaning, even abusive, but that would not necessarily have been classified as crimes. The crucial point is that Jesus concluded his discussion of the law of retribution by summoning his followers to love both their enemies and those who persecute them.

With regard to the law of retribution, the transformative initiative urged by Jesus is usually translated as "Do not resist one who is evil" (RSV). This translation conveys the practical wisdom of prudently accommodating prevailing social conditions. For the bulk of Jesus's followers, such a stance would probably have been viewed as the only realistic option. The faithful were, of course, sustained by hope that the "evil ones" would ultimately be held accountable for their wrongdoing. At the same time, the Gospels make clear that Jesus boldly stood up to persons in power, especially Temple priests and scribes, who in his judgment were implicated in evil. Stassen and Gushee call attention to translation difficulties with this particular verse. The Greek verb for "resist," *anistenai*, can itself be translated as "retaliate." Indeed, *anistenai* is the term normally used in the Septuagint to translate the Hebrew verb for "retaliate." Thus, Jesus's message was not "do not resist" but rather "do not retaliate." Second, the Greek word that is usually translated as "evil," *to ponero*, is itself ambiguous. It can refer either to "evil means" or to an "evil person." Taking into account the triadic structure of Jesus's teachings, the translations suggested by Stassen and Gushee are quite persuasive: "Do not retaliate or resist violently or revengefully by evil means."[15]

The underlying difficulty with retaliatory practices is the fact that they are commonly ineffective in resolving the problems they are supposed to address. Instead of giving people incentives to stop performing harmful acts, they frequently unleash continuing cycles of conflict, making matters worse than they were before. Thus, Jesus was urging transformative initiatives that could potentially open possibilities for reconstructing flawed social practices in healing ways. If someone strikes you on the right cheek, turn the other cheek as well. This response would create an awkward situation for a right-handed person, for he would normally deliver a rebuke with the back of his hand. By turning your cheek, you deliver a challenge in return, though without committing any wrong. If someone sues you for your coat, then offer your cloak as well. In giving up your cloak, you might be stripped naked, an awkward circumstance that would dramatize the excessive action of the one who demanded the coat. If you are forced to go one mile as a burden bearer for someone who wields power over you, offer to go a second mile. While this action might appear generous, it could violate established procedures, thereby creating a problem for the one who imposed the demand. The summons to give to those who beg and lend to those who borrow reinforces Jesus's call to include the vulnerable (Matt. 5:38–42; cf. Isa. 50:4–9).[16]

The central message is that Jesus was urging his followers to claim their dignity by taking initiatives of their own, initiatives that presented a moral challenge to those who abused them or made excessive demands of them. He repudiated retaliation unequivocally, even just retaliation, because retaliation normally does little more than provoke further cycles of violence. Jesus called instead for a witness that would break this cycle. The point was not simply to submit to ruling powers but to expose their unjust practices, speaking the truth boldly and without fear. The ideal outcome would be a process of reconciliation that could lead to fundamental changes in well-established patterns of social interaction, a social equivalent to the efforts of brothers to resolve their conflicts in a peaceful manner. Even in the worst-case scenario, the prophetic calling would have been fulfilled, for what was hidden would have been revealed and what was concealed would have been uncovered (cf. Matt. 10:26–27; Luke 12:2–3). Jesus reminded his followers, moreover, that they had nothing to fear even from those who could kill the body, for thereafter, there would be nothing more that they could do.

Jesus concluded his discussion of human relationships by directing attention to enemies and persecutors. With regard to enemies, he cites the traditional teaching as "Love your neighbor and hate your enemy" (Matt. 5:43). The Old Testament contains no such statement. Was such a view circulated in the first-century Palestinian world? The Dead Sea Scrolls contain a text that admonishes the faithful to "love all the sons of light, each according to his lot among the council of God, but to hate all the sons of darkness, each according to his guilt in the vengeance of God."[17] Sons of light and sons of darkness are not the same as neighbors and enemies, yet this text does suggest that ideas similar to those Jesus called into question were discussed in the first-century Palestinian world. Jesus called on his followers not simply to love their neighbors but to love their enemies as well and to pray for those who persecuted them. Luke's version elaborates the central idea: "Love your enemies, do good to those who hate you, bless those who curse you, pray for those who abuse you" (Luke 6:27–28; Matt. 5:43–44; cf. Rom. 12:20–21). By such love, Jesus declared, we become sons (and daughters) of our Father who is in heaven, for he causes the sun to rise on the evil and on the good and sends rain on the just and the unjust.[18] If we only love those who love us, do good to those who do good to us, lend to those from whom we hope to receive, and salute our own brethren, then our actions are no different from the typical practices of sinners everywhere. Jesus set a radically higher standard for his followers (Matt. 5:45–47; Luke 6:32–36).

Jesus's discussion of anger and personal insults moved incrementally from addressing broken relationships with brothers to seeking reconciliation with accusers, to venturing transformative initiatives toward those who harm or abuse us, and finally to responding compassionately even to our enemies and persecutors. If we are to fulfill the commandment that prohibits killing, we must be prepared to reach out to others, even our enemies, and to work toward harmonious relationships with all of our fellow human beings, including those who have threatened or abused us in some manner. Otherwise, we will simply continue to participate in routinized patterns of violence and oppression that are themselves driven by anger and hatred. In the midst of a world of endless conflict, Jesus calls us to become peacemakers. "Blessed are the peacemakers," he declared to those gathered around him, "for they shall be called the sons [and daughters] of God" (cf. Matt. 5:9). How then shall we fulfill the instructions of the law and the prophets regarding killing, deceit, and acts of violence? We must ourselves become peacemakers. It is hardly surprising that Jesus's vision of peacemaking has fostered strategies of nonviolent resistance to oppressive social structures. Both Nelson Mandela in South Africa and Martin Luther King Jr. in the civil rights movement embodied this vision in their struggles for freedom, and Mahatma Gandhi provided a Buddhist example. Equally important, this vision has inspired attempts to reconcile parties long divided by extreme enmity and hatred. Commitments to "restorative justice," that is, attempts to compensate for past wrongs, have often been crucial components of these undertakings.[19] Drawing on Jesus's teachings in the Sermon on the Mount, Glen Stassen has promoted practical and realistic commitments to "just peace-making," calling for creative initiatives that can enable us to move beyond impulsive commitments to war in responding to deep-seated international conflicts or violent clashes between rival religious and ethnic parties. Stassen's vision is not an unqualified commitment to pacifism. He recognizes that resort to military force, even to war, may at times be necessary in order to prevent greater harm to vulnerable people. At the same time, the process of "just peacemaking" outlines concrete measures that can increase our chances of making sure that war is at least a last resort. It also provides a fruitful model for just postwar peacemaking, that is, strategies aimed at addressing underlying conflicts that initially provoked military action after war has come to an end.[20]

In the next section of the Sermon on the Mount, Jesus challenges both public displays of piety and virtue and the accumulation of earthly treasures (Matt. 6:1–7:6). He provides multiple examples of the former: giving alms with a sounding trumpet, praying in public places, offering lengthy prayers filled with empty phrases, and presenting a dismal appearance while fasting (Matt. 6:1–18). Almsgiving, public prayers, and fasting were practices well-grounded in traditional teachings. Indeed, individuals who conscientiously observed these practices could have claimed that they were honoring Jesus's own summons: "Let your light shine before your fellow human beings that they may see your good works and give glorify to your Father who is in heaven" (Matt. 5:16, author paraphrase). Yet Jesus characterized their behavior as a hypocritical attempt to gain recognition, honor, and esteem. In effect, they were taking the Lord's name in vain (Exod. 20:7; Deut. 5:11). These teachings are extensively elaborated in Jesus's woes against the Pharisees and scribes (Matt. 23; cf. Luke 11:39–52, 20:45–47; cf. Mark 12:37–40). Jesus did acknowledge that scribes and Pharisees sat on Moses's seat, so he counseled his followers to "practice and observe whatever they tell you, but not what they do," for "they preach, but do not practice"; "they do all of their deeds to be seen by men"; "they love the place of honor at feasts," "the best seats in the synagogues," and "salutations in market places" (Matt. 23:2–3, 5–7). Jesus advised his followers to give alms, to pray, and to fast in secret, counsel that reinforced his earlier comments about appropriate forms of prayer (Matt. 6:5–15).

Those who seek public attention for their piety and virtue invariably become judgmental toward others, even when their own behavior is worse. In Jesus's words, they see the speck in the eye of a brother but fail to see the log in their own eyes (Matt. 7:1–5; cf. Luke 6:37–42). To address these tendencies, Jesus urged his followers to begin by removing the logs from their own eyes. They would then be able to see more clearly how to take the speck out of a brother's eye. The eye is the lamp of the body, Jesus observed. If the eye is sound, the body will be full of light; if the eye is not sound, the whole body will be immersed in darkness. Jesus warned of false prophets in sheep's clothing who are actually ravenous wolves preying on others (Matt. 7:15–16; cf. Matt. 7:21–23; Luke 11:33–36). Prophetic pretenders, he insisted, gain no standing simply by calling on the name of the Lord. They must do the will of the Father who is in heaven (Matt. 7:21–22).

In a similar manner, Jesus challenged human preoccupations with accumulating earthly possessions. Such endeavors do not simply disclose human greed; at a deeper level, they amount to idolatry. It is not possible, Jesus observed, to serve God and mammon. Where your treasure is, Jesus declared, there will your heart be also (Matt. 6:19–21, 24, 12:13–21). In Luke's Gospel, Jesus reinforced this point by telling the parable of the rich fool. Relishing an abundant harvest, a rich man planned to tear down his barns and build larger ones for storing his crops. He could then say to himself, "Soul, you have ample goods laid up for many years; take your ease, eat, drink, be merry." But God said to the man, "You foolish man! This night your soul shall be required of you." So it is, Jesus concluded, for those who lay up treasures for themselves and are not rich toward God (Luke 12:13–21). Jesus called on his followers to lay up treasures in heaven, trusting God to provide for their earthly needs: food, water, clothing (Matt. 6:25–34). They should ask, seek, and knock, for "everyone who asks receives, and he who seeks finds, and to him who knocks it will be opened." He added that the Father knows how to give good gifts to those who ask (Matt. 7:7–8, 11; cf. Luke 11:9–13). In discussing these matters, Jesus said nothing about human obligations to work in order to provide for basic needs, a point that Paul emphasized during his gentile mission. Jesus's insistence on total trust in the heavenly Father reflected the counsel he gave his disciples when he sent them forth to advance his mission. In the setting of the Galilean mission, he instructed his disciples to take nothing as they traveled, relying for their subsistence on households that received them. The crucial message is that we should seek first the kingdom of the Father and his righteousness, trusting that our essential bodily needs will be met.

Jesus's concluding words in the Sermon on the Mount centered on the fundamental choice that he presented to those gathered to hear him: the narrow and demanding way that leads to life or the wide and easy way that leads to destruction. Jesus conveyed the urgency of this choice with a parable. Those who hear and follow his words are like the wise man who built his house on a rock; those who hear his words but do not follow them are like the foolish man who built his house on the sand. When heavy rains, winds, and floods came, the wise man's house withstood the assault, while the foolish man's house fell, and great was the fall of it (Matt. 7:24–27; cf. Luke 6:46–49). The parable emphasizes two key principles: (1) Jesus addresses human beings who are capable of exercising discriminating personal judgments and of making free choices about the meaning and purpose of their lives, and (2) states of honor and shame that accompany basic life choices are themselves intrinsic to the ways of living that derive from those choices. In regard to the first principle, God does not exercise complete and total control over everything that happens. God rather empowers us as creatures made in his image to take personal responsibility for our own lives. In regard to the second principle, the honor or shame that ultimately accompanies our life choices does not derive from extrinsic rewards or penalties that God imposes on us by employing his sovereign power. They disclose states of mind that are ingredient in the ways of life that are formed by our choices. Our lives do remain finite and limited, and because God does sustain free space for relatively independent human initiatives, we do have to cope with the destructive impact of perverse human choices and with systemic patterns of evil that invariably pervade human societies. Consequently, even choices that are profoundly wise can and do make us vulnerable to the powers of evil, at least within the limits of the present age. Yet the sufferings we endure when we challenge the powers of evil can themselves become blessings, for we will know that we have done what is right.

Jesus's Sermon on the Mount is thus congruent with Deuteronomy's repeated declarations of the Lord's steadfast love for the people of Israel and the corresponding summons to the people to love the Lord in return. In contrast to Deuteronomy, Jesus did not give priority to the challenges of displaying the pertinence of these teachings for an established form of social and political order. To be sure, he did acknowledge Caesar's dominion, and he displayed respect for Pharisees, scribes, and Temple priests even though he called them to account for abusing privileges associated with their offices. Nevertheless, his primary focus was to generate a grassroots movement devoted to renewing and transforming Israel's formative traditions in ways that would enable people to orient their lives toward God's ultimate redemptive purposes. In important respects, this movement embodied Israel's prophetic legacy, revealing what had been hidden and uncovering what was concealed. Equipping people to become active participants in a movement of this kind required attention to the underlying moral and spiritual substance of the law and the prophets, potentially transforming human lives and interpersonal relationships. Only through such processes could people comprehend the full significance of the love commands, commands that embrace not simply love for God and for neighbors and strangers, but also love for enemies and prosecutors. Such love finds expression in concrete initiatives to address and to resolve deep-seated divisions and conflicts among human beings. The implication is that authentic social change requires active participation in social movements that bear promises of healing and renewal in the lives of people. Jesus recognized that his followers would face persecution and hardship, but he summoned them to live truthfully and uphold their life commitments despite the hardships they might endure. He reminds us that self-righteous arrogance and material wealth do not contribute to our quest for human dignity and worth. On the contrary, they distort and corrupt our lives, undermining our prospects for an authentic sense of wholeness. He calls us to place our trust in the gracious love of the heavenly Father, who knows what we need and how to give good gifts to his children.

Notes

1. The reference in Exodus is to Mount Sinai (Exod. 19–20). Biblical scholars have traced the origins of the book of Deuteronomy to the northern kingdom of Israel, before its destruction by the Assyrians. Deuteronomy links a ceremony of covenant renewal to Mount Gerizim and Mount Ebal, both of which overlooked the city of Schechem, the locus of a northern Israelite shrine (Deut. 11:26–32). Deuteronomy also provides an account of the covenant process that reflects Assyrian diplomatic treaties, most notably in an extended list of curses that would befall a disobedient people (Deut. 27:15–26). Likewise, Deuteronomy condemns pagan practices that had been prevalent in northern Israel, in particular, the worship of Baal of Peor (Deut. 4:3; cf. Num. 25:1–13). Cf. Norman Gottwald, *The Hebrew Bible: A Socio-Literary Introduction* (Philadelphia: Fortress Press, 2002); Walter Brueggemann, *An Introduction to the Old Testament: The Canon and Christian Imagination* (Louisville, KY: Westminster John Knox Press, 2003); and John J. Collins, *Introduction to the Hebrew Bible* (Minneapolis: Augsburg Fortress, 2004).

2. Carolyn Sharp has directed attention to substantive links between Deuteronomy and Jeremiah in her book *Prophecy and Ideology in Jeremiah: Struggles for Authority in the Deutero-Jeremianic Prose* (London: T&T Clark, 2003). It is noteworthy that Isaiah delivered a similar message, declaring the Lord's dismay that his people would come before him "with their mouths" and honor him "with their lips" while their hearts remained far removed. In effect, the people turned their acts of worship into nothing more than rote performances (Isa. 29:13).

3. References to the Sabbath in Exodus explicitly cite the text in Genesis that reports the Lord's day of rest following the completion of creation (Exod. 20:8–11, 31:12–17; cf. Gen. 2:1–3).

4. There are exceptions to the death penalty. An engaged woman raped in open country whose cries for help could not be heard would not be punished, although her male rapist would be slain (Deut. 22:25–27). Likewise, a man who seizes a virgin who is not engaged will not be slain. Instead, he must pay a penalty to the father and then take the woman as his wife, and he will not be permitted to divorce her as long as he lives (Deut. 22:28–29).

5. Deuteronomy refers to the Temple as the "Place." Though it reflects a period in history when the Temple was a central institution in the kingdom of Judah, it seeks to portray that period from the perspective of the Mosaic legacy when a Temple did not yet exist. Thus, Moses anticipated the future establishment of a "place" for the sacral practices of the people, a future that was realized when King Solomon constructed the Temple (1 Kings 8–9).

6. The Gospel of Matthew contains only three terms to describe the command to love God: we must love God with heart (*kardia*), soul (*psuche*), and mind (*dianoia*). Matthew omits the term for strength (*ischuos*), which is contained in both Mark (12:29–30) and Luke (10:27). Luke places Jesus's discussion of the

love commands in the context of his journey toward Jerusalem. It names a "lawyer" as the one who put Jesus to the test (Luke 10:25). This exchange set the stage for Jesus's parable of the Good Samaritan.

7. K. C. Hanson, "How Honorable! How Shameful! A Cultural Analysis of Matthew's Makarisms and Reproaches," *Semeia* 68 (1996): 83. For a succinct description of the social and cultural implications of honor and shame in the context of the first-century Mediterranean world, see Bruce J. Malina and Richard L. Rohrbaugh, *Social Science Commentary on the Synoptic Gospels* (Minneapolis: Fortress Press, 2003), 369–70. Christina McRorie, one of my former students, directed my attention to these resources.

8. There are no references to woes or shame in the Sermon on the Mount, though these declarations are central to Jesus's final challenges to scribes and Pharisees in Jerusalem (Matt. 23). He charges them with hypocritically portraying themselves as righteous while inside they are full of iniquity. They neglect weightier matters of the law—justice, mercy, and faith—and they persecute prophets, a message common to the Synoptic Gospels.

9. Glen Stassen and David Gushee provide charts that display parallels between the beatitudes in the Sermon on the Mount, prophetic teachings in the book of Isaiah, and portraits of faithfulness in the letters of Paul. Cf. Glen Stassen and David Gushee, *Kingdom Ethics: Following Jesus in Contemporary Society* (Downers Grove, IL: InterVarsity Press, 2005), 35, 48–49.

10. Cf. Joseph Fitzmyer, *The Gospel According to Luke, X–XIV. The Anchor Bible* (New York: Doubleday, 1985), 118.

11. These triads have been elaborated in relation to a wide range of contemporary issues in Stassen and Gushee, *Kingdom Ethics*. For the basic framework, see pp. 125–48. Interpreters of the Sermon on the Mount have typically referred not to "triads" but to "antitheses," i.e., contrasts between "traditional teaching" and Jesus's own words. The reference to "triads" emphasizes Jesus's observations about negative consequences that follow from adherence to traditional teachings. The list of triads provided by Stassen and Gushee makes clear, however, that these consequences are not always explicitly stated.

12. Matthew records a parallel case regarding a man coping with harm caused by a brother. The resolution of this conflict finally required action by a general assembly, cited as *ecclesia* in the Greek text. This term could refer to a synagogue or a church (Matt. 18:15–20; cf. Luke 17:3–4; cf. also Deut. 19:15–20; I Cor. 6:1–6; Gal. 6:1; James 5:19–20). In Luke's version of this story, the focus is on settling the complaint rather than making friends (Luke 12:57–59). In effect, Luke offers a legal version of penitence, i.e., a public acceptance of responsibility for a personal misdeed.

13. Cf. Dale C. Allison, *The Sermon on the Mount: Inspiring the Moral Imagination* (New York: Herder & Herder, 1989), 73–74. Cf. also Stassen and Gushee, *Kingdom Ethics*, 269. Dallas Willard aptly characterizes Jesus's words as referring to "the look." Cf. Dallas Willard, *The Divine Conspiracy: Rediscovering Our Hidden Life in God* (San Francisco: HarperSanFrancisco, 1998), 161. The "look" in question effectively turns a fellow human being into an object.

14. Cf. W. F. Albright and C. S. Mann, *The Anchor Bible: Matthew* (New York: Doubleday, 1971), 68–70. Cf. also Josephus, *Antiquities* (Cambridge, MA: Loeb Classical Library), 13.52.

15. Stassen and Gushee, *Kingdom Ethics*, 138. Stassen and Gushee cite Clarence Jordan, *The Substance of Faith and Other Cotton Patch Sermons*, ed. Dallas Lee (New York: Association Press, 1972), 69; John Ferguson, *The Politics of Love: The New Testament on Nonviolent Revolution* (Nyack, NY: Fellowship Publications, 1979), 4–5; Donald A. Hagner, *Matthew 1–13, Word Biblical Commentary 33A* (Waco, TX: Word, 1993), 130–31; Pinchas Lapide, *The Sermon on the Mount* (Maryknoll, NY: Orbis, 1986), 134; Willard Swartley, "War and Peace in the New Testament," in *Aufstieg und Niedergang der Romischen Welt*, ed. Wolfgang Haase (Berlin: Walther de Gruyter, 1996), 2298–408; and Walter Wink, "Beyond Just War and Pacifism: Jesus' Nonviolent Way," *Review and Expositor* 89, no. 2 (1992): 197–214.

16. Cf. Walter Wink, *Violence and Nonviolence in South Africa* (Philadelphia: New Society Publishers, 1987), 13–20; cf. also Daniel L. Buttry, *Christian Peacemaking: From Heritage to Hope* (Valley Forge, PA: Judson Press, 1994), 13–18.

17. Cited by O. J. F. Seitz, "Love Your Enemies," *NTS* 16 (1969): 44. This text is quoted by Victor Paul Furnish is his book, *The Love Command in the New Testament* (Nashville: Abingdon Press, 1972), 46–47.

18. In a similar vein, Paul spoke of how we have been reconciled to God by the death of his son even though we were enemies of God (Rom. 5:10). God's love draws us into the body of Christ, where in the power of the Spirit we are enabled to love one another (Rom. 12; 1 Cor. 12–13).

19. See Donald W. Shriver Jr., *An Ethic for Enemies: Forgiveness in Politics* (Oxford: Oxford University Press, 1995); and Lisa Cahill, *Love Your Enemies: Discipleship, Pacifism, and Just War Theory* (Minneapolis: Fortress Press, 1994).

20. Cf. Glen Stassen, *Just Peacemaking: Transforming Initiatives for Justice and Peace* (Louisville, KY: Westminster John Knox Press, 1992) and *Just Peacemaking: Ten Practices for Abolishing War* (Cleveland: Pilgrim Press, 1998); and Stassen and Gushee, *Kingdom Ethics*, sec. 3, chaps. 7 and 8, 149–93. Lisa Cahill has reinforced this vision in her book, *Love Your Enemies*, pp. 210–30, where she distinguishes between Christian perspectives that portray nonviolence as an obligatory rule and those that actively promote nonviolence as a way of discipleship. The latter stance, she suggests, is the one that accords most closely with Jesus's teachings and practices.

2

Conceptions of Love, Greek and Christian

MY TASK IS TO DISCUSS Christian love with special reference to one part of the tradition from which it develops—Plato and Aristotle. I will pursue this task by discussing a controversy about love within Christian thought. Even a sketch of this controversy will help us to appreciate more justly the role of Platonic and Aristotelian views in the formation of Christian views about love.

This description of my task, aims, and procedure already commits me to some controversial claims. I begin with a sketch of how I understand "love" for the purposes of this essay.

It would be rash to assume that the ordinary uses of the English "love" mark out a single philosophically significant genus. But since we need to start somewhere, let us assume that love for a person requires disinterested concern for the well-being of the person. I use "disinterested concern" so that it implies, in Aristotle's terms, wishing good to the person for the person's own sake, not simply for one's own sake.[1] By "concern," I mean that love for persons requires some specific mental state directed toward them. It is not simply a behavioral tendency to promote their good, nor is it just any attitude that tends to lead to actions that promote their good. The relevant mental state is concentrated specifically on their good. When I speak of "disinterested" concern, I mean that love is not to be identified with concern for the good of another person exclusively because of the causal results of benefit to the other. If, for instance, I care about you only because your good will also cause some further benefit to me or to some third person, such concern is insufficient for love of a person.

This initial description of love does not capture all common views about the extent of love:

1. According to this description, it would be self-contradictory to claim to love another person simply for one's own benefit. But—one might argue—such a claim is not self-contradictory because there are purely selfish or instrumental forms of love.
2. Mere concern for another or caring about another may be thought insufficient for love. We could show concern for someone without any further feeling of liking or any tendency to seek or to enjoy their company. But this further affective element may seem to be necessary for love.

These objections may be correct, so that our initial description of love may be in one respect too narrow and in another respect too wide. But the initial description is useful for our comparison of Greek and Christian conceptions, even if it does not exactly capture everything we might say about love of persons. If the initial description raises questions, the Greek and the Christian conceptions raise similar questions.

My initial description suggests that Greek and Christian conceptions are different accounts of the same thing. But this suggestion may be challenged. Some discussions of Christian love deliberately speak of agape rather than of love more generally.[2] One might prefer to do this if one supposed that "love," or any other English word, offers only a misleading translation of "agape," so that the outlook designated by "agape" cannot be accurately designated by any English word. Alternatively, one might contrast "agape," "eros," and "philia" by saying that they can all be rendered by "love," but they distinguish different senses of the English word. If this is the right way to relate the Greek words to the English word, we cannot say that the Greek terms mark different kinds of love that are species of a single genus. If "love" designates the genus of which the three loves are species, the genus has to be called "love" univocally; if it were not, it would not be a single genus but three different genera, and the three loves would not be species of one genus.[3] We will see later whether it is appropriate or inappropriate to treat Greek and Christian conceptions as accounts of one and the same thing or as accounts of different species of the same genus.

A further preliminary warning is necessary. In my discussions of Greek and Christian conceptions, I use "Greek" simply as an abbreviation for "Platonic and Aristotelian." If I were to survey the views of different Greek philosophers on love, I would certainly have to look beyond Plato and Aristotle, and much of what I am going to say would need to be modified. In particular, any consideration of Neoplatonic views would introduce further questions and complications. Since I restrict my discussion of Greek views to Plato and Aristotle, I do not assume that what I say about the "Greek" conception really applies to all Greek conceptions. But consideration of Plato and Aristotle may help us to understand some of the alleged contrasts between the Greek and the Christian conception. Plato provides one pole of the contrast that some critics assert between Greek eros and Christian agape.[4] Some reflection on Aristotle may cast doubt on this contrast. Though I do not think the conclusions would be different if we considered Plato rather than Aristotle, I have not argued for this claim.[5]

Not all Christian reflections on love assert a sharp contrast with the Greek. We can roughly distinguish a "moderate" tradition, which denies the sharp contrast, and a "radical" tradition, which affirms it. Moderates belong to a Scholastic tradition that runs from Aquinas to Bossuet. Radicals belong to a tradition that begins with Scotus and continues to Luther, Fénelon, Kierkegaard, and Nygren.[6] Both traditions might claim support from Augustine. I will not discuss these traditions in detail. But I will try to isolate some of the philosophical disputes that divide them, and then I will try to decide who has the better of these disputes. Though I do not claim that these different Christian views of love rest entirely on philosophical rather than theological disputes, I believe that some questions can be answered once we have made a little progress with the philosophical questions.

The radical tradition claims to find a sharp contrast because it takes the Christian conception to reject three central elements in the Greek conception: (1) Love is oriented to value because it is an attitude toward some antecedently valuable property that is already present in the beloved. (2) It is oriented to the self because friendship is founded on one's desire for one's own well-being. (3) It is selective, not directed to everyone without distinction. According to the radical tradition, the Christian conception makes love indifferent to value, indifferent to one's own well-being, and entirely nonselective.

First, I will try to explain why one might be inclined to agree with the radical tradition. Then, I will argue in favor of the moderate tradition.

Christian Asymmetry

Since it is difficult to present the main questions clearly without some reference to specific texts, I will mention a little of the evidence that Christian reflection on love needs to explain. Some elements in the Johannine doctrine of divine and human love provide a starting point.

Christian views of love need to explain the asymmetries of attitude that St. John describes in his comparison of divine and human love.[7] He advises Christians to love one another because love is from God (*ek tou Theou*, 1 John 4:7), and indeed, love is part of the divine nature. The divine love does not consist in a response to human love but in God's first loving us (1 John 4:10) and thereby making us children of God (1 John 3:1). The love of God toward human beings is not earned by human love of God. It is gratuitous insofar as "God began it himself and did not wait for us to begin to love" (Aquinas, *in Ioann.* 13, lec. 7.3). As Paul says, God establishes his love for us in the fact that Christ died for us while we were still sinners (Rom. 5:8). While ordinary human love is restricted to worthy objects (Rom. 5:7), divine love is not restricted in the same way. This love of God toward us is the reason why we ought to love one another (Rom. 4:11). The requirement (*opheilomen*, Rom. 4:11) is also presented as a command that the one who loves God should also love his brother (Rom. 4:21). Jesus presents this as a part of his new commandment "that you love one another, even as I have loved you, that you also love one another" (John 13:34).[8] The new element in this commandment is not the requirement to love one another; the Gospels never suggest elsewhere that the commandment to love one's neighbor is new. The clause "as I have loved you" introduces the new element. Jesus took the initiative in love, and so we ought also to love without waiting for someone else to take the initiative (*Catena Aurea*, ad loc.). Moreover, when Jesus returns to this command, he explains the "as" clause by saying that the greatest love is shown by laying down one's life for one's friends (John 15:13). We ought to follow this example (1 John 3:16). If we love other people, God is present in us and God's love is completed in us.[9] The basic reason for observing the command to love one another is that God's love is completed by human love. This fact gives us a reason to love if we care about completing the divine love by imitating it. This is why we love, because God first loved us.[10] But we cannot love God without also loving what God loves, and so anyone who claims to love God but does not love his brother is a liar.

The divine command to love one another does not simply require some favorable attitude to other people. We know that we love the children of God insofar as we love God and carry out his commands.[11] In this case, "commands" in the plural refers not simply to the command to love but to the more specific commands that specify the content of love for another. Love for God consists in keeping these commands (1 John 5:3). John does not say what they are; he only assures his readers that they are not heavy, because God gives us the ability to fulfill them. We have this ability because whatever is born from God has overcome the world (1 John 5:4). Elsewhere, however, John says how we fulfill the command to love by fulfilling more specific commands. We will not behave as Cain behaved toward Abel (1 John 3:11), but we will practice justice (1 John 3:10–12).[12] On this basis, we can judge that someone who is well-off and looks with indifference on a brother in need cannot have the love of God remaining in him (1 John 3:17).[13] This degree of concern for the welfare of the less well-off is taken to be a simple requirement of justice. The opposite of such concern is marked by irrational appetite and boastful arrogance (1 John 2:16).

The Greek Conception

These Johannine claims about love mark an apparent contrast with the Greek conception. A survey of the Greek conception will show how it is oriented to value, oriented to the self, and selective in its attitude to others.

It is oriented to value because it treats love as an attitude toward some antecedently valuable property that is already present in the beloved. Plato describes this property as "the beautiful" or "the fine" (*kalon*) in the beloved. Aristotle speaks of the best friendship as a relation between virtuous people, each of whom admires the character of the other. To form the appropriate sort of love, we need to recognize valuable properties in other people. These properties are not the product of love for another but starting points for love. Similarly, the fact that these properties are valuable is not a result of love but antecedent to it. If we could not grasp the relevant sort of value, we could not love the appropriate people in the appropriate way that is founded on the valuable properties.

This Greek conception of love is also oriented to the self, because friendship is founded on one's desire for one's own well-being or happiness (eudaimonia). Both Plato and Aristotle affirm that the ultimate end of rational human action is one's own happiness, and love is one of the attitudes that are justified by reference to this ultimate end. In this respect, the Platonic and Aristotelian conception of love is egoistic.

Orientation to value and to the self makes love selective in principle. If not everyone has the valuable properties that are the appropriate basis of love for others, not everyone will be loved. And if not everyone makes a difference to my happiness, because many people do not affect me at all, not everyone will be loved.

We have now said enough about the Greek conception to introduce some of the main questions about Christian love. In the light of the Johannine claims, Christian moralists examine these features of the Greek conception of love, and they ask what is wrong with the Greek conception. The moderates answer, "Nothing." The radicals answer, "Everything." According to the radicals, the three features of the Platonic and Aristotelian conception make it unfit to express a Christian view of love because the whole point of the Christian view is to repudiate and to replace any conception of love that has these features.

Our description of the Greek conception implies that the radicals interpret the Greek conception correctly if they attribute these features to it. If they are wrong, it is not because their interpretation is wrong on these points but because they are wrong to suppose that such a conception cannot be reconciled with Christian views about love.

Christian Love and Voluntarism

The first feature of the Greek conception, its orientation to value, appears to some Christian critics to be inconsistent with a Christian view. According to these critics, God "first loved us" because God does not respond to the recognition of value in the object of love but creates the value by will. Only a voluntarist conception of love does justice to the crucial difference between divine love and ordinary human love.[14] Though some types of human love begin from the recognition of value in the object of love, divine love is not confined in this way by the nature of the object.

This voluntarism about the love of God may be defended from the more general claims about divine mercy that underlie the doctrines of grace and justification.[15] God does not justify sinners because he owes them something. God's treatment of us manifests divine mercy. God's righteousness is not righteous because it responds to our goodness. Any attempt to explain divine grace as a response to the goodness of human beings would introduce a Pelagian error. John, as we have seen, emphasizes the priority of divine love. Paul emphasizes that this divine love is not determined by, and does not respond to, human merit.

If, then, we have to accept a voluntarist account of divine love, how are we to understand the command to love others as God has loved us? We might try to weaken the force of the "as" so that we take John to mean "Since God has loved us, we ought to love others," rather than "We ought to love others in the way God has loved us." If we take the first view, the character of divine love may not be the pattern for the character of human love. But if we take "as" to indicate the character of the appropriate sort of human love, we accept a voluntarist account of Christian love for other human beings. For the salient character of divine love is indifference to the value of the object. If Christian love for others retains the character of divine love, it is also indifferent.

These voluntarist claims—about divine love, Christian love for other people, or both types of love—do not require a voluntarist conception of value as a whole. We need not say that all value is the creation of will, either divine or human. We might grant that good and evil, right and wrong, are not constituted by acts of anyone's will but still affirm that love is indifferent to these features in its objects. The distinctively Christian (according to this view) conception of love does not commit us to wider claims about the relation of value to will.

Christian Love and Egoism

We can also reject egoism by appeal to divine love as the paradigm for human love. The idea that a perfect and self-sufficient God needs anything that might either motivate or justify love for human beings is difficult to make intelligible. The truth about divine love seems to be the exact opposite; Christ emptied himself in becoming human (Phil. 2:7). Saint Paul treats this aspect of divine love as an explicit pattern for Christian love (Phil. 2:6, *touto phroneite* [. . .]) and tells his readers not to pursue their own interest but the interest of others.[16] Following Moses, he expresses this indifference to his own interest in his attitude to his own people (Rom. 9:3; cf. Exod. 32:32).

This strongly anti-egoist view might be defended by reference to the voluntarist conception of Christian love. If love is indifferent to value, it should also be indifferent to the relation between love for another person and one's own interest. For a connection between that person and one's own interest would be a valuable feature of the other person, and so concern for our own interest would preclude indifference to value. The indifference to value required by Christian love requires indifference to prudential value as well as to every other sort of value.

A further argument against egoism may be derived from a distinct aspect of Christian love. If the love of God for human beings elicits a response of human love toward God, what sort of love should this be? God's supreme goodness seems to make it inappropriate to limit our love for God by consideration of our own interest. God, therefore, seems to require the sort of love that renounces self-interest.[17] That is why Augustine speaks of the love of God that goes as far as contempt for oneself. The City of God is opposed to the earthly city because in one city the love of self takes precedence, in the other the love of God.[18] If the love of God demands forgetfulness of oneself and one's own interests, the love of one's neighbor that results from the love of God is also selfless, and so it conflicts with the natural self-love of sinful human beings.

Christian Love as Nonselective

These arguments contend that Christian love has to reject the orientation to value and the orientation to the self that are characteristic of the Greek conception. They also cast doubt on the third element of the Greek conception: its selective character. If we are not constrained by the value present in other people, or by their relation to our interest, we lack two reasons for loving some people rather than others. If we are not moved by these two grounds for selection, discrimination in our love to other people would apparently be capricious. While capricious discrimination may have a place in some forms of human love, it seems inappropriate in divine love. Divine love, therefore, seems to be wholly nonselective. If God loves without regard to the value of the object loved, God seems to love all persons without distinction. God manifests this indiscriminate love in making his sun rise on the just and the unjust and in redeeming those who are still sinners. That is why God wills that all human beings be saved and come to the knowledge of truth (1 Tim. 2:3).

If we treat divine love as a pattern for Christian love among human beings, love for human beings should also be indiscriminate. While the Christian outlook need not reject selective attitudes altogether, the distinctive type of love that it requires is essentially nonselective. This is the point of the command to love our enemies and to benefit those who cannot repay us (Matt. 5:43–48). This command requires us to interpret the command to love our neighbor as ourselves in the light of an expanded conception of the neighbor who is the appropriate object of this love (Luke 10:25–37). All this may seem familiar enough to be a commonplace of Christian views about love.

Questions about Disinterested Concern

When I described love as disinterested concern for another person, I explained "disinterested" through Aristotle's conception of love (*philein*) as wishing for the good of another for the other's own sake. Though this is a plausible and, one might suppose, intuitively clear aspect of love for other people, it does not apply without controversy either to the Greek or to the Christian conception. If we explore this question a little further, it will help us to evaluate the contrasts that have been set out.

Disinterested concern may appear to conflict with the Greek conception insofar as Greek theories are egoistic and eudaimonistic. If my ultimate reasons for action have to refer to my own happiness, what I choose for its own sake is ultimately some state of myself. Hence, any concern for another is ultimately concern for myself, and so my concern for the other is always subordinate to concern for myself. Hence, apparently, it cannot be concern for others for their own sake because it is really concern for others for my sake.

A critic might infer that the Greek conception cannot explain and cannot justify love for other people for their own sake. Only the strongly anti-egoistic conception of divine and human love justifies genuine love of persons for their own sake. Someone who is willing to lay down his life for his friends cares about them for themselves and not for any further benefit that he hopes to gain from them.

But if this argument proves that disinterested love is impossible in the Greek conception, it may have proved too much. For a similar argument rules out disinterested love within the Christian conception. As I explained disinterested concern, the mere absence of self-interest does not imply disinterested concern for people. A fanatic about art might not care about the welfare of any human beings except insofar as they are needed to design and build the Parthenon. A revolutionary who hates capitalists, Muslims, or Americans might not care about the interests of people for their own sake, but he may be completely selfless in his enthusiasm for his cause. Though his attitude to other people is not self-interested, he does not display disinterested concern for others. We might say that he is concerned about them only for the sake of his greater cause.

This attitude of the fanatic or revolutionary is similar to the outlook of Christian love, according to one description of it. The Christian cares about other human beings quite selflessly, insofar as he imitates the selfless attitude of God to human beings. But one might argue that he does not care about them for their own sakes. John tells us to love other people because anyone who loves the father loves the child also (1 John 5:1). He explains that we know we love the children of God whenever we love God and fulfill his commands. If we love other people only for God's sake, and only because we seek to fulfill God's commands, God is the only being whom we love for his own sake. Love for anything or anyone else is entirely derived from our love for God.

If this description of the Christian attitude to disinterested concern is correct, the Christian critic cannot reasonably object to the Greek conception on the ground that it has no room for disinterested concern for persons in their own right; for it turns out that neither conception has room for such concern. Perhaps the idea of disinterested concern is an intuitive element of love of persons that has no place in a sound theoretical account, philosophical or theological, of the character of love.

Alternatively, we might regard the absence of disinterested concern as a flaw in both the Greek and the Christian conceptions. The belief that love of persons requires concern for them for their own sake is inseparable from the more general belief that persons matter in their own right and that their value is not merely derivative from, or instrumental to, the value of some other person or nonperson. If either the Greek or the Christian conception denies that persons deserve concern for their own sake, we have some reason to question it.

But should we concede that either conception precludes disinterested concern for persons?

Disinterested Concern in the Greek Conception

On behalf of the Greek conception, we can rely on the familiar point that not everything we choose for the sake of our own happiness is a merely instrumental means to it. We may choose some things as parts of our happiness and not simply because their causal results promote our happiness. And so the mere fact that our account of rational action is eudaimonistic does not preclude a conception of happiness that treats disinterested concern for persons as a part of our happiness.

Still, even if this argument shows that the eudaimonistic aspect of the Greek view allows disinterested concern, it does not yet prove that a true account of one's own good requires disinterested concern as a part. To prove this further point, we need to set out some plausible features of a component of happiness, and we need to argue that disinterested concern has these features.

For present purposes, we can only state Aristotle's answers to these questions, without defense or criticism. In his view, happiness consists in the activities that are essential to a rational agent. We develop and extend these activities insofar as we extend our deliberative capacity. We extend this capacity insofar as we can treat the deliberation of others as equivalent to our own. We can treat it in this way if and only if we are concerned for other people for their own sake. Hence, the disinterested concern that belongs to friendship is a part of the rational activity that constitutes one's happiness.

While many questions can be raised about this argument, it suggests that the hope of finding a place for disinterested concern within the Greek conception is not clearly misguided. We ought not to dismiss the Greek conception, therefore, on the ground that it is clearly wrong about the possibility and importance of disinterested concern.

Disinterested Concern in the Christian Conception

This argument for the possibility of disinterested concern within the Greek conception applies equally to the Christian conception. Previously, I assumed that the attitude of the Christian would be similar to the attitude of the fanatic or the revolutionary who does not care about persons for their own sake. But this assumption is unjustified. If we love God, and we love other persons for God's sake, we may still love them for their own sake. For if we love God and if God reveals to us that other people are worth loving for their own sake, love for God gives us a reason to love other people for their own sake. Our love for them, according to this view, is derived from our love for God, but we do not love them only for God's sake. On the contrary, if we imitate the love of God, we love them for their own sake for God's sake. Love of other persons is in one respect secondary to love for God, but it is not purely instrumental to love for God.

This argument shows how love of other persons for their own sake might be understood within this Christian view of love. Whether this is the right way to understand it depends on how we understand the divine love for human beings. Does God love human beings for their own sake or simply as manifestations of his wisdom and skill? A carpenter might make a table not in order to function as a table but simply as visible evidence of his skill. If he decided to make a different one that would display his skill as well or better, he would have no reason to care about the first table any longer. In that case, we might say he does not care about either table for its own sake but values them only as evidence of his skill. If this is the whole of God's attitude to human beings, neither God nor an imitator of God has any reason to care about human beings for their own sake.

The comparison with artifacts fits some biblical contexts quite well. The Flood results from God's decision to scrap his old artifacts and to start almost from scratch. He makes a similar proposal to Moses, who has to intercede for the people, just as Abraham had to intercede for Sodom and Gomorrah (Exod. 32:7–14; cf. Gen. 18:17–33). The comparison of the clay and the potter is used by both Jeremiah and Saint Paul to illustrate the complete dependence of human beings on God's choices about the sort of product he will make (Jer. 18:4–10; Rom. 9:20–23). If human beings can be replaced, and if God so readily contemplates their replacement, perhaps they do not matter to God in their own right but only as evidence of his skill. In that case, they are disposable if God is inclined to replace them with something better.

But though this inference would be easy, it would not be legitimate. For God's plans for destruction—fulfilled or unfulfilled—do not result simply from his desire for improvement or for variety. They have some punitive and retributive basis. If destruction is allowed only as a punishment for wrongdoing, God allows human beings to survive as long as they avoid wrongdoing, even if they could be replaced by something better or by something interestingly different. He therefore takes himself to have created beings who have some moral standing of their own and so are appropriate objects of concern in their own right.

We have reached this conclusion without casting any doubt on the moral legitimacy of the divine punishments that are threatened. A full treatment of these passages and of other relevant biblical evidence would recognize and exploit the fact that God does not only threaten punishment but also forgives and shows mercy. These further divine attributes strengthen the argument to show that God regards human beings as appropriate objects of concern for their own sakes. Though they depend on God for their existence, God does not assume that he is morally free to discard them in favor of something better or different. God aims to make human beings better, not to replace them with superior creatures. If they cannot legitimately be destroyed simply to suit the purposes of God, they must matter in their own right.

These fairly evident features of the Christian outlook show that it allows, and indeed affirms, love for persons that includes disinterested concern. Neither the Greek nor the Christian conception, therefore, rejects or ignores disinterested concern.

Does Christian Love Require Voluntarism?

This role for disinterested concern within the Christian conception of love casts doubt on our earlier description. We need to review the case for the radical tradition that contrasts the Christian with the Greek conception on the points we have mentioned.

What we have said about disinterested concern may count against a voluntarist interpretation of Christian love. God's attitude to human beings, as objects of punishment or mercy, presupposes that God attributes value to them in their own right. This is consistent with a voluntarist account of value, provided that we take this attribution of value to result from God's choice and not from God's recognition of the value that they possess apart from God's choice. If it results from God's choice, it should also be revocable by God's choice, without reference to whether human beings have done anything wrong. In the instances we have discussed, however, God recognizes human beings as deserving just treatment, and he does not revoke this recognition. To explain this, the voluntarist has to appeal to the difference between ordered and unqualified ("absolute") power. The noninstrumental value of human beings, therefore, is irrevocable by God's ordered power, though revocable by God's unqualified power. If we ask why God treats the fact about value as irrevocable by ordered power, we cannot give any further answer.

Does the Christian outlook require this voluntarist claim about unqualified divine power? The most general defense of voluntarism appeals to the Christian doctrine of creation. But this defense is unreliable. Though the existence of anything that instantiates value depends on God's creative will, it does not follow that the fact that it is valuable also depends on God's will. God's creative will may agree with distinct facts about value; if so, the fact that it is better to create one situation than another is not a product of God's will. The divine will that is relevant to questions about value and voluntarism is not God's creative will but God's legislative will. Acceptance of a doctrine of creation does not require voluntarism. Hence, we cannot argue that this basic Christian doctrine commits us to a voluntarist doctrine about the nature of value and about the basis of love of persons.

We might, however, argue that belief in divine sovereignty and unmerited grace requires voluntarism because they exclude any "boasting" on the basis of merit.[19] If human beings had some inherent value, not entirely dependent on the divine will, would they not deserve something that would give them a claim on God, and therefore a ground for boasting? According to this argument, we have to choose between voluntarism and some form of Pelagian error.

This argument can be resisted, however. The exclusion of boasting is the exclusion of any appeal to "works of the law." These are voluntary actions of human beings that might establish a claim based on merit. According to Pauline doctrine, no merit that results from voluntary actions can constrain divine grace. But not all value is merit that results from voluntary action. Other facts besides voluntary actions may make some sorts of treatment more appropriate than others. To say that human beings, simply by being rational agents, deserve consideration in their own right is not to say that they have done anything to merit such consideration; on the contrary, if they deserve it in their own right, it is due to them apart from what they do. And so it is not a basis for the sort of boasting that Paul excludes.

We may still not be satisfied with this way of explaining value apart from merit. The doctrine of unmerited grace rejects any claim of justice. Divine grace is gratuitous insofar as it is not required on the basis of justice. If we deserved something, even apart from any merit acquired by our actions, what we deserve would not be given to us on the basis of grace. We may still, therefore, be suspicious of any appeal to the inherent value of human beings apart from the divine will.

Such suspicion is unjustified. Inherent value is not only a basis for claims about justice but also a basis for claims about generosity. If we think people are valuable in their own right, we can argue for various sorts of treatment that may be appropriate and justified, even though they are not required by justice. When the Prodigal Son went away with his inheritance, his father had (one might argue) done for his son all that was required by justice and was not obliged to do anything more for him. Still, the son was an appropriate object for his father's generosity because he was a son. In return for injustice, either punishment or mercy is appropriate, but in either case, the value of the recipient is relevant.

And so the fact that God is merciful rather than narrowly just is not a good enough reason for voluntarism. At the very least, the central Christian doctrines that might appear to require voluntarism do not require it. Moreover, the acknowledgment of inherent value in the objects of divine justice and mercy makes it unnecessary to assume arbitrary exercises of divine unqualified power. The Christian outlook does not differ from the Greek by being committed to a voluntarist conception of value.

This conclusion makes it easier to treat divine love as a pattern for human love of God or of other human beings. If we take divine love to be independent of any value in its objects and to create value by willing it, we have to admit that human love is necessarily quite different. We do not love God without reference to his inherent goodness, and we do not create the goodness that belongs to God. Moreover, it is difficult to see why we should love other human beings in the way that God loves them; for we do not create their value, but we ought to recognize and to respond to the value that (according to the voluntarist) God has created in them by his will.[20]

Egoism and Christian Love

We found that the egoist aspects of the Greek conception are compatible with, and may even support, disinterested concern for other people. We ought not to be surprised, therefore, that Aristotle expects the best kind of friendship to encourage self-sacrifice; when someone judges it finer to die in place of his friend, that is what he will do, both out of friendship and for the sake of his own happiness (*EN* 1169a18–b2).

We cannot, therefore, appeal to Christian approval of self-sacrifice in order to show that the Christian conception is not egoistic in the way that Aristotle's eudaimonism is. Jesus's remark that the greatest love is shown in laying down one's life for one's friends does not rule out Aristotelian eudaimonism. We might even argue that eudaimonist egoism is no less central to the Christian than to the Aristotelian outlook. Jesus never discourages or attacks those who are seeking their well-being through eternal life. The story of the Good Samaritan is provoked by someone who wants to know what he has to do to inherit eternal life. Jesus tells him that if he keeps the Great Commandments, requiring the love of God and of his neighbor, he will get what he wants.[21] He assures those who lose their life for his sake and the Gospel's that they will save it. Similarly, Paul does not advise imitators of Christ to ignore their own well-being but to think of others as well as themselves.[22]

If, then, Aristotle faces some difficulty in reconciling his demand for self-sacrifice with his eudaimonist assumptions, this Christian conception of love must face the same difficulty since it accepts the same eudaimonist assumptions. We have found, however, that the alleged difficulty is not insuperable, because a eudaimonist outlook allows self-sacrifice. Similarly, the Christian conception faces no insuperable difficulty, because the basic pursuit of well-being does not necessarily conflict with the demand for self-sacrificing love.

If this is so, a defender of this Christian conception has no reason to be embarrassed by its eudaimonist aspects and no reason to suggest that they are misleading or superficial. Opponents of eudaimonism have not shown that the genuinely Christian conception is the outlook of purely self-sacrificing love without reference to one's own well-being. It would be legitimate to insist that Christianity requires an attitude that may be described as "self-sacrificing love that does not count the cost to one's own happiness." This description implies that love of other persons does not include any thought about one's own happiness. But it does not follow that someone who displays self-sacrificing love does not think of his own happiness, for even if this thought is not part of self-sacrificing love, it may be part of the thought that persuades us that we ought to practice the sort of love that does not include thought about one's happiness.[23]

This division between two roles for thought of one's happiness is familiar from mundane contexts. It may be best for me if I absorb myself in, say, playing chess or painting a picture without asking whether this is the best way to spend my life. If I am always asking this more general question, I may make my life worse by gaining less than I could gain from this activity. But the general question is appropriate on occasions when I am not engaged in an activity that demands my absorbed attention. Similarly, the appropriate sort of reflection on one's own well-being does not exclude selfless and even self-sacrificing concern.

If this is so, a defender of the Christian conception ought not to reject eudaimonism simply on the ground that it conflicts with self-sacrificial love. I have not proved that a defender of the Christian conception ought to accept eudaimonism. Perhaps eudaimonism is open to objection on grounds that I have not considered, and perhaps a eudaimonist basis for Christian love is inappropriate for reasons that I have not considered. I have considered only one objection to the reconciliation of eudaimonism with the Christian conception. Still, this objection is worth considering because some Christian critics reject eudaimonism on the ground that it is incompatible with the disinterested love of God and of other people.[24] This is an insufficient ground for rejection.

We have found no good reason, then, to contrast Christian rejection of egoism with Greek egoism. Christian sources, no less than Greek sources, take the eudaimonist starting point to be reasonable, and they do not hesitate to appeal to life after death as a basis for confidence that we will be better off through Christian belief and the corresponding action. If this unquestioning acceptance of the egoist starting point implied that self-interest is the only reason for fulfilling the law of mutual love, we might be surprised to find that Christian writers accept egoism. But since eudaimonist egoism does not require this restriction on possible motives for mutual love, it is not at all surprising if Christian writers accept both egoism and a non-self-interested motive for mutual love.

Selectivity and Christian Love

Something similar may be said about the view that Christian love is necessarily nonselective. Just as we have found in the case of egoism and self-sacrificial love, the impression of a sharp contrast between this Christian and Greek view results partly from misunderstanding.

We can identify the misunderstanding if we consider the basis of selection. The Greek conception is necessarily selective in principle because it is oriented toward value in the objects of love. Insofar as the virtuous character of a friend is a proper basis of friendship, as Aristotle argues, this type of love selects the virtuous over others. Members of a family and citizens of a state are also proper objects of the relevant type of friendship. The extent of friendship depends on the number of those who have the features that are the appropriate basis of friendship. If, as we have argued, the Christian conception of love is also oriented to value, it should in principle be selective in the same way. And this is indeed what we find in the passages that have most to say about divine and human love. Jesus speaks of laying down one's life for one's friends and speaks of his disciples as his friends, in contrast to the world. Similarly, John speaks of love for one's brothers and of mutual love within a Christian community. Paul tells his readers to do good to everyone, especially to those who belong to the household of faith.[25] Christian writers who maintain an "order of charity," and hence recognize a place for differential love, legitimately cite these passages in their support.[26]

If we thought that such remarks conflict with the clear requirements of universal love for other human beings, we might discount them as misleading but isolated distortions of the genuinely Christian view. But we have no good reason to discount them. The demand for universal love is quite compatible with a selective conception of love. Even if the principle of selection is based on value in the object of love, it still requires universal love if the appropriate value belongs to every person alike. As we have seen in discussing voluntarism, the presence of value in every person does not mean that everyone is equally good or equally meritorious in every way. Hence, the presence of one property that warrants universal love is compatible with the differential presence of properties that warrant love of some people more than others. This Christian conception is not indifferent to value; hence, it warrants differential love, based on some valuable properties, no less than it warrants universal love, based on other valuable properties. While we have good reason to say that the Christian conception requires universal love in addition to differential love, we have found no good reason to say that it requires the replacement of all differential love with universal love.

Conclusion

We began with a sharp contrast between the Christian and the Greek conception of love, in line with the radical tradition. But further examination has blurred the contrast. Attention to the Christian sources of the supposedly distinctive conception has not supported the contrast that some critics have maintained. Their belief in the contrast rests not on a clear Christian affirmation of the contrast but on the unwarranted assumption that different elements of the Greek conception are incompatible with Christian demands about love.

This is not a new conclusion. The moderate tradition in Christian reflection on love of God and human beings affirms a Christian conception that agrees with the Greek conception. This tradition emphasizes the legitimate place for concern for one's own happiness, allows some degree of selectivity in love (the "order of charity"), and takes love to be oriented to value. The radical tradition maintains that this moderate tradition takes over too much of the Greek conception without recognizing the fundamental contrast with the Christian conception. This radical tradition relies, explicitly or implicitly, on the questionable philosophical arguments that we have discussed.

I have not argued that Christians have no distinctive claims about love for God and for other people or about the specific demands of love. But I have argued that these claims do not rest on a distinctive conception of the nature of love, or of its relation to value, or of its relation to one's own happiness. On these points, we have found good reason to support the moderate tradition that sees continuity rather than contrast between the Greek and the Christian conceptions.

Notes

1. "Let loving (*philein*) be wishing to someone what one thinks to be good things, for his sake, but not for one's own, and being active, as far as one can, in doing these things." Aristotle, *Rhetoric* 1380b36–1381a1.

2. Hence, Gene Outka (*Agape* [New Haven, CT: Yale University Press, 1977], 7n) says he will use the Greek word "because it is conspicuously prevalent in the New Testament and in current usage is almost uniformly the referent for any alleged distinctiveness in Christian love."

3. See G. B. Matthews, "Senses and Kinds," *Journal of Philosophy* 69 (1972): 149–57.

4. The most familiar statement of this contrast appears in Anders Nygren, *Agape and Eros* (London: SPCK, 1953).

5. Different views on Plato are defended by G. Vlastos, "The Individual as Object of Love in Plato," in *Platonic Studies*, 2nd ed. (Princeton, NJ: Princeton University Press, 1981), chap. 1; A. W. Price, *Love and Friendship in Plato and Aristotle* (Oxford: Oxford University Press, 1989); T. H. Irwin, *Plato's Ethics* (Oxford: Oxford University Press, 1995), chap. 18.

6. Some of the relevant sources are discussed by J. Burnaby, *Amor Dei* (London: Hodder & Stoughton, 1938); M. C. D'Arcy, *The Mind and Heart of Love*, 2nd ed. (London: Faber & Faber, 1954); P. Rousselot, *Pour l'histoire du problême de l'amour au moyen age* (Münster: Aschendorff, 1933); R. A. Knox, *Enthusiasm* (Oxford: Oxford University Press, 1950).

7. "In this the love of God was made manifest among us, that God sent his only Son into the world, so that we might live through him. In this is love, not that we loved God but that he loved us and sent his Son to be the expiation for our sins. Beloved, if God so loved us, we also ought to love one another" (1 John 4:9–11).

8. The relation of the two "that" (*hina*) clauses to the "as" (*kathôs*) clause is not clear. The RSV resolves the ambiguity by placing a semicolon before "as." A similar construction (*hina . . . kathôs . . . hina*) appears in John 17:2, 21.

9. This paraphrase assumes that "*hê agapê autou*" in 1 John 4:12 is to be taken as a subjective genitive. See A. E. Brooke, *The Johannine Epistles* (Edinburgh: T&T Clark, 1912), ad loc. I normally follow his explanation of the Greek text.

10. This paraphrase takes "*agapômen*" in 1 John 4:19 to be indicative rather than subjunctive.

11. I take "*en toutô(i)*" in 1 John 5:2 to look forward and to be explained by "*hotan . . . poiômen*."

12. The relation between *agapê* and *dikaiosunê* in these verses is not clear. I have taken *dikaiosunê* to specify the demands of *agapê* more precisely and hence have rendered it as "justice." Alternatively, we might (as Brooke, in *Johannine Epistles*, does) take *dikaiosunê* to refer to righteousness very generally and take *agapê* to be more "one special form of righteousness which is in fact the basis of the whole." Brooke cites Rom. 13:9, which, however, does not tell clearly in favor of his interpretation.

13. Here "of God" is an objective genitive (Brooke, *Johannine Epistles*). The point is the same as in 1 John 5:1–2.

14. Luther states his voluntarism in a contrast between divine and human love, in *Heidelberg Disputation* §28, quoted with approval and discussed by Nygren, *Agape and Eros*, 233, 724–37.

15. "For neither is it because something is good or just that God wills it, but it is because God wills it that it is thereby good and just. For the divine will does not depend on our goodness, but our goodness depends on the divine will, and nothing is good except because God has accepted it as such." Gabriel Biel, *Canonis Missae Expositio*, ed. H. A. Oberman and W. J. Courtenay (Wiesbaden: Steiner, 1963), 1:212, Lect. 23E. See H. A. Oberman, *The Harvest of Medieval Theology* (Cambridge, MA: Harvard University Press, 1963), 96ff.

16. *mê ta heautôn hekastoi skoupountes, alla kai ta heterôn hekastoi*, Phil. 2:4. I will return to the significance of the "*kai*" later; see n. 22.

17. "These words will appear strange and even foolish to those who regard themselves as holy and who love God with a covetous love, i.e., for the sake of their own salvation and eternal rest, and for the purpose of avoiding hell, in other words: not for God's sake but for their own sake. They are the ones who babble that ordered love begins with itself and that everyone must first of all wish his own salvation and then his neighbour's as his own. . . . But as a matter of fact, to be blessed means to seek in everything God's will and his glory, and to want nothing for oneself, neither here nor in the life to come" (Luther, *Lectures on Romans*, on 9:3).

18. "And certainly this is the great difference which distinguishes the two cities of which we speak, the one being the society of the godly men, the other of the ungodly, each associated with the angels that adhere to their party, and the one guided and fashioned by love of self, the other by love of God" (Augustine, *CD* 14.13). "Two loves have made two cities; the earthly city is the product of love of self going as far as contempt for God (*amor sui usque ad contemptum Dei*), and the heavenly city is the product of the love of God going as far as contempt for self" (*CD* 14.28).

19. "Then what becomes of our boasting? It is excluded. On what principle? On the principle of works? No, but on the principle of faith. For we hold that a man is justified by faith apart from works of law" (Rom. 3:27–28).

20. This question of whether Christian love requires voluntarism is also implicit to C. K. Barrett's comment in *The Gospel According to St John* (London: SPCK, 1955), on 13:34: "The Father's love for the Son, unlike his love for sinful humanity, is not unrelated to the worth of its object." Barrett also acknowledges that love of Christians for one another is not unrelated to the worth of its objects. But he does not question the assumption expressed in "unlike . . . ."

21. And behold, a lawyer stood up to put him to the test, saying, "Teacher, what shall I do to inherit eternal life?" He said to him, "What is written in the law? How do you read?" And he answered, "You shall love the Lord your God with all your heart, and with all your soul, and with all your strength, and with all your mind; and your neighbour as yourself." And he said to him, "You have answered right; do this, and you will live" (Luke 10:25–28).

22. This is the force of "*alla kai*" in Phil. 2:4. See n. 16 above. Some manuscripts omit the "*kai*," but it is unlikely to be a later interpolation. Since the effect of the "*kai*" is to make the sentence a little irregular, one might expect an interpolator to have produced something less irregular (e.g., by inserting "*monon*" in the previous clause as well).

23. Some of the relevant points are helpfully discussed by P. Pettit and M. Smith, "Backgrounding Desire," *Philosophical Review* 99 (1990): 565–92.

24. On this dispute between Fénélon and Bossuet, see Knox, *Enthusiasm*, 271–82. The Quietist attitude to self-conscious virtue reflects a rejection of backgrounding (see n. 23).

25. Gal. 6:10 . . . *malista de pros tous oikeious tês pisteôs.* We might give "*oikeious*" a more general sense of "close," "proper," or "akin." It suggests that they are "one's own" people. E. D. Burton (*Galatians* [Edinburgh: T&T Clark, 1921], ad loc.) finds this remark difficult: "The qualification of the exhortation to do good to all men, . . . if intended as a general principle, represents a lapse from the universalistic principle of 5:13." Since Burton relies on a view that rejects any order of charity, he tries to restrict the scope of "doing good" to purely physical welfare.

26. See, e.g., Aquinas, *ST* II-II.44.8 ad 2.

3

"Repellent Text"

The Transition from Wisdom to Ethics in Augustine's *Confessions* 10

OLIVER O'DONOVAN

JAMES O'DONNELL HAS CHARACTERIZED Book 10 of the *Confessions*, with a measure of irony perhaps, as a "repellent and frustrating text."[1] The reason has to do with the book's structure: "bright mystical vision, culminating in luminous and often-quoted words . . . is suddenly derailed by an obsessive and meticulous examination of conscience." The structural difficulty is, however, also a material one. The whole character of Augustine's ethics as presented in this book is put in question for O'Donnell by the sudden transition from the luminous to the meticulous. To understand the ethics of *Confessions* 10 then (which means, as with everything ethical in Augustine, to understand how love is ordered), we must reach some understanding of the book's structure.

Great issues of interpretation in Augustine are frequently structural. Augustine was a self-conscious architect, a designer of literary structures large and small—we recall that letter giving instructions as to how *City of God* was to be organized and bound in codices. This was one of the ways in which he innovated on literary traditions of antiquity, which favored a loosely structured style of philosophical argument, either in Ciceronian dialogue form, which imitated the relaxed and digressive conversation of gentlemen at leisure, or in the probing, exploratory manner of a Plotinus. Augustine liked to think through an intellectual problem organizationally. Not that his structures are always self-evident, or even successful, but they are never insignificant or extraneous. Recent work on *de Trinitate* has underlined how profoundly expressive the structure of that work is of its Trinitarian theology.[2]

The later books of the *Confessions* pose a special problem in this regard, since the textual surface has such a high gloss of reiterative meditation that the reader's eye is quickly blinded to the structural moves that support it. Two major questions confront us directly in Book 10. One of these has to do with its position in the overall structure of the work, mediating between two unequally sized and materially contrasted blocks of material in Books 1–9 and Books 11–13. In his account of the *Confessions* in the *Retractationes*, Augustine groups Book 10 together with the first nine books, which are said to be "about me," as distinct from last three which are "about Holy Scripture" (Augustine, *Retr.* 2.6). The translator F. J. Sheed in 1944 followed this note of guidance in assigning the tenth book a title that must surely have bewildered his readers, "Concludes Augustine's Confessions."[3] At first glance, Augustine's analysis seems slightly superficial, as those retrospective comments on his earlier works could sometimes be. Book 10 looks as much like the opening of the second block as the conclusion of the first. The autobiographical narrative is suspended; the light falls on universal questions of the soul's relation to God. The "I" of Book 10 is Augustine, to be sure, but also—and with a vengeance—Everyman. Self-interrogations about why he enjoys eating, why he finds music helpful in worship, why temptations of smell are less pressing than those of other senses all present "anthropological" questions, feeling out the perplexing texture of human experience as such.

First impressions on this point are reinforced by the opening exordium. Only four of the thirteen books of the *Confessions*, all from the narrative block, lack an exordium altogether, but the nine exordia that remain are by no means equal in length and weight. The longest of them, longer even than the famous opening of Book 1, is that of Book 10. It serves two purposes, intricately woven together: it situates the book in relation to the preceding autobiography, as concerned with "what I now am" rather than "what I was" (4.6), and it poses a question about the social and pastoral value of publishing the *Confessions*. This question looks digressive when first we meet it but in fact anticipates the whole direction of the second block of the work, which will end with Augustine's earliest systematic approach to the theme of the City of God. But to render this indication less conclusive, the third longest exordium, after those of Books 10 and 1, is that of Book 11, marking another new beginning with its shift of theme to the hermeneutics of creation in Genesis 1. The "Janus-like" position of Book 10 has been the subject of a sensitive exploration by Pamela Bright,[4] and I shall not retrace that ground here, though in pursuing questions about the internal structure of the book, we cannot allow its setting in the *Confessions* to drop out of sight.

The second structural question, then, has to do with the way the book is organized internally, and it is this that attracted O'Donnell's acerbic epithet. Let us sum up what presents itself to the eye. As commonly identified, there are two major sections (the passage on the desire for happiness treated as part of the section on memory, not, as by Bright, as a separate middle section). How we describe these two sections may prejudge important questions, so let us refer to them severely by their leading Latin terms, *Memoria* and *Continentia* (*M* and *C*). *M* takes us in search of God, beginning with the material contents of the universe that declare "he made us" and proceeding to an exploration of the memory. *C*, under the guidance of the biblical text 1 John 2:16, "the lust of the flesh, the lust of the eyes, the pride of life," engages in a process of moral self-scrutiny. Each of the two sections is framed by introductory and concluding passages. The framing of *M* is so discreet that we may miss it: the exordium concluded, Augustine addresses God with a brief but striking declaration, "My love for you, Lord, is not an uncertain feeling but a matter of conscious certainty" (6.8). The meaning of "you" is then unfolded in terms of "a light, voice, odour, food, embrace of my inner man." Whereupon Augustine asks, understandably enough, What is this? And with that question, the word "love" disappears from sight and remains more or less invisible until it bursts out again dramatically at the conclusion of *M* in the famous ecstatic invocation, "Late have I loved you, beauty so old and so new!" (27.38).

The framing of *C* is more obvious. Its fronting is the passage immediately following the address to God as beauty, sharply contrasting the state of this life with full possession and articulating for the first time the famous prayer to which Pelagius took exception, "Grant what you command and command what you will" (29.40). At the far end of *C*, we have another fine rhetorical apostrophe: "Truth, when did you ever fail to walk with me, teaching me?" (40.65). A brief recapitulation of the journey of the book then leads to a concluding discussion of the "true Mediator" (43.68)—or, perhaps, "truthful," since the epithet is *verax*, not *verus*—who is both God and Man and makes atonement for sin. Provisionally, we may describe the book as composed of two long self-interrogations: a *cognitive* self-interrogation framed by an *emotional* confession of God as beauty and a *moral* self-interrogation framed by a confession of *faith* in God's truthful provision for our need. Spelled out like this, the structure of Book 10 can be seen to have a chiastic form. The cognitive substance of the first part anticipates the cognitive framework of the second; the voluntative framework of the first part anticipates the voluntative substance of the second. We shall return to this shortly.

In his *Commentary*, O'Donnell suggested that "if [the *Confessions*] were merely the story of A's ascent to God, the work could well end with 10.27.38," that is, with "Late have I loved you." It is worth asking how such a reading with such a conclusion would truncate our understanding not only of the *Confessions* as a whole, nor even of Book 10 as a whole, but of the *M* section of Book 10 in particular. *M* would then have to be read exclusively as an exercise in *negative* theology. The mind, passing upward through the things of creation and the contents of memory, would treat each in turn as a springboard to leap from, canceling out one thing after the other. That is, in fact, more or less the way O'Donnell, like others, presents it. I take his view to be that though the *Confessions* as a whole is concerned with more than Augustine's ascent to God, the first section of Book 10 is not. It revisits the vision of Ostia in Book 9. "What A. learned to do at Ostia," O'Donnell tells us, "he now *does*, in writing this text. This is no longer an account of something that happened somewhere else some time ago; the text itself becomes the ascent."

Now, there are many telling points of comparison between the *M* section and the vision at Ostia—unsurprisingly so, since a broad set of neo-Platonic metaphysical assumptions lie behind them both. But what a very different text the first section of Book 10 really is! For one thing, it goes on much longer. It is infinitely more curious about the contents of the mind and the psychology of recollection. It strikes a note, we must surely think, *less* existentially immediate than the narrative of Book 9. The high poetry with which it ends, far from forming a natural climax to it, seems to break in across its path—witness the sudden reappearance of the verb *amare*—intruding on what has mainly been a philosophical exploration, analytic, even scientific in character, in which Augustine has laid the groundwork for Western philosophical and psychological investigation as well as for his own epoch-making treatment of time in Book 11. Nowhere, not even in his most extended essay in psychology, *de Trinitate*, does he so effectively convey the philosophical bewilderment of the mind as it attends to its own operations. Some recent translators give Book 10 (as a whole) the heading, "Memory"; both Henry Chadwick and Maria Boulding have taken this course, followed by Philip Burton with his witty title "Remembrance of Things Present," and though one-sided, this does draw attention precisely to the features of *M* that are only remotely connected with the vision at Ostia.[5] In sum, if *M* is intended to relive the rapture of Ostia, it does so very digressively and prosily. On the other hand, how very selective an account of *M* the perspective from Ostia affords!

Let me tentatively propose a way of refocusing the question about the internal structure of Book 10. The puzzle, in my view, is not that the second half of the book follows "frustratingly" on a first half perfectly in keeping with a "bright mystical vision" of the earlier books. The real puzzle is the first half itself. Why does it take the shape it does? What service can a philosophical treatment of memory render the tenth book of the *Confessions*? Of course, it offers a reflection on the psychology of the autobiographical experiment itself. But that hardly accounts for the distinction between "what I am now" and "what I was," for the ascending pursuit of a God who remains tantalizingly out of cognitive reach, for the interest in philosophical concerns such as a priori truths, memories of past emotions, and so on. *M* stands framed by the certainties of love that dictate the ultimate direction of the journey, but its contribution seems to be a tediously negative one: the beauty so ancient and so new is present *not* as the memory's vast content of impressions and ideas is present, *not* as the mind is present to itself. Why go so far to establish so little?

Let us begin our answer with a proposition that will probably not be controversial: Book 10, taken as a whole, adopts something of a revisionist stance toward the mystical elements in the narrative block of the *Confessions*. Years ago, Professor Andrew Louth pointed out to me that the sequence of the book reverses the order in which *askesis* and ascent are arranged in Eastern Christian speculative theology of the period, in which the mind first purifies itself by moral self-interrogation, separating out the *nous* from the lower soul, and is only then ready to begin its ascending quest. The inversion of this sequence in *Confessions* 10 corresponds to the way Augustine has come to rethink the mystical project in the light of Paul's teaching on grace. Since John Burnaby highlighted this crucial development seventy years ago, much has been written about it, and we need not delay over the details.[6] It is enough to say that the second half of Book 10, the *C* section, is Augustine's first major attempt at spelling out what it means for the believer to live as the divided sinner of Romans 7, in hope of perfection but still awaiting the attainment. And that recalls the opening sentences of the book, which state, as a kind of program, "In this hope I am placing my delight when my delight is in what it ought to be" (1.1). Mystical experience is viewed from the sober perspective of one bound by the "habit," *consuetudo*, of sin.

> Sometimes you cause me to enter into an extraordinary depth of feeling marked by a strange sweetness. If it were brought to perfection in me, it would be an experience quite beyond anything in this life. But I fall back into my usual ways under my miserable burdens. I am reabsorbed by my habitual practices. I am held in their grip. I weep profusely, but still I am held. Such is the strength of the burden of habit. (40.65)

The vision of Ostia is "what I was," but this is "what I am now"—hence the importance of the concluding paragraphs of the book, with their unexpected engagement with Christ's two natures and the Paschal mystery. Christ enters precisely as God's solution for the custombound state; his death and resurrection stamp the praise and confession of the Christian pilgrim with a note of triumph not dependent on the mind's success in breaking free.

What light does this shed on *M*? The ladder of ascent is recast in terms dictated by the need to understand the Christian life as an *ethical* task. The goal of the book is set in the quotation from St. John's Gospel in the opening paragraph: "He who does the truth comes to the light" (John 3:21 at 1.1). *M* therefore takes the shape it does in order to provide a foundation for *C*. Augustine's understanding of the Christian life as lived under grace requires that Book 10 comes finally to rest in continence and in the Incarnation rather than in wisdom. But for continence to be intelligible, there must be a cognitive encounter with reality to found it on. Not an ascent to wisdom (which is why *memory* takes the part that *mind* is often assigned elsewhere, since as a capacious receptacle it reflects the universality of truth while making no proprietorial claims), but an engagement with "Truth," the summit of reality synonymous with God himself, "everywhere presiding over all who ask counsel" (26.37). Truth enters dramatically toward the climax of the ascent in *M* (23.23) and is apostrophized for the first time immediately before the great address to Beauty (26.37).

⁖ Let us recapitulate some familiar generalizations about Augustine's approach to ethics. It is marked by a recurrent polarity: on the one hand, the human agent, psychosomatically constructed, is in search of fulfilment; on the other, the *ordo rerum*, an objective structure of reality with God at its summit, demands existential conformity. Ethics is a striving for subjective completion within terms set by objective reality. This pattern appears in a variety of ways in Augustine's writings before the *Confessions*. Most common, perhaps, and most enduring—for it provides the structure for the mighty nineteenth book of *City of God*, written more than two decades later—is to begin with the desire for happiness. Uncertain of the real content of happiness, the questing soul encounters God's authoritative directions for pursuing it and finally makes the discovery that happiness is God himself or (in the mature formulations) eternal life at peace with God. A variant on this uses the terms of the twofold love command, a text of critical and distinctive importance to Augustine. We love ourselves without being told to, he often tells us, but we need instruction on *how* to do so effectively. God has given us a "rule" for self-love, which is himself as our true good, and our neighbor alongside us, our "measure." In the first book of *de doctrina Christiana*, written shortly before the *Confessions*, the order of reality is presented first. But reality is ordered in terms of its demands on us: there are things "to be loved with enjoyment" and things "to be loved with use." We are called to distinguish: "The person who lives a just and holy life is one who is a sound judge (*aestimator*) of these things."[7] But from whichever angle it is approached, there is a subjective and an objective pole to ethical normativity, and the life we are given to live with God requires the two poles to be seen as mutually elucidatory. Fulfilment *is* the reality of the God who demands all of us; the God who is the highest reality of all realities *is* the fulfilment we seek without knowing it.

Love, correspondingly, has two aspects, subjective and objective. It is seeking or striving; it is appreciating or valuing. If *Confessions* 10 with its stress on appetition and satisfaction lays greater weight on subjective striving initially, we should not miss the significance of the climax of *C*. Having dealt with the temptations of the senses, Augustine names the temptation of the soul as *curiositas*, by which he does not mean, as we might, a healthy tendency to ask questions, but the diversion of attention from things of first importance to trivialities. This leads on to the temptation of the mind, which turns out, remarkably, to be about justice. Temptation to injustice takes an unusual form. It consists of love of praise—not, since praise is a fitting response to well-doing, a love of being praised appropriately but a love of praise regardless of its proportion to our desert. We note the reappearance of the verb *aestimare* in this context. Augustine is discontent with praise, he tells us, when people "estimate at more than their true value good things which are of slight importance" (38.61). An early signal was given in the opening sentences of the book: "As to the other pleasures of life, regret at their loss should be in inverse proportion to the extent to which one weeps for losing them."

Confessions 10 moves, then, from the subjective to the objective pole of the Christian moral life. It begins with the love of God, the first subjective certainty (*certa conscientia*); it ends with the just relation of the self to the neighbor, the objective "measure" that shows up complacency. Its starting point, the "conscious certainty" of love of God, sets it apart from those other ascending arguments in the Augustinian canon whose aim is primarily apologetic. The certainties from which they begin are a priori certainties about life in the world: that we wish to be happy; that we wish to know the truth; that we, who wonder whether the world exists, exist ourselves; and so on. Love of God is the end, not the beginning of their arguments. The shape of this exploration, however, takes the narrative of grace in Books 1–9 as its presupposition. And so it requires us to qualify our initial impression that Augustine in Book 10 is Everyman. Everyman, yes, but not in the state of nature. Everyman is now downstream from his awakening to grace. Book 10 concerns "what I am now" as opposed to "what I was" (4.6). Everyman is the pilgrim soul in the wake of conversion, knowing that it loves God because God has loved it first. Everyman's question now is, how can the love of God take form in a well-ordered life?

The answer takes us first through an encounter with the order of reality reflected in the mind, second through a discipline imposed by reality on the emotions, bringing us at the end to the decisive saving reality, the Mediator between God and man. But the two major sections of the book do not simply represent the subjective and the objective poles of experience as such. That is the sequence of the two *framework* structures, love and truth. *Within* the two frameworks, chiastically organized, the first quest is for cognition, the second for emotional control. Once again, the program has, in fact, been stated in the very opening sentences of the book: "May I know you, who know me," points forward to the first section; "power of my soul, enter into it and fit it for yourself, so that you may have and hold it 'without spot or blemish,'" points forward to the second.

The "order of things" (*ordo rerum*) is the objective pole of the moral life. It is grasped at first not directly but mediated subjectively through reflections and impressions of reality seated in the memory. Through these Augustine must travel in pursuit of the God he loves, but that is not all: he must place them in their due order. Great care is taken over the order; twice after the section is apparently over, Augustine goes back to refresh our memories about it. As will tend to happen within the constraints of literary composition by dictation, the three presentations do not coincide exactly, but the changes themselves reveal something of his intention. At 25.36, the steps through the memory are identified as follows: first, "images of physical objects" shared with the beasts; second, our affections; third, "the very seat of my mind." The review at 40.65 is broadly comparable: first, the "external world . . . the life of my own body and . . . my own senses"; second, the "recesses of my memory, manifold vastnesses full of innumerable riches"; and third, "the ego (*ego ipse*), that is the power by which I was doing it (*vis mea*)."

The original sequence (6:9–16:25) had been more complex. First, there was the earth and its contents, including the physical self, the "force" that ties the soul to the body and the "force" that commands the senses, in common with the beasts. Second, there was memory, involving (i) "images"; (ii) the contents of an *interior locus*, which make up the categories of the liberal arts, the truths and laws of mathematics and reason; and (iii) the reflective memory of memory itself and of emotion, which comes complete with its own organizing categories. Augustine then retrospectively announces that this last element of the memory is the third step, the self as such (16.25). The most notable disparity is the identification of remembered affection with the self, which seems then to be contradicted in the two reviews when the agent-self is separated from the affections and other memories that "have something of myself in them." From this we conclude that what Augustine intended to emphasize was that the self, though transcending its experiences, is still the object of its own remembering. It is not immutable; it is not God. Remembered affection is one foreshadowing of the remembered self, but the capacity of the self to hold itself before its own eyes is the central core of memory, the point furthest removed from the empirical images that are drawn into the memory from outside. The key to the ascent through memory is the extraordinary phenomenon of self-objectification by which the self takes its own place as a thing among the things of the world while simultaneously contemplating itself as such. The temporal logic of this will be systematically unpacked in Book 11.

The goal of the ascent is to become clear that the self is not God but a thing within the world, an object "under" God. And that prepares the way for the *moral* self-examination and self-direction of continence. The *M* section reaches beyond the self's self-presence to the distinctive mode in which God is present to it, a fundamental categorical assumption of the memory, the undefined "happiness" that makes sense of all active life. In this way, memory represents divine transcendence, the object of striving always beyond memory while it lurks within it, which cannot be held by the memory within the focus of its eye.

The *C* section too is planned as an ascent through the order of reality, following a three-fold anthropological division, of body, soul, and spirit. First John 2:16 does not immediately suggest this interpretation, but Augustine has no hesitation in imposing it, treating "the lust of the eyes" in terms of the soul's inordinate "curiosity." The trichotomous ascending scheme—the "song of ascent," as Augustine liked to call it, with reference to the heading of certain Psalms—was a favorite of his. It is not often noticed that the well-known three goods of marriage—*proles*, *fides*, and *sacramentum*—follow this pattern (*De bono conjugali* 24.32). In interpreting these threefold schemes, one must always be aware of the ascending sequence; much trouble could have been avoided if the first of the goods of marriage had never been called the "primary" good. The climax of this sequence is "the pride of life," and it is here Augustine takes occasion to introduce justice and, with it, the neighbor.

The late appearance of the neighbor maximizes the effect when he finally does arrive. But this is not the only striking feature of the climax. At the earlier climax of the *M* section, Augustine reached the conclusion that the content of happiness was *gaudium de veritate*, delight in the truth. At that point, apparently interrupting the direction of the argument, God was apostrophized as *beauty*, an object of emotional attraction accompanied by no clear cognitive grasp. But now, at the climax of the *C* section, when Augustine has reached the conclusion that the pinnacle of self-discipline is *non complacere de se*, "not to take satisfaction in oneself," God is powerfully apostrophized as *truth*. We have already observed the chiastic organization of the book that weaves emotion and reality together into a single cord. The relation between happiness and truth having been grasped at the culmination of *M*, arrival at the truth is deferred until the culmination of *C*. And that is the very point at which the neighbor finally steps forward. The twin poles that set up the magnetic field of moral endeavor are the self, wholly present in its action, and the truth of things needed to give form and shape to that action. Moral consciousness is an exertion of the self toward its own innermost realization and, at the same time, a "seizure," as the phenomenologists like to call it, of the innermost self by God for his own objective ordering of things. The world of reality, which we have been prepared to see in terms of the created order, in terms of ourselves, even, as one among the creatures of an ordered creation, now presents us with our neighbor. He is doubly mediated to us when we finally encounter him. He is not only the provisional form of our own fulfilment until that time when we finally stand face to face with the primary object of our love, but he is the demand made on us by the Creator of a reality that is truly outside ourselves and other to us. The appearance of the neighbor, then, and with him of justice, is the climax not only of the second section of Book 10 but of the book as a whole.

The neighbor was, as we said, a striking absentee from the earlier *M* section. For commentary on this absence, there are many passages in Augustine's discussion of the twofold love command to which we might turn. One highly typical passage, which has the merit of belonging to a sermon apparently composed in 397, more or less contemporary with the *Confessions*, comes from the newly discovered Mainz collection:

> There needed to be two commands given us. One, perhaps, might have done—"You shall love your neighbour as yourself"—were it not for the danger that having first gone wrong in loving ourselves we might go wrong in loving our neighbor, too. So the Lord resolved to give you a form for your love of yourself through the love of God; and only then did he entrust you with your neighbor, to love him as yourself. (*Sermo* Mainz 40.12)

There is danger, this sermon tells us, in trying to get to neighbor love too quickly, taking it too much for granted, assuming we know just what the neighbor needs. Until we have a true sense of our own need, a developed self-awareness shaped to the love of God, we cannot be trusted with our neighbor's welfare, for we have no reliable standards by which to judge this. So there is a logic of progressing in two stages, from the love of God—"with *all* your heart, soul, mind and strength," Augustine repeatedly emphasizes—to the true love of self first and then second, by reference to love of self, to the love of the neighbor. Why was there no presence of the neighbor within the memory? It was to highlight the fulfilment of the self in God, which is the *precondition* for arranging the self alongside the neighbor in a just equality. The logic by which Augustine weaves desire and reality together in the chiastic patterns of *Confessions* 10 turns out to be precisely the logic he finds in the two commands of love presented by Jesus as the summary of all the moral law.

Notes

This essay was intended to be dedicated to the Reverend Professor Sir Henry Chadwick, KBE FBA, in gratitude for many years' contribution to scholarship on Augustine and for the supervision of my own early work on the author, but since his death in June 2008, the dedication must be *in spe resurrectionis*. Quotations from *Confessions* 10 are taken from Henry Chadwick's translation (Oxford: Oxford University Press, 1991). With this volume, I have a welcome opportunity to combine that dedication with a word of gratitude to another of my teachers with whom I learned to read Augustine. It was under the influence of Gene Outka's Princeton class in 1970 that I returned to Oxford to tell Dr. Chadwick that I wanted to understand the problem of self-love in Saint Augustine.

1. James O'Donnell, *Augustine, Sinner and Saint* (London: Profile, 2005), 36. We may justifiably read this remark in the light of the author's observation in his introduction to the book: "Bk. 10 is only scandalous to those whose view of *conf.* as a whole is partial and one-sided" (Augustine, *Confessions*, vol. 3, *Commentary, Books 8–13 and Indexes*, ed. James O'Donnell [Oxford: Oxford University Press, 1992]). The scandalized interpreters, O'Donnell tells us, are overdependent on Neoplatonic mysticism as the matrix of interpretation.

2. Luigi Gioia, *The Theological Epistemology of Augustine's "De Trinitate"* (Oxford: Oxford University Press, 2008).

3. Augustine, *Confessions*, trans. F. J. Sheed (London: Sheed & Ward, 1944).

4. Pamela Bright, "Book Ten: The Self Seeking the God Who Creates and Heals," *A Reader's Companion to Augustine's Confessions*, ed. Kim Paffenroth and Robert P. Kennedy (Louisville, KY: Westminster John Knox Press, 2003), 155–66.

5. Augustine, *Confessions*, trans. Maria Boulding (New York: New City Press, 1997); Augustine, *Confessions*, trans. and ed. Philip Burton (London: Everyman's Library, 2001).

6. John Burnaby, *Amor Dei: A Study of the Religion of St Augustine* (Eugene, OR: Wipf & Stock, 2007).

7. Augustine, *De doctrina Christiana* 1.27.59, trans. R. P. H. Green (Oxford: Oxford University Press, 1995).

4

The Desire for Happiness and the Virtues of the Will

Resolving a Paradox in Aquinas's Thought

JEAN PORTER

NEAR THE BEGINNING of the *prima secundae, secunda pars* of the *Summa theologiae*, Aquinas says that every rational agent necessarily desires and seeks his or her own happiness (*ST* I-II 5.4 *ad* 2, 5.8). This was a commonplace for Aquinas and his interlocutors, and it might seem that he only affirms it out of deference to a long-established tradition.[1] But Aquinas is very well able to distance himself from traditional claims when his overall position requires him to do so, and that is not what we see him doing here. On the contrary, he takes this claim as the starting point for the extended analysis of human actions that comprises the *secunda pars*, in accordance with the program set out in the prologue to I-II 1.6. What is more, he interprets it in terms of the metaphysical analysis sketched in the *prima pars*, in such a way as to integrate the doctrine of God with the analysis of the actions through which the rational creature returns to God—thus following the program set out at the beginning of the *Summa theologiae*, in the introduction to I 1.2. Finally, as we will see further on, Aquinas maintains this claim even though it generates internal difficulties for his overall analysis. Briefly, he says at different points that the agent necessarily aims at her own happiness in every act, and that the virtuous will, informed by justice or charity, is disposed in such a way as to aim at something beyond the agent's own good as an individual. Aquinas is the most systematic of thinkers, and even a *prima facie* inconsistency of this sort indicates that he has something of some importance at stake in these claims.

Until recently, it was hard to see what this might be. Aquinas's remarks about happiness place him at odds with a widespread modern view, associated with Kant as well as with some strands of Reformed theology, according to which the desire for happiness is at best distinct from and secondary to moral commitment, or at worst, sinful and reprehensible.[2] In this context, it has proved hard for some interpreters even to acknowledge that Aquinas says what he plainly does say about the universal desire for happiness, much less to try to understand why he says it.[3] However, recent developments in moral philosophy have opened up possibilities for a fresh appraisal of Aquinas's remarks on happiness. Specifically, there is a growing

A version of this essay, which was originally commissioned for this book, also appears in the *Journal of Moral Theology* 3, no. 1 (2013), edited by David M. Cloutier and William C. Mattison III. Reprinted by permission.

sense among our contemporaries that we have exaggerated the difference between Aristotelian and Kantian theories of morality.[4] Whatever we may say about Aristotle and Kant themselves, their followers do at least share commitments to the rationality of morality, the normative or constitutive function of practical reason, and the importance of the unity of agency as an ideal, or perhaps a precondition, for moral judgement and choice. Precisely because they share these key commitments, Aristotelian and Kantian moral philosophers have disagreed, deeply and yet fruitfully, about what each means and how they should be fitted together. But these disagreements, while deep, are not radical—on the contrary, they share common roots in very long-standing traditions of normative reflection on reason, activity, and the overall shape of one's life.

The Aristotelian Aquinas, who also anticipates some key elements of Kant's moral thought, is plainly part of this extended tradition. In common with contemporary Aristotelian and Kantian moral philosophers, he is committed to an account of moral judgement which displays its rationality, on the one hand, and its integral connection to rational agency and action on the other. Recent developments in moral philosophy open a space within which to see the point and significance of these commitments, for Aquinas himself and for moral thought generally. Seen in this light, his more specific claims about the centrality and pervasiveness of the desire for happiness make sense, and indeed, emerge as necessary elements within his overall theory. At the same time, contemporary work on practical reason offers new perspectives on these claims, suggesting a way to resolve the internal tension mentioned above. This will call on an extended interpretation that goes beyond what Aquinas says, but not in such a way as to undermine or distort the overall contours of his account.

In this paper, I will accordingly offer an analysis of Aquinas's treatment of the universal desire for happiness, focusing on his remarks in the *Summa theologiae*, within which the idea of happiness plays a central organizing role. My aims will be primarily interpretative—I hope to illuminate what Aquinas himself says, and to draw out the immediate implications of his views. The scope of this paper will not allow for a more extended examination of Aquinas's overall position and its significance for theological as well as philosophical debates. However, this paper is motivated by the conviction that Aquinas is, fundamentally, right on the key questions. His metaphysically informed analysis of the unity of agency leaves ample room for what our contemporaries call self-constitution and the determination of one's own aims, and in addition it offers what they cannot, namely, a well-grounded and systematic account of the givens, the starting points and parameters, without which practical reason could not function in a coherent way at all. What is more, he interprets the universal desire for happiness in such a way as to show that this desire is in no way contrary to Christian charity, which is oriented outwards, toward God and neighbor. Again, a defense, or even a full explication of these larger claims would go well beyond the scope of this paper, but I do hope to at least lend them plausibility by what follows.

In the first section of this paper, I will argue that Aquinas's claim that the will is necessarily oriented toward the agent's happiness follows from his overall account of the metaphysics of agency, not only human agency, but causal agency of any kind. He says that all men and women necessarily desire happiness, because otherwise, human beings would not be causal agents at all. At the same time, Aquinas interprets happiness in such a way as to identify connatural happiness with the practice of the virtues. This line of analysis implies that the universal desire for happiness is not inconsistent with virtuous dispositions, but it does not account for the distinctively other-regarding orientation that is characteristic of the virtues of the will. In the second section, I attempt to lay the groundwork for resolving this problem through an analysis of the objective and subjective components of inclination, choice, and motivation, taking advantage of recent work on practical reason, virtue, and motivation in order to draw out what I take to be implicit in Aquinas's own thought. In the third section, I will apply these distinctions to Aquinas's account of virtues of the will, in order to show how the virtuous will can be said to incline toward the agent's own perfection, understood in one sense, while genuinely desiring the good of the other for her own sake, in another sense.

Perfection, Happiness, and Virtue: Framing the Issues

In the first question of the *prima secundae*, Aquinas unequivocally says that every human being acts for some one end, toward which all his actions are directed (I-II 1.5, 6). Formally considered, this end is the same for all—namely, the individual's own perfection, or equivalently, his beatitude, or happiness (I-II 1.6, 8). This presupposes that the individual is in fact capable of acting in a characteristically human way, that is to say, rationally, implying that he is capable of directing his own activities in accordance with a reasoned idea of goodness (I-II 1,2; cf. the prologue to the *prima secundae*). It might seem that the reasonable character of human action as Aquinas understands it implies only that the agent acts in accordance with some reasoned grasp of what is good, *tout court*. But Aquinas's claim is stronger than that— every human agent acts in accordance with his best conception of his own good, understood by reference to the kind of entity he takes himself to be (I-II 1.7, II-II 25.7).

Aquinas lays out the main lines of his argument at the beginning of the *prima secundae*, in which he identifies the fundamental categories in terms of which human action is to be analyzed. Human action, we read, is a kind of activity, stemming from the causal principles proper to a creature of a specific kind, and thus intelligible as an actualization of a specific form (I-II 1.2,3, 5). This is the point behind the seemingly artless question with which the *prima secuandae* begins, namely, is it proper to the human agent to act for an end?

He responds that it is. Not only is it proper for the human agent to act for an end—every causal agent pursues an end in its proper operations, namely, the expression, development, and preservation of its form as a creature of a specific kind (I-II 1.2; cf. I 5.1, 2, 5; II-II 123.7). This is what agency most fundamentally means—the intelligible exercise of causal powers, in accordance with the principles structuring a specific kind of existence (I 77.3; I 80.1). Thus understood, agency presupposes neither sentience nor rationality—rather, the conscious activities of animals, and human action properly so called, represent distinctive ways of exercising agency in accordance with the mode of functioning proper to the creature. Human action, like every other kind of activity, thus stems from a specific form, actualizing it in some comprehensible way—if this were not so, it would make no sense to regard the putative act as an action, an intelligible expression of proper causal powers. Correlatively, to the extent that the creature actualizes the proper potentialities of its form, it is perfected, made actual, as a creature of a certain kind. Again, this is true of the human person, as much as for any other kind of creature. Thus, Aquinas can say that there is a sense in which the human creature shares the same end with all other creatures—namely, perfection, meaning the complete actualization of the potentialities proper to it as a creature of a specific kind (I-II 1.8). At the same time, the human person acts and pursues her perfection in a distinctive way, in accordance with some reasoned conception of what it is that constitutes perfection for the kind of creature that she is.

On its face, this is implausible. Does Aquinas really believe that ordinary men and women even think in terms of activity and perfection, much less direct their affairs accordingly? But he has already established that for the rational or intellectual creature, perfection is equivalent to beatitude or happiness (I 62.1). Formulated in these terms, the claim that everyone seeks perfection understood as happiness, while still controversial, is at least credible. He goes on to say that objectively considered, happiness in the fullest sense consists in the unqualified and supreme perfection brought about through union with God (I-II 2.8, 3.8). This kind of perfection exceeds the capacities of human nature, or indeed any created nature, and can only be brought about through God's direct action on the creature through grace and the conferral of glory (I-II 5.1, 5; cf. I 12.4, 62.2). But there is also a kind of perfection, complete on its own level, which is connatural to the human creature—namely, virtuous activity, sustained over the course of a lifetime (I-II 5.5; cf. I-II 65.2). Again, this is an ancient commonplace, associated above all with the Stoics. On its face, again, it seems implausible, or at best, stipulative—indeed, it often seems that no virtue goes unpunished in this world. But placed within the context of Aquinas's overall analysis, this claim offers a substantive and fruitful interpretation of connatural happiness and its relation to human perfection more generally considered. In order to see what he is driving at, we need once again to consider what is distinctive about rational functioning, seen in contrast to the modes of operation proper to other kinds of animals.

Non-rational animals are capable of perception, apprehension, and self-initiated activities. But the relevant capacities or faculties, constituting the form or soul of a given kind of living creature, are keyed to particular targets and outcomes in fairly specific ways. The animal's capacities for perception and response are structured in such a way that it apprehends specific objects as desirable and attractive, or noxious and threatening, and reacts accordingly. If all is well, these apprehensions will more or less correspond to objects and situations that are good for the animal, or potentially harmful, with little or no need or room for judgement and action in terms of general categories. In contrast, the human person characteristically judges and acts in accordance with general categories, that is to say, in accordance with reason, and it is a sign of immaturity or defect to be incapable of a reasoned spontaneity of judgement and activity. (The terms of this contrast are set out in I 83.1, I-II 6.1, 2.)

For this very reason, the faculties of the human soul stand in need of a kind of development that is unnecessary for other animals, if the individual is to be capable of functioning in accordance with distinctively human modes of operation. This development requires education and training, leading to the formation of *habitus*, that is to say, stable dispositions toward certain kinds of apprehensions and activities (I-II 49.3, 4).[5] General capacities for apprehension, concept-formation, discursive reasoning and judgement need to be developed through instruction in language, modes of inquiry, forms of reasoning and ideals of sound judgement, in order for the maturing child to begin actually to think. In much the same way, the child's natural faculties of desire and aversion stand in need of development, through which certain kinds of satisfactions and activities become salient or attractive, while others are flagged as problematic. Assuming that these dispositions are well-formed, stable, and grounded (at some point) in the agent's own reasoned reflection, these are virtues, that is to say, dispositions of intellect, passions, and will mediating between the individual's native capabilities, and the specific exercise of her faculties in particular exercises of intellect, or particular choices (I-II 55.1).

The virtues are thus actualizations of the faculties of the soul, insofar as they comprise developments of undifferentiated capacities which mediate between the unformed potential of the rational agent, and the full actualization of its capacities through active use. For example, in the process of acquiring a language, a child's capacities for speech are developed, in such a way that they can then be exercised in specific utterances, verbal comprehension, and the like. In the terms of Aquinas's metaphysics, it follows that the virtues are perfections, singly perfections of the faculties they inform, and jointly, perfections of the individual considered as an agent (I-II 55.3). The intellectual virtues perfect the agent in his distinctively human operations of inquiry, understanding, and the like (I-II 57.1). At the same time, Aquinas, in accordance with long-standing tradition, identifies the perfection of the agent above all with the operation of the moral virtues (I-II 58.1). These, the traditional cardinal virtues of practical wisdom, justice, fortitude and temperance are perfections of the agent's capacities for practical reasoning, desire and action, which shape her judgements, sensibilities, and will in such a way as to lead her to desire what is truly good, and to act accordingly (I-II 61).

This brings us back to Aquinas's claim that connatural happiness consists in the sustained practice of the virtues. Because happiness as such is equivalent to the perfection, that is to say, the full, proper, and integral development and exercise, of the rational agent's faculties, it follows that a life of virtuous activity will be in some way constitutive of, and not simply an instrumental means to, happiness. It is true that Aquinas identifies happiness in the most unrestricted sense with direct union with God in the beatific vision (I-II 2.8). Yet subjectively speaking, this vision is also a kind of sustained activity which perfects the faculties of the soul (I-II 3.1, 2). Perfection at this level is thus subjectively equivalent to the exercise of a virtue, namely the theological virtue of charity, which is brought to its fullest development through the love elicited by the beatific vision (I-II 67.6; in addition, the infused moral virtues remain as principles of operation, even though they have no scope for exercise in heaven, I-II 67.1).

Does it follow that for Aquinas, the universal desire for one's own perfection or happiness implies a universal desire to practice virtue? If only it were so—but as we all know full well, not everyone grasps the point that happiness consists in the practice of the virtues, and even those who get the general point may have a badly skewed sense of the true ideals or standards for virtuous activity (I-II 1.7, 5.8; cf. II-II 25.7). Yet even though Aquinas does not explicitly say so, his analysis implies that in a qualified sense, every developmentally normal individual can be said to aim at the sustained practice of virtues broadly so called, albeit not under that description. Keep in mind that Aquinas regards the reflectively formed *habitus* of the intellect as virtues in a broad but legitimate sense (I-II 49.3, 4; 56.3). These include the virtues of art—skills, crafts, artistic and athletic abilities, and the like—and it does not seem too much of a stretch to include as well the ensemble of social skills and capabilities employed by a good administrator, or therapist, or parent (I-II 56.3, 57.3, 4). A life of virtuous activity, comprehensively understood, is thus tantamount to a life of sustained activity, engaging the individual's capabilities in some appropriate way, in pursuit of worthwhile aims. And while this point too would be controversial, it is again at least credible that all normal persons do desire a life of sustained, fulfilling activity of this kind—which is to say, all persons desire a life of virtue, not necessarily under that description, and allowing for a broad, non-moral sense of "virtue."

At any rate, Aquinas claims that true connatural happiness is equivalent to a life of virtue properly understood, implying that happiness has a positive moral value. If this is so, then we cannot simply dismiss the desire for happiness as unworthy or selfish. Some men and women do desire selfish or distorted forms of happiness, but the desire for happiness as such is not morally problematic, and can be directed toward a praiseworthy end. Even so, we are likely to have reservations about Aquinas's claim. For one thing, it may seem that there is still something problematic about a concern for one's own virtue. We have all known people so preoccupied with their own virtue or integrity that they are prepared to sacrifice almost any advantage or interest, those of others as well as their own, in order to maintain standards of purity or rectitude. These tend not to be terribly attractive people, even though there can be something admirable in such a fierce devotion to goodness. What is more, we may well question whether this solicitude for one's own virtue is appropriate for a Christian. Is it consistent with charity, which does not seek its own advantage—even, presumably, its advantages as a moral agent (I Cor. 13.5)?

Dispositions of Desire and Descriptions of Choice

The terms of this problem presuppose an oversimplified account of desire and choice, and if we are to do justice to Aquinas's claims regarding happiness, virtue, and the aim of activity, we must find a way to reformulate the issues at stake. In order to do so, we need to move beyond the explicit terms of his analysis, in such a way as to distinguish more carefully among the different senses in which activities, objects, and states of affairs can be regarded as aims of activity. At this point, we can usefully draw on recent work on practical reason and choice, which points the way toward an expanded account of choice and its relation to aims and motivations. As I hope to show, this expanded account allows us to interpret Aquinas's claim that the perfection or happiness of the agent consists in the practice of the virtues, without implying that a virtuous agent is necessarily motivated by a concern for her own virtue. In the next section, I will draw out the implications of this line of analysis for Aquinas's account of the virtues of the will, in order to show how the inconsistency between the desire for happiness and the other-regarding orientation of justice and charity is only apparent, not real.

While this account of practical reason and choice goes beyond what Aquinas explicitly says, it relies on key elements within Aquinas's analysis of action, seen in relation to its originating principles and defining ends, and I believe that it captures his central concerns. The first such element is the most fundamental. As we have already noted, Aquinas begins the *prima secundae* with the claims that everyone necessarily acts for one final end, in accordance with some reasoned grasp of her overall good, in such a way as to direct all her actions in some way toward this end. The terms of this analysis will be unfamiliar to many readers, and so it is worth noting that Aquinas's concerns are not all that different from those motivating much recent work on practical reason and agency. If our contemporaries do not typically speak in terms of a final end, or much less interpret this in terms of a metaphysics of agency, they do nonetheless give considerable attention to the ways in which practical reason itself cannot operate, apart from some overarching commitment or broad conception of the good. Without some such general principles, the familiar operations of practical reasoning—applying general norms to specifics, resolving incommensurable values and commitments, judging when to set aside one obligation in view of another—cannot proceed in orderly, discursively defensible ways.[6] Thus, without some overarching principles of interpretation, application, and judgement, practical reason, so called, would not really be a form of reasoning. These general principles are given by the agent's core commitments, by his sense of the duties incumbent on him as a rational agent, by some reflective sense of what she cares about and why it matters, his inductive sense of what gives him the deepest happiness—these represent diverse (not incompatible) recent proposals for understanding the overarching conception that gives structure and point to practical reason, and renders the actions chosen intelligible as acts of one unified agent.

Aquinas would have no difficulty with any of this—for him, the agent's apprehensions of her obligations, her sense of what matters and where her deepest happiness lie would all be comprehended in her conception of the overall good, and her choices and actions would correlatively reflect a human life held together by a unified and coherent will. Admittedly, Aquinas's claims at the beginning of the *prima secundae* stand in need of qualification to be fully persuasive. However, if we take these as setting out the key components of an ideal of fully rational and free action, while allowing that most of us will more or less approximate these rather than attaining them, then they are not only credible, but widely shared.[7]

This brings us to a second element of Aquinas's account of happiness as perfection. We noted above that for Aquinas, the unity of human agency would be one instance of a more general principle of unity of agency, according to which every causal agent operates out of the ordered potentialities constituting its form. An exercise of agency is nothing other than the active expression of the causal powers proper to a kind of creature, and it is intelligible as an operation of the creature, one of its acts, only in those terms. Seen from this vantage point, human action is a causal operation, stemming from the agent's form and aimed in some way or other at the continuance and expression of that form (I 80.1; I-II 8.1; II-II 123.7). This implies that human actions are only intelligible as such, as operations of the agent, insofar as they can be analyzed in some way as expressions of the agent's specific form, and the dynamic ensemble of causal faculties constituting that form. Correlatively, the choice to act in any way at all implies a readiness to actualize one's causal powers, governed by some overall conception of the kinds of activities that promote, safeguard, or render actual whatever it is that the individual takes himself to be. To put the same point in less forbidding terms, the agent necessarily acts for Aquinas in such a way as to pursue her happiness, understood as perfection through activities in accordance with her best conception of her true nature and identity—or alternatively, her sense of her own fulfillment, her overall purpose, or her self-identification with overarching projects or ideals.

But of course, nobody, not even a Thomist, normally thinks in such terms. While it is true that the choice to act necessarily implies a desire to bring about what is in fact a perfection of one's self as an agent, that does not mean that the activity in question is desired under that description, or much less, desired because it represents a perfection of the agent. Rather, the desire to act in some particular way is targeted on some state of affairs that the agent hopes to bring about, or to forestall—what in Aquinas's terms would be identified as the formal object, the description under which the act is a voluntary act of the agent (I-II 18.2, 6, 7). The agent's choice is properly described in terms of this object, and his reasons for acting—the aims for which he acts, in terms of which his behavior is intelligible as an intentional action—can only be characterized in terms of some aspect of the state of affairs at which he aims.

Over the course of a series of important essays on Kant's theory of practical reason, Barbara Hermann proposes a way of dealing with a similar problem in Kant's theory that can usefully be applied at this point.[8] If I have understood her correctly, Hermann's interpretation goes as follows. Kant seems to say that our actions are morally good only if they are done out of respect for the moral law—implying that morally good actions cannot be motivated directly by any kind of concern for other persons, communities, and the like. But as Herman reads him, Kant's overall position is more subtle and persuasive. That is, he holds that the good will is informed by a commitment to morality, in such a way that the agent cares about certain kinds of things and not others, commits herself to acting in some ways rather than others, and rules certain kinds of behavior out, or at the very least regards them as problematic. Thus, the overall ensemble of reasons governing the actions of a morally good person will be determined by norms of rational consistency and equal regard implied by the categorical imperative, in such a way that the reasons governing her choice in any specific instance will stem from this overall ensemble in some way. But that does not mean that the person of good will necessarily acts in order to respect the moral law—that is to say, this stance does not imply that the morally good person always acts for the reason that her act fulfills the requirements of morality. The commitment to duty enters in at an earlier level, so to speak, structuring the agent's motives in accordance with an overarching commitment to live in accordance with the requirements of morality. In her day to day actions, the moral agent will act for a diverse range of reasons, just like everyone else—but the particular reasons for which she acts, the way she acts, and the constraints she observes, will all reflect her overarching commitment to the moral law in some way or other. As Hermann remarks, the morally good individual, confronted by someone in urgent need, "acts to provide help: this is what he ought to do. Moral rules describe what our duties are; they are not the objects of dutiful actions."[9]

I suggest that much the same can be said about the agent's rational love for some final end, as Aquinas understands it. He is committed by the overall logic of his analysis to say that ideally, the human person acts in accordance with some explicit conception of a final good, which she has reflectively adopted as in some way for her good, the overarching principle or aim governing all her actions. This is tantamount to willing her happiness, understood as her perfection as whatever she takes herself to be, but that need not imply that she reflectively grasps and wills the final good under this description. Nor does this claim, by itself, imply that the agent always acts for the reason that this or that course of activity will in some way promote her final end. The agent's conception of the final end, and her sense of who and what she is in relation to it, will determine the kinds of reasons for which she acts, the ways in which she acts, and the kinds of things she will avoid doing, but in such a way as to leave space for her to act, directly and immediately, on reasons of a more specific kind. The conception of the final end provides the ultimate justification for regarding this or that as a proper reason for choice, but that does not mean that the final end is itself, immediately and directly, the reason for which the agent acts in each particular instance.

Admittedly, this account goes beyond what Aquinas says. Yet we do have grounds for thinking that it offers a legitimate extension of his overall view. He does say that every agent directs each of his acts toward the attainment of some final end, identified subjectively with the perfection of the rational agent. At the same time, he recognizes that intentional states (broadly so called) can truly be attributed to an agent under some descriptions, but not others, and he explicitly makes this point with respect to the universal desire for happiness (I 2.1 *ad* 1, I-II 8). Given the overall terms of his analysis, this implies that the desire for happiness, construed as one's perfection as an agent, is implied by a desire to act at all, since action *is* perfective of the agent. What is more, the desire to act will necessarily imply a desire to act in a fitting and efficacious way, in accordance with whatever best accords with and sustains the ensemble of faculties constituting the ongoing life of the creature. Even so, the necessary link between action and perfection need not imply that the agent is even aware of this link, or much less that he desires and acts in order to perfect his causal powers as an agent. Thus, Aquinas's overall analysis need not imply that every action of the rational agent is intentionally directed toward happiness—that the attainment of his final end is the reason for which he acts. It seems consistent with Aquinas's overall view to read this as saying, again, that whatever the agent chooses, he regards this activity (state of affairs, etc.) desirable because he regards it as being in some way consonant with his overall good—as an appropriate activity, given the kind of creature that he considers himself to be.

Keep in mind, second, that the virtues, regarded as *habitus* of the faculties of the soul, are themselves perfections—they perfect, that is to say, they bring to actuality, the faculties they inform, in such a way as to orient them toward further perfection, in and through actions of a characteristic kind. That, as we saw, is why Aquinas identifies connatural happiness with the practice of the virtues, sustained over a lifetime. If the agent in question is genuinely virtuous, then his choices will be targeted on what will in fact be the attainment of his perfection as a human agent through the practice of the virtues. But that does not mean that he chooses to act under the description of acting virtuously, or perfecting himself or attaining happiness—much less, that these constitute the reasons for which he acts. Rather, the virtuous agent, like everyone else, acts for reasons bound up with the state of affairs he hopes to bring about or to forestall, a state of affairs constituting the formal object under which his act is intelligible as an intentional act of a given kind. Very often, the desired (or feared) state of affairs will be bound up with the attainment or continued enjoyment of the necessary and proper goods of human existence—nourishment, shelter, sexual enjoyments, fruitful procreation, and the like (I-II 10.1).

The virtues of the passions, including temperance, fortitude, and their related virtues, are perfections of sensate faculties for desire and aversion, in the case of temperance, or for spirited engagement, in the case of fortitude. But precisely because these virtues are perfections of natural faculties for responsiveness and desire, and engagement, they are properly expressed in activities targeted on enjoying natural desiderata and avoiding their contraries (I 82.5; I-II 22.1).[10] The virtuous person is not distinguished from someone who is immature or vicious by the kinds of activities and enjoyments that he pursues—rather, what sets him apart are distinctive ways in which he pursues and enjoys the good things of life (I-II 56.4). More specifically, through temperance and fortitude and their associated virtues, an agent's undifferentiated desires for the pleasures of taste and touch are transformed in such a way as to track the agent's genuine good, as determined through reasoned reflection (I-II 56.6). Like everyone else, the virtuous person spontaneously desires what he finds appealing, and dislikes what he finds unpleasant—but at least to a considerable extent, his perceptions of the appealing and the unpleasant track his overall judgements concerning his overall good.

Thus, the virtuous person need not be distinguished by the particular reasons for which she acts, or the states of affairs at which she aims in any given choice. Rather, the virtuous agent is distinguished by the way in which she pursues her aims, out of passions which have been shaped and integrated through her overall, reflective judgements. Once a passion has been informed in the proper way by the relevant virtue, the disposition in question will normally be expressed in the immediate exercise of the passion itself—otherwise, the virtuous disposition would not be a perfection of the passion, shaping its own immediate exercise. Virtuous dispositions of the passions are such, genuinely admirable and perfective, because they dispose the agent to feel in accordance with an ensemble of reasoned considerations which are, so to speak, built into the disposition itself. Someone who acts out of the *habitus* of virtue, as a virtuous person, acts out of this ensemble of reasonable considerations—thus, the temperate agent is disposed to like wholesome food, in part because it is wholesome. But it does not follow that whenever he has a nice bowl of oatmeal (let's say), he does so out of a choice to eat something wholesome, or much less, that he has breakfast in order to be a virtuous person. The genuinely temperate individual will really like his oatmeal, and he will find it a tasty, appealing option when he is feeling peckish. Normally, this will be reason enough for him to fix himself a bowl. The broader ensemble of reasons and dispositions that distinguishes virtuous actions from those actions done out of unformed, though generally good tendencies, will be integrated into the agent's overall character through the virtues themselves, in such a way that the agent will not normally need to act immediately and directly for these broader reasons—or much less, to act for the sake of actualizing virtue.

What has just been said about the dispositions motivating the temperate and courageous individual also applies to the individual who is virtuous, *tout court*. Indeed, the commitment to the unity of agency shared by Aquinas and many of our contemporaries implies that the virtuous agent's passions are informed by, *inter alia*, a reflective sense of the relative weight of the diverse reasons for which she acts, the appropriate ways in which different aims can be pursued, and the constraints that she should respect. Thus, the virtuous agent cannot simply be well-disposed with respect to her desires for wholesome food, or courageous on the battlefield, or disinclined to cheat on her income taxes. In order to be truly virtuous, the agent must be able to bring together a diverse range of considerations, bearing immediately on distinct elements of human capacities and circumstances, but unified in action, just as the distinctive faculties of the agent are unified into one form. Were this not the case, someone would not be able to act as a unified agent, someone whose particular choices stem from a consistent set of judgements and commitments in some intelligible way. We sometimes say that someone who is immature or inconsistent—in Aristotle's terms, an akratic individual— is not always the same person, and while this may not be ontologically true, it does capture a human reality. Someone whose overall judgements are unformed or inconsistent cannot take responsibility for past acts or commit to the future in any reliable way. What is worse, when faced with practical dilemmas or genuinely unprecedented situations, he will be unable to muster the resources needed to deal with these in a reasoned way—precisely because he lacks a framework within which diverse considerations can be placed into some kind of order and evaluated accordingly.[11]

Thus, on Aquinas's view, the particular virtues are necessarily connected in their proper operations (I-II 65.1; cf. I-II 61.3, 4). This does not imply that all the virtues are expressions of one quality, reasonableness or love or something similar. Aquinas allows that this, the classical thesis of the unity of the virtues, is true if we take "virtue" in its most general sense, but he nonetheless insists that the particular virtues are distinctive dispositions, immediately characterized as dispositions of some specific faculty. At the same time, the particular virtues themselves are, in part, dispositions which shape the relevant faculty to be responsive to the wider context of reasons informing what we might call the field of virtuous behavior. Thus, Aquinas explains that the passions, as faculties of sensual desire and aversion, stand in need of virtues because in their unformed state, the passions are responsive to whatever is immediately appealing or unpleasant. Of course, these initial reactions may not track the agent's actual good at all, and so the passions need to be shaped in such a way as to respond, more or less, to whatever is good for the individual, comprehensively considered. That is why the virtues of the passions can be said to be perfections of the faculties they inform—through these virtuous dispositions, the individual's native, unformed tendencies toward desirable and undesirable objects are extended and shaped, so as to tend to what is desirable or undesirable comprehensively considered, in reality and not just in immediate appearance.

Let us return now to Aquinas's claims that every rational agent necessarily aims at perfection, which is to say happiness, in everything that she does, and his further claim that seen from one perspective, true happiness consists in the practice of the virtues. If the line of analysis set out above is consistent with his virtue theory, then we can say of the pursuit of happiness and virtue what has just been said about acting out of (for example) temperance. Certainly, a truly virtuous agent will act in accordance with reasoned judgements about what is good, fitting, praiseworthy, or perhaps obligatory, for a creature of her kind—that is part of what it means to be a mature, appropriately rational person, for Aquinas and for many others. But it does not follow that the virtuous agent's every choice and action will be self-consciously directed toward the attainment of her own perfection, happiness, or virtue. Rather, she cares about those states of affairs, activities, and values that she regards as components of a good human life, in key part because these are fitting for her, required of her, or something similar. But what she cares about will normally be whatever it is that provides the immediate reasons for her actions. The reasons out of which she acts, the way in which she pursues her aims, the constraints she respects and the overall ordering of priorities that she observes, have all been integrated into her faculties for desire and judgement through the processes through which the virtues are acquired or (in the case of infused virtues) brought into active use.

The Desire for Happiness and the Virtues of the Will

At this point, we come back to the problem flagged at the beginning of this paper. Because he is rational, the agent is capable of apprehending his own good as an instantiation of an abstract category, the good in general—indeed, qua rational, he cannot apprehend it at all, except in these terms. But the abstract category of the good extends beyond the individual's good, and indeed, the human good as such. We can make sense of the good of all kinds of objects—non-human animals and plants, a political community, an artistic work, an ecosystem, even the universe itself, regarded as a structured cosmos. What is more, if we can conceive of these as good, then it would seem to follow that they too are possible objects of the will, constituting meaningful reasons for choice and action.

Indeed, not only is this possible, Aquinas seems to say as much. At any rate, he insists that every creature naturally loves some greater good (I 60.5; I-II 109.3; II-II 26.3). This natural orientation is presupposed by the virtues of general justice and charity, each of which orients the will toward something greater than individual good, namely, the common good or the supreme goodness of God (I-II 56.6; II-II 23.1, 4, 24.1, 58.9, 12).[12] The virtue of justice presupposes that the human person naturally loves the common good of her political community more than she loves herself, or more precisely, that she would do so, if her natural capacities for love were not constricted by the general effects of sinfulness. The love of the commonwealth as a greater good can be identified as an integral component of human nature at its best, even though we find it difficult to achieve it—otherwise, justice would be a perversion, rather than a perfection of the will. The love of God for God's own sake is the distinctive mark of charity (II-II 23.5 *ad* 2), and charity toward the neighbor requires us to try to promote her good, for her sake and not our own (II-II 31.1).

Now here is the critical point. These kinds of love and activity stem from the distinctively human, rational faculty of desire, namely, the will, and they are only possible because the will is informed by our reasoned capacity to grasp the good as such, in abstraction from our own individual perfection. Yet Aquinas insists that the individual necessarily acts in pursuit of her own perfection, her happiness, in everything that she does. Why is he committed to this claim, even though it generates difficulties within his system? To answer this question, we need to take account of one further aspect of Aquinas's overall theory. That is, for him the will is the overarching causal principle of the human person, giving rise directly or indirectly to all her actions.[13] We have already emphasized this point in connection with the unity of agency, but now I want to focus on another element of this analysis—that is, the will is an operative principle, an appetite giving rise to characteristic actions (keeping in mind that the inclinations of the will are among its acts; I-II 50.5 *ad* 1, 51.1). It is true that

Aquinas distinguishes between the will and the faculty of freedom of judgement, which is oriented toward choice, but this is a rational distinction between two elements of one and the same faculty—the will as such is the appetite for the end, toward which the choices stemming out of free judgement are oriented (I 83.4).

Thus, whatever overarching good the agent loves as her final end, she must regard it as in some way a meaningful goal for her own actions. The inclination of the will toward any final end whatever implies a commitment to judge, choose, and act in accordance with that end (I 83.4; I-II 8.2, 9.3). The agent need not know exactly what she ought to do out of love for whatever she identifies as her end, but unless she is committed to do something, and has a general idea of what that practically means, her protestations of love are empty. At this point, we recall that every agent perfects itself in and through appropriate activities, bringing actuality to the potentialities of its form. This implies that any choice to act is *ipso facto* directed toward one's own perfection, and the commitment to an overarching final end, seen as a commitment to a consistent pattern of activity, implies a commitment to seek one's own perfection through appropriate activities, which in some way place the agent in a right relation with whatever she most loves.

This brings us to a second point. The problem at hand only arises for Aquinas because he holds that the greater objects of love are all realities—there really are goods that are greater than the good of the individual, and they call for an appropriate response. Aquinas could readily admit that the universal good, abstractly considered, is greater, more comprehensive, even more lovable than the particular good of some individual—indeed, he would seem to be logically compelled to say as much. But this abstract claim, in itself, would have no purchase on anyone's sentiments or actions. The tension between self-love and the love of greater goods creates a real problem for Aquinas because there really are greater goods for him— objects of the will calling for concrete responses and corresponding actions, which may be at least *prima facie*, inconsistent with the individual's own well-being. But posed in this way, it becomes apparent that the terms of the problem point toward its solution. That is, Aquinas's analysis implies that there may be something about the substantive character of the greater goods in question, or about the structures of the will, or both, which resolves the dilemma at hand. I want to argue that this is in fact the case—Aquinas's way of construing the greater goods informing the virtues of the will, and his analysis of the will itself, operate in such a way as to forestall this as a real, exigent dilemma.

In order to move forward, we need first to look more closely at the way in which Aquinas analyzes greater, general, or universal good. As we would by now expect, Aquinas construes the general or universal good at every level in the terms of his own metaphysics—which is to say, general good is instantiated through some system of orderly, intelligible interrelationships. As she considers a general good of this kind, the individual sees that she herself plays a part in this dynamism—otherwise, it would not be a comprehensive, general good, within which all the particulars falling within its scope have their proper place (I-II 92.1; II-II 47.10–12, 58.7). She sees that she herself is a part of the community, playing a role in its common good, that she is one active entity in a dynamic cosmic order, and finally—given the transforming effects of grace—that she has a place in the fellowship of God's friends. What is more, she naturally grasps that her own good as an individual depends on her standing in right relation to these more comprehensive goods. Even though the claims of the commonwealth, or the wider demands of natural reverence or grace, may go contrary to her immediate interests, they cannot ultimately come into conflict with her true good, her perfection and (therefore) her happiness. The integral link between the good of the individual and more general goods opens up a conceptual space within which the agent's practical reason and will can operate in a unified, coherent way.

Yet while this may seem to resolve the problem on one level, it sharpens it on another. For thus understood, isn't the love of the commonwealth, the cosmos, or even God himself, just another form of self-love? Aquinas rejects this claim (II-II 26.3 *ad* 4), and so should we. As we observed in the last section, we should distinguish between the reasons that inform a given set of dispositions or commitments, and the reasons out of which an agent chooses or acts at any particular point. The genuinely temperate person is disposed to enjoy the kinds of foods that are really good for her, and some consideration of what these are will have shaped her preferences. But that does not mean that she chooses a cup of plain yogurt because she wants to eat something healthy; she really likes it, and that is reason enough, here and now, to have some. In the same way, the just or charitable individual has come to love the commonwealth, or to cherish friendship with God, out of considerations which include, necessarily but not only, some reflection on the ways in which his own individual good is constituted by his relation to these wider goods. But once these dispositions have been formed, he does not act out of devotion to his community or to God because this places him in right relation to a wider good—he cares about these objects of love for their own sakes, and that is all the reason he needs to act accordingly.

This brings us to a further point. Because the will is a principle of activity, its operations cannot be completely detached from some orientation toward choice and action. Once again—Aquinas understands perfection and happiness on every level in terms of some activity, perfective of the agent. This implies that the agent's desire for its own perfection cannot be understood apart from a consideration of the agent's proper activities, through which it expresses its form. In the case of the rational agent, this implies that the desire for perfection or happiness, under whatever description the agent would recognize, can only be conceptualized in terms of the kinds of activities that would constitute its perfection. Certainly, activity as such would not count as anyone's idea of a happy life, including Aquinas's—the activity in question must be correlated with something, some ideal or satisfaction or set of relationships, that the agent serves, brings about, or enjoys through appropriate operations. This "something" would be identified by Aquinas as happiness in the objective sense, the attainment (in some sense) of which constitutes the subjective perfection or happiness of the individual. In its genuine forms, whether connatural or bestowed by grace, objective happiness always corresponds to something transcending the individual, whether that be the common good or God's own goodness—thus, the agent necessarily loves the object of her happiness more than she loves herself. But she cannot meaningfully express that love, except through choices and actions placing her in some right relation to the higher objects of her love.

My point is this. The perfection and happiness of the rational agent, subjectively considered, cannot be understood apart from sustained activities through which she stands in right relation to some greater good. Her love and loyalty to this greater good may well lead her to sacrifice her individual good, considered from some limited perspective. We should not minimize what might be very great sacrifices indeed, yet even in such cases—perhaps especially in such cases—the choice to sacrifice oneself for the object of one's supreme love implies choosing some pattern of activities which perfects the individual by bringing her into right relation with a more comprehensive whole. This is the case even when someone chooses to give up any actual enjoyment of the greater good, as for example, when someone willingly dies for the commonwealth, without expecting any kind of posthumous awareness of having done so. Even this is a choice to attain one's perfection as an agent through appropriate activities—not necessarily formulated under that description, or much less chosen for that reason.

What has just been said about the meaning and limits of self-sacrifice on behalf of the commonweal can also be applied to the friendship with God proper to charity. It might seem to be the height of Christian love to will one's own damnation, if God has in fact predestined the individual in that way.[14] And there can be little harm, from Aquinas's standpoint, in assenting to the proposition, "If God has predestined me to damnation, then it is good that I be damned." What I cannot coherently do, however, is to choose to act in a damnable way, out of the love of God, because a damnable action is precisely an action done in disregard or defiance of the claims that God's love places on me. In order to be intelligible as a stance of the will, a practical specification of the first principles of practical reason which eventuates in a series of choices and acts, what I say I love and what I actually do, or propose doing, must come together in some coherent way. If I take up my own damnation as a project to be carried out through my own activities, out of the conviction that this is God's predestining will for me, then I am choosing to undertake a pattern of activities contrary to, and destructive of the love of God bestowed on me through charity. And that I cannot coherently do—or to be more precise, I cannot choose to do so *out of charity*, as an intelligible expression of the love of God that supposedly, by hypothesis, motivates my actions. I cannot choose to love God, which implies placing myself in right relations to God through my actions, by means of actions chosen for the sake of placing myself out of right relation to God—sins, in other words, damnable acts. Of course, I could very well pursue such a course of activity out of some other motivations—despair or angry defiance, for example. But in that case, I would not, even nominally, be acting in such a way as to express my love for God.

A qualification is in order here. I am well aware that this line of analysis can lead to egregious impositions on individuals in the name of the common good, or indeed in the name of the church. It is important to keep in mind, as Aquinas himself says, that the common good itself presupposes, at a minimum, commitments to the well-being of individuals and the claims of particular justice, which rule out any strategy of simply sacrificing individuals to any polity (see, for example, II-II 62.6). These qualifications imply that the relation between communal and individual goods is more complex than the preceding remarks suggest. I cannot pursue this issue here, but it would be centrally important in any comprehensive treatment of political theory or ecclesiology.[15]

In this paper, I have focused on clarifying the different elements of Aquinas's comprehensive account of happiness, virtue, and the will, in order to bring out the consistency and cogency of that account and to defend it from some common objections. Consistency and relative freedom from errors are central intellectual virtues, certainly, but we should not lose sight of the wider significance of Aquinas's account of happiness and virtue in these processes of analysis. Aquinas offers us a compelling, humane, and at the same time inspiring vision of what human life at its best might be. On his showing, the genuinely virtuous individual lives a life of ongoing connections with others, grounded in the natural ties that structure every human life and given further direction through the pursuit of shared ideals. This kind of life may well include much suffering and loss, and yet we can readily see how we might regard this as the kind of life we would want to live, a life that satisfies our deepest needs for meaning and connection, which we can live with enthusiasm and look back on without regrets. Those of us who work within the field of virtue ethics, especially Thomist virtue ethics, do not need to minimize or apologize for this aspect of his thought. On the contrary, Aquinas's ideal of virtuous happiness represents one of the most powerfully attractive, and at the same time admirable and inspiring, aspects of his overall thought, which lends credence to his overall theory of the virtues and draws us to further inquiry.

Notes

1. For an excellent overview of the classical origins of this tradition, and specifically the link between happiness and virtue, see Julia Annas, *The Morality of Happiness* (Oxford: Oxford University Press, 1993), 27–47.

2. For a comprehensive analysis of modern philosophical and theological perspectives on self-love and the desire for happiness, see Gene Outka, *Agape: An Ethical Analysis* (New Haven, CT: Yale University Press, 1972), 55–74.

3. See, for example, John Finnis, *Aquinas: Founders of Modern Political and Social Thought* (Oxford: Oxford University Press, 1998), 103–10. On his view, the happiness that Aquinas identifies as the proper end of life would be equivalent to a condition of secure, unrestricted participation in the basic goods, which constitute the genuine, and irreducibly plural aims of human action. It is difficult to see how this analysis can be squared with Aquinas's insistence that happiness itself, considered both as a subjective state and in terms of its objective target, is the ultimate, unitary end of human life.

4. In addition to the authors discussed below, see the essays collected by Stephen Engstrom and Jennifer Whiting in *Aristotle, Kant, and the Stoics: Rethinking Happiness and Duty* (Cambridge: Cambridge University Press, 1996). Their introductory essay, "Introduction," 1–18, offers a good overview of the issues at stake in this reappraisal.

5. *Habitus* is frequently translated "habit," or "habits"—the Latin noun can be either singular or plural—but this implies a tendency towards mechanical, thoughtless behavior, which is not at all what Aquinas and his interlocutors would have meant.

6. This point is frequently made. I am especially indebted to Elijah Millgram's cogent arguments defending it and drawing out its implications for the possibilities of reasoned practical induction; see *Practical Induction* (Cambridge, MA: Harvard University Press, 1997), especially 43–66 and 87–104.

7. I would thus take issue with Candace Vogler, who remarks that Aquinas's claims regarding a unifying end of human life are motivated, and perhaps presuppose, theological commitments (*Reasonably Vicious*, Cambridge, MA: Harvard University Press, 2002, 26–52). Certainly, Aquinas's analysis is informed by his theological aims, but it is also the case that he has independently compelling philosophical reasons for asserting the necessity of some final end, and at least some of those reasons would be widely shared today. However, she is quite right that basic considerations of practical reasonableness do not, in themselves, imply that the rational agent necessarily grasps what his (objectively true) last end is, or even that he fixes on an admirable or morally defensible last end. Aquinas does recognize this; see, for example, I-II 78, II-II 25.7.

8. Collected in *The Practice of Moral Judgement* (Cambridge, MA: Harvard University Press, 1993). In what follows, I rely especially on "Integrity and Impartiality," 23–44, but my thinking on these issues is indebted to her other essays as well. In what follows, I am also indebted to the analysis of reasons for action proposed by Michael Thompson, *Life and Action: Elementary Structures of Practice and Practical Thought* (Cambridge, MA: Harvard University Press, 2008), 85–96, 106–19. Needless to say, I don't presuppose that either Hermann or Thompson would agree with the following arguments.

9. *Practice of Moral Judgement*, 27.

10. The will is also a natural faculty of desire, which both incorporates the objects of the other appetites into its inclinations, and inclines towards those kinds of enjoyments and satisfactions which presuppose rationality (I-II 10.1). Thus, the following observations would apply to the will as well, with some qualifications. For simplicity's sake, I have focused on the virtues of the passions in this section.

11. This point is well made by Millgram; see *Practical Induction*, 43–66. Rosalind Hursthouse explicitly defends a modified version of the thesis of the unity of the virtues on similar grounds in *On Virtue Ethics* (Oxford: Oxford University Press, 1999), 153–57.

12. General or legal justice directs the individual rightly towards the common good, whereas particular justice directs the individual towards right relations to other individuals—to a good outside the self, in other words, if not precisely to a good greater than oneself (II-II 58.5, 7).

13. I owe this observation to Robert Pasnau, *Thomas Aquinas on Human Nature: A Philosophical Study of Summa theologiae Ia 75-89* (Cambridge: Cambridge University Press, 2002), 45.

14. I am grateful to John Hare for calling this problem to my attention and pressing me on it.

15. I want to say a special word of thanks to John Hare, with whom I discussed these and related issues at some length during the 2008–9 academic year, while he was on sabbatical at Notre Dame. I am afraid that these remarks do not fully express the extent to which I benefitted from our conversation, but I am very much in his debt. I also want to express my appreciation to a remarkable group of graduate students, with whom I read through a selection of contemporary work on practical reason during the spring semester of 2010.

5

Kant on Practical and Pathological Love

JOHN HARE

IMMANUEL KANT SAYS, in a section of his second critique called "Of the Drives of Pure Practical Reason," that we are subjects, not sovereigns, in the moral realm. He interprets the love command in light of this.

> The possibility of such a command as, "Love God above all and thy neighbor as thyself," agrees very well with this. For, as a command, it requires esteem for a law which orders love and does not leave it to arbitrary choice to make love the principle. But love to God as inclination (pathological love) is impossible, for He is not an object of the senses. The latter is indeed possible toward human beings, but it cannot be commanded, for it is not possible for a person to love someone merely on command. It is, therefore, only practical love which can be understood in that kernel of all laws. To love God means in this sense to do His commandments gladly, and to love one's neighbor means to practice all duties toward him gladly. The command which makes this a rule cannot require that we have this disposition but only that we endeavor after it. To command that one do something gladly is self-contradictory. For a law would not be needed if we already knew of ourselves what we ought to do and moreover were conscious of liking to do it; and if we did it without liking but only out of respect for the law, a command which makes just this respect the drive of the maxim would counteract the disposition it commands.[1]

In what follows, I will call this "the practical love passage." It tells us a good deal about what Kant thinks the different kinds of love are and how they relate to the moral life. In the present essay, I am going to try to lay out what Kant sees as the relation of emotion and reason in practical love. I am going to propose a set of stages through which moral deliberation goes, for Kant, and this will enable us to see how emotion contributes to the process in both helpful and unhelpful ways. I will end by contrasting what I take to be Kant's view of practical love with the view that Jean Porter attributes to Aquinas in her excellent article in the present volume.[2] I will call the contrast position "Aquinas-Porter," and I will urge that Kant's position is better.

Kant on Practical Love, Reason, and the Emotions

Practical love of God, Kant says, is to do God's commandments gladly. Kant's teaching, throughout his published work, is that we have to recognize our duties as God's commands.[3] I will not try to discuss here the parts of our proper bearing to God that are beyond our duties to other people, though Kant does discuss these other parts.[4] My interest in this essay is in the part of practical love of God that coincides with our practical love of the neighbor, where we love God *by* loving the neighbor. I want to look at the relation of emotion and reason in this practical love, at what it means *to do our duty gladly*.

The first thing to say—and this will be the major contrast with Aquinas-Porter—is that practical love is expressed in choices that meet the requirements of duty in that they make no essential reference in their object or end to the person making the choice. This exclusion of self-indexing is required by Kant's categorical imperative procedure, which I will not try here to describe except to say that it requires continuing to will the maxim of one's action (which is the prescription of the action together with one's reason for the action) when it is willed as universal law. In other work, I have tried to trace the connection backward from Kant to Duns Scotus, five hundred years before.[5] Scotus is the first person to work out a theory of the two fundamental motivations behind human action, though he takes his terms for them— "affection for justice" and "affection for advantage"—from Anselm. The affection for advantage is for my own happiness and perfection and is thus self-indexed. The affection for justice is for what is good in itself, independently of my happiness and perfection, and is thus not self-indexed. Scotus, like Kant after him, holds that we humans are characteristically moved by both affections, and there is nothing wrong with this, but the key question is the ranking. We should be willing, if God required it (which happily God does not), to sacrifice even our salvation for the sake of the glory of God.[6] Scotus and Kant are not disagreeing here with Aquinas-Porter about the centrality of reason in the moral life, but they have a fundamentally different account of the nature of reason.

The second thing to say—and here the contrast with Aquinas-Porter is much less than one would expect—is that Kant has a significant place for the emotions in practical love.[7] He is concerned that he is misunderstood as advocating a "morose" ethics, which sets morality in opposition to all pleasure and renounces all concern of moral persons for their own happiness.[8] It is important to see that Kant is not simply arguing in the practical love passage that love is commanded and therefore is a matter of rational will, not feeling or desire.[9] The command is not simply to do one's duty but to endeavor after the disposition that takes pleasure in doing it. There are two mistakes Kant wants to avoid here, each an exaggeration of one side of his own position. He does not want to say that we already have this disposition after which we should endeavor, for then it would not make sense to say we are commanded to endeavor after it. On the other hand, he does not want to say (like the Stoics, as he construes them) that we should merely do our duty and not care about the disposition to take pleasure in it. The destination for limited creatures of need like ourselves is that our inclinations should be in line with our duty, not that we should stop having inclinations.[10] We will always (even in heaven) pursue happiness: "To be happy is necessarily the desire of every rational but finite being, and thus it is an unavoidable determinant of its faculty of desire."[11] The key question is not whether we desire to be happy but how we *rank* this desire with respect to the moral law. In *Religion within the Boundaries of Mere Reason*, Kant acknowledges in the end only two such rankings: the good maxim, which puts duty above happiness, and the evil maxim, which puts happiness above duty.

Kant classes all inclinations under the desire for happiness and thus, I shall say, regards them as self-indexed, by which I mean that the agent's desire is for some state of the agent and that this self-reference is salient in the agent's deliberation. I do not mean that the self-indexing is explicit or articulated as such but that it makes a difference to what the agent counts as satisfying the desire. My desire to achieve something for a neighbor can be self-indexed, for example, if I am not satisfied by that same result being achieved for the neighbor by somebody else. A qualification is needed here. Since the two affections, or streams of motivation, will often be concurrent, the agent can be both satisfied and not satisfied at the same time. But the *inclination* will not be satisfied unless *the agent* accomplishes the benefaction. Again, self-indexing does not require that the agent *articulate* that the object is self-indexed.

Kant's account of the inclinations is, I think, defective because it is too dichotomous. I will mention briefly two defects resulting from two dichotomies. First, regarding all motivation as *either* self-indexed inclination *or* universal-moral principle is a mistake, though an easy one. It is interesting that Scotus makes very much the same mistake. After he has worked out the distinction between the two affections, Scotus proceeds to argue that every motivation that is for justice in the sense of the distinction is for God, and so the choice is always God or self. But surely I can be motivated to achieve something for Peter without this being self-indexed either by Peter being in some special relation *to me* or by my caring that the result be achieved *by me*. My motivation here is indexed to a particular, to Peter, and I may not be motivated to pursue similar good things for other similar people. In the same way, Kant moves too quickly from the premise that morality requires elimination of self-reference to the conclusion that it requires elimination of reference to any particular. We need an intermediate category of inclinations that are not universal (since they contain reference to individuals) but are indexed not to the self but to some other individual.[12] Seeing this omission in Kant is important in part because it helps us to explain the gap that many people feel between the formulation of the categorical imperative in terms of universal law and the formulation in terms of human beings as "ends in themselves."[13] It is natural to think (though this is not Kant's own explication of the second of these formulations) that I could treat another person as an end in herself without universalizing the maxim of my action toward her.

The second defect in Kant's account of the inclinations is that he insists that they are all sensuous. The contrasting term here is "intellectual," as where Kant says in his discussion of the feeling of respect, "For that reason the lowering (humiliation) of the pretensions to self-esteem on the sensuous side is an elevation of the moral, i.e. practical, esteem for the law on the intellectual side."[14] One sign that Kant is in difficulty here is that he has just said that humiliation is "intellectual contempt."[15] The problem is that Kant wants to say both that respect is something that we feel and that its object is something we apprehend by reason alone. He is committed to the dichotomous view that every feeling of pleasure and displeasure, and every inclination based on this feeling, is sensuous and not intellectual.[16] But pleasures are too various for this kind of dichotomy, and respect is the kind of feeling that makes the need for an account of intellectual pleasures acute.

Kant on Affect and Passion

I said I wanted to look at the relation of emotion and reason in practical love and have used here the term "emotion," which Kant does not usually use.[17] To get at what he would say about the place of emotion in practical love, we need to look at the relations among four terms that he does use: "feeling," "affect," "inclination," and "passion."[18] Kant contrasts "practical love" with "pathological love," and this suggests that the contrast is with passion (since *pathos* in Greek is often translated as "passion"). But this is not Kant's usage. There is an instructive difference here with Aristotle. For Aristotle, only *some* passions are "named together with the bad" (*NE* 2.6. 1107a10f). He lists spite, shamelessness, and envy. Other passions are constitutive of virtue so that courage, for example, consists in the disposition to fear in the way that reason prescribes. Aquinas-Porter preserves the Aristotelian usage here: "Virtues, that is to say, dispositions of intellect, passions, and will mediating between the individual's native capabilities, and the specific exercise of his faculties in particular exercises of intellect, or particular choices" (Aquinas, *ST* Ia–IIae.55.1).[19] For Kant, by contrast, *all* the passions are by definition an obstacle to reason, and an inclination that was properly trained by virtue would not count as a passion at all. But it is important to see that this is so far merely a difference in usage, not a difference in doctrine.

In *Metaphysics of Morals*, Kant distinguishes affects and passions, which are both resistant to reason, on the grounds that affects are *feelings* that are resistant and passions are *inclinations* that are resistant.[20] Inclinations are desires that have become settled habits of mind. The difference between feelings and desires is that the faculty of desire is the faculty of choice. Kant says in the *Anthropology*, "Desire is the self-determination of a subject's power through the representation of something in the future as an effect of this representation."[21] We have a mental picture of what we desire to achieve, and this picture itself motivates us to achieve it. Feeling does not, qua feeling, have representational content. But desires and inclinations are given their content by some representation that itself relates back to the feeling of pleasure and displeasure, which will be different for different people, since different people take pleasure and displeasure in the thought of different things.[22]

Both affects and passions can be turbulent or calm (as, in the case of affects, lassitude or weariness and, in the case of passions, cold hatred). But one difference is that whereas affects make reflection more difficult or impossible, passions allow it: "The calm with which one gives oneself up to a passion permits reflection and allows the mind to form principles upon it and so, if inclination lights upon something contrary to the law, to brood upon it, to get it rooted deeply, and so to take up what is evil (as something premeditated) into its maxim."[23] This difference between affect and passion is what makes Kant say that passions enter into kinship with vice more readily than affects do.

Kant sometimes says things that sound as if he thinks inclinations are themselves the source or ground of evil. For example, in *Metaphysics of Morals*, he says, "Since the basis of great crimes is merely the force of inclinations that weaken reason."[24] But even here, he is not saying that inclinations as such are the basis; rather, those that weaken reason (e.g., the "passions") are the basis. When he is careful about this, he says that we only get imputability, and so "crimes," when the inclinations are incorporated into deliberation under what he calls "the evil maxim," which subordinates duty to inclination. The clearest text here is *Religion within the Boundaries of Mere Reason*, where he says that it is tempting to locate the ground of evil "in the sensuous nature of the human being, and in the natural inclinations originating from it."[25] But the truth is, rather, that "the difference, whether the human being is good or evil, must not lie in the difference between the incentives that he incorporates into his maxim (not in the material of the maxim) but in their subordination (in the form of the maxim): which of the two he makes the condition of the other." In other words, is the agent committed to doing her duty *only* if she thinks it will make her happy, or is she committed to making herself happy *only* if she sees it is consistent with her duty? Here we have the Kantian descendant of

Scotus's point about the ranking of the two affections, which I mentioned earlier. Kant is no doubt drawing from Luther, who makes a similar point in *The Bondage of the Will*. Luther says that the source of evil is not "in the flesh, in the sense of the lower and grosser affections, but in the highest and most excellent powers of man, in which righteousness, godliness, and knowledge and reverence of God, should reign—that is in reason and will, and so in the very power of 'free-will,' in the very seed of uprightness, the most excellent thing in man."[26] In Kant's terms, the same material of the maxim, namely, the inclination, can be incorporated in two fundamentally different ways or can be given two fundamentally different forms: one (the good maxim) that allows willing the maxim as universal law and the other (the evil maxim) that does not.

Kant compares himself to the Stoics on this point. He endorses apathy (lack of *pathos*) both about affects and passions but not about feelings or inclinations more generally. In the *Anthropology*, he says that the wise person must never be in a state of affect because affect makes us blind.[27] For example, fear is a feeling but not yet an affect, but a panic attack (*Schreck*) is an affect, preventing us temporarily from seeing our situation as reason would present it to us. Affect prevents the wider view of one's situation that reason provides.[28] Kant also recommends apathy with respect to the passions because passion is "an inclination that prevents reason from comparing it with the sum of all inclinations in respect to a certain choice."[29] Wisdom admits of no passions at all.[30] Again, an example is helpful. Ambition (*Ehrbegierde*, literally the desire for honor) is an inclination that can be approved by reason but only if reason is also taking cognizance of all sorts of other desires, such as the desire for love from others and for the maintenance of financial security.[31] When ambition becomes a passion, it is blind to these other ends, and it does not care about being hated by others or becoming impoverished through the required expenditure. Passion thus, like affect, prevents the wider view (in this case, of one's interests) that reason provides.

Kant on the "Friend of Man"

There is a famous passage about the "friend of man" in *Groundwork of the Metaphysics of Morals* that often misleads readers about Kant's intentions in contrasting reason and inclination. He describes persons "of so sympathetic a temper that, without any further motive of vanity or self-interest, they find an inner pleasure in spreading happiness around them."[32] This would be a case of pathological love, as described in the practical love passage I started with. This person is "conscious of liking to do" what duty in fact prescribes, namely, spreading happiness. Note that pathological love is not to be equated with "vanity or self-interest." I am going to follow Barbara Herman's clarifying exegesis of this passage.[33] We need to understand what Kant intends by denying that the action of such a person, a "friend of man," has moral worth. He says that this person's action, "however right and amiable it might be, still has no genuinely moral worth. It stands on the same footing as [action from] the other inclinations—for example, the inclination for honor, which if fortunate to hit on something beneficial and right and consequently honorable, deserves praise and encouragement, but not esteem; for its maxim lacks moral content, namely, the performance of such actions, not from inclination, but *from duty*." Surely, I find my students say when they read this, the conscientious people who visit me in the hospital merely because it is their duty are *less* admirable than the people who like to do it and get pleasure in cheering me up in this way. People who find an inner pleasure in spreading happiness around them can be more stable, more reliable, than those acting only from guilt or because they think they have to. The students' unease increases when Kant goes on to imagine that the friend of man loses the inclination to help and becomes what we would call "depressed" but nonetheless "tears himself out of this deadly insensibility and does the action without any inclination for the sake of duty alone; then for the first time his action has its genuine moral worth." My students find this account of moral worth grim and unattractive, in Kant's own term "morose."

Herman points out, however, that the friend of man has the same character in both cases, both before the depression and during it. He used to help others because he was stirred by their need, but when depressed, this is not enough; the inclinations are not there to get him to act. Of *him* it was true that when he did have the inclination, he did not act from duty. But there is no implication that for *others* the motive of duty requires the absence of inclination. Kant is saying just that there are two different kinds of worth.[34] Sympathetic inclinations like those of the friend of man should occasion praise and encouragement, he says, but not esteem, which is appropriate for moral worth. This makes it clear that Kant is not recommending the elimination of the inclinations. What gives moral worth, and so what occasions esteem, is where the inclination is incorporated into a maxim that is willed as a universal law. The inclination to help needs to be tested; I do not need to help those with immoral ends. Using the formulation of the categorical imperative in terms of human beings as ends in themselves, we could put the point this way. I am required to share the ends of those affected by my actions, and so make them my ends, but only if those ends are themselves morally permitted.[35] Reason requires us to take account of the inclinations of *all* those affected by what we do, counting our own, but only because we, like all the others, have the dignity of persons.

Perhaps an analogy would help. The inclinations give us goals to pursue, and this is like driving a car to some destination. Usually there is no point in driving unless there is somewhere we want to get to, and usually "going for a drive" is not a sufficient incentive. But we need to make sure that our driving to our destination is consistent with the morally permissible goals of the other drivers on the road. We have to check in our rearview mirrors, stay a safe distance behind the vehicle in front, signal our intentions when we change lanes, and so on. This is because our getting to our destination is no more important than their getting to theirs, if we look at the situation from what Henry Sidgwick calls "the point of view of the universe." There is nothing inconsistent with morality in starting from an inclination, and indeed most actions are only intelligible on such a basis. But there is a distinct kind of worth that resides in testing those inclinations against the moral law, and in particular against all the other inclinations (our own and others') that are morally permissible and are at play in the situations in which we act.

Kant and the Five Stages of Deliberation

This brings us to the five stages of deliberation that I have claimed can be distinguished in Kant's account of agency.[36] The first stage is the desire or inclination from which the action starts. Moral agents are not different in this respect from any other kind of agent. Agents who were concerned only with their own happiness would also start from a desire or inclination. We should acknowledge here the mistakes I pointed to earlier in Kant's account of inclination. They do not invalidate the structure I am laying out. Moral agents process this inclination through the categorical imperative procedure, and I will not try to say more about this than that it is initially (in the second stage) an intellectual process, a testing for one of two different kinds of consistency. It would be possible for a person to determine that a maxim could be willed as universal law without thereby *willing* it as universal law. An immoralist who had merely vestigial respect for the moral law could still recognize that the moral law commanded something.[37] The theological counterpart of this view is that even the demons in hell can recognize that something is commanded by God, but this does not lead them to obey the command but to repudiate it. The third stage is that the recognition that the moral law commands something occasions the feeling of respect in us. Respect is, Kant says repeatedly, a feeling, but it is unique in that it is occasioned only by the presentation by reason of the pure practical law. It is like a radio tuned to only one frequency. This feeling is not the ground of morality, but it is a consequence of our apprehending the moral demand in our reason. But there is, so to speak, a feedback mechanism; the feeling of respect "promotes the influence of the law on the will."[38]

What does Kant mean by this? He cannot mean that the feeling of respect has a causal impact on the rational will, because he cannot allow causation from the phenomenal to the noumenal. His explanation is ingenious but leaves some important difficulties unresolved. What we feel, he says, is that an obstacle to the influence of the moral law on the will is removed. The obstacle is what he calls "self-esteem" or "self-conceit," by which we regard ourselves, and so the satisfaction of our self-indexed inclinations, as supremely valuable. We are attached in this way to the satisfaction of our inclinations as a sum. What happens when we feel respect in the presence of the law is that our sense of the worth of this satisfaction is lowered in comparison with our sense of the elevated worth of the law. Kant calls the lowering "humiliation," a negative effect or a feeling of pain. But the image of lowering and elevating suggests a pair of scales, where putting a greater weight on one pan raises the level of the other. As I quoted earlier, "The lowering (humiliation) of the pretensions to self-esteem on the sensuous side is an elevation of the moral, i.e. practical, esteem for the law on the intellectual side." The feeling of respect is thus like the feeling of the sublime, which also has two moments, the first negative (e.g., a sense of one's own smallness or weakness in comparison with the size or might of the ocean) and the second positive (a sense of something in oneself of higher worth, namely, reason or freedom). Because of this positive moment of respect, we can say that "respect for the law is not the drive to morality; it is morality itself, regarded subjectively as a drive, inasmuch as pure practical reason, by rejecting all the rival claims of self-love, gives authority and absolute sovereignty to the law."[39]

Respect (the third stage) "promotes the influence of the law on the will." The willing of the morally good maxim as the agent's own maxim, as a maxim *for her*, is the fourth stage. Kant talks of willing that the law be *my* law, which is what it means for the law to be *practical*. The respect is taken up or incorporated into the agent's maxim. But we have not yet got to the fifth and final stage, the action itself. There can be external obstacles. I make it my maxim to keep my promise to water your garden, and I am prevented by circumstances beyond my control; the local government declares a drought and forbids the use of the hose. But what is conceptually harder to see is that there can also be internal obstacles to an action *with moral worth*. Kant discusses what he calls "impurity," "where although the maxim is good with respect to its object and perhaps even powerful enough in practice, it is not purely moral, i.e. it has not adopted the law *alone* as its *sufficient* incentive."[40] It is helpful to construe impurity in terms of degrees of respect. Kant's language of "lowering" and "elevating" and "promoting the influence" suggests that we can have more and less respect. I may have enough respect for me to adopt a maxim that is good in its object (e.g., keeping the promise by watering your garden) but not enough so that it would lead to action if this incentive were to be alone. Perhaps what is required to get me to keep the promise is a mixture of respect for the moral law and fear of your wrath. This teaching about impurity does not imply that I cannot (if pure) have concomitant inclinations but that if I do, they are not necessary to get me to action. If there is enough respect, there will not be impurity, and the resulting action will have moral worth strictly speaking.[41]

We can now venture a conclusion about how feelings and inclinations enter into moral deliberation in both helpful and unhelpful ways. The first thing to say is that desires (and the feelings on which they are based) are usually the starting point and provide the material of the maxim from which the agent acts. Desires are what I called the first stage. As I said earlier, this is no different for moral agents than it is for agents who are concerned only with their own happiness. But the matter provided by some inclinations is recalcitrant to the form provided by the categorical imperative procedure, just as in Aristotelian metaphysics, the matter of a jellyfish is recalcitrant to the form of an armadillo. So one way in which desires and feelings can be an obstacle is that they provide matter that resists the moral form so that the maxim that incorporates it cannot be willed as universal law. "Passions," in Kant's usage, are inclinations that are recalcitrant in this way. The second way in which feelings and desires enter into moral deliberation is at what I called the third stage. We human beings, though this is not true of all rational beings, need something sensuous in addition to the mere intellectual recognition that something is morally required. We need what Kant calls "respect," and moreover, we need enough respect so that the moral incentive needs no more than that respect in order to get us to action. Kant probably thinks that all humans have *some* respect for the moral law because of the predisposition to good, which is intrinsic to human nature.[42] But not all humans have enough respect so that they will a maxim that is good in its object, or even if they do this, enough respect so that the moral incentive is sufficient. So the second way feelings and desires enter into deliberation unhelpfully is that we have deficient respect or admiration, or in general deficient feelings and desires that we can class under what Kant calls "the aesthetic of morals."

Kant and Aquinas on Practical Love

We can now go to the second task of this paper, which is to compare the picture of Kant I have just offered with the picture of Aquinas offered by Jean Porter in her contribution to the present volume. I am not going to try to pass judgment on whether her picture of Aquinas is accurate. She suggests a three-part solution to the paradox that Aquinas both affirms eudaimonism and asserts that charity loves God for the sake of God and the neighbor for the sake of the neighbor, and not for our own sakes. The eudaimonism is expressed in his statement that all human beings act for some one end, toward which all their actions are directed, and formally considered, this end is the same for all—namely, the individual's own perfection, or (which she regards as equivalent) his beatitude, or happiness (Aquinas, *ST* I–II.1.5, 6, 8). Porter says, "Aquinas begins the *prima secundae* with the claims that everyone necessarily acts for one final end, in accordance with some reasoned grasp of her overall good, in such a way as to direct all her actions in some way toward this end." All of this sounds like a clear denial of the picture I attributed to Scotus and Kant at the beginning of this paper, that there are *two* fundamental motivations behind human action. But Aquinas also says that the love of God for God's own sake is the distinctive mark of charity and that charity toward the neighbor requires us to promote the neighbor's good for the neighbor's sake and not our own (*ST* II–II.23.5 ad 2, 31.1). There is a paradox here, and Aquinas-Porter proposes a way to resolve it in three steps.

The First Part of the Solution

The first part of the solution comes in the following key paragraph:

> Whatever overarching good the agent loves as her final end, she must regard it as in some
> way a meaningful goal for her own actions. The inclination of the will toward any final end
> whatever implies a commitment to judge, choose, and act in accordance with that end (*ST*
> I 83.4; I-II 8.2, 9.3). The agent need not know exactly what she ought to do out of love for
> whatever she identifies as her end, but unless she is committed to do something, and has
> a general idea of what that practically means, her protestations of love are empty. At this
> point, we recall that every agent perfects itself in and through appropriate activities, bring-
> ing actuality to the potentialities of its form. This implies that any choice to act is ipso facto
> directed toward one's own perfection, and the commitment to an overarching final end,
> seen as a commitment to a consistent pattern of activity, implies a commitment to seek
> one's own perfection through appropriate activities, which in some way place the agent in
> a right relation with whatever she most loves.

This point is not yet a solution to the paradox all by itself, but it provides an account of the
fundamental motivation behind the eudaimonism. What is a Kantian going to say about this
point? She is going to say that it begs the question. What we have here are two fundamentally
different accounts of human agency. I will put this point in language from Scotus, but it could
just as well be put in language from Kant. There are two basic affections or drives of the will:
the affection for justice and the affection for advantage. For Aristotle, and for Aquinas-Porter,
there is just one. The final end, the only one, the "overarching" one, is the individual's own
perfection or happiness, and therefore, "any choice to act is ipso facto directed toward one's
own perfection." Scotus and Kant do not deny that, in Kant's language, "to be happy is necessarily the desire of every rational but finite being."[43] But as I tried to show in the first half of
this paper, this incentive is contrasted with an independent incentive, which is also operative
in every rational but finite being. On this view, the key question, because humans are free, is
how they will rank these two incentives. Humans are in this way unlike other animals. The
Aquinas-Porter account of action depends on the premise that action is an activity, and
therefore, like all natural activities, it is the actualization of an individual's telos. But the
Scotus-Kant account is that human action is not in this sense natural, but free. Scotus, following Anselm, says that if an angel had the affection for advantage but not the affection for
justice, its actions would not be free. To assert that we know, just on the basis of understanding human agency, that there is one final end, begs the question.

What I have said about respect helps to forestall one objection to Kant's position as I
have described it. It is tempting to say, "But if the action is to be *my* action, it is only intelligible if it is directed towards *my* good, and so the inclination has to be toward a self-indexed
object." On Kant's picture, respect is *my* feeling (even, he says, a sensuous feeling, though not
a pathological one). But it does not follow that it is occasioned by a self-indexed object.
Rather, it is occasioned by the moral law, which has no reference to me at all. It is important
to distinguish here the question of whether the object is self-indexed and the question of
whether the description under which the object is loved is self-indexed. The Aquinas-Porter
position and the Scotus-Kant position have common ground in denying the latter. Porter
distinguishes between "the reasons that inform a given set of dispositions or commitments
and the reasons out of which an agent chooses or acts at any particular point." But what is at

issue between the two positions is the former question: Must the object of one's own action be self-indexed if it is to be intelligible to an agent? Aquinas-Porter says yes (though the object may not be articulated as such), and Scotus-Kant says no.

The Second Part of the Solution

Aquinas-Porter gives a second step in the solution to the paradox by pointing to the fact that the individual belongs in a nested series of more and more general goods: the political community, the natural world, and God's friends.

> She sees that she herself is part of the community, playing a role in its common good, that she is one active entity in a dynamic cosmic order, and finally—given the transforming effects of grace—that she has a place in the fellowship of God's friends. What is more, she naturally grasps that her own good as an individual depends on her standing in right relation to these more comprehensive goods. Even though the claims of the commonwealth, or the wider demands of natural reverence or grace, may go contrary to her immediate interests, they cannot ultimately come into conflict with her true good, her perfection, and (therefore) her happiness. The integral link between the good of the individual and more general goods opens up a conceptual space within which the agent's practical reason and will can operate in a unified, coherent way.

I will proceed by asking what a Kantian would say about this nested series, starting with the political community and going on to the natural world and then the community of the redeemed. I will go somewhat beyond Kant in the details of my responses, but Kant himself would reject the overall claim that there cannot be a conflict of true interest in any of these cases. One difficulty here is that Kant and Aquinas (and Aristotle) do not mean the same thing by "happiness." For Kant, my happiness is the satisfaction of my inclinations as a sum. For Aquinas, it is my chief good. A direct comparison of texts, therefore, on the question whether it is possible for me to will to sacrifice my happiness is going to be misleading. But we can take our cue from Porter in the previous quotation and ask whether it is possible for me to will to sacrifice my own ultimate (not just my immediate) interests. It is important here to bear in mind the modal nature of the claim that is in dispute, that there *cannot* be a conflict. It will not be enough in any of the three cases just to say that there is not a conflict. The claim is one of necessity, a necessity that applies even to the divine will.

First, is it right to say that the interest of the individual necessarily coincides with the "true interests" of the polis? For Aristotle, there is a tension here that emerges in the tension between books 1 and 10 of the *Nicomachean Ethics*.[44] In book 1, Aristotle's position is that nobility (*to kalon*) requires ruling: "For while the good of an individual is a desirable thing, what is good for a people or for cities is a nobler and more godlike thing" (*NE* 1.2.1094b9–10). The knowledge of the statesman is the knowledge of this good under which all goods produced by action are ranked. The highest good is a life of action by which one realizes this good; in other words, it is the life of the statesman. The best life, in this view, is the life of the leader. As Meno says, when Socrates asks what human excellence is in Plato's dialogue, "it is simply the capacity to govern human beings, if you are looking for one quality to cover all the instances" (Plato, *Meno* 72d1–2). This generates a problem. What if it is best for the city if I do not rule but hand over the rule to someone else and retire from public life? The situation will then be like what Aristotle says about friendship, and this is not a coincidence, because

Aristotle thinks of fellow citizens as the broadest class of friends. I want good for my friends, Aristotle says, for their sake and not for my own. But I do not want the highest good for my friend, which is to become a god (*NE* 8.7.1159a5–12). For that will put my friend too far above me, and I will no longer be able to maintain the special relation. So the good I want for the friend is contingent on the maintenance of the special relation, and the same is true for the good of the polis; it is my highest good contingently on my being one of the leaders who rule it.

The nature of the state changes between Aristotle and Aquinas and equally radically between Aquinas and Kant. Is the tension between *Nicomachean Ethics* 1 and 10 recapitulated in a disagreement between Aquinas-Porter and Kant about the relation of the individual and the state? I think so, but to show this, I will need to go beyond Kant's own texts and discuss what is sometimes called "the problem of dirty hands."[45] The state needs, in its leadership, people who are willing to compromise moral standards in a way that is inappropriate for private individuals. This leads, it can be argued, to a corruption of individual moral character that is to the advantage of the state but to the disadvantage (morally speaking) of the individual. To argue that it is advantageous to the state for our leaders to have, to some degree, dirty hands may seem a cynical view of politics. But I am not urging that morality simply be abandoned; rather, I am arguing that moral compromises have to be made and that is a cost to moral character that our leaders have to bear.[46] Consider the analogous case of surgeons who have to cut into living tissue on a regular basis and who have to develop a certain kind of hardness of mind if they are going to do their jobs. This too is a kind of sacrifice of moral sensitivity they make. Or consider the case of soldiers who, even if one believes in a just-war theory, have to be willing to become hardened to some degree about killing other people. For a Kantian, the sacrifice of some degree of individual moral character is a sacrifice of one's highest interest. Kant himself might take the absolutist position that such a sacrifice is never justified under any circumstances, just as he sometimes says that lying is never justified. But remember again the modal claim that is in dispute: that there *cannot* be a conflict. It seems highly plausible that the state could have an interest in this kind of sacrifice by an individual. Kant's own position on the union of individuals into a state is that coincidence of interest is not thereby achieved without divine assistance; there is no natural harmony, in Kant's sense of "natural," because we are all, even after political union, under radical evil. We can only hope for this harmony through the establishment and spread of a society constituted in accordance with, and for the sake of, the laws of virtue. "We can already see that [the duty to work toward a universal republic based on laws of virtue] will require the presupposition of another idea, namely, that of a higher moral Being through whose universal dispensation the forces of separate individuals, insufficient in themselves, are united for a common end."[47]

The second level in the nested series is the level of the natural world, or cosmos. Is it true that the interests of the individual necessarily coincide with the interests of the natural world? Here again, we need to go beyond Kant, but this time because Kant did not know about the theory of evolution. Kant thought that God had the overriding purpose in the entire natural order of creating human moral character.[48] It is interesting that here too Kant agrees with Scotus that the highest object is a state of the will, not of the intellect.[49] But even if we accept that and suppose that God accomplishes this end through evolution, can we say that the interests of all the individuals who suffer and die in the course of evolution are somehow realized in the development of human beings?[50] Whole species have had to be terminated. In any case, it seems doubtful that the whole natural order exists for our sake. If we grant that species other than ours have interests independent of ours, it seems that we have had an impact on the biosphere that is to a significant extent negative. Hundreds of species are dying out because of our activities. Can we say that the interests of the human inhabitants of Washington, DC, for example, are necessarily coincident with the interests of the individual birds and insects and mammals that occupy the same territory? Or if we think that individual members do not have interests but species do, then we can ask whether the interests of human beings necessarily coincide with the interests of all other species, or would many species be better off if human beings had never existed?

Kant's own position is again one that sees no *natural* coincidence of interest, though he agrees that humans cannot survive or flourish without the laws of nature in place. In the *Critique of Judgment*, he mentions Spinoza, a righteous man who does not (in Kant's view) believe in God:

> For while he can expect that nature will now and then cooperate contingently with the purpose of his that he feels so obligated and impelled to achieve, he can never expect nature to harmonize with it in a way governed by laws and permanent rules (such as his inner maxims are and must be). Deceit, violence, and envy will always be rife around him, even though he himself is honest, peaceable, and benevolent. Moreover, as concerns the other righteous people he meets: no matter how worthy of happiness they may be, nature, which pays no attention to that, will still subject them to all the evils of deprivation, disease, and untimely death, just like all those other animals on the earth. And they will stay subjected to these evils always, until one vast tomb engulfs them one and all (honest or not, that makes no difference here) and hurls them, who managed to believe they were the final purpose of creation, back into the abyss of the purposeless chaos of matter from which they were taken.[51]

Aquinas-Porter does not seem to have looked into this abyss or been terrified by it. There is no disagreement between Aquinas-Porter and Kant that God maintains the natural order, but Kant has a view of "nature" by itself that Aquinas-Porter does not. Kant follows Scotus here too in denying final causes to nature in itself, though preserving the purposiveness of nature in God's intention for it.

The third level in the nested series is the community of the redeemed, the "friends of God." Here we need to go back to the counterfactual thought experiment I mentioned in the first part of this paper in connection with Scotus. Again, we go beyond Kant because he has grave doubts about the doctrine of election.[52] But suppose we accept, with Aquinas, that God can predestine some for salvation and some for reprobation. Is it possible that the loss of salvation by the latter might be to the glory of God and that someone might accept that if she *were* among that number, charity would therefore require accepting that? Note that this is not the same as "choosing to act in a damnable way, out of the love of God." Porter is right to deny that this is coherent. But this is not what is at issue. In previous generations, Calvinist congregations would regularly contain people who thought they were among the reprobate but nonetheless attended divine worship with devotion. Is such a frame of mind incoherent? If not, then surely there is not a necessary coincidence between *my* greatest good, in this case my salvation, and the glory of God. Again, because of the modal nature of the claim under dispute, it is not necessary to argue that God in fact predestines some to reprobation but that God could, that this is within the scope of God's sovereignty.

Even though Kant does not endorse the doctrine of double predestination, he does have a place in his system for God's discretion. In the *Critique of Practical Reason*, he argues that reason in its practical employment requires the postulation of the immortality of the soul. Even though we do not see holiness of the will at the time of death, and will never in fact reach it, "nevertheless in this progress toward a goal infinitely remote (a progress which in God's sight is regarded as equivalent to possession) he can have prospect of a blessed future." Kant sees this "regarding as equivalent to possession" as God's grace.[53] There are many obscurities here that I am not going to go into.[54] My point is just that God is not constrained here by necessity any more than we have necessity at the other two levels of the nested series. About all three levels we can say that Kant does believe there is a harmony, but it is a contingent harmony established because God is both, in Leibniz's terms, which Kant also uses, sovereign of "the kingdom of nature" and sovereign of "the kingdom of grace."[55]

The Third Part of the Solution

Finally, the third part of the solution to the paradox in Aquinas-Porter is given in the following passage:

> My point is this. The perfection and happiness of the rational agent, subjectively considered, cannot be understood apart from sustained activities through which she stands in right relation to some greater good. Her love and loyalty to this greater good may well lead her to sacrifice her individual good, considered from some limited perspective. We should not minimize what might be very great sacrifices indeed, yet even in such cases—perhaps especially in such cases—the choice to sacrifice oneself for the object of one's supreme love implies choosing some pattern of activities which perfects the individual by bringing her into right relation with a more comprehensive whole. This is the case even when someone chooses to give up any actual enjoyment of the greater good, as for example, when someone willingly dies for the commonwealth, without expecting any kind of posthumous awareness of having done so. Even this is a choice to attain one's perfection as an agent through appropriate activities—not necessarily formulated under that description, or much less chosen for that reason.

This passage ties together the two previous points and is open to the previous objections. I can deal with it briefly by summarizing the claims I have already made. First, for Kant, our interests as individuals may or may not coincide with the "true interests" of the political units to which we belong. So the "right relation" to these units may or may not produce the fulfillment of our own interests. The only way we can be sure that there is harmony of this sort is if we have achieved an "ethical commonwealth" in which all members live their lives not just in accordance with but for the sake of the laws of virtue. But while Kant thinks we do already belong to a kingdom of ends, the ethical commonwealth is at this point still an object of aspiration. Now we can add, from the earlier treatment of Aquinas-Porter's first point, that even if there is not a coincidence of interest, there can still be a moral obligation to obey. Duty does not, in Kant, have a necessary coincidence with self-interest but one mediated by the free choices of the sovereign of the kingdom of ends. Second, the "true interests" of the natural world may or may not coincide with the interests of the individual humans who live in it, and so the "right relation" to it may or may not produce the fulfillment of our own interests. Consider the choices of whether to put up a cell-phone tower or a string of colossal windmills to produce energy or to launch a satellite into space. The right picture here seems to be one in which the interests of humans are in tension with the interests of the rest of the natural world, and what choices we should make depends on how important the interests of humans are within this tension. There is not a necessary harmony. But again, we can add the key point that the existence of a duty toward the natural world does not depend on its relation to our self-interest. Finally, even in our relation to God through salvation, there seems to be a possible tension unless we believe that God is required by some kind of necessity to save us all. It is possible that God's "true interest" (though this is an odd expression) does not include some individual's eternal happiness.[56]

None of this discredits Porter's claim, at the beginning of her essay, that "there is a growing sense among our contemporaries that we have exaggerated the difference between Aristotelian and Kantian theories of morality." Both theories stress the role of reason within practical love, and both give a significant place also to emotion. Thus, both Aquinas-Porter and Kant hold, if I am right, that the standard case of action is one that starts from inclination and that the best kind of human life is one in which inclinations have been trained to fit with moral law. Both see God as central to the moral life. This is easier to see in Aquinas-Porter, but it is true also in Aristotle and Kant.[57] Both have significant place also for duties as well as virtues, though the Aristotelian account of the virtues is much richer and more fully worked out. Some of the traditional attributions of tension between the two can be seen to result from differences in usage or terminology rather than differences in doctrine. This is true, for example, with the terms "passion" and "happiness." Having said all that, there remain significant differences, and this paper is designed as a contribution to articulating more carefully where these reside.

Notes

I would like to express my gratitude to Gene Outka, who taught me my first course in theological ethics, at Princeton, and whose book *Agape: An Ethical Analysis* has been a continuing source of illumination for me.

1. Immanuel Kant, *Critique of Practical Reason*, in *Practical Philosophy*, ed. and trans. Mary J. Gregor (Cambridge: Cambridge University Press, 1999), 5:83.

2. I would like to record here my gratitude to Jean Porter. I was able, through the generosity of the Notre Dame Center for the Philosophy of Religion, to spend a year at Notre Dame in 2008–9, and Jean Porter and I met regularly and discussed each other's work. I have learned a great deal from her, and this paper is a fruit of our discussion.

3. E.g., Immanuel Kant, *Religion within the Boundaries of Mere Reason*, in *Religion and Rational Theology*, ed. and trans. Allen W. Wood and George di Giovanni (Cambridge: Cambridge University Press, 1996), 6:154.

4. E.g., Immanuel Kant, *Lectures on Ethics* (Collins), in *Lectures on Ethics*, ed. Peter Heath and J. B. Schneewind, trans. Peter Heath (Cambridge: Cambridge University Press, 1997), 27:322.

5. See John Hare, *God and Morality* (Oxford: Blackwell, 2007), esp. chaps. 2 and 3.

6. See Samuel Hopkins, "To Be Willing to Be Damned," in *The Nature of True Holiness* (1770), in *The Works of Samuel Hopkins* (Boston: Doctrinal Tract and Book Society, 1852), 3:147. But see also Moses at Exod. 32:32, Paul at Rom. 9:3, and perhaps Jesus at Matt. 27:45.

7. For Aquinas's view of the passions, see Jean Porter, *Nature as Reason* (Grand Rapids, MI: Eerdmans, 2005), 252–65. There is also an excellent account of Aquinas on the passions in Eleonore Stump, "The Non-Aristotelian Character of Aquinas's Ethics: Aquinas on the Passions," *Faith and Philosophy* 28 (2011): 29–43.

8. Kant, *Lectures on Ethics*, 27:302–4.

9. The treatment of practical love in Kant, *Groundwork of the Metaphysics of Morals*, in *Practical Philosophy*, 4:399, is less accommodating: "Such love resides in the will and not in the propensities of feeling, in principles of action and not in tender sympathy."

10. Kant says in ibid. (4:400), "Now an action done from duty must altogether exclude the influence of inclination and therewith every object of the will." But he should be interpreted here as denying that the

inclinations enter into the *moral* motivation, not that they enter into the motivation *tout court*. For he does not mean to deny that actions have objects of the will. I say more about this when discussing 4:398 later.

11. Kant, *Critique of Practical Reason*, 5:25.

12. I have discussed this more in John Hare, *The Moral Gap* (Oxford: Clarendon Press, 1996), chap. 6, and defended one version of particularism against the Kantian claim that universalizability is a *necessary* feature of moral judgment in all term positions in the judgment.

13. Kant, *Groundwork of the Metaphysics of Morals*, 4:430.

14. Kant, *Critique of Practical Reason*, 5:79.

15. Ibid., 75.

16. Ibid., 26.

17. His closest term to our "emotion" is *rührung* (e.g., Kant, *Critique of Judgment*, in *Critique of the Power of Judgment*, ed. Paul Guyer, trans. Paul Guyer and Eric Matthews [Cambridge: Cambridge University Press, 2000], 5:273–74), but "emotion" in its current sense is an invention of the nineteenth century. See Thomas Dixon, *From Passions to Emotions: The Creation of a Secular Psychological Category* (Cambridge: Cambridge University Press, 2003).

18. I have discussed the material in sections 1b–1d in more detail, covering more of Kant's relevant texts, in John Hare, "Kant, the Passions, and the Structure of Moral Motivation," *Faith and Philosophy* 28 (2011): 54–70. This article also discusses the relation of the five-stage account of moral deliberation to the question of whether Kant is an internalist about moral motivation.

19. For Jean Porter's take on this, see *Nature as Reason*, 254n.

20. Kant, *Metaphysics of Morals*, in *Practical Philosophy*, 6:408.

21. Immanuel Kant, *Anthropology from a Pragmatic Point of View*, in *Anthropology, History, and Education*, ed. Guenter Zoeller and Robert B. Louden, trans. Mary J. Gregor et al. (Cambridge: Cambridge University Press, 2007), 7:251.

22. Kant, *Critique of Practical Reason*, 5:25.

23. Kant, *Metaphysics of Morals*, 6:408.

24. Ibid., 384–85.

25. Kant, *Religion within the Boundaries of Mere Reason*, 6:35.

26. Martin Luther, *The Bondage of the Will* (New York: Fleming H. Revell, 1957), 280.

27. Kant, *Anthropology*, 7:253.

28. Kant allows two exceptions in the *Anthropology* to the general prohibition on affect. The first (7:257) is that "courage as affect (consequently belonging in one respect to sensibility) can also be aroused by reason." The second example (7:261) is when "he who thoughtfully and with a scrutinizing eye pursues the order of nature in its great variety falls into *astonishment* at a wisdom he did not expect: an admiration from which he cannot tear himself away. . . . However, such an affect is stimulated only by reason." See also Kant, *Metaphysics of Morals*, 6:406, where he talks of "an aesthetic of morals," in which "the feelings that accompany the constraining power of the moral law (e.g. disgust, horror, etc., which make moral aversion sensible) make its efficacy felt."

29. Kant, *Anthropology*, 7:265.

30. Ibid., 271.

31. Compare Aristotle's discussion of *philotimia* (the love of honor) at *NE* 2.7.1107b25f.

32. Kant, *Groundwork of the Metaphysics of Morals*, 4:398–99.

33. Barbara Herman, *The Practice of Moral Judgment* (Cambridge, MA: Harvard University Press, 1993), 2–40. She is responding to Richard Henson, "What Kant Might Have Said: Moral Worth and the Overdetermination of Dutiful Action," *Philosophical Review* 88 (1979): 45–46.

34. Compare Aristotle, *NE* 1.12, where he contrasts two kinds of worth, namely, what we commend and what we honor. We honor the gods, but we do not commend them.

35. Kant, *Groundwork of the Metaphysics of Morals*, 4:430.

36. I am replying here to an important paper by Karl Ameriks, "Kant and Motivational Externalism," in *Moralische Motivation*, ed. H. Klemme, M. Kühn, D. Schönecker (Hamburg: Felix Meiner Verlag, 2006), 3–22. See also Ameriks, *Kant and the Historical Turn* (Oxford: Oxford University Press, 2006), chap. 4.

37. I say "vestigial respect" because Kant's view is that morality itself requires us to recognize in all humans, insofar as they are human, the predisposition to the good, even if it does not become actualized in

the fruit of a morally good life. Whether Kant is right about, for example, psychopaths is a question for a different essay.

38. Kant, *Critique of Practical Reason*, 5:75.

39. Ibid., 76.

40. Kant, *Religion within the Boundaries of Mere Reason*, 6:30.

41. There is a formal inconsistency that is worth noting here, but I think it is not troubling. Kant says both that the moral incentive has to be sufficient if the action is to have moral worth and that we need something in addition to it (namely, respect). But we can revise the first claim by noting that respect "cannot be compared with any pathological feeling," and we can say that the moral incentive has to be enough so as not to need anything else except respect for the law. See Kant, *Critique of Practical Reason*, 5:76.

42. Kant, *Religion within the Boundaries of Mere Reason*, 6:28.

43. Kant, *Critique of Practical Reason*, 5:25.

44. There is a large body of literature here, but I have given a summary in the first chapter of Hare, *God and Morality*, 7–72.

45. There is a characteristically nuanced and historically informed account in Michael Walzer, "Political Action: The Problem of Dirty Hands," in *War and Moral Responsibility*, ed. Marshall Cohen, Thomas Nagel, and Thomas Scanlon (Princeton, NJ: Princeton University Press, 1974), 62–82.

46. I should probably divulge that I spent some time working on the staff of the House Foreign Affairs Committee in Washington, though I do not mean to imply that it is only American politicians who compromise in this way.

47. Kant, *Religion within the Boundaries of Mere Reason*, 6:97. See John Hare, "Kantian Ethics, International Politics, and the Enlargement of the *Foedus Pacificum*," in *Sovereignty at the Crossroads*, ed. Luis E. Lugo (London: Rowman and Littlefield, 1996), 71–92.

48. Kant, *Critique of Judgment*, 5:436.

49. See Porter, *Nature as Reason*, 255, where the foundational virtue is faith.

50. Note that this would not require "guided evolution" of the kind that seems *not* to be the case, namely, where mutations occur selectively for the benefit of the species in which they occur.

51. Kant, *Critique of Judgment*, 5:452.

52. E.g., Kant, *Religion within the Boundaries of Mere Reason*, 6:143–44.

53. Kant, *Critique of Practical Reason*, 5:123.

54. See Hare, *God and Morality*, 160–61. My interpretation is controversial, but it is not controversial that Kant says this is God's grace.

55. Kant, *Critique of Pure Reason*, A812–B840.

56. The Aquinas-Porter argument can be revised in a way that is not liable to the objections I have made. We can suppose that what the agent identifies with as her good is not some more *general* good, like the good of the polis or of the natural world or of God's friends, that necessarily *includes* her individual good, but the divine itself, which is by its own nature self-transcending. We have both a self-perfecting and a self-transcending love, but the second comes out of the first because we identify in perfecting ourselves with a being that is itself self-transcending. See Shelley's couplet, "True love in this differs from gold and clay / That to divide is not to take away." I discuss this in John Hare, *God's Command* (Oxford: Oxford University Press, 2015), and reply that on this revision we again end up with a non-self-indexed and therefore a double-source account of motivation.

57. See Hare, *God and Morality*, chaps. 1 and 3.

6 ⦂•

Kierkegaard and Kant on the "Duty to Love"

M. JAMIE FERREIRA

ATTEMPTS TO COMPARE and contrast Kant's ethics with Kierkegaard's ethics usually use Kant's *Groundwork for the Metaphysics of Morals* and Kierkegaard's pseudonymous writings *Either-Or* and *Fear and Trembling*. It seems to me that a more fruitful comparison of their ethics is possible by drawing on the more mature ethical accounts of both thinkers: in Kant's case, the later and fuller *Metaphysics of Morals* and, in Kierkegaard's case, *Works of Love*, signed in his own name. In particular, I suggest that a study of their views of the scriptural commandment to "love your neighbor" can be mutually illuminating.[1]

It is clear that Kierkegaard's *Works of Love* is a lengthy and detailed analysis of the scriptural commandment to love your neighbor, which he affirms. It is, as we shall see, part of an ethic that is unconditionally binding, universal in scope, and resolutely anti-consequentialist. In these respects, the potential for comparison with Kant's own unconditional, universal, and anti-consequentialist ethic is apparent. But Kant claimed (as is well-known) that "love as an inclination cannot be commanded" and (as is less-known) that "a duty to love is an absurdity" because "love is a matter of feeling, not willing."[2] So it might seem that a direct comparison of Kant and Kierkegaard on this issue is impossible. However, two considerations mitigate this apparent impasse. First, Kierkegaard too was aware that there was at least an "apparent contradiction" in the notion that "to love is a duty,"[3] and he too claimed that love as an inclination cannot be commanded. Second, Kant wrote at great length in his *Metaphysics of Morals* about "die Pflict der Nächstenliebe" and "Liebespflicten" in explaining and affirming what he thought was the true meaning of the scriptural commandment of the Abrahamic religious traditions to love your neighbor (e.g., *MM*, 199, 201). An examination of these two works thus allows a direct comparison (and contrast) of their understandings of our "duty" to "love" others.

I propose to consider the dimensions of the ethical revealed in their respective treatments of the duty to love others: first, with respect to the scope and bindingness of the obligation as well as its content; second, with respect to the relation of the obligation to our instinctive predispositions; and finally, with respect to the precise way in which the obligation is to be fulfilled. I begin with a brief sketch of Kierkegaard's position on love of neighbor and then present those aspects of Kant's position that provide points of contact with Kierkegaard's.[4] My aim is to consider what seem like obvious similarities and dissimilarities, in the

91

hope of clarifying and qualifying both. In particular, I will analyze what seem to be differences between them on the question of the obligation we have.

Kierkegaard on the Duty to Love Others

Kierkegaard admits that the commandment to love the neighbor "contains this apparent contradiction: to love is a duty."[5] He goes about resolving this apparent contradiction in two ways. First, he appeals to what he considers our common experience by suggesting that binding ourselves to love is a fulfillment of our nature's need to love—that is, the joyousness of spontaneous love "feels a need to bind itself, if possible, even more securely" (*WL*, 29). Whether or not we find that convincing, he offers another, a philosophical, response—namely, that the love that is commanded is neither feeling, nor inclination, nor attraction since these are spontaneous and cannot be commanded (*WL*, 50); rather, the love that is commanded is a responsibility to *care for* others in ways that respect the "equality" and "kinship of all human beings" (*WL*, 69), even if it involves different physical and psychological expressions given the particular context. In what follows, I will unpack this philosophical response in ways that will facilitate a comparison with Kant's view.

First, Kierkegaard affirms an *unconditional and universal obligation* to fulfill the scriptural commandment to "love your neighbor" (*Du skal elske din Naesten*). The unconditional "shall" of the commandment is explained by him in terms of a universal scope: "The Christian doctrine is to love the neighbor, to love the whole human race, all people, even the enemy, and not to make exceptions, neither of preference nor of aversion" (*WL*, 19). That is, "everyone is the neighbor" (*WL*, 44) because "Christianity teaches us to love all people, unconditionally, all." (*WL*, 49). In short, "the neighbor is one who is equal"; "he is your neighbor on the basis of *equality* with you before God, but unconditionally every person has this equality and has it unconditionally" (*WL*, 60). The universality of the obligation is a function of acknowledging a "*kinship* with all people, with unconditionally every person" (*WL*, 74), as well as an equality with all: "In being king, beggar, rich man, poor man, male, female, etc., we are not like each other—therein we are indeed different. But in being the neighbor we are all unconditionally like each other. . . . The neighbor is eternity's mark—on every human being" (*WL*, 89). It is this equality that is guaranteed by the requirement of closing one's eyes to distinctions that deny kinship (*WL*, 75). The universal scope of the commandment is found not only in the claim that the neighbor is all people (none can be excluded) but also in the way in which no one is exempt from being bound unconditionally by the commandment.

Second, our duty in fulfilling the commandment is *not a duty to have a feeling or inclination or attraction*; what he calls "instinctive and inclinational love" or "spontaneous love" (*WL*, 29, 35) cannot be commanded. He notes, "The poet idolizes inclination, and therefore is quite right . . . in saying that to command love is the greatest fatuousness and the most preposterous talk" (*WL*, 50).

Third, the "love" to which we are obligated is a *practical* love. Kierkegaard contrasts both wishes and empty platitudes with active works: "one should not love in words and platitudes" (*WL*, 12). Christian love, "which is the fulfilling of the Law . . . is sheer action" (*WL*, 98)—in Christ, "love was sheer action" (*WL*, 99). Although such action does not necessarily mean public behaviors—forgiveness, for example, is as much an action as feeding the hungry and tending the sick—the "works" or "fruits" of love must be "recognizable": "this hidden life of love is *recognizable by its fruits*—indeed, to be able to be known by its fruits is a need in love" (*WL*, 10). Love's fruits or works are the actualization of the potential of love, which is placed in us by God who is Love, and that actualization must be "recognizable." That is, he distinguishes between a "fruit" or work and a mere wish or inner feeling. For example, love's fruit of forgiveness must be more than an idle wish or warm feeling.

Fourth, at the same time as the love commandment demands practical expression, the duty of love is *anti-consequentialist*. Kierkegaard distinguishes between love's works or fruits and any external achievement. Fruits are distinguished from external accomplishments or success because "what a person will or will not achieve is not within his power" (*WL*, 84). Just as the fruit of forgiveness can be present even if the external expression of forgiveness is not successful, so too a fruit or work of love can be actualized even if its intention is thwarted by others or by natural impediments.

Fifth, the general *content* of neighbor love is the "beneficence" of helping the other to stand alone before God. Kierkegaard's exemplar of practical love is the Good Samari-tan—"Christ does not speak about knowing the neighbor but about becoming the neighbor oneself, about showing oneself to be a neighbor just as the Samaritan showed it by his mercy" (*WL*, 22). We are obligated to be "God's co-workers in love" (*WL*, 63), contributing to the ability of the other to be independent, free, because "in the world of spirit, precisely this, to become one's own master, is the highest—and in love to help someone toward that, to become himself, free, independent, his own master, to help him stand alone—that is the greatest beneficence" (*WL*, 274). Without doubt, "the greatest, the only beneficence one human being can do for another, [is] to help him stand by himself, to become himself, to become his own master" (*WL*, 277–78), and this can be done in countless different ways; contributing to the other's independence will involve eliminating obstacles to its expression (e.g., poverty, oppression, and despair).

Sixth, such commanded love is an "infinite debt" that can never be repaid. Kierkegaard puts before us the challenging notion of love as infinite debt with decisive typographical emphasis: "*the one who loves by giving, infinitely, runs into infinite debt*" (*WL*, 176). Kierke-gaard's Lutheran heritage accounts for his commitment to the idea that commanded love is *owed* to the other.[6]

Seventh, the commandment *can be fulfilled by us* ("ought implies can"): "Eternity, which speaks of the highest, calmly assumes that every person can do it and therefore asks only if he did it" (*WL*, 79).

Eighth, although the obligation is unconditionally binding and infinite, it has *limits*. The commandment is to "love your neighbor as yourself," and Kierkegaard insists repeatedly that the "as yourself" requires a "proper" self-love (*WL*, 18). Contempt of oneself is excluded because the self is a part of creation to be valued and cherished, like all other parts. Sacrifice is not an end in itself. Nevertheless, self-denial will be part of any attempt to allow others their own autonomy; as Kierkegaard notes, "The rigid, the domineering person lacks the pliability to comprehend others; he demands his own from everyone, wants everyone to be transformed in his image, to be trimmed according to his pattern for human beings" (*WL*, 270).

Ninth, *gratitude* for our love of others is not precluded. There is no reason our loving efforts cannot both benefit the neighbor and be recognized as doing so—the model of God's love for us shows that the gift is not invalidated because it is responded to with gratitude but only if it is conditional on the response of gratitude.

Tenth, the *how* of fulfilling the commandment is crucial: "the greatest beneficence is specifically the *way* in which the one and only true beneficence is done" (*WL*, 274). "The greatest benefaction, therefore, cannot be done in such a way that the recipient comes to know that it is to me that he owes it. . . . By hiding his help, [he] has helped him to stand by himself" (*WL*, 275). That is, the loving one is the "hidden benefactor," the one who "chose lovingly to stay in the background," although "he had the power *unlovingly* to make the seeker specially obliged to him" (*WL*, 278). "Love does not seek its own; it rather gives in such a way that the gift looks as if it were the recipient's property" (*WL*, 274)—it gives in such a way that the other is not made to feel indebted, humiliated, condescended to (*WL*, 338, 342, 343). "The one who loves hides himself" (*WL*, 340) as much as possible, knowing that it is a "difficult task" to "be as rigorous as truth requires and yet as gentle as love desires" (*WL*, 339). The how is especially important in forgiving: it is "unloving" to forgive while making "myself important by being able to forgive" or by being reluctant to forgive or by increasing the other's sense of guilt (*WL*, 295). One must have "solicitude" for the wrongdoer (*WL*, 340), avoiding pride, conceit, arrogance, and so on (*WL*, 332, 334).

Eleventh, the human potential for love is an endowment, a gift of God at creation. There is only one source of the potential for human love; it is the gift of God who is *Kjerlighed*, and so all human potential for love is *Kjerlighed*: "God is Love [*Kjerlighed*], and therefore we can be like God only in loving, just as we also . . . can only be *God's co-workers*—in love" (*WL*, 63). *Kjerlighed* is the source of all human expressions of love because *Kjerlighed* is the energy of love, the love potential, placed in us by God. As the love potential, *Kjerlighed* is expressed in both preferential and non-preferential love. Preferential loves are romantic love (*Elskov*) and friendship (*Venskab*); non-preferential love is *Kjerlighed*.

In other words, *Kjerlighed* can be expressed in two ways, either simply without restriction (non-preferentially, *Kjerlighed*) or with restrictions (preferentially, *Forkjerlighed*). There is one underlying love insofar as the only love potential (energy, ability) we possess is the *Kjerlighed* that God gifted us with at creation. What is being expressed in *Forkjerlighed* is *Kjerlighed* with a narrow focus.

Twelfth, Kierkegaard insists that both preferential and non-preferential love are valuable; indeed, he suggests that "erotic love is undeniably life's most beautiful happiness" (*WL*, 267). Normatively, the relation between them is that preferential loves like romantic love and friendship must "preserve" *Kjerlighed* in them: the commandment requires that "in erotic love and friendship, [we] preserve love for the neighbor [*Kjerlighed til Naesten*]" (*WL*, 62). What is commanded is *Kjerlighed*, not *Elskov* or *Venskab*. But they are not mutually exclusive.

Since this is often a source of misunderstanding, it is worth examining in detail.[7] It is a contradiction to say that we should treat people as both preferred by us and not preferred by us, but the problem disappears if we imagine a concrete case and not a question of fitting two logically contradictory terms together. So what does Kierkegaard mean? Preserving *Kjerlighed* (non-preferential love) in these preferential loves amounts to maintaining the sense of the other's dignity in their own right as an equal before God, refusing to use the preferred one simply for our pleasure. Preferential and non-preferential loves are therefore not mutually exclusive. Kierkegaard insists repeatedly that preserving *Kjerlighed* in erotic love and friendship does not need to militate against their distinctive expressions: "If someone thinks that the difference between paganism and Christianity is that in Christianity the beloved and the friend are loved faithfully and tenderly in a quite different way than in paganism, this is a misunderstanding" (*WL*, 53). It is a confusion to think that Christianity teaches "a higher love but in addition praises erotic love and friendship"—it is foolishness "to talk like a shopkeeper who carries the best grade of goods but in addition has a medium grade, which he can also very well recommend as almost as good" (*WL*, 45). Preferential love and non-preferential love are not related as something less high to something higher—they are related as a restriction of *Kjerlighed* to a nonrestricted *Kjerlighed*. It is all *Kjerlighed* because that is the potential with which we are gifted at creation.

That erotic love and friendship should "preserve" love for the neighbor means that our preferential attractions (our special relations) should preserve in them the same appreciation for the dignity and autonomy of our beloved and friend as of all human beings. Kierkegaard explains, "No person is an exception to being a human being because of his particular dissimilarity but is a human being and then what he is in particular. Thus Christianity has nothing against the husband's loving the wife in particular, but he must never love her in particular in such a way that she is an exception to being the neighbor that every human being is" (*WL*, 142). The preferential relation should never be allowed to exist without being informed by the acknowledgment of the other's genuine alterity (dignity, equality, autonomy)—or it would be a way of making of our preferred other an object for our use or exploitation.

In other words, the expressions of the love that is commanded will take different forms. The neighbor love that is commanded in the case of a needy spouse or child or friend will be a warm and intimate caring—but it will be warm, intimate, or passionate because that is the nature of the relation, not because warmth or intimacy or passion is commanded. The neighbor love that is commanded in the case of a stranger we meet in physical distress will be a benevolence that will address the stranger's distinctive needs rather than some abstract, formulaic attitude, but it need not have the same tenderness that we would show to an intimate relation. We are not commanded to feel the preference we feel in the case of an intimate relation, but we are commanded not to let the lack of preferential feeling militate against our responsibility to help the other. Where there is neither passionate love nor friendship, what is commanded is best seen in terms of our responsibility to the other, the infinite debt we owe. The nature of the relationship will shape the response. The commandment cannot command the partiality of inclination, but it does not exclude its presence so long as that partiality does not undermine our appreciation that the debt we owe has no exceptions. Loving the other does not amount to the same thing in every case: in some cases, but not all, beneficence will be extended with warmth, emotion, or intimacy.

Finally, love of neighbor is tied to love of God; for Kierkegaard, there is no question but that the *command to love the neighbor comes from God*. However, the command is embedded in the order of creation; creation includes the commandment to love without exclusion, so there cannot be a question of God commanding us not to love. It would be a "contradiction" for us to be commanded by God not to love someone (*WL*, 61).

This is, admittedly, a rough sketch of Kierkegaard's position on the love commandment in *Works of Love*, but it can serve as a framework that allows us to consider Kant's points of contact with it. The question I am addressing is whether Kant's understanding of the duty to love others is comparable to Kierkegaard's. The short answer is that, as we shall see, Kant, like Kierkegaard, believes that "love for our neighbor" (*Nächstenliebe*) is "incumbent on us as a duty" (*Pflict*) (*MM*, 207). A long answer is necessary, however, because a more precise examination will also reveal that certain differences and similarities in their accounts of the duty of love are significant.

Kant on the Duty to Love Others

The Scriptural Commandment—*Praktische Liebe* and *Wohltun*

One way to begin to reveal the relation between Kant and Kierkegaard on the love commandment is to reconsider Kant's numerous interpretations of the scriptural neighbor-love commandment. Kant saw references to the love commandment as a perfect opportunity to make
a crucial contrast between inclination and duty. His most well-known reference to this commandment is found in the *Groundwork for the Metaphysics of Morals* (1785)—the claim there
is that because "love as an inclination [*Liebe als Neigung*] cannot be commanded," we should
"understand those passages of Scripture which command us to love our neighbor and even
our enemy" as requiring "beneficence from duty [*Wohltun aus Liebe selbst*]" or "practical love
[*praktische Liebe*]."[8] The only "love [*Liebe*]" that can be commanded, he goes on, is "practical
love"—which resides in the "will" and "principles of action" rather than in the "propensities
of feeling" or "tender sympathy." When Kant later considers the scriptural love commandment in his *Critique of Practical Reason* (1787), he claims that "inclination" or "pathological
love" "cannot be commanded, for it is not within the power of any human being to love
someone merely on command," and he concludes, "It is, therefore, only *practical love* [*praktische Liebe*] that is understood in that kernel of all laws."[9] He repeats this same rejection of a
duty to love-as-inclination/feeling in his mature *Metaphysics of Morals* (1797): when we
speak of "the duty of love for one's neighbor [*die Pflict der Nächstenliebe*]," "love is not to be
understood as *feeling* [*Gefühl*], that is, as pleasure in the perfection of others; love is not to be
understood as delight in them (since others cannot put one under obligation to have feelings). It must rather be thought as the maxim of benevolence (practical love) [*Wohlwollens
als praktische*], which results in beneficence [*Wohltun*]" (*MM*, 199). These are all examples of
Kant's rejection of the relevance of the notion of love-as-inclination/feeling in the context of
the love commandment, and in this respect, Kant and Kierkegaard would be in agreement.

The possibility of a difference between them, however, arises because in addition to the
three preceding examples in which Kant clearly insists that love-as-inclination/feeling cannot
be commanded, there is one place where Kant seems to restrict "love" as such to "love-as-
feeling": he writes, "Love is a matter of *feeling*, not of willing, and I cannot love because I *will*
to, still less because I *ought* to (I cannot be constrained to love); so a *duty to love* is an absurdity," adding that "unselfish benevolence toward human beings is often (though very inappropriately) also called *love*" (*MM*, 161). As a result, some commentators have suggested that
Kant does not really endorse a "duty of love"; they argue that *praktische Liebe* is not *Liebe* at
all, but something else—for example, a kind of respect. The question is whether Kant thinks
(a) that love *is* (restricted by definition to) feeling and therefore cannot be commanded (*MM*,
161) or (b) that there is a kind of love that *is not* feeling but, rather, beneficence (*MM*, 199),
and we will see that the answer depends on an appreciation of context.

In principle, a rejection of love-as-inclination as the content of the love command does
not amount to a rejection of the relevance of the notion of *Liebe* as such. To say that love as
feeling, spontaneous preference, or affection toward another cannot be commanded is simply
to make the claim that a command to do something not under your control does not make
sense—it is not necessarily to look for an alternative to "love" when explicating what the love
commandment entails. I would argue that Kant does not look for an alternative. First, in the
three examples first cited, Kant turns to *praktische Liebe*. The retention of the word "*Liebe*" is
in line with his earlier claim in his *Lectures on Ethics* (1775–81) that "well-wishing love to

one's neighbor [*die Liebe des Wohlwollens gegen seinen Nächsten*] can be enjoined upon everyone."[10] Moreover, in the much appealed-to *Groundwork* passage, Kant's German phrase "*Wohltun* aus *Liebe*" is obscured by the English translation of it as "beneficence from duty"— the German phrase raises the question what kind of *Liebe* is present in *Wohltun aus Liebe*.

Finally, the notion of the duty as one of "*Liebe*" finds its greatest support in *Metaphysics of Morals*, where "Doctrine of Virtue" introduces the category of a "*Liebespflict*" and includes a discussion of "*die Pflict der Nächstenliebe*." Since Kant introduces and examines the notion of a "duty to love" in the very same text in which he claims that "a duty to love is an absurdity," there is clearly interpretive work to be done. In what follows, I am arguing that *Metaphysics of Morals* provides an important development of the truth in the *Groundwork* formulation of "*Wohltun aus Liebe selbst*"; it makes clear why Kant thinks that *praktische Liebe* is still rightly worth calling *Liebe*, even though it is contrasted with "inclination" or "feeling."[11]

"Duty of Love" in *Metaphysics of Morals*

"Doctrine of Virtue" develops the references to the commandment to love your neighbor already found in the earlier works, but it also goes beyond them. There are three main places in "Doctrine of Virtue" where Kant addresses the scope, bindingness, and content of our duty to other human beings. The first two discussions occur in the introductory section, which (in prolegomena-like fashion) presents a generic analysis of "duties of virtue" and of the presuppositions involved in being subject to such duty at all: the first of these offers a rationale for the duty of "beneficence" and an account of it as a "wide" duty; the second offers an account of the "endowment" or "predisposition" of "love of neighbor" (*Liebe des Nächsten*). The third discussion—the one most directly relevant to the scriptural love commandment—is found in "Elements of Ethics" and analyzes the kind of obligation involved. Here is where Kant explicitly insists on the "duty of love for one's neighbor" (*die Pflict der Nächstenliebe*) (*MM*, 199) and announces three ethical "duties of love" (*Liebespflicten*)— namely, beneficence, gratitude, and sympathy (*MM*, 201). I will consider these discussions in the order in which they occur in Kant's text to show how he develops his concern, and in the process, I will try to point out where a comparison with Kierkegaard on the love commandment is possible.

Duty of Virtue: Beneficence (Wohltun, Wohltätigkeit)

The first discussion of our duty concerning the "natural welfare" (*Wohlfahrt*) of others occurs in section 8 of the introduction, "Exposition of Duties of Virtue as Wide Duties" (*MM*, 155). In the sections immediately preceding section 8, Kant recapitulates the contrast between "duty of virtue" (or "ethical" duty) and "duty of right" (or "juridical" duty) he made in the beginning of the book (*MM*, 20–22, 31). Here he says, "What essentially distinguishes a duty of virtue from a duty of right is that external constraint to the latter kind of duty is morally possible, whereas the former is based only on free self-constraint" (*MM*, 148). "Duties of right" are obligations to avoid infringing on the rights of others, with respect to which external constraint can be applied (civil or criminal laws); such duties can be fulfilled simply by conforming our actions to the law; they do not require that they be done out of respect for the moral law. "Duties of virtue" must be done out of respect for the moral law in order for fulfillment to have moral worth; because duties of virtue are unconditional duties to adopt an obligatory end (*MM*, 148), they are not supererogatory. One such obligatory end is the end of "promoting the happiness of other human beings, whose (permitted) end I thus make my own end as well" (*MM*, 151), and in section 8, Kant develops the notion of "The Happiness of Others as an End That Is Also a Duty."

He now makes a sharp distinction concerning our duty to adopt the end of promoting the happiness of others, a distinction between *Wohlwollen* and *Wohltun*: "Benevolence [*Wohlwollen*] can be unlimited, since nothing need be done with it. But it is more difficult to *do good* [*Wohltun*], especially if it is to be done not from affection (love) [*Nuneigung (Liebe)*] for others but from duty [*Pflicht*]" (*MM*, 155). In short, the duty we have to others is specifically a duty of *Wohltun* or *Wohltätigkeit* (doing good, beneficence), and this initial contrast between benevolence and beneficence is important since through it Kant affirms that our duty is a *practical* one—the content is the welfare of others, which involves their human (embodied) well-being—what Kant calls their "natural happiness."[12] Moreover, in saying that only benevolence could in principle be unlimited, since it requires no action, he implies that the duty of "beneficence" (he equates *Wohltun* with *Wohltätigkeit*) will have practical limitations.

In this section of "Doctrine of Virtue," Kant does not emphasize the absolute unconditionality of an ethical law, but rather offers a rationale for the duty: he suggests that *Wohltätigkeit* (beneficence) is a duty at all only because "since our self-love cannot be separated from our need to be loved [*geliebet zu werden*] (helped in case of need) by others as well, we therefore make ourselves an end for others, and the only way this maxim can be binding is through its qualification as a universal law, hence through our will to make others our ends as well" (*MM*, 156). Thus, while Kant agrees with Kierkegaard that the duty is universal in its bindingness (on everyone) and in its scope (toward everyone), for Kant, unlike Kierkegaard, such universalization implies the relevance of a kind of reciprocity implicit in an ethic based on the demands of reason.

Admittedly, in contrast to Kierkegaard, Kant does not consider the unconditionality of a duty of love an obligation generated by an external lawgiver; we do not have duties to God. Kant cannot affirm an external author of the command; the needs of morality do not entitle us "to *assume* that such a supreme being *actually exists* outside [ourselves]" (*MM*, 190). But that difference need not preclude a fruitful comparison of Kant and Kierkegaard on the love command insofar as Kant concedes that "a law that binds us *a priori* and unconditionally by our own reason can also be expressed as proceeding from the will of a supreme lawgiver, that is, one who has only rights and no duties (hence from the divine will); but this signifies only the idea of a moral being whose will is a law for everyone, without his being thought of as the author of the law" (*MM*, 19).[13] Moreover, Kant adds that the "idea" to which "conscience unavoidably guides" us is that of "an omnipotent moral being" (*MM*, 189–90) and that "we cannot very well make obligation (moral constraint) intuitive for ourselves without thereby thinking of *another's* will, namely God's (of which reason in giving universal laws is only the spokesman)" (*MM*, 229). Although this is not a duty to God, but rather "the duty of a human being to himself" (*MM*, 229), the duty is legitimately construed as a command from God: we have "the *duty of religion*, the duty 'of recognizing all our duties as (*instar*) divine commands'" (*MM*, 193). In other words, the question of the unconditionality of the command is more nuanced for Kant than for Kierkegaard,[14] but a comparison of them is nevertheless possible and fruitful.

One of the ways in which Kant's account is nuanced is in terms of the detail he provides about the conceptual limitations of fulfillment of duties of virtue: their unconditionality does not prevent duties of virtue from being "wide" duties, which because they concern the maxims of our actions leave latitude concerning "precisely in what way one is to act and how much one is to do" by way of adopting an end (*MM*, 153, 168, 195) (as opposed to duties of right, which require particular actions and are of "narrow" obligation). Beneficence is a "wide" duty—that is, "the duty has in it a latitude for doing more or less, and no specific limits can be assigned to what should be done" (*MM*, 156). Although this does not warrant an "exception" to the obligatory maxim (*MM*, 153), there are some limits to what I am bound to do.[15] For example, one cannot, without contradiction, be asked to have a maxim of promoting others' happiness "at the sacrifice of one's own happiness and one's true needs" (*MM*, 156). Kant takes pains to make clear that the determination of the extent and kind of sacrifice required involves a determination by the agent of his own "sensibilities"—that is, his "own happiness" and "true needs." This judgment, which aligns with Kierkegaard's notion of "proper self-love," is definitely the prerogative of the agent. Later, Kant announces another kind of limitation on our duty generated by the legitimacy of the determination of his own needs by the person we help (*MM*, 151). It is not clear that Kierkegaard could accept the degree of latitude Kant allows to duties of love, but they both agree that there are legitimate limits. Whether duties with limits could ever be considered "infinite" duties is a question Kant doesn't address, although duties of respect may count as such.[16]

In any case, despite their limits, wide duties like beneficence involve (as they do for Kierkegaard) genuine self-denial without hope of return—"I ought to sacrifice a part of my welfare to others without hope of return," "forgoing the satisfaction of concupiscence" (*MM*, 156). Moreover, Kant and Kierkegaard are in agreement about our ability to fulfill an unconditional command; for Kant, everyone "can do what the law tells him unconditionally that he ought to do" (*MM*, 146).

Love of Human Beings as an "Endowment" (Liebe des Nächsten and Menschenliebe)

The second place Kant discusses our duty to further the "happiness" of others introduces the category of "neighbor love" (*Liebe des Nächsten*) as such. In the section "Concepts of What Is Presupposed on the Part of Feeling by the Mind's Receptivity to Concepts of Duty as Such" (*MM*, 159), Kant announces that "love of one's neighbor" (*Liebe des Nächsten*) is a "moral endowment" (*moralische Beschaffenheit*), a "predisposition" (*Anlage*), which, like "moral feeling," "conscience," and "respect for oneself," "lies at the basis of morality," for it is only "by virtue of [these predispositions—"moral feeling," "conscience," and "respect for oneself"] that [one] can be put under obligation."[17] So this kind of love of neighbor cannot be commanded; it recalls the "instinct for benevolence" (*Instinct zur Gütigkeit*) treated in Kant's *Lectures on Ethics*.[18] This, by the way, is the only context in which Kant's restriction of love to "feeling" occurs—neighbor love is not inclination, but it is a non-empirically recognizable kind of feeling.[19]

For Kierkegaard, "*Kjerlighed til Naesten*" is likewise an endowment insofar as *Kjerlighed* is the gift God creates us with. Whereas for Kant our endowment or predisposition to neighbor love is what allows us to be susceptible to the duty to fulfill it, in Kierkegaard's case, this endowment is what allows us to fulfill the commandment. For Kierkegaard, love (*Kjerlighed*) is placed in us by God as a potential that seeks to actualize itself. Love is a "need" (*Trang*) that is "*deeply* rooted in our human nature," a "need to love and be loved" (*WL*, 154, 155); it needs to express itself or it will wither and die (*WL*, 11). It does not need to be commanded as such (*WL*, 375); rather, the command "guides this great need" so that it is not merely restrictive (*WL*, 67). With Kant, there seems to be no sense of drive or urge to express itself as there is in Kierkegaard—no *Trieb* to correlate with Kierkegaard's *Trang*.[20]

After first listing love of one's neighbor as one of four endowments, or forms of receptivity to the concept of duty, Kant goes on to discuss it in the section titled "Love of Human Beings" (*Menschenliebe*). *Liebe des Nächsten* seems to equal *Menschenliebe*—that is, every human being is the neighbor; no one is excluded from the scope of the predisposition or the duty.

A Duty of Love (Liebespflict)

The third place in which Kant explicitly examines neighbor love is in "Doctrine of the Elements of Ethics," in part 2, "On Duties of Virtue to Others," where he writes "On the Duty of Love [*Liebespflict*] to Other Human Beings." This is where he equates the ethical law of perfection "Love your neighbor as yourself" with the "maxim of benevolence (practical love of human beings [*praktische Menschenliebe*])" (*MM*, 200) and reminds us that "love for our neighbor" (*Nächstenliebe*) is "incumbent on us as a duty [*Pflict*]" (*MM*, 207). Here he specifically identifies "beneficence" (*Wohltätigkeit*) as a "duty of love" and adds "gratitude" (*Dankbarkeit*) and "active sympathetic participation" (*Teilnehmung Empfindung*) (*MM*, 198–201).

Duty of Love versus Duty of Respect

Having earlier considered the duty to promote the happiness of others as a "duty of virtue" (as contrasted with a "duty of right") as well as love of neighbor as an uncommandable endowment that allows us to be susceptible to the obligation of *Menschenliebe*, Kant now begins a more specific analysis of a "duty of love" by contrasting it with another kind of duty of virtue, namely, a duty of "respect" (*MM*, 199). Heretofore he had lumped together duties of love and duties of respect as a single category ("duties of virtue") to be contrasted with "duties of right." Now, when he is contrasting duties of love with duties of respect, he is far more specific about the particular characteristics of duties of love.

In addition to repeating a number of points he had made earlier (duties of love are "meritorious," "wide," and positive duties; they are practical as opposed to "*benevolence* in our wishes for others [which costs us nothing]" [*MM*, 201]; our duty excludes "hoping for something in return" [*MM*, 202]—i.e., reciprocity is not incompatible but it cannot be the condition of doing our duty), Kant explains that the rationale for "beneficence toward those in need" as a "universal duty" is "just because they are to be considered fellowmen, that is, rational beings *with needs*, united by nature in one dwelling place so that they can help one another" (*MM*, 202; my italics). This particular expression of the rationale of this duty of love here (we are rational beings "with needs") is significant. The earlier emphasis on "promoting the happiness of other human beings" is now explicitly contrasting happiness and rationality as such.

Happiness versus Rationality

That the content of a duty of love is directed toward the happiness (needs, natural welfare) of others (as contrasted with their rationality as such) is clear from Kant's formulation. Duties of respect require "recognition of a dignity in other human beings, that is, of a worth that has no price, no equivalent for which the object evaluated could be exchanged" (*MM*, 209). They address our "dignity" as rational free humans who cannot be used "merely as a means" to an end (*MM*, 209) and who never lose their "predisposition to the good" (*MM*, 210). Duties of respect are "narrow" and negative duties "analogous to the duty of right not to encroach upon what belongs to anyone" (*MM*, 199). Kant insists on the contrast between the duty of love and the duty of respect: whereas the "duty of love for one's neighbor" is "the duty to make others' *ends* my own (provided only that they are not immoral)" (*MM*, 199) (e.g., the duty "to promote according to one's means the *happiness [Glückseligkeit] of others in need*, without hoping for something in return" [*MM*, 202; my italics]), the duty of respect "is contained in the maxim not to degrade any other to a mere means to my ends" (*MM*, 199).

This contrast is absolutely clear in his discussion of a duty of love to act on sympathetic feelings, where Kant makes explicit the way in which duties of love address us not specifically as rational beings but as rational "animals"; he writes that there is a "duty of humanity (*humanitas*) because a human being is regarded here not merely as a rational being but also as an animal endowed with reason" (*MM*, 204). A concern with human happiness thus qualitatively distinguishes duties of love from duties of respect.

Separability of Duties

The status of Kant's contrast between duties of love and duties of respect has been the subject of much debate among Kant scholars, and often the result is the suggestion that the two duties are not really different—either love is really a species of respect or love "includes" respect.[21] I disagree with these attempts to collapse the distinction between the two kinds of duty because I think this would run afoul of two Kantian commitments that support his explicit claim that they are separable duties—first, his commitment to the importance of human happiness and, second, his commitment to a significant difference between the duties in terms of failure to perform them.

Given the critical difference in the concerns addressed in both cases, it should not be surprising that Kant insists that duties of love and duties of respect "can be considered separately (each by itself) and can also exist separately" (*MM*, 198).[22] That is, they are *separable* both in theory and in practice—a concern with human happiness has different aims than a concern with recognition of our dignity as rational agents. Consider the precise character of Kant's examples of the different duties. The clearest example of a duty of love is "beneficence"—promoting the natural happiness or fulfilling the human needs of others. The duty of "sympathy" or "sympathetic participation" is the "duty to sympathize actively" in "the fate of others" and therefore includes the "indirect duty to cultivate the compassionate natural feelings in us, and to make use of them as so many means to sympathetic participation" (*MM*, 205). Vices opposed to love are "envy," "ingratitude," and "malice" (*MM*, 206–7).

On the other hand, examples of violations of duties of respect are "arrogance" (contempt), "defamation," and "ridicule" (e.g., of the other's logical use of reason). This is a very restricted category for Kant. There may be times when it is difficult to know whether our concern for another is addressing a recognition of them as rational agent as such or their need for happiness, but there are other times when it is clear that the help we offer addresses the other's need for happiness and natural welfare (e.g., binding up his wounds, feeding her when she is hungry) or the other's recognition as of a priceless dignity because of their rational agency (e.g., abstaining from ridicule or condescension). In any case, for Kant, separable duties "in one duty" means two distinguishable duties in one performed duty.

Obligation: Difference in the Failure to Fulfill a Duty of Love

Moreover, any attempt to collapse the distinction between the two kinds of duty would also run afoul of Kant's contrast between them in terms of "obligation." The question of obligation comes up in two forms: first, the way in which we are bound to these duties—that is, at fault for failing to do them—and, second, the way in which our performance of duties of love will "put others under obligation" (*MM*, 198).

First, Kant distinguishes duties of love from duties of respect in terms of the character of our failing. He writes, "Failure to fulfill mere duties of love is lack of virtue [*Untugend*] (*peccatum*),"[23] for "no one is wronged if duties of love are neglected," whereas "failure to fulfill the duty arising from the respect owed to every human being as such is a vice (*vitium*)" and "infringes" on another's "lawful claim" (*MM*, 211).[24] Although Kant had earlier suggested that failure to perform duties of virtue was not "culpable (*demeritum*)" (*MM*, 19),[25] he did this in his contrast between duties of virtue and duties of right; this does not commit him to seeing all duties of virtue as homogenously nonbinding. The attribute of "non-culpability" has meaning only in terms of the contrast between duties of virtue (as unenforceable) and duties of right (as enforceable); it does not rule out the presence of either *peccatum* or *vitium*. The difference between duties of love and duties of respect will be significant as long as failing to fulfill a duty of respect and failing to fulfill a duty of love have different results, so the difference between duties of respect and duties of love will be significant so long as *vitium* (vice) is different from *peccatum* (transgression).[26]

Difference in the Way of Putting People under Obligation

A second but related way in which Kant maintains the conceptual contrast between duties of love and duties of respect is by claiming that only in the case of the former do we "put others under obligation." Kant divides "duties of virtue to others" into two kinds: "duties to others by the performance of which you also put others under obligation and duties to others the observance of which does not result in obligation on the part of others" (*MM*, 198). Kant repeats this important point: "By carrying out the duty of love to someone I put another under obligation: I make myself deserving from him. But in observing a duty of respect I put only myself under obligation" (*MM*, 199).

This claim that the performance of duties of love puts the other "under obligation" to us and makes us "deserving from him" serves as a way of keeping duties of love conceptually distinct from duties of respect, but it looks like it signals a major difference between Kant and Kierkegaard. For Kant, duties of love are not "owed" to people, as are duties of respect (*MM*, 198) (and duties of right); moreover, we put *others* under obligation when we fulfill duties of love to them. Kierkegaard, on the contrary, insists that loving others places *us* in debt, not them, and that it would be wrong to place them under any sense of obligation. But is this a substantive difference between them? I suggest that two commitments held by Kant mitigate the difference between Kant and Kierkegaard in this respect. The first commitment is to the normative unity between the duties, and the second is Kant's concern with actively engaging with others on the basis of our sympathetic feeling.

Normative Unity of Love and Respect

Kant's claim that when we fulfill duties of love we place others under obligation is qualified by his sensitivity to the how of fulfilling a duty of love. He maintains the conceptual and the de facto separability of duties of love and respect at the same time as he upholds a sort of ideal or normative unity between the two: "They are basically always united by the law into *one duty*, only in such a way that now one duty and now the other is the subject's principle, with *the other joined to it as accessory*" (*MM*, 198; my italics). But the recommendation of such a normative unity of love and respect depends on the substantive difference between duties of love and respect. When Kant writes that "they are basically always united by the law into *one duty*" (*MM*, 198), his example illustrates their normative unity in a single performance: "So we shall acknowledge that we are under obligation to help someone poor; but since the favor we do implies that his well-being depends on our generosity, and this humbles him, it is our duty to behave as if our help is either merely what is due him or but a slight service of love, and to spare him humiliation and maintain his respect for himself" (*MM*, 198). This does not mean that there is no distinction between helping the poor through love and respecting them. There are still two duties, and at any given time, one is "accessory" to the other.

One of the most striking aspects of Kierkegaard's *Works of Love*, as we noted earlier, is his extremely sensitive appreciation that so-called works of love can be done unlovingly: doing a work lovingly depends on the how. Kant too reveals a very sensitive appreciation of how we ought to perform our duties of love, and this paradoxically involves our willingness to be put under obligation by those we put under obligation.

As we saw previously, Kant insists, "It is our duty to behave as if our help is either merely what is due him or but a slight service of love." Although a duty of love is not "owed" in the sense that a duty of right or a duty of respect is "owed," it is our duty to "behave as if" it was "owed." Moreover, Kant insists that a person must "carefully avoid any appearance of intending to bind the other by it; for if he showed that he wanted to put the other under an obligation (which always humbles the other in his own eyes), it would not be a true benefit that he rendered him. Instead, he must show that *he is himself put under obligation by the other's acceptance* or honored by it, hence that the duty is merely *something that he owes*, unless (as is better) he can practice his beneficence in complete secrecy" (*MM*, 202; my italics). The parallel with Kierkegaard's construal of our debt of love and of hiding ourselves is striking.

In other words, Kant justifies such sensitivity to the other by acknowledging that we "owe" the other in some sense; the claim that we put the other under obligation is balanced by the claim that we also put ourselves under obligation. Kant says this explicitly in his *Lectures on Ethics*: "All moralists and teachers should therefore see to it that, so far as possible, they represent acts of benevolence [*Gütigkeit*] to be acts of obligation [*Schuldigkeit*], and reduce them to a matter of right [*Recht*]."[27] Another example of this normative unity is found in Kant's discussion of "the duty of being benevolent as a friend of human beings," which includes "thought and consideration for the *equality* among them, and hence the idea that in putting others under obligation by his beneficence he is himself under obligation, as if all were brothers under one father, who wills the happiness of all" (*MM*, 217).

The point is that Kant goes to some lengths to put important restrictions on the way in which we are to understand how we put another under obligation and how we make ourselves deserving from the other. He suggests that a duty of love needs to be fulfilled in a way that at the same time respects the other's dignity and freedom; such freedom is "the only innate right" we have, and it involves both one's innate "equality" and that one be his "own master" (*MM*, 30). That the normative ideal is both love and respect at the same time does not preclude them being two different duties. Kant first radically distinguishes what he wants to ultimately join together in one performance. Since we are all embodied centers of rationality, seeing others as "ends in themselves" requires fulfilling both duties of love and duties of respect. One could construe Kant's appreciation of the ideal unity of the duty of love and the duty of respect as the ideal unity of the what and the how. I suggest that Kant's nuanced discussion of the way in which fulfilling a duty of love puts others under obligation at the same time as it puts us under obligation is a rich and much-neglected aspect of Kant's moral theory.

Sympathetic Participation

Although there is latitude with respect to the fulfillment of a duty of love, there is a clear how required in the sense that it should be done in union with fulfillment of the duty of respect.

However, another dimension of Kant's appreciation of the how of fulfilling a duty of love supports the attribution of *Liebe* to it—namely, a normative unity between beneficence and sympathetic participation.[28] That is, I am arguing that there is a how in the performance of a duty of love that is not reducible to performance of a duty of respect.[29] Kant expresses a deep appreciation of the sensitivity to the particular happiness and inclinations of others with which duty should be performed. He writes that when I fulfill my duty to promote "the happiness of *other* human beings," "it is for them to decide what they count as belonging to their happiness" (*MM*, 151). He adds the qualification that "it is open to me to refuse them many things that they think will make them happy but that I do not, as long as they have no right to demand them from me as what is theirs" (*MM*, 151), but later insists again that "I cannot do good to anyone in accordance with *my* concepts of happiness (except to young children and the insane), thinking to benefit him by forcing a gift upon him; rather, I can benefit him only in accordance with *his* concepts of happiness" (*MM*, 203). I suggest that this reveals a dimension of how that is not the same as the dimension of "respect" for dignity and equality but rather a sensitivity to the concrete embodiedness of the other. This sensitivity keeps the beneficence from being practiced as one would practice it toward a disembodied rational agent.

Kant points to this second sense of "how" when he suggests that the way to "cultivate one's love of human beings" is to "combine the *cordiality* of a benevolent disposition with *sensitivity* to benevolence (attentiveness to the smallest degree of this disposition in one's thought of duty)" (*MM*, 204). The phrase "sensitivity to benevolence" signals something different from sensitivity to the other's status as rational agent—it points to a sensitivity concerning the other's happiness or needs. This may loosely be considered a kind of respect, but it is definitely not the same as the respect covered by Kant's duties of respect. It is the other's difference, their embodiedness, their individual distinctiveness, rather than their sameness and equality, that is being attended to in this how of love.

In other words, the normative unity of love and respect is more than simply the normative unity of beneficence and the refusal to be arrogant or condescending in the sense required by technical duties of respect. There is a normative unity of love—that is, of beneficence and sympathetic participation. The sensitivity of sympathetic participation—"the will to share in other's feelings," "to sympathize actively in their fate" (*MM*, 204, 205)—is to be normatively joined to beneficence. The duty "not to avoid the places where the poor who lack the most basic necessities are to be found but rather to seek them out" (*MM*, 205) involves a sensitivity to the other that should be distinguished from the respect Kant highlights in his account of duties of respect. We cannot be obligated to feel "compassion" (*Mitleidenschaft*), but we are obligated to seek out places where our "compassionate natural (aesthetic) feelings" can be cultivated (*MM*, 205). If this sensitivity is not attributed to the restricted category of respect shown to the other, one might see it as a reason why Kant can call them duties of "love."

Conclusion

Rather than provide a tedious reiteration of the comparison and contrast between Kant and Kierkegaard that I have been drawing in the paper, I want to end by rephrasing the contrast between them in a way that builds on my examination but takes a kind of meta-level perspective. One could say that for Kant the domain of the love commandment is the domain of duties of love (especially beneficence and sympathetic participation)—in fact, the domain of concern with human happiness—and that it is important that these duties of love be carried out in ways that respect the rational dignity and equality of the other—hence, have respect as an "accessory" duty. This would result in a tripartite picture: Kant contrasts love as "inclination" with duties of virtue, which he divides into duties of love and duties of respect that are conceptually distinguishable because of the difference in the concerns they address. For Kierkegaard, on the other hand, there seems to be a simpler two-part picture: namely, love as "inclination" is contrasted with *Kjerlighed til Naesten*. The category of *Kjerlighed til Naesten* includes both love (caring for) and what Kant apportions to a duty of respect. Kant first radically separates what he then joins together; for Kierkegaard, however, these duties are not radically separated to begin with because our potential to fulfill both of them rests on a love potential given to us by God, who is love (*Kjerlighed*). If, however, we concentrate on Kant's insistence on the normative unity of love and respect, his becomes a two-part picture much like Kierkegaard's, although it has the added important detail of distinguishing (1) love from respect and (2) beneficence from sympathetic participation.

Kierkegaard does not separate duties of love from duties of respect but insists that *Kjerlighed til Naesten*—a combination of duties of love (caring for) and respect—be "preserved" in our special relationships (those based on inclination). Inclination, for Kierkegaard, is not incompatible with caring respect—there are, in a sense, "special relations."[30] Kant explicitly allows for special ethical relations when he writes, "In wishing I can be *equally* benevolent to everyone, whereas in acting *I can, without violating the universality of the maxim, vary the degree greatly in accordance with the different objects of my love* (one of whom concerns me more closely than another)" (*MM*, 201; my italics). For Kant, the universality of the maxim and the unconditionality of the obligation are not necessarily prejudiced by variation in the "degree" of my beneficence.

Kierkegaard's suggestion that we preserve neighbor love in erotic love and friendship raises for many the question of their compatibility—how is nonpreferential preserved in preferential love? In the light of Kant's account, it is easier to see what Kierkegaard assumed—namely, that the nonpreferential *Kjerlighed* was the caring-respect that keeps inclinational/preferential loves from being exploitative. Kierkegaard's talk about preserving neighbor love in erotic love and friendship highlights the respect due to the other, but Kant's discussion of sympathy is actually more developed in relation to the love dimension that is neither merely inclination nor respect, and this reveals a way in which Kierkegaard's category of *Kjerlighed til Naesten* is the normative unity of beneficence, sympathetic participation, and respect.

Both thinkers evidence a deep sensitivity to the how of the performance of love, but as an analytic philosopher, Kant makes distinctions and contrasts that Kierkegaard does not bother to make explicitly. Kant writes a doctrine of virtue, with its countless details about "wide" and "narrow" obligation and about embodied happiness as distinct from pure rationality. Kierkegaard has an exemplary account—he points to Christ and the Good Samaritan as concrete examples of the holistic love (caring-respect) to be practiced.

Notes

1. I see myself as building on Ronald Green's fine essay, "Kant on Christian Love," in *The Love Commandments: Essays in Christian Ethics and Moral Philosophy*, ed. Edmund Santurri and William Werpehowski (Washington, DC: Georgetown University Press, 1992).

2. Immanuel Kant, *Groundwork of the Metaphysics of Morals*, ed. Mary Gregor (Cambridge: Cambridge University Press, 1997), 16; *Metaphysics of Morals*, ed. Mary Gregor (Cambridge: Cambridge University Press, 1996), 161 (hereafter cited in the text as *MM*).

3. Søren Kierkegaard, *Works of Love*, vol. 16 of *Kierkegaard's Writings*, trans. Howard V. Hong and Edna H. Hong (Princeton, NJ: Princeton University Press, 1995), 24.

4. For further detail and development of any part of the summary of Kierkegaard's position, see M. Jamie Ferreira, *Love's Grateful Striving* (Oxford: Oxford University Press, 2001).

5. Kierkegaard, *Works of Love*, 24 (hereafter cited in the text as *WL*).

6. Luther cites St. Ambrose: "If your enemy needs you and you do not help him when you can it is the same as if you had stolen what belonged to him, for you owe him your help" (Martin Luther, "Treatise on Good Works" (1515–16), in *Luther's Works*, vol. 44, ed. James Atkinson [Philadelphia: Fortress Press, 1966], 109).

7. For further detail on this issue, see M. Jamie Ferreira, "The Problematic Agapeistic Ideal—Again," in *Ethics, Love, and Faith in Kierkegaard: Philosophical Engagements*, ed. Edward F. Mooney (Bloomington: Indiana University Press, 2008).

8. Kant, *Groundwork of the Metaphysics of Morals*, 16.

9. Immanuel Kant, *Critique of Practical Reason*, ed. Mary Gregor (Cambridge: Cambridge University Press, 1997), 71.

10. Immanuel Kant, *Lectures on Ethics*, ed. Peter Heath and J. B. Schneewind (Cambridge: Cambridge University Press, 1997), 181.

11. The lectures on ethics are a rich resource, and the distinctions Kant makes there deserve fuller consideration; at the very least, my view is supported by his early contrast there between "love from obligation" and "love from inclination" (*Liebe aus Verbindlichkeit als auch aus Neigung*) (Kant, *Lectures on Ethics*, 181).

12. The positive duty we have concerns their "natural happiness" as opposed to their "moral happiness" (*MM*, 151). Nevertheless, since another's "moral well-being" is included in their happiness, we have a "negative" and "wide" duty to promote their moral well-being too.

13. The contrast is between God as author of the law and reason as spokesman of the law inscribed by God in our hearts; true, one crucial difference would obtain if Kierkegaard has to allow that God can change the moral law and command us not to love, but I do not think he does.

14. Kant goes into detail about wide, narrow, perfect, and imperfect duties, and he makes a distinction between the result of a failure to fulfill a duty of love and the result of a failure to fulfill a duty of respect.

15. For discussion of how dire the "need" must be, how much we must do, and how we choose to help one person rather than another, see Marcia Baron and Melissa Seymour Fahmy, "Beneficence and Other Duties of Love in *The Metaphysics of Morals*," in *The Blackwell Guide to Kant's Ethics*, ed. Thomas E. Hill Jr. (Chichester, UK: Blackwell Publishing, 2009), 216–22.

16. Gratitude is the closest he comes to speaking of an "infinite" duty, and this may be because he brings it close to a species of respect: "Gratitude must also be considered, in particular, a sacred duty, that is, a duty the violation of which (as a scandalous example) can destroy the moral incentive to beneficence in its very principle. For, a moral object is sacred if the obligation with regard to it cannot be discharged completely by any act in keeping with it (so that one who is under obligation always remains under obligation). One cannot, by any repayment of a kindness received, *rid* oneself of the obligation for it, since the recipient can never win away from the benefactor his *priority* of merit, namely having been the first in benevolence" (*MM*, 203).

17. Kant is not here drawing the fine distinctions he makes in *Religion within the Limits of Reason Alone*, where he contrasts propensity, inclination, and predisposition.

18. Kant, *Lectures on Ethics*, 179.

19. Allen Wood, "The Final Form of Kant's Practical Philosophy," supplement, *Southern Journal of Philosophy* 36 (1997): 1–20; pp. 15–18 discuss the difference between endowment and "inclination."

20. Kant's lectures on ethics do address the question of "need" to some extent.

21. On love as a species of respect, see Robert Johnson, "Love in Vain," supplement, *Southern Journal of Philosophy* 36 (1997): 45–50; on love as including respect, see Marcia W. Baron, "Love and Respect in the Doctrine of Virtue," supplement, *Southern Journal of Philosophy* 36 (1997): 33, 42.

22. The remainder of the quotation makes clear that Kant is talking about the separability of duties of love and respect rather than merely feelings of love and respect.

23. Elsewhere he simply calls this lack of virtue "moral weakness" (*MM*, 148).

24. This dimension of duties of respect makes them like "duties of right" in terms of their relation to a "lawful claim" (although they remain unlike "duties of right" in terms of the "constraint" involved and the way in which the law is given).

25. It is perhaps still a legitimate question why a failure in a duty of respect is a vice, whereas the earlier judgment was that failure in duties of virtue in general was not culpability.

26. It is true that at one point Kant seems to consider vice simply a habitual form of *peccatum* (*MM*, 153).

27. Kant, *Lectures on Ethics*, 180. Why would Kant think this? He believes that where there has been systematic injustice, acts of benevolence are "acts of duty and indebtedness, arising from the rights of others" (Kant, *Lectures on Ethics*, 179), and he says that "for the most part," inequality of wealth arises from "the injustice of the government" (*MM*, 203).

28. I omit "gratitude" (which Kant says concerns "honoring a person because of a benefit he has rendered us," which is "connected" with the "feeling" of "respect" [*MM*, 203]) here because Kant later expresses his own doubt about whether it is really a duty of love (*MM*, 206).

29. See Melissa Seymour Fahmy, "Active Sympathetic Participation: Reconsidering Kant's Duty of Sympathy," *Kantian Review* 14, no. 1 (2009): 31–52.

30. See Ferreira, "Problematic Agapeistic Ideal."

Part II
THEORY

7

The Problematic Love for God

"Love the Lord, All You Saints" (Psalm 31:23)

EDWARD COLLINS VACEK

SINCE JESUS DECLARED that love for God was the first and greatest commandment, we might expect that theologians would long ago have developed a standard account of this love. Not so. Of course, many theologians write about God's love for us. And contemporary Christian ethicists, such as Gene Outka, have done marvelous, if still contested, work on the connection between love for God and love for neighbor or love for self.[1] In various ways, these ethicists hold that "love for God subtends or affects all one's goals and projects, not simply the moral ones."[2] But they seldom focus on love for God itself.[3] Indeed, most Christian ethicists, dealing as they do with this-worldly problems, write as if Jesus's first great commandment itself is irrelevant to their work.[4]

Anders Nygren, almost eighty years ago, complained about the opposite phenomenon: "Men have started from the conviction that love for God is in the last resort the only legitimate form of Christian love. They have therefore thought it necessary to justify the demand for love to one's neighbour by showing that it is only another way of speaking of love for God."[5] Nygren, among the most influential twentieth-century writers on the topic of love, then tried to show that love for God was either a mistake or sinful. He boldly proclaimed that Paul replaced love for God with faith, thereby, it would seem, improving not only the central creed of Judaism, the Shema (Deut. 6:5–9), but also Jesus's own summary of the law.[6] He extolled Paul, who wrote that love for neighbor is the sum of the law (Gal. 5:14). Nygren's view so captured the imagination of theologians that, forty years later, Gene Outka raised the question: "Why not explicitly conclude . . . that the principle of neighbor-love is *all* the content that 'love for God' possesses?"[7] As we will see, Karl Rahner, writing about the same time, often argued in a way that seemed to draw that very conclusion.

As Nygren's comments about Paul indicate, right from its beginning Christianity offered various interpretations of the first great love commandment.[8] Similarly, according to historian Bernard Brady, Martin Luther, reacting to the medieval quest for God, redirected theological ethics: "The drama of life is not humans moving up the scale of love, but God's love moving down to humans. . . . The immediate effect of God's love of us is that we are to love others. . . . In place of contemplation in the monastery, Luther calls us to direct service of others in the world. In a way, Luther identifies love of God as love of neighbor."[9] The social gospel and liberation theologies often continue this pattern.

111

The goal of this essay is to describe a direct love for God. I use Nygren and Rahner among others as examples of how Christian ethics tends to reject, ignore, or subordinate the first commandment. Next, I try to show how various incomplete understandings of love further distort the meaning of love for God. After that, I show that widely divergent understandings of God make the theology of love for God anything but obvious. Still, I conclude by describing three different forms of love for God.

Traditioned Experience

For not a few Christians, God's love for them is a matter of dogma that they believe, not an experience they have.[10] They may simply rely on Jesus's testimony: "God so loved the world" (John 3:16). A Christian's own love for God, however, cannot be outside experience: "Love is neither theory, nor principle nor an object of belief."[11] Rather, love is an emotion that manifests itself in innumerable kinds of practices but is not identical with those practices. Our love for God is a matter of immediate (though possibly mistaken) experience. Love for God requires believers to have some kind of "religious experience," that is, an experience whose "object" is God.

Descriptions of love for God require that at least some people first have had such an experience. For the rest of us, the description may come before, be simultaneous with, or be subsequent to the experience. By receiving from others various descriptive accounts of the experience, we can prepare for, more clearly see, or foster our own experience of love for God.[12] By naming our own experience, we make it more available to our mind and heart.[13] By reflecting on it afterward, we can integrate it more into our lives as well as make it available to still others. Of course, our descriptions and the experiences they express will have been significantly formed by our personal history and especially by the various traditions that form our lives.[14] In turn, our descriptions can and should be evaluated by others both inside and outside our traditions. If someone's particular description or narrative fails to illuminate or engender in us an experience of love for God, the problem may lie with us, but it also may mean that the account is no longer disclosive, if it ever was.[15]

Love for God can be problematic. To say that one believes that God exists is not yet love. It is also not enough to love Jesus, deducing that since Jesus is God, one who loves Jesus ipso facto loves God. Rather, love for Jesus is just love for another human being unless one experiences loving God in that act of loving Jesus. And in the two great commandments, Jesus himself tells us to love God, referring not to himself but to his Abba. Similarly, one may love a neighbor out of love for God, but that presupposes that one has a love for God.

Two Substitutes for Love of God

Love for God is a positive duty. In the objective order, a lack of love for God is the greatest failure in being human. The atheist—taken as a pure type and setting aside questions of responsibility—is objectively the ultimate sinner.[16] That so few take this point seriously testifies to how incidental the first great commandment has become, at least in our conversation.

One appropriate reason for neglecting to speak of love for God is that, as Gene Outka observed, there is "a natural reticence . . . about direct giving to God. Indeed, such talk strikes many as anomalous and quickly presumptuous."[17] It has been commonly supposed that we can do nothing for a perfect God. Thus, any desire to do good must of necessity turn toward creatures, since we can do good things for them.[18] Theologians may claim that such love for neighbor is a test, a sign, a condition, or a consequence of love for God.[19] Still, these claims presuppose that love for God is intelligible in its own right.

Another reason for theological silence on love for God is that the New Testament itself stresses the second great commandment more than the first commandment (e.g., Matt. 7:12; John 15:12–16; 1 John 4:7–12). Even if, as Pheme Perkins surprisingly claims, there was no need in New Testament times to encourage love for God,[20] in an era such as ours when the very meaning of loving God seems obscure (though I prefer to presume that people practice better than what they say), it is not surprising that substitutes for love of God have been found. I consider two very common substitutes.

First Substitute: Obedience

When we consider Nygren's view of agape, it is easy to see why he could find no place for love for God. Agape, he wrote, is directed to that which is worthless. It creates value rather than responds to value. It is spontaneous, not motivated by the good but directed to what is inferior.[21] Hence, Nygren concluded, we should not have agapic love for God.[22] (Nygren did allow that we will have an eros love for God, but this, he thought, was sinfully selfish, and he peremptorily excluded the very possibility of a caritas or philia love because, he claimed, such love requires equality.)[23]

Nygren held that "love towards God" should rather be understood as to be "under His absolute lordship, and it finds expression primarily in obedience to his will."[24] Love for God is "obedience to God, without any thought of reward."[25] Similarly, Timothy Jackson writes, "Individuals are to love God with an utterly unqualified obedience, whereas they are to love their neighbors as themselves."[26] Jackson quotes the second part of Jesus's declaration exactly as Jesus gave it but skews considerably Jesus's text on love for God. Though Jesus uses the same word "love" in both commandments, rightly Jackson doesn't say that love of neighbor means even qualified obedience to the neighbor.

It is common to equate love and obedience when it is "love" for a sovereign. The problem, however, is that obedience is quite compatible with despising the sovereign, with fearing his punishments, or with cooperation out of pure self-interest. Of course, if we love others, including God, we want their will to be fulfilled. But we should not confuse wanting what another wants with obedience. For example, we can also want to do another's will out of a desire to get a reward, to avoid the burden of having to make our own decision, or to please a third party.

Thus, love and obedience are very different personal acts.[27] Obedience has to do with fulfilling a command given by an authority.[28] Not only can we obey persons we do not love, but we usually do not obey persons we do love. Parents do not obey the child whom they love, and God does not obey a creature whom God loves. Indeed, the opposite is generally true: if we love someone, we ordinarily would not think in terms of obedience.[29]

Furthermore, if God loves us, God wills our good, and a major part of our own good is the exercise of our own judgment and freedom.[30] Thus, God's love for us should lead not to obedience but to a dependent exercise of our own self-determining agency. Still, attitudes and practices such as obedience, surrender, wonder, trust, submission, delight, worship, and so forth all can also be appropriate responses to God. Some are compatible with love. The point here is that they are not the same as love for God.

Second Substitute: Love for Neighbor

If Nygren may serve as a prime example of a theologian who replaces love for God with obedience, Karl Rahner may serve as a leading example of a theologian whose writings have had the effect of reducing love for God to love for neighbor. Two qualifications are immediately necessary. The first is that Rahner's views on the topic shifted over the course of his long career away from his better known and more influential position.[31] Second, even when he emphasized love for neighbor, he claimed that this was at the same time, though implicitly, also love for God.[32]

Rahner boldly announced his thesis: the "categorized explicit love of neighbor is the primary act of the love of God." By comparison, explicit love for God is secondary.[33] He wrote that the tendency to preach "not about God, but about one's neighbor" was appropriate for our times.[34] He claimed, "The act of personal love for another human being is therefore the all-embracing basic act of man which gives meaning, direction and measure to everything else." He held that love for God does not exist without love of neighbor, that the two are really the same thing, point to the same reality, and that "the *whole* truth of the gospel," though hidden, is found most easily in love for neighbor.[35] As a consequence, he asserted, "The only way in which man achieves self-realization is through encounters with his fellow man."[36]

When Rahner describes the love of God, his primary concern is to assert that God communicates or bestows God's self to us; he was not, however, inclined to talk of our return love as communicating our self to God. In fact, like Nygren, he too suggests that Jesus should not have given us two distinct commandments and especially should not have said that the second only resembles the first. Rather, Rahner goes on, St. John is more to the point when he implied that God loved us "not so that we might love him in return but so that we might love *one another*."[37]

These claims by the most famous Catholic theologian of the twentieth century authorized for many a nearly exclusive focus on love for neighbor.[38] After all, if love for neighbor is the most and the only fully fulfilling personal act, and if an explicit love for neighbor is more profound than an explicit love of God, and if love for God is "inescapably given" with love for neighbor,[39] then explicit or direct love for God seems quite dispensable. If, as Rahner concluded in his most famous essay on the topic, "one can love God whom one does not see only *by* loving one's visible brother,"[40] then explicit love for God, say, in private prayer, seems superfluous, possibly even a sinful deviation from social activity.

The most obvious, even if simplistic, objection to this line of theologizing is that our neighbors are not God. As Timothy Jackson writes, "One should no more conflate love of God with love of others than one should conflate love of others with love of self. Because God, others, and self are distinct and to be loved for themselves, the vertical and horizontal axes of ethics remain discrete, however closely related."[41] Many people, who are agnostic or despairing or indifferent to ultimates or angry at the absurdity and unfairness of life, nevertheless love their children, their spouses, their work, and so forth. Humans, like other animals, can find great significance in their activities, even when they are not affirming any ultimate meaning in such activities.

A second objection is that Rahner's proposal dangerously suggests that love as complete surrender due to God will occur in complete surrender to a particular neighbor, thus idolizing the neighbor.[42] Outka rightly noted that we ought not show our neighbor the same devotion we show God, for example, worship. Outka insists, "The great and first commandment—to love God with all your heart, soul and mind—retains a necessary discreteness."[43] Indeed,

Rahner's close uniting of love of neighbor with love of God makes it hard to explain how idolatry is possible.[44] Rahner himself, later in his career, wrote that it was apostasy to hold that Christianity consisted in neighbor love—a position which he had espoused but which he now described as a radical horizontalism that had suddenly appeared in the church.[45] He added that once we do attain an explicit awareness of God's presence in our love of others, it would be a denial of God to let God slip from our explicit awareness.[46]

A third mistake is the uncritical assumption made by many that we can have no direct relationship with God. For example, John Whittaker writes, "Since God is not a person one can thank directly," one should show gratitude by acting generously to another human.[47] Likewise, Germain Grisez discourages explicit expressions of "I love you, God."[48] It is an anomaly that theologians who write this way belong to Christian communities that at the Eucharist regularly say "Thank you" and give praise to God in word and song. Similarly, Jean Porter criticizes Rahner's position because it implies we have no good reason to take up the teaching and practices of the Christian faith, including worship and other forms of prayer.[49]

A fourth problem, central to this essay, is underestimating the moral significance of freely affirmed and explicit intention.[50] For most of Rahner's career, God is the necessary horizon in terms of which we understand and appreciate finite goods. He concludes from this not only that love for this ultimate accompanies necessarily every deep love of neighbor but also that it need not and perhaps cannot be explicit. The advantage of this approach is that it makes clear God is not one thing among other things. It preserves the mystery of God—God is not an object. Nevertheless, there is an enormously significant moral and religious difference between doing something implicitly and doing it explicitly as well as between doing it necessarily and doing it willingly. As Rahner himself argued,[51] I can love a person and deny the God who is the origin and destiny of that person. This is sin, but it is possible. More positively, loving a child, loving the child as a child of God, loving God as present and active in the child, and loving God are four distinct activities. To love God with our whole mind and heart requires that—at least at some points and with growing frequency and depth—we explicitly and freely affirm the affection of love for God.

Misunderstanding the Participation in Love

What is love? In earlier work, I have explained at length that love is an emotional, affirming participation in the dynamic tendency of a being (or Being) to realize its full goodness.[52] I begin with the idea of "participation."

Love is not a zero-sum game.[53] While that may seem obvious, the language used by many theologians to describe the relationship between God and humans often reflects a zero-sum mentality, thus making love impossible. Out of a desire to acclaim God and God's grace as all, these authors describe humans and human contributions as nothing.

Nygren is typical: to have a relationship with God, he writes, everything in us must be destroyed.[54] If God's love of us is to be sovereign, there can be no place for "our" love for God or even for neighbor.[55] Nygren describes our proper relationship to God variously as that of obedient slave to sovereign, as empty tube to the life-giving fluid running through it, and as inert possession used by its owner.[56] Nygren writes, "The Christian has nothing of his own to give; the love which he shows to his neighbour is the love which God has infused into him."[57] Again, "'all things are of God'—nothing is of man."[58] Werner Jeanrond similarly describes this tradition: "The total annihilation of the self in the mystical tradition is mirrored here in the total destruction of the human will."[59]

Nygren fails to understand that love is a form of personal participation, a unity that differentiates and thereby enhances both the lover and the beloved. Like Plato before him, he rightly recognizes that we humans are needy. When it comes to spiritual goods, however, we need to participate in them, not acquire them. When we leave the art museum, we may "take" the Renoir painting with us, but it remains for millions of other viewers. It is not egocentric or selfish to take what we have seen with us; indeed, it would take an egoist not to do so.

The basic idea of this participation derives from the experience of how a person can share in something or someone in a way that unites the two while enhancing each. Intellectual knowledge is one form of personal participation. In the act of knowing, (some aspect of) the known becomes part of the knower. The knower becomes more fully developed and thereby differentiated. At the same time, the known is not diminished but now has an "intentional" existence in the knower. Similarly, the lover participates in the value or goodness of the beloved. The lover has an "intentional" focus on the beloved's value. The good of the beloved makes a difference to the lover, and the lover is inclined toward realizing ever greater goodness in the beloved. This living for the beloved also enriches the lover.[60]

Outka insightfully observes that at stake here is the doctrine of grace, in particular the stereotypical Protestant and Catholic divide.[61] Put simplistically, in much Protestant theology, following one strand of Augustine, God acts in us without us. For the Catholic tradition that follows Aquinas, God acts in us with us (*ST* II-I.111.2). Thus, Rahner, who emphasized God's love for us rather than God's sovereignty over us, argued that God's love for us proportionally increases rather than decreases our freedom to love God in return, the opposite of Nygren's position. The dialectical either-or is changed not only to a both-and but also to a proportional relationship: the more we are involved with God the freer and more fully developed we are.[62] Similarly, LeRon Shults remarks, "There is no sense of competition here but a recognition that true human loving is an abiding *in* God, which is itself a gift *from* God."[63] In this sense, being "possessed" by a loving God is desirable and liberating since it affirms union with the mystery that is God in whom we move and have our being, that is, in whom we flourish.[64]

Outka notes that in a strictly theocentric view, we cannot save ourselves.[65] While surely orthodox, this claim is one-sided. God also cannot save us, that is, cannot save us without our cooperation (Aquinas, *ST* II-I.111.2). I have elsewhere proposed that we ought to take a theanthropocentric view. There is, to be sure, an asymmetry between God and ourselves, but not the asymmetry of all to nothing. As Outka notes, "Our love for God remains dependent and responsive in a manner that God's love never is."[66] Still, the cooperation is wholly our own work and wholly God's work.[67] We must do our "part" within our own capacity, just as God does God's "part." Our freedom is essential because our responsive love for God is salvation and must be our free act.[68] Still, because the Spirit prays in us (Rom. 8:16), our love for God is—by God's grace in us—also God loving God in us.[69]

Misunderstanding the Emotion in Love

Love for God is an affective participation in God. Indeed, as Lonergan noted, God can be loved (affectively) before he is known (conceptually).[70] Let me briefly explain what I mean by love as an emotion.

Emotions, in their fullness, include four aspects.[71] The first aspect involves a general openness to value. Specifically, we have a capacity for affective religious experience, for being graced by God so that we can respond to God. As Augustine put it, we are made to love God. When this openness is not filled, we are restless.

The second aspect of an emotion is being affected by a particular value, akin to Aquinas's "complacency."[72] In a religious context, it is sometimes described as being possessed by God. In interpersonal relationships, love is an emotion that commonly takes the form of attunement. We "resonate" with the beloved. Similarly, when we love God, we are in attunement with God.[73] For us, revelation is not primarily propositions about God but, in the first place, being moved by God's own self to which we become attuned.[74] Thus, when we engage in discernment, we "sense" we are in harmony or out of harmony with God. In interpersonal relationships, we feel attuned or conformed to that other, even if we are not able to put this relation into words.[75]

The third aspect is an appreciation of the goodness (or badness) of the beloved. God is revealed. Because God is not a finite object, any apprehension of God's value will have a sense that the value perceived is really present though not in a delimitable form. It will be objective, though not objectifiable. Even the description that Rahner sometimes gives for the experience of God—namely, a terrifying, unreal, empty, refusing, silent, distant darkness[76]—still has within it, if it describes an experience of God, what Rudolf Otto added, namely, a quality of *fascinosum*.[77] Hence, it is still possible to love even this darkness as revealing the transcendence of God.

The fourth aspect completes the emotion, though it can be withheld. In love, we say yes not primarily to our own self-transcending emotion but to the valuable "object" of the emotion. Even if love for God is already implicit in someone's life, for example, she affirmatively feels there is an ultimate meaning to her life, this love becomes properly her own when she endorses it with a second-order consent.[78] To take a this-worldly example, it is one thing for her to enjoy doing things with a friend, another to realize that she has become a friend, a third to assent to "I want to be a friend," and a fourth finally to say to the friend, "I love you." Friendship may be implicit in the beginning, but it becomes more her own the closer she moves to freely avowing an explicit love.[79] As Francis de Sales noted, following the Council of Trent, this love properly includes an explicit choice or election.[80]

Usually, those who write on love omit one or more of these four aspects. For example, even when talking about love for neighbor, Rahner focuses attention on the self who loves. He describes love in negative terms as forgetting self and losing self.[81] Similarly, he asserts that love is the best way to find ourselves, and he points to how a lack of love harms us.[82] He writes that freedom itself is described as the possibility of saying yes or no to our own self,[83] and love is described as accepting ourselves in our a priori orientation to neighbor and God.[84] Love for God is described as opening ourselves and accepting that God accepts us.[85]

Opening, affirming, accepting, forgetting, and losing self do describe aspects of an affection for God.[86] Still, accepting God's self-gift or forgetting our self is not the same as offering ourselves in return to God, nor is it the same as actually loving God in God's own self. The likely reason that Rahner focuses on the self is that, for him, God, the term of our love, "remains absolutely beyond and absolutely untouched by our love."[87] Rather than understanding love as an affective affirmation or personal participation in God, Rahner describes it as surrendering our self to the single movement of our existence that is through neighbor toward God.[88]

By contrast, when love is a full emotion, the lover actively and explicitly is directed to the beloved, typically wanting to enrich the beloved.[89] Love for God includes a growing affirmation and appreciation of the goodness of God. Accordingly, what is going on in the beloved makes a difference to and becomes a concern of the lover who shares in the life of the beloved. That is, what matters to God now matters to us. As Paul Wadell writes, "We become more like God because we learn to love what God loves."[90] I would add that God loves God, and thus so can we.

Problem of God

The greatest difficulties in describing love for God arise from one question: Who is God? The difficulty arises because the experience of love changes with the object we love: "Love and the beloved condition each other mutually, and the description of one implies a proposition about the other."[91] The love we have for our spouse, for example, is and should be different from love for our children. The same can be said of love for strangers, for an enemy, for a pet cat, for roses, for chocolate, for deep dark woods, for "life," or for beauty—a fortiori, for God.

Further, the love we have even for one particular "object" is intricately modified by the multiple, complex, and often contrary, if not also contradictory, qualities and relationships of the beloved. A wife may love her husband's thoughtfulness, but not his fits of anger. She may appreciate his anger when it is directed at protecting the family, but not when it is directed at the children. Particular loves are richly complex. This complexity is exponentially increased by the number and kinds of relationships the beloved is involved in—a fortiori, for our love of God, who is maximally related.

Who is the God that people love? Diverse answers come from devout children and desert monks and dogmatic popes. The answers come from atheists with their objections, from Hindus with their innumerable gods, and from mystics with their dark nights. Owing to their different histories, each Christian will have one or more preferred descriptions of God.[92] For example, Jonathan Edwards describes God as Beauty and Sweetness, while Rahner describes God as terrifying darkness. I will consider three types of answers that here I will call "spiritual experiences," "religious practices," and "theological conceptualizations." What is contained in these three types helps explain why polytheism rather than monotheism has been attractive down through the ages.

Spiritual Experiences

People experienced God in ordinary life long before they had sacred scriptures. Similarly, many of us today experience God in starry skies, the endless ocean, a shiny leaf, the majesty of a sequoia redwood, the intricacy of DNA, the birth of a child, our bodily vitality, the events of history, and so forth.[93] In these experiences, "a sense of God's presence, power, and grace accompanies and shines through."[94] These spiritual experiences tacitly or explicitly include a "more" that is felt as "in-finite," that is, not limited to the particular sunset or infant that evokes such wonder.[95]

In our age, with its great preoccupation with the self, in addition to finding God in nature or history, we often discover God in existential concerns about the meaning of our lives.[96] We may experience God in exercises of conscience, as when we refuse to tell a lie that would make us look good or when we feel contrition for betraying a friend or when we witness self-sacrifice for another human being.[97] These sacramental moments in our lives cannot be simply willed to happen, but they flow from a capacity that is in us and that must be cultivated.[98]

While these religious experiences may have only a transient effect on us, commonly they evoke a sense of attachment to God that lasts long after the specific experience has passed. That is, a love for God, like a love for a human being, tends to outlast, even through a lifetime, the initial experience that gave rise to it. Indeed, it often continues despite contrary experience. We Christians may lose the very things, such as health, success, or friends, that once sparked a love-engendering encounter with God. We do not deny God when we experience such losses because we interpret these losses within the love relationship with God that has outlived the original religious experiences.

Thus, even experiences of evil, such as natural disasters or disease or injustice, which raise for many the question of theodicy, can occasion for religious people a further encounter with and love for God. We may experience God as one who has mercifully spared us in a tornado. We may experience the tornado, when we are affected by it, as God's way of chastising us or shaking us so that we can move into a deeper life.[99] Even the prospect of our own death can be part of our relationship with God, as the resurrection attests. Or more actively, we may experience all forms of natural, social, or institutional evils as what God opposes and thus as what God invites us to participate in rectifying.[100]

Much less dramatically, the God experienced in daily life is normally more like a companion who is just there with us. The "practice of the presence of God" readily brings this God near to the heart. In this everyday practice, as Vincent Brümmer notes, "the believer's love 'loses all thought of the greatness of its object' and overcomes all reticence in approaching God. The believer takes the risk of setting aside all such restraint, in the confident expectation of not being turned away by God."[101] We may wake, saying "Good Morning, God," or, in a moment of gratitude, "God, I love you." When we do so, we do not have a sense we are casting our thoughts into the wind. We are aware that our "categorical" images are insufficient.[102] We are aware that God, whom we relate to as if a familiar friend, is in fact the unmanipulable Ever-More. Nevertheless, we sense this God is near, loveable, and loving.

Religious Practice

Many of us Christians likely feel the presence of God through various specifically religious practices such as the rosary or the liturgy of the hours. We may set aside specific periods in the day for quiet so that we can explicitly raise our minds and hearts to God.[103] We may experience the otherness of God by worshiping in a space that is separate from ordinary life and by prayers and ritual actions that are formulaic.[104] God may become for us more spatially and temporally focused when we receive the Eucharist.[105] Through a host of such activities, we establish a distinct part of our life as specifically devoted to growing in union with, that is, love for, God.[106] All this is commonplace. Still, in much moral theology these activities, though they may be said to have consequences for our moral life, have not seemed to be themselves part of our moral life.[107]

We have seen that the trusted God of everyday life can be experienced not only in beautiful sunsets but also in encounters with evil. Similarly, many of us Christians go through periods of darkness or emptiness in our religious practices. At the limit, we may experience only dark nights.[108] Less painfully, we also may experience the namelessness of God when we close our eyes and go within ourselves during prayer. More exuberantly, we might experience the transcendence of God when singing "Holy, Holy, Holy."[109] Through such experiences, we grow in love for the transcendent God.

One religious practice that helps many Christians encounter God is reading or listening to the Bible. The scriptures highlight a narrative account of God interacting with us, usually to our benefit.[110] Some strands of scripture, however, present a God who is hard to love, which helps explain why obedience to God, fear of God, or even forgetfulness of God, not love for God, is often prominent. For example, let us consider two central books of the bible, Exodus and Romans, which speak profoundly if disturbingly of a God whom we would want to keep very distant but also whom we welcome as more intimate to our selves than we are to ourselves.

When asked who God is, God responds with a statement that evokes the otherness, mystery, and sovereignty of God: "I am who I am" (Exod. 3:14). When asked how God decides, God replies, "I show favors to whom I will, and I grant mercy to whom I will" (Exod. 33:19; Rom. 9:18). This God is full of perplexing paradoxes: God endures with much patience (Rom. 9:22), but he executes his sentence quickly and decisively (Rom. 9:27). To those who ask God to be with them, God threatens genocide because no one can look on his face and live (Exod. 33:5, 20), except that God speaks with Moses face-to-face as with an intimate friend (Exod. 33:11, 17). On the one hand, this God kills the firstborn children and animals of all Egyptians from royalty down to prisoners (Exod. 12:12); on the other hand, this God provides breakfast and dinner to hungry Israelites (Exod. 16:12). God executes vengeance and repays people according to their deeds (Rom. 2:6, 12:19), yet God reckons righteousness apart from deeds and indeed welcomes those weak in faith (Rom. 4:6, 14:3). This God hardens the Egyptians hearts and then kills them for having a hard heart, and does so to gain glory for himself (Exod. 14:17; Rom. 9:17, 22–23, 11:25–26); still, this God makes us children and heirs, his people, his beloveds, and so God makes all things work together for our good (Rom. 8:16–17, 28, 31, 9:24–25).

Each of these traits of God (and many more that could be drawn from the two testaments) represents aspects of God that make love for God anything but straightforward. Just as those who experience God in the goodness of ordinary life must also reckon with evil and just as those whose religious practices bring light also have to reckon with darkness, so also those who are inspired by the uplifting graciousness of the biblical God have to reckon with the God who is unpredictable and kills. The tension well demonstrates Otto's description of the holy: at once attractive and terrifying. An adequate love for God includes not only intimacy but also fear of the Lord.

Philosophical Theology

Perhaps surprisingly, the descriptions of God given by the most profound theologians greatly contribute to the problematic of loving God. These theologians try to speak about God less poetically and more literally. For them, much of classical "mythic-agential theories of the divine" found in "spiritual experiences" and in "religious practices" gives way "to highly de-anthropomorphized understandings of God."[111] To Thomas Aquinas, God is Pure Act and Primary Cause; to Rudolf Otto, God is the *mysterium tremendum*; to Paul Tillich, God is the Ground of Being and Ultimate Concern; to Robert Adams, God is goodness itself; and to Rahner, God is "holy mystery" or the "Whither" of our transcendentality.[112]

The religious problem is that the God named by these theologians and philosophers does not easily evoke love. It is doubtful that religion could survive on such thin gruel. By contrast, popular religions, with their prayers and rituals and texts and holy places, speak of God as someone(s) who talks with people and performs miracles, who can be pleased or appeased by certain prayers or rites, who can be found in specific places, and so forth. Rahner observes that a religion that would avoid all this particularity in favor of an abstract view "seems to evaporate into a mist which perhaps does exist, but in practice it cannot be the source of religious life."[113] Nevertheless, humans can and do have affections that are not limited to concrete sensuous objects, and love can attain to a non-objectifiable God.

Writing quite abstractly as a philosophical theologian, Rahner describes three experiential modes of relating to God. First, God is present to us as "the distant, incomprehensible and asymptotic term of our transcendence," a transcendence present not only in knowledge but also in the dynamism of love. In this mode, human transcendence seeks for an ultimate both as the horizon of its questions and knowledge and as the ultimate, meaning-giving term of its desire.[114] This search may be filled with anxiety, since this transcendence toward "an infinitely distant horizon" meets or includes "a remote judgment" on the seeker and tends to "frighten him away and back into the narrow confines of his everyday world."[115] Nevertheless, we can love this infinitely distant God because the human mind can participate in "infinity," not by an endless series of advances from this good plus more good and more good, and so on until we reach some "highest good," but by a leap from a few instances to the infinite good. This is so because the infinite good lies on a different plane than any series of finite goods.

Second, God is present in the mode of closeness through an absolute "self-communication,"[116] a mode that envelops us and in that way invites love. In this mode, we experience God's nearness within us and around us, and we are aware that thus we are loved. We feel our lives do have meaning since we are "connected" and share in the totality of reality or in mystery.[117] Here God is present as "a hidden closeness, a forgiving intimacy, . . . a love which shares itself, something familiar which [we] can approach and turn to."[118] In this experience, we may find comfort and even joy in realizing that we belonged to God long before we could appreciate this belonging.

Third, though much less prominent in Rahner, God is a partner who enables our cooperation with God's action in the world.[119] God, "in the implanting of his divine Spirit in the innermost heart and centre of man, becomes a direct partner of man himself."[120] In this mode, which elsewhere I have more thoroughly elaborated,[121] we experience God acting in and through us such that we are created cocreators with God. Such a privilege. The infinity of God takes flesh in us and in our world. Just as the narratives of Israel's exodus are also the narratives of God's involvement with Israel, so too the narratives of our lives continue God's involvement as creator, redeemer, and sanctifier. We experience ourselves, of course, as dependent on God.[122] We cooperate with God in creation by admiring it, by maintaining it, and by bringing novelty into it, especially the novelty that is human existence. We cooperate with God as redeemer who enters into our own chaos, especially when we oppose or overcome disorder in our material world, by repentance and forgiving or by institutional reform. We cooperate with God as sanctifier, for example, when we help others engage in religious practices.[123] Love for God, then, means to affirm and cooperate with God in this activity.

Let me conclude with a contentious point. Does our love for God make any difference to God? Most lovers hope to enrich the beloved. One school of theology so emphasizes God's sovereignty or God's perfection that our loves, indeed our very selves, do not—because they cannot—make a difference to God.[124] Here, it seems, the only enrichment that can occur is in our appreciation of the beloved. Another school, frequently using the name "process theology," imagines that our love makes a difference to God. This school, to which I loosely subscribe, has a different understanding of perfection, such that if God could not relate and respond to humans, God would be less than perfect.[125] Benedict XVI says that a theology of a God who cannot change and has no external relations is formula for despair.[126] As Daniel Day Williams describes this God, "The love God offers is responsive love, in which he takes into himself the consequences of human actions, bears with the world, and urges all things toward a society of real freedom in communion."[127] Similarly, the First Letter of John says God's own love is perfected through us (4:12). One reason why I favor a process understanding of God is that if love includes being affected by what affects the beloved, then in this sense the immutable God cannot love us.

Types of Love for God

The English language uses the word "love" to point to a great variety of experiences. This lack of differentiation reappears in the many different ways that theologians use the words "agape," "eros," and "philia." Elsewhere, I have stipulatively distinguished these three by the criterion of "for whose sake" we love.[128] Agape is love for the sake of the beloved. Eros is a genuine love of the beloved, but for the sake for the lover. Philia, for example, friendship, is the love that unites two or more for the sake of their relationship. Here I use these three types to describe love for God, even as I readily admit all three are in play most of the time. As suggested previously, our actual experiences of these loves will vary depending both on the aspect of God we focus on and on the aspect of ourselves most engaged. For example, an aesthetic love of God's sublimity is differently experienced than a grateful love of God as merciful, though both are part of our love for God.

Outka provides an important corrective to the emphases of Nygren and Rahner and many others who write as if we are only receptive in relationship with God: "Justice must be done to an active as well as a passive element in response. . . . For while it may be true that the agent cannot give any*thing* to God, he can meaningfully withhold *himself*. And if he can be said to withhold . . . his final loyalty, his heart, soul, and mind, he can also plausibly be said to give them."[129] All three loves I will describe involve "giving" of self to God, though in different ways.

Eros

Historically, it seems, the predominant love for God has been an eros love that turns to God for safety, support, miracles, rescue, bountiful harvests, and the like. We genuinely love God, but for our own sakes. The Psalms, for example, regularly plead for God's assistance. Saint Paul reassures Christians: "All things work together for good for those who love God" (Rom. 8:28). Nygren describes eros rather well: "Man reaches up towards God and seeks to secure participation in His riches and blessedness. Here the upward-striving tendency of Eros comes into its own: human want and need seek for satisfaction, in the Divine fullness. . . . It is natural that He should attract to Himself all desire and love."[130] In Nygren's opinion, Catholic doctrine privileges this love. Also, in his view, it thereby promotes "an egocentric perversion," alien to the Gospel.[131]

Instead, I propose that eros is a genuine love for God, found in everyday prayer, encouraged in scripture and liturgy, and represented in such theological titles for God as "Ultimate Concern" or Highest Good. Even Rahner, who speaks of "faith in a wintry season,"[132] writes of the comforting nearness of God when God gives God's own self to us. Eros love participates affirmatively in God's life and wants God to be supremely great, but does so in view of

God's goodness to us individually and to our community. Without eros, we cannot be grateful to God.[133]

Because of our eros love, we are able to see all things as, in one way or another, gifts from God, the Giver of all good gifts. Of course, love for God cannot fulfill all our needs and cannot make us fully satisfied or happy. God's goodness is a divine goodness, not a creaturely goodness. A deep love for God will not of itself replace our need for oxygen or medical cures or human companionship. If God is the highest good, God is so in the sense of source of all good, not as the summation of all goods.[134] When we love this good, we are primarily enriched in the sense that our own vocation to be in relationship with God is fulfilled. With that fulfillment comes peace and security, even if on the level of creation, there is no peace or security. A strong eros love for God expects that no matter how many good things are absent, we still love the one who fulfills our deepest spiritual and religious hungers.

Agape

Weaver notes, "The erotic tenor of classical and medieval accounts of the divine-human relation shifted in the Reformation to an emphasis on God's agape and subsequently, to agape as the norm for Christian life."[135] The problem the Reformation addressed is that classical Catholic ethics seems to be "a kind of theological ethical egoism." That is, it makes the norm of one's action to be one's own fulfillment.[136] Still, between eros and agape, we do not in practice have an either-or choice. That is, "loving God as one's good is compatible with loving God for God's own sake."[137]

An agapic love for God, as I have defined it, is directed to God for God's own sake. We look not to the consolations or goods that may come with loving God; rather, we affectively affirm God's own good. One extreme form of agape is to be so focused on God that one loses awareness of self.[138] This type of mysticism tends, unfortunately, to be articulated as complete self-annihilating merging that leads to the loss of human selfhood.[139] Another difficult form of agape is forced on us when our prayer goes through periods of dryness, desolation, or darkness; any ostensible eros is extinguished. These periods make clear that "prayer is properly about expressing and growing in love for God, not about those benefits."[140]

Karl Rahner at times advocated an exclusively agapic love: "The love of God . . . is what it must be only when God is loved for his own sake—when love for him is produced and experienced not with a view to human self-assertion and interior self-fulfillment, . . . when human beings, ultimately without self-seeking, go out of themselves, forget themselves because of God, and really lose themselves in the ineffable mystery to which they willingly surrender."[141]

The term "surrender" is common among those who write of an agapic relation to God.[142] In this context, surrender suggests the sort of self-subordination that occurs when we are deeply invested in others. We allow ourselves to be swept up in and flow with their own dynamism. The language of surrender, however, still lacks that aspect of emotion that is an active affirmation of the beloved. Also missing is the sense of explicitly committing ourselves. Similarly, agapic lovers commonly use exaggerated language, describing it as abrogating or annihilating the self. In this vein, Rahner describes even marital love not as a communion or friendship but as a love in which "one thus abandons oneself."[143] A fortiori, he described love for God as if it were an "ecstatic bursting forth from self" that "never more permits the human being to return to self."[144]

Needless to say, humans always do return to themselves, and they should do so. To be sure, in ecstatic love, we do momentarily "lose" ourselves, but we therein also experience how a dimension of ourselves is enriched and we freely consent to this.[145] Sometimes this happens suddenly, as when we "fall in love with God." Then, a person "falls, as it were, into the absolute, infinite and incomprehensible abyss of all being."[146] Usually, the process is more gradual. No matter whether suddenly or gradually, we yield to an affective movement initiated by God but then take up that movement as our own in devoting ourselves to God.

Philia

Jesus taught us to call God "Father" (Matt. 6:9), and Paul described us as children of God (Rom. 8:14). These biblical images point to a love that is not agape or eros, nor is it a combination of the two (Aquinas, *ST* II-II.23.1, 6). Rather, they name an interpersonal relationship between God and us.[147] I use "philia" to name the love we have for those that we love for the sake of our relationship to them. We have a philia relationship or covenant with God. This philia relationship is given before we are able to affirm it, similar to the way children have a family before they choose it and their usual role is to grow into this relationship.[148] As in a family, this philia need not be, pace Nygren, a relationship of equals.[149] Rather, it is a love in which the members have their own cherished role.

Experientially, a philia love for God includes a sense of belonging to God. This manifests itself prominently in experiences we have of cooperating with God, as we have seen previously. We not only act, but we also experience God acting in and through us. Both Nygren and Aquinas promote fellowship with God, but the difference in their approaches could hardly be greater. For Nygren, "Our fellowship with God, then, rests for us on the basis not of holiness but sin."[150] For Aquinas, it is grace that makes us friends of God (*ST* II-II.24.2).

We can reject or gradually grow into this fellowship with God. Weaver wisely writes, "Love for God is a relationship of profound personal intimacy. Like all relationships, it consists in a particular history—seasons of sweetness and of difficulty, movements into deeper intimacy and evasions of it. Because the person's relationship is with a living God, love for God has an open-ended character."[151] This philia demands purification,[152] in particular, "renouncing any independent choice" or any separately "established relation with the world."[153] It is not enough if we just happen to promote the good that God wants to promote.[154] Rather, we want to promote it in concert with God. This fellowship significantly includes our own personal interests, such as cooperating with God in procreating and then raising a family.[155] It also involves activities such as liturgy that are mainly engaged in for the sake of expressing the relationship.

In a quiet way, this philia love is the religious experience of "thousands of unpretending Christians." They live in an "easy" relationship with God. Rather than largely being a religion of visions and ecstasies, Brümmer observes, Christianity arguably has "this continuous relationship with God" at its "heart and centre."[156]

Conclusion

I have tried to present a critique of contemporary culture both inside and outside the church. Rahner suggests that "*the* real and central problem" for us today is whether it is even possible to address and "achieve a personal relationship" with God.[157] To the degree that this problem is real, our culture is a major failure. Still, I am confident that countless Christians, however fragmentarily, do practice love for God. Theologians, nevertheless, have had a hard time explaining the first commandment, and for quite serious reasons. It is hard to describe love. It is vastly harder to describe God. However falteringly, this essay has tried to put the two together because of the importance of love for God. Love for God is an emotion through which we affirmatively participate in God's goodness and activity. When we so live in this love, the first commandment is first.

Notes

1. Gene Outka, "Universal Love and Impartiality," in *The Love Commandments: Essays in Christian Ethics and Moral Philosophy*, ed. Edmund Santurri and William Werpehowski (Washington, DC: Georgetown University Press, 1992), 2.

2. Ibid., 59.

3. See Edward Vacek, "Love for God—Is It Obligatory?," *Annual of the Society of Christian Ethics* 16 (1996): 221–47; "Divine-Command, Natural-Law, and Mutual-Love Ethics," *Theological Studies* 57, no. 4 (December 1996): 633–53; "Religious Life and the Eclipse of Love for God," *Review for Religious* 57, no. 2 (March–April 1998): 118–37; "The Eclipse of Love for God," *America* 174, no. 8 (March 9, 1996): 13–16.

4. As James Keenan shows, Catholic moral theology often focused on sin and behavioral norms, not love. *A History of Catholic Moral Theology: From Confessing Sins to Liberating Consciences* (New York: Continuum, 2010); also Darlene Fozard Weaver, *Self Love and Christian Ethics* (New York: Cambridge University, 2002), 4–5, 66.

5. Anders Nygren, *Agape and Eros* (New York: Harper & Row, 1969), 98.

6. Ibid., 123–27.

7. Gene Outka, *Agape: An Ethical Analysis* (New Haven, CT: Yale University Press, 1972), 45.

8. Raymond Moloney, "The Freedom of Christ in the Later Lonergan," *Theological Studies* 70 (2009): 819. For a superb survey of exceedingly diverse interpretations of the second great commandment, see Garth Hallett, *Christian Neighbor-Love* (Washington, DC: Georgetown University Press, 1989).

9. Bernard Brady, *Christian Love: How Christians through the Ages Have Understood Love* (Washington, DC: Georgetown University Press, 2003), 181; see also Daniel Day Williams, *The Spirit and the Forms of Love* (New York: Harper & Row, 1968), 78.

10. Klaus Demmer, *Living the Truth: A Theory of Action* (Washington, DC: Georgetown University Press, 2010), 17; Karl Rahner, *Foundations of Christian Faith* (New York: Seabury, 1978), 16.

11. Werner Jeanrond, *Theology of Love* (New York: T&T Clark, 2010), 246; Andrew Tallon, "The Heart in Rahner's Philosophy of Mysticism," *Theological Studies* 53 (1992): 710; Robert Merrihew Adams, *Finite and Infinite Goods: A Framework for Ethics* (New York: Oxford University Press, 1999), 210–11.

12. William J. Wainwright, *Reason and the Heart: A Prolegomenon to a Critique of Passional Reason* (Ithaca, NY: Cornell University, 1995), 3; James Martin, "More Than a Feeling: A Desire for God," *US Catholic* 75, no. 7 (July 2010): 37–38. Rahner, in *Foundations of Christian Faith* (pp. 44–51), reversed his standard practice; he begins with the word "God" and then seeks to discover what it might point to. This linguistic starting point is, in fact, a common pattern for most people. Still each person must have some kind of real apprehension of the referent if "God" is not to be like "ghosts." For a debate on the relationship between experience and language, see Shannon Craigo-Snell, *Silence, Love, and Death: Saying Yes to God in the Theology of Karl Rahner* (Milwaukee: Marquette University Press, 2008), 32–35, 59–75.

13. Karl Rahner, *Theological Investigations* (New York: Crossroad, 1974), 11:152; *The Love of Jesus and the Love of Neighbor* (New York: Crossroad, 1983), 11.

14. Michael Barnes, *Stages of Thought: The Co-Evolution of Religious Thought and Science* (New York: Oxford, 2000), 207–9.

15. Rahner, *Theological Investigations*, 11:155.

16. Vacek, "Love for God," 221–47.

17. Outka, *Agape*, 45.

18. For reasons of stylistic simplicity, I focus, as Rahner and Nygren do, on human beings. Any theory of love should be able, mutatis mutandis, to be applied to the extra-human cosmos.

19. Carlo Maria Martini, *Letting God Free Us* (New Rochelle, NY: New City Press, 1993), 127; Rahner, *Love of Jesus*, 71; Outka, *Agape*, 52.

20. Pheme Perkins, *Love Commandments in the New Testament* (New York: Paulist, 1982), 24. Matthew Elliott, in *Faithful Feelings: Rethinking Emotion in the New Testament* ([Grand Rapids, MI: Kregel, 2006], 156), concurs but notes several places where Paul describes believers as those who love God.

21. Nygren, *Agape and Eros*, 75–80.

22. Ibid., 93–94.

23. Ibid., 92.

24. Ibid., 148; also Germain Grisez, *Way of the Lord Jesus* (Chicago: Franciscan Herald, 1983), 603.

25. Nygren, *Agape and Eros*, 95.

26. Timothy Jackson, *Love Disconsoled: Meditations on Christian Charity* (Cambridge: Cambridge University Press, 1999), 142. Outka's phrase is "unqualified obedience or adoration." Outka, *Agape*, 53. See also Elliott, *Faithful Feelings*, 138–40; Bernhard Häring, *Law of Christ* (Westminster, MD: Newman, 1961), 1:317.

27. Vacek, "Divine-Command, Natural-Law," 633–53; Gary Chartier, *Analogy of Love: Divine and Human Love at the Center of Christian Theology* (Charlottesville, VA: Imprint Academic Philosophy Documentation Center, 2007), 112–21.

28. Vincent Brümmer, *The Model of Love: A Study in Philosophical Theology* (New York: Cambridge University Press, 1993), 222, also 214.

29. Dietrich von Hildebrand, *Nature of Love* (South Bend, IN: St. Augustine Press, 2009), 87.

30. Brümmer, *Model of Love*, 217.

31. For some of the changes that occurred in his theology, see Edward Vacek, "Development within Rahner's Theology," *Irish Theological Quarterly* 42, no. 1 (January 1975): 36–49; Craigo-Snell, *Silence, Love, and Death*, 33.

32. When he was more cautious, Rahner said this unity occurred when this love of neighbor "attains it proper nature and its moral absoluteness and depth," a qualification that by definition makes it love for God. *Theological Investigations* (Baltimore: Helicon, 1969), 6:237. For an excellent explication and defense of Rahner's often contrary claims, see Gerald Beyer, "Karl Rahner on the Radical Unity of the Love of God and Neighbour," *Irish Theological Quarterly* 68, no. 3 (2003): 251–80.

33. Rahner, *Theological Investigations*, 6:241, 246–47. However, in the same essay, it should be noted, Rahner wrote that explicit prayer to God was an act of love for God and not for neighbor, and it had a higher dignity than an explicit love of neighbor because of its categorized object ("God" versus "another human"). Both loves have God as transcendental horizon (238, 246).

34. Rahner, *Foundations of Christian Faith*, 64.

35. Rahner, *Theological Investigations*, 6:232–33. These teachings, I propose, formed the take-away message from Rahner's writings, amplified in his doctrine of the anonymous Christian. Still, in the same essay, Rahner allows that one could have an interpersonal love restricted to its "merely human" dimension (236), and he says "of course" prayer to God is not love of neighbor. A different—and in my mind also mistaken—claim is that those who love God necessarily love their neighbor. This "metaphysical" claim is different from a moral claim that lovers of God *ought* to love at least some neighbors. One obvious problem with the claim is that our neighbors number into (an ever changing) billions of people. A second is that most if not all people do not love at least one of their immediate neighbors, and that would imply that—contrary to the evidence—they have no love for God.

36. Karl Rahner, *Theological Investigations* (New York: Crossroad, 1975), 13:127; Mark Taylor, *God Is Love: A Study in the Theology of Karl Rahner* (Atlanta, GA: Scholars Press, 1986), 403.

37. Rahner, *Theological Investigations*, 6:234–35.

38. Subsequently, Rahner variously qualified these claims, writing, for example, that this neighbor love must reach its "moral absoluteness and depth," which raises the bar quite high. *Theological Investigations*, 6:237. Later, he wrote that sinful humans rarely if ever achieve such a deep love. *Love of Jesus*, 45. Near the end of his career, Rahner alters his position in another way, saying that love of neighbor must develop into an explicit acceptance of God. *Foundations of Christian Faith*, 309.

39. Rahner, *Theological Investigations*, 6:238; also Rahner, *Love of Jesus*, 71.

40. Rahner, *Theological Investigations*, 6:247.

41. Jackson, *Love Disconsoled*, 13, 26.

42. Outka, *Agape*, 46–47; Craigo-Snell, *Silence, Love, and Death*, 93–94; Weaver, *Self Love and Christian Ethics*, 144; Jeanrond, *Theology of Love*, 150; Beyer, "Karl Rahner on the Radical Unity," 264; Rahner, *Theological Investigations*, 14:305. However, in *Foundations of Christian Faith* (p. 120), Rahner says that God is really accessible only in worship.

43. Outka, "Universal Love and Impartiality," 73.

44. Chartier, *Analogy of Love*, 84, 87–88. A similar overstatement of a profound insight occurred when Rahner held that to dialogue with God means that we listen to ourselves since we are God's word spoken to us. See Craigo-Snell, *Silence, Love, and Death*, 43–44, referring to Karl Rahner, *Christian at the Crossroads* (New York: Seabury, 1975), 67. Such identifications beg for qualifications.

45. Compare Rahner, *Theological Investigations*, 6:234, with Rahner, *Theological Investigations* (New York: Seabury, 1976), 14:295, 298.

46. Rahner, *Theological Investigations*, 14:305.

47. John Whittaker, "'Agape' and Self-Love," in Santurri and Werpehowski, *Love Commandments*, 237.

48. Grisez, *Way of the Lord Jesus*, 603.

49. Jean Porter, "Salvific Love and Charity: A Comparison of the Thought of Karl Rahner and Thomas Aquinas," in Santurri and Werpehowski, *Love Commandments*, 240–41.

50. Thomas Oord, "The Love Racket: Defining Love and Agape for the Love-and-Science Research Program," *Zygon* 40, no. 4 (December 2005): 924–25. Rahner tended to write as someone describing from the outside, not from a phenomenological viewpoint. For example, he wrote that the command to love is simply the command to fulfill oneself. Karl Rahner, *Theological Investigations* (Baltimore: Helicon, 1966), 4:456. Loving God or neighbor does fulfill oneself, but to love with the intention of fulfilling one's self is quite different. Cf. John Crosby, "Introductory Study," in Hildebrand, *Nature of Love*, xxi.

51. Rahner, *Foundations of Christian Faith*, 100.

52. Edward Vacek, *Love, Human and Divine* (Washington, DC: Georgetown University Press, 1993), 34, 44.

53. F. LeRon Shults, "That Than Which Nothing More Lovely Can Be Conceived," in *Visions of Agapé: Problems and Possibilities in Human and Divine Love*, ed. Craig Boyd (Burlington, VT: Ashgate, 2008), 131–32.

54. Nygren, *Agape and Eros*, 682.

55. Ibid., 93.

56. Ibid., 93–94.

57. Ibid., 129.

58. Ibid., 132.

59. Jeanrond, *Theology of Love*, 93, 100; see also Rahner, *Foundations of Christian Faith*, 83.

60. Dietrich von Hildebrand, *Ethics* (Chicago: Franciscan Herald, 1953), 196.

61. Outka, *Agape*, 49.

62. Karl Rahner, *Theological Investigations* (New York: Herder & Herder, 1973), 10:280–81.

63. Shults, "That Than Which Nothing," 131–32.

64. Constance Fitzgerald, "From Impasse to Prophetic Hope: Crisis of Memory," *Proceedings of the Sixty-Fourth Annual Convention—Catholic Theological Society of America* 64 (June 2009): 31. Perhaps needless to say, living for another can in some ways lead to loss of self when sacrifices, especially the sacrifice of life, for the beloved, is invited or required. In such cases, the "flourishing" may only be the greatness of making the sacrifice.

65. Outka, "Universal Love and Impartiality," 62, 65.

66. Ibid., 88.

67. Edward Vacek, "Inquiring after God when Working," in *Inquiring after God: Classic and Contemporary Readings*, ed. Ellen Charry (Malden, MA: Blackwell, 2000), 89–107; Aquinas, *ST* I:105.5.

68. Brümmer, *Model of Love*, 196; Aquinas, *ST* II-I.111.2.

69. Karl Rahner, *Theological Investigations*, 4:97; Rahner, *Foundations of Christian Faith*, 125. Even when Rahner uses communion or partner language, he generally describes this as a state that God creates, with the supposition that humans can accept or reject this offer. Rahner, *Foundations of Christian Faith*, 120–21; Karl

Rahner, *Theological Investigations* (London: Darton, Longman, and Todd, 1963), 1:123; Rahner, *Theological Investigations*, 6:245; Rahner, *Theological Investigations*, 14:304; Rahner, *Theological Investigations*, 10:282; also Weaver, *Self Love and Christian Ethics*, 211.

70. Rahner, in *Theological Investigations* (5:209), makes a similar point, though he overstates the depth of most spiritual activities. Our attunement with God, he writes, "though not allowing us to grasp it completely in a reflective manner, is nevertheless the permanent basis for all other spiritual activities and which, on this account, is always more 'there' and less objectively 'there' than anything else."

71. Vacek, *Love, Human and Divine*, 11–16.

72. Stephen Pope, *Evolution of Altruism and the Ordering of Love* (Washington, DC: Georgetown University Press, 1995), 56; Francis de Sales, *Treatise on the Love of God*, trans. Henry Mackey (Rockford, IL: Tan Books, 1997), 30–34.

73. Boyd Taylor Coolman, "Gestimmtheit: Attunement as a Description of the Nature-Grace Relationship in Rahner's Theology," *Theological Studies* 70 (2009): 782.

74. Coolman, "Gestimmtheit," 798.

75. Coolman, "Gestimmtheit," 784, 798; Tallon, "Heart in Rahner's Philosophy," 708.

76. See Craigo-Snell, *Silence, Love, and Death*, 45–54.

77. Rudolf Otto, *The Idea of the Holy* (New York: Oxford, 1977), 1–39.

78. Brümmer, *Model of Love*, 233–34.

79. Hildebrand, *Ethics*, 202–3, 220–22, 233–35.

80. de Sales, *Treatise on the Love of God*, 425; Pope, *Evolution of Altruism*, 57.

81. Rahner, *Love of Jesus*, 70; Rahner, *Foundations of Christian Faith*, 125.

82. Rahner, *Theological Investigations*, 4:229–30, 6:242.

83. Ibid., 6:185.

84. Ibid., 241, 246; Karl Rahner, *Theological Investigations* (New York: Crossroad, 1983), 19:143; Rahner, *Foundations of Christian Faith*, 100.

85. Rahner, *Theological Investigations*, 1:123; Rahner, *Foundations of Christian Faith*, 128.

86. Rahner, *Theological Investigations*, 4:52, 11:156.

87. Rahner, *Foundations of Christian Faith*, 122.

88. Rahner, *Theological Investigations*, 1:123, 14:309.

89. Mark Taylor, rightly I think, extends this claim to development in God. He writes of "the mutual participation of God and the creatures in each other's act of self-creation. The individuals of the world play a role in the divine self-creation in that they are included within the divine actuality. God, in turn, plays a role in the self-creation of the creatures in that God provides the conditions and the material for creaturely self-creation. This relationship is most appropriately symbolized as love. The relationship has no goal or purpose other than the facilitation of the full, authentic self-realization of both God and the creatures. God opens Godself to the creatures, allows the creatures to make a real difference to God and to influence the self-creation of God. Likewise, the creatures open themselves to God and let the product of the divine self-creation influence their own self-creation. Then, the creatures bestow themselves upon God; they literally live unto God and for God's greater glory, in that the product of their acts of self-creation becomes a part of the divine actuality." See *God Is Love*, 389–90.

90. Paul Wadell, *The Primacy of Love: An Introduction to the Ethics of Thomas Aquinas* (New York: Paulist, 1992), 77.

91. Rahner, *Love of Jesus*, 25.

92. Adams, *Finite and Infinite Goods*, 210–11; Rahner, *Theological Investigations*, 14:309.

93. Adams, *Finite and Infinite Goods*, 192, 194; Kendra Hotz and Matthew Mathews, *Shaping the Christian Life* (Louisville, KY: Westminster John Knox Press, 2006), 14; Denis Edwards, "Exploring How God Acts," in *God, Grace, and Creation*, ed. Philip Rossi (Maryknoll, NY: Orbis, 2010), 136.

94. Hotz and Mathews, *Shaping the Christian Life*, 17.

95. Adams, *Finite and Infinite Goods*, 194; Rahner, *Foundations of Christian Faith*, 52.

96. Demmer, *Living the Truth*, 11–12, 17; Rahner, *Theological Investigations*, 11:162.

97. Hotz and Mathews, *Shaping the Christian Life*, 9–11, 15.

98. Timothy O'Malley II, "The Hermeneutic Sacramentality of Augustine: Learning to Contemplate the Invisible Reality of God in the Visible Creation," in Rossi, *God, Grace, and Creation*, 39.

99. Paul Tillich, *Shaking of the Foundations* (Harmondsworth, Middlesex: Penguin, 1962), 66.

100. Ethan Regan, *Theology and the Boundary Discourse of Human Rights* (Washington, DC: Georgetown University Press, 2010), 156; Edwards, "Exploring How God Acts," 136; Wynn, *Emotional Experience and Religious Understanding,* 172;

101. Brümmer, *Model of Love,* 180–81.

102. Rahner, *Theological Investigations,* 11:161.

103. Karl Rahner, *Theological Investigations,* vol. 3 (Baltimore: Helicon, 1982), 30; Karl Rahner, *Everyday Faith* (New York: Herder and Herder, 1968), 24–25.

104. Wynn, *Emotional Experience and Religious Understanding,* 172.

105. Edward Vacek, "Two Types of Eucharistic Piety," *Emmanuel* 86, nos. 8 and 9 (September–October 1980): 439–46, 491–99.

106. de Sales, *Treatise on the Love of God,* 127, 232–33, 281–84.

107. Craigo-Snell, in *Silence, Love, and Death* (p. 87), writes that it is impossible "to love God directly, apart from the world." The earlier Rahner clearly wrote we can have a direct presence to God. Rahner, *Theological Investigations,* 6:209.

108. Fitzgerald, "From Impasse to Prophetic Hope," 22.

109. Otto, *Idea of the Holy,* 1–39.

110. Amy Hollywood, "Spiritual but Not Religious: The Vital Interplay between Submission and Freedom," *Harvard Divinity Bulletin,* Winter/Spring 2010, 21, 25; also see Weaver, *Self Love and Christian Ethics,* 140; Williams, *Spirit and the Forms of Love,* 20–22.

111. Weaver, *Self Love and Christian Ethics,* 6.

112. Brady, *Christian Love,* 17–18; Aquinas, *ST* I.9.1, 105.5; Otto, *Idea of the Holy*; Paul Tillich, *Systematic Theology* (Chicago: University of Chicago, 1957), 3:9, 87; Paul Tillich, *Love, Power, and Justice: Ontological Analyses and Ethical Applications* (New York: Oxford University Press, 1976), 109; Adams, *Finite and Infinite Goods,* 13–49; Rahner, *Foundations of Christian Faith,* 65; Rahner, *Theological Investigations,* 4:48–50.

113. Rahner, *Foundations of Christian Faith,* 82.

114. Rahner, *Love of Jesus,* 52–53; Rahner, *Theological Investigations,* 11:163.

115. Rahner, *Foundations of Christian Faith,* 70, 131.

116. Ibid., 119; Rahner, *Theological Investigations,* 11:153.

117. Rahner, *Theological Investigations,* 6:242; Rahner, *Love of Jesus,* 70.

118. Rahner, *Foundations of Christian Faith,* 131.

119. Rahner tends to stress only human passivity before God; thus, for him, human subjectivity listens, does not control, is overwhelmed, and is opened by God. Ibid., 58.

120. Rahner, *Theological Investigations,* 14:304.

121. Vacek, *Love, Human and Divine,* chap. 4; Edward Vacek, "God's Action and Ours," *Emmanuel* 90, no. 7 (September 1984), 370–76; Edward Vacek, "John Paul II and Cooperation with God," *Annual of the Society of Christian Ethics* 10 (1990): 81–108.

122. Rahner, *Theological Investigations,* 4:97; Rahner, *Foundations of Christian Faith,* 125. Even when Rahner uses communion or partner language, he generally describes this as a state that God alone creates. Rahner, *Foundations of Christian Faith,* 120–21; Rahner, *Theological Investigations,* 1:123, 14:304.

123. Jeanrond, *Theology of Love,* 33.

124. Aquinas, *ST* I.13.7; de Sales, *Treatise on the Love of God,* 444.

125. Thomas Jay Oord, "A Relational God and Unlimited Love," in Boyd, *Visions of Agapé,* 142. In this text also is a long list of those who reject God's impassibility. See also the Teilhardian view: Illia Delio, "Is 'The World' a Problem? A Teilhardian Response," *Teilhard Studies,* no. 60 (Spring 2010): 15; John Haught, *God after Darwin: A Theology of Evolution* (Boulder, CO: Westview Press, 2008), 44–47, 54–55, 122–23.

126. Benedict XVI, "Meditation during First General Congregation," at Special Assembly for the Middle East Synod of Bishops, October 11, 2010, Rome.

127. Williams, *Spirit and the Forms of Love,* 137. See also Adams, *Finite and Infinite Goods,* 134; Brümmer, *Model of Love,* 227; Taylor, *God Is Love,* 338, 389–90; Jackson, *Love Disconsoled,* 161; Edward Vacek, "God's Gifts and Our Moral Lives," in *Method and Catholic Moral Theology,* ed. Todd Salzman (Omaha, NE: Creighton University, 1999), 105–6.

128. Vacek, *Love, Human and Divine,* 157–58.

129. Outka, *Agape*, 51.

130. Nygren, *Agape and Eros*, 212.

131. Ibid., 94, 100, 213, 217, 681–83.

132. Paul Imhof and Hubert Biallowans, eds., *Faith in a Wintry Season: Conversations and Interviews with Karl Rahner in the Last Years of His Life* (New York: Herder & Herder, 1989).

133. Vacek, "God's Gifts and Our Moral Lives," 103–24; Edward Vacek, "Gifts, God, Generosity, and Gratitude," in *Spirituality and Moral Theology: Essays from a Pastoral Perspective*, ed. James Keating (New York: Paulist, 2000), 81–125.

134. Nygren, *Agape and Eros*, 212–13; Rahner, *Theological Investigations*, 1:116; Brady, *Christian Love*, 117–18.

135. Weaver, *Self Love and Christian Ethics*, 4–5.

136. Ibid., 3–5.

137. Ibid., 138.

138. Brümmer, *Model of Love*, 64–66.

139. The loss of selfhood, however, does not refer to this-worldly energy and creativity. Fitzgerald, "From Impasse to Prophetic Hope," 30, 37; Brümmer, *Model of Love*, 214.

140. Weaver, *Self Love and Christian Ethics*, 139; Fitzgerald, "From Impasse to Prophetic Hope," 29–30.

141. Rahner, *Love of Jesus*, 70, also 52–53.

142. William James, *Varieties of Religious Experience* (Rockville, MD: Manor, 2008), 158; Nygren, *Agape and Eros*, 94; Rahner, *Love of Jesus*, 45, 52–53, 70; Rahner, *Theological Investigations* (New York: Crossroad, 1983), 18:101.

143. Rahner, *Love of Jesus*, 16–17.

144. Ibid., 41–42; Rahner, *Foundations of Christian Faith*, 66. This claim of not returning to the self is strange in Rahner's thought, which exulted in the return to self. Similarly, in a rare and more sober moment, Rahner wondered whether a human being ever can or does make such an unconditional commitment (Rahner, *Love of Jesus*, 40), and he also noted three basic ways that people can avoid the self-transcendence that he had taught to be constitutive of being a human (Rahner, *Foundations of Christian Faith*, 32–33).

145. Hollywood, "Spiritual but Not Religious," 26; Aquinas, *ST* II-II.23.2.

146. Rahner, *Foundations of Christian Faith*, 308–9; Karl Rahner, "Thomas Aquinas on the Incomprehensibility of God," supplement, *Journal of Religion* 58 (1978): S123.

147. Brümmer, *Model of Love*, 33.

148. This paragraph is my too-brief response to the gentle criticisms of my earlier work by Jackson in *Love Disconsoled*, 79–88.

149. Nygren, *Agape and Eros*, 92.

150. Ibid., 687, 684.

151. Weaver, *Self Love and Christian Ethics*, 134.

152. Ibid.; Aquinas, *ST* II-II.24.4–8.

153. Jeanrond, *Theology of Love*, 59.

154. Adams, *Finite and Infinite Goods*, 197–98.

155. Ibid., 196–97.

156. Brümmer, *Model of Love*, 77.

157. Rahner, *Theological Investigations*, 11:162.

8

Empathy, Compassion, and Love of Neighbor

JOHN P. REEDER JR.

ARTHUR SCHOPENHAUER ASKS, "How is it possible for *another's* weal and woe to move my will immediately, that is, in exactly the same way in which it is usually moved only by my own weal and woe?"[1] He answers that this is possible "only through that other man's becoming *the ultimate object* of my will in the same way as I myself otherwise am." This in turn "necessarily presupposes that, in the case of his *woe* as such, I suffer directly with him, I feel *his* woe just as I ordinarily feel only my own; and, likewise, I directly desire his weal in the same way that I otherwise desire only my own."[2] And this desire "requires that I am in some way identified with him, in other words, that this entire difference between me and everyone else, which is the very basis of my egoism, is eliminated, to a certain extent at least."[3]

Contemporary writers may accept some features of Schopenhauer's account of compassion: for example, that the other becomes an object of my will along with myself, that I in some sense feel the suffering of the other and desire their well-being, and that this desire requires some form of identification with the other. But they may reject his view that compassion is innate and indestructible and his "metaphysical explanation" of the "phenomenon" of compassion, the "doctrine" that "teaches that all plurality is only apparent; that in all the individuals of this world, however infinite the number in which they exhibit themselves successively and simultaneously, there is yet manifested only one and the same truly existing essence, present and identical in all of them."[4]

My intention here is not to interpret Schopenhauer but to look at three other efforts (Diana Cates, Edith Wyschogrod, Søren Kierkegaard) to describe, explain, and justify compassion: as an extension of self-love, as a form of other regard entirely independent of self-love, and as an expression of equal love. I will then draw on all these accounts in order to make a few points of my own. I will make a distinction between empathy and normative identifications that conceptions of compassion presuppose. I will look at accounts that explain how identification is accomplished, and finally, I will argue that the tension between self-sacrifice and the good of the self can be explained as two facets of an underlying ideal: the self-giving of a parent or friend and the equal inclusion of siblings or friends within that love.

Self-Love: Cates

Diana Cates makes friendship the constitutive presupposition of compassion: friends make the good of others part of their own good; the suffering of the other affects my self-interest.[5] This is not a "eudaimonistic judgment" that makes the good of the other one of my interests, an interest of the self that is not self-interested because the object of the interest is the good of the other.[6] For Cates, when I have compassion,[7] my self-interest—self-love—has been expanded to include the other.[8] The "good of the self is extended to include the good of others as partly its own";[9] "wishing and doing of good to others for their own sake is . . . an extension of affection for ourselves and doing of good to ourselves for our own sakes."[10] Each friend has an expanded self that "partly" envelopes the other, but the friends do not become a single entity.[11]

Friends, then, are "another self." One loves the other in the same *manner* that one loves oneself in the sense that the good of the other is an object of desire just as one takes one's own to be. One loves both self and other in the expanded self for their own sake (*mode*). One dislikes and desires to alleviate the other's suffering to the same *degree* as one does one's own (in the unexpanded sense of the self) since the other's good is now one's own (in the expanded sense of the self). But how wide the *scope* of our compassion will be depends on the sort of friend at hand. If friendship rests on mutual liking, admiration, and a desire to share lives with those we know personally, and if compassion were limited to this sort of friendship, then by definition the scope of compassion is narrow indeed.[12]

Cates, however, thinks that compassion can be expanded from the matrix of "character-friends" to the stranger and the enemy who may not even recognize, much less return, love. Cates begins with the recognition of similarity: "The stranger, and even the enemy, is more like us than he/she is unlike us in morally significant respects."[13] For Cates, the self legitimately seeks its fulfillment, but that constitutively involves the well-being of others: "We are relational creatures who have a personal stake in the flourishing of every other 'human being.'"[14] We extend friendship from special relations to the relation to God (mutatis mutandis), and friendship with God is the bridge to friendship with the stranger, even the enemy: we "befriend" friends of God on the assumption that we extend love to the friends of friends.[15]

But Cates notes that our resources are finite and that in any case when we relate to strangers in compassion as "other ourselves," we do so differently than we do with "character-friends": "Clearly character-friends are 'other ourselves' in a sense that strangers and enemies are not."[16] The love we form for strangers, moreover, does not replace our special relationships, in which we have our primary responsibilities.[17]

Thus, Cates's normative view is that other regard for the near and dear and the stranger is best rooted in the expanded self-love of friendship in which the good of the other becomes part of one's own. Cates does not hold the doctrine of psychological egoism, that is, the thesis that all our motives are self-regarding. But she does seem to hold the psychological thesis that even if some of our motives are other-regarding, we always have self-regarding ones as well.[18] The ideal of pure self-giving love is prone to self-deception and is especially bad for women who have been denied legitimate self-love in the name of the care and nurture of others.[19]

One loves the other, then, for one's own sake since the good of the other becomes part of one's own, and one loves others for their own sake in the sense that they are separate centers of sentience, unique irreplaceable selves. One loves, then, not only "private goods" but also "shared goods"—goods wanted with or for you—and one loves the good of the relation itself.[20] Shared goods and the relation are both part of expanded self-love.[21] Cates suggests that friends aim to maximize their joint good (not in a utilitarian sense but in the sense of weighted goods) on the assumption that each self is of equal value.[22]

What are the difficulties with Cates's view? If the stranger does become part of the self (part of one's self-love), then is the life of the stranger more important than enhancing the lives of the near and dear who are part of the self? Once the stranger is part of the self, then does one maximize, weighted for importance, and give to Oxfam instead of enriching the lives of one's children? Cates makes two fundamental replies: special relations must be preserved as the matrix of the moral life, including regard for the stranger, and regard for the stranger does not release us from our primary duty to the near and dear.[23] My sense is that for Cates, we are required to privilege the near and dear as far as necessities go, but whether luxuries—enhancements—are permitted is a question agents have to determine in their own situation, and there is no one right answer.[24]

Another objection is to making regard for the stranger along with regard for the near and dear part of self-love. If we do have the capacity for an independent other regard, then one could argue for an other-regarding love of the stranger. This sort of love would be an interest of the self, but not part of self-love. Other regard of this sort would have an independence, a distinctiveness, that sets it apart from any form of self-love, even an enriched self-love of friendship. One would preserve a strong phenomenological difference between types of other regard.

Radical Other Regard: Wyschogrod

Whereas Cates anchors compassion in the bonds of *friendship*, extended even to the stranger, Edith Wyschogrod posits a *saint* who responds to the demand of any other. In the friendship model, the self brings the other into its own self-love, but the saint is emptied of its own interests and takes on the interests of the other. Thus, Wyschogrod argues that saints "put themselves totally at the disposal of the Other."[25] The saint aims at "the dissolution of self-interest."[26] One puts one's "own body and material goods at the disposal of the Other";[27] "a saintly life is defined as one in which compassion for the Other, irrespective of cost to the saint, is the primary trait."[28]

Wyschogrod sometimes speaks as if she means that self-interest is set aside and replaced by other regard; among the interests of the self, other-regarding ones drive out self-regarding ones. But I read her to say overall that all my prior interests—self-regarding or other-regarding—are to be supplanted by the interests of the other. The other's interests are *substituted* for my own. What competes with the demand of the other is not a particular or general desire for my self-regarding good but a desire for and an attachment to my projects, whether self-regarding or other-regarding.

But the other does not simply replace the self.[29] The self does not absorb the other, for that would still make the other "part of the self's conative, affective, or cognitive structure"; nor does one lose one's own agency, for that would leave only the other.[30] Rather, the self that is morally "at the disposal of the Other . . . forgoes self-interest claims . . . empties itself of self."[31] The self simply responds to the other's need;[32] the saint strips itself of wealth in order to respond to the need of the destitute.[33] The other for Emmanuel Levinas—who guides Wyschogrod's thought—is "experienced as . . . a drawing nigh, a nearness that is not a merging with the self."[34]

Moreover, the relationship is not a "transcendental structure of the moral life," at least in the sense that "responsibility . . . is an attribute of the subject."[35] Rather, for Levinas, there is a primordial claim made by the other: "Before it knows or acts, egoity is already hostage to the Other."[36] For Wyschogrod, then, responsibility is not an a priori principle but a nonconceptualizable bond before "thematization."[37] Wyschogrod argues that if we encounter the other *only* as interpreted, if we see the other as analogous to ourselves, we grasp the other conceptualized in the categories of similarity and difference we use to understand ourselves and our relation to the world; in this sense, we reduce the other to the same.[38] Further, if an ethic of equality encompasses the other who is like me in crucial respects, then "under duress," that is, in situations where loss to the self is likely to be severe, I will prefer the self that *is* me as opposed to the self (the other) that is *like* me. Thus, "rational" arguments that purport to establish equality might be logically successful but would not always motivate us.[39]

Wyschogrod therefore sets aside reason-based views of a moral bond that gives self and other the same moral status and reduces the other to the categories by which the self sees itself.[40] Wyschogrod also criticizes modern emotion-based views. Against a sympathy-based approach, such as Cates's I assume, she objects both to the linking of the good of the other to the good of the self and to the limited scope of the affections of special relations.[41] The only alternative to both sorts of theories is a nonconceptual bond.[42]

Thus, she argues that the "order of experience precedes the order of reflection": "the prescriptive character of the human face . . . is prior to the *concept* of fairness or justice, and the saint's healing actions are prior to the *concept* of compassion."[43] With Levinas, she says that one is always already related to the "third," to more than one other neighbor. Hence, the demand of the Face has to be rendered in justice and compassion where comparison and concept enter in.[44] The Face demands a saintly altruism on my part that exceeds measure and limit; all my interests are set aside, and the interests of others fill my firmament,[45] but I interpret and relate to the interests of others in and through the categories of justice and compassion.[46]

Wyschogrod's claim that the bond with the other is nonconceptual, and only secondarily expressed in concepts, runs up against the theory that "all experience is interpreted." Even if one says that others are unique and irreplaceable, that judgment is within the ken of the knowing subject. But Wyschogrod wants to affirm the other as "singular," as not capturable in the net of categories at all. In reply, one might argue that saintly exemplars are different because they are differently interpreted and hence that one cannot abstract a nonconceptualizable demand from particular narrative contexts. Even the putative commonality of a deep commitment to the other presupposes a conception of self and other in relation in the world.

Wyschogrod, however, insists on a form of cognition that is deeper than concept and language,[47] a form of "bodily knowing" that is not linguistically formulated, that cannot be captured in the totalizing categories of the self but serves as the functional analogue of a supreme principle.[48] Even if one grants that this sort of experience is possible—not *all* experience is interpreted—the difficulty remains that we might also discover a deep nonlinguistic way of relating to others as enemies rather than as others who demand our devotion. Why *endorse* the one rather than the other?[49]

As for the argument that if we judge the needs of the other by our own lights, if we posit an analogous other, then we elide the alterity of the other, Wyschogrod has to face what Gene Outka calls the "blank check" problem: (1) Are we prepared at any cost to ourselves to act for the other?[50] Wyschogrod says that the self is not required to lose its self-respect or integrity. I think this means that one is not required to do wrong on behalf of the other. Wyschogrod does seem prepared to issue a blank check, however, as regards nonmoral cost to the giver. (2) Is she willing, moreover, to forgo any judgment of our own about the best interests of the sufferer? Is our willingness to set aside our interests limited to cases of "destitution," of "serious" suffering in Martha Nussbaum's vocabulary?[51] Or do we respond to any need or wish of the other no matter how trivial? Even in cases of destitution, do we defer to the destitute to tell us what they need? Cates, in contrast, calls for a mutual adjustment of views between friends; in some cases, one will defer to the friend, but in others, one will have to follow one's own judgment about what is essential to the flourishing of the other.[52]

Moreover, the problem about motivation would seem to apply to Wyschogrod's view as well. Even if the demand of the Face is inherently motivating, that is, even if Wyschogrod is an "internalist" about the relation of obligation and motivation, the question remains whether the demand of the Face in reality overcomes other motives. Wyschogrod does not explain why radical altruism (my prior interests—the interests of a self—are to be replaced by the interests of the other) should prove any more powerful or effective than equality, why it should bridge the gap to actual motivation that "theory" cannot provide. For both equality and substitution, there is still the question of how either form of moral motivation can overcome the contrary pull of other motives.[53]

Finally, there is a moral objection to the model of the saint. Taken as the basic moral demand, the model seems to instrumentalize the self in the service of the other.[54] The self gives no inherent moral weight to its own good independent of the interests of the other that have become its own. An ethic of equal regard in contrast holds that total divestment neglects legitimate attention to the self (by self and other).[55] Wyschogrod, however, combines the notion of a regard for persons as such that (1) is independent of merit or attractiveness, (2) does not make a recognition or return of love a condition,[56] and (3) is unalterable with (4) a notion of self-giving that empties the self and fills it with the other; no interests should remain other than the interests of the other.[57]

Equal Love: Kierkegaard

Søren Kierkegaard can be read as a middle way between Cates and Wyschogrod.[58] Drawing on ancient images in Christian tradition, he constructs a notion of human-to-human love (agape) that is modeled on God's equal love for each creature or child of God. One is to love oneself as one is to love the neighbor.[59] One loves neighbor and self equally *as* they are loved by God; in this sense, God is the "middle term" between self and other. But Kierkegaard also insists, as we will see, that agape is "inward self-denial" and outward "self-sacrifice."[60]

Agape is equal love, then, but it does not necessarily require identical treatment. The Good Samaritan attends to a person as such, a neighbor, who has particular needs, whom we are to recognize in their "distinctiveness." Agape is equal love, but it is not a matter of equal justice, of equal claims. In agape, there is no "mine and thine" in the sense of what we possess or own. When we love, we do not give a gift of what is ours, for what God has given us already belongs to the neighbor. Or better expressed, what God has given us belongs neither to self or neighbor; it is a common provision to be shared.[61] Agape is equal love, but it calls for service to the other even at great cost to ourselves.[62] Moreover, one is not even to *seek* a return of love, for only God can seek a return without seeking "his own";[63] we cannot seek a return of love without making the return a *condition*. But the good of the self is eternally secure, for love itself is already—it will be perfected in the *eschaton*—a participation in God, who is love and the highest good. Thus, love itself brings a return, "like for like."[64]

M. Jamie Ferreira considers some important objections to *Works of Love*: Kierkegaard does not seem to provide for attention to the concrete situation of the neighbor; his notion of love does not require efforts to change unjust social structures; agape replaces eros and philia as forms of self-love.[65] She argues in response that the Good Samaritan, which Kierkegaard cites frequently, attends to the concrete needs of a particular person.[66] Kierkegaard did not intend to say that one should rest content with injustice but that one can and should love the neighbor from any station, even within unjust hierarchies. Moreover, agape is to "permeate" eros and philia, not supplant them. Agape ensures first that one loves others in eros and philia also as children of God and second that one's loves are never entirely preferential but leave some room for the stranger;[67] in these senses, agape removes the "selfishness" in preferential love but allows both chosen and unchosen relations to remain.[68]

In eros and philia, then, one loves others as particular persons—in this sense, in their difference—but also simply as persons—in this sense, in their sameness.[69] Drives and inclinations "remain in force" in the sense that they can be encompassed within an agapistic framework, but they are "dethroned" as the sole determining ground of the will.[70] Agape is to be "present in every other expression of love."[71] Thus, for Kierkegaard, agape "permeates" in the sense that it protects the friend and the beloved as neighbor, as child of God, and that it demands that one not exclude the stranger.[72] Agape provides a new sense of the identification of interests over and beyond the friend or beloved as another self.[73]

But there seems to be a residual tension between equal love and self-sacrifice.[74] If equal love is the norm, if I am to love the self as I love the neighbor, then some measure of temporal good for the self seems appropriate. Equal love arguably sets limits to self-sacrifice. It could call, for example, as Alan Gewirth argues, for sacrifice *below* the level of comparable cost to the giver (e.g., limb for life), but not, however, *at* the level of comparable cost (limb for limb or life for life), much less *beyond* comparable cost (life for limb).[75]

A defender of equal love might say that to give *one* life for *many* other lives does meet the criterion of *below* comparable cost. Another defender, however, would say that to give one life for many is still a sacrifice *at* the level of comparable cost: life for life as a *type* of good. I do not, this defender of equal love would say, have a duty to let my body be fatally used to harvest organs to save five others. The defender of equal love arguably objects in any case to requiring sacrifice *at* comparable cost, because that merely substitutes my loss for yours, and also to requiring sacrifice *beyond* comparable cost, because in making my loss greater than your gain it departs from equality.

My sense is that Kierkegaard is endeavoring to combine the notion of equality before God with commands and exemplars from scripture.[76] The self who imitates the divine exemplar devotes his or her resources, body, or life. The agent gives not only below but at or beyond comparable cost. The self who loves the other as another self in eros and philia may exhibit "unlimited giving," but agape now adds its own demand of sacrifice, both in special relations and in relations with strangers.

I do not think, however, Kierkegaard held the view that one should pay any cost (however great) to meet any need or wish (however small).[77] He presumably assumes a limit on self-giving—great sacrifices only for goods important to flourishing. He might also grant that the agent may seek her own good for her own sake in cases where seeking the good of the self does not stand in the way of seeking the good of others.[78] He also may assume as well an instrumental proviso—preserve oneself (seek one's own good, e.g., health and life) in order to be able to continue to aid neighbors.[79] Kierkegaard's giver would nonetheless *in some cases* give life for the neighbor's life or even their limb. God's equal love seeks the eternal good of all, but Jesus's sacrificial death sets the standard for temporal existence.

Empathy, Compassion, and Normative Identifications

Thus, we have three different conceptions of the identification of interests underlying compassion:[80] for Cates, it is in friendship that the interests of the other become included in my self-love; for Wyschogrod, the nonconceptual demand of the other requires that the interests of the other are substituted for my interests; and for Kierkegaard, equal status before God links love of neighbor and legitimate self-love. I argue in this section (small, tentative steps from now on toward an account) that the transition from empathy to sympathy (compassion) requires a normative identification of interests.[81] Empathy is a necessary but not sufficient condition.[82] In the next section, I discuss how identification is accomplished, and finally, I discuss the relation of equality and self-sacrifice.

Empathy, or better, one type of empathy, is an imaginative grasp of another's suffering.[83] To have such a grasp, one must have experienced suffering but not necessarily the sort of suffering the other endures. We do not imagine only what the other feels, or only what we would feel in the circumstances, but a compound of both.[84] We imagine a drama in which we play the other's role; we imagine how we would feel were we the other.[85] If the other is known to us as a particular person, we project ourselves into the other's identity. If the other is a stranger, we imagine the other's experience as a human being in certain circumstances, for example, as a starving child. The pain we imagine in the other is a pain we would ordinarily dislike in our case and as such desire to alleviate.[86] In empathy, we imagine how the other dislikes and desires to alleviate their pain.[87] Our imagination creates a vicarious sense of the emotional turmoil of the sufferer.[88]

It may be that we can sometimes also experience to some extent, independent of imaginative empathy or in some cases accompanying it, the same sort of pain as the sufferer (another sort of empathy). Our evolved brain structures actually can produce in us a form of the sort of pain we perceive the other to endure.[89] The vibration, as it were, in one person sets off an involuntary vibration in another.[90] Thus, while we do not feel the other's pain in a numerical sense, that is, we do not feel the other's pain itself as if our minds were melded, it may be that on occasion we feel a similar sort of pain in a qualitative sense.[91] Cates says that qualitative sameness is rare but that "something of the same" sort of pain is often shared.[92]

Even if I am empathetic in either sense, however, it does not follow, as Nussbaum observes, that I will have compassion. I could imaginatively dislike and desire to alleviate the pain of the other *as if* I were the other, but I may not actually dislike and desire to alleviate his or her suffering.[93] If I feel something of the same sort of pain in a qualitative sense, I may for the moment not distinguish self and other, but I will do so soon enough and realize that the pain is finally the other's. It is a separate step then from empathy to disliking and desiring to alleviate the suffering of the other.[94] In empathy, we shudder when the hand of the child touches the stove, and in compassion, we dislike and desire to alleviate that pain itself.[95] I have a dislike of the pain and a desire to alleviate it that parallels the child's own.[96]

When I "feel with" you in compassion or sympathy, then, I dislike and desire to alleviate your painful sensation: I make your pain (in light of a normative identification) a parallel object within my own experience (in the same way or *manner* as I do or would my own).[97] Moreover, I desire your good for your own sake, although not necessarily only for your sake: I do not desire your good simply as a means to mine (*mode*). I might desire your good less than, as much as, more than, or instead of my own (*degree*). The objects of compassion may be persons in special relations or persons as such (*scope*).[98] Manner and mode I define as essential features of compassion; degree and scope can vary according to the sort of normative identification in which compassion is embedded.

Compassion, then, is a step beyond empathy.[99] In the patterns of normative identification we have looked at, we find in effect three familiar senses of "as yourself" in the command to love the neighbor as oneself: the neighbor as part of myself, the neighbor instead of myself, and the neighbor as equal to myself.[100] For Cates, the suffering of the other becomes a parallel object of dislike and desire for me because the other is my friend; since the good of the other becomes part of my good, I love the other to an equal degree. For Wyschogrod, the desire is parallel to a desire for my own good in a subjunctive sense: I desire your good as I would desire my own were I to have retained interests independent of yours; I desire your good instead of my own. For Kierkegaard, although my ultimate good is eternally secure, the temporal good of the other is an interest of the self that I am commanded to prefer over self-regarding interests; in this sense (and only in this sense) am I commanded to love the other more than self.

In sum, compassion does not *provide* an identification of interests; it *presupposes* one.[101] Compassion is not a freestanding moral sentiment. It functions within a web of role relationships (friend, saint, child of God). The pattern of normative identification underlies and shapes compassion.

Build On

If we adopted Schopenhauer's distinction between the "phenomenon" and the "explanation," then we could treat the differences among Schopenhauer's metaphysical monism, Cates's friendship, the Face in Wyschogrod, and the theological bridge in Kierkegaard simply as alternative accounts of a compassion that is experienced commonly at the phenomenological level.

But the phenomenon-explanation distinction seems dubious here. We find different identifications and different "genealogies," that is, psychosocial accounts of how an identification is accomplished. For Cates, to extend friendship to persons as such, we build on the matrix of special relations; we develop an expanded relation to God as friend and to strangers as friends or children of God. As I read Cates, one utilizes capacities learned in special relations to construct a different sort of love. We "build on," we do not "build up" or "build out," in the sense that we simply extend the *same* love, or "draw in," in the sense that we bring others into the circle of the *same* concern we have for self or near and dear.[102] In other words, the identification of interests provided by friendship is reconstructed; in this sense, compassion for friends in the paradigm sense is for Cates not the same as compassion for befriended strangers.[103] But the latter arises on the basis of the former.[104]

Kierkegaard also uses the metaphor of children of God but would insist that the affections of special relations are not so much used as they are governed—"permeated"—by a commanded love for creatures as such.[105] This sui generis love grounds a basic bond of equality among persons as such. The basic bond then penetrates special relations. Kierkegaard would thus insist that agape is not constitutively formed out of the materials of special relations but as a function of the God relation and proceeding from a different experiential matrix, the encounter with God, agape permeates from above. No less than Kierkegaard, Wyschogrod would resist any account in which the demand of the Face is built on the desires, emotions, or rational capacities of the empirical self; the demand of the Face constrains aims and attachments.

I believe Cates is correct. A process can occur in which the conceptual and psychological capacities learned in special relations furnish the building blocks of compassion for persons as such (the stranger and the near and dear regarded as persons). We can develop empathetic capacities and the ability to desire the good of others as well as our own in special relations. But we do not simply build out or extend these relations. We undergo a transformative process in which we build on these capacities to construct a new form of love.

Consider, for example, coming to see oneself as child or creature of God. Presumably this experience is both empowering and authorizing. Coming to see oneself—experiencing oneself—as child of God both opens a new door and authorizes one's passage. The new way of seeing oneself both makes the construction of the new love possible and gives reasons for it. Compassion does not just "overflow" from special relations to the stranger. Rather, a special experience or process (whether theologically or nontheologically interpreted) constructs a new love with old materials. On the one hand, then, the transformative process provides the categories one needs to construct the new love: self and other as children or creatures of God, for example. On the other hand, the experience provides authorizing reasons for the construction: one should love as God loves.

If we amend Cates in one respect, however, I think we can incorporate an insight from Kierkegaard. Instead of thinking of compassion for persons or creatures of God as an extended form of friendship, even a friendship that differs, as Cates says, from the paradigm sense, I suggest that the transformative process furnishes us with empowering and authorizing reasons to construct a new love that is an interest of the self but not a form of self-love. While the other is another oneself in philia and eros, the good of the other in compassion for persons or creatures of God is an independent interest. Over and above compassion for those who are friends, who are part of us, and hence part of our self-love, we are empowered and authorized to have compassion for those who are not part of us. We have learned empathy and love of others as well as ourselves in special relations. These capacities of self-transcendence, as it were, are used in an empowering and authorizing process that constructs a new interest of the self.[106] Kierkegaard is right then to suggest that the good of persons as such is a new and distinct interest of the self. Where he goes seriously wrong is not seeing, as Cates so clearly does, that the new love builds on the materials of special relations.

Equality and Sacrifice

A distinctive form of love for persons for their own sakes is reflected in both Kierkegaard and Wyschogrod: it is *unqualified* in the sense that it does not depend on attraction or merit;[107] *unconditional*, requiring neither recognition or return of love; *unalterable*, that is, "everlasting"; and *unlimited*, that is, there are no nonmoral limits on costs to the one who loves (except perhaps a restriction to serious needs, i.e., "destitution"; an instrumental proviso; and an exception for cases where the good of the self does not compete with the good of the other).

We are familiar with a similar ideal as it appears in some images of parental love. A parent does not love offspring because of attraction or merit; a parent desires but does not make mutuality a condition; his or her love is unbreakable; a parent seeks his or her own good, when it competes with the good of others, only in order to serve (the instrumental proviso for life and health), and is prepared to give in other cases not only below comparable cost but at or beyond. In some versions, the self-giving of the parent is not limited to cases of destitution but extends to what some would call "trivial" wants or needs. In some variants, moreover, the instrumental proviso may even be set aside, and the parent gives life for life or life for limb.[108] In any case, the ideal parent can seek her own good for her own sake only if it does not interfere with seeking the good of others.[109]

The notion of giving at great cost also appears in friendships or similar relationships that are arguably not unqualified, unconditional, or unalterable—for instance, in the classic sacrifice of the soldier who falls on a grenade to save the lives of comrades.[110] One way to read this case is that self-sacrifice can be rendered to friends as a love based on qualities, which depends on recognition and return and is alterable. Jesus's sacrifice in one source is for *friends*: "Greater love has no one than this, that a man lay down his life for his friends" (John 15:13).[111]

In any case, the ideal of love as not only unqualified, unconditional, and unalterable, but unlimited is sometimes transmuted by the religious imagination into a notion of divine love and love of neighbor. One can acknowledge this process without saying that the religious imagination is the source of illusory projections.[112] Moreover, even if we explain the evolution of the love of parents and friends as forms of "kin" and "group" altruism, as forms of behavior selected for because they promote survival and reproduction, we can recognize how the religious imagination has used these forms of love in special relations as images of divine love for persons as such. Patterns that have their origin in special relations are changed (perhaps modified) by the religious imagination into a normative paradigm of divine and human love.[113] Once imagined, the divine love for each creature or child of God provides the categories and authorizing reasons, as I argued earlier, that transform capacities learned in special relations into a love of neighbor that extends to the stranger as well as the near and dear.

Where unqualified, unconditional, unalterable, and unlimited love is imagined as divine, however, it can be read in two ways as a pattern for human relationships. Often conceived in Christian traditions as the divine parent's equal love, this love includes self as well as other. Thus, Kierkegaard says loving oneself as one is loved by God is legitimate self-love. The relation to God establishes a common moral status for the siblings as persons. Their equal status is taken as the basis for their duties to one another. In a sense, Wyschogrod would not disagree. Her functional substitute for the inclusive divine love is simply the bedrock moral fact that just as neighbors are a Face to me, I am a Face also to neighbors. In this sense, the self *is* included. Even if there are de facto reasons not to insist in interhuman relations that I am also a Face, the basic de jure equality remains: each is equally a Face to others.[114]

But if one takes the divine action itself as the norm for the siblings in their relationships, the giver's love is to be not only unqualified, unconditional, and unalterable, but unlimited. And this is indeed what Kierkegaard says: agape is inward self-denial and outward self-sacrifice.[115] Temporal self-regard is suspended in the name of other regard. Legitimate self-love is displaced into hope for eternal good. Just as the parent's love is self-giving, so is the sibling's in relation to other siblings. Thus, the divine love includes the self, but the human-to-human imitation of that divine love requires unlimited devotion. Self-giving is primary; equality becomes a secondary norm of distribution between recipients.

The self then is included in the ultimate love, but the self in the earthly sphere is prepared to set aside its self-regarding good. With eternal good secure, siblings are to imitate the parental love; they are to disregard their own temporal good (assuming the restriction to serious needs, an overridable instrumental proviso, and exceptions where self-love does not compete) in favor of the other siblings. For Kierkegaard, the disregard of the good of the self—the prioritizing of imitation over equal status—is apparently based on scriptural teachings. For Wyschogrod, the disregard seems to rest on the psychological claim that the inclusion of the self—its equal claim as a Face—would detract from attention to the neighbor.

What should we say about this ideal of unlimited love from special relations and its transmutation into divine love and love of neighbor?

First, there is an unanswered question—an aporia—in the ideal, at least as I have described it so far. The parent, for example, is to subordinate his or her good. He or she gives not only below but at or beyond comparable cost, even to the point *in some cases* of setting aside the instrumental proviso (which is overridable) and giving life for life or life for limb. If the parent is prepared to set aside the instrumental proviso, when? What are the *cases* in which the parent sacrifices life or even health? The parent may well sacrifice his or her own violin lessons for a child's (comparable cost) or even his or her boat for a child's summer camp (beyond comparable cost). But if the parent, overriding the instrumental proviso, gives life for life or life for limb, then he or she can no longer continue to be a giver.

In what circumstances should the unlimited lover, then, override the instrumental proviso? Even if the parent's sacrifice is not just for one child but for all, the problem remains: the parent is no longer in a position to give. The problem also remains if we extend unlimited love to all children of God: if I give my life, then I can no longer be a giver. So the question is, when should I give life: whenever my child or a stranger needs it, or only in *some* of these cases?

Second, would we want to endorse the notion of unlimited love even in special relations? Perhaps the parent should put limits on sacrifice: his or her violin lessons instead of the child's or his or her boat instead of camp for the child. One argument against unlimited love as a parent is that when parents set aside their interests, they are likely to repress resentment and children are likely to be burdened with unnecessary guilt. The earthly task instead is to relate love of the near and dear, love of the stranger, and love of self.[116]

My inclination, however, is to argue for unlimited love as a feature of some special relations. The soldier is prepared to give at or beyond, even life. Even if some cases are "beyond the call of duty," that is, supererogatory, in others one is required to make the "supreme sacrifice." Moreover, the John 15 tradition suggests that "friends" are sometimes prepared to give life, whether as requirement or supererogation. Even if we think of the parent's giving as supererogatory in some cases, it seems to belong to the experience of parenting for many.

Third, even if we retain the model of unlimited love for parents or friends or soldiers, should we transpose it into our notion of what we owe any neighbor? Another alternative is to let equal status define love of neighbor and self. Unlimited love should be relegated at least as requirement to one or more special relations. It is one thing to give at or beyond for a child, especially if the instrumental proviso is removed, but another for a stranger. But even if our standard for love of the stranger is below comparable cost, it can still be very demanding: arguably no luxuries for me or my child until all have necessities.[117]

It may be—a historical thesis I am not competent to support—that in some strands and strata of Christian traditions, the ideal of the Parent or Friend who shows unlimited love and the notion of Jesus's death as substitutionary atonement coalesce to shape a notion of neighbor love: as Jesus dies for all, so we should live for others. But perhaps we should disentangle what was necessary (if we think it was necessary) for the salvation of humankind from the love of each child of God for the other.[118] If so, then we could maintain below comparable cost as the standard for neighbor love while relegating at or beyond (at least as requirement) to certain special relations.[119] Love of neighbor, even if it should be unqualified, unconditional, and unalterable, should be limited in cost, even to alleviate serious suffering, not only by the duties of special relations but by legitimate self-love. Sacrificial love in the sense of a love that gives at or beyond comparable cost may be required in some special relationships, or even there remain in some cases a matter of supererogation, but it should not become a requirement of neighbor love. Here too, however, the ideal can remain as supererogation.[120]

How would one choose between these two views of neighbor love, one that takes the divine love itself as a model and the other that takes the equal status established by God as basic?[121] My unsurprising suggestion is that an answer will reflect fundamental theological commitments. In the end, the difference may lie in how a theological ethic understands the human-to-human vocation, the task given by God to earthly pilgrims.

Conclusion

My purpose has been to show that compassion presupposes not only empathy but also a meta-bond that identifies interests. I have argued that love of neighbor builds on capacities learned in special relations. I have also discussed two ways of understanding the role of unlimited love.

When an ideal of love is imaged as divine, or even when, as for Wyschogrod, it simply becomes the demand of the human, it is often taken as the basic principle or virtue. Thus Wyschogrod, for example, takes the demand of the Face as the moral demand simpliciter; justice has a subordinate role as what this demand does with the "third" (who is always present). For Kierkegaard, justice has a role in those "outward" relations that remain in place.[122] In this sense, as for Wyschogrod, justice is what the one who loves does in the world when dealing with more than one neighbor. My sense, however, is that justice is more than a derivative tool, application, or approximation of love as self-sacrifice.[123] I stay, therefore, with a "horizontal" model of justice and love (respect and compassion) as twin virtues.[124]

I would also try, however, to reformulate a "vertical" model. Instead of thinking of a utopia where there is no justice-based sense of claims and shares, but rather a relation of mutual love that unites its members,[125] I suggest that we think of a utopia where there is no role for either justice or compassion as we know them.[126] If justice specifies "mine and thine" in the sense of due claims or rights, compassion on the account I have given here presupposes not only me and you, as Kierkegaard says, but my good and yours. The distinction of goods is presupposed in the very process of uniting them in a bond of compassion. Would a utopia not only transcend justice but the need to make the neighbor's interests our own through an affective bond? Would not all be in God and God be all to all?

Notes

In addition to acknowledgments in the text, I would like to thank Vaughn Allen, Matthew Bagger, Diana Fritz Cates, Andrew Flescher, Maria Heim, Curtis Hutt, Jianshe Kong, Paul Lauritzen, Charles Lockwood, Jung Lee, Thomas Lewis, David Little, Alissa Macmillan, Richard Miller, Gene Outka, Melissa Proctor, Bharat Ranganathan, Terrence Reynolds, Donald Swearer, James Swan Tuite, Rachel White, and David Wills for their help over the years, as well as my Brown colleagues Wendell Dietrich and Sumner Twiss. The late Giles Milhaven influenced me more than he knew.

1. Arthur Schopenhauer, *On the Basis of Morality*, trans. E. F. J. Payne (1841; Indianapolis: Bobbs-Merrill Educational Publishing, 1981), 143.

2. Schopenhauer says, "In exactly the same way," but "not always in the same degree" (ibid., 144); sometimes, "I more or less subordinate . . . my own weal and woe" (ibid., 143). Cf. Bishop Butler: "The same kind of pleasure in their prosperity, and sorrow in their distress, as we have from reflection on our own" ("On Compassion," Sermon V in *Butler's Fifteen Sermons*, ed. T. A. Roberts [London: SPCK, 1970]). See M. Jamie Ferreira, *Love's Grateful Striving: A Commentary on Kierkegaard's* Works of Love (New York: Oxford Univer-

sity Press 2001), 197; and Sarah Moses, "'Keeping the Heart': Natural Affection in Joseph Butler's Approach to Virtue," *Journal of Religious Ethics* 37, no. 4 (December 2009): 615.

3. Schopenhauer, *On the Basis of Morality*, 143–44.

4. Ibid., 207. Taking up Kant's distinction between things in themselves and "phenomenal appearance," Schopenhauer argues, "But if *time* and *space* are foreign to the thing-in-itself, to the true essence of the world, so too must *plurality* be" (207). One could reply, however, that both plurality and oneness are categories of thought; hence, one cannot predicate oneness of things in themselves any more than one can predicate plurality. See George Simmel, *Schopenhauer and Nietzsche*, trans. Helmut Loiskandl, Deena Weinstein, and Michael Weinstein (1907; Urbana: University of Illinois Press, 1991), 37–39; Bernard Reginster, *The Affirmation of Life: Nietzsche on Overcoming Nihilism* (Cambridge, MA: Harvard University Press, 2006), 291n2; Brian Leiter, *Nietzsche on Morality* (London: Routledge, 2002), 55–57, 84.

5. Concern for the other's overall good as Nietzsche taught may require that some suffering not be eliminated (Reginster, *Affirmation of Life*). Cates can grant that compassion need not aim at the wholesale rejection of all forms of suffering.

6. Martha C. Nussbaum, *Upheavals of Thought: The Intelligence of Emotions* (Cambridge: Cambridge University Press, 2001), 319. I assume that one can have self-regarding and other-regarding interests in the same object, person, or state of affairs; for example, one can seek the good of another person both for their sake and one's own sake. I can even desire to be the one who is of service to you (Robert Merrihew Adams, *A Theory of Virtue: Excellence in Being for the Good* [Oxford: Clarendon Press, 2006], 79); see also M. Jamie Ferreira, "The Problematic Agapeistic Ideal—Again," in *Ethics, Love, and Faith in Kierkegaard*, ed. Edward F. Mooney (Bloomington: Indiana University Press, 2008), 100–101, 258n41). To have dual motives, however, is not the same as loving the other only as a means to one's self-interest. See Andrew Michael Flescher and Daniel L. Worthen, *The Altruistic Species: Scientific, Philosophical, and Religious Perspectives of Human Benevolence* ([Philadelphia: Templeton Foundation Press, 2007], 52–53, 147, 238), who argue that the good of the other is the altruist's "ultimate aim." Altruism can be defined simply as desiring and acting to benefit another. Some definitions add for the other's sake, expense to the giver, and lack of self-regard. See Flescher and Worthen, *Altruistic Species*, chap.1; Stephen G. Post, Lynn G. Underwood, Jeffrey P. Schloss, and William B. Hurlbut, eds., *Altruism and Altruistic Love: Science, Philosophy, and Religion in Dialogue* (New York: Oxford University Press, 2002), 3, 8, 10; and Stephen Pope, *Human Evolution and Christian Ethics* (Cambridge: Cambridge University Press, 2007), chap. 9.

7. As with Nel Noddings, *Caring: A Feminine Approach to Ethics and Moral Education* (Berkeley: University of California Press, 1984), for Cates there is first "engrossment" or reception of the other and then a "motivational displacement" (in my terminology, empathy and compassion, respectively).

8. I use "self-regard" (self-interest, self-love) and "other regard" (interest in others for their own sake, love of others) sometimes to refer to particular desires ("particular passions" in Butler's terminology) for a good of self or other, e.g., my health or your health. I also use self-regard and other regard to refer to generalized desires for the good of the self overall ("self-love," in Butler's terminology) or for the good overall of the other ("benevolence," in one interpretation of Butler, "On Compassion"; see Adams, *Theory of Virtue*, 95, 96n2, 99n9, 100–101, 258n41).

9. Diana Fritz Cates, *Choosing to Feel: Virtue, Friendship, and Compassion for Friends* (Notre Dame, IN: University of Notre Dame Press, 1997), 64.

10. Ibid., 52. See Frederick A. Olafson, *Heidegger and the Ground of Ethics: A Study of Mitsein* (Cambridge: Cambridge University Press, 1998), 70 and 85, on the well-being of others as part of, or as a necessary condition of, our own; and Nicholas Wolterstorff, *Justice in Love* (Grand Rapids, MI: Eerdmans, 2011), 4–5, 111–12, on eudaimonism (seeking the good of the other for their own sake and as a component of one's own good).

11. Alan Soble, "Union, Autonomy, and Concern," in *Love Analyzed*, ed. Roger E. Lamb (Boulder: Westview Press, 1997), 66, 68, 78, 91–92 passim, argues that a "robust" benevolence ("x desires for y that which is good for y, x desires this for y's own sake, and x pursues y's good for y's benefit and not for x's") is not possible in "union" views of love in which the lovers, their interests, and their good are fused or merged. But Cates's notion of union does not amount to a fusion that would eliminate distinct selves.

12. I use the notion of stranger to mean someone not in a special relation with you, someone who is for you only a person as such. Friends are also persons as such, a point of great importance in Kierkegaard's account as we will see. Cates uses friendship in a broad sense to include family.

13. Cates, *Choosing to Feel*, 204, 217, 231.

14. Ibid., 221–24, 227.

15. Ibid., 232–33. We are also commanded to love: "*You shall* be disposed to regard and treat every person in pain, *in* her particularity, *as* 'another yourself'" (ibid., 235; see 275n76 on Kierkegaard).

16. Ibid., 230–31, 234–35.

17. Ibid., 233–35.

18. Soble ("Union, Autonomy and Concern," 78n24) comments that even though Aquinas says that in friendship the other is "another self," "one wants good things for him as one does for oneself" and the "beloved remains separate" (78n24). Cates says that self and other are distinct persons, but she wants to include in friendship what Soble takes Aquinas to contrast with it, namely, a desire for something "contributing in some way to one's own wellbeing" (Soble, "Union, Autonomy, and Concern," 78n24; Aquinas, *ST* la2ae.28.1). See also Adams, *Theory of Virtue*, 78.

19. Cates, *Choosing to Feel*, 221–23. One can have a legitimate interest in particular in being a certain sort of self (83); moral virtue is part of flourishing. See Neera Kapur Badhwar, "Altruism versus Self-Interest: Sometimes a False Dichotomy," in *Altruism*, ed. Ellen Frankel Paul, Fred D. Miller Jr., and Jeffrey Paul (Cambridge: Cambridge University Press, 1993), 92–93, 92–93n8, on self-interest in a "kind of moral excellence" as a moral motivation. One acts for the sake of the other but also to express one's moral identity (112–13). See also Arthur J. Dyck and Carlos Padilla, "The Empathetic Emotions and Self-Love in Bishop Joseph Butler and the Neurosciences," *Journal of Religious Ethics* 37, no. 4 (December 2009): 581–82, 588–96, 608–10, on love of others contributing to self-love; and Flescher and Worthen, *Altruistic Species*, 240–44, 255–57, on altruism having good effects on the giver.

20. Cates, *Choosing to Feel*, 58–59.

21. Shared goods, e.g., a piece of candy, are still individually possessed or consumed. But the relationship, which is part of the good of each, is an indivisible good.

22. Cates, *Choosing to Feel*, 82–83, 191–95.

23. Care for the stranger has limits for several other reasons: maintaining ourselves as givers, scarce resources, and the need to monitor for effectiveness (127–29, 202–7, 233, 260n50).

24. Julia E. Judish, "Balancing Special Obligations and the Ideal of Agape," *Journal Religious Ethics* 26, no. 1 (Spring 1998): 17–46, argues that as long as some lack necessities, impartial love would require that we forgo special relations entirely. Given that we do, however, have moral commitments to special relations, Judish also argues that there is no meta-rule to use in resolving the conflict.

25. Edith Wyschogrod, *Saints and Postmodernism: The Revisioning of Moral Philosophy* (Chicago: University of Chicago Press, 1990), xiv.

26. Ibid., xiv, xxiv, 33.

27. Ibid., xxii.

28. Ibid., xxiii.

29. Ibid., 33–34.

30. Ibid., 33–34. M. Jamie Ferreira, "'Total Altruism' in Levinas's 'Ethics of the Welcome,'" *Journal of Religious Ethics* 29, no. 3 (2001): 433–70, argues that Levinas does not elide "ethical agency"; to be "host" as well as "hostage," one must be a self. Even if responsibility is constitutive of selfhood, precisely as responsible I am an agent (452–55, 468). See also John J. Davenport, "Levinas's Agapistic Metaphysic of Morals: Absolute Passivity and the Other as Eschatological Hierophany," *Journal of Religious Ethics* 26, no. 2 (Fall 1998): 349–52; Sylvia Walsh, "Kierkegaard's Philosophy of Love," in *The Nature and Pursuit of Love: The Philosophy of Irving Singer*, ed. David Goicoechea (Amherst, NY: Prometheus, 1995), 179n13; and Merold Westphal, *Levinas and Kierkegaard in Dialogue* (Bloomington: Indiana University Press, 2008), chaps. 5 and 6.

31. Wyschogrod, *Saints and Postmodernism*, 33.

32. Ibid., 84–85.

33. Ibid., 96–99.

34. Ibid., 148.

35. Ibid., 149–50.

36. Ibid., 154.

37. Ibid., 49–52, 160–61.

38. Ibid., 70–71; see Margaret Farley, "How Shall We Love in a Postmodern World?," *Annual of the Society of Christian Ethics* 14 (1994): 17–18.

39. Wyschogrod, Flescher points out, seems to object both to the positing of an analogous other and to the inadequate motivational force of an ethic of equality (Andrew Flescher, *Heroes, Saints, and Ordinary Morality* [Washington, DC: Georgetown University Press, 2003], 202, 229n111). If we take the other as like the self, we try to know according to our own lights what the other needs (230n12). And if we normatively regard the other just as we regard the self, then in conflict situations we will tend to prefer the self. Flescher says that we can know basic needs before encounters, but he is inclined to accept Wyschogrod's point about motivation (203–4, 230n112, 114). I am also indebted to Danielle Novetsky for my interpretation of Wyschogrod.

40. Wyschogrod, *Saints and Postmodernism*, 160. Davies argues that consciousness, mediated by language, is intersubjective, a self-other relation ab initio (Oliver Davies, *A Theology of Compassion: Metaphysics of Difference and the Renewal of Tradition* [London: SCM Press, 2001], 37–40). The self can "affirm" or "occlude" the other, but the former reflects the nature of consciousness, whereas the latter denies it. (See also Olafson, *Heidegger and the Ground of Ethics*). Moreover, affirmation of the other in its richest form is "self-emptying and self-giving" (32–33, 35–38). In compassion, one will risk one's life, not in every act, but when there is sufficient risk to the other (42, 44). I differ at two points. First, I think that consciousness is intersubjective but that it does not determine the psychological or normative relation of self-regard and other regard. Second, I do not think that compassion reaches its fullest realization in self-sacrifice. Compassion as such does not determine the normative question of the cost of aiding others. See "Equality and Sacrifice."

41. Wyschogrod, *Saints and Postmodernism*, 242; Flescher, *Heroes, Saints, and Ordinary Morality*, 204–5. Wyschogrod argues that sociobiology reduces the body to an object in contrast to the "lived" sentient body that makes a moral claim before interpretation ("Pythagorean Bodies and the Body of Altruism," in Post et al., *Altruism and Altruistic Love*, 29–39). Empathy and sympathy make the other into another "me" according to "the measure of one's own consciousness" (29–30, 35–36).

42. See Merold Westphal, "The Empty Suitcase as Metaphor," in *Saintly Influence: Edith Wyschogrod and the Possibilities of Philosophy of Religion*, ed. Eric Boyton and Martin Kavka (New York: Fordham University Press, 2009), 51, 59. The demand of the other is latent, not immediately given (Wyschogrod, *Saints and Postmodernism*, 149–50; Flescher, *Heroes, Saints, and Ordinary Morality*, 208, 210–211). We have a predisposition to saintly altruism that can be elicited and developed by saintly practices and narratives. See Westphal, "Empty Suitcase as Metaphor," 51–52; and Boyton and Kavka, *Saintly Influence*, 7–8.

43. Wyschogrod, *Saints and Postmodernism*, 160 (second italics mine).

44. John J. Davenport, "Levinas's Agapistic Metaphysic of Morals: Absolute Passivity and the Other as Eschatological Hierophany," *Journal of Religious Ethics* 26, no. 2 (Fall 1998): 344–45.

45. See Westphal, *Levinas and Kierkegaard in Dialogue*, 5–6, 38–39, 83–84, on Levinas: "The *conatus essendi* of our egoistic self-assertion must be inverted or converted."

46. Levinas, as Ferreira ("'Total Altruism' in Levinas's," 455, 464–66) notes, sees the relation of total self-giving take shape not only in compassion but in justice. Evidently, Levinas thinks that justice includes the self, but this seems incompatible with the idea that the prior interests of the self have already been put aside. The inclusion of the self in justice would not in any case follow from the presence of the third. Justice can be conceived as how the self deals with more than one neighbor without including the self in its scope (Paul Ramsey, *Basic Christian Ethics* [1950; Chicago: University of Chicago Press, 1978]). Justice is "what Christian love does when confronted with two or more neighbors" (243). Quoted in Gene Outka, "Universal Love and Impartiality," in *The Love Commandments: Essays in Christian Ethics and Moral Philosophy*, ed. Edmund Santurri and William Werpehowski (Washington, DC: Georgetown University Press, 1992), 19–20, 25–30.

47. Wyschogrod says that just as the James-Lange theory of emotions holds that bodily reactions are interpreted after the fact, so the claim of the other is prior to interpretation ("Pythagorean Bodies and the Body of Altruism," 37). Nussbaum rejects James-Lange and holds that emotions are cognitive judgments, but she does not insist on cultural-linguistic interpretation; the emotions of dogs, for example, are cognitive albeit not linguistic (*Upheavals of Thought*). See also Paul Lauritzen, *Religious Belief and Emotional Transformation: A Light in the Heart* (Lewisburg, PA: Bucknell University Press, 1992).

48. See Westphal, *Levinas and Kierkegaard in Dialogue*, 14, 17ff., 23–24, 36–37,154–55n18. The call of the other cannot be a function of an "onto-theology" with which the self connects thought and world; it is an irruption from "beyond being."

49. Christine M. Korsgaard et al., *The Sources of Normativity*, ed. Onora O'Neill (Cambridge: Cambridge University Press, 1996).

50. Gene Outka, *Agape: An Ethical Analysis* (New Haven, CT: Yale University Press, 1972); and Outka, "Universal Love and Impartiality," 1–103.

51. Nussbaum, *Upheavals of Thought*.

52. Cates, *Choosing to Feel*, 161–62. See Garth L. Hallett, *Christian Neighbor-Love: Six Rival Versions* (Washington, DC: Georgetown University Press, 1989), 42.

53. Ferreira argues that Levinas recognizes that the motivational force of the demand does not necessarily win out over conflicting desires ("The Misfortune of the Happy: Levinas and the Ethical Dimensions of Desire," *Journal of Religious Ethics* 34, no. 3 [2006]: 461–69). Levinas postulates, however, a desire that is not eros or concupiscence based on need but an insatiable appetite for the infinite as other, as "inexhaustible exteriority"; we can seek the infinite other, however, only in the finite (473–74). In this sense, the ethical relation itself is a good, an excellence, which motivates us (474). This good of ethical relation can be an "incentive" without making a return a condition (474–78). Moreover, the relation is a type of ethical motive or incentive that is generically different from all other incentives (478–79, 481–82). But even if generically different, why would the desire for the infinite trump self-interested motives?

54. Jung Lee, "Neither Totality nor Infinity: Suffering the Other," *Journal of Religion* 79, no. 2 (1999): 250–79. While Levinas famously sees a trace of God in the Face (the demand) of the other, others would make the religious objection that total devotion—loving the other ultimately more than self—is reserved for God alone. See Outka, "Universal Love and Impartiality," and Ferreira, *Love's Grateful Striving*, 205, 231nn130, 131, 132.

55. Outka, *Agape*; and Outka, "Universal Love and Impartiality."

56. John Milbank characterizes Wyschogrod's radical altruism as having "no expectation" of return ("The Ethics of Self-Sacrifice," *First Things* 91[March 1999]: 33–38). He wants an ethic of "complex reciprocity." Only when we interact with interpreted others can they be "genuinely other." See Wyschogrod's reply: "Pythagorean Bodies and the Body of Altruism," 31, 34, 37–38.

57. Post says that Wyschogrod might take natural self-love and family ties for granted, but she seems to empty the self of any interests (*Altruism and Altruistic Love*, 174–75, 178).

58. Søren Kierkegaard, *Works of Love*, ed. and trans. Howard V. Hong and Edna H. Hong (Princeton, NJ: Princeton University Press, 1995).

59. Paul Ricoeur, *Fallible Man*, trans. Charles A. Kelbley (New York: Fordham University Press, 1986), 124, argues that my regard for my own worth is a regard for humanity in my neighbor and myself: "I love myself as if what I loved were another."

60. Let me acknowledge my debt to M. Jamie Ferreira (*Love's Grateful Striving* and "Problematic Agapeistic Ideal") and Gene Outka (*Agape*; "Equality and Individuality: Thoughts on Two Themes in Kierkegaard," *Journal of Religious Ethics* 10, no. 2 [Fall 1982]: 171–203; and "Universal Love and Impartiality") for this interpretation of Kierkegaard in *Works of Love*, without suggesting that either would endorse it. I do not attempt to relate *Works of Love* to other works of Kierkegaard or to place him in historical context. Even if my reading of *Works of Love* is faulty, I hope the argument is useful.

61. We do not *repay* God by loving the neighbor, but love of neighbor itself generates a sense of infinite indebtedness to the other. I think Kierkegaard uses debt here only in a metaphorical sense, for otherwise agape would become justice.

62. See Outka (*Agape*; "Universal Love and Impartiality," 2–44, 94n28), who makes sacrifice in some situations a tactical expression of agape but rejects the thesis that agape in principle sets aside self-love. The return of love, moreover, can be desired and hoped for without being a condition; mutuality is the internal telos of agape. Thus, one acts for the sake of the other in the sense that one does not benefit the other *only* to benefit the self, but it is not necessary to desire *only* the good of the other. See also Christine Gudorf, "Parenting, Mutual Love, and Sacrifice," in *Women's Consciousness, Women's Conscience: A Reader in Feminist Ethics*, ed. B. Andolsen, C. Gudorf, and M. Pellauer (New York: Harper & Row, 1985), 186, 190–91. Timothy Jackson affirms agape as equal regard that includes the self (*The Priority of Love: Christian Charity and Social Justice* [Princeton, NJ: Princeton University Press, 2003], 3n7, 55–56, 138n6, 143–44) but insists that Jesus's sacrificial death is the final norm; believers should love according to the standard of "as you have been loved," not "as yourself" (23n64, 55, 143–44).

63. As Ferreira renders this argument, only if we were beings like God, a "being who is love," could we "directly seek love without seeking our own" (*Love's Grateful Striving*, 152; Kierkegaard, *Works of Love*, 265, 268).

64. But in effect does not one make one's relation to the highest good a condition? One way to reply to this objection is to sharply distinguish trust from motivation; one trusts one's good is secure, but one does not love the neighbor for the sake of one's own good. But Kierkegaard could have made a stronger reply: I affirm proper self-love; hence, so long as one does not make recognition and return a condition, one can love the neighbor for their own sake, and for one's own, that is, for the sake of one's participation in the highest good.

65. Ferreira, *Love's Grateful Striving*. "Just as self-love selfishly embraces this one and only *self* that makes it self-love, so also erotic love's passionate preference selfishly encircles this one and only beloved, and friendship's passionate preference selfishly encircles this one and only friend. For this reason the beloved and the friend are called, remarkably and profoundly, to be sure, the *other self*, the *other I*—since the neighbor is the *other you*. . . . That it is self-love when an unfaithful person wants to jilt the beloved . . . this paganism saw. . . . But that the devotion with which the lover gives himself to this one . . . is self-love—this only Christianity sees. But how can *devotion and unlimited giving of oneself* be self-love? Indeed, when it is devotion to the *other I*, the *other self*" (Kierkegaard, *Works of Love*, 53–54, 55). See Amy Laura Hall, *Love's Treachery* (Cambridge: Cambridge University Press, 2002), 28, 43–45, 81. Cf. Cates, *Choosing to Feel*.

66. Kierkegaard recognizes that sometimes one will not be able to help, but one's commitment to the neighbor remains as "mercifulness," which is a work of love (*Works of Love*, 315ff.). See Ferreira, "Mutual Responsiveness in Relation: The Challenge of the Ninth Deliberation," in *International Kierkegaard Commentary: Works of Love*, ed. Robert L. Perkins (Macon, GA: Mercer University Press, 1999), 193–209; and Louise Carroll Keeley, "Loving 'No One,' Loving Everyone: The Work of Love in Recollecting One Dead in Kierkegaard's *Works of Love*," in Perkins, *International Kierkegaard Commentary*, 211–48, on remembrance of the dead as a work of love.

67. See also Gilbert C. Meilaender, *Friendship: A Study in Theological Ethics* (Notre Dame, IN: University of Notre Dame Press, 1981), 7, 27–28, 35, 41–47, 53, 62–64, 84; and C. Stephen Evans, *Kierkegaard's Ethic of Love: Divine Commands and Moral Obligations* (New York: Oxford University Press, 2004), 108–9, 112, 150, 187, and chap. 9, who, like Ferreira (*Love's Grateful Striving* and "Problematic Agapeistic Ideal"), argue for a "permeate" interpretation. Other authors argue for a "negate but fulfill" interpretation: Green and Ellis say that agape "achieves the unconditional acceptance of the other to which marriage aspires, but which its basis in preference sometimes threatens" ("Erotic Love in the Religious Existence-Sphere," in Perkins, *International Kierkegaard Commentary*, 358); "by resolving to love the beloved for this shared humanness more than for all the features that elicit passion, Christian love therefore fulfils what erotic love promises" (359). Alastair Hannay says that agape puts philia and eros into a "new perspective" in which we progress from self-regard to other regard ("Kierkegaard on Natural and Commanded Love," in Mooney, *Ethics, Love, and Faith*, 118). Sylvia Walsh argues that agape is a "new form of immediacy" that integrates duty, passion, and inclination ("Forming the Heart: The Role of Love in Kierkegaard's Thought," in *The Grammar of the Heart*, ed. Richard H. Bell [New York: Harper & Row, 1988], 244–46); "while we certainly love persons in our special relations differently from the way we love others, this difference is not essential, since we love them fundamentally as we love others, that is, as a neighbor" (241; Walsh, "Kierkegaard's Philosophy of Love," 170–73; Sylvia Walsh, "On 'Feminine' and 'Masculine' Forms of Despair," in *Feminist Interpretations of Soren Kierkegaard*, ed. Céline Léon and Sylvia Walsh [University Park: Penn State University Press, 1997], 214n4; Sylvia Walsh, *Living Christianly: Kierkegaard's Dialectic of Christian Existence* [University Park: Penn State University Press, 2005], 97–100). Wolterstorff also says that for Kierkegaard "preferential forms of love . . . are to be so formed and shaped that they become manifestations of one's agapic love" (*Justice in Love*, 25–37, 39–40, 92, 94, 111–16). See also C. S. Lewis, *The Four Loves* (1960; New York: Harcourt, 1988), 133. If all loves become manifestations of the equal love of agape, however, then it is hard to see how one could love one's child more than others; but if agape "permeates" or "is present in," then one can combine agape and partiality. For a constructive "permeate" account, see William Werpehowski, "'Agape' and Special Relations," in Santurri and Werpehowski, *Love Commandments*, 146–52.

68. Sharon Krishek argues that there is a strong case for taking Kierkegaard to hold, or at least to say sometimes, that there are two incompatible loves: in preferential love, one loves one person more than others, while agape loves all equally ("Two Forms of Love: The Problem of Preferential Love in Kierkegaard's *Works of Love*," *Journal of Religious Ethics* 36, no. 4 [December 2008]: 602–6; see also Judish, "Balancing Special Obligations," 17–46). The two selves become one self (the friend as another self), and thus, this love reduces to self-love, while in agape God is the middle term that relates self and other. Krishek ("Two Forms

of Love," 60) notes the place where Kierkegaard (*Works of Love*, 55) says that even if one removed any other selfishness in preferential love, it would still be a form of self-willfulness and hence incompatible with self-denial (see also Amy Laura Hall, *Love's Treachery* [Cambridge: Cambridge University Press, 2002]). Thus, Krishek proposes to amend Kierkegaard: there is one love that paradoxically both affirms the neighbor as such and can also be preferential ("Two Forms of Love," 611–16). Krishek, however, comes close to Ferreira's interpretation: even if preferential love is a different sort of love, not just a "manifestation of *agape*," it "should not conflict with *agape*'s recognition of intrinsic value" (609–10).

69. Ferreira, "Problematic Agapeistic Ideal," 101; Kierkegaard, *Works of Love*, 62.

70. Hannay, "Kierkegaard on Natural and Commanded Love," 104.

71. Ferreira, "Problematic Agapeist Ideal," 108; Kierkegaard, *Works of Love*, 143, 146.

72. See Outka, *Agape*, 273–74; "Universal Love and Impartiality," 90, on agape that "sets boundaries" around special relations: never mistreat outsiders for the sake of the near and dear, and never fall below for the near and dear what is prohibited or required as regards any neighbor. See Meilaender on "build down," "build up," and "build around" (*Friendship*, 22, 31; and "Friendship," in *The Westminster Dictionary of Christian Ethics*, ed. James Childress and John McQuarrie [Philadelphia: Westminster Press, 1986], 241). See also Judish, "Balancing Special Obligations," 18–23, on Outka.

73. Kierkegaard does not seem to deal in *Works of Love* with the question of whether one's agapistic duties to strangers might conflict with one's preference for the near and dear (save your child or the children of strangers) or whether one is permitted to give luxuries to the near and dear when others lack necessities (see Judish, "Balancing Special Obligations"; Krishek, "Two Forms of Love"). Sylvia Walsh says that Kierkegaard elsewhere views ordinary sympathy (compassion) as often cruel, for it suggests that "things are not so bad" or "will improve" (Walsh, *Living Christianly*, 73–75, 142, 145–47). But Christ is the pattern of true compassion (123–29).

74. We should keep in mind various senses of sacrifice or self-sacrifice. Of course, *any cost* to the giver from trivial to serious could be said to be a sacrifice on the part of the self. Self-sacrifice also often refers to giving one's life. Self-sacrifice can also refer to the substitution of the interests of others—whether one's prior interests are self-regarding or other-regarding—or to the idea that self-regarding interests in this world are to be supplanted. I hope that when I speak of sacrifice, the meaning will be clear in context.

75. Alan Gewirth, *Reason and Morality* (Chicago: University of Chicago Press, 1978); Alan Gewirth, "Ethical Universalism and Particularism," *Journal of Philosophy* 85, no. 6 (1988): 291; Judish, "Balancing Special Obligations," 26. Gewirth's standard, it might be argued, is too strong even for equal love. For if I give limb for life, the outcome is that the one saved is better off than the one doing the saving; we are both alive, but I have lost a limb. My aiding the other does not restore us to equality.

76. On the question whether love (as desire or emotion) can be commanded as duty, Ferreira says that agape is not a "feeling or inclination" that is not "subject to will," but rather "the assumption of a responsibility to take care of another who needs care" ("Problematic Agapeistic Ideal," 106–7). Roberts takes another tack: insofar as love is an emotion, it has a cognitive dimension, and if we can change beliefs and judgments, then we can cultivate emotions. Thus, the natural repertoire of emotions is reshaped in the God relation. Just as agape has no continuity with pagan conceptions of duty but is entirely filled with Christian content, so emotion and desire (Robert C. Roberts, "Kierkegaard and Ethical Theory," in Mooney, *Ethics, Love, and Faith in Kierkegaard*, 85–88). If emotions are inherently connected to natural goods and evils, however, as Nussbaum would argue, then the emotions are not simply old wineskins to be filled with new wine (*Upheavals of Thought*). There would have to be substantive continuity somehow with "desire and inclination." See Hall (*Love's Treachery*, 12–13n7, 201–2), who says that this is just what Kierkegaard denies, but see Pope for a defense of the theme that grace heals nature (*The Evolution of Altruism and the Ordering of Love* [Washington, DC: Georgetown University Press, 1994], and *Human Evolution and Christian Ethics* [Cambridge: Cambridge University Press, 2007]). I will not discuss here the related but distinct question whether Kierkegaard espouses some version of a divine command ethic (see Evans, *Kierkegaard's Ethic of Love*; Philip L. Quinn, "The Divine Command Ethics in Kierkegaard's *Works of Love*," in *Faith, Freedom, and Responsibility*, ed. Daniel Howard-Snyder and Jeffrey Jordon [Lanham, MD: Rowman and Littlefield, 1996]; Philip L. Quinn, "Kierkegaard's Christian Ethics," in *The Cambridge Companion to Kierkegaard*, ed. Alasdair Hannay and Gordon D. Marino [Cambridge: Cambridge University Press, 1998], 349–75; and Roberts, "Kierkegaard and Ethical Theory," 72–92). I am indebted to Leo Ungar on these issues.

77.   Robert M. Adams says that it would be "absurd" to "always prefer the slightest benefit for another person to the greatest benefit for herself" (*Theory of Virtue,* 81). For Kierkegaard, one has in mind always the recipient's ultimate good, loving God and neighbor (Walsh, "Kierkegaard's Philosophy of Love," 175).

78.   Hallett distinguishes several positions: (1) Self-preference: sacrifice your own good when the good of the other ("collective or individual") is greater, but prefer your own good if it is equal to or greater than the good of others. (2) Other-preference: sacrifice your own good when the good of the other is greater and also when it is equal; prefer yourself only when your good is greater. (3) Parity: maximize the good counting each as one. (4) Self-subordination: seek your own good only if it does not compete with the good of others. (5) Self-forgetfulness: take no thought for your own good. (6) Self-denial: never seek your own good except as a means to the good of others (*Christian Neighbor-Love,* 3–6 passim). (1) is the view I have linked to equal regard.

79.   Gewirth, *Reason and Morality;* Hallett, *Christian Neighbor-Love;* and David Little, "The Law of Supererogation," in Santurri and Werpehowski, *Love Commandments,* 157–81, use the model of a relation where commensurable costs and benefits are distributed to giver and receiver. Cates (*Choosing to Feel*), however, primarily refers to what is appropriate in certain *relationships.* Others distinguish certain types of *resources* and *needs* (see David Little, "Natural Rights and Human Rights: The International Imperative," in *Natural Rights and Natural Law: The International Imperative,* ed. Robert P. Davidow [Fairfax, VA: George Mason University Press, 1986], 67–122, on Locke; see also "Law of Supererogation," 174, 178; and Pope, *Evolution of Altruism,* on Aquinas on senses of "superfluities" and "necessities"). Sometimes the motifs are combined.

80.   One could say that there are different "conceptions" of the "concept" of the identification of interests (John Rawls, *A Theory of Justice* (Cambridge, MA: Harvard University Press, 1971).

81.   Some sentences are drawn from John Reeder, "Extensive Benevolence," *Journal of Religious Ethics* 26, no. l (Spring 1998): 47–70; and John Reeder, "What Kind of Person Could Be a Torturer?," *Journal of Religious Ethics* 38, no. 1 (March 2010): 67–92. My definitions are stipulative and heuristic.

82.   Nussbaum thinks that empathy can be an aid to compassion, but it is not necessary (*Upheavals of Thought,* 304, 312, 330–35): we have compassion for animals "whose experience we know we can never share," sometimes the suffering is "remote" and "hard to reconstruct," and we could take it on authority that someone is suffering without perceiving it ourselves (330). My sense, however, is that we take some animals to have emotions, as Nussbaum argues (*Upheavals of Thought*), and to that extent, we can imagine their pain. As for remoteness, we can imagine a stranger simply as a human being with characteristic vulnerabilities (Nussbaum, *Frontiers of Justice: Disability, Nationality, Species Membership* [Cambridge, MA: Belknap Press of Harvard University Press, 2006]; and *Creating Capabilities: The Human Development Approach* [Cambridge, MA: Belknap Press of Harvard University Press, 2011]). And as for authority, we can form an imaginative picture of someone's suffering even if we hear about it from someone else. Nussbaum also says that a compassionate god might be omniscient and not need imagine human suffering. I grant this, but the god simply has a better form of cognition; some awareness is still a necessary precondition. Cf. Flescher and Worthen, *Altruistic Species,* 139–40, 141, on C. Daniel Batson, *The Altruism Question: Toward a Social-Psychological Answer* (Hillsdale, NJ: Lawrence Erlbaum Associates, 1991).

83.   See Nancy E. Snow's broader definition: "S empathizes with O's experience of emotion E if and only if: (a) O feels E; (b) S feels E because O feels E; and (c) S knows or understands that O feels E" ("Empathy," *American Philosophical Quarterly* 37, no. 1 [January 2000]: 68). A further condition (d)—"S understands S feels E because O feels E" —is present only in a "cognitively sophisticated form of empathy." Snow grants that the responses of some children may not satisfy (c), but she prefers to call these "precursors of empathy" (see 71–72). However we draw the borders of empathy, I want to distinguish it from the identification that is part of compassion or sympathy (cf. Snow, "Empathy," 71).

84.   See Ferreira on Butler, Smith, and Hume (*Love's Grateful Striving,* 196–97, 291–92nn25–30); see also "Hume and Imagination: Sympathy and 'the Other,'" *International Philosophical Quarterly* 34, no. 1333 (March 1994): 39–57. See Sherman, "Empathy and Imagination," *Midwest Studies in Philosophy* 22 (1998): 100–103, and "Empathy and the Family," *Acta Philosophica* 13 (2004) (fasc. 1): 28, 38, on the compound.

85.   See Karen Lebacqz for the view that empathy should not be cast either as "projection" or as direct "reception" but as an imaginative interpretation that draws both on our own experience and on input from the other ("The Weeping Womb: Why Beneficence Still Needs the Still Small Voice of Compassion," in *Secular Ethics in Theological Perspective,* ed. Earl Shelp [Dordrecht: Kluwer Academic Publishers, 1996], 92–93).

See also Michael Slote, *The Ethics of Care and Empathy* (London: Routledge, 2007), 12ff. See John J. Davenport on Levinas's objection to empathy as seeing others as ourselves ("Levinas's Agapistic Metaphysic of Morals: Absolute Passivity and the Other as Eschatological Hierophany," *Journal of Religious Ethics* 26, no. 2 [Fall 1998]: 339–40), and Wolterstorff's version of agapism, which does not "give centrality to empathy" (*Justice in Love*, 103–4).

86. Cates defines physical pain as a bodily sensation, an emotional reaction of dislike (a negative evaluation), a desire to stop or escape the pain, and an "agitation" as the sufferer imagines its "larger significance" (*Choosing to Feel*, 137–38). Note that pain as Cates describes it is an interpreted experience; in this sense, "pain" and "suffering" are equivalent.

87. Could we have imaginative empathy for the masochist who likes and desires his or her own suffering? I think so. Since the masochist *suffers*, we can assume that at some level he or she dislikes and is averse to pain, although liking and desiring is overriding.

88. Nussbaum, *Upheavals of Thought*. Cf. Diana Fritz Cates, "Conceiving Emotions: Martha Nussbaum's Upheavals of Thought," *Journal of Religious Ethics* 31, no. 2 (Summer 2003): 336–38, and Dyck and Padilla, who define empathy as an "emotional capacity accurately to perceive" the distress of the other, in distinction from "feeling with," which they call "sympathy," and responding with concern, which they call "compassion" (Arthur J. Dyck and Carlos Padilla, "The Empathetic Emotions and Self-Love in Bishop Joseph Butler and the Neurosciences," *Journal of Religious Ethics* 37, no. 4 [December 2009]: 579, 581–82, 604–5). I think of empathy as an act of imagination based in perception, but not identical with it. Compassion (which I take as synonymous with sympathy) is the dislike and desire to alleviate (as one's own). (Here I amend John Reeder, "Extensive Benevolence," *Journal of Religious Ethics* 26, no. 1 [Spring 1998]: 47–70). But compassion can be normatively overridden; it does not necessarily lead to beneficent action. Nussbaum holds that compassion is not appropriate when suffering is deserved, but I think we can have compassion even when the desire to alleviate is overridden by justice or other considerations (*Upheavals of Thought*). See Dyck and Padilla, "Empathetic Emotions and Self-Love," 579–80; and Moses, "'Keeping the Heart,'" 619–20.

89. When we recognize others as having an emotion (by "mirror neurons"), Jeffrey Stout points out, we do not *infer* that a person is having a particular emotion, but we do interpret it linguistically (*Blessed Are the Organized: Grassroots Democracy in America* [Princeton, NJ: Princeton University Press, 2010], 152–54, 162, 228, 313n81). Martin Hoffman, however, says that some forms of empathy have little or no linguistic content (*Empathy and Moral Development: Implications for Caring and Justice* [Cambridge: Cambridge University Press], 5). However, see Reeder, "What Kind of Person?," 71n17.

90. Sherman argues that empathy in this sense developmentally precedes imaginative empathy; we are "pre-wired to mimic," for example ("Empathy and Imagination," 82, 87–88, 103–6; and "Empathy and the Family," 33–36). See also Hoffman, *Empathy and Moral Development*. But I don't think that qualitative similarity necessarily accompanies imaginative empathy in adults.

91. Nussbaum says that Smith and Scheler take the view that one experiences in one's person not merely the same suffering in a qualitative sense but the same suffering in a numerical sense. For Smith, one becomes "in some measure the same person," and for Scheler, "the entire distinction" between self and other is "to a certain extent removed" (Nussbaum, *Upheavals of Thought*, 327–28, 327nn45, 46). However we interpret Smith and Scheler, a sense of numerical distinctness is the presupposition of Cates's insistence that even when we include the friend in our own flourishing, we desire their good for their own sake (*Choosing to Feel*). See Sherman ("Empathy and Imagination" and "Empathy and the Family") on Smith.

92. Cates, *Choosing to Feel*, 140–44. See Slote, *The Ethics of Care and Empathy* (London: Routledge, 2007), 14–15, on Hoffman, *Empathy and Moral Development*. Slote seems to take empathy as involuntary and, like Nussbaum, makes it an aid rather than a necessary condition of compassion (13; but cf. 27). Stephen Darwall, however, distinguishes "contagion" from imaginative empathy ("Empathy, Sympathy, Care," *Philosophical Studies* 89, no. 2–3 [March 1998]: 264–72). Stanley Milgram may be referring to contagion, i.e., a qualitatively similar experience: "The cries of pain issuing from the learner strongly affected many participants, whose reaction to them is immediate, visceral, and spontaneous" (*Obedience to Authority: An Experimental View* [1974; London: Pinter and Martin, 1994], 157).

93. Nussbaum, *Upheavals of Thought*, 323, 330. See also Stephen G. Post, *Unlimited Love: Altruism, Compassion, and Service* (Philadelphia: Templeton Foundation Press, 2003), 146–47; Reeder, "What Kind of

Person?," 71–75. As Hoffman points out, even empathetic reactions can be suppressed. He cites a study of "weak empathizers," whom he compares with the androids in *Blade Runner* who were "incapable of empathy" (*Empathy and Moral Development*, 35–36). He also notes (198ff.) that empathy can be deflected by "overarousal" (personal distress), "egoistic drift" (thinking about oneself instead of the victim), and "habituation" (cumulative exposure) (206). Richard B. Miller, *Friends and Other Strangers: Studies in Religion, Ethics, and Culture* (New York: Columbia University Press, 2016), 117–22, also discusses ways in which empathy could be morally problematic.

94. Wyschogrod says that empathy is "ethically neutral" ("Pythagorean Bodies and the Body of Altruism," 8). The empathetic person can be indifferent or like the suffering of the other and want it to continue for its own sake (cruelty or sadism) or as a means to an end. Thus, the sadistic torturer's empathy can be an aid to producing the suffering the torturer likes (Nussbaum, *Upheavals of Thought*, 323). The torturer can even communicate to the victim what empathy reveals as another way to cause pain (cf. Sherman, "Empathy and Imagination," 96). On torturers, see Reeder, "What Kind of Person?"

95. The compassionate agent can also have a second-order desire to be a compassionate person. See Harry G. Frankfurt, *The Importance of What We Care About: Philosophical Essays* (Cambridge: Cambridge University Press, 1988); and Reeder, "What Kind of Person?"

96. Nancy E. Snow argues that imaginative identification is not necessary for compassion since there are cases where we are not able to imagine the experience of the other, e.g., anencephalic infants or the comatose ("Compassion," *American Philosophical Quarterly* 28, no. 3 [July 1991]: 195–99). I think that we often have an immediate dislike of sickness or misfortune. Let us call this "pity" ("he is in a pitiful condition; I pity him") and reserve "compassion" for the experience in which one dislikes and desires to alleviate the suffering of the other as one does one's own. Cates, however, makes both disliking that you are in pain and disliking your pain part of compassion (*Choosing to Feel*).

97. Compassion today usually refers to the woe of others, but its meaning could be extended to liking and desiring to promote their weal. In some Buddhist traditions, there is apparently a separate category of "sympathetic joy."

98. Darwall accepts the thesis that there is a psychological connection between imaginative empathy and sympathy (concern for an individual's well-being for his or her own sake) ("Empathy, Sympathy, Care," 261, 272ff.): an imaginative identification with "Carol" passes over into "distress *at* Carol's plight *and* on her behalf . . . *for her own sake*" (273–74). I argue, however, that some normative reason must identify interests in order to make the transition from empathy to sympathy. The idea that any person's suffering is an agent-neutral *reason* for anyone to relieve it is a normative bridge (274–78; see also Korsgaard et al., *Sources of Normativity*; Little, "Natural Rights and Human Rights"; and Charles Larmore, *The Autonomy of Morality* [Cambridge: Cambridge University Press, 2008]).

99. Sherman thinks that altruistic emotions presuppose empathy, but she also says that empathy predisposes us to these emotions (subjects who are empathetic are more likely to want to help) ("Empathy and Imagination," 110–13). Even if this is so, the torturer can also have empathy (Reeder, "What Kind of Person?").

100. "As yourself" is also sometimes used to mean universalizability or to furnish guidance as to what the neighbor needs or wants.

101. See Korsgaard et al., *Sources of Normativity*, 148–49, on Thomas Nagel, *The Possibility of Altruism* (Princeton, NJ: Princeton University Press, 1970), 80n1. See also Olafson, *Heidegger and the Ground of Ethics*, 10–12, 48–49, 48n16, 68.

102. See Nussbaum, *Upheavals of Thought*, 388, on Hierocles. Others are drawn in, become "like oneself," but Nussbaum also uses the metaphor of "build on."

103. We do not necessarily experience the mutual liking or desire to share lives that we do in the paradigm sense of friendship. Judish argues that "friendship and *agape* do not differ merely in range; the love that friendship shows is typically different from the love commanded by *agape*" ("Balancing Special Obligations," 22). Judish, like Cates, stresses that friends want to be, if possible, in each other's presence, while agape focuses on the other whether present or absent. See also Darlene Fozard Weaver, *Self Love and Christian Ethics* (Cambridge: Cambridge University Press, 2002), 75–76, 229, on Edward Collins Vacek, *Love, Human and Divine: The Heart of Christian Ethics* (Washington, DC: Georgetown University Press, 1994), on differences in intention (in the sense of consciousness of a particular sort of object) in different kinds of love. David Velleman,

"Love as Moral Emotion," *Ethics* 109, no. 2 (1999): 338–74, argues that it is possible to love a particular other, but not want to be in their presence, but his "love" is a recognition of "rational nature" (365). We see the "person" through the empirical "persona" (371). My sense is that this view is not unlike Kierkegaard's idea that with God as the middle term, one relates to the child of God through the empirical self.

104. See Pope, *Evolution of Altruism*, 134, and *Human Evolution and Christian Ethics*, 173, on Gustafson, *Ethics from a Theocentric Perspective*, vol. 2, *Ethics and Theology* (Chicago: University of Chicago Press, 1984); and Pope, *Human Evolution and Christian Ethics*, 215, on Cahill, *Sex, Gender, and Christian Ethics* (New York: Cambridge University Press, 1996). See Pope, "'Equal Regard' vs. 'Special Relations'? Reaffirming the Inclusiveness of Agape," *Journal of Religion* 77, no. 3 (July 1997): 359–60, 374, 376–77, on special relations as the matrix of universal love. See also Don S. Browning, "Science and Religion on the Nature of Love," in Post et al., *Altruism and Altruistic Love*, 342, on an "analogical extension"; and Flescher and Worthen, *Altruistic Species*.

105. Evans, *Kierkegaard's Ethic of Love*. God's love, it is widely said, makes us all brothers and sisters, but this is not a literal kinship unless one defines kinship broadly as species membership.

106. See Nussbaum, *Upheavals of Thought*, 319, on the "eudaimonistic judgment": "The person must consider the suffering of another as a significant part of his or her own scheme of goals and ends. She must take that person's ills as affecting her own flourishing." The good of the other becomes an interest of the self that affects the self's flourishing in the sense of the fulfillment of the goals of the self. The good of the other is one of the self's interests, an interest of the self that is not self-interested because the object of the interest is the good of the other. Thanks to David Golemboski.

107. See Gene Outka on "unqualified" in "Comment," *Journal of Religious Ethics* 26, no. 2 (Fall 1998): 435–40.

108. Even taking a short rest can compete with meeting some need of the other. But this can be justified as a means to continue to be of service. The "good parent," however, can read a book when there is nothing he or she can do for others, or he or she can listen to music at the same time that he or she labors for others (both are cases in which seeking one's own good for one's own sake does not compete with seeking the good of others). On the relation of patriarchy to images of love or care, See Barbara Hilkert Andolsen, "*Agape* in Feminist Ethics," *Journal of Religious Ethics* 9, no. 1 (Spring 1981): 69–83; Marilyn Chapin Massey, *Feminine Soul: The Fate of an Ideal* (Boston: Beacon Press, 1985). See also Sara Ruddick, *Maternal Thinking: Towards a Politics of Peace* (London: Women's Press, 1989).

109. Post (*Unlimited Love*, chap. 6 passim) traces his notion of "unlimited" love to the evolved character of parental love (his sense of unlimited refers to scope—any person—and he also discusses other features in chap. 9). See the essays in Post et al., *Altruism and Altruistic Love*. On various forms of evolved altruism, see Flescher and Worthen, *Altruistic Species*, and Pope, *Human Evolution and Christian Ethics*.

110. See David Little, "Law of Supererogation," 168–79; see also 180n9.

111. The question of how to interpret the Jesus material in its historical context remains. What is the notion of friendship at work? And of course, interpretations in later traditions are another matter.

112. John Reeder, "Religion and Morality," in *The Oxford Handbook of the Sociology of Religion*, ed. Peter B. Clarke (Oxford: Oxford University Press, 2011), 336–59. The *ordo cognoscendi* is not necessarily the *ordo essendi*.

113. Pope, *Human Evolution and Christian Ethics*.

114. See Westphal, *Levinas and Kierkegaard in Dialogue*, 56, and Westphal, "Empty Suitcase as Metaphor," 53, 265–66n22.

115. Kierkegaard, *Works of Love*, 2.X.

116. Vacek, *Love, Human and Divine*. See Amélie O. Rorty, who says that a "historical" love may even end precisely because the lovers have affected each other ("The Historicity of Psychological Attitudes: Love Is Not Love Which Alters Not When It Alteration Finds," in *Friendship: A Philosophical Reader*, ed. Neera Kapur Badhwar (Ithaca, NY: Cornell University Press, 1993), 73–88. In some cases, a parent's love remains, even if it takes the form of "tough love." But some special relations, I believe, can and should come to an absolute end. Cf. Steven G. Post, "Conditional and Unconditional Love," *Modern Theology* 7, no. 5 (1991): 435–46.

117. One can "love" a child more than a stranger without it being the case that one should in every instance prefer or be partial to the child. I may have a duty to provide necessities first for my child—to prefer

my child—but I may also have a duty to withhold enhancements or luxuries until the starving in my group or in humanity at large are fed.

118. If the life and teaching of Jesus are the embodiment of divine love, what should we take as normative in our relations with others, "given the patterns he singularly enacts on our behalf"? Gene Outka, "Following at a Distance: Ethics and the Identity of Jesus," in *Scriptural Authority and Narrative Interpretation*, ed. Garrett Green (Eugene, OR: Wipf & Stock, 2000), 145. The disciple seeks to love inclusively and to preserve personal uniqueness (155–57), but our need for response distinguishes followers from Jesus (157–58). Outka notes that some, however, have argued directly from Jesus's "forness" to a pattern that is "sheerly other-regarding."

119. Cf. Stephen G. Post, "The Inadequacy of Selflessness: God's Suffering and the Theory of Love," *Journal of the American Academy of Religion* 56 (Summer 1988): 213–28, which contrasts mutual love with a theology of self-abnegation or absence of self-love. In 2003 he rejects self-abnegation and called for a love that includes the self (*Unlimited Love*, 41, 144). But while love seeks a response, it does not make return a condition (151). Care for the self is a means to caring for others (153). Moreover, love is willing to be self-sacrificial as Jesus was (152–53).

120. On an *ordo amoris*, see Cates, *Choosing to Feel*; Flescher, *Heroes, Saints, and Ordinary Morality*; Hallett, *Priorities and Christian Ethics* (Cambridge: Cambridge University Press, 1998); Judish, "Balancing Special Obligations"; Outka, "Universal Love and Impartiality"; Pope, *Evolution of Altruism*; Pope, "Love in Contemporary Christian Ethics," *Journal of Religious Ethics* 23, no. 1 (Spring 1995): 165–97; Pope, *Human Evolution and Christian Ethics*; Post, *Spheres of Love: Toward a New Ethics of the Family* (Dallas: Southern Methodist University Press, 1994); Post, *Unlimited Love*; Bharat Ranganathan, "On Helping One's Neighbor," *Journal of Religious Ethics* 40, no. 4 (2002): 653–77; Vacek, *Love, Human and Divine*; and Werpehowski, "'Agape' and Special Relations." There are at least two questions: What is the *ranking* of duties of special relations, within themselves and in relation to duties to strangers, and what is the *cost* to self in both spheres? See Flescher, *Heroes, Saints, and Ordinary Morality*, on duty and supererogation. See Pope, "'Equal Regard' vs. 'Special Relations'?," 353–79, on Outka, "Universal Love and Impartiality"; Post, *Spheres of Love*; and Werpehowski, "'Agape' and Special Relations."

121. Hastings Rashdall, *The Idea of Atonement in Christian Theology* (London: Macmillan, 1919), 37, 45–46, argued that in the teaching of Jesus, the Messiah gives his life to save his friends from persecution and death, not to pay the penalty for sin. Rashdall also argued in *Conscience and Christ: Six Lectures on Christian Ethics* (New York: Charles Scribner's Sons, 1916), 139–40, that the central concept of neighbor love is that "each individual human life . . . possesses an intrinsic value. . . . Each man should treat himself as of no less value than his neighbor. . . . It cannot be reasonable that an individual should sacrifice a larger amount of his own good for a smaller amount of another's." I read Rashdall to say that one should give below comparable cost, and also at comparable cost, e.g., life for life, but not beyond comparable cost. Rashdall seems to combine an emphasis on equality and the imitation of Jesus's sacrifice for his friends. His view could be read as a middle ground between the two alternatives I have suggested. Cf. Hallett, in *Christian Neighbor-Love*, on "other-preference" and on Rashdall (106, 165).

122. Kierkegaard, *Works of Love*, 265.

123. Reinhold Niebuhr, *The Interpretation of Christian Ethics* (1935; New York: Harper and Bros, 1955).

124. I argue for justice and love as distinct and possibly conflicting virtues (they are conceptually different, can be concretely incompatible, and can differ in psychological strength in or between persons) (John Reeder, "Are Care and Justice Distinct Virtues?," in *Medicine and the Ethics of Care*, ed. Diana Fritz Cates and Paul Lauritzen [Washington, DC: Georgetown University Press, 2001], 3–40). See also Moses, "'Keeping the Heart,'" 619–20, which argues that for Butler, justice can sometimes trump compassion. Other models include remedy and deficiency (Carol Gilligan, *In a Different Voice: Psychological Theory and Women's Development* [1982; Cambridge, MA: Harvard University Press, 1993]), irreducible perspectives (Carol Gilligan, "Moral Orientation and Moral Development," in *Women and Moral Theory*, ed. Eva Feder Kittay and Diana T. Meyers [Totawa, NJ: Rowman and Littlefield, 1987], 19–33), dialectic (Paul Ricoeur, "The Logic of Jesus, the Logic of God," in *Figuring the Sacred: Religion, Narrative, and Imagination*, trans. David Pellauer, ed. Mark I. Wallace [Minneapolis: Fortress Press, 1995], 279–83; Paul Ricoeur, "Ethical and Theological Considerations in the Golden Rule," in *Figuring the Sacred*, 292–302; and Paul Ricoeur, "Love and Justice," in *Figuring the Sacred*, 315–29), distinct but interdependent concepts (Margaret Farley, *Compassionate Respect: A Feminist Approach to Medical Ethics and Other Questions* [New York: Paulist Press, 2002]; Margaret Farley,

Just Love: A Framework for Christian Social Ethics [New York: Continuum, 2006]), and incorporation (Wolterstorff, *Justice in Love*).

125. John Reeder, "Analogues to Justice," in Santurri and Werpehowski, *Love Commandments*, 281–307.

126. Cf. Eric Gregory, *Politics and the Order of Love: An Augustinian Ethic of Democratic Citizenship* (Chicago: University of Chicago Press, 2008), 111n63, on Augustine.

Forgiveness in the Service of Love

MARGARET A. FARLEY

IN A VOLUME that aims to expand our understandings of Christian love by clarifying love's meaning in theory and practice, a chapter devoted to "forgiveness" may appear marginal to the task. Yet the opposite is the case. There is no genuine Christian forgiveness without love, and love is sometimes tested in its ultimate possibility and imperative by the forgiveness it generates. Moreover, the construals of forgiveness that are central to much of Christian theology slip into caricature unless they include love in their foundation, framework, and movement. Christians believe that God's love for humans is revealed—perhaps centrally—in God's forgiveness of sinners, and that God's people (all of them sinners) are to be like God in their love and forgiveness of one another. The sin that requires divine forgiveness is the refusal of God's love; and the sins of humans against humans that require human forgiveness are the falsities and inadequacies that betray or distort our loving and being-loved. My focus on Christian forgiveness is primarily on human forgiveness. Yet forgiveness cannot be understood Christianly apart from its relationship to divine forgiveness or apart from its context in human community and history.

In this essay I consider ways in which love and forgiveness are intertwined, and ways in which both divine and human forgiveness are themselves forms of love. I want ultimately to show how forgiveness offers a way to a form of "de-centering," better known in Christian circles as an other-centered love, needed in a conflict-driven world. I do this in five steps: (1) description of the context in which new interest in forgiveness has arisen; (2) analysis of the challenges to forgiveness that are part of this new interest; (3) placement of Christian love and forgiveness in a matrix of Christian beliefs; (4) descriptive examination of the experience of forgiveness and the meanings it yields; and (5) resolution of tensions between forgiveness and justice through a proposal for "anticipatory" as well as "actual" forms of Christian forgiveness. I begin with some preliminary observations.

Introduction

Forgiveness is a preoccupation not only of the Christian tradition, but of other world religions as well—in particular Judaism and Islam. The Hebrew Bible is replete with stories of

A version of this essay, which was originally commissioned for this book, also appears in Margaret Farley's *Changing the Questions: Explorations in Christian Ethics* (Maryknoll, NY: Orbis Books, 2015). Reprinted by permission.

God's merciful forgiveness granted to human beings (as in the promises to Noah) and in particular to the Israelites despite their infidelities (as in the provision of new tablets of the law after Moses, in response to the idolatry of the people, had destroyed the originals). The Psalmist, along with cries for God's wrath against enemies, still sings and sings again of the quality of divine forgiveness. Prophets threatened divine punishment, yet they combined lamentation with hope for forgiveness. Between and among humans, too, there are paradigmatic cases of astonishing forgiveness (as in Joseph's response to the brothers who betrayed him). Liturgically throughout the centuries, Yom Kippur, a High Holy Day for many Jews, is a day of atonement (in memory of God's merciful re-giving of the law of the covenant to the Israelites). On this day divine pardon can be attained, and reconciliation among individuals may be sought.[1]

In the Qur'an, too, Allah is continually named "The Most Forgiving," or "The Most Merciful and Compassionate." Followers of Muhammed Ibn Abdallah were to believe in divine mercy, and also to imitate it.[2] The Qur'an describes Believers as "those who avoid major sins and . . . when they are angry they forgive" (Al-Shura 42:37). Buddhism, on the other hand, recognizes no personal God, but in general addresses harms imposed by one human on another as requiring transcendence. The response to harm consists therefore in spiritual efforts at patience, peace, detachment, not forgiveness. Yet in a later form, Mahayana Buddhism, compassion becomes more important than psychological or spiritual equanimity. The bodhisattva offers a form of radical forgiveness precisely for the sake of the one who has caused harm.

The importance of forgiveness to various world religions notwithstanding, multiple ambiguous interpretations of its meaning and apparent inconsistencies in its practice suggest that there are many questions to be pursued, and more than proof-texts to be drawn from traditional writings. Although there is not the opportunity here to probe more fully the questions raised and insights offered from religious traditions other than Christianity, they remain on the horizon for anyone concerned about the role of forgiveness in a fractured and conflicted world.

In the last three decades, an impressive body of literature has developed regarding human forgiveness. A kind of urgency of inquiry has emerged not only among religious thinkers, but among philosophers, historians, political theorists, psychologists, as well as biological and social scientists.[3] Research and analysis in these many secular fields have advanced particularly important issues regarding the meaning of human forgiveness, its required elements, its appropriateness in some contexts but not in others. To the forefront have come questions of the compatibility between forgiveness and justice, the conditionality of forgiveness, the potential corruption of the concept of forgiveness when it becomes primarily a therapy for victims, and the dependence of forgiveness on the expressed repentance and remorse of perpetrators of harm. Once again, it is not possible to probe here the results of these many studies or the ongoing scholarly conversations they promote, although I will endeavor not to leave them completely behind. I turn, then, to questions of Christian forgiveness by attending briefly to the contemporary context in which they and their secular counterparts arise.

Context for Forgiveness: Conflict, Injury, and Pain

What has awakened so much recent interest in questions of human forgiveness? No doubt many catalytic forces have been at work, but one of them might be described as a new and searing recognition of the lengths to which the inhumanity of humans against humans can go. The context for new interest in forgiveness, human and divine, is overall one in which poverty, oppression, exploitation, and violence seem to grow exponentially. Perhaps it has always been so. Humans have struggled throughout history for justice and for peace, for fairness and freedom, for healing of the pain in both body and spirit. Still the suffering goes on: violence begetting violence, exploitation escalating seemingly beyond remedy. New issues of race, class, and gender fuel worldwide conflicts; anger, resentment, and intractable greed fracture human relationships; religious and cultural imperialisms undergird human battles of devastating proportion—whether between or within nations, corporations, tribes, families, and even churches. Everywhere visible are both the causes and the consequences of these conflicts: destitution, war, abuses of power, systemic evils hidden behind "business as usual," and relentless but unnecessary injury and dying.

More particularly, ours is a time and a world in which "crimes against humanity" may have shaken the thick complacency that allowed toleration of unspeakable assaults on humans as human. Such crimes are perhaps not new in the 20th and 21st centuries, but we are far removed from the ancients who could interpret them as a function of fate. The atrocities revealed in the Nuremberg Trials after World War II constituted a milestone in human history, one that showed to many a coming fork in the road for radical choice regarding human affairs. In experiences around the world, however, these kinds of atrocities have continued—whether in Argentina, the Balkans, Rwanda, the Democratic Republic of Congo, Iraq, or anywhere— auguring (as some maintain) the end of the history of human forgiveness or a new beginning.

The strides of contemporary globalization make it almost impossible today to isolate or ignore crimes against humanity itself. Hence, it is not surprising that as these very phenomena appear to increase, or at least become more widely visible, they have also occasioned new clarity about the rights of all humans, and they have roused on a global scale new stirrings of human concern, movements of human compassion. It would be a mistake to think in some naive way that these correlative phenomena can be identified simply as forces of evil and forces of good. We are all probably implicated in both, not the least because our opposition to perpetrators of injury and harm is an opposition more often shaped by goals of punishment than of the restoration of human relationships and societies. Western cultures in particular seem to have become more and more punitive in their response to perpetrators, ostensibly on behalf of victims. Nonetheless, it is in the midst of this complex context that new and sustained interest in forgiveness has emerged.

To some, this interest in forgiveness is dangerous, likely to mask what is "premature reconciliation" and to burden yet further the ones among us who are already most vulnerable. Others, however, find in the concept of forgiveness some inkling of the kind of "de-centering" required of ourselves if we are ever to offset the worst forms of fear, ambition, resentment, and self-righteousness that divide us. In any case, the rise in concern for forgiveness and reconciliation may signal new energy for fashioning the "conditions of possibility" for *recognition* and *respect* of one individual for another, one group toward others, one generation for all humanity. There is some suffering that does not have to be, that can be ended in change not in death.

Dramatic and Everyday Challenges to Forgiveness

Between and among humans the need for forgiveness is commonplace in our experience. As Hannah Arendt observed, "willed evil" may be rare, but "trespassing is an everyday occurrence," and it needs forgiveness.[4] Why else, she asks, are we enjoined to forgive not seven times but seventy times seven? (Matthew 18:22) Only through this "constant mutual release" from what we do, from the harmful consequences of actions that are otherwise irreversible, are we freed to live into the future.[5] For beings who are free, forgiveness is a necessary part of the fabric of human life. Small offenses may indeed be commonplace among us, but the fabric of relationships may be torn nonetheless.

Moreover, as we have already noted, there are uncommon offenses as well, some of which are considered so horrific that they cannot be forgiven, at least not in this world. However, it has never been easy for Christians or anyone else to identify with certainty what is meant by an "unforgivable sin." It is a sin against the Spirit, says Jesus (Mark 3:28–30; Matthew 12:30–32; Luke 12:8–10); and philosophers like Hegel have followed suit—though not necessarily with a univocal meaning for Spirit. Somehow what is at stake is an offense that blocks the movement of the Spirit, a crime against that which gives the power to forgive. But what or how could this be? On the one hand, there is some presumption that it occurs when the *agent* of the crime (the offense) chooses to refuse the forgiveness offered by the victim through the grace of the Spirit. But on the other hand, it may also be an injury that so incapacitates, destroys, the *victim* that she or he is rendered incapable of forgiving the perpetrator. Such an injury would be unforgivable because the power of the Spirit could not any longer be received by the victim. These descriptions approach the question of the meaning of "unforgivable," but they seem not to settle it.

In the 20th and into the 21st century, the paradigmatic case for the unforgivable sin has been the Holocaust, that unspeakable crime primarily against Jews (though others as well) under the National Socialist regime in Germany during World War II. There have been additional claims about cases comparable to this, whether on behalf of other genocidal events or even the terrifying destruction of the psychological humanity of individuals in very particular situations.[6] Yet the consistent probing of the possibility and the meaning of forgiveness—in the face of the "unforgivable"—that has followed the experience of the Holocaust is unparalleled, and it serves as a challenge to any other efforts at understanding human forgiveness. A close rendering of this analysis, with a stark joining of its issues, is dramatically portrayed in the writings of two French philosophers, Vladimir Jankélévitch (1903–1985) and Jacques Derrida (1930–2004), both of whom were Jewish. Jankélévitch, at one point in his writings, argues for the view that the Shoah was an *inexpiable* crime—that is, irreparable, irremediable, and on a human scale unforgivable. With this sort of crime "One cannot punish the criminal with a punishment proportionate to his crime. . . . The penalty [therefore] becomes indifferent; what happens is literally *inexpiable*."[7] This is why, Jankélévitch maintains, the human history of forgiveness has ended, for "forgiveness died in the death camps."[8] Jacques Derrida cautiously questions this view, but he also embraces the notion of "unforgivable" sin as central to an understanding of forgiveness.[9]

Both Jankélévitch and Derrida identify "crimes against humanity" as in some sense "unforgivable." Both consider these crimes to be not just against one's political or ideological enemies, but crimes against what makes humans "human." They are crimes so massive, so monstrous, that they cross the line of radical evil.[10] They aim at the destruction of not only the human body but the human spirit. Their motivation is the conviction that the object of their attacks has no right to be "human" or treated as human. In the Holocaust these were attacks against the very *existence* of Jews (or gypsies or homosexuals or any despised minorities) as "human." Such crimes say: "We do not want you to *be*." For Jankélévich, in the face of this kind of assault, forgiveness is impossible. For Derrida, crimes like these, precisely as "unforgivable," reveal the deepest core of the concept of forgiveness—an impossible possibility.

Derrida searches for a conceptual genealogy of forgiveness in the "heritage" of Western concepts and practices of forgiveness, based largely in the traditions of the Abrahamic religions (especially Judaism and Christianity) and in the philosophies and judicial systems they have helped to shape. He concludes that this inheritance is permeated with a view of forgiveness as something that must be earned and deserved. Although in this "heritage" forgiveness is considered a free "gift" from God, when it is exercised by humans it is nonetheless practiced and therefore continually conceptualized as "conditional." Only those can be forgiven who become worthy of forgiveness by fulfilling, at a bare minimum, certain conditions: (1) acknowledgment of fault, (2) reasonable repentance and remorse, (3) request for forgiveness, (4) expression of intent to transform their behavior, and (5) some effort at reparation.[11] Such conditionality, Derrida maintains, is in profound tension with the "unconditionality" of forgiveness that also belongs to the traditions but transcends their history. The tension between unconditionality and conditionality is analogous, he suggests, to the tension between justice and the law.

Thus on Derrida's interpretation there is in the "heritage" a conditional imperative, proportioned to expected requirements. But there is also an unconditional imperative, a "pure" concept of forgiveness which stabilizes its essential core. The latter is revealed particularly in forgiveness of the unforgivable, forgiveness offered to the guilty as guilty—a core that must be in every act of "true" forgiveness, even though it is hidden by and within a complex web of historical conditions. The rationale of this core in human forgiveness is grounded not in the virtue of the one who forgives, nor in the offender's fulfillment of conditions, but in the sacredness at the heart of the human, even at the heart of the human wrongdoer,[12]—that same sacredness that crimes against humanity aim to destroy. This dual imperative—conditional and unconditional—is not finally contradictory, though it must deal with what appear to be contradictions, or at least aporias, and ongoing tremendous tensions.[13] Yet it alone, with its two sides, can sustain both the concept of forgiveness and its power to restore human relationships in concrete historical contexts.

What makes Derrida dissatisfied with the conditional imperative is his profound suspicion that conditional forgiveness slides all too frequently into an economic exchange—corrupted by calculation, bargaining, and negotiation ("if you agree to this, I will agree to that"). When forgiveness is wholly based on the fulfillment of conditions, it is easy to "forgive," the power of forgiveness having been trivialized and dissipated. That is, the guilt of the guilty is so mitigated by agreed upon conditions, that there is little left to forgive. There is nothing that requires or even fosters conversion of heart. In the end, then, there is nothing about conditional forgiveness that is, by itself, true forgiveness.

For Derrida, the unforgivable, the inexpiable, is what really needs unconditional forgiving. Like a "gift," unconditional forgiveness is given without strings attached. It appears at the center of the meaning of forgiveness as "a force, a desire, an impetus, a movement, an appeal (call it what you will) that demands that forgiveness be granted, if it can be, even to someone who does not ask for it, who does not repent or confess or improve or redeem himself. . . ."[14] But the two imperatives, unconditional and conditional, must be held together, neither one reducible to the other nor dissociated from the other. Insofar as this can be done, the core unconditional imperative will help to anchor the conditional imperative so that forgiveness remains forgiveness all the while it is inscribing itself in the political, legal, and religious structures of human history.[15] We must see if these kinds of understandings of forgiveness have any heuristic value for understanding Christian forgiveness in the context of Christian love.

Christian Love and Forgiveness

I began this essay with a twofold claim: that there is no Christian forgiveness without love; and that the imperative to love that is central to the Christian life includes an imperative to forgive. I also averred at the start that Christian understandings of forgiveness include and depend upon insights into the relationship between human forgiveness and divine. My aim now is to place these claims within a pattern of Christian beliefs that may render them more accessible to the questions of forgiveness that have become urgent today,[16] and then to press issues particular to Christians regarding the meaning, possibility, and norms of human forgiveness. Although I use the term "pattern," and even "stages," my focus is not necessarily on temporal sequence but on the layers of meaning in the experience of Christian love and the forgiveness that can be within it.

A. Creative Love

The pattern I have in mind does not begin with divine or human forgiveness. It begins with God's creative love. No matter how strongly Christian theologies may emphasize the profound need of humans for "justification," for forgiveness and redemption from their sins, for reconciliation with God and with one another, all of this depends on and implicitly incorporates the first part of the pattern—that is, God's initial (and eternal) decision to share God's own "being" with utterly new entities that we call "creatures." As Karl Rahner suggested near the end of his theologizing and his life: "A Christian theologian is not prevented from thinking that the theme of human sinfulness and forgiveness of guilt through pure grace is, in a certain sense, somewhat secondary compared to the theme of God's radical *self*-communication."[17] It is God's giving of existence, bringing into being *ex nihilo*, and sustaining in creative love, not more Being but more beings, that constitutes the first and ongoing movement of all that follows. More specifically, among God's creatures humans receive a gift of existence that includes the possibility of knowing and being-known, loving and being-loved, by God who offers to them a direct and intimate share—a "personal" share—in God's own life and love. This in a sense holds the whole gift of God, the "pure grace" that helps us to understand the importance of all grace as it continually unfolds.

B. Commanded Love

Out of God's creative love comes the command to human persons to love God with their whole heart and soul and mind and strength, and to love one another as they love themselves.[18] Neighbor love is to be universal in scope and in its unexceptionable regard for the dignity of each individual. The command to such love is an obligating imperative but also a liberating call, since it accords with and calls forth what is at the heart of the "human." The dual command to love God and neighbor is ultimately able to be experienced by humans as an imperative, a call, and an inner yearning toward "other-centered" love. This is the love whereby a human person at least wants, desires, to center her being and action in relation to God above all else; and love whereby she wants to love other persons and all creation in a way that is integral with her love for God. God's own creative and inviting love awakens the possibility in humans of a responding love—not only as an intellectual affirmation of the good that the Creator *is* and the good that the created can *become*, but as an affective affirmation which is also a *unio affectus*, a union with and dwelling in what is loved, both Creator and created.

C. Forgiving Love

However, humans also experience within themselves resistance to God's command and appeal. Within humans, individually and together, are multiple barriers, conflicting yearnings, that prevent harmonious responses. The context of their lives and the order in their hearts appear broken in significant respects. Call it (literally or metaphorically) a catastrophic "fall" from an original set of capabilities for true and just love; or an evolutionary struggle to learn to love; or social malformations that perpetuate themselves from one generation to another; or let it be too obscure to name at all, except as the mystery of human freedom in the face of the mystery of the "human condition." Whatever characterizes the situation, humans have been estranged from God, from one another, and from their own selves. And some form of responsibility for this appears to attach to all humans, since all are both free (even if in "bondage") and estranged.

Yet God's creative and sustaining love continues. Like God's free decision to create out of love, so does this same love modulate into a love of compassionate forgiveness. On God's part, it is still infinite love, still pure grace, in presence and action, dwelling by *unio affectus* in and with humans. This eternally forgiving love is enacted and revealed in and through the life, death, and resurrection of Jesus Christ. God "has delivered us from the dominion of darkness and transformed us to the kingdom of God's beloved Son, in whom we have redemption, the forgiveness of sins" (Col. 1:13–14). The almost un-believable good news for all humans is that "in him all the fullness of God was pleased to dwell, and through him to reconcile to himself all things, whether on earth or in heaven, making peace by the blood of his cross" (Col. 1:19–20).[19]

There is here no room for Christian theologies about a wrathful father-god exacting blood sacrifice from his son, and no room for preoccupation only with death.[20] There is only room for a story of forgiving love. Within the life, suffering, death, and resurrection of Jesus Christ, the reality and meaning of the cross is not finally suffering and death, but a relationship that holds; love and forgiving love hold. The relationship between Jesus and God forever holds; within this, the relationship between God and humanity is forever restored, and it holds. Whatever the forces of evil against him, the utter love in Jesus's heart was not plucked out, not damaged or changed—neither his love for the God he called Abba, nor the love he embodied and revealed from God for all humans, nor the love he made forever newly possible among humans. A covenant was eternally sealed, a love crucified but not destroyed. And it is this love that has lived and poured out life and love and forgiveness ever since. From here on, human struggles for just and truthful loves, and just and truthful forgiveness, continue; but the conditions for their possibility are now in place.

D. Missioned Forgiveness

In the Gospel attributed to John, we find the post-Resurrection Jesus meeting with his disciples, greeting them with peace, showing them the scars from his wounds, breathing his Spirit upon them, and giving them a mission of forgiveness (John 20:19–23). As some theologians have argued (though not necessarily commenting on this particular text), the message of forgiveness encompasses in a sense the Christian message in its entirety. It is the decisive gift of the Holy Spirit.[21] For Christians, it is what makes possible a "new heart," dying and living with Jesus Christ, partaking of God's own being and life, restoring relationships otherwise without hope. Christians are taught to ask for it every day: "Forgive us our sins, as we forgive those who sin against us." It reaches to communities as well as individuals. It is to be offered to all who desire to drink of the waters of the Spirit, to all who desire to come to the table of the Lord. The mission, then, is to forgive, and to reveal the forgiveness of God, in and through Jesus Christ.

Moreover, this is a mission not given only to a designated few but to all who share in the gift of the Spirit, all who gather to receive God's mercy along with the mission to reveal it to others. As Paul proclaims: "So if anyone is in Christ, there is a new creation. . . . All this is from God, who reconciled us to himself through Christ, and has given us the ministry of reconciliation. . . . So we are ambassadors for Christ, since God is making God's appeal through us . . ." (2 Corinthians 5:17–20).

The mission of forgiveness as Christians have understood it since Paul's ministry to the gentiles goes out to all humans—to neighbors near and far, even to neighbors that are enemies. As a reconciling mission it incorporates the call to respond to God's creative love, hear God's commandments to love, accept God's forgiving love, and make visible the new forgiveness offered by Jesus Christ. It is therefore a mission informed by a universalist love, aimed at reconciliation, forged in the hope of new relationship with God and among all human persons. Yet forgiveness is a complex concept (as we have seen), and the concept of Christian forgiveness bears further analysis. In particular, issues of context, conditionality or unconditionality, and relationship to justice are, in our efforts to understand this form of forgiveness, neither trivial nor moot. A biblical query may sharpen or intensify some of these issues and perhaps even the nature of the mission.

Forgive Them: In the Fourth Gospel, the words recorded of Jesus when he gives the mission of forgiveness to his disciples are these: "As the Father has sent me, so I send you. . . . Receive the Holy Spirit. If you forgive the sins of any, they are forgiven them; if you retain the sins of any, they are retained" (John 20:21–23). This text has sometimes been interpreted, and often popularly understood by Christians, to refer to the granting of authority to judge, and out of this the power to forgive or not, to open the gates of heaven or to keep them closed. Sometimes it is put together with Matthew 16:18–20: "On this rock I will build my church. . . . I will give you the keys of the kingdom of heaven, and whatever you bind on earth will be bound in heaven, and whatever you loose on earth will be loosed in heaven." Together the texts have been thought by many to establish not only authority to judge on the part of the disciples of Jesus, but beyond this also a structure for authority in the Christian community that followed.

But what if there is another meaning to this text in the Gospel attributed to John? It is after all not like Matthew 16 where there is reference apparently to technical rabbinic procedures. And the situation is very different—with now the risen Christ commissioning his disciples to carry on his own ministry of forgiveness. What, then, if the primary meaning of the text is not that the disciples of Jesus, and the Christian community, are to sit in judgment on individuals and groups, but that they are to *forgive* and thereby to *free* people, and if they do not do so, the word of God is somehow blocked, left silent? What if the force of the mission is this: "If you forgive them, they are forgiven and freed; but if you do not forgive them, they remain bound. So then, *forgive* them, because if you do not, they will remain bound and unfree."

But can such an interpretation hold? Is this indeed the truth that Jesus said the Spirit would teach in his name, reminding his followers of all he had said? Jesus himself, after all, did make judgments; he did not offer instant forgiveness to all. Yet those he judged and challenged seem to have been only the self-righteous, those whose hearts were hardened with their own self-assurance, those who recognized no need to drink of new waters or ask for greater mercy. Others—so many great sinners—Jesus did not examine for the worthiness or perfection of their repentance; he simply forgave them when they approached him. He rejected no one—not tax collectors and not adulterers; not Peter, who had his troubles; not James and John who needed a long time to learn humility; not any of those who betrayed him; not even Judas, with whom he shared a life and a table (and who today may shine in heaven as a blazing testimony to the power of a forgiven love).

It is difficult not to hear in Matthew's Gospel the multitude of "judgment" texts.[22] Yet these have more to do with judgment as a dramatic preliminary to entering the reign of God than they do with Jesus's own mode of judging. And it is Matthew who reports Jesus's response to his critics (those who questioned his eating with tax collectors and "sinners"): "Go and learn what this means: 'I desire mercy, not sacrifice.' For I have come to call not the righteous but sinners" (Mt 9:13). John's Gospel has little about judging, although judgment takes place in some circumstances simply because Jesus is present. Luke is clearly more concerned with forgiveness than judgment. As part of the Sermon on the Plain, Luke has Jesus listing all the ways in which God is merciful, and bidding his hearers to imitate God: "Be merciful just as your Father is merciful" (Lk 6:36). And Jesus follows this with: "Do not judge, and you will not be judged; do not condemn, and you will not be condemned. Forgive, and you will be forgiven" (Lk 6:37–38; also Mt 7:1–2). Beyond even this form of conditionality, and in the context of describing Jesus's mission of forgiveness, Paul proclaims that ". . . in Christ God was reconciling the world to himself, *not counting their trespasses against them*, and entrusting the message of reconciliation to us" (1 Cor 5:19, my italics).

Many texts in the Gospels and in the writings of Paul could be gathered to show either that Jesus came to forgive and not to judge, or that Jesus took the matter of judgment extremely seriously. Moreover, in many cases, one and the same text can be interpreted both ways. I am not so much interested, however, in once and for all adjudicating the importance of judgment as part of forgiveness versus the importance of forgiveness offered seemingly without judgment.[23] Clearly anyone who forgives another must have some knowledge of why forgiveness is relevant and needed—some knowledge and assessment, therefore, of the wrongdoing that is being forgiven. But just as clearly, when "judgment" becomes an overall "judgmentalism," it drains the meaning of forgiveness, obscuring the potential for the freeing of others from the burden of their offenses and dissipating the power of forgiveness for the restoration of relationships. Hence, my ultimate point here is that the mission of forgiveness—the mission given through the power of Jesus's Spirit to those who follow him—is a mission of forgiveness more than it is one of judgment.

No doubt it is the social as well as individual context that ought to determine to some extent where emphases should be placed. In a world marked by conflict and fear, by violence and hatred, the message of forgiveness will hold judgment and forgiveness together—in part prophetic against perpetrators of harm, in part offering a "new creation" because of the ministry of forgiveness. Among people oppressed and dominated, the message will refuse to "break the bruised reed" by burdening it too much with judgment. But when spoken to the powerful, if they care little for the poor and the marginalized, the message may come like lightning, striking the hearts of the agents of misery. At the same time, the message may give light to those who struggle for justice, and offer hope in forgiveness even to those who have caused the injustice.

What does all of this mean for the significance of forgiveness in our world? Can experiences of forgiveness really bear witness to a ministry of forgiveness—given by God in Jesus

Christ and empowered by the Spirit? This is too large a question to be resolved here, but it suggests preliminary questions to be addressed in furthering our understanding of forgiveness. The first of these is about our experiences of forgiveness—both of being-forgiven and forgiving—and the insights they suggest. What, for example, "happens" when forgiveness is either given or received?

Meanings of Forgiveness

Human persons experience forgiveness, or the need for forgiveness, in many ways. Whether we are harmed by or we have harmed another, our interest in forgiveness depends on how much we care about the other, about our own selves, about the relationship that has been damaged or lost. It is easy to understand the necessity and the role of forgiving when treasured personal relationships are at stake. We reach out to the one we love, participating in the restoration of the bond between us, by hoping for forgiveness, by offering forgiveness. Or at the very least, we wait patiently, holding on to the love and the hope that the relationship represents. In either case, our experience is different from simply despairing of any possibility of healing the breach—worn out from our trying or our waiting, taking a realistic view of what is impossible, or walking away in anger or disgust, shame or fear, irritation and indifference. But if restoration of the relationship and loving affirmation of the beloved Other are what we want, what do we do when we "forgive," and what happens to us and what do we do when we are "forgiven"?

When the situation is not one of person-to-person, individual-to-individual, forgiveness, how do we comprehend the necessity or possibility or even strategy for forgiving? Despite many thinkers' insistence that forgiveness can take place only between singular individuals, it is possible between individuals and groups, or even between one group and another. After all, in this era of forgiveness, it is not unusual for heads of state, leaders of world religions, owners of companies, to *ask for* forgiveness from institutions and whole populations, as well as from the individuals within them. It is perhaps not so usual for individuals to *offer* forgiveness to larger entities, but it seems thinkable at least. So, when we are harmed by or we harm an institution or a group, what can forgiveness mean at all? What would we be doing in such situations if we either forgave or were ourselves forgiven? Perhaps at its core, forgiveness is the same whether offered to or received from individuals or groups.[24]

A descriptive analysis of the experience of forgiveness yields something like the following. To forgive is above all not to be passive in the face of injury, betrayal, persecution, abuse. Forgiveness may, in fact, be one of the most active responses possible in the face of whatever sort of breach occurs in human relationships. It is linguistically a "performative"—an utterance or gesture that signifies an action which accomplishes or at least aims to accomplish something. Moreover, to forgive is a complex action, for it is a choice to act in a certain way in regard to one's own self as well as in regard to the recipient of one's forgiveness. Put simply, forgiveness is a decision to "let go" of something within one's self, and to "accept" anew the one by whom we have been harmed. But what do we "let go" of? In regard to ourselves, we do not (and ought not) let go of our sense of justice, nor a sense of our own dignity as a person (I shall return to this particular issue shortly). Yet in forgiving another, we do let go (at least partially) of something *in* ourselves—perhaps anger, a desire to win in some conflict, resentment, perhaps building-blocks of stored up pain. And we let go (at least partially) of something *of* ourselves—perhaps our self-protectedness, our selves as desiring renewed self-statement in the face of misjudgment or exploitation by another. In regard to the other—that is, the recipient of our forgiveness—we choose to "accept" the other once again, to affectively sustain and renew our loving affirmation of the other, to be again in *unio affectus* with the other by whom we have been wronged and to whom we offer our forgiveness.

To fathom our experiences of forgiving—whether by gaining insight into our reasons to forgive or into the elements of the experience itself—it is useful to consider also our experiences of being-forgiven. Being-forgiven, like forgiving, involves action, in this case by the recipient of forgiveness. The action is again complex, including both "acceptance" and "letting go." If anything is actually going to "happen" in response to the offer of forgiveness, the one who can be-forgiven must choose to receive the offer and to accept the one who offers. There can be no being-forgiven without this. The form of acceptance involved is acceptance of the "word" of the one forgiving, believing in the genuineness of the intention to forgive. In the recipient it requires a "letting go" not only of shame and all that it might entail, but also of the objections and fears that may arise in the one to-be-forgiven. Since the full efficacy of forgiveness has to do with relationship, it will not "take," it cannot accomplish its purpose, unless it is actively received. When we recognize our own responsibility for injuring another, marring a relationship, losing what we treasured in the other and in our way of being with the other, we are afraid of the future which we had taken for granted and in which we had hoped. To experience being-forgiven, then, is to experience being-accepted and affectively affirmed, in spite of ourselves. To repeat: accepting forgiveness is an action on our part—not just a passive forgetting of our offense, but a choice to accept being-forgiven. It generates relief in the recipient, but more than this, joy and gratitude that his or her failure has not finally broken the bonds of friendship, colleagueship, or family. The greater the infraction and the realization of its gravity, the greater the possibility of gratitude and a new or renewed love in response. One who has been forgiven much, as Jesus observed, loves more than one who has been forgiven only a little (Lk 7:41–47); or at least that is the possibility opened to us when we are indeed forgiven.

Although we learn what it means to be-forgiven within human relationships, the potentially paradigmatic experience for humans is the experience of being-forgiven by God. To experience the forgiveness of God is to experience one's self accepted by the incomprehensible source of one's existence and life, accepted even without becoming wholly innocent, without being completely turned around in one's ways; accepted even "while we still were sinners" (Rom. 5:8). Some human persons in history (persons like Paul, Augustine, Martin Luther) bear witness to this out of their own overwhelming experience of divine forgiveness. They testify, too, to their need to respond—in acceptance, letting go of their doubts and objections, actively surrendering to unconditional forgiveness and love. They call their responses trust, or faith, or gratitude, or love. Others whose life stories are less dramatic or well-known report similar experiences of forgiveness and response. Still others hope in such grace, and if they are poets, they sometimes give us language for our own understanding. The often wry and ever-enigmatic Emily Dickinson is among the latter, speculating about another world but translating her language into this one, foreshadowing an ultimate experience of which she has only inklings: receiving and accepting eternal Acceptance:

> I think just how my shape will rise—
> When I shall be *"forgiven"*—
> Till Hair—and Eyes—and timid Head—
> Are *out of sight*—in Heaven—

> I think just how my lips will weigh—
> With shapeless—quivering—prayer—
> That you—*so late*—*"Consider" me*—
> The *"Sparrow" of your Care*—
>
> I mind me of that Anguish—sent—
> *Some* drifts were moved away—
> Before my simple bosom—broke—
> And why not *this*—*if they*?
>
> And so I con that thing—*"forgiven"*—
> Until—delirious—borne—
> By my long bright—and *longer*—*trust*
> I *drop* my Heart—*unshriven*![25]

Others, like philosophers Jankélévitch and Derrida, appear to have hints not only of the need for divine forgiveness—for sins that cannot be forgiven "in this world" or offenses that are "on a human scale unforgivable." They also search for an understanding of "unconditional" forgiveness that may be possible only from God. If, for example, Derrida's concept of unconditional forgiveness (which is not unlike what can be found in Jankélévitch's writing before him) resonates anywhere, it ought to resonate here. In Dickinson's rhetorical interpretation, there is a kind of "pure" forgiveness, not a deal-maker, not one that lessens the force, desire, impetus, movement, appeal "that forgiveness be granted." It is unconditional, uncompromised by any form of negotiation, or anything else except God's desire and decision to forgive—individuals as well as whole peoples. It is, in alternate language, wholly other-centered even as it responds to human creatures God has made. The question of whether such unconditional other-centered forgiveness can be granted also by humans to humans, may be lodged more fruitfully in the mysterious ways that Christians and others experience and understand, however obscurely, the willingness, decision, and desire of God to heal creation through the graced agency of God's creatures.

But when we turn back now to experiences of human forgiving and being-forgiven, it helps to ponder something like a "dropping of the heart" that is active surrender, letting go of, whatever would bind us to past injuries inflicted on us by others, or whatever would prevent our acceptance of the new life held out to us in the forgiveness of those we have injured. In both there is a letting go of our very selves, a kenosis, that alone frees us to become ourselves; and there is an acceptance, an affective affirmation and *unio affectus*, of the one to be forgiven and the one who forgives. "Dropping our hearts," surrendering our selves, in forgiveness or in trust of being-forgiven, is the beginning choice that makes renewed relationships possible. It comes full circle in the mutuality that restored relationships promise.

One more question remains to be attended to, however, in our "preliminary" questions of forgiveness. It has been framed frequently thus: What if those who injure us continue to injure us? Whether knowing or not knowing "what they do," what if there is no regret or remorse, no willingness or ability to accept our forgiveness? What if the perpetrators of oppression believe their actions are justified—by whatever twisted stereotyping, judging, stigmatizing? There are, of course, countless situations like these in which injury is ongoing; abuse, violence, and exploitation do not stop. How, then, is forgiveness possible, and what would be its point? How shall we forgive in the context of the new killing fields of the century, this era's tangled webs of enslavement and new levels of destitution? In regard to *current* oppressors, must our focus be not on forgiveness, but on justice? Not on "dropping our hearts," but on a struggle against the evils that cry out to heaven for change?

The challenge in each of these questions is not to be taken lightly. I want to argue, however, that even in situations where injustices prevail, where the rights of individuals and groups continue to be violated, the disposition in the heart of the oppressed and violated (as well as those who stand in solidarity with them) ought to include (insofar as this is possible[26]) forgiveness. Or more precisely, it ought to include a "readiness" to forgive. To argue this in no way contradicts a need for resistance—against exploitation, abuse, or whatever threat there is to the human physical, relational, or moral integrity of others. If we think that forgiveness all by itself is a sufficient antidote to injustice, this is a mistake. But if we think that struggles for justice are sufficient, no matter what is in our hearts, this, too, is a mistake. The challenge and the call to forgiveness in situations of ongoing humanly inflicted evil and suffering is a call to forgive even those we must continue to resist. Forgiveness in such situations is what I call "anticipatory" forgiveness.

Anticipatory Forgiveness: The Greatest Challenge of All?

Forgiving and being-forgiven have nothing to do with tolerating grave wrongs, or (as I indicated earlier) with being passive in the face of massive (or even small) injustices. Neither the forgiveness offered by God in Jesus Christ, nor the forgiveness that can be a graced and glorious human action, is to be equated with "premature reconciliation" or a covering over of exploitation and ongoing violence, large or small. Christian and even human forgiveness can include a radical "No!" to the world as a place of injurious conflict, gross injustice, and needless destruction. Indeed, forgiveness, and a Christian obligation to forgiveness, can require that we resist the forces of evil until we can do no more. Nevertheless, an attitude of forgiveness, the disposition of heart required for forgiving and being-forgiven, does entail that we not return lies for lies, violence for violence, domination as a supposed remedy for domination. In relation to such evils, a stance of forgiveness can mean "Never again!"

Anticipatory forgiveness shares the characteristics of any human forgiving. That is, it involves a letting go within one's self of whatever prevents a fundamental acceptance of the other, despite the fact that the other is the cause of one's injuries. It is grounded in a basic respect for the other as a person, for what Derrida calls the "sacredness at the heart of the human." For Christians, it can be explicitly grounded, too, in love for the other as held in being and forgiven by God. It does not mean blinding oneself to the evil that is done to oneself or to others. It does not mean passive acquiescence or silence when it comes to naming the injury that is imposed, or the perpetrator of the injury. It does not mean failing to protect victims or to struggle with all one's might to prevent the "breaking of the bruised reed." It does mean being ready to accept the injurer, yearning that he or she turn in sorrow to whoever has been injured; it means waiting until the time that the enemy may yet become a friend. It is "anticipatory" not because there is as yet no disposition for acceptance and love, but because it cannot be fulfilled until the one who is forgiven (the perpetrator) acknowledges the injury and becomes able to recognize and accept, in turn, a forgiving embrace. This is not to make anticipatory forgiveness "conditional"; on the contrary, anticipatory forgiveness comes closer to "unconditional" forgiveness than most forms of human forgiveness. It can be truly other-centered, though until it is received by the other, it cannot as forgiveness be finally fulfilled.

Perhaps nowhere is the challenge and call to anticipatory forgiveness more clearly issued to Christians than in the community of the church. It is here that the moral imperative comes forth to love one's enemies. It is here that grace should be passed from one to the other, making possible the melting of hearts and the acceptance of friend and enemy, neighbor and stranger alike. It is here that Christians are marked by the encomium, "See how they love one another." It is here where Christians can learn of the model of God's anticipatory as well as infinitely actual love and forgiveness—whether as expressed in the parable of the "Prodigal Son" (or "Merciful Father") where the son is awaited and greeted with open arms, seemingly without judgment, seemingly with only yearning desire for the son's return; or as depicted in the story of salvation historically enacted in the forgiveness of Jesus Christ, which holds out for our recognition and acceptance the forgiveness of God.

It may be that forgiveness, the very possibility of forgiveness, dies in countless human assaults on individuals and groups within countless human relationships. Yet it remains, or can remain, at least for some, a matter of hope. It could have been that forgiveness died in the death camps of Germany or on the slaughtering hills of Rwanda. But it did not, at least not for everyone—although its power for holding human lives together was shattered, crucified, in such terrible ways. Rather than the end of the history of forgiveness, contemporary crimes (great or small) against humanity may have—as Derrida suggested and Jankélévitch finally agreed might be the case—brought unprecedented urgency to its possible new beginnings.

Notes

Since this essay focuses on questions of love and Christian ethics, I dedicate it to my longtime colleague and friend Gene Outka. I indicate in the essay particular writings of his that have helped to inform my own insights on the issues of Christian love and forgiveness. This dedication carries with it my tribute and my great gratitude.

1. Multiple interpretations and commentaries on the place of forgiveness in the Jewish tradition mark the history of rabbinical texts. For an intriguing and succinct, though not uncontroversial, overview of a pattern discernible in the Hebrew Bible, see Jonathan Sacks, *The Dignity of Difference: How to Avoid the Clash of Civilizations* (New York: Continuum Publishing Co, 2002), 182–88. An elegant contemporary introduction to and translation of the liturgy for Yom Kippur can be found in Rabbi Jules Harlow, ed., *Mahzor for Rosh Hashanah and Yom Kippur: A Prayer Book for the Days of Awe* (New York: Rabbinical Assembly, 1972), 325–783.

2. For a brief but pointed English introduction to themes in Islam relevant to forgiveness, see Laleh Bakhtiar, "Becoming a Fair and Just Person: Sufism and Mental Health," *Park Ridge Center Bulletin* 25 (Jan–Feb, 2002).

3. Important religious writings include: Miroslav Volf, *Free of Charge: Giving and Forgiving in a Culture Stripped of Grace* (Grand Rapids, MI: Zonvervan, 2005); Donald W. Shriver, *An Ethic for Enemies: Forgiveness in Politics* (New York: Oxford University Press, 1995); Desmond Mpilo Tutu, *No Future Without Forgiveness* (New York: Doubleday, 1999); Raymond G. Helmick and Rodney L. Peterson, eds., *Forgiveness and Reconciliation: Religion, Public Policy, and Conflict Transformation* (Philadelphia: Templeton Foundation Press, 2001). For contributions from other fields, see for example: Robert D. Enright and Joanna North, eds., *Exploring Forgiveness* (Madison, WI: University of Wisconsin Press, 1998); Martha Minow, *Between Vengeance and Forgiveness: Facing History after Genocide and Mass Violence* (Boston: Beacon Press, 1998); Herbert W. Helm, Jonathan R. Cook, and John M. Berecz, "The Implications of Conjunctive and Disjunctive Forgiveness for Sexual Abuse," *Pastoral Psychology* 54 (September 2005): 23–34; Loren Toussaint and Jon R. Webb, "Gender Differences in the Relationship Between Empathy and Forgiveness," *Journal of Social Psychology* 145 (2005): 673–85; Erwin Staub, et.al., "Healing, Reconciliation, Forgiving and the Prevention of Violence After Genocide or Mass Killing: An Intervention and its Experimental Evaluation in Rwanda," *Journal of Social and Clinical Psychology* 24 (2005): 297–334; Steven J. Sandage, Peter C. Hill, and Henry C. Vang, "Toward a Multicultural Positive Psychology: Indigenous Forgiveness and Hmong Culture," *The Counseling Psychologist* 31 (2003): 564–92; Teresa Godwin Phelps, *Scattered Voices: Language, Violence, and the Work of Truth* (Philadelphia: University of Pennsylvania Press, 2004).

4. Hannah Arendt, *The Human Condition* (Chicago: University of Chicago Press, 1958), 240. Arendt elsewhere acknowledges that the cumulative effect of "commonplace" offenses can constitute enormous evil. See her *Eichmann in Jerusalem: A Report on the Banality of Evil*, revised edition (New York: Penguin Books, 1965).

5. Arendt, *Human Condition*, 240.

6. In addition to well-known claims that widespread oppression and killing are in themselves unforgivable crimes against humanity, contemporary psychological studies conclude that what counts as "unforgivable" is not only context-relative, but relative to the particular experiences of individuals—and the level of their traumatization. Practically speaking, an injury is "unforgivable" when it assaults the very worldview, fundamental belief systems, of the victim. See Beverly Flanagan, "Forgivers and the Unforgivable," in *Exploring Forgiveness*, ed. Robert D. Enright and Joanna North (Madison, WI: University of Wisconsin Press, 1998), 95–105. For significant theological background to interpretations of such experiences, see Gene Outka, "On Harming Others," *Interpretation* 34 (October, 1980): 381–93; and Jennifer Erin Beste, *God and the Victim: Traumatic Intrusions on Grace and Freedom* (Oxford: Oxford University Press, 2007).

7. Jankélévitch, "Shall We Pardon Them?," trans. Ann Hobart, in *Critical Inquiry* 22 (Spring, 1996): 558; also cited in Jacques Derrida, "To Forgive: The Unforgivable and the Imprescriptible," in John D. Caputo, Mark Dooley, and Michael Scanlon, eds., *Questioning God* (Bloomington, IN: Indiana University Press, 2001), 30.

8. Jankélévitch, "Shall We Pardon Them?": 567; originally in Jankélévitch, *L'imprescriptible: Pardonner? Dans l'honneur et la dignité* (Paris: Seuil, 1986). Jankélévitch offers a different view in an earlier work, *Forgiveness*, trans. Andrew Kelley (Chicago: University of Chicago Press, 2005); originally published as *Le Pardon* (Paris: Aubier-Montaigne, 1967). As Derrida later points out, these two works are inconsistent, since *Le Pardon* does allow forgiveness of the otherwise unforgivable crimes in the Holocaust on the condition that forgiveness is at least asked for by the perpetrators and appropriate remorse is exhibited. Derrida also notes that at the end of his life Jankélévitch acknowledged that perhaps the history of forgiveness did not have to end with the Holocaust (a statement occasioned by correspondence with a young German who did, in effect, ask for forgiveness). Even then, however, Jankélévitch said of himself that it was too late for him to forgive. See Derrida, "To Forgive," 38–41.

9. Derrida, "To Forgive," 21–51.

10. "Radical evil" in the sense in which Jankélévitch and Derrida intend it is not to be equated with the use of the term in, for example, Kant, for whom "radical" refers to the "root" of all moral evil, not to its "monstrosity." See Immanuel Kant, *Religion Within the Limits of Reason Alone*, trans. Theodore M. Greene and Hoyt H. Hudson (New York: Harper Torchbooks, 1960), I:15–39.

11. These are readily recognizable as conditions incorporated in some Christian traditions of "confession," or the "Sacrament of Reconciliation." They are also visible in many Western legal and judicial processes.

12. Derrida, "On Forgiveness," in *On Cosmopolitanism and Forgiveness*, trans. Mark Dooley and Michael Hughes (New York: Routledge, 2001), 27–60.

13. Very rarely does Derrida refer to the duality of these two moral imperatives as "paradoxical." He does so, though somewhat indirectly, in "To Forgive," 30.

14. Derrida, "To Forgive," 28.

15. Ibid. Derrida refers to this as a "hyperbolic ethics," or "ethics beyond ethics," a concept that Jankélévitch had also introduced in his first major work on forgiveness, *Le Pardon*, but moved away from in *"Shall We Pardon Them?"*

16. My articulation of this pattern needs here to be extremely brief, hence drastically elliptical. It therefore risks serious challenges not only to its details but to the pattern as such. Nonetheless, it is necessary to attempt something, however brief, that situates stages of love, command, divine forgiveness, and human forgiveness in a way that the meaning of the last is tied to and held within the meaning of the previous three. Thus will the connection between Christian love and forgiveness be relevant to my claims about forgiveness.

17. Karl Rahner, "Experiences of a Catholic Theologian," in *The Cambridge Companion to Karl Rahner*, ed. Declan Marmion and Mary E. Hines (New York: Cambridge University Press, 2005), 303.

18. It is not possible here to clarify adequately the relationships among these loves (for God, self, and neighbor), although understanding them is crucial to discerning the moral questions they entail. Here the work of Gene Outka offers stunningly comprehensive and profound analyses and insights. See especially Outka, *Agape* (New Haven: Yale University Press, 1972); and Outka, "Universal Love and Impartiality," in

The Love Commandments: Essays in Christian Ethics and Moral Philosophy, ed. Edmund N. Santurri and William Werpehowski (Washington, DC: Georgetown University Press, 1992), 1–103.

19. I am rendering these beliefs in Christian terms, though I do not exclude ways of articulating a central part of their meaning in other terms, by those whose lives, situations, and traditions have been revelatory in other symbols and terms.

20. For a telling critique and reconstruction of the Christian doctrine of atonement, see Martha Schull Gilliss, "Resurrecting the Atonement," in *Feminist and Womanist Essays in Reformed Dogmatics*, ed. Amy Plantinga Pauw and Serene Jones (Louisville, KY: Westminster John Knox Press, 2006), 125–38.

21. See, for example, Walter Kasper, "The Church as a Place of Forgiveness," *Communio* 16 (Summer, 1989): 162.

22. On one count, there are sixty pericopes regarding judgment in the Gospel of Matthew. See Thomas W. Buckley, *Seventy Times Seven: Sin, Judgment, and Forgiveness in Matthew* (Collegeville, MN: The Liturgical Press, 1991), 17.

23. I clearly take a different view, however, from those who make blame, judgment, and condemnation essential and even central to both secular and Christian notions of forgiveness, as for example Miroslav Volf appears to do. See Volf, *Free of Charge*, chap. 2. Nor do I suggest that it is only Christians who can free one another and others from guilt or fear or ignorance. I am trying both to broaden the call to forgive and to find in it a fuller meaning than the conditionality that Derrida thought so inadequate.

24. Although there are a growing number of excellent theories regarding the place of forgiveness in political and social life, the one that combines Christian and secular ethics most effectively is Donald W. Shriver's *An Ethic for Enemies*. The relevance of collective forgiveness to individual forgiveness is indicated in his insistence that "our teachers have to be the victims," 67.

25. Emily Dickinson, in *The Complete Poems of Emily Dickinson*, ed. Thomas H. Johnson (Boston: Little, Brown and Company, 1987), n. 237, italics original. Dickinson, of course, always found a profound ambiguity in the mystery of God, yet sustained a deep belief in the reality of God. I take this poem to express a profound trust in God, even without explicit "forgiveness." Biographers suggest that whatever "scandal" lurked in her life at some point, she did not regret her choices, but believed that she was a child, a "sparrow" of God, who loved as she could love.

26. "Ought" may be too strong a term here. By using it, I do not want to impose yet another burden on those who suffer under ongoing oppression of whatever kind. I simply mean that it is an appropriate disposition, one that can be freeing and strengthening, even under these circumstances. And there is the matter of the second love commandment, which I have been at least suggesting up to now can include an obligation to forgive. I do not want to back away from this. Yet I acknowledge fully that every obligation is tempered, and may even be waived, according to capacity and circumstance.

10

Agape as Self-Sacrifice

The Internalist View

EDMUND N. SANTURRI

> This is my commandment, that you love one another as I have loved you. No
> one has greater love than this, to lay down one's life for one's friends.
>
> —John 15:12–13

> Her last act was selfless, Christlike in laying down her life for her children.
>
> —Spoken of Sandy Hook Elementary School teacher Victoria Soto
> on the day of her funeral

HERE I OFFER A CONTENTIOUS PROPOSAL: Christian love is essentially *self-sacrifice*, however else that love must be described. More particularly, Christian love—*agape* in the most frequently employed New Testament designation—marks a quality of character, a theological virtue, one incorporating precisely an agent's disposition to sacrifice the interests of the self for the good of the neighbor, whatever else such love may say about the identity of the neighbor or the nature of the good in question.[1] Note especially that in this account, the relation between agape and self-sacrifice is *essential* rather than accidental, *necessary* rather than contingent, *intrinsic* rather than extrinsic. Christian love is not something else, which then *remains open* to self-sacrifice should the need for it arise fortuitously—as though such love in principle could do what it does or be what it is apart from self-sacrifice.[2] Neither is the relation between agape and self-sacrifice a matter simply of the former's conferring on the latter an "*instrumental* warrant" given conditions required in fact for meeting the ends that agape ratifies.[3] The connection between agape and self-sacrifice is not merely or centrally instrumental, not solely or primarily constituted by the fact that self-sacrifice can serve as a means to bringing about what is mandated by a Christian love conceived independently of such sacrifice. Rather self-sacrifice is *internal* to the concept of agape. Christian love *just is* the agent's disposition so to sacrifice the interests of the self for the sake of the neighbor. Without such disposition, there is no Christian love. Call this account the *internalist view of the relation between agape and self-sacrifice* or simply *the internalist view*.

This view is defensible, as I shall argue, on theological grounds but is also contentious because it collides with a range of contemporary accounts that deny an essential connection between agape and self-sacrifice. The worries stimulating these alternative accounts are manifold.[4] Among other things, it is said that defining Christian love as self-sacrifice (a) makes it

171

impossible to distinguish from the point of view of agape a morally commendable altruism from a morally pernicious servility; (b) makes agape irrelevant to the resolution of conflicts between second and third parties when in fact agape enjoins the agent's preference for innocent victims against unjust perpetrators;[5] (c) ignores the fact that in some instances, self-sacrifice is vicious rather than virtuous, for example, the case of the suicide terrorist or Nazi soldier who sacrifices his life for the cause;[6] (d) permits agape's exploitation as an ideological instrument of domination impeding rightful self-assertion by the unjustly oppressed against their unjust oppressors;[7] (e) leaves insufficient normative space for a theologically legitimate self-love;[8] (f) fails to account for the agapic deficiency in relations when agent sacrifice goes unreciprocated;[9] and (g) obscures Christian love's proper focus, which ought to be on the neighbor's good rather than on the agent's sacrifice.[10] Such concerns and others have prompted two general normative responses to construals of agape as self-sacrifice—either outright denial that self-sacrifice is ever a virtue (e.g., Mary Daly[11]) or, more typically, relegation of self-sacrifice to a subsidiary role in the general economy of love. Given the second strategy, self-sacrifice is instrumentally justified at best and that only to the degree it promotes what is required by genuine agape, which is understood essentially in terms other than agent sacrifice, for example, as equal and unconditional regard for the neighbor or full mutuality in the communion of persons.[12]

While these worries about self-sacrifice reflect significant normative concerns, the theoretical alternatives the worries generate fail to do full justice to the cruciform and kenotic normative patterns of the New Testament witness. Moreover, in rejecting for reasons typically cited and *tout court* an essential connection between agape and self-sacrifice, these alternative accounts miss the nuances of the internalist view proposed here.

As we shall see, the principal theological warrants for the internalist view are Christological, rooted specifically in theologies of the cross, atonement, and incarnation, and the scriptural locations of the warrants are predominantly Johannine and Pauline. Such predominance should not surprise, of course, since the most extensive and elaborate New Testament accounts of Christian love generally are found in Johannine and Pauline sources. Still, while the strongest biblical case for self-sacrificial love is Johannine and Pauline in inspiration, that case is also compatible with the larger New Testament witness and, indeed, is supported by key normative patterns of that larger witness. In any event, the argument I offer for the internalist view is part exegetical demonstration, part ethical defense of a normative line plausibly reconstructed from the relevant scriptural materials. The intended yield is a position that forges an essential connection between agape and self-sacrifice and meets standard theoretical objections to defining Christian love of neighbor in radically self-sacrificial terms.

Johannine Trajectories

In articulating the internalist view, I proceed inductively by identifying a range of relevant Johannine and Pauline motifs. I begin with the Johannine.[13] Centrally for the Johannine witness "God is love" (1 John 4:16), and whatever one makes of Trinitarian or proto-Trinitarian construals of that proposition, there is in the Johannine account intimate enough association between "Father" and "Son" in divinity to ground richly Christocentric renderings of agape. As the Son is one with the Father (John 10:30) and as the Word "was with God" and "was God" (John 1:1), Jesus, qua Son and incarnate Word, reveals the essential character of the love God is and thus the essential character of agape as such. That revelation is accomplished through Jesus's teaching and example. "Just as I have loved you," Jesus enjoins, "you also should love one another" (John 13:34), and the practical illustration leading to this injunction is Jesus's own action of washing his disciples' feet, an action resisted at first by Simon Peter as incommensurate with Jesus's dignity but presented finally by Jesus as an exemplum of loving behavior: "So if I, your Lord and Teacher, have washed your feet, you also ought to wash one another's feet. For I have set you an example, that you also should do as I have done to you" (John 13:14–15). Of course, Jesus's self-denying gesture here serves as a kind of proleptic emblem of his quintessentially loving act of atonement, his self-sacrificial acceptance of death on the Cross, an act that functions in the Johannine account as epistemic standard. "We know love by this, that he laid down his life for us" (1 John 3:16). And, "In this is love, not that we loved God but that he loved us and sent his Son to be the atoning sacrifice for our sins" (1 John 4:10). This supreme act of divine love provides the Christian additionally with warrant for loving behavior. "Since God loved us so much, we also ought to love one another" (1 John 4:11)—particularly, "we ought to lay down our lives for one another" (1 John 3:16). In Jesus's own summation, "This is my commandment, that you love one another as I have loved you. No one has greater love than this, to lay down one's life for one's friends" (John 15:12–13).

In the Johannine account, then, Jesus both exemplifies and enjoins love as self-sacrifice, and Christology is linked thereby to epistemic identification and normative justification of agape. That is, Jesus both reveals love's nature as self-sacrifice and affords justifying reasons for self-sacrificial behavior, reasons grounded either in the sheer fact of his divine injunctions to love or in his own loving action, which generates an obligation on the part of beneficiaries to respond in kind by loving one another in self-giving ways. But in the Johannine witness, Jesus not only exemplifies and enjoins love. He also empowers his disciples to love through his communication of the divine love incarnate in his loving action. Because of Jesus's own love shown to them, the disciples now can love one another in a way they could not have apart from Jesus's love. Incarnate love transmits "a new motive and power for the love command,"[14] a novel motivational impulse to sacrifice one's life for others.

This motivational impulse, or perhaps better, motivational complex, admits of rendering in ordinary moral-psychological terms even if the terms are implicit rather than explicit in the Johannine account. For instance, recognition or memory of Jesus's sacrifice for others inspires imitation, and gratitude for that sacrifice on one's own behalf or compassion for the one who bears the sacrifice stimulates reciprocation or response in kind. Yet for the Johannine, such moral-psychological descriptions must be taken finally as elaborations of a more basic theological or metaphysical claim, namely, that the motivational impulse to love signifies in its deepest reality the presence of divine love within the agent or the dwelling of the agent within that divine love. "God is love, and those who abide in love abide in God, and God abides in them" (1 John 4:16). Christologically put, in loving one another, the disciples abide in the love of Jesus, who abides in the love of the Father (John 15:10). It is this abiding in love that Jesus mediates as teacher and exemplar and that the Spirit sustains in the life of the Christian community after the Son has returned to the Father (John 14; 1 John 3:24, 4:13–16).

We can infer reasonably that this Johannine abiding in love is a spiritual state intimately connected with the disposition to perform self-sacrificial actions for the sake of the other. But neither the spiritual state nor the disposition is reducible to habitual action as such. A person might be in a loving state or so disposed to sacrifice—might "abide in love"—without having occasion for such sacrifice. Should the occasion arise, of course, agape will manifest itself as self-giving action. But the love that gives rise to the action is equivalent neither to the action itself nor to the empirically marked tendency toward the action. Rather, for John, agape designates centrally a loving spirit resident in or present to the agent, a spirit that motivates self-sacrificial action in the relevant contexts.[15] Johannine "abiding in love," then, marks primarily the agent's relation to that spirit and the most immediate consequence of that relation, the agent's empowered spiritual state, a quality of character constitutive of a kind of person, and only derivatively a kind of action or observed tendency toward a kind of action.[16] To say as much is not to deny that in the Johannine account human persons develop this loving character partly through habitual action informed and sustained by Christological memory, devotional practice, and communal pedagogy. Indeed, in moments one might be tempted to read the Johannine Jesus himself as a kind of Aristotelian, linking the cultivation of loving virtue to the formation of loving habit by loving practice: "If you keep my commandments, you will abide in my love, just as I have kept my Father's commandments and abide in his love" (John 15:10). But whatever the score on that matter, for John abiding in love or love as virtue is not just another way of talking about loving practice or even the inferred tendency toward loving practice as certain behaviorist accounts of virtue might insist.[17] We shall see later on that this distinction between character or spiritual state and action or practice is particularly important for deflecting certain criticisms of love as self-sacrifice.

At this point, however, it might be objected that the stress on self-sacrifice in the account elaborated thus far is misleading. "[In John's Gospel,] the mission of the Father's love toward the world begins and continues with self-sacrificing love, but it marks its success by mutual love, and that is John's focus both in proclamation and in exhortation."[18] After all, the Johannine Jesus instructs his disciples to love *one another* and commends as love's greatest expression laying down one's life *for one's friends*, both the instruction and the commendation accentuating "mutual love within the community of faith, not 'unilateralism.'"[19] That mutuality indicates particularly the interest of Johannine love in reciprocal response, a fact obscured if not rendered unintelligible by defining that love as self-sacrifice. It is better to say, according to the present objection, that Johannine love identifies a relation among persons in community, a relation marked by mutual giving and receiving. Where the giving is one-sided and unreciprocated, that is something less than Johannine love. Thus self-sacrifice sans phrase falls short of the Johannine love ideal.[20]

But as Gene Outka has observed generally against certain mutualist views of agape, to hope for response in kind as love's "ideal fruition" is neither to expect such response necessarily nor, more important, to condition one's own loving initiative on an anticipated response.[21] Implied by Outka's observation is that sincerely altruistic motivations are fully compatible in principle with genuine aspirations to reciprocity, and that seems right. One might be prepared to sacrifice for the other come what may, all the while hoping for mutual relationship. Accordingly, it is reasonable to hold both that Johannine love is essentially a disposition to self-sacrifice and that such love seeks reciprocal community as ideal outcome. Moreover, whatever normative role is assigned mutuality in the Johannine perspective, it would be implausible to suggest that a self-sacrificial attitude gone unreciprocated cannot by the very lack of reciprocation count as Johannine *love*. To take the paradigm case for John, the loving self-sacrifice of the Father and Son certainly retains its identity *as love* even when offered to a world (John 3:16) that meets the sacrifice with hatred (John 15:18–25). Similar considerations apply to love within the community of discipleship. Jesus *loves* Peter, in this moral cosmos, despite Peter's denial of him, though love's hope for reciprocity is impeded provisionally by that denial (John 18:25–27). Neither does certification of Jesus's love for Peter *as love* await Peter's eventual reciprocation or action in kind. To be sure, Peter's denial does mark a failure to love, but the failure is Peter's, not Jesus's, and the dereliction precisely is Peter's unwillingness *to lay down his life* for his friend (John 13:36–38).[22]

Pauline Trajectories

We have seen that the Johannine doctrine of incarnation plays a *formal* role in the Johannine rendering of agape inasmuch as the doctrine authorizes Jesus as unique teacher, exemplar, and progenitor of love in the world. Since, for John, God is love and Jesus is divinity incarnate, Jesus's words and actions in the world are definitive and generative of love. More particularly, Jesus, as incarnate deity, reveals, exemplifies, validates, and empowers love as self-sacrifice. Still, while Johannine incarnation doctrine establishes Jesus's supreme authority and power in love's domain, the doctrine *in itself* seems not to determine or shape the meaning of Johannine agape apart from Jesus's explicit instruction and example in the world. Rather, for John, love is established *as self-sacrifice* precisely because Jesus qua incarnate God *teaches and exemplifies love as self-sacrifice in the world.* There is, in other words, no clear indication in John that the sheer fact of incarnation, of God's becoming human, presents *in itself* an act of sacrifice revelatory of love's essential nature. For such a *substantive* connection between incarnation and agape *made explicit*, one must look to Pauline theology and particularly to Paul's "kenotic" Christology.[23]

That Christology emerges famously in Paul's Philippians, an epistle addressed to a Christian community marked by internal dissension, the apparent consequence of unidentified opposition from without (Phil. 1:28). Paul urges the Philippians to set aside their differences (Phil. 2:14, 4:2); to "be of the same mind, having the same love, being of full accord and of one mind" (Phil. 2:2); to abandon egocentric or prideful preoccupation; and more, to adopt an altruistic attitude utterly unqualified by self-concern: "Do nothing from selfish ambition or conceit, but in humility regard others as better than yourselves. Let each of you look not to your own interests, but to the interests of others" (Phil. 2:3–4). To assume the loving disposition commended is to have "the same mind . . . that was in Christ Jesus who, though he was in the form of God, did not regard equality with God as something to be exploited, but emptied himself [*heauton ekenosen*], taking the form of a slave, being born in human likeness" (Phil. 2:5–7). This divine *emptying—kenosis—*is understood best not as a construct that explains the incarnation metaphysically (i.e., as in one strain of "kenotic theology," Christ's literally emptying himself of divine properties or divinity as such) but rather as a metaphor that captures vividly the moral and spiritual attitudes of humility and self-renunciation reflected in that incarnation.[24] In becoming human for humanity's sake, Christ empties himself of concern for what is rightfully his—the full "prerogatives" of divinity.[25] Incarnational kenosis is then in Pauline theology a prototype of love as self-sacrifice for the good of the neighbor. To be Christianly loving is to assume the kenotic disposition, to "let the same mind be in you that was in Christ Jesus" (Phil. 2:5).

Thus, incarnation doctrine shapes the normative content of agape in Paul's Philippians.[26] But even in Philippians, divine *kenosis* reaches beyond incarnational to cruciform expression: "Being found in human form, he humbled himself and became obedient to the point of death on a cross" (Phil. 2:8).[27] And more generally, Pauline theology finds love's prototype, rationale, and empowerment not only in incarnation but also in Christ's atoning sacrificial death: "God proves his love for us in that while we still were sinners Christ died for us" (Rom. 5:8). For Christian believers, of course, that sacrificial atonement along with Christ's resurrection yields the benefit of salvation but also the reality of a new life for love.

Christians are "justified by his blood" (Rom. 5:9; also, 3:24–25) through "faith" (Rom. 5:1, 3:25); in baptism, their old selves, enslaved to sin, *die* with Christ and their new selves, released from sin for sanctification (Rom. 6:22), *rise* with Christ (Rom. 6:3–11). These new selves are beings into whose hearts God's love is infused (literally "poured") by way of the Holy Spirit (Rom. 5:5). Through faith and baptism, then, Christians are liberated from sin into morally empowered lives marked by radically new prospects for kenotic service. Thus, as is often remarked, Paul's moral exhortations delicately and intricately combine imperative and indicative, prescription and description. In urging to love, Paul is saying: *Burnish fully in sanctification what you now are in substance—justified and faithful kenotic selves, the gifted consequence of Christ's incarnation, sacrificial death, and resurrection.*

These theological convictions frame Paul's love casuistry, which illuminates further the meaning of Pauline agape by identifying concrete expressions of kenotic virtue, including particular instances of the disposition to surrender or waive prerogative modeled on divine kenosis. As illustration, consider Paul's exhortations on eating "unclean" (unkosher) foods (Rom. 14–15:6) or meat sacrificed to idols (1 Cor. 8, 10–11:1).[28] Given the principles of Pauline theology, such eating is intrinsically a matter of religious indifference—*adiaphoron*—unless tied to pagan temple communal meals or other worship practices that compromise devotion to the one true God or Christ as Lord (1 Cor. 11:14–23, 8:6.). After all, idols refer to nothing real, and thus, food sacrificed to them is not transformed in any spiritually significant way (1 Cor. 10:19, 8:4, 8). Moreover, Jesus taught "that nothing is unclean in itself" (Rom. 14:14). Consequently, Christians in principle are at liberty to eat unkosher foods and foods sacrificed to idols either purchased on the open market or offered by an unbelieving host "without raising any question on the ground of conscience, for 'the earth and its fullness are the Lord's'" (1 Cor. 10:25–27). At the same time, some Christians with "weak" consciences mistakenly *believe* that eating such food defiles, and thus, if *they* eat that food, their consciences *are* defiled (1 Cor. 8:7). While nothing is unclean in itself, "it is unclean for anyone who thinks it unclean" (Rom. 14:14). Thus, those who know better and can eat with good conscience still should abstain in circumstances when eating might offend the weak or tempt them to violate *their* consciences (1 Cor. 10:28–29, 8:7–13). "'All things are lawful,' but not all things are beneficial. 'All things are lawful,' but not all things build up. Do not seek your own advantage, but that of the other" (1 Cor. 10:23–24). To seek one's own advantage on grounds of superior knowledge is spiritually prideful as well as egoistic. "Knowledge puffs up, but love builds up" (1 Cor. 8:1). Dissolve the pride and egoism in humility and self-giving, Paul urges. Surrender what is in some sense rightfully yours, the liberty or prerogative of eating certain foods, for the sake of the weak neighbor's spiritual welfare. Such is the particular determination of love (Rom. 14:13), a determination linked explicitly by Paul to Christ as kenotic exemplar: "We who are strong ought to put up with the failings of the weak, and not to please ourselves. Each of us must please our neighbor for the good purpose of building up the neighbor. For Christ did not please himself; but, as it is written, 'The insults of those who insult you have fallen on me'" (Rom. 15:1–3; also, 1 Cor. 8:9–13).

This understanding of agape as the waiving of prerogative for the neighbor's sake goes a long way toward explaining Paul's love casuistry. Paul himself draws an analogy between forgoing eating prerogatives out of concern for the weak neighbor and his own waiving of the apostolic "right" to economic assistance, making "the gospel free of charge" to enhance the prospects of salvation (1 Cor. 9:4, 18–19; generally, 9:1–23). And the same principle is operative in Paul's urging the Corinthians to donate to the collection for the Jerusalem church. That contribution is not strictly mandated by Paul: "I do not say this as a command, but I am testing the genuineness of your love," and the testing is an invitation to follow the example of Christ, who, "though he was rich . . . for your sakes . . . became poor" (2 Cor. 8:8–9; generally, 2 Cor. 8–9). In this case, the call to Christian love is a call to sacrifice, "not reluctantly or under compulsion," the benefits and prerogatives of wealth for the sake of the neighbor in need. Of course, it would go too far to argue from such instances that the meaning of Pauline kenotic love *simply is* the disposition to set aside the self's *just* claims for altruistic reasons. Such a disposition for Paul seems reflective of a deeper inclination and resolve to sacrifice *any* personal interest or preference for the neighbor's sake.[29] Thus, in Philippians, Paul, writing from prison, contemplates the possibility of his own death, which he desires "to be with Christ, for that is far better" than continued existence. But he realizes that his remaining "in the flesh is more necessary" for the Philippians, and his accepting that fact combined with his warm reassurances that he will be with them again certainly strikes the Pauline agapic attitude even though it would be implausible to say that Paul believes he has a *just* claim to his own death (Phil. 1:21–26). Notwithstanding, for Paul, an important dimension of agape *is* that it urges the agent's surrender of just prerogative out of concern for the neighbor's well-being, and such surrender has as its central paradigms Christ's incarnation and sacrificial death.

Though the precise terms are different, the logic of the Pauline argument for love generally maps the logic of the Johannine argument for love described previously. For Paul, as for John, Christ both reveals love as self-sacrifice and warrants self-sacrificial behavior. In the Pauline account, Christ *reveals* love's character predominantly in the narratives of incarnation and atonement via cross, and Christ *warrants* self-sacrificial action centrally by prescribing it as law.[30] But as in John, there is in Paul at least the strong suggestion too that apart from Christ's injunctions embedded in his *law* of love, Christ's *act* of love in incarnation and atonement generates an obligation on the part of beneficiaries to respond in kind by sacrificing themselves for others—though the spirit of meeting the obligation should be one of joyful willing service and not grudging sense of indebtedness or oppressively bonded reciprocation. Christians are to imitate Christ's loving sacrifice, that is, out of grateful appreciation for what he has done on their behalf and—in the true spirit of *imitation*—out of genuine benevolence toward the neighbor.

Finally, for Paul, as for John, Christ does not simply reveal and warrant love. Christ also empowers love, though, as noted already, the empowerment in Paul's case is tied distinctively to baptismal transformation. What baptism brings forth is a new disposition to sacrifice for the good of the neighbor, a disposition that reflects at the deepest metaphysical level a spiritual state of the agent variously described by Paul but typically designated as "living in Christ" or "living in the Spirit" (Rom. 8).[31] Indeed, this living in Christ or the Spirit stands as the Pauline analogue to John's abiding in love. Like the Johannine "abiding in," Paul's "living in" comprehends a motivational complex that is reasonably associated with ordinary moral-psychological states (e.g., gratitude, inspiration, compassion, empathy) but finally is not reducible to such states. Rather, "living in Christ" or "in the Spirit" marks fundamentally for Paul a spiritual quality of the agent's *being*, a quality that expresses itself as self-sacrificial *doing* in the appropriate contexts but is something more than such doing in such contexts and something more than the ordinary moral-psychological motivations linked with such doing. In sum, love for Paul is a virtue of character, a disposition connected to a kenotic power indicative of a divine reality—Christic and pneumatic—present in or to the agent transformed by grace through faith in baptism.

Overall, this account of Pauline kenotic love is traditional and resists especially certain contemporary revisionist readings. According to one such reading, offered by Anna Mercedes, it may be mistaken to interpret Philippians 2:5–11 primarily as an ethical commendation of self-emptying. Instead Paul's invocation of the kenotic hymn may have been "pastoral"—to offer hope to a divided, troubled, and suffering community by reminding it of its "ontological" connection with Christ, whose obedient acceptance of humiliation and suffering in crucifixion was rewarded by God ultimately with cosmic exaltation and honor (Phil. 2:9). In this rendering, Paul was about a "kenotic identity politics" that "may have brought the strength of renewed identity to a vulnerable people," a "power of identity 'in Christ'" that reinforced "the dignity of generous and humble postures under and against oppressive regimes." Read in that fashion, Paul's "kenotic ontology" offers "fortification against exploitation."[32] This interpretive line then opens the way to normative extrapolations accentuating the liberative dimensions of kenotic love. In such accounts, kenotic "self-abandon" can be a "form of resistance" to oppression, a form reflective of genuine agency and "subversive subjectivity."[33] Indeed, in this perspective, kenotic "self-giving" may be seen in certain contexts as "resistance strategy" morally and spiritually akin to the strategy of a nonviolent political resistance that evinces genuine self-determination in self-restraint. Thus, a woman's kenotic refusal to leave an abusive relationship or to meet violence with violence within the relationship may signify a mode of creative resistance, an expression of kenotic power, indicative of active, courageous "self-determination" rather than passive, diffident self-surrender.[34]

Of course, Mercedes's principal concern here is to defend kenotic love against the feminist criticism that urging women to self-sacrifice impedes their self-determination, and there is much to be valued generally in Mercedes's rich, subtle, complex, and often powerful account. But one has to be wary of its tendency, as a reading of Paul, to slip into terms of normative justification closer in spirit to the feminist liberation theology Mercedes is trying to challenge than the Pauline kenotic theology she is trying to reclaim (at least at a certain level). While Paul does see honor and dignity in Christian self-sacrifice, an honor and dignity signaled in Christ's exaltation, and while his proclaiming that exaltation in Philippians strikes notes of consolation and solidarity, he does not commend kenotic love finally as a strategy of resistance to oppression or as a personally, politically, or socially liberative power. Such love for Paul does reflect liberation from sin and does promise liberation from death. But those are spiritual liberations divinely instigated, something other than personal, political, or social self-determinations. Similarly, for Paul, love as self-sacrifice is not valued ultimately because it reflects, assists, or advances agent autonomy. It is valued rather as imitation of Christ, an imitation itself legitimated as response to Christ's loving injunctions and loving actions, an imitation empowered, not by the "erotic" energies of embodied selves that re-instantiate incarnation as Mercedes proposes, but by graceful transformation of the self effected through Christ's sacrificial death and resurrection and through the Spirit's operation in the Christian's baptismal dying and rising with Christ.[35]

And as genuinely mimetic of Christ, kenotic love for Paul is altruistic all the way down. It is the other rather than the self that is ever in love's view. In her discussion of women in oppressive relationships, Mercedes comes closest to capturing the sensibility of Pauline kenotic altruism when she describes the "ethics of care" often embraced by women in these circumstances.[36] Such an ethics might be directed toward their own children or toward a wider class of vulnerable persons. In any event, "care" in these contexts is marked decisively by a heroic resolve to sacrifice for the sake of others. Mercedes sees in such resolve an active resistance against exploitative persons and structures and thus a sense of self as well as an impressive power of agency. But for Pauline theology, it is neither the self-awareness nor the agential power that marks such care as kenotic or, more important, certifies kenosis as normative. Pauline kenotic love just is the disposition to sacrifice for the neighbor, and its standing as normative derives not from its connection with agential self-realization or self-determination but from its fidelity and responsiveness to Christological example, injunction, and loving initiative. In fairness to Mercedes, one must admit that she does occasionally register her sense of possible distance from Paul on these matters.[37] If this distance is real (as I think it is in moments), is it rightful given moral or theological considerations that somehow prove Pauline kenotic love unacceptable? In other words, is Pauline kenotic love in fact, servile, unconscionably self-abnegating, masochistic, or otherwise morally offensive such that it ought to be rejected or radically revised as some contemporary critics suggest? We take up variations on these questions eventually. But for now enough has been said to establish the indispensable centrality of self-sacrifice in Paul's vision of agape.[38]

Synoptic Reverberations

The preceding argues strongly to the conclusion that both the Johannine and Pauline accounts of agape authorize what I have called the internalist view of the relation between Christian love and self-sacrifice. This view reverberates in varying degrees throughout the New Testament as a whole, stakes a reasonable claim as the New Testament's deep theory of agape, and finds corroboration in a range of normatively isomorphic New Testament theological patterns and paradigms. I can hardly make the full case for the larger New Testament corroboration here but offer as brief illustration the Synoptic Gospel account of Christian discipleship.

The Synoptics unite in affirming that Christian "discipleship" has a "cost" and that the cost is borne in service to others.[39] The particular notes of this Synoptic theme are familiar enough and thus need only brief mention here. Just as the Son of Man surrenders "his life" as "a ransom for many," so "whoever wishes to be first among" Christian disciples "must be slave of all" (Mark 10:44–45, 9:35). Followers of Christ must "deny themselves and take up their cross," must "lose their life" to "save it" (Mark 8:34–35) since "the last will be first," "many of the first, last," and so forth (Mark 10:31). Such general injunctions to costly service set a theological context for specific ethical prescriptions and commendations. Thus, the rich young ruler is charged to sell all he owns and give the proceeds to the poor as a condition for inheriting eternal life (Mark 10:17, 21), and the widow's gift, though meager relative to the donations of the rich, is valued more highly precisely because she has given all she has (Mark 12:41–43).[40] "Lend," the Lukan Jesus commands in similar spirit, "expecting nothing in return" (Luke 6:35).[41]

But the Synoptic cost of discipleship reaches beyond material sacrifice to the cultivation of various spiritual and moral attitudes of self-limitation and self-denial. For instance, as Dietrich Bonhoeffer observed, the gospel call to radical forgiveness of sin is itself a call to cruciform sacrifice.[42] After all, to forgive "seventy-seven times" (Matt. 18:22) is to waive unconditionally a prerogative or power of moral leverage born of having been offended, to forgo a right or privilege of continued indignation or resentment. Thus, we can say with Bonhoeffer that "forgiveness is the Christlike suffering which it is the Christian duty to bear" for the neighbor's sake.[43] Similarly, to turn the other cheek in response to unprovoked assault, to love the enemy, to pray for those who persecute you, to bless those who abuse you, as Jesus enjoins in Matthew and Luke, is to forswear a prudential recourse or retaliatory attitude allowed by certain standards of fairness or to relinquish interests and desires whose satisfaction is permitted if not required by certain equalitarian conceptions of justice (Matt. 5:38–48; Luke 6:27–36). In the words of Reinhold Niebuhr, "The absolutism and perfectionism of

Jesus' love ethic sets itself uncompromisingly not only against the natural self-regarding impulses, but against the necessary prudent defenses of the self, required because of the egoism of others. It does not establish a connection with the horizontal points of a political or social ethic or with the diagonals which a prudential individual ethic draws between the moral ideal and the facts of a given situation."[44]

As the command to *love* one's enemies indicates, the Synoptics in moments link their calls to self-renunciation explicitly with love. To cite one other instance, Luke presents the Good Samaritan parable expressly as a midrash on the command to love your neighbor as you love yourself, a midrash identifying the Samaritan as the one who "proved neighbor" to the man in need and commending the Samaritan's self-sacrificial beneficence precisely as an example of neighborly love (Luke 10:25–37). But overall, the Synoptic connections between self-sacrifice and Christian love are implicit rather than explicit. Certainly such connections are plausibly inferred. In the Synoptic outlook, the command to love the neighbor is with the command to love God reckoned as the greatest of all, and "on these two commandments depend all the law and the prophets" (Matt. 22:40). Thus, any Synoptic injunctions with decisive moral weight are reasonably construed as elaborations or derivatives of the neighbor-love command, including the discipleship injunctions to costly service.

Admittedly, there might appear to be some tension between the radically altruistic character of those injunctions and the prudential presumptions of the Synoptic love commandment, which requires that you love your neighbor *as you love yourself* or—in the Golden Rule variation—that you do to others *as you would be done by* (Matt. 7:12; Luke 6:31). But any appearance of tension dissipates if one takes the love commandment as addressed to auditors inclined already to advancing and protecting their own interests. In this account, the commandment's prudential recognitions do not legitimate self-regard; rather, they offer from what is naturally familiar guidance for determining the character of other regard—to wit, you are to love others *as you do now in fact love yourself.* The purpose of the commandment, then, is not to authorize prudence even secondarily, derivatively, or implicitly but to awaken and direct altruism. Read in this way, the commandment's prudential notes are fully compatible with the radically self-sacrificial character of the discipleship injunctions. And overall, it seems clear that the Synoptic rendering of agape, viewed against the background of the Synoptic interpretation of discipleship, corroborates the Johannine and Pauline accounts of love as self-sacrifice.[45]

Normative Assessment

I have proposed *that* and have shown *how* the internalist view of the relation between Christian love and self-sacrifice stakes a reasonable claim to standing as the New Testament's deep theory of agape. More could be said on that matter, and I shall take up a number of related points in what follows, but here I shift the primary emphasis of discussion to normative assessment. Can the internalist view meet objections posed by standard ethical and theological criticisms of construing Christian love as self-sacrifice?

It should be noted at the outset that some of these objections can be met simply by precise formulation of the internalist view. To reiterate, Christian love, in this view, is essentially a virtue incorporating the disposition to sacrifice the interests of the self *for the genuine good of the neighbor.* The neighbor-good codicil wards off certain stock criticisms of agape as self-sacrifice. Thus, as mentioned earlier, some object to defining Christian love essentially in self-sacrificial terms because certain instances of self-denial are vicious rather than virtuous and hence cannot plausibly be commended as loving, for example, the case of the "Balkan commander" who follows "all orders to engage in ethnic cleansing out of selfless obedience."[46] Indeed, it has been argued recently that the spirit of self-sacrifice is at the heart of a peculiarly virulent form of evil whose uniqueness is signaled precisely by a perverse willingness to sacrifice self in a malignant cause. Such perversity allegedly is more pernicious than egoism and closer in spirit to idolatry than to love.[47] Thus, love cannot be reduced to self-sacrifice *simpliciter*. But the internalist view denies that simple reduction. For the internalist, Christian love marks necessarily a disposition to sacrifice self *in morally, religiously, and spiritually appropriate contexts discerned and certified as appropriate by agape itself.*[48] The criteria governing agape's discernment and certification here are tied in principle to a range of neighborly considerations with distinctive theological warrants, for example, equal regard of all neighbors, never treating neighbors simply as means, concern for the neighbor's moral character and spiritual well-being as well as material welfare. Some proposed considerations (or their particular implications) will be debatable; others will be beyond contention. But the main point here is that to admit that agape judges some self-sacrifice inappropriate given such considerations is not to deny that agape *essentially is* the disposition to *appropriate self-sacrifice*. Ruling out certain expressions of sacrifice as inconsistent with Christian love, then, does not entail rejection of the internalist view, which, to repeat, insists that *self-sacrifice for the neighbor's sake* is *internal* to the concept of agape.[49]

Yet some standard criticisms of self-sacrificial love cannot be handled simply by precise formulation of the internalist view. In what follows, I consider three of these recast explicitly as criticisms of the internalist view and defend that view in response to the reconstructed criticisms.

Criticism 1: Because it downgrades the agent's moral standing, the internalist view fails to capture fully the egalitarian or universal thrust of Christian love. That thrust is indicated in key New Testament moments, for example, the command to love the enemy, which widens love's scope beyond concern for "those who love you," or the Good Samaritan parable, which extends love's neighborhood beyond traditionally adversarial ethnic boundaries. These New Testament moments presumably reflect in turn a deep "theocentric" logic underwriting interpretations of agape as equal and unconditional regard. According to this logic, since God loves all persons equally and unconditionally, Christians in principle are to love all persons likewise. Since the self is a person loved by God, so the self requires consideration commensurate with that equal standing before God. Thus, a theocentrically warranted universal love justifies an agent's *self-love* at least at a certain level of generality. For the agent to deny a legitimate self-love is incompatible with recognizing God's universal love and offends against certain logical principles of consistency and universalizability. If the enemy and the Samaritan are to be loved equally and unconditionally because they are loved by God, as a matter of consistency, the self, also loved by God, should be loved equally and unconditionally. Moreover, certain practical submissions by an agent reflect a self-denigration that is morally and religiously offensive precisely because it fails to value what God prizes. But the radical altruism of the internalist view leaves no normative space for the agent to refuse such submissions *out of self-love or self-regard or self-respect*. A morally and religiously pernicious servility, then, is countenanced in theory by the internalist view, which should be rejected therefore as incompatible with a theocentrically comprehended universal love.[50]

In assessing this criticism of the internalist view, there are a number of things to keep in mind. First, in the wisdom of the world, the way of the cross is foolishness (1 Cor. 1:19–31), and what the Christian venerates as loving service, the world may revile as abject servility. Indeed, even the disciples initially resist Jesus's paradigm of servanthood as dishonorable (e.g., John 13:8; Mark 8:32). Thus, Christian love is bound to collide with conventional expectations, particularly in a world that prizes autonomy, independence, self-expression, self-realization, individual achievement, and public recognition. Such a world may judge a mother's lifelong sacrifice for family as a failure to achieve selfhood or self-respect even as the Christian commends that life as an instance of virtuosity in love's domain. And unless one is a Nietzschean or Randian or a Kantian of a particular stripe, it's not obvious that the Christian commendation is wrong despite enormous cultural pressures to insist that it is. Second, as Outka has underscored, there are altruistic reasons for a loving agent to resist self-exploitation; innocent third parties (e.g., children) also may be harmed by such exploitation, and it is in the *moral* interest of an unjust perpetrator to be resisted.[51] Third, to juxtapose an agent's resistance to exploitation with sacrifice of self as simple either-or obscures the potential complexity of act descriptions in these contexts. A spouse's leaving an abusive relationship may be motivated substantially by self-protection and self-respect, but such leaving might also require, for instance, the sacrifice of relative economic security and comfort, a sacrifice willingly embraced for the sake of others (e.g., children) as well as self.

Having said all this, we are still left with the question whether in principle the internalist view of love as self-sacrifice can accommodate the judgment that some resistance to exploitation can be grounded in self-regard. I think such accommodation is possible, though its way is indirect and, as we shall see presently, the accommodation is most convincing when rooted in an appeal to other regard as a kind of meta-value. At the very least, it should be made clear that there is no necessary connection between even a systematic willingness to sacrifice self for others and a morally offensive self-denigration.[52] For the internalist, the attitude of the loving agent is not "I don't count in principle" but, rather, "In the eyes of God I do count, but for the sake of others, I choose not to press my equal standing." On this matter, the kenotic Christology of Philippians is instructive: Again, there it is said that Christ "did not regard equality with God as something to be exploited." There is no denial of Christ's equality with God; there is only the claim that Christ practically waived the prerogative of divine equality in sacrificing himself for others and set thereby the self-sacrificial standard for Christian love. Admittedly, Paul complicates things somewhat when he urges the Philippians to "regard others as better than yourselves," but here the Christological reference should control interpretation, and we should read Paul as prescribing the agent's practical deference without compromise of the agent's equal standing. At any rate, generally speaking, there is no contradiction between the internalist view's essential commendation of self-sacrifice and recognition of the loving agent's equal standing.

And an agent's insistence on her or his own equal standing can provide justification for resisting exploitation. Yet for the internalist, the justification approaches Christian love as it reaches toward a larger altruistic rationale—*the blunt moral education of those bent on the violation of persons.* To resist exploitation on grounds of equal standing is to instruct potential violators through moral confrontation, and this is to their own good. Such confrontation is an expression of justice. Whether it is also an expression of love proper, in the internalist view, will depend on whether it is an expression of the disposition *to sacrifice* for the neighbor's good. And it is not implausible to suggest that self-sacrifice indeed may be a key element in these instances since confronting perpetrators of injustice even on one's own behalf often comes knowingly at great personal cost. In such cases, the internalist can say reasonably that resistance on behalf of the self is also a way of *loving* the enemy.[53]

Criticism 2. Because it defines Christian love essentially as self-sacrifice, the internalist view restricts love's possibility to a morally imperfect world. Yet certainly agape reigns in the perfectly redeemed community of heaven or the Kingdom of God. Thus, love cannot be defined essentially as self-sacrifice. In this critique, the normative force of any injunction to *sacrificial* love depends on the existence of conditions less than ideal. Self-sacrifice is allegedly the cost of loving initiative in a world marked by "conflict and sin" when, for example, such initiative is met with indifference or outright hostility. That cost must be borne since, after all, even the enemy must be loved if always in the hope that full equality and mutuality might be restored. But the ethic of self-sacrifice is a "transitional ethic," a postlapsarian provisional compromise. In a world without conflict and sin, there would be no need for such sacrifice. Love as equal and unconditional regard for the neighbor would elicit response in kind.[54] In a second version of the argument, leaning toward self-sacrifice as a general policy is said to be justified to counterbalance the sinful human tendency to favor self unduly. Under such circumstances, even love understood as *equal* regard underwrites a "practical *swerve*" in altruism's direction, a "bias . . . toward the well-being of the other against inconvenience or cost to the self."[55] Self-sacrifice, then, has "instrumental warrant" as "ameliorative strategy."[56] But in a world without sin, presumably no such strategy would be necessary since agents would not be inclined to disproportionate self-regard in practical deliberation. More generally, in the present objection, all moral justifications for self-sacrifice are contingent on sin in this way, and therefore, none of these justifications could apply in a world fully redeemed. If Christian love is quintessentially self-sacrifice, then agape can have no place in heaven or the Kingdom of God. But agape does have such a place *as preeminent virtue.* Thus, the internalist view of love as self-sacrifice must be rejected.

This line of argument is questionable at a number of points. For one thing, it is difficult to see how exactly the "ameliorative strategy" warrant for self-sacrifice advanced in the second version of the criticism comports with the New Testament depiction of Christ as sacrificial love's divine exemplar. While Christ is definitive of love in that depiction, it would be odd to suggest that his willingness to sacrifice is indicative of a general policy aimed at checking his sinful inclination to disproportionate self-regard. Noting as much still leaves us with the criticism's first version, which argues that self-sacrifice is warranted as the cost borne by loving initiative in a world that sinfully fails to reciprocate. This version avoids the Christological problem identified but assumes controversially that sacrificing self is occasioned *only* by sinful conditions absent in a world fully redeemed. It is not at all clear, however, that self-sacrifice is occasioned exclusively by the conditions of a *sinful* world; such sacrifice may also be occasioned by the conditions of a *finite* world: witness the case of parents who suffer sleepless nights caring for children.[57] Of course, it is fruitless to speculate in detail how human finitude might be transformed in a heavenly realm or divine kingdom, but it is not obvious that the transformation must do away with all occasion for self-giving. Indeed, in light of the New Testament witness, one might expect, as C. S. Lewis once proposed, that a fully redeemed life involves precisely the mystery of an eternal self-realization *constituted by an eternal self-giving.*[58]

At any rate, whatever occasions one admits for *sacrificial action* in a fully redeemed world, it is still possible to say that the denizens of that world are marked by *the spirit or virtue of sacrificial love,* that they possess a *loving character* incorporating *a genuine disposition to sacrifice the interests of the self for the sake of others.*[59] Saying as much is neither to reduce the neighbor for whom one would sacrifice to a "generalized other which can only be a projection of ourself,"[60] nor to declare that self-sacrifice "is simply expressive of something resident in the agent,"[61] but rather to affirm that citizens of the redeemed community are *loving persons* in the sense that they are the *kind* of persons who *will the good of others with self-sacrificial resolve.* Given such considerations, it should be clear that there is no need to deny the possibility of sacrificial love in a world without sin, and thus, we can continue to say with the internalist that love is *essentially* self-sacrifice even as we agree that agape is the preeminent virtue in a fully redeemed world.

Criticism 3. The internalist view cannot account adequately for the role mutual love must play in any comprehensive treatment of Christian love. For those who advance this criticism, "mutual love" designates most generally *a relation* among persons, one marked by mutual affection, appreciation, enjoyment, benevolence, and support. There is a tendency in such relations toward coincidence of interests or shared goods without suppression of individual identities, and in the ideal case, each participant in the relation finds fulfillment in the fulfill-ment(s) of the other(s). Most important, participants in the relation both give to *and receive from* each other. This reciprocity shows itself in action as well as in attitude and is genuinely cooperative in spirit; in other words, entering into the process of reciprocal exchange is not motivated by a concern to secure a narrowly egocentric personal advantage (I'll scratch your back if you scratch mine) but by a sense of shared purpose or prospective enjoyment in the gain for all, even if personal advantages do come the agent's way as a matter of fact and even if the agent does find *self*-fulfillment in the gain to others. In some sense, according to the present criticism, this *mutuality* or *reciprocity* or *giving and receiving* is at the heart of Chris-tian love, a fact that cannot be explained by the internalist view, which puts *unilateral self-giving* at the center of that love.

Proponents of Christian love as mutual love typically challenge self-sacrificial accounts of agape with a welter of scriptural, theological, phenomenological, and anthropological appeals. It is sometimes said, for instance, that the New Testament warrants mutuality in commending things like community, fellowship, brotherhood, friendship, or family;[62] that understanding love as mutuality comports best with the phenomenology of moral experi-ence[63] or with Thomistic theologies of nature, grace, and charity supplemented by evidence drawn from the "kinship altruism" theories of evolutionary biology;[64] or that love as mutual-ity is confirmed supremely by Trinitarian interrelationality or biblical visions of "conviviality" at the "eschatological banquet."[65] I can hardly cover the whole terrain of argument in detail here but will reiterate, in general response to mutualist claims, the observation made earlier in discussion of Johannine love: to affirm mutual relationship as an ideal aim of agape is not to deny that agape is essentially a disposition to self-sacrifice for the neighbor's sake.

Thus, as noted earlier, even if one grants that Jesus's commendation of laying down life for "friends" implies his approval of a general *mutuality* endemic to friendship, this granting neither denies that Jesus identifies *the sacrifice itself* as an essential dimension of love nor asserts that he regards sacrifice as something other than love should the "friend" fail to respond in kind. Neither is the *altruism* of *sacrificial* love compromised or nullified by hope for an eschatologically consummated mutuality or self-realization via resurrection since, again, it is still reasonable to say that the attendees at the "eschatological banquet" will be those who love each other for all eternity *with self-sacrificial resolve*. Similarly, though "God is love" may be said to signify a Trinitarian *mutual* love within divinity that serves as a general theological paradigm for interpreting agape, that Trinitarian love need not lack a sacrificial dimension. On the contrary, it is still possible to say, and there is every scriptural reason to say, that what is shared in the triune life is exactly an eternal disposition to self-giving among the triune persons: "This love is perfectly present in the Holy Trinity where each divine Per-son totally surrenders Himself to the others. . . . The self-donation of each divine Person to the others unites all three in a *communion of persons*."[66] An affirmation of Trinitarian mutuality, then, is wholly consistent with the internalist view of agape as self-sacrifice since Trinitarian love can be seen as constituted essentially by the eternal spirit of self-giving that marks each of the triune persons in relation to the others.

Of course, proponents of agape as mutual love also offer more mundane considerations in criticism of sacrificial love, for example, that "ought implies can" and that "extreme self-sacrificial formulations of the concept of love" demand of human beings *in this world* what is unnatural to them.[67] In this account, evolutionary biology shows that human love is constituted by natural affections like erotic attraction or empathy rooted in biologically determined kinship relations structured in turn by reciprocal expectations and prospects for desire fulfillment or self-gratification. Visions of self-sacrificial love, it is said, float high above such empirical realities, and proposals for mutual love are presented as more adequate to the task of rendering theological ethics compatible with plausible naturalistic accounts of human behavior. Yet however one assesses the general relevance of evolutionary biology to Christian ethical reflection, even some of the most ardent mutualists concede that biological reductionism must be resisted and that an adequate theology of grace must allow for moral behavior that moves beyond the narrow confines of natural inclinations and basic drives.[68] Such concessions pave the way to agreement with Reinhold Niebuhr's observation: "Sometimes the act of complete self-abnegation, the pouring out of life for other life, is the consequence of pressures of a given moment which endow the individual with resources beyond his natural capacities. . . . There are . . . forces in life which can only be described as the grace of God."[69] And here the examples of Victoria Soto and others like her come inexorably to mind.

Finally, it should be noted that with respect to scriptural interpretation, both "mutualist" and simple "equal-regard" constructions of agape face a difficult problem that the internalist view avoids. The problem, as exegetes commonly observe, is that there exists a tension in the New Testament between accounts of love stressing mutuality within the restricted circle of Christian discipleship and those emphasizing equal and unconditional regard of all human beings, including Samaritans and other enemies. Indeed, some New Testament scholars have gone so far as to suggest that there is irremediable conflict between, say, Johannine sectarian depictions of love as mutual relation among the brethren and Synoptic inclusivist depictions of love as unconditional regard for all humans.[70] Whatever the score on that last proposal, it should be clear that the internalist view identifies as essential to Christian love a dimension about whose importance there is comparatively little New Testament disagreement, namely, the dimension of self-sacrifice for the neighbor's sake *whoever counts as neighbor*. That canonical agreement underwrites in an especially powerful way the claim of the internalist view to standing as the New Testament's deep theory of agape.

Epigraphs

The first epigraph and all subsequent scriptural quotations are taken from *The New Oxford Annotated Bible: New Revised Standard Version with the Apocrypha* (New York: Oxford University Press, 2010).

The second epigraph is from "Remembering the Passion of a Teacher Who Died Protecting Students," *New York Times*, December 19, 2012, http://www.nytimes.com/2012/12/20/nyregion/remembering-the-passion-of-victoria-soto-a-sandy-hook-teacher.html?_r=1&.

Notes

This essay is dedicated to three women who have been or were living sacrifices for others: Norma E. Santurri, Ruth Jacobson, and Jolene Barjasteh.

1. Throughout I use the terms "Christian love," "love of neighbor," "neighbor love," "agape," and sometimes simply "love" as interchangeable designations of the same theological virtue. My definition of love here modifies an earlier undeveloped suggestion. See Edmund N. Santurri, "Introduction" to Reinhold Niebuhr, *An Interpretation of Christian Ethics* (Louisville, KY: Westminster John Knox Press, 2013), xviii. In an important way my argument in this essay amounts to a defense of Niebuhr's view of Christian love.

2. On agape as open to self-sacrifice in this contingent way see Timothy P. Jackson, *The Priority of Love: Christian Charity and Social Justice* (Princeton, NJ: Princeton University Press, 2003), 24–25; and Timothy P. Jackson, "Judge William and Professor Browning: A Kierkegaardian Critique of Equal-Regard Marriage and the Democratic Family," in *The Equal-Regard Family and Its Friendly Critics*, ed. John Witte Jr., M. Christian Green, and Amy Wheeler (Grand Rapids, MI: Eerdmans, 2007), 143–44.

3. Pace Gene Outka. The quoted phrase is his. See Gene Outka, *Agape: An Ethical Analysis* (New Haven, CT: Yale University Press, 1972), 278.

4. The summary that follows in this paragraph adapts, with significant changes, my earlier account. See Santurri, "Introduction," xvii–xviii.

5. Outka advances these first two concerns. See his *Agape*, 274–79; also, 21–24. Cf. his "Universal Love and Impartiality," in *The Love Commandments: Essays in Christian Ethics and Moral Philosophy*, ed. Edmund N. Santurri and William Werpehowski (Washington, DC: Georgetown University Press, 1992; repr., Eugene, OR: Wipf & Stock, 2009), 1–103.

6. Stephen J. Pope, *Human Evolution and Christian Ethics* (Cambridge: Cambridge University Press, 2008), 227–28; Peter Geach, *The Virtues* (Cambridge: Cambridge University Press, 1977), 82–83.

7. This concern has been central to a wide range of feminist, womanist, and liberationist critiques of Christian love as self-sacrifice. See, e.g., Barbara Hilkert Andolsen, "Agape in Feminist Ethics," *Journal of Religious Ethics* 9, no. 1 (Spring 1981): 69–83; Susan Nelson Dunfee, "The Sin of Hiding: A Feminist Critique of Reinhold Niebuhr's Account of the Sin of Pride," *Soundings* 65, no. 3 (Fall 1982): 316–27; Margaret Daphne Hampson, *Theology and Feminism* (Oxford: Basil Blackwell, 1990), 121–26; Judith Plaskow, *Sin, Sex and Grace: Women's Experience and the Theologies of Reinhold Niebuhr and Paul Tillich* (Lanham, MD: University Press of America, 1980); Traci C. West, *Disruptive Christian Ethics: When Racism and Women's Lives Matter* (Louisville, KY: Westminster John Knox Press, 2006), 23–35. A principal inspiration of the feminist critique is Valerie Saiving Goldstein, "The Human Situation: A Feminine View," *Journal of Religion* 40, no. 2 (April 1960): 100–12.

8. Outka, "Universal Love and Impartiality." Also, Nicholas Wolterstorff, *Justice in Love* (Grand Rapids, MI: Eerdmans, 2011), 95.

9. Stephen G. Post, *A Theory of Agape: On the Meaning of Christian Love* (Lewisberg, PA: Bucknell University Press, 1990).

10. Paul Ramsey, *Nine Modern Moralists* (Englewood Cliffs, NJ: Prentice-Hall, 1962), 146. Cf. C. S. Lewis, *The Weight of Glory* (New York: HarperCollins, 2001), 25–26.

11. See Mary Daly, *Gyn/ecology: The Metaethics of Radical Feminism* (Boston: Beacon Press, 1978), 137–39.

12. On self-sacrifice as justified in promoting equal regard, see Outka, *Agape*, 278–79. On self-sacrifice as supportive of Trinitarian mutuality, see Margaret Farley, "New Patterns of Relationship: Beginnings of a Moral Revolution," in *Women: New Dimensions*, ed. Walter Burghardt (New York: Paulist Press, 1975), 51–70; and Andolsen, "Agape in Feminist Ethics," 76–80.

13. By "Johannine" or "John," I mean essentially the Gospel and Epistles of John—though, for the purposes of this discussion, I focus on the Gospel and First Epistle. My account abstracts from issues of authorship, and nothing in the argument turns on the question of single authorship. "Johannine" or "John" here is a term of convenience demarcating what New Testament scholars commonly identify as the "Johannine School," a school inclusive of the Gospel and three Epistles of John and exclusive of the Book of Revelation, itself attributed to a John of Patmos. In any event, the normative force of Johannine proposals for Christian ethics derives from their presence in the New Testament canon and not from any identification with a particular author or school.

14. Richard A. Burridge, *Imitating Jesus: An Inclusive Approach to New Testament Ethics* (Grand Rapids, MI: Eerdmans: 2007), 327. My overall accounts of both Johannine and Pauline love are indebted to Burridge's general discussion, though my analysis carries distinctive accentuations, proposals, extrapolations, and reconstructions. Cf. Burridge, *Imitating Jesus*, 81–154 (Pauline), 285–346 (Johannine). My views

of Johannine and Pauline love are also along the lines of Nygren's classic treatment—though there are important differences. See Anders Nygren, *Agape and Eros*, trans. Philip Watson (New York: Harper & Row, 1969), 105–59.

15. For current purposes, I set aside questions of the relation of this motivation to free human agency and divine grace.

16. In John's Gospel, Jesus casts this account of "abiding in love" in the image of vine, branch, and fruit. "Just as the branch cannot bear fruit by itself unless it abides in the vine, neither can you unless you abide in me. I am the vine, you are the branches. . . . As the Father has loved me, so I have loved you; abide in my love" (John 15:4–5, 9). Victor Furnish takes the vine, branch, fruit analogy as indicative of "love's 'ethical' and 'metaphysical' sides . . . where . . . abiding in love (metaphysical) and bearing the fruit of love (ethical) are vitally interrelated" but distinct. Victor Paul Furnish, *The Love Command in the New Testament* (Nashville: Abingdon, 1972), 141. Put in these terms, my general position is that the metaphysical claim in John is primary and the ethical claim secondary, though intimately connected with the metaphysical.

17. For a penetrating discussion of "being and doing" as they relate to agape as virtue, see Outka, *Agape*, 137–45.

18. Allen Verhey, *The Great Reversal: Ethics and the New Testament* (Grand Rapids, MI: Eerdmans, 1984), 144.

19. Pope, *Human Evolution and Christian Ethics*, 232.

20. Gail R. O'Day, "Gospel of John," in *Women's Bible Commentary*, 3rd ed., ed. Carol A. Newsom, Sharon H. Ringe, and Jacqueline E. Lapsley (Louisville, KY: Westminster John Knox Press, 2012), 525–26.

21. Outka, *Agape*, 37. Admittedly, in arguing against the strict mutualists, Outka is not arguing for agape as self-sacrifice, but his observation still assists the point I am making here mutatis mutandis.

22. Thus, the Johannine view is to be distinguished from one radically mutualist position identified by Outka: "[A mutualist] may hold that agape unrequited is not fully agape, that some mutuality is a necessary condition. In [that] case, one might say for example of a man who remained one's enemy not 'I loved him,' but rather 'I *tried* to love him.'" Outka, *Agape*, 36.

23. I leave open the possibility that a substantive connection between incarnation and agape is *implicit* in the Johannine literature. At any rate, such a connection seems *compatible* with Johannine theology.

24. On this point, I am in agreement with Gordon Fee's reading of Philippians 2:6–8. Fee's interpretation challenges metaphysical construals of kenosis advanced to explain Incarnation. See Gordon D. Fee, "The New Testament and Kenosis Christology," in *Exploring Kenotic Christology: The Self-Emptying of God*, ed. C. Stephen Evans (Oxford: Oxford University Press, 2006), 25–44, but especially 33–34. On Philippian kenosis and Christian ethics generally, see Stephen Fowl, "Christology and Ethics in Philippians 2:5–11," in *Where Christology Began: Essays on Philippians 2*, ed. Ralph P. Martin and Brian J. Dodd (Louisville, KY: Westminster John Knox Press, 1998), 140–53; Richard B. Hays, *The Moral Vision of the New Testament* (San Francisco: HarperSanFrancisco, 1996), 28–32; and Burridge, *Imitating Jesus*, 145–46.

25. Fee, "New Testament and Kenosis Christology," 34.

26. My reading of Philippians 2:5–11 stakes a claim in territory overrun with competing interpretations. For one account of some options and a singular reading, see Sarah Coakley, *Powers and Submissions* (Oxford: Blackwell, 2002), 3–39.

27. On the incarnational-cruciform kenotic progression, see Karl Barth, *Epistle to the Philippians*, trans. James W. Leitch (Louisville, KY: Westminster John Knox Press, 2002), 60–65.

28. My general account of Paul's love casuistry is shaped by Burridge's reading. Cf. his *Imitating Christ*, 144–48.

29. On the different senses of self-sacrifice that might be associated with kenotic theology, see Ruth Groenhout, "Kenosis and Feminist Theory," in Evans, *Exploring Kenotic Christology*, 296–98. Groenhout's "taxonomy" draws on and adapts that of Sarah Coakley. See Coakley's "Kenosis: Theological Meanings and Gender Connotations," in *The Work of Love: Creation as Kenosis*, ed. John Polkinghorne (Grand Rapids, MI: Eerdmans, 2001), 203.

30. "Bear one another's burdens, and in this way you will fulfill the law of Christ" (Gal. 6:2). Moreover, since bearing such burdens is love's determination ("through love become slaves to one another") and since "the whole law is summed up" in the command to love the neighbor (Gal. 5:13–14), the reasonable inference is that Christ commands self-sacrifice as love. In equating the "law of Christ" in Paul with the love

commandment, I follow the dominant scholarly line. See David Wenham, *Did Paul Get Jesus Right? The Gospel according to Paul* (Oxford: Lion Hudson, 2010), 65. See also Burridge, *Imitating Jesus*, 107–13; Furnish, *Love Command in the New Testament*, 95–102.

31. Cf. Hays, *Moral Vision of the New Testament*, 43–46; Burridge, *Imitating Christ*, 102–3.

32. Anna Mercedes, *Power For: Feminism and Christ's Self Giving* (London: T&T Clark International, 2011), 20.

33. Ibid., 109, 101.

34. Ibid., 114–21.

35. Cf. ibid., 129–53, for Mercedes's account of kenotic love as erotic power exerted in reiterated divine *incarnations*. In challenging this position as a reading of Pauline kenotic love, I am not denying, of course, that for Paul, the Incarnation serves as a model for love's *imitation* of incarnation.

36. Ibid., 117–20.

37. "As part of the flow of Jesus' christic self-giving, Jesus' death comes not as the exemplary instance of Jesus' *kenosis* (though Paul may have it so), but rather as the realizing of one possible result of Jesus' passionate life. Jesus need not suffer the Roman cross for us, but Jesus could not be other than for us, and that *forness* was in one vital instance met with the cross." Ibid., 151–52. Incidentally, it should be pointed out that even if it is true that Jesus *need not* have been crucified for us, this observation would not undermine the view that the crucifixion is an exemplary expression of Christian love understood as *the disposition* to sacrifice the self for the neighbor's sake when such is called for.

38. This reading is consistent with Paul's soaring homily on love in 1 Cor. 13, a homily that, despite its reputation, rhetorical power, and summative form, ought not to be taken, in any event, as Paul's singularly definitive or comprehensive statement of agape's normative content. Paul's main project here is to criticize Corinthian hubris over claimed spiritual gifts (e.g., speaking in tongues, prophesying) and to commend love as the greatest spiritual gift as well as one among three spiritual gifts that perdure (with faith and hope). Still, what Paul does say about agape's normative content in this homily distinguishes love sharply from various expressions of Corinthian self-centeredness and associates love generally with an altruistic attitude and willingness to assume burden for the sake of others. Thus, "Love is patient; love is kind; love is not envious or boastful or arrogant or rude. It does not insist on its own way" (1 Cor. 13:4–5). In addition, Paul here exposes certain Corinthian pretensions to radical self-sacrifice as deep-down self-serving: "If I give away all my possessions, and if I hand over my body so that I may boast, but do not have love, I gain nothing" (1 Cor. 13:3). The strong suggestion is that genuine love expresses itself as sacrifice *for the good of the neighbor*.

39. Dietrich Bonhoeffer, *The Cost of Discipleship* (New York: Macmillan, 1959).

40. The Synoptic sensibility here is captured nicely in C. S. Lewis's remark: "I am afraid the only safe rule is to give more than we can spare. . . . If our charities do not at all pinch or hamper us, I should say they are too small." *Mere Christianity* (New York: HarperCollins, 2001), 86.

41. Cf. the Lukan Acts 2:44–45, 4:32–37.

42. "The law of Christ, which it is our duty to fulfill, is the bearing of the cross. My brother's burden which I must bear is not only his outward lot, his natural characteristics and gifts, but quite literally his sin. And the only way to bear that sin is by forgiving it in the power of the cross of Christ which I now share. Thus the call to follow Christ always means a call to share the work of forgiving men their sins." Bonhoeffer, *Cost of Discipleship*, 80.

43. Ibid.

44. Niebuhr, *Interpretation of Christian Ethics*, 39. "Jesus' love ethic" in Niebuhr's usage is largely a token for the *Synoptic* representation of that love ethic and especially as that ethic is presented in the Sermon on the Mount.

45. Here I take issue with Gail R. O'Day, who distinguishes John radically from the Synoptics precisely on the matter of love as self-sacrifice and "emptying." According to O'Day, Johannine love lacks the Synoptic dimensions of radical self-denial and self-emptying. See "Gospel of John," 525–26.

46. Pope, *Human Evolution and Christian Ethics*, 238.

47. "The moral drama and its psychology have to be reformulated: *misguided self-transcendence is morally more problematic and lethal than a disproportionate attachment to self-interest.* In line with a long philosophical tradition, I think that self-transcendence does constitute the moral act. But from that fact itself, self-sacrifice also derives its corrupting force. Misdirected self-transcendence falsely [simulates] a noble

moral act. . . . The religious sensitivity to such a phenomenon is the reason why misguided self-transcendence constitutes the ultimate sin of idolatry. Idolatry, in this sense, is the utmost surrender to a cause that is not worthy of the corresponding sacrifice." Moshe Halbertal, *On Sacrifice* (Princeton, NJ: Princeton University Press, 2012), 78.

48. Cf. Santurri, "Introduction," xviii.

49. A similar logic can be employed to respond to the criticism that defining love as self-sacrifice makes agape irrelevant to the resolution of conflicts between second and third parties when in fact agape enjoins the agent's preference for innocent victims against unjust perpetrators. The internalist view can justify that preference given the criteria for appropriate sacrifice certified by love itself. Of course, the internalist view insists that agape is, nonetheless, *the disposition to sacrifice* for the neighbor in contexts where innocent victims are preferred.

50. Cf. Outka, "Universal Love and Impartiality," 40–44, 81–82; also Thomas Hill, "Servility and Self-Respect," *The Monist* 57 (January 1973): 87–104.

51. Outka, *Agape*, 21–23, 275–76.

52. In moments, Wolterstorff seems to conflate the two. See *Justice in Love*, 95.

53. None of this is to deny the claim of feminists, womanists, and other liberationists that in certain circumstances appeals to self-sacrificial love can serve as an ideological instrument of domination impeding rightful self-assertion by the unjustly oppressed against their unjust oppressors. But in such cases, what we find is an abuse of normative principles, not their appropriate application. To acknowledge that a principle may be abused is not to rule out all possibility of its valid application.

54. Don S. Browning, *Christian Ethics and the Moral Psychologies*, 2nd ed. (Grand Rapids, MI: Eerdmans, 2006), 143–44; Don S. Browning and Terry D. Cooper, *Religious Thought and the Modern Psychologies* (Minneapolis: Fortress Press, 2004), 135–38. Both discussions draw on Louis Janssens, "Norms and Priorities of a Love Ethics," *Louvain Studies* 6 (Spring 1977): 228.

55. Outka, "Universal Love and Impartiality," 82. The quotation within the quotation is from James M. Gustafson, "Mongolism, Parental Desires and Right to Life," in *On Moral Medicine: Theological Perspectives in Medical Ethics*, ed. Stephen E. Lammers and Allen Verhey (Grand Rapids, MI: Eerdmans, 1987), 488.

56. Outka, *Agape*, 278–79; Outka, "Universal Love and Impartiality," 82.

57. Cf. Bonnie J. Miller McLemore, "Generativity, Self-Sacrifice, and the Ethics of Family Life," in Witte et al., *Equal Regard Family*, 28–29.

58. C. S. Lewis, *Problem of Pain* (New York: Macmillan, 1948), 139–40.

59. On this matter, recall earlier observations about love as a spiritual state irreducible to action. See pp. 173–74, 177.

60. John Milbank, "The Ethics of Self-Sacrifice," *First Things*, March 1999, www.firstthings.com/article/1999/03/004-the-ethics-of-self-sacrifice.

61. Outka, *Agape*, 278. Cf. Ramsey, *Nine Modern Moralists*, 46; and Lewis, *Weight of Glory*, 25–26.

62. Post, *Theory of Agape*, 85–89; Pope, *Human Evolution and Christian Ethics*, 242–43.

63. Edward Collins Vacek, *Love, Human and Divine: The Heart of Christian Ethics* (Washington, DC: Georgetown University Press, 1994), xiv, 287–95.

64. Pope, *Human Evolution and Christian Ethics*, 214–49; Browning, *Christian Ethics*, 106–45.

65. M. C. D'Arcy, *The Mind and Heart of Love* (New York: Henry Holt, 1947), 15–16; Farley, "New Patterns of Relationship," 66; Andolsen, "Agape in Feminist Ethics," 77–79; Milbank, "Ethics of Self-Sacrifice."

66. Richard H. Hogan and John M. Levoir, *Covenant of Love: Pope John Paul II on Sexuality, Marriage, and Family in the Modern World* (Garden City, NY: Doubleday, 1985), 37.

67. Browning, *Christian Ethics*, 128–29.

68. Pope, *Human Evolution*, 248–49; Browning, *Christian Ethics*, 122.

69. Niebuhr, *Interpretation of Christian Ethics*, 216–17.

70. J. L. Houlden, *Ethics and the New Testament* (New York: Oxford University Press, 1977), 35–41, 58, 72.

11

Eudaimonism and Christian Love

FREDERICK V. SIMMONS

THE RELATIONSHIP BETWEEN eudaimonism and Christian love is a vast and vexing topic, in part because both notions have been taken to mean so many things. Of course, eudaimonia itself has been variously understood.[1] Indeed, as the transliteration of the term from Greek into English suggests, eudaimonia is notoriously difficult to translate, reflecting long-standing disagreements about the content of this abstract idea.[2] Furthermore, apart from controversy regarding the nature of eudaimonia, eudaimonism has signified several positions in its own right. Eudaimonism often denotes theories describing the connection between eudaimonia and morality, although not always.[3] Moreover, there is considerable diversity among the forms of eudaimonism that concern this connection. For example, eudaimonism sometimes designates the thesis that the moral life aims at one's own eudaimonia.[4] Others conceive eudaimonism as the doctrine that moral obligation is justified by its contribution to the eudaimonia of those who comply with it.[5] More modestly, eudaimonism may refer to the conviction that attainment of eudaimonia corresponds to fulfillment of moral duty.[6] Finally, still others interpret eudaimonism as a method of ethics in Henry Sidgwick's sense of a rational procedure to determine what individual human beings ought to do, namely, seek eudaimonia.[7] Thus, while these forms of eudaimonism that address the connection between eudaimonia and morality all link the right to the individual's good, they do so differently.

Christian conceptions of love have been similarly manifold. Love per se is obviously a protean phenomenon; indeed, musing on the difficulty of defining love has long been trite. As a consequence, Christians and others often distinguish multiple kinds of love. Here again transliteration is common, with "eros," "agape," "philia," "caritas," and "storge" among the most prominent terms that Christians now use to mark these multiple kinds. Yet despite the precision these labels may provide, there is no Christian consensus on whether all, one, or some combination of these loves are properly Christian; on the sorts of things that should be loved in these ways; or even on what these words mean. Accordingly, aside from their divergences on other pertinent matters, Christians' differing understandings of eudaimonia, eudaimonism, and love have led them to construe the relationship between eudaimonism and Christian love in myriad ways.

Nevertheless, some initial generalizations are possible before specifying particular senses of eudaimonia, eudaimonism, and Christian love. After all, to at least some degree, love and eudaimonia are inherently linked for Christians since Christians commonly consider love of God and neighbors crucial for human flourishing.[8] Further, basic Christian commitments connect love of God and neighbors with morality.[9] Taken together, Christians have good reason to couple eudaimonia and morality. Indeed, Christian scripture is replete with references to rewards for loving God and neighbors and thus repeatedly asserts a tie between eudaimonia and morality.[10] Moreover, Christians typically believe that God both morally obligates and saves human beings and that God is at once just and loving. The Christian doctrine of sanctification integrates these convictions and so naturally connects the moral life with each person's flourishing, just as eudaimonism maintains.

Yet despite these captivating convergences, Christian love and eudaimonism also seem at odds. While eudaimonism posits a connection between morality and one's own eudaimonia, Christians in particular apparently have good reason to believe love is—or at least should be—about benefiting the beloved. After all, Jesus's life and teaching so consistently present love as service that Paul admonishes Christians not to seek their own advantage but that of others (e.g., 1 Cor. 10:24). In fact, the Gospels do not merely portray Christian love as willing to serve others but insist on love's disposition to sacrifice itself for others and depict Jesus as abjuring the quest for one's own happiness as self-defeating.[11] Hence, although Christian scripture frequently links love and one's own eudaimonia, as on many other topics it apparently advocates multiple positions concerning that connection.[12]

However, on closer consideration, these Christian convictions about love may not contravene the relationship eudaimonism propounds between the moral life and eudaimonia and might even presuppose it. Indeed, Christian scripture does not simply promise that loving others conduces to the lover's ultimate happiness but persistently declares that it does so precisely when that love is concerned with serving others rather than oneself (cf., e.g., Matt. 25:31–40). Similarly, Aristotle did not interpret his insistence that reason might require death for one's friends as challenging eudaimonism but instead as following from it (*NE* 9.8 1169a.18–1169b.2). Obviously, Aristotle was not attempting to reconcile eudaimonism with a distinctively Christian understanding of love, and so his account does not demonstrate their compatibility. Nevertheless, it is striking that the Johannine Jesus identifies his love of his friends as the love that is to characterize the new law distinguishing Christian morality and that he describes the acme of such love as laying down one's life for one's friends (cf., e.g., John 13:34–35, 15:12–15; 1 John 3:16). Moreover, Aristotle maintained that the moral life may enjoin dying for one's friends without invoking eschatological rewards for the righteous. Even more arresting, the Gospels consistently present Jesus as rejecting self-seeking specifically because it is self-defeating and, thus, as evidently teaching that the love Christian morality commands should benefit the lover (cf., e.g., Mark 8:34–36; Matt. 10:39–42, 16:24–26; Luke 9:23–25, 17:33; John 12:25–26). If so, Christian scripture's myriad passages obligating service of others would not gainsay Christian eudaimonism's link between love and the lover's eudaimonia but rather indicate the character of Christian love that makes Christian morality eudaimonist.

Certainly, many major Christian thinkers have thought as much. Augustine, for example, assumed throughout his writings that the Christian moral life is tightly tethered to the eudaimonia of those who lead it. For instance, in *Of the Morals of the Catholic Church*, Augustine states, "Clearly, when we treat of morals . . . we inquire what manner of life must be held to obtain happiness."[13] Augustine further believed that God sanctions happiness as the reason to live morally: "People who are good, after all, are good in order to be happy. . . . The happy life is the reward of the good; goodness is the work, happiness the reward. God orders the work, offers the reward. He says, 'Do this, and you will get that.'"[14] Thomas Aquinas too staunchly affirmed a close connection between eudaimonia and the moral life. Negatively, he maintained, "We offend God only by doing something contrary to our own good."[15]

Positively, he contended, "Virtue's true reward is happiness itself, and good men aim at this. To act for honour would be ambition, not virtue."[16]

Of course, other influential Christian thinkers have disagreed. For example, Martin Luther vehemently rejected any suggestion that the moral life is ordered to the eudaimonia of its adherents as incompatible with genuine neighbor love, declaring, "This is a truly Christian life. Here faith is truly active through love, that is, it finds expression in works of the freest service, cheerfully and lovingly done, with which a man willingly serves another without hope of reward."[17] Luther also dismissed eudaimonism as inconsistent with proper relationship to God, asserting, "The children of God do good with a will that is disinterested, not seeking any reward, but only the glory and will of God, and being ready to do good even if—an impossible supposition—there were neither a kingdom nor a hell."[18] Similarly, John Calvin is customarily interpreted as disavowing eudaimonism, on the basis of such claims as

> The whole law is contained under two heads ["that we should love the Lord our God with all our heart, and with all our soul, and with all our powers"; and "that we should love our neighbor as ourselves"]. Yet our God, to remove all possibility of excuse, willed to set forth more fully and clearly by the Ten Commandments everything connected with the honor, fear, and love of him, and everything pertaining to the love toward men, which he for his own sake enjoins upon us.[19]

Likewise, in a chapter of his *Institutes of the Christian Religion* titled "The Sum of the Christian Life: The Denial of Ourselves," Calvin admonishes, "You can find no other remedy [for vice] than in denying yourself and giving up concern for yourself, and in turning your mind wholly to seek after those things which the Lord requires of you, and to seek them only because they are pleasing to him."[20]

Just as Christian scripture seems to offer varying assessments of eudaimonism, then, there is great—at times polarizing—diversity on the matter within Christian tradition.[21] Accordingly, rather than attempt to provide a putatively generic analysis of eudaimonism and Christian love, I shall specify a sense of each term to explore central aspects of their relationship with greater precision. While this delimits the topic somewhat, I select relatively broad, widely accepted senses of eudaimonism and Christian love involving minimal commitments so that my discussion remains relevant to many principal, particular conceptions of both notions. Although this approach enables me to draw provisional conclusions concerning the nature of the connection between eudaimonia and love for Christians, it does not settle the adequacy of Christian eudaimonism even granting the senses of these terms I select since other factors decisively affect that assessment as well. Nevertheless, this approach also allows me to identify a couple of these factors and delineate a few of the reasons eudaimonism has proved so vexing and controversial for Christians. In particular, I suggest that given common Christian understandings of eudaimonia, eudaimonism, and love, the Christian moral life better promotes its adherents' eudaimonia if it seems only somewhat eudaimonist, can be effectively eudaimonist even if not strictly so, and may come closer to eudaimonism at one stage of salvation history than another.

Eudaimonia and Eudaimonism

In what follows, I treat eudaimonism as the thesis that the moral life aims at one's own eudaimonia. Taking eudaimonism in this first of the four senses of the term concerning connections between eudaimonia and morality that I distinguished at the outset has several benefits. To begin, as I noted, this is Aristotle's understanding of eudaimonism, and his is a definitive classical statement of the view.[22] Next, this is a moderate form of eudaimonism: not as broad as the third sense of the term I initially distinguished—the conviction that attainment of eudaimonia corresponds to fulfillment of moral duty—nor as narrow as the second—the doctrine that moral obligation is justified by its contribution to the eudaimonia of those who comply with it.[23] Finally, I believe interpreting the moral life as aiming at one's own eudaimonia poses many of the most stimulating questions for Christian understandings of love.

For example, if Christian morality is aptly summarized by the duty to love God unreservedly and our neighbors as ourselves, is it appropriate to conceive Christian morality as aiming at one's own eudaimonia as this interpretation of Christian eudaimonism claims? After all, this summary of Christian morality makes no mention of eudaimonia and stipulates duties to God and neighbors rather than oneself. Of course, the answer to this question depends in part on the meaning of eudaimonia, and as I observed at the outset, this is a formal term admitting of various specifications. Moreover, I noted that it is plausible for Christians to maintain that loving God and neighbors is central to human flourishing. Accordingly, assuming this understanding of eudaimonia, it may seem fitting to construe Christian morality as aiming at one's own eudaimonia.

However, even granting this sense of eudaimonia, does a eudaimonistic interpretation of Christian ethics imply improper orientation to God and our neighbors? Specifically, even supposing that loving God unreservedly and our neighbors as ourselves is central to eudaimonia, if the moral life is conceived as aiming at one's own eudaimonia, it seems that morality enjoins loving God and neighbors this way for the sake of one's own eudaimonia. Yet surely Christian morality cannot advocate loving God or neighbors as a means to eudaimonia. On the contrary, Christians must reject any pretension to love God instrumentally as sacrilegious and futile, and as I have previously indicated, Christian scripture abounds with admonitions to love one's neighbors without regard for oneself. In short, even if Christians may consistently accept that love of God and neighbors is vital for eudaimonia, they cannot countenance eudaimonism if it treats eudaimonia as God.

Once again, the answer to this question is partially axiological, this time requiring further specification of the relationship between eudaimonia and love of God and neighbors. It is not enough for Christian eudaimonists to affirm that love of God and neighbors is central to eudaimonia, since such love may be central merely as a principal external means to eudaimonia. Instead, Christian eudaimonists must insist that love of God and neighbors is central to eudaimonia because it is a primary constituent of eudaimonia. Here again, such an interpretation of eudaimonia is not simply an expedient to which Christians need recur if they are determined to reconcile eudaimonism with their faith, but plausible for Christians in its own right. Indeed, since Christians typically affirm that God is the greatest good, it is natural for them to interpret love of God as intrinsically good and so integral to eudaimonia.

More broadly, eudaimonia need not denote a single, distinct, best thing for human beings so that eudaimonism treats all that morality values besides eudaimonia as ultimately a means to this final end. Instead, eudaimonia may be conceived as an ordered assembly of good things valuable as ends in themselves that is not itself valued for the sake of something else or missing anything essential to a life worthy of pursuit. Julia Annas calls this interpretation of eudaimonia inclusivism, and although she discusses the position with respect to ancient Greek ethics, it allows Christian eudaimonists to hold both that love of God and neighbors is valuable for its own sake and that Christian morality obligates human beings to love God and neighbors for the sake of their own eudaimonia.[24] By embracing multiple goods as constitutive of eudaimonia, then, eudaimonists can consistently interpret the moral life as aiming at each individual's eudaimonia without reducing all moral goods other than eudaimonia—such as love of God and neighbors—to merely instrumental value.[25] Indeed, if loving God and neighbors is constitutive of eudaimonia, eudaimonism interprets the moral life as aiming at such love, not as using it to attain something else, precisely because it also interprets the moral life as aiming at eudaimonia.[26] Thus, Christian eudaimonists can endorse and powerfully motivate the insistence, sometimes posited as an objection to eudaimonism and other major types of normative ethics, that loving God and neighbors as an extrinsic means to eudaimonia is self-defeating since it traduces proper ends into instruments, impairing our relationship to them and thereby diminishing the eudaimonia that would have been realized by loving God and neighbors as ends in themselves integral to eudaimonia.[27]

Accordingly, examining the possibility of eudaimonistic interpretations of Christian morality offers insights into Christian conceptions of eudaimonia. In particular, it is inclusive, encompassing love of God and neighbors as central, constitutive aspects of eudaimonia. Christian eudaimonia is therefore more than organismal well-being. Here again, this is not unique to Christian understandings of eudaimonia; as Annas notes, "All the ancient theories greatly expand and modify the ordinary non-philosophical understandings of happiness, opening themselves to criticism from non-philosophers on this score."[28] Nevertheless, this reinterpretation of the meaning of eudaimonia has important implications. For Christian eudaimonists, it signifies that the moral life is not a means to an end distinct from it but part of the reward to which it leads. To the extent that embracing the moral life in this way transforms one's values and goals, the life that is found by losing it through Christian discipleship is not the same as the life that was lost (cf., e.g., Matt. 10:39 and 16:25).

At the same time, eudaimonism also imposes limits on the extent to which it can recalibrate conceptions of eudaimonia. After all, since eudaimonism interprets the moral life as aiming at one's own eudaimonia, morality is necessarily eudaimonist if eudaimonia is simply a matter of realizing morally appropriate ends, but then eudaimonism approaches tautology. Of course, given a concrete set of moral obligations, such an interpretation of eudaimonia would not be vacuous. For example, assuming the command to love God unreservedly and one's neighbors as oneself, eudaimonia would mean actualizing this love. Nevertheless, assuming these commands and this meaning of eudaimonia, nothing is added by affirming that morality is eudaimonist since these commands completely define eudaimonia, and the moral life necessarily aims at fulfillment of moral obligation, however deliberately. Thus, while commitment to eudaimonism rightly enriches understandings of eudaimonia, it cannot wholly determine the meaning of eudaimonia if eudaimonism is to be more than a doctrine of the good or trivially true.

Fortunately, other considerations in addition to eudaimonism tend to influence the meaning of eudaimonia. For instance, independent of reflection on morality or eudaimonism, people usually have ideas about what it is to flourish. In particular, organismal well-being is generally assumed to be an aspect of flourishing, and perhaps even more strongly, acute organismal distress—whether agony, despair, or even just persistent pain or deprivation—is commonly regarded as inconsistent with it.[29] Certain subjective states are also usually associated with flourishing—among them enjoyment or satisfaction—since it seems impossible to flourish wholly against one's will.[30] Inclusivist interpretations of eudaimonia accommodate treating these further factors as ends in themselves partially constitutive of eudaimonia. Yet however they are thought to relate to eudaimonia, most plausible understandings of eudaimonia must include organismal well-being and satisfaction along with fulfillment of moral duty, and this tempers the concern about tautology that arises if eudaimonia were solely defined by reference to morality's aims.

Nevertheless, mitigating this worry about tautology hints at another potential problem for Christian eudaimonism. A more than moralistic interpretation of eudaimonia means that eudaimonism conceives the moral life as aiming at more than each individual doing their moral duty. In particular, as just noted, the aims of the moral life are likely to include aspects of organismal well-being and certain subjective states, at least to some degree. While these additional dimensions of eudaimonia keep eudaimonism from tautology, they also highlight eudaimonism's inherently self-referential character. To be sure, the notion that the moral life aims at each individual fulfilling moral duty conceives morality as oriented to the self, although in a potentially incidental way since the duty each individual is to fulfill may be oriented to others, as in the case of the commands to love God unreservedly and one's neighbor as oneself. However, the notion that the moral life also aims at each individual's organismal well-being and satisfaction, at least to some degree, renders morality robustly self-referential, for these aims are states of the individual. Yet is it appropriate for Christians to construe morality as more than incidentally self-referential? The answer depends in part on a more determinate understanding of properly Christian love.

Eudaimonism and the Character of Christian Love

My discussion thus far has already indicated that for Christians, an adequate conception of eudaimonia involves love for God and neighbors as ends in themselves. Even so, questions remain about the nature of properly Christian love that are decisive for Christian assessments of eudaimonism. In particular, does Christian morality obligate love of God and neighbors as ends in themselves for the sake of the lover, the beloved, both of them, or for some other reason, like God's will or God's and neighbors' worth? These rationales need not be mutually exclusive, and Christian eudaimonism can endorse a variety of them. Nevertheless, because eudaimonism interprets the moral life as aiming at each individual's own eudaimonia, Christian eudaimonism must construe such love as contributing at least to the good of the lover. However, is this always an accurate or constructive portrayal of properly Christian love? I have noted that there is no Christian consensus on the meaning of love, and as a consequence, there are no generic answers to these questions. Instead, they require assumptions about Christian love that exclude some Christian perspectives. Conceiving properly Christian love as open to self-transcendence is one such assumption, and I shall adopt it here to explore Christian eudaimonism in greater depth.

The notion of a love open to self-transcendence itself requires clarification. To begin, self-transcending love does not merely refer to loving something other than oneself; any credible Christian conception of love involves loving God and neighbors, and hence, there must be more to self-transcending love if it is to specify a subset of Christian perspectives. Further, in this context, self-transcending love does not simply designate loving something other than oneself as an end in itself either since as I observed in the previous section, it is possible to love something as an end in itself for additional reasons, including self-regarding ones such as one's own sake or the sake of one's relationship with the other. Instead, self-transcending love in the sense that I shall consider denotes love of another simply for the sake of the other.

As with the type of eudaimonism I have chosen to examine, by treating proper Christian love as able to accommodate self-transcendence in this sense I intend to select a moderate and capacious position.[31] After all, this is scarcely an idiosyncratically rigorous interpretation, for given Christian scripture's multiple hard teachings about discipleship and identification of Jesus's exemplary love with his sacrificial death, Christian love has frequently been construed as requiring self-denial rather than merely openness to self-transcendence.[32] Indeed, even those who allow that Christian love need not be self-denying sometimes maintain that it must be completely self-transcending and not simply open to self-transcendence.[33] At the same time, interpreting properly Christian love as open to self-transcendence rather than ruling out self-regard altogether is not a conspicuously self-indulgent account of properly Christian love either since Christians often consider robustly self-referential ends integral to the highest form of love.[34] In fact, construing properly Christian love as merely open to self-transcendence poses a prima facie challenge to Christian eudaimonism, for by depicting the moral life as aiming at one's own eudaimonia, eudaimonism seems to present moral obligation as necessarily self-regarding. Nevertheless, interpreting properly Christian love as open to self-transcendence does not beg the question against Christian eudaimonism since it does not determine the relationship of such love to the self's eudaimonia. On the contrary, Christian eudaimonists could maintain that self-transcending love of God and neighbors is constitutive of eudaimonia.[35] I will argue, however, that assuming other basic Christian commitments, interpreting properly Christian love as open to self-transcendence shapes the sort of eudaimonism Christians can consistently accept, and that assuming other beliefs about eudaimonia and the world, this interpretation of such love affects the circumstances under which Christians can consistently accept eudaimonism at all.

To appreciate how understanding the moral life as aiming at its adherents' eudaimonia might nonetheless afford a central place to a love of others that may be simply for their own sakes, it helps to specify the apparent dissonance between eudaimonism's self-reference and such love's potential self-transcendence more precisely. In particular, interpreting properly Christian love as open to self-transcendence need not conflict with eudaimonist conceptions of the substance of the moral life, since as I have noted, such love may be conceived as integral to one's own eudaimonia. Instead, interpreting properly Christian love as open to self-transcendence is evidently difficult to reconcile with eudaimonist depictions of the moral life's orientation, since understanding the moral life as aiming at one's own eudaimonia—whatever that is taken to be—portrays that orientation self-referentially while self-transcending love in the sense of the notion that I am considering is not self-referential—however much it may benefit the lover. As such, although the various virtues and activities of the moral life may focus on others supposing eudaimonism, because eudaimonism casts the aim of the moral life self-referentially, Christian eudaimonists seem compelled to interpret love and other moral duties as ultimately for the sake of the self. Hence, if properly Christian love must be open to self-transcendence, eudaimonism appears inadequate as a framework for Christian ethics.

Worse, if potentially self-transcending love is indeed an aspect of eudaimonia, eudaimonism may prove self-limiting—not yielding as much eudaimonia as another moral theory would—or even self-defeating. I have noted that by construing the moral life as aiming at one's own eudaimonia, eudaimonism disposes its adherents to attribute self-referential ends to their moral duties that seem to preclude them from accepting that they could have an obligation to love that is simply for the sake of the beloved. Accordingly, supposing openness to such self-transcending love partially constitutes eudaimonia, eudaimonism appears not only unable to regard this love morally requisite but thereby to impede realization of the eudaimonia at which it conceives the moral life to aim.[36] After all, while self-transcending love of God and neighbors may partially constitute one's own eudaimonia, loving them for that reason is no longer self-transcending love in the relevant sense. Nevertheless, if self-transcending love of God and neighbors is partially constitutive of one's own eudaimonia and Christian morality obligates such love, then at a minimum the Christian moral life aims at an aspect of one's own eudaimonia and thus seems eudaimonist all the same. So how then should Christians who make these assumptions interpret their morality, as eudaimonist or not?

Classical utilitarians' theories of the good and the right both pose a similar puzzle, and Christian eudaimonists may adopt one of their solutions to it—self-effacement.[37] Specifically, in cases where it is not possible to accept a moral theory's depiction of the aim of an action without precluding a motive that is necessary to perform the action, the theory has reason to disclaim itself and thus be self-effacing.[38] As applied to Christian eudaimonism, if acceptance of eudaimonism's interpretation of the moral life as aiming at one's own eudaimonia precludes Christians from acknowledging a moral duty to love God and neighbors with the openness to self-transcendence that is partially constitutive of their eudaimonia—because it implies that such love must contribute to the lover's eudaimonia and so imposes self-regarding constraints on that love—then Christian eudaimonism has cause to disclaim itself and deny that the aims of the moral life are necessarily self-referential.[39] After all, unlike forthrightly eudaimonist accounts, depicting the moral life as accommodating non-self-referential ends allows its adherents to accept that a love for God and neighbors open to self-transcendence may be morally obligatory. Accordingly, supposing such love partially constitutes the lover's eudaimonia and does not thwart it, a life ordered by this love in fact aims at one's own eudaimonia and so remains eudaimonist, albeit self-effacingly. Indeed, given these assumptions, this depiction of the moral life disavows the self-referential aims of that life precisely in order to further them and hence has eudaimonist reasons to deny eudaimonism.

Self-effacing eudaimonism thus maintains that the moral life rewards its adherents but requires those who lead it to concentrate on their duties to others rather than the rewards for oneself. Given the Gospel records of Jesus's repeated rejection of self-seeking and call to disinterested service explicitly in terms of their boon for those who heed his words, many Christians have agreed.[40] Moreover, interpreting the love of God and neighbors that Christians often regard partially constitutive of eudaimonia as open to self-transcendence not only prompts them to characterize the Christian moral life as self-effacingly eudaimonist but allows them to specify the nature of that self-effacement. In particular, since such love must simply be able to accommodate self-transcendence rather than dismiss all concern for oneself, self-effacingly eudaimonist depictions of the Christian moral life that assume this account of love and eudaimonia need not deny that the moral life has self-referential aims. Instead, they must merely deny that its aims are necessarily self-referential. Similarly, so long as Christians believe such love partially but not fully constitutes eudaimonia, there may be other aspects of eudaimonia, like basic organismal well-being, that there is no reason not to acknowledge as aims of the moral life. Consequently, given this conception of properly Christian love and eudaimonia, it seems Christians could construe the moral life as aiming at one's own eudaimonia without compromising that life or the realization of its end, provided that they do not depict that life as necessarily aiming at one's own eudaimonia. Since self-effacement per se could connote a theory's categorical self-disavowal—in this case denying not just that the moral life necessarily aims at one's own eudaimonia but that it so aims at all—I refer to this more refined account of how the ends of the Christian moral life may be presented as somewhat self-effacing eudaimonism.

Characterizing the Christian moral life as somewhat self-effacingly eudaimonist tempers the astringency of fully self-effacing eudaimonism in pivotal ways. It avoids depicting the moral life as requiring complete indifference to its implications for the eudaimonia of those who live morally. It also averts commitment to a severe conception of Christian love that cannot countenance any self-concern, as well as a wholly moralistic interpretation of eudaimonia that seems impoverished in its own right and renders eudaimonism effectively tautological.[41] Nevertheless, characterizing the Christian moral life as somewhat self-effacingly eudaimonist also represents that life as amenable to aims besides one's own eudaimonia. To be sure, that amenability allows this life's adherents to embrace a possibly self-transcending love of God and neighbors coherently, and thus, supposing eudaimonia is partially constituted by such love, that amenability is necessary if the Christian moral life is in fact to aim at its adherents' eudaimonia and so remain eudaimonist. Yet by depicting the Christian moral life as amenable to non-self-referential aims, somewhat self-effacing Christian eudaimonism implicitly adumbrates non-eudaimonist interpretations of that life in which it does not just appear amenable to aims that may not contribute to one's own eudaimonia but actually is.

Accordingly, while self-effacement allows Christians to reconcile eudaimonism's self-referential framework with conceptions of properly Christian love as open to self-transcendence, it also harbors potential responses to those perplexed by the prospect of interpreting the Christian moral life as anything other than eudaimonist. For example, in a review of Nicholas Wolterstorff's *Justice: Rights and Wrongs*, Nigel Biggar states,

> This Augustinian, eschatological eudaimonism does imply, it seems to me, a prudential reading of the love commandment. Wolterstorff finds this "offensive". I do not. This is partly because the flourishing for which I hope is constituted by my giving myself in love; and partly because I know of no better way to answer the questions, "Why love? Why render the respect due to another?" than to say, "Because it is good for me, ultimately". Besides, if we do not have faith in the love of God to bring us to flourish as beings who give themselves in love, then I do not know what we have faith in the love of God for.[42]

Eudaimonists are hardly confined to Biggar's answers to his questions and can instead consistently contend that "I should love because it is good for my neighbor, ultimately," and that "I ought render the respect due another because it is his or her due."[43] Likewise, eudaimonists can straightforwardly maintain that Christians may have faith in the love of God to bring other people to flourish. In short, although eudaimonism interprets the moral life as aiming at one's own eudaimonia, it does not imply that one's own eudaimonia is the only reason to live morally. Indeed, assuming eudaimonia is partially constituted by potentially self-transcending love of God and neighbors, eudaimonism naturally suggests that we are to live morally for God and our neighbors' sakes as well. Moreover, while eudaimonism interprets the moral life as aiming at one's own eudaimonia, it does not even entail that we are to live morally for our own sakes. The aim of the moral life is one thing, the motive for living that life another.[44] Nevertheless, although eudaimonism need not finally reduce moral motivation to concern for one's own eudaimonia as Biggar implies, it cannot exclude morality's reference to one's own eudaimonia either. For the eudaimonist, reverencing God, benefiting the neighbor, and respecting another can all constitute good reasons to live morally and make it right to do so, but morally obligatory actions must also contribute to one's own eudaimonia; otherwise, the moral life would not aim at its adherents' eudaimonia as eudaimonism claims.

*[handwritten note in top margin: * vice versa – aim at other's good, + in fact this is/may be good for self + motive eg. go to hell if for God's + pleasure]*

Conversely, even Christians who interpret morality as self-effacingly eudaimonist can consistently accept Biggar's confidence that loving God and neighbors is good for the lover and trust that God's love will bring human beings to eudaimonia. Although fully self-effacing eudaimonism does not portray the moral life as aiming at each individual's eudaimonia, it nonetheless maintains that the moral life in fact contributes to each individual's eudaimonia while ostensibly pursuing other aims. A fortiori, if Christian morality is only somewhat self-effacingly eudaimonist, it can even portray the moral life as aiming at each individual's own eudaimonia so long as it also affirms that the moral life may have other aims. Hence, self-effacing Christian eudaimonism can naturally treat reverencing God, benefiting the neighbor, and respecting another not simply as good reasons to live morally but as aims of the moral life. Still, eudaimonism—self-effacing or not—cannot concede that the moral life does not in fact aim at each individual's eudaimonia. Thus, Christians' assessments of eudaimonism turn on whether they believe the moral life may ever be fully realized yet fail to deliver the agent's eudaimonia or perhaps even impede it, and so I conclude by exploring that question.

Christian Love, Eudaimonia, and Christian Eudaimonism

The character of the connection between the moral life and each moral agent's eudaimonia obviously depends on the nature of both. I have been interpreting the Christian moral life as involving potentially self-transcending love of God and neighbors, and I have argued that Christians who accept this interpretation of the moral life have reason to regard such love partially constitutive of eudaimonia. I have also noted the desirability of attributing other elements to eudaimonia and suggested that minimal conditions of organismal well-being are plausibly among them. These considerations help delineate the relationship between the Christian moral life and its adherents' eudaimonia, but without specifying the constitution of eudaimonia further, they are insufficient to determine whether that life might ever compromise the eudaimonia of those who live it.

For example, if eudaimonia is not principally moral excellence but decisively consists in conventional goods like wealth, status, beauty, power, pleasure, family, and friends, then the Christian moral life may at times jeopardize its adherents' eudaimonia and perhaps even lead them to renounce it, for in a world of great disparity and need, love of God and neighbors open to self-transcendence may forsake such things to help other people. This is hardly surprising; I have observed that eudaimonists frequently revise prevailing understandings of eudaimonia. Moreover, while consideration of these conventional goods illustrates the importance of defining eudaimonia for assessments of eudaimonism, it is far from a conclusive objection to Christian eudaimonism since Christians often regard these goods as subordinate to love of God and neighbors. Of course, such mundane goods are not the only reason to question whether moral excellence is the decisive element of eudaimonia; perhaps aesthetic expression, the pursuit of truth, cultural refinement, or other personal or collective achievements might be crucial components of eudaimonia potentially at odds with a love of God and neighbors open to self-transcendence.[45] Nevertheless, even with respect to these putatively higher goods, eudaimonists generally extol moral excellence as the core of eudaimonia and thus they do not interpret the possibility that the moral life may impede them as an obstacle to eudaimonism.[46] As I have noted, this is not without cost, for it can reduce eudaimonism per se to the trivial truth that the moral life aims at the moral excellence of those who lead it.[47] Still, interpreting eudaimonia as overwhelmingly a matter of moral excellence remains a robust and controversial claim, even if interpreting the moral life as eudaimonist given that claim is not.[48]

Christians might seem particularly disposed to embrace this definition of eudaimonia. After all, Christians often prize spiritual over material goods—at least nominally—and frequently correlate God's judgment, with its attendant blessings and curses, to moral performance.[49] Moreover, I have noted that Christians have reason to regard love of God and neighbor partially constitutive of eudaimonia, and such love is undoubtedly central to the Christian moral life. However, I do not think Christians can rightly interpret eudaimonia as tantamount to moral excellence. I have indicated that basic conditions of organismal well-being or at least freedom from intense suffering and protracted privation are plausibly aspects of a complete conception of eudaimonia, but Christians need not put them on a par with moral excellence. Instead, I expect Christians regard blessedness, understood as joyous participation in a loving relationship with God and others with God, as central to eudaimonia, and indeed a more comprehensive characterization of it than moral excellence. By participation in a loving relationship, I do not intend simply being loved or loving but their combination—a dynamic, reciprocal partnership that actively gives and receives. Accordingly, participating in a loving relationship with God and others with God necessarily includes love of God and neighbors, and hence, from this perspective, that is precisely why Christians commonly regard such love partially constitutive of eudaimonia. Yet there is more to participation in a loving relationship with God and others with God than such love—in particular, awareness that one is loved by God and others with God so that their love may be actively received—and thus that is why from this perspective love of God and neighbors is only partially constitutive of eudaimonia.

Given this interpretation of eudaimonia, eudaimonist conceptions of the Christian moral life are not tautological, for while it is necessarily true that the moral life aims at its adherents' moral excellence, it is not necessarily true that this life aims at its adherents' blessedness. Specifically, love of God and neighbors open to self-transcendence need not aim at the lover's active reception of their love. Of course, participation in a loving relationship with God and others with God may be the ideal outcome of a potentially self-transcending love of them, not simply in the platitudinous sense that blessedness—as the objectively best state for human beings—is always the ideal outcome for the agent, but in the substantive sense that a potentially self-transcending love of God and neighbors inherently prizes participation in a loving relationship with them. Thus, the Christian moral life may lead its adherents to hope for eudaimonia as its fitting fruition. Nevertheless, if self-transcending love denotes love of another simply for the sake of the other, as I have been supposing, then love of God and neighbors open to self-transcendence could be fully realized without awareness of its reciprocation.[50] Consequently, if the Christian moral life fundamentally involves such love, that life might not aim at the eudaimonia of those who lead it.

Yet if such potentially self-transcending love of God and neighbors in fact fosters awareness of its reciprocation, among other things, the Christian moral life would be effectively eudaimonist assuming this interpretation of eudaimonia.[51] So, then, does this love foster such awareness? No doubt many Christians have generally thought as much. After all, the conviction that God loves human beings is commonly at the heart of Christian faith, and many seeking to lead a Christian life do so as a response to God's love. What's more, Christians often contend that they are able to love God and neighbors only because God first loved them and that nothing can separate human beings from God's love.[52] Hence, Christians frequently maintain that a love of God and neighbors open to self-transcendence does not simply cultivate appreciation for God's reciprocal love but understands itself as reciprocating God's own. Both affirmations link such potentially self-transcending love of God and neighbors with awareness of God's love and thereby connect the aim of the Christian moral life with eudaimonia granting my interpretation of them.

However, although a potentially self-transcending love of God and neighbors may often contribute to participation in a loving relationship with God and others with God, Christians ought not simply assume that it must. After all, principal Christian authorities have suggested that such love could forfeit the lover's blessedness. For example, in telling the story of the golden calf, Exodus presents Moses as asking God to forgive the people's sin and then entreating God "to blot" him out of the book God has written if that is necessary to reconcile God and the people (Exod. 32:30–33).[53] Here Moses's love for God's people is self-transcending yet does not aim at his own eudaimonia, for it is fulfilled by restoring their relationship with God even if Moses must forfeit his own. Similarly, Paul was so anguished that many of his people failed to recognize Jesus as the Christ that he tells the church in Rome, "I could wish that I myself were accursed and cut off from Christ for the sake of my own people, my kindred according to the flesh" (Rom. 9:3). Like Moses's, Paul's love for God's people in this case would not aim at his own blessedness but surrender it to facilitate others'. While potentially self-transcending love of God and neighbors would not conduce to the lover's eudaimonia in these instances, they do not show that the Christian moral life does not effectively aim at the eudaimonia of those who lead it, for Exodus portrays God as declining Moses's appeal and Paul frames his willingness to sacrifice his relationship with God for his fellows' relationship with God as a possibility. Still, since a love open to self-transcendence may offer itself in these ways, these examples illustrate that such love need not aim at the lover's participation in a loving relationship with God and thus that a life suffused by this love might not be eudaimonist.

Further, Jesus's crucifixion may indicate that this possibility has been actualized. Christians often interpret Jesus's death on a cross as a manifestation of Jesus's love for God and human beings that helped restore human beings' relationship to God. The ordeal was undoubtedly excruciating and shameful. More challenging for Christian eudaimonism, Christians frequently contend that it placed Jesus under God's curse.[54] If so, perhaps this rent in their relationship is reflected in Jesus's cry from the Cross as recorded in Matthew and Mark: "My God, my God, why have you forsaken me?" (Matt. 27:46; Mark 15:34). In any case, it is implausible to suppose Jesus was enjoying eudaimonia as he uttered these final words before dying.

I suggest this is not primarily because he was in agony and on the verge of death. Although I have observed that the basic conditions of organismal well-being, or at least freedom from severe anguish, are likely elements of eudaimonia, I have also indicated that Christians commonly regard other aspects of eudaimonia far more important, for example, love of God and neighbors. Yet there is also no reason for Christians to think that Jesus ceased to love God and neighbors, even under such severe distress. As his agonized question attests, Jesus does not ignore—much less defy—God but beseeches God, and the surprise evident in his expression of abandonment implies not that he had stopped loving God but that he thought God no longer reciprocated his love. Nor does Jesus's sense of dereliction show that his love was incomplete or thwarted, since assuming such love was open to self-transcendence, it could attain its aim without being returned. Instead, I propose that Jesus's cry reveals that he was not then enjoying eudaimonia principally because it registered his inability to perceive God's love for him at that moment, so that whether accursed or not, Jesus was not then participating in a loving relationship with God in a way that constitutes blessedness. If this is accurate, the Christian moral life is not eudaimonist in this case, for Jesus is loving God and neighbors fully without realizing his eudaimonia, and thus his life and that love are not aiming at it. Indeed, since eudaimonia does not accompany moral excellence for Jesus, the Christian moral life is not effectively eudaimonist in this case either.[55]

However, even if this analysis is accurate, it is only partial, for Christians who celebrate Easter have reason to insist that Jesus's participation in a loving relationship with God and others with God—and thereby his eudaimonia—was restored through Jesus's resurrection. Accordingly, given such Christian eschatological commitments, the Christian moral life ultimately seems to lead to the blessedness of those who live it even in this torturous instance. After all, Christians commonly believe potentially self-transcending love of God and neighbors partially constitutes and often realizes participation in a loving relationship with God and others with God. Consequently, while this love may not facilitate participation in a loving relationship with God and others with God under extreme conditions that can obtain before God's salvation and consummation are wholly actualized, many Christians confess that when God is all in all, such conditions will be overcome and those who love in this way will participate in that sort of loving relationship.[56] If so, then although the Christian moral life may not be eudaimonist now, in the end it effectively is. As a result, the adequacy of eudaimonism as a framework for Christian morality proves sensitive to the stage of salvation history in which it is assessed.

Moreover, although this sensitivity may only have affected Jesus in extremis since his participation in a loving relationship with God and others with God was sufficiently robust to withstand lesser challenges, it has quotidian significance for Jesus's disciples, given the greater instability of their participation in that relationship. For example, potentially self-transcending love of God and neighbors leads some to the social margins, hoping to help the suffering, vulnerable, oppressed, displaced, and despondent. It prompts others to study and reflect, seeking to understand God and their faith more fully. Such love moves others to ministry or religious life in its myriad forms. For many, these experiences and vocations deepen their feeling of God's presence and love and hence enhance their participation in a loving relationship with God and others with God. However, others' perception of God's love—and therewith their participation in a loving relationship with God and others with God—evanesces in these endeavors and thus for them, the Christian moral life does not lead to eudaimonia. As in Jesus's case, this need not be because their love of God failed or was frustrated; some continue to love God and neighbors despite ceasing to sense God's love, and since it is open to self-transcendence, the success of this love does not depend on cognizance of its return—or even its return at all. Such return is surely desirable and a fitting outcome of this love, but a love open to self-transcendence is open to love simply for the sake of the other and so open to aiming at something other than its return—for instance, affirmation of the other. In short, if there is more to eudaimonia than moral excellence, the moral life may not deliver eudaimonia. If moral excellence involves openness to self-transcendence, the moral life may be fulfilled without delivering eudaimonia. Christians who accept both conditionals should therefore conclude that the Christian moral life may not be eudaimonist. Given Jesus's ordeal on the Cross and many others' more mundane loss of awareness of God's love despite loving God and neighbors, I argue that Christians who accept these conditionals should conclude that at this stage of salvation history, the Christian moral life may sometimes not even be effectively eudaimonist.

Still, although failure to bring eudaimonia to its adherents need not signal incompletion of the Christian moral life if that life involves potentially self-transcending love of God and neighbors and eudaimonia is principally participation in a loving relationship with God and others with God, it is by definition an unhappy result. What's more, it may jeopardize the moral life. Naturally, by involving potentially self-transcending love of God and neighbors in a world of great disparity, fragility, and injustice, the Christian moral life is often costly and difficult. It is also risky, for such love in this sort of world may lead to just the experiences and circumstances in which God's love seems to disappear. If so, the Christian moral life would not only aim at something other than its adherents' eudaimonia but could now imperil it. Of course, seeking to love God and neighbors is hardly the only human pursuit that endangers a sense of God's love. Nevertheless, if participation in a loving relationship with God and others with God is the greatest human good, then losing a sense of God's love is quite a loss. Worse, losing a sense of God's love may undermine faith in God's eschatological consummation—or at least one's participation in it—so that the Christian moral life ceases to seem eudaimonist ultimately, not only proximately. Perhaps most harrowing of all, those who lose the sense of God's love may cease loving God and others in God. This is especially ominous because supposing such love is a central, constitutive aspect of eudaimonia as Christian eudaimonists reasonably maintain, the failure to bring eudaimonia that may jeopardize the leading of a moral life might thereby preclude realization of eudaimonia since leading that life is integral to it. In such cases, the Christian moral life would not merely fail to be even effectively eudaimonist but could seem practically anti-eudaimonist, for by drawing its adherents to pursuits and perspectives that may prompt them to question the presence and reality of God's love, that life does not simply risk but could impede the eudaimonia of those who lead it.

This is obviously a far cry from my contention that the Christian moral life is effectively eudaimonist in the end. However, I do not think accepting that the Christian moral life may not be even effectively eudaimonist at this stage of salvation history need have such subversive effects. Regarding the Christian moral life potentially thwarting its adherents' eudaimonia, Christians have reason to be cautious about the inference that those now lacking a thematized love for God will not finally participate in a loving relationship with God.[57] Thus, even if the Christian moral life were to lead some of its adherents to stop loving God deliberately, that life may yet prove effectively eudaimonist for them in the end. That the Christian moral life may cease to seem eudaimonist ultimately and not simply proximately need not belie interpreting it as effectively eudaimonist in the end either. After all, I have argued that if the Christian moral life includes a love open to self-transcendence and is to be eudaimonist, its eudaimonism has reason to be self-effacing. Nevertheless, recognition of the riskiness of the Christian moral life on this interpretation is significant, for it reveals that a potentially self-transcending love is open not simply to a love that is not for one's own sake but to a love that may not seem to be in one's own interest. If so, and supposing the Christian moral life involves such a potentially self-transcending love of God and neighbors, eudaimonist interpretations of that life depend not only on ethical argument but Christian faith and hope as well.

Notes

I would like to express my gratitude to John Hare and Jennifer Herdt, from whom I have learned much about the meaning and adequacy of Christian eudaimonism. I would also like to thank the Princeton religious ethics discussion group, and in particular, Neil Arner, John Bowlin, Liane Carlson, Jesse Couenhoven, Emily Dumler, Clifton Granby, Eric Gregory, Thomas Lewis, Robin Lovin, Joshua Mauldin, Jeffrey Stout, Andrea Vicini, William Werpehowski, and Derek Woodard-Lehman, for helpful comments on an earlier draft of this essay.

1. Aristotle observes that although all agree that eudaimonia is a matter of living and faring well, there is widespread disagreement about what it is to live and fare well (*NE* 1095a.15–22). In fact, Augustine reports that Varro differentiated 288 possible interpretations of eudaimonia (*CD* 19.1).

2. For example, eudaimonia was once frequently translated into English as happiness, but with the subjective connotations of that word given the influence of classical utilitarianism's identification of happiness with pleasure, eudaimonia is now often translated as flourishing. Either way, such English terms are indeterminate and so scarcely specify the substance of eudaimonia.

3. For instance, psychological eudaimonism simply refers to the descriptive thesis that human beings invariably seek eudaimonia and thus does not reference morality; cf., e.g., Gregory Vlastos, *Socrates: Ironist and Moral Philosopher* (Ithaca, NY: Cornell University Press, 1991), 203.

4. Aristotle frames his account of ethics this way in *NE* 1.1–4.

5. Oliver O'Donovan concentrates on this sense of eudaimonism in *The Problem of Self-Love in St. Augustine* (New Haven, CT: Yale University Press, 1981), 195. Stephen Pope implicitly appeals to the same understanding of eudaimonism in advocating for a version of natural law theory in "The Evolutionary Roots of Morality in Theological Perspective," *Zygon* 33, no. 4 (December 1998): 554.

6. For instance, Joseph Butler posits such a link between eudaimonia and morality; see his *Fifteen Sermons Preached at the Rolls Chapel and a Dissertation of the Nature of Virtue* (London: SPCK, 1970), 39.

7. Henry Sidgwick, *The Methods of Ethics*, 7th ed. (Indianapolis: Hackett, 1981), 1; cf. Stephen Darwall, *Philosophical Ethics* (Boulder, CO: Westview, 1998), 195.

8. For example, both the Hebrew Bible and New Testament repeatedly contend that love of God and neighbors is essential for human well-being; from among innumerable passages, cf., e.g., Deut. 6:3–5 and John 15:11–12. Of course, the Judeo-Christian tradition is hardly unique in affirming the value of loving others; even egoists tend to emphasize it.

9. For instance, the Synoptic Gospels portray Jesus as identifying love of God and neighbors as the greatest commandments, on which all the law and the prophets depend (Matt. 22:34–40; Mark 12:28–31; Luke 10:25–28).

10. Amid countless examples, cf., e.g., Deut. 28:1–14 and 1 Cor. 2:9.

11. Concerning Christian love's distinctive disposition to sacrifice itself for others, cf., e.g., Matt. 5:43–46 and John 15:12–13. Regarding Jesus's rejection of self-seeking as counterproductive, cf., e.g., Mark 8:35 and John 12:25.

12. Kenneth E. Kirk puts the point particularly sharply, noting that throughout the Synoptic Gospels, "the disinterestedness of Christian discipleship is emphasized as fully as it well can be. In flat contradiction to this doctrine of ethical disinterestedness, or self-forgetfulness, are the passages [stressing recompense]. The two strains of thought appear to contradict and neutralize one another beyond all hope of reconciliation; and the 'mercenary' sayings are at least as prominent as the others. . . . Nothing would be left of Jesus' teaching if the references to reward and punishment were struck out as inauthentic," and yet, "the main tendency of Jesus' teaching . . . was to help men to forget themselves by focussing [*sic*] all their aspirations upon God and the kingdom of God, and upon the needs of men as seen with the eyes of God." *The Vision of God: The Christian Doctrine of the Summum Bonum* (London: Longmans, Green, 1931), 142 and 141, respectively.

13. Philip Schaff, ed., *A Select Library of the Nicene and Post-Nicene Fathers of the Christian Church*, trans. Richard Stothert, vol. 4 (Grand Rapids, MI: Eerdmans, 1983), 5 §8.

14. *Sermon 150*, vol. 5 in pt. 3—Sermons of Augustine, *The Works of Saint Augustine: A Translation for the 21st Century*, ed. John Rotelle, trans. Edmund Hill (New Rochelle, NY: New City Press, 1992), §4. Indeed, Augustine later even insisted, "Felicity is not a goddess, but a gift of God; and therefore no god is to be worshipped by men except the God who can make men happy. If Felicity were in fact a goddess, then she would rightly be called the sole divinity worthy of worship" (*City of God*, trans. Henry Bettenson [London: Penguin, 1984], bk. 5, preface).

15. Thomas Aquinas, *Summa Contra Gentiles*, trans. Vernon Bourke (Notre Dame, IN: University of Notre Dame Press, 1991), 3.122.

16. Thomas Aquinas, *Summa Theologiae*, trans. Thomas Gilby (London: Blackfriars, 1969), I-II.2.2r.1.

17. Martin Luther, *The Freedom of a Christian*, vol. 31 in *Luther's Works*, ed. Helmut Lehmann and Harold Grimm (Philadelphia: Muhlenberg Press, 1957), 365.

18. Martin Luther, *The Bondage of the Will*, vol. 33 in *Luther's Works*, ed. Helmut Lehmann and Philip Watson (Philadelphia: Fortress Press, 1972), 153. In fact, as early as his 1517 *Disputation against Scholastic Theology*, Luther explicitly repudiated Aristotle's *Ethics* and his "statement concerning happiness" as "the

worst enemy of grace" and a contradiction of proper Christian doctrine (§40–§42, in vol. 31 of *Luther's Works*, 12).

19. John Calvin, *Institutes of the Christian Religion*, ed. John McNeill, trans. Ford Lewis Battles, bk. 2, chap. 8.12 (Louisville, KY: Westminster John Knox Press, 1960), 1:377.

20. Ibid., bk. 3, chap. 7.2, 1:689, 692.

21. Despite the illustrations I have just adduced, Western magisterial Christian disagreement about eudaimonism should not be conflated with division between Catholics and Protestants. For example, Duns Scotus denied eudaimonism, and as I noted earlier, Joseph Butler maintained that enjoyment of eudaimonia corresponds to fulfillment of morality. Neil Arner further dispels any facile correlation of advocacy and criticism of eudaimonism with the split between Catholics and Protestants in "Theological Voluntarism and the Natural Law: The Integrated Moral Theories of John Duns Scotus, John Calvin, and Samuel Pufendorf" (PhD diss., Yale University, 2012).

22. Indeed, according to Julia Annas essentially all ancient Greek ethical philosophers were eudaimonists in this sense except the Cyrenaics, who were not eudaimonists at all (*The Morality of Happiness* [New York: Oxford University Press, 1991], 440–47).

23. For example, Kant famously insisted that we are entitled to believe that attainment of eudaimonia corresponds to fulfillment of moral duty and so would effectively commend a eudaimonistic account of morality in this broader sense of the term. However, Kant is generally not classified as a eudaimonist since he attributes moral obligation to the requirements of pure practical reason without any appeal to eudaimonia (cf., e.g., *Religion within the Boundaries of Mere Reason*, in *Religion within the Boundaries of Mere Reason and Other Writings*, ed. and trans. Allen Wood and George di Giovanni [Cambridge: Cambridge University Press, 1998], 6:3–4) and maintains that an action's moral worth depends on motivation by respect for the moral law rather than the desire for eudaimonia or another inclination (cf., e.g., *Groundwork of the Metaphysics of Morals*, ed. and trans. Mary Gregor [Cambridge: Cambridge University Press, 1997], 4:397–403). As such, this broader sense of eudaimonism can be misleading; it also assimilates types of connections between eudaimonia and morality I seek to distinguish to examine the relationships between eudaimonism and Christian love.

Conversely, interpreting eudaimonism as the doctrine that moral obligation is justified by its contribution to the eudaimonia of those who comply with it can be misleading because it excludes thinkers commonly considered eudaimonists. For instance, although Augustine conceives of moral obligation in this way (cf., e.g., O'Donovan, *Problem of Self-Love*, 195), Aquinas does not. Aquinas affirms that a right, good will is necessary for happiness because the comprehension of God that constitutes happiness requires repose in God with delight, which is possible only when the will is duly bent on God, as is a right, good will (*ST* I-II.3.4, 4.3, 4.4, 5.7). Aquinas does not claim that a will duly bent on God is right and good because it is necessary for happiness. Nevertheless, Aquinas forthrightly aligns his interpretation of morality with Aristotle's and is widely regarded a eudaimonist (cf., e.g., *ST* I-II.Foreword). Moreover, this narrower sense of eudaimonism obscures its relationship with the facet of Christian love I emphasize.

24. Annas, *Morality of Happiness*, 36–42. See also John Ackrill, "Aristotle on *Eudaimonia*," *Proceedings of the British Academy* 60 (1974): 339–59; and Terence Irwin, *The Development of Ethics: A Historical and Critical Study* (Oxford: Oxford University Press, 2007), 1:128–31.

25. For instance, David Brink argues for a formally similar interpretation of Plato's and Aristotle's understandings of eudaimonia and love to defend their ability to warrant intrinsic and not simply instrumental concern for other people on eudaimonist grounds in "Eudaimonism, Love and Friendship, and Political Community," *Social Philosophy and Policy* 16, no. 1 (Winter 1999): 273–77.

26. The same may be said of eudaimonist moral agents. For example, Scott MacDonald contends that "the claim that one seeks the good of others as a part of one's own good does not mean that one does not seek the good of others for its own sake but only for the sake of one's own good. One can seek the constituents of one's own good for their own sakes, and also for the sake of the good of which they are constituents. Constituent parts of one's own good, then, will be goods identified by Plato, Aristotle, and Aquinas as things sought for their own sake and for the sake of something else." Scott MacDonald, "Egoistic Rationalism," in *Christian Theism and the Problems of Philosophy*, ed. Michael Beaty (Notre Dame, IN: University of Notre Dame Press, 1990), 352 #35.

27. For example, Michael Stocker poses a version of this objection to prevalent forms of ethical egoism, utilitarianism, and deontology in his much discussed "The Schizophrenia of Modern Ethical Theories," *Journal of Philosophy* 73, no. 14 (August 1976): 453–66. Indeed, so understood eudaimonism proves an alternative to these forms of modern ethical theories—differing from such ethical egoism and utilitarianism by denying their brand of consequentialism and instead insisting that the moral life aims at certain actions, not merely valuable consequences of actions. Stocker does not define the sort of deontology he seeks to criticize, but eudaimonism differs from forms of deontology that present rightness as specifiable apart from goodness since it maintains that rightness necessarily refers to goodness. Cf., e.g., Thomas Hurka, "Teleological Ethics," in *Encyclopedia of Philosophy*, 2nd ed., vol. 9, ed. Donald M. Borchert (Detroit: Thomson Gale, 2006), 382–84.

28. Annas, *Morality of Happiness*, 331.

29. Cf., e.g., James Gustafson, "The Transcendence of God and the Value of Human Life," in *Christian Ethics and the Community* (Philadelphia: Pilgrim Press, 1971), 139–49; and Aristotle, *NE* 1153b.19–21. Of course, the Stoics are famous for excluding organismal well-being from eudaimonia strictly speaking, confining it to living in accord with virtue.

30. Indeed, the contributions of organismal well-being and these sorts of subjective states to eudaimonia are among the reasons I suggest that Christian eudaimonists interpret unreserved love of God and love of neighbors as oneself as constitutive rather than exhaustive of eudaimonia.

31. For example, even Aristotle, who of course was not accountable to Israel's prophetic witness or Jesus's example and teaching, explicitly defined love "as wishing for [the beloved] what you believe to be good things, not for your own sake but for his, and being inclined, so far as you can, to bring these things about" (Aristotle, *Rhetoric* 2.4 1380b.36–1381a.2, in *The Works of Aristotle: Translated into English under the Editorship of W. D. Ross*, trans. W. Rhys Roberts, vol. 11 [Oxford: Clarendon Press, 1924]).

32. For instance, Garth Hallett identifies over three dozen authors across Western church history who characterize Christian love as self-denying (*Christian Neighbor-Love: An Assessment of Six Rival Versions* [Washington, DC: Georgetown University Press, 1989], 6).

33. For example, Anders Nygren contends, "Christianity does not recognise self-love as a legitimate form of love. Christian love moves in two directions, towards God and towards its neighbour; and in self-love it finds its chief adversary, which must be fought and conquered. It is self-love that alienates man from God, preventing him from sincerely giving himself up to God, and it is self-love that shuts up a man's heart against his neighbour" (*Agape and Eros*, trans. Philip Watson [London: SPCK, 1953], 217). Likewise, Reinhold Niebuhr maintains that love "does not carefully arbitrate between the needs of the self and of the other, since it meets the needs of the other without concern for the self" (*The Nature and Destiny of Man: Human Nature* [Louisville, KY: Westminster John Knox Press, 1996], 295). Here too even Aristotle's account of love is illustrative, for he insists that a "friend is the sort of man who shares your pleasure in what is good and your pain in what is unpleasant, for your sake and for no other reason" (*Rhetoric* 2.4 1381a.3–5).

34. For example, in his magisterial *Love, Human and Divine: The Heart of Christian Ethics*, Edward Vacek argues that philia, understood as loving others for the sake of one's relationship with them, "is the most complete Christian love[,] . . . holds pride of place among Christian loves," and is "the foundation and goal of Christian life" (Washington, DC: Georgetown University Press, 1994), xvi, 280.

35. Influential Christian eudaimonists have gone further. For example, Augustine famously commended not just self-transcending love of God but "love of God carried as far as contempt of self" (*CD* 14.28).

36. Colin Grant also assumes that properly Christian love is open to self-transcendence and states the claim succinctly: "The biggest barrier to self-fulfillment is its deliberate pursuit. Just as happiness happens when we are involved in something, rather than seeking to be happy as such, so self-fulfillment happens when we are engaged from beyond ourselves. Self-fulfillment ultimately depends on self-transcendence . . . the meaning of our lives is to be found beyond ourselves" (*Altruism and Christian Ethics* [Cambridge: Cambridge University Press, 2000], xviii–xix). Cf. e.g., Darlene Fozard Weaver, *Self-Love and Christian Ethics* (Cambridge: Cambridge University Press, 2002), 159; and Timothy Jackson, *The Priority of Love: Christian Charity and Social Justice* (Princeton: Princeton University Press, 2003), 11.

37. In simplified form, since hedonists claim that pleasure alone is valuable and often contend that people enjoy more pleasure when they pursue things besides pleasure, hedonists have reason to disavow hedonism. Likewise, since maximizing consequentialists claim that the right action produces the most value

and often contend that people generally produce more value when they act for reasons besides producing the most value, maximizing consequentialists have reason to disavow consequentialism.

38. Cf. Derek Parfit, *Reasons and Persons* (Oxford: Oxford University Press, 1984), 23–24. To explain self-effacement, I follow Parfit's convention and personify morality.

39. O'Donovan uses a similar strategy to explain Augustine's Christian eudaimonism, according the moral life's contribution to one's own eudaimonia a justifying role in moral obligation but denying it an epistemological one (*Problem of Self-Love*, 8, 155–58).

40. As simply two examples, O'Donovan is fond of the dictum, "Heaven is full of people who are not particularly concerned with being there" (ibid.). Likewise, Kirk contends, "Jesus constantly promised reward only to those who were prepared to follow and obey him from some other motive . . . 'For my sake and the gospel's' is to be the motive of the Christian's renunciations; if he renounces the joy and associations of this world merely for the sake of blessedness in the next, his blessedness will be forfeit" (*Vision of God*, 144).

41. No doubt potentially self-transcending love of God and neighbors delivers more than moral goods. Still, so long as Christians believe such love morally obligatory, interpreting eudaimonia as completely constituted by that love leaves eudaimonia an entirely moral matter and trivializes the eudaimonist notion that the moral life aims at the eudaimonia of those who lead it.

42. Nigel Biggar, review of *Justice: Rights and Wrongs*, by Nicholas Wolterstorff, *Studies in Christian Ethics* 23, no. 2 (2010): 136.

43. For example, while Irwin acknowledges that Aristotle "tries to derive [the requirements of justice and fairness] from self-regarding and self-centered concerns," Irwin also notes that according to Aristotle, "the most general form of concern [for the other] will still be concern for the other for his own sake" (*Development of Ethics*, 231). Indeed, in interpreting Aristotle's ethics, Sarah Broadie explains that acting "'for the sake of the noble' refers to a spirit in which the person does whatever he has independent reason to think it right or good to do. . . . The agent who does A because it is noble to do it does A as one who, by the doing of this independently right action, renders *himself* noble or fine" (*Ethics with Aristotle* [New York: Oxford University Press, 1991], 92–93; italics original). See also Annas, *Morality of Happiness*, 123, 127–28; and Vlastos, *Socrates*, 205–6, especially n. 27.

44. Here again, Broadie's exposition of Aristotle's understanding of the moral life is clarifying: "Aristotle does not introduce the conception of the supreme end [eudaimonia] in order to provide us with a motive for valuing those things which well-brought-up people value" (*Ethics with Aristotle*, 23). The reason is that "the *aiming* which is the central notion of [eudaimonism] is not intending, seeking, or purposing in a psychological sense. . . . Aristotle's argument attaches aims and ends to . . . abstract entities[,] crafts, activities, practices, projects. They cannot have motives, and the 'aim of' each is defined by the end whose achievement is the mark of *success* for that kind of craft, activity, etc." (*Ethics with Aristotle*, 16; italics original). Thus, Broadie insists, "Aristotle's notion of happiness is not designed to answer the question 'Why should I be moral?'" (*Ethics with Aristotle*, 56, #41).

However, this interpretation is contested. For example, Irwin offers an alternative, psychological account of the aim in Aristotle's eudaimonism (cf., e.g., Irwin, *Development of Ethics*, 124–26). By contrast, Annas contends that Aristotle "does not have the means to make such a sharp separation between the external way of looking at the action, in terms of actual success in the result, and the internal way of looking at the action, in terms of the agent's aiming at the kalon . . . [and thus] an important ambiguity is left in [Aristotle's] notion of aiming" ("Aristotle and Kant on Morality and Practical Reasoning," in *Aristotle, Kant, and the Stoics: Rethinking Happiness and Duty*, ed. Stephen Engstrom and Jennifer Whiting [Cambridge: Cambridge University Press, 1996], 246–47). Accordingly, Annas advocates an avowedly pluralist interpretation of Aristotle's conception of aiming that incorporates elements of Broadie's and Irwin's positions without distinguishing sharply between them (cf., e.g., Annas, *Morality of Happiness*, 29–35).

45. Cf., e.g., Bernard Williams, *Moral Luck* (Cambridge: Cambridge University Press, 1981), 20–39.

46. For example, Broadie explains that according to Aristotle "it is of the nature of human virtue to value its own activity above all else" (*Ethics with Aristotle*, 52).

47. For instance, Rosalind Hursthouse observes that "according to eudaimonism, the good life is the *eudaimon* life, and the virtues are what enable a human being to be *eudaimon* because the virtues just are those character traits that benefit their possessor in that way, barring bad luck" ("Virtue Ethics," in *Stanford Encyclopedia of Philosophy*, Fall 2013 ed., ed. Edward Zalta, http://plato.stanford.edu/archives/fall2013

/entries/ethics-virtue/). Thus, if eudaimonia is interpreted principally as virtuousness (moral excellence), then the eudaimonist thesis that the virtues enable a human being to be *eudaimon* effectively reduces to the affirmation that the virtues enable a human being to be virtuous. While this assertion is surely right, regarding eudaimonia principally as virtuousness precludes eudaimonism per se from specifying the substance of virtue significantly or constituting a meaningfully distinctive account of the moral life. Hence, Broadie insists that "the notion of [eudaimonia] in Aristotle cannot serve to explain why qualities like justice and generosity should count as human virtues or excellences, nor to justify our regarding them as such. On the contrary, the empirical content of the notion [eudaimonia] is drawn from the standard virtues" (*Ethics with Aristotle*, 42).

48. Indeed, Broadie contends that by beginning the *Nicomachean Ethics* by declaring that the moral life aims at the eudaimonia of those who lead it, Aristotle is not attempting to characterize the virtues or even explicate the moral life but instead "is intend[ing] to establish a certain definition of *the* good, a definition in terms of 'aiming'" (*Ethics with Aristotle*, 9; italics original).

49. The diversity of Christian soteriology challenges even such qualified generalizations. Nevertheless, given my interpretation of Christian moral life as involving love of God and neighbors open to self-transcendence, it is worth noting that no less an advocate of faith's soteriological importance than Paul asserted the insignificance of faith without love (e.g., 1 Cor. 13; cf. Augustine, *On Faith and Works*, chap. 14).

50. Some commentators interpret aspects of the relationship between agape and philia in a formally similar fashion, cf., e.g., Gene Outka, *Agape: An Ethical Analysis* (New Haven, CT: Yale University Press, 1972), 18–19, 34–44, 174–80, 209–14; Gilbert Meilaender, *Friendship: A Study in Theological Ethics* (Notre Dame: University of Notre Dame Press, 1981), 45–52, 65; Gene Outka, "Universal Love and Impartiality," in *The Love Commandments: Essays in Christian Ethics and Moral Philosophy*, ed. Edmund N. Santurri and William Werpehowski (Washington, DC: Georgetown University Press, 1992), 8, 66, 70, 88–89, 102n166; Colin Grant, "For the Love of God: Agape," *Journal of Religious Ethics* 24, no. 1 (Spring 1996): 3–21; Edward Vacek, "Love, Christian and Diverse," *Journal of Religious Ethics* 24, no. 1 (Spring 1996): 29–34; Gene Outka, "Theocentric Agape and the Self: An Asymmetrical Affirmation in Response to Colin Grant's Either/Or," *Journal of Religious Ethics* 24, no. 1 (Spring 1996): 35–42; Colin Grant, "A Reply to My Critics," *Journal of Religious Ethics* 24, no. 1 (Spring 1996): 43–46; Gene Outka, "Agapeistic Ethics," in *A Companion to Philosophy of Religion*, ed. Philip Quinn and Charles Taliaferro (Cambridge, MA: Blackwell, 1997), 481–88; Stephen Pope, "'Equal Regard' versus 'Special Relations'? Reaffirming the Inclusiveness of Agape," *Journal of Religion* 77, no. 3 (July 1997): 353–79; Gene Outka, "Comment," *Journal of Religious Ethics* 26, no. 2 (Fall 1998): 435–40; Stephen Pope, "The Author Replies," *Journal of Religious Ethics* 26, no. 2 (Fall 1998): 440–44.

51. I characterize this interpretation of the Christian moral life as effectively eudaimonist because in depicting eudaimonia as accompanying moral excellence, it portrays the moral life as de facto ordered to the eudaimonia of its adherents. This interpretation of the Christian moral life is not strictly eudaimonist in the sense I have been examining in this chapter, however, because it does not regard moral excellence as incomplete without eudaimonia and so does not conceive the moral life as aiming at the eudaimonia of its adherents.

52. Among many scriptural texts, cf., e.g., Rom. 5:1–8; 1 John 4:7–21; Rom. 8:38–39, respectively.

53. This and all scriptural quotations are taken from the New Revised Standard Version of the Bible.

54. For example, Paul states as much in Gal. 3:13, referencing Deut. 21:23, and makes effectively the same claim in 2 Cor. 5:21.

55. Of course, canonical Christian scripture includes four gospels, and the differences in their account of Jesus's passion would affect this interpretation. For example, by presenting Jesus as explicitly enjoining his disciples to love one another as he has loved them and extolling his death on their behalf as the acme of such love (John 15:12–17), the Gospel of John may appear to broaden my analysis and show that the Christian life generally, and not simply Jesus's own, is not eudaimonist. However, John's Gospel does not depict Jesus as experiencing dereliction on the Cross but instead as displaying a serenity and self-control that—given his otherwise terrible condition—may attest to his ongoing, active participation in God's love and so enjoyment of eudaimonia. Indeed, immediately preceding his claim that there is no greater love than sacrificial death for one's friends, John's Gospel presents Jesus as saying, "If you keep my commandments, you will abide in my love, just as I have kept my Father's commandments and abide in his love. I have said these things to you so that my joy may be in you, and that your joy may be complete" (15:10–11).

Luke's Gospel also omits any reference to the crucified Jesus's perception of dereliction and instead portrays him as convinced of God's presence and blessing throughout the ordeal. Rather than record any doubts or questions, Luke attributes only these three statements to Jesus on the Cross: "Father, forgive them; for they do not know what they are doing"; "Truly, I tell you, today you will be with me in Paradise"; "Father, into your hands I commend my spirit" (23:34, 43, 46, respectively). Actively loving God and others with God until the end, in Luke's Gospel it appears Jesus continues to enjoy eudaimonia even from the Cross.

Finally, Christian scripture does not only present Jesus's submission to crucifixion as an expression of self-transcending love for God and neighbors. Instead, the book of Hebrews exhorts those who would be Christian to look "to Jesus the pioneer and perfecter of our faith, who for the sake of the joy that was set before him endured the cross, disregarding its shame" (12:2). Moreover, this passage apparently portrays the exemplary Christian life as aiming at the eudaimonia of those who lead it. Accordingly, just as there is no consensus on the meaning of eudaimonia, eudaimonism, or proper Christian love, there is seemingly no single biblical position on the relationship between the moral life and its adherents' eudaimonia. Indeed, such scriptural polyphony on these matters may be one reason that assessments of Christian eudaimonism remain contentious.

56. Cf., e.g., 1 Cor. 15:20–28 and the ecumenical creeds.

57. Cf., e.g., Matt. 25:31–46; and Karl Rahner's notion of anonymous Christianity, rooted in the Johannine promise that "those who abide in love abide in God, and God in them" (e.g., 1 John 4:7–16; Karl Rahner, "Reflections on the Unity of the Love of Neighbour and the Love of God," in *Theological Investigations: Concerning Vatican Council II*, vol. 6, trans. Karl Kruger and Boniface Kruger [Baltimore: Helicon, 1969], 231–49).

Admittedly, these considerations would not avail if losing a sense of God's love leads one to cease loving altogether. However, there is no reason that this loss should have that effect. Besides, even if it does, that would not gainsay the contention that the Christian moral life is effectively eudaimonist in the end, for eudaimonism concerns the aim of the moral life; it does not pledge that all who live that life earnestly will ultimately realize that aim (among multiple recent discussions of this point, cf., e.g., John McDowell, "Eudaimonism and Realism in Aristotle's Ethics," in *The Engaged Intellect: Philosophical Essays* [Cambridge: Harvard University Press, 2009], 32). More broadly, Christians' common conviction that with God all things are possible is also germane in this connection (cf., e.g., Mark 10:27, parallels in Matthew and Luke, and antecedents in Gen. 18:14, Job 42:2, and Zech. 8:6).

12

Christian Love as Friendship

Engaging the Thomistic Tradition

STEPHEN J. POPE

IN RECENT YEARS, Christian ethics has begun to recover an appreciation for the moral and religious significance of friendship. While much of Christian ethics in the twentieth century tended to regard friendship with a somewhat skeptical eye, important insights in the last twenty years or so have helped us come to a greater appreciation for its positive contribution to the moral life. The recovery of friendship has taken place primarily within Aristotelian and Thomistic circles but also within feminism, Augustinian ethics, Lutheran ethics, narrative theology, phenomenological and personalist ethics, and elsewhere.[1]

While most Christian ethicists now appreciate the value of friendship and recognize the poverty of life devoid of friends, most also continue to assume that friendship is different from Christian love. Friendship at its best is still preferential and, therefore, Timothy Jackson insists, ought not to have the central place within Christian ethics.[2] Friendship at its worst falls into either egoism that subordinates the friend's good to that of the self or into favoritism, an unjust bias toward the friend over the rightful claims of others. Jackson observes, "Jesus became convinced that human beings do not normally know how to love themselves,"[3] but if so, it is also the case that we do not normally know how to love our friends or, more generally, how to affirm others in self-giving generosity. The purpose of the church is precisely to teach us how to love properly, first God and then all human beings, and indeed all creatures, in light of this love.

This essay provides an explication of the main lines of how the tradition flowing from Thomas Aquinas contributes to our understanding of friendship in a way that not only avoids the dangers of egoism and favoritism but also does not categorize Christian love as a "type" of love that is separate from other "types" like friendship and desire. The main point of this chapter will spring from a fundamental Thomistic conviction that grace heals and enhances the deepest moral capacities of our humanity. I will argue first that Christian love is found wherever human beings authentically love one another and second that the quintessential expression of authentic human love lies in true friendship. In this view, it is neither theologically appropriate nor ethically helpful to say that "Christianity puts charity first, higher even than friendship,"[4] because Christianity calls us to life in an ecclesial community marked by the deep bonds of the most important kind of friendship, that based on the love of God. Fellowship lies at the very core of the covenant and the Kingdom of God, the calling of the disciples and the Last Supper, the Resurrection and Pentecost.

This essay begins with an overview of the main lines of the Thomistic account of friendship and its interpretation of charity as friendship and then turns to examine three particularly important topics for the contemporary ethics of friendship: joy as an effect of charity, love for the poor as an effect of mercy, and civic friendship as the basis for balancing group solidarity with respect for the dignity of the person and the value of subsidiarity. These three topics underscore the importance of friendship for contemporary Christian ethics.

Love

Aquinas viewed love in its most elemental sense as a passion and, more precisely, as the first principle in the movement of an appetite toward an object of love (*ST* I-II.26.1).[5] Love is a complex reality that includes an aptitude for (or "connaturality" with or "complacency" in) the good, a purposive movement toward the good, and a delight in possessing the good.[6] In Aquinas's moral anthropology, every human act is moved by interior acts of willing, and every act of willing begins with love of some kind. As philosopher Josef Pieper put it, loving is the "primal act of willing that permeates all willing-to-do from its very source."[7] Because human actions always reflect some kind of love in the agent, theologian Paul Wadell observes, Thomistic morality "begins in love, works through desire, and is completed in joy."[8]

Love always implicitly affirms some good. Love in every case is a response to a perceived good of some kind, whether natural (which, in Aquinas's sense, encompasses what is inanimate), sensitive (related to animality), or intelligent and rational (*ST* I-II.27.1–2). Rational or intellectual love is the aptitude of the "intellectual appetite," or will, toward its suitable good. Pieper maintains that, for Aquinas, love of every kind involves some kind of approval: "loving someone or something means finding him or it *probus*, the Latin word for 'good'. It is a way of turning to him or it and saying, 'It's good that you exist; it's good that you are in this world.'"[9] Pieper did not maintain that we ought to love because we like the neighbor or admire certain traits the neighbor possesses. Yet he did claim that we love the neighbor because we acknowledge the neighbor's attractiveness as a human being made in the image of God. As *imago Dei*, each person possesses a fundamental dignity and an inherent ontological and created goodness. Pieper echoed Genesis 1:31, Yahweh's announcement that the existence of humanity, along with fullness of creation, is very good. "Approval" in the sense Pieper intended, moreover, does not refer primarily to an emotional response to the beloved but rather to an activity of the will that implicitly affirms the friend: "I want you (or it) to exist!"[10] Pieper elaborated on this claim by citing Gabriel Marcel on the intentionality underlying love: "To love a person means to say: 'You will not die.'" This is of course not a predictive claim but a statement of what Pieper called the will's intense "partisanship for the existence of the beloved."[11] Yet this partisanship is not unjustly arbitrary. Characteristically human love ("dilection" from *dilectio/diligo*; Aquinas, *ST* I-II.26.3) is a matter of both striving for the goodness that is not yet attained and assenting to a goodness already possessed.

Friendship Love

Aquinas understood human love to be marked by two major dimensions, one indirect and the other direct. He employed Augustine's famous distinction between enjoyment (*frui*) and use (*uti*), but his language managed better to avoid the misleading suggestion that we ought to "use" our neighbors as a way of pleasing or growing closer to God, let alone "making them a means to one's own happiness."[12] What Aquinas called the "love of concupiscence" is directed to any object seen as good that one wants for oneself or another. Love in a qualified sense loves an object because it is good for another (Aquinas *ST* I-II.27.3); for example, we love the gym because it helps us maintain our health. The "love of friendship," on the other hand, is love for someone to whom or for whom one wants some good; for example, because we love our friends and ourselves, we value our friends' and our own health and so we love the gym. This "love of friendship" constitutes love in an unqualified sense because it loves friends for their own sakes (Aquinas, *ST* I-II.24.4).

Concupiscent love is not to be confused with the negative sense of "concupiscence" as disordered appetite; it is simply a necessary instrument of friendship love. Love in both senses—as either concupiscent or intrinsic—pertains in some way to friendship, and both are praiseworthy when virtuous as well as blameworthy when vicious. Drawing from Augustine's notion of sin as disordered love, Aquinas interpreted the fundamental human problem to lie in the confusion of these dimensions of love such that we treat those whom we ought to embrace with a friendship love with mere concupiscent love. Philosopher Alan Donagan thus regarded Thomistic friendship as one of the historical antecedents of Kant's personalist formula of the categorical imperative according to which we are to treat others as ends and never merely as means.[13]

Friendship love is not a feeling that fluctuates spontaneously but rather a choice to affirm the good of the friend for his or her own sake. On this particular point, Aquinas appreciated the need for stability and consistency in a way that has a certain resonance with Gene Outka's claim that "agape is a regard for the neighbor which in crucial respects is independent and unalterable."[14]

Aquinas's concupiscent love included Aristotle's friendships of both utility and pleasure. They preserve one core trait of friendship in that they involve wanting some good for a friend, yet because they essentially relate the good to the agent's own pleasure or utility, they fall short of the full meaning of friendship (Aquinas, *ST* I-II.26.4 ad 3). (Aristotle himself described these inferior forms of friendship as "incidental."[15]) It is crucially important to recognize that Aquinas did not confine friendship love to a small circle of like-minded intimate associates who more or less share the same tastes. Friendship love is not to be identified with the "lifestyle enclave" of expressive individualism.[16] What Pieper said about philia equally applies to Aquinas's *amicitia*: it stresses a broad "fellow feeling, the solidarity among human beings, and not only of friends, but also of spouses, fellow countrymen and people in general."[17]

We might thus distinguish personal friendships within the broader category of relationships embraced by Thomistic friendship love. Friendship love is inclined to move beyond superficial acquaintance and to grow in greater knowledge and affective appreciation of friends (Aquinas, *ST* I-II.28.2). This movement gives rise to an important effect that Aquinas calls the "mutual indwelling" of the lover in the beloved and vice versa (*ST* I-II.28.2). Mutual indwelling occurs in both the cognitive power by which we apprehend one another and in the appetitive power by which we affectively appreciate one another. It is important to recognize that for Aquinas the end of this movement is a relationship in which the lover considers the good or evil undergone by the beloved to be *his or her own good or evil*. This affirmation sharply contrasts with the prevalent, modern Anglo-American ethical reading of human action as zero-sum competition, according to which gain for the self is loss for the other and vice versa.[18] In Christian ethics, as Jackson points out, love is "not a zero-sum game, with someone's gain inevitably entailing another's loss."[19]

Aquinas had additional ways of talking about the characteristic effects of charity. Charity creates a kind of "ecstasy," a going outside of oneself. Cognitive and affective focus on the beloved leads the agent to suspend self-concern (Aquinas, *ST* I-II.28.3). Charity also generates a "zeal" that resists whatever threatens the good of the friend (Aquinas, *ST* I-II.28.4), for example, as illustrated in the protective attitude of parents toward their children. Finally, charity can become so powerful that it "wounds" the self, as felt, for example, even in negative bodily conditions like chronic sleeplessness, ulcers, and the like. Friendship love, in short, transforms the self into someone who comes to identify deeply with the beloved and who is willing to accept the negative as well as positive effects of such love. Friendship love suffers over, as well as celebrates, the friend's condition.

Charity as Graced Friendship Love

The Thomistic term "caritas" is simply the Latin translation of the Greek "agape." Aquinas defined charity as a certain kind of friendship with God and with all persons in God (*ST* II-II.23.1). The offer of friendship in grace is initiated and made possible by God, not by human beings. Jackson rightly reminds us that friendship with God is "impossible without unmerited divine favor,"[20] but Aquinas goes further in seeing that since this friendship is both the foundation and the goal of the Christian moral life, it is first among the virtues as well as the animating spirit of the other virtues. Friendship with God makes possible the generous, non-reciprocal love of neighbor. God's gracious love, in other words, always takes the form of ongoing, self-giving communication that invites us to share in the divine life, a participation that enables us to communicate and share in the lives of one another.

Depicting our relation with God as potentially one of friendship decisively broke with Aristotle's belief that the vast gulf between human beings and God made friendship between us impossible. Aquinas conceived of divine transcendence as expressed in divine imminence, even to the point of Incarnation. Aquinas here concurs with Outka's conviction that as made in the image of God, "we are capable of intentional activity, moral accountability, and friendship, in relation both to God and to one another."[21] Outka's "theocentric frame" focuses on "obedient willing" and fidelity to God in ways that provide a helpful corrective to our inconstancy, favoritism, and self-bias, yet he also regards his position as "wholly compatible with the affirmation that communion *is* the fulfillment of love."[22] Aquinas differs from Outka, however, in regarding every act of charity as friendship love as *already* a kind of communion with (or "participation" in) God and so not only its future ideal fruition. Communion, and more precisely communion with God as friend, is constitutive of every act of charity and not only, as Jackson puts it, its ideal consummation in heaven.[23] This does not of course gainsay Outka's proper insistence that our love for God is responsive to God's love but not "reciprocal" in the ordinary interpersonal sense in which "mutual needs are met, assistance rendered, or enrichment provided."[24]

The conceptual foundation for Aquinas's account of friendship as charity resides in his Trinitarian theology, according to which the meaning of friendship is most powerfully displayed in the eternal procession of the Holy Spirit from the radically self-giving and mutual love of the Father and the Son. The love that is the Holy Spirit flows from the divine goodness and embraces all creatures (Aquinas, *ST* I.37.2 and ad 3). God loves every person as a rational creature but also offers to each an even greater gift, divine grace, the indwelling of the Holy Spirit that creates friendship between God and the person.

Edward Vacek thus unfortunately mischaracterizes Aquinas when he depicts him as claiming, "We creatures can do nothing for God . . . [and] we sinners cannot really share divine life . . . [and] any love for God is God's action in us, not really ours."[25] While as sinners we do not share the divine life, for Aquinas, the grace of conversion is an invitation to participate in the divine life, though in concretely human ways. This offer of grace initiates a transformative process in which the cooperative respondent becomes rooted in the Holy Spirit's gift of a "created habit" or "infused virtue" (cf. Rom. 5:5). Divine love does not, for Aquinas, replace our powers of human agency but rather provides a gracious support for the development of our created capacity for self-transcending love. This dynamism is thus both "really" ours and also "really" God's. The more we cooperate with the divine invitation of grace, in other words, the more we love authentically.

There is, of course, a danger that this theology of grace will tempt us to pride, or that, as Outka worries, "the more we seek to merge our standing with God's, the more we aggrandize in our own world."[26] Yet Thomistic theology envisions cooperation, not merging. Authentic charity differs from idolatrous self-love in that it is constituted by a union that respects the differences between God and creatures. As Paul Wadell points out, "If charity is truly friendship, . . . it makes us more fully ourselves."[27] As such, it gives the freedom to love others without self-seeking. Authentic charity is marked by self-gift rather than self-aggrandizement: those who wish to retain their lives will lose them, and those who seek to lose their lives will gain them (Luke 17:33).

Love in its most basic form, as we have seen previously, is not a virtue but simply a constitutive affective force of human nature. Love that is wise and otherwise virtuous is good; love that is foolish or otherwise vicious is bad. As human love that has been healed and ordered by grace, charity is an "infused virtue" (i.e., not acquired by human effort) that can be expressed in any rightly ordered love. Mistaken impressions could have been avoided if some theologians in the past century could have refrained from assuming a basic opposition of charity (agape) to either eros or philia (or both). Charity is best understood as sublating— retaining in a healed and reordered form—both human desire and friendship.

Adopting and modifying Augustine's notion of the order of love, Aquinas's order of charity maintained that we ought to love God first, then ourselves (spiritually), then our neighbors, and finally, at least in an analogous way, our own bodies. Aquinas's treatment of the order of charity should not be read as an attempt to offer a script for how love of neighbor ought to be applied in one's life. It provides, rather, a set of considerations about how different relationships can inform one's moral deliberation. Rather than reduce the multiplicity of love to one "kind" of love, Aquinas distinguished various modalities of love, including love of honor, love of intimacy, and love of care, in order to indicate the complexity of love and our need for practical wisdom, the virtue that quintessentially puts order into things. Charity observes different priorities under varied contingent circumstances and does not simply adhere to the rules of a legal system directing us how and whom we ought to love.

Aquinas maintained that grace-inspired friendship love does not violate the fundamental ordering of nature given to us by our Creator. Charity complexifies and deepens this natural order by expanding its range and intensifying its meaning: friendship love for God leads one to extend friendship love to all human beings but also presents personal and family relationships as special contexts for the growth of grace in one's life. Aquinas was clear that we ought to love all human beings without exception, and he thus agrees with Outka that to be human is to be a neighbor.[28] At the same time, because of the particular kind of creatures we happen to be, human flourishing depends on caring for some people more than others.

Thus, whereas Outka endorses equal consideration but not identical treatment,[29] Aquinas maintained that we ought to have neither identical consideration nor identical treatment of all people (beyond the equal minimal requirements of basic benevolence and justice).

Grace perfects the natural ordering of love that leads us, in different ways, to love, say, our mother, sister, or daughter more than a stranger's mother, sister, or daughter. The Christian ought to will everyone the good but, other things being equal (and, in the concrete, they are often not), to will the good to one's own children with a special care not found elsewhere and to treat them with greater solicitude and concern than others. The same is true of the love that honors one's parents and the intimate love of one's spouse. In this regard, our friendship love is decidedly unlike God's, while still conforming to God's will for us. We are to imitate divine love in willing the greater good to those who are more virtuous than those who are less so (Aquinas, *ST* II-II.26.7), but our love is complicated by a host of other considerations that include affective proximity and what sociologists call "role responsibilities." Aquinas here would have concurred with Outka's claim that while we are committed to recognizing the equal dignity of every person, we are not bound to equal inclusion: that is, to "invariably protect and promote the neighbor's well-being and the self's well-being in exactly the same way."[30] The same is true of the self vis-à-vis multiple neighbors.

Friendship Love and Anti-eudaimonism

Dialectical works like Anders Nygren's *Agape and Eros* and, more recently, Timothy Jackson's *The Priority of Love* argue that the order of love in both Augustine and Aquinas justifies a subtle (or not so subtle) egoism that either loves God instead of (or "in") the neighbor or subordinates both neighbor and God to the self's interests.[31] Jackson does not want to "vilify" either friendship or self-love. He moves beyond Nygren in seeing that "there is, finally, no competition between *agape* and [*eros* and *philia*],"[32] but his accent falls sharply on the word "finally" in a way that suggest he has softened but not jettisoned Nygren's moral dualism. The eudaimonist seeks above all happiness, the self's own good, Jackson worries, and so cannot help but subordinate neighbor and even God to the self's individual quest for happiness.

These "hyper-Augustinians," as Charles Taylor might call them, are actually deeply suspicious of Augustine, whom they decry as the archpriest of the eros-infiltrated "caritas synthesis." They invoke Aquinas's paradigm of friendship—Aristotle's description of the friend as "another self"—as the prime exhibit in the case against friendship as the antithesis of the self-sacrificial love expressed on the Cross. A complete response to this kind of criticism cannot be developed here, but we must note the essential but sometimes misunderstood point that charitable friendship involves a *transformation* of the agent from one who is, in one way or another, marked by a fundamental egoistic self-centeredness to one who is at least on the way to being more capable of self-giving love. Thomistic charity transcends "long-term self-interest" in the usual egoistic meaning of this phrase.[33] Vacek

Vacek rightly points out that "the phrase 'another self' can . . . obscure the self-transcending quality of philia,"[34] yet it is possible to avoid this problem by keeping in mind the fundamentally transformative character of Thomistic charity. Proper self-love refers to the rightly ordered self, not the sinful self. The same is true of eros: charity is motivated by a grace-transformed desire that seeks to give itself away, not a sinful, egoistic desire that seeks to possess. Aquinas had in mind what William Werpehowski describes as a "non-possessive eros" that desires "to enter a relation that fulfills one joyfully in self-giving response to God's love."[35] Conversion affects a radical alteration in our understanding of friendship and reveals that authentic happiness is found only in self-transcending friendship with God and every creature in relation to this friendship with God.[36]

Aquinas thus did not identify charity with complete self-sacrifice, unconditional self-denial, indiscriminate giving, or purely disinterested concern. These phrases express a kind of Christian radicality but fail to acknowledge the limits of human moral agency. The fundamental human problem according to the Thomistic tradition lies in learning how to consent to and cooperate with divine grace so that we can learn to love properly as the concrete and particular human beings we happen to be. Aquinas's assumption that grace works in and through our human nature differs sharply from Nygren's description of Christians as mere "tubes" through whom God's love flows to others.[37] Whereas Nygren's agape is solely "God's own love,"[38] Thomistic charity is always human love that has been reformed by divine love.

Recognizing the human matrix of Christian love enables Aquinas to acknowledge that even those saints traveling the road to God in the right way must serve others in light of multiple demands and trade-offs. The moral challenges forced on us by finitude cannot be met by goodwill alone or even by grace alone. The good person must exercise the virtue of prudence to know when, how, and how much we are to care for others in any particular context. In some circumstances, for example, it can be perfectly legitimate for one to make a claim of justice against one's neighbor. Consider a recent case of an undergraduate who in a moment of temptation decided to steal her roommate's credit card, charged hundreds of dollars of gifts for her friends, and then surreptitiously returned the credit card with the assumption that her roommate was too wealthy to notice the new debits. The roommate did soon notice the new charges and in fact discovered the identity of the thief thanks to the store's video-recording technology. The victim and her family now have to decide whether to press charges, a decision that pivots on a host of circumstances that include the relationship between the roommates, an assessment of what would be best for the victim and what would be best for the offender, and the way the potential courses of action would affect others. The question of what to do cannot be reduced to discerning the most impartial or self-sacrificial course of action. Whether one wants to press for justice is a matter of concrete assessment of what is good for all concerned, given the particular circumstances of the case.

Thomistic ethics appreciates that mutually complementary relation of proper friendship and proper self-love. True friendship is reducible neither to pure selflessness nor to pure selfishness but rather is sustained by virtuous and appropriate self-love. Virtuous friendship is, in fact, the context for the development of proper self-love, and vice versa. False self-love regards others primarily as aids for the attainment of egoistic wants. True self-love, in contrast, seeks the good of one's friends for their own sakes and, as we have seen, culminates in a deeply "ecstatic" love that identifies the friend's goods as one's own.

Consider another example taken from university life. Contrast the attitude of a faculty member who feels envy toward the accomplishments of a hardworking colleague with another professor who delights in her friend's success. The former can see his peer's success only as casting his own work in a dim light; the latter experiences her friend's good as her own. Identifying with the friend does not draw the friend into the self, to be put at the service of the self's own wants, but rather draws the self into the life of the friend, to be in the service of the friend's good. The key point here is that true friendship requires a *transformation* of the self away from egocentrism and toward goodwill to, identification with, and availability to one's friend. Friendship radically expands one's sense of what counts as one's good and what one takes to be worthwhile activity.

Thomistic theology accents human transformation: grace makes it possible for us to exercise a friendship love that would have been otherwise unattainable. This friendship and mutual indwelling is *primarily* between the divine Trinity and the human person (Aquinas, *ST* II-II.23.1). The vertical emphasis at the center of Aquinas's account of charity distinguishes it from the horizontal focus in Nygren, Jackson, and Outka. Thomistic charity begins with God's utterly gracious offer of unconditional love, that is, of friendship. Grateful acceptance of this offer leads to a love for all other human beings as embraced within it, which in turn generates a unilateral concern that is neither dependent on nor controlled by other attractions.

True neighbor love always participates in the agent's friendship with God. Outka has consistently worried that friendship lacks the stability of agape because of the way it "depends at least in part on mutual liking, and usually on admiration and esteem as well."[39] Yet the friendship love of God is founded on the most stable of all foundations: the eternal procession of love within the Trinity that is poured out onto creation in divine grace. This unalterable divine stability grounds goodwill for the neighbor that is, as Outka puts it, a combination of "agent-commitment" and "recipient-evaluation" good for both friends.[40]

The centrality of mutual indwelling means that benevolence is necessary but not sufficient for friendship. In friendship, benevolence is reciprocal and maintained by mutual communication (in the broad sense of having goods in common; Aquinas, *ST* II-II.23.1). Through grace, God shares the divine life with us and allows us to participate in divine happiness: "I no longer call you servants, but friends" (John 15:15; Aquinas, *ST* II-II.23.1). Just as the effect of love is union, so the effect of charitable friendship love is a spiritual union with God that constitutes the greatest attainable human happiness in this life (Aquinas, *ST* II-II.180.7). This participation is imperfect in this life, when we see merely "through a glass darkly" (1 Cor. 13:12), but will become perfect in the next.

Aristotle, as noted previously, held that paradigmatic friendship is between equals (*NE* 1157b37). While he allowed for friendship between those who are unequal (e.g., parents and their children), he also held that the greater the inequality, the more limited the friendship (*NE* 1158b33–1159a3). Aquinas maintained that grace has the capacity to elevate the person to intimate ways of knowing and loving God and that it even affects a "certain sharing in the divine nature" (*ST* I-II.112.1, I-II.110, I-II.113.2). Fergus Kerr explains that in this kind of friendship, there is no "annihilation of the self in submission to, or submersion in, the absolute other. The relationship is modeled on the kind of 'space' that friends accord one another: koinonia, conversation, even a kind of 'symposium.'"[41]

As we have seen, the order of charity supports a legitimate ordered loyalty to the common good of one's own political community, but it is a patriotism bounded by charity that insists on justice for "outsiders" as well as "insiders." Justice in this context thus fulfills some of the functions that Outka associates with equal regard, particularly the way a proper sense of impartiality and fairness ought to frame the treatment of any neighbor and, in a wider social context, shape the structure and execution of civil laws. Thomistic justice, like equal regard, resists any illicit grasping, as Outka puts it, at "arbitrary privilege and [any] failure to count each individual as one and no more than one."[42]

Friendship with God inspires a friendship love for every person as belonging to God, made for divine love, and called to goodness and virtue.[43] While insisting on minimal conditions of justice as an expression of basic benevolence, charity intends to move well beyond these conditions and into true communion. Charity is marked by a spectrum that runs from a special intensity of love for those close to us through an extensive love for neighbors who are more remote. As Wadell puts it, "Neither philia nor agape can be defined apart from the other; not only is agape learned in Christian friendship, agape is a kind of friendship extended to the world, to those whom Jesus called our neighbors, even if those neighbors be our foes."[44] Even though, then, fellow feeling might be absent, we ought to and can love enemies with a friendship love at least in the minimal form that wills the good to them. To be sure, charity as friendship love views mutuality as the "final ideal fruition of neighbor-regard."[45] Nevertheless, friendship love exists when one treats any neighbor (including an offensive one) as a friend "in God," and this can take place whether or not there is mutuality or shared religious belief.

Thomistic friendship love, as we have seen, carries broad connotations that extend well beyond what we consider personal friendships and so stands in contrast to modern conceptions that confine friendship to nonfamilial emotional bonds shared in the private sphere. Charity as friendship for God works against the tendency to exclusiveness that tempts ordinary friendships, yet its ordering also resists the Stoic reading of *philanthropia*, friendship for humanity as such, as the paradigmatic moral duty. Charity as friendship love encompasses personal life and public life, familial relations and social activities, local communities and cosmopolitan love for humanity as such. It inclines us to extend friendship love to any fellow human beings with whom we interact, indirectly and directly. While we will the good to everyone, however, whether or how we decide to act depends on a host of circumstances, especially within the specific contours of our particular moral lives and communities.

Some Christian theologians in the patristic era (e.g., Gregory of Nazianzus, John Chrysostom, and John Cassian) conceived of charity in terms of friendship, but Aquinas was the first to draw systematically from the conception of friendship made available by the recovery of Aristotle's *Nicomachean Ethics*.[46] Aquinas's account of charity retained the marks of Aristotelian friendship—goodwill, communication in some good, and mutuality—but in a way that understood charity, in an ontological sense, as fundamentally directed to God and only derivatively to human persons. Aquinas, moreover, understood mutuality, or concord, as conformity of the human will to the divine will, rather than as the union of wills that takes place in human friendship.[47]

Aquinas, like Aristotle, regarded friendship as based on virtue and as an essential part of temporal flourishing (*ST* I-II.4.8). Friends help one another to act virtuously and to enjoy doing so. Aquinas accepted the broad range of Aristotelian friendship (e.g., fellow soldiers, farmers, citizens) but departed from the notion that complete friendship involves an equality of power, intelligence, status, and shared activities and judgments. Friendship with God, as we have seen, radically expands the range of those embraced with friendship love to include not only those with whom we share deep affective bonds but also the socially marginalized (e.g., biblical lepers, prostitutes, tax collectors, the poor).

Whereas Aristotle thought that a virtuous person has friendship in the full sense only for other virtuous persons, Aquinas believed that friendship love as charity is extended to the morally unstable and even the vicious. He brought an Aristotelian virtue consideration back, however, in recognizing that other things being equal, virtuous people will tend to be closer in friendship to those who are virtuous than to those who are vicious (Aquinas, *ST* II-II.26.7; also, II-II.24.4, 10, 11).

Charity is not dependent on interpersonal reciprocity but neither is it simply neutral with regard to the response of the neighbor. Aquinas in this regard goes well beyond the early Outka's somewhat grudging concession that "so far as I can see, there is nothing to preclude an acceptance [of reciprocity]."[48] Thomistic friendship resonates much more with Martin

No = Agape

Luther King Jr.'s goal of converting enemies into friends.[49] It is furthermore anything but the case, as Vacek claims, that charity "does not care about developing a relation with the beloved" and, for this reason, "might be attractive to those who don't want to 'be involved' even when they 'get involved.'"[50] Such love is a problem, but it is not what Aquinas meant by charity.

The thin edge of the boundary of charity is found in Aquinas's treatment of heretics, those Christians whom Aquinas thought stubbornly and proudly chose not to assent to some truths clearly taught by Christ (*ST* II-II.11). The church in mercy ought to work for the salvation of such "wanderers," yet when their obstinacy reveals a refusal to be corrected, Aquinas reasoned, the church, concerned for the salvation of the faithful, ought not only rightly excommunicate them but also hand them over to the civil authority to be executed (*ST* II-II.11.3). Relapsed heretics who recant should be forgiven, he held, but still executed for the good of other souls since excessive leniency might embolden relapsed heretics to "infect" the body of Christ and even tempt other reformed heretics to relapse (Aquinas, *ST* II-II.11.4). God might save them (we of course have no idea of whether this is the case), but out of concern for the common good, the church ought not to shield them from the death sentence (ad 2). Contemporary readers will find cold comfort in Aquinas's reminder that the church trusts that God wills the correction and salvation of heretics, even when they are deprived of their temporal (bodily) lives.

Effects of Charity: Joy and Almsgiving

Charity produces the interior effects of joy, peace, and mercy and the exterior effects of beneficence, almsgiving, and fraternal correction. We will now concentrate on two effects of charity that are particularly relevant for Christian ethics today—joy and mercy—and then move to examine the social dimension of charity in civic friendship.

First, charity is not primarily a matter of fulfilling the duties of the moral law but rather of living in joy. This topic is particularly important today when charity, self-sacrifice, and self-denial are derided as the products of a guilt-ridden and overly negative church bent on suppressing human freedom. The lineage of this critique goes back at least as far as Sigmund Freud's *Civilization and Its Discontents*, gathered popular momentum in the cultural stream Robert Bellah calls "expressive individualism,"[51] and gained more academic respectability with the growth of the research agenda of "positive psychology."[52]

In the Catholic tradition, the reduction of charity to the fulfillment of duty and of Christian motivation to guilt avoidance was common among the neo-scholastic manuals that dominated the field of moral theology from the mid-nineteenth to the mid-twentieth century.[53] Yet in Aquinas's ethics, agents who consistently act out of settled habits of the good experience a kind of pleasure in acting rightly. Every act of genuine love that produces some kind of union (either real or affective) gives rise to delight or joy. Charity produces spiritual joy in the one loved but also sorrow when the beloved is deprived of any good. Thus, whereas common sense regards joy and sadness as mutually exclusive experiences, Thomistic ethics regards them as potentially coexisting simultaneously in the same agent.

The interior effect of spiritual joy suggests that true friendship is motivated neither by neurotic guilt feelings, nor by a desire to impress others, nor by Nietzschean ressentiment. The heart of Christian joy lies in charity. While our "most perfect and enduring joy is found in God,"[54] charity regards creation as a gift from the Creator for which we ought to feel gratitude and in which we ought to take delight. This "ought" is not to be understood moralistically, as produced by a strenuous act of the will, but rather as the spontaneous result of loving what is absolutely and unconditionally good. Charity thus gives rise not only to spiritual joy but also, in appropriate ways, to more ordinary dispositions of friendliness, cheerfulness, and sharing in the pleasures of conversation with one another. These "positive emotions," as positive psychologists call them, flow from a theocentric gratitude, not egoistic optimism.

Second, Aquinas's notion of mercy is also of particular interest today. To love the neighbor in its most obvious and simple sense, as Outka puts it, is "to aid a person or persons in distress."[55] Mercy produces three general kinds of exterior effects: beneficence, or doing the good for others; almsgiving, or caring for the needy; and fraternal correction, in which friends gently challenge one another by speaking the truth in love (Aquinas, *ST* II-II.31–33; based on Eph. 4:15). Mercy expresses charity when it faces the needs of those who are unable to care for themselves in particular ways. The corporal works of mercy are to feed the hungry, give drink to the thirsty, clothe the naked, harbor the harborless, visit the sick, ransom the captive, and bury the dead. The spiritual works of mercy are to instruct the ignorant, counsel the doubtful, admonish sinners, bear wrongs patiently, forgive offenses willingly, comfort the afflicted, and pray for the living and the dead (see Aquinas, *ST* II-II.32).

Moderns have sharply criticized mercy and almsgiving for paternalism, and indeed, Aquinas's treatment of almsgiving did typically envision a have helping a have-not. This relation can amount to a form of self-aggrandizement that reinforces dependency and subordination. One does not find in Aquinas much of anything like Jean Vanier's recognition of the fact that the disabled have something to teach us or that friendship with them can be deeply enriching.[56] And while Aquinas understood every Christian act of the virtue of justice as informed by charity, he did not grasp that, as Pedro Arrupe, SJ, puts it, "it is the oppressed who must be the principal agents of change."[57] This observation is not meant to be a criticism based on an ahistorical moralism but simply an indication of Aquinas's distance from some of our own moral sensibilities.

Having said this, Aquinas's notion of friendship also contains the seeds of a deeper identification with the needy, especially to the extent that we become more aware of our many weaknesses, dependencies, and vulnerabilities. Aquinas's theology of charity is rooted in our common status as made in the image of God, our common neediness as material as well as spiritual creatures, and our common destiny in grace. As Amy Laura Hall points out, Aquinas's account of the virtue of mercy is best interpreted in light of a "wise regard for our common dependence" and in our sharing a "fundamental kinship of neediness and giftedness in grace."[58] Economically and psychologically impoverished people are, in this context, not "the other," but friends in Christ. Thomistic charity as friendship love rather than as philanthropic giving resonates with, and can be enriched by, some contemporary interpretations of hospitality (as in the work of Dorothy Day and the Catholic Worker movement), solidarity (as in the liberation theology of Albert Nolan, OP), accompaniment (as displayed by the Jesuit Refugee Service), or friendship itself (as illustrated by the Sant'Egidio community).

Civic Friendship

The account of charity as grace-inspired friendship love bears significant social and political implications. Thomistic charity stands in sharp contrast with most contemporary reductions of friendship to private interpersonal bonds. Some recent scholarly efforts have been dedicated to recovering something of the premodern appreciation of the political significance of friendship.[59]

The final section of this chapter will merely attempt to point to, rather than describe in any detail, the political significance of Thomistic charity as friendship love. As the graced perfection of nature, charity embraces and elevates the social nature of the person in community. It positively values our natural social interdependence, our need for community as the context of human flourishing, our natural orientation to social virtues and civic friendship, our natural inclination to justice as the primary basis for promoting the common good, and our individual and communal need for law as a guide for ordering our conduct to the common good (Aquinas, *ST* I-II.90.4).

Aquinas's profoundly social understanding of the human person recognized that we always exist as dependent parts of communities that we did not create. As Herbert McCabe observed, even the most basic will to live together—not only biologically but also culturally, spiritually, linguistically—is itself a will to friendship.[60] Thomistic appreciation of the social basis of friendship—the fact that all forms of friendship are based in a shared love of specific kinds of human goods—supports a balanced devotion to the common good that is sorely lacking in the ethos of contemporary Western societies.[61] Besides highlighting the importance of social networks and community as the context of human flourishing, Aquinas's account of friendship love highlights the ethical primacy of the common good (consistent of course with the other requirements of justice) within political and social deliberation.

Aquinas was obviously in no sense a proponent of liberalism, yet some of his recent intellectual descendants have sought critically and selectively to appropriate the political insights of liberalism without falling prey to its shortcomings.[62] The general character of the following comments is meant not to glide over complex debates but simply to indicate the attempt of some modern Thomists, particularly the philosophers Jacques Maritain, Yves Simon, and John Courtney Murray, to understand liberal democracy in terms of Thomistic civic friendship.

Twentieth-century Thomistic liberalism accepted constitutional democracy as the best form of government for the modern age.[63] It endorsed a limited view of the power of the state, legal protection of religious freedom to all citizens and to every religious community, constitutional separation of church and state as superior to the confessional state, and a view of politics as instrumentally valuable for the protection of the equal dignity of every person. It came to recognize the value of procedural justice in liberal democracy without reducing justice to pure proceduralism.

Some creative Thomistic thinkers sought critically to appropriate the characteristic structures and procedures of liberal democracy without also adopting the ideology of liberalism and its agenda of secularizing society as a whole. They embraced liberal democracy through a moral filter marked by a dual focus: the equal dignity of every person as protected by a robust doctrine of human rights and the primacy of the common good fostered by active citizens organized in the pursuit of shared purposes.[64] Civic friendship plays a particularly important role in inspiring virtues of civic republicanism necessary for the promotion of the common good. Liberal Thomists distanced themselves from some of Aquinas's own hierarchical, elitist, and paternalistic assumptions while avoiding both the atomistic individualism that often besets political liberalism and the romantic communalism that undergirds various totalitarianisms and authoritarianisms.

Liberal Thomism advocated a Christian humanism that underscored the responsibilities of civic friendship and the political obligation to human rights and the common good. It supported legal protection for cultural diversity and individual particularity within pluralistic societies.[65] At the same time, it offered an important reminder of the fact that the endorsement of tolerance and the avoidance of paternalism do not by themselves provide sufficiently for collective human flourishing. The critical retrieval of civic friendship can play an important role in promoting every citizen's political participation and socioeconomic contribution to the common good. It also provides grounds for encouraging local community organizations to exert their agency in ways that both resist entrenched socioeconomic and political elites and that promote constructive visions of the concrete good available in particular times and places.

Thomistic friendship here is useful for correcting any exclusive focus on individual rights that erodes the possibility of healthy and just communal solidarity, and it appreciates the moral significance of the public square in a way that provides an alternative to the modern tendency to restrict moral considerations to the private sphere.[66] It balances respect for the limited but real moral responsibility of the state and political institutions with an appreciation for the principle of subsidiarity, which is based on a recognition of our human capacity for multifaceted and differentiated civic friendship.[67] Understanding that intermediate associations within civil society provide much of the energy for our collective life, advocates of subsidiarity hold that social challenges should be met by the most socially local agency that can efficiently address them.[68] As legal scholar Thomas Kohler explains, subsidiarity recommends that "social institutions of all types be ordered so that decision-making can occur at the lowest capable level."[69]

The state and powerful social institutions thus ought to assume responsibility only if smaller associations cannot address the operative challenges. The central feature of subsidiarity is the "continuous and active involvement of those directly affected in an ongoing discourse about the way their lives should be ordered." Proper promotion of subsidiarity depends on being "flexible rather than dogmatic, and emphasizes practice over programmatic versions of theoretical certainty and structural uniformity." Subsidiarity is positive as well as negative: it both limits the responsibility of government and requires the engagement of government when necessary.[70] Subsidiarity is thus not concerned with simply restricting government, as it is often assumed, but rather with either limiting *or empowering* any forms of social organization as needed for the common good. It seeks neither a maximal nor a minimal but rather an appropriate exercise of social responsibility in various specific contexts.

Conclusion

Thomistic understanding of charity as grace-inspired friendship love continues to shed light on the fundamental features of Christian love. The core of the chapter argued that a theology of grace as working to heal and redirect the human person to the love of God and neighbor can help us to avoid the distracting and misleading tendency to separate charity (or agape) from other "types" of love (particularly eros and philia). It argued that charity is displayed in ordered and healed acts of philia and eros as well as in all the acts of the other virtues. Related to the New Testament, one can say that Jesus's actions of healing, forgiving, and calling for justice are all expressions of his charity, but so are his acts of praying, table fellowship, and teaching. In fact, every act done in gracious love is rooted in the virtue of charity.

This position helps us move beyond debates over whether self-sacrifice has priority over friendship in Christian ethics or whether equal regard comes before mutuality. Viewing charity as the transformation of all our motivations, attitudes, and actions enables us to concentrate on conversion of our disordered love of God, disordered love of neighbor, and disordered love of self. It prods us to differentiate the love of God that is distorted by our idolatries from the pure love of God for God's sake, the love of friendship based on ulterior motives from virtuous friendship, narcissistic self-love from rightly ordered self-love, and corrupted solidarity rooted in bias and expressed through out-group exploitation from solidarity ordered to justice and inclusive concern. Thomistic charity concurs with Outka's claim that the basis for neighbor love is the love of God. In viewing the love of God as fundamentally a matter of friendship, charity seeks to love all human beings as most fundamentally belonging within the circle of divine friendship.

Notes

1. See, for example, Liz Carmichael, *Friendship: Interpreting Christian Love* (London: T&T Clark, 2004); Edward Collins Vacek, *Love, Human and Divine: The Heart of Christian Ethics* (Washington, DC: Georgetown University Press, 1994); Gilbert Meilaender, *Friendship: A Study in Theological Ethics* (Notre Dame, IN: University of Notre Dame Press, 1981); and Paul Wadell, *Friendship and the Moral Life* (Notre Dame, IN: University of Notre Dame Press, 1991).

2. See Timothy Jackson, *The Priority of Love: Christian Charity and Social Justice* (Princeton, NJ: Princeton University Press, 2003), 55.

3. Ibid.

4. Timothy Jackson, *Love Disconsoled: Meditations on Christian Charity* (New York: Cambridge, 1999), 65.

5. The key texts from Thomas Aquinas for this chapter are *Summa Theologiae* I-II.26–28 (love) and II-II.23–27 (charity). References to this work are from Thomas Aquinas, *Summa Theologiae*, 4 vols. (Rome: Marietti, 1948). I have consulted the three-volume translation of the Fathers of the English Dominican Province (New York: Benzinger Brothers, 1947).

6. See Frederick E. Crowe, "Complacency and Concern in the Thought of St. Thomas Aquinas," in "Three Thomist Studies," ed. Fred Lawrence, supplement, *Lonergan Workshop* 16 (2000): 71–203.

7. Josef Pieper, *Faith, Hope, Love* (San Francisco: Ignatius, 1962), 166.

8. Paul J. Wadell, *The Primacy of Love: An Introduction to the Ethics of Thomas Aquinas* (Mahwah, NJ: Paulist Press, 1992), 3.

9. Pieper, *Faith, Hope, Love*, 163–64.

10. Ibid.

11. Ibid., 169.

12. Jackson, *Love Disconsoled*, 78. For this controversy and a subtle resolution in Augustine's favor, see Eric Gregory, *Politics and the Order of Love* (Chicago: University of Chicago Press, 2008), chap. 6.

13. Alan Donagan, *The Theory of Morality* (Chicago: University of Chicago Press, 1979).

14. Outka, *Agape: An Ethical Analysis* (New Haven, CT: Yale University Press, 1972), 9. While Aquinas sometimes used friendship love interchangeably with benevolence, the former is more than the latter. Aquinas drew from Aristotle's notion that friendship is like love for another self in which willing the good to a friend is in some significant ways like willing the good to the self (*ST* I-II.26.4). A friend esteems her friend as another self, i.e., insofar as she wills the good to her friend as to herself (*ST* I-II.28.1).

15. Aristotle, *Nicomachean Ethics*, trans. Martin Ostwald (Indianapolis: Bobbs-Merrill, 1962), 1156a6–21.

16. See Robert Bellah et al., *Habits of the Heart: Individualism and Commitment in American Life*, 3rd ed. (Berkeley, CA: University of California Press, 2007).

17. Pieper, *Faith, Hope, Love*, 156.

18. See David Gauthier, *Morals by Agreement* (Oxford: Clarendon, 1986); and Thomas Nagel, *The Possibility of Altruism* (Oxford: Clarendon, 1970). For criticisms and alternative views of altruism, see Lawrence A. Blum, *Friendship, Altruism, and Morality* (London: Routledge & Kegan Paul, 1980); and Stephen G. Post, Lynn G. Underwood, Jeffrey P. Schloss, and William B. Hurlbut, eds., *Altruism and Altruistic Love: Science, Philosophy, and Religion in Dialogue* (New York: Oxford University Press, 2002).

19. Jackson, *Priority of Love*, 47.

20. Jackson, *Love Disconsoled*, 79.

21. Gene Outka, "Faith," in *The Oxford Handbook of Theological Ethics*, ed. Gilbert Meilaender and William Werpehowski (New York: Oxford University Press, 2005), 279.

22. See Outka, "Universal Love and Impartiality," in *The Love Commandments*, ed. Edmund N. Santurri and William Werpehowski (Washington, DC: Georgetown University Press, 1992), 88.

23. See Jackson, *Priority of Love*, 56.

24. Outka, "Universal Love and Impartiality," 88

25. Vacek, *Love, Human and Divine*, 116.

26. Outka, "Faith," 283, 284.

27. Wadell, *Friendship and the Moral Life*, 139.

28. See Gene Outka, "Augustinianism and Common Morality," in *Prospects for a Common Morality*, ed. Gene Outka and John P. Reeder Jr. (Princeton, NJ: Princeton University Press, 1993), 124.

29. Ibid., 20.

30. Outka, "Universal Love and Impartiality," 87.

31. Anders Nygren, *Agape and Eros*, trans. Philip Watson (Chicago: University of Chicago Press, 1982), pt. 2, chap. 2, the "caritas-synthesis," and chap. 4, the "medieval doctrine of love." One of the clearest critiques is found in Outka, *Agape*, 47–50 passim. For a more recent treatment that is both sympathetic and critical, see William Werpehowski, "Anders Nygren's Agape and Eros," in Meilaender and Werpehowski, *Oxford Handbook*, 447–48. Jackson, *Love Disconsoled*; and *Priority of Love*. Jackson makes it clear that he is both deeply influenced by Nygren and wants to distance himself from Nygren's extreme rejection of any forms of Christian self-love and friendship, however chastened. See *Priority of Love*, 8n25, 11n31. Jackson disputes the Augustinian and Thomist equation of caritas with agape in *Love Disconsoled*, 11n25. For a friendly critique of Jackson's position, see Eric Gregory, *Politics and the Order of Love: An Augustinian Ethic of Democratic Citizenship* (Chicago: University of Chicago Press, 2010).

32. Jackson, *Love Disconsoled*, 23.

33. Pace Vacek, *Love, Human and Divine*, 296.

34. Ibid.

35. Werpehowski, "Anders Nygren's Agape and Eros," 442.

36. Once again, see the excellent treatment of these topics from an Augustinian point of view in Gregory, *Politics and the Order of Love*, chap. 6.

37. Nygren, *Agape and Eros*, 735.

38. Ibid., 736.

39. Outka, *Agape*, 282.

40. Ibid., 10.

41. Fergus Kerr, "Charity as Friendship," in *Language, Meaning and God*, ed. B. Davies (London: Geoffrey Chapman, 1987).

42. Outka, *Agape*, 301. This is not to suggest that Aquinas's ethic either accorded with that based on an impartial spectator or supposed political egalitarianism, only that he provides strong grounds for the equality of basic justice. See Jean Porter, *The Recovery of Virtue* (Louisville, KY: Westminster John Knox Press, 1990), 135ff.

43. See Paul J. Wadell, *Friends of God: Virtues and Gifts in Aquinas* (New York: Peter Lang, 1991).

44. Wadell, *Friendship and the Moral Life*, 74.

45. Outka, *Agape*, 37. Also "Universal Love and Impartiality," 89.

46. See Carmichael, *Friendship*, chaps. 1–2.

47. See Daniel Schwartz, *Aquinas on Friendship* (New York: Oxford University Press, 2007).

48. Outka, *Agape*, 280.

49. See Martin Luther King Jr., *Strength to Love* (Cleveland, OH: Williams Collins, 1963), chap. 4, "Love Your Enemies."

50. Vacek, *Love, Human and Divine*, 299–300.

51. See Robert Bellah et al., *Habits of the Heart: Individualism and Commitment in American Life* (San Francisco: Harper & Row, 1981), chap. 6.

52. See Martin E. Seligman, *Authentic Happiness: Using the New Positive Psychology to Realize Your Potential for Lasting Fulfillment* (New York: Free Press, 2004). More scientific treatment of the important

themes is provided by Christopher Peterson and Martin E. P. Seligman, eds., *Character Strengths and Virtues: A Handbook and Classification* (New York: Oxford University Press, 2004).

53. See James F. Keenan, *A History of Moral Theology in the Twentieth Century: From Confessing Sins to Liberating Consciences* (New York: Continuum, 2010), chaps. 1 and 2.

54. Wadell, *Primacy of Love*, 3.

55. Outka, "Universal Love and Impartiality," 1.

56. See Jean Vanier, *Becoming Human* (Mahwah, NJ: Paulist Press, 1998). See also Stanley Hauerwas and Jean Vanier, *Living Gently in a Violent World: The Prophetic Witness of Weakness* (Downers Grove, IL: IVP Books, 2008).

57. Kevin Burke, ed., *Pedro Arrupe: Essential Writings* (Maryknoll, NY: Orbis Press, 2007), 187.

58. Amy Laura Hall, "Love: A Kinship of Affliction and Redemption," in Meilaender and Werpehowski, *Oxford Handbook*, 313.

59. See, for example, John von Heyking and Richard Avramenko, eds., *Friendship and Politics: Essays in Political Thought* (Notre Dame, IN: University of Notre Dame Press, 2008), especially chap. 5, Jeanne Heffernan Schindler, "A Companionship of Caritas: Friendship in St. Thomas," 139–62.

60. See Herbert McCabe, *The Good Life: Ethics and the Pursuit of Happiness* (New York: Continuum, 2005), 37–38.

61. See Jonathan Sacks, *The Home We Build Together: Recreating Society* (New York: Continuum, 2007).

62. See R. Bruce Douglass and David Hollenbach, eds., *Catholicism and Liberalism: Contributions to American Public Philosophy* (New York: Cambridge University Press, 1994).

63. See Clifford G. Kossel, "Thomistic Moral Philosophy in the Twentieth Century," in *The Ethics of Aquinas*, ed. Stephen J. Pope (Washington, DC: Georgetown University Press, 2002), 385–411.

64. See Jacques Maritain, *Man and the State* (Chicago: University of Chicago, 1951); Yves Simon, *Philosophy of Democratic Government* (Chicago: University of Chicago Press, 1951); and John Courtney Murray, *We Hold These Truths* (Kansas City, MO: Sheed and Ward, 1988). For a helpful analysis of the Catholic context of this debate, see Joseph A. Komonchak, "Vatican II and the Encounter between Catholicism and Liberalism," in Douglass and Hollenbach, *Catholicism and Liberalism*, 76–99; and for a clear discussion of rival approaches to liberalism among contemporary Thomists, see John P. Hittinger, *Liberty, Wisdom, and Grace: Thomism and Democratic Political Theory* (Lanham, MD: Lexington Books, 2003). Robert P. George, *The Clash of Orthodoxies: Religion, Law and Morality in Crisis* (Wilmington, DE: Intercollegiate Studies Institute, 2002), finds a fundamental harmony between Aquinas and the "ordered liberty" of American liberalism, properly construed.

65. As in, for example, Eberhard Schockenhoff, *Natural Law and Human Dignity*, trans. Brian McNeil (Washington, DC: Catholic University of America Press, 2003).

66. See Charles Taylor, *Modern Social Imaginaries* (Durham, NC: Duke University, 2004).

67. See Clifford Kossel, "Global Community and Subsidiarity," *Communio* 37 (1981): 37–50.

68. See Aquinas, *ST* II-II.58.5. See also F. H. Mueller, "The Principle of Subsidiarity in the Christian Tradition," *American Catholic Sociological Review* 4, no. 3 (1943): 144–57; Nicholas Aroney, "Subsidiarity, Federalism, and the Best Constitution: Thomas Aquinas on City, Province and Empire," *Law and Philosophy* 26, no. 2 (2007): 161–228.

69. This and the following two quotations appear in "Lessons from the Social Charter: State, Corporation, and the Meaning of Subsidiarity," *University of Toronto Law Journal* 43, no. 3 (1993): 614–15.

70. See Paolo G. Carozza, "Subsidiarity as a Structural Principle of International Human Rights Law," *American Journal of International Law* 97 (2003): 38–79.

13

Evolution, Agape, and the Image of God

A Reply to Various Naturalists

TIMOTHY P. JACKSON

> If this life be not a real fight, in which something is eternally gained for the universe by success, it is no better than a game of private theatricals from which one may withdraw at will. But it feels like a real fight, —as if there were something really wild in the universe which we, with all our idealities and faithfulness, are needed to redeem; and first of all to redeem our own hearts from atheisms and fears. For such a half-wild, half-saved universe our nature is adapted.
>
> —William James

IN CHAPTER 4 of *On the Origin of Species*, Charles Darwin briefly discusses why birds sing. It is often, he notes, a function of "the severest rivalry between the males of many species to attract by singing the females."[1] A particularly strong or melodious song will contribute to reproductive success both by inducing females to mate and by announcing territoriality to other males. Darwin was unaware of modern genetics, but neo-Darwinians would say that a strikingly robust or appealing song makes it more likely that the male will be able to get his genes into the next generation and, over time, natural selection will reinforce or even palpably augment such "fitness."[2] Call this the naturalistic explanation of why birds sing.

In chapter 10 of *To Kill a Mockingbird*, Atticus Finch says to his son, Jem, whom he has given an air-rifle for Christmas: "I'd rather you shot at tin cans in the back yard, but I know you'll go after birds. Shoot all the bluejays you want, if you can hit 'em, but remember it's a sin to kill a mockingbird." Miss Maudie explains to Scout, who has also received a rifle, "Your father's right . . . Mockingbirds don't do one thing but make music for us to enjoy. They don't eat up people's gardens, don't nest in corncribs, they don't do one thing but sing their hearts out for us. That's why it's a sin to kill a mockingbird."[3]

Now, is the singing of birds any less beautiful, any less a cause for Jem's and Scout's appreciation and respect, when we know the naturalistic explanation? In the novel, the mockingbird is a metaphor for innocence, but scientifically, of course, it is no more altruistic than the blue jay, no more singing for our enjoyment. Presumably, the mockingbird's song is sparked by the same evolutionary forces as that of any other bird. Is there an either-or, then, between Darwin's finches and Harper Lee's Finch? I suspect that many of us would say, "Not at all. One may actually enjoy birdsongs all the more when one knows the complex evolutionary dynamics behind them. Who cares *why* birds sing, biologically speaking? It's the aesthetic *result* that matters, it's the melody that moves us, and we should want to conserve wildlife for the sake of its intrinsic delicacy and loveliness, independently of anthropocentric (or theocentric) reasons."

Fine; I agree . . . at least for the sake of argument.

But is the tale the same in ethics? Do only consequences count, as arguably in aesthetics— at least regarding the "productions" of nature—or are results only part of the ethical story? What about the motive of the agent and the form of her action, what moral philosophers call "aretology" and "deontology"?[4] Can love of neighbor, for instance, be accounted for purely in terms of evolutionary utility and still be itself? In *The Voyage of the Beagle*, Darwin himself wonders about moral motive, asking whether the self-immolation of a slave he witnessed manifested "the noble love of freedom" or "mere brutal obstinacy"; and in *On the Origin of Species*, he recognized that the reality of self-sacrifice was a major challenge to his theory of "success in the battle for life."[5] Have we made real advances on these matters since Darwin's time?

I examine in this essay the ways in which reductively naturalistic explanations of human sentiments and behaviors undercut or preclude Christian agape. In the process, I argue against various forms of neo-Darwinism and in favor of purposeful agency, both human and divine. In particular, I maintain (1) that Stephen Jay Gould's account of evolution is incompatible with Christian convictions about charity and the image of God, but (2) that Gould's account is not the only one possible and is in fact mistaken. The problem with Gould's position is twofold: (a) he erroneously considers science and religion to constitute "non-overlapping magisteria," with the former concerned exclusively with "facts" and the latter solely with "values," and (b) he fails to appreciate the significance of convergence in genetically unrelated species. Even as I criticize Gould, I nevertheless make use of a distinction that he (and Richard Lewontin) popularized: that between a spandrel and an adaptation. My main thesis is that pure consequentialism in ethics, pan-adaptationism and pan-selectionism in biology, and hard (in)determinism in physics cannot do justice to agapic love. Happily, however, these three "isms" do not exhaust the alternatives.

Once we recognize that the moral meaning of human behaviors cannot be determined independently of self-conscious motives—what William James calls "our idealities and faithfulness"—we must surrender a mechanistic picture of the world and make room for both actions and events.[6] Once we realize that not all traits or patterns of behavior emerge because of their adaptive benefit to the individual, we must admit, as did Darwin, that natural selection is not the only mechanism driving evolution. Once we see that historical contingency is not antithetical to progress (even purpose) in nature and its laws, we must let go of any simple dichotomy between chance and necessity. Once we do these three things, we can affirm the compatibility of a form of evolution with Christian agape. This form is commonly called "teleological evolution" or "teleological theism."

The Importance of Intentionality

Imagine that I extend help to the needy because I am mad at my wife and I know that such "philanthropic giving" upsets her, or because I am on a scavenger hunt and assistance to a derelict is part of the amusing challenge to bring in "a forgotten man."[7] Would we call this altruism? I think not. *The Oxford English Dictionary* defines altruism as "devotion to the welfare of others, regard for others, as a principle of action; opposed to egotism or selfishness."[8] *Merriam-Webster Online* (2016) defines the term as "(1) unselfish regard for or devotion to the welfare of others; (2) behavior by an animal that is not beneficial to or may be harmful to itself but that benefits others of its species." Reference to "regard" in both texts suggests that a certain motivational structure is a necessary condition for real altruism, though it is not a sufficient one. Actions and effects matter too, of course. (In fact, agent character, forms of action, and consequences of action are the three dimensions of the moral life, and without attention to all three, ethical theory is severely stunted.) If I proclaim that I care about the poor and victimized but never lift a finger to help them, or if my efforts to aid them are rife with swindles and snafus, then one might plausibly doubt my supposed care. Even if I sincerely tell myself that I am a compassionate person, without the appropriate behaviors and even some modest positive results, one would rightly suspect self-deception. Still, an other-regarding motive is crucial and cuts against calculations of reward. Even a saint may be partly inspired by the thought that God is watching and storing up treasures for her in heaven, but that can't be the *main* motive. If my thinking and acting is mostly "about me," I just am not altruistic. In general, the truly altruistic don't let the left hand know what the right hand is doing.

I do not mean to neglect or vilify reciprocity, mutual aid pacts, and related forms of rational cooperation and fair-mindedness; neither do I want to erase eros or erode self-love. Life would not be livable without justice and healthy instinctual desire, and upholding them is a real achievement. I am simply saying that altruism—aka agape—has priority as a distinct and more fundamental virtue. No other good can supplant charity in this regard. Economies of exchange and self-interested desires are dependent on altruism—self-interested persons emerge only because they are given an unearned and costly care by others—and altruism itself requires more than a particular set of external results. We are comparatively untroubled by the thought that the sweet trilling of a titmouse is undesigned and instinctive, but without irreducible subjectivity, no *moral* action is possible *for a human person*. Ethics inescapably involves intentionality. That moral action known as generosity or self-sacrifice is, once more, not synonymous with delayed gratification, kin altruism, or indirect reciprocity—as though shifting from now to later or from the individual to a group makes self-interest less self-interested. Animals certainly experience morally meaningful pain, and some even behave self-sacrificially (e.g., for their young). Moreover, all sentient life can profit from acts of charity. But only self-conscious persons with intentions are "generous" in the fullest sense.

Perhaps the most troubling implication of reductive evolutionary biology is that the human person is herself seemingly epiphenomenal to her genes and their replication strategies. If the problem with Cartesian dualism is that it makes the soul seem like a "ghost in a machine," the problem with reductive naturalism is that it eliminates the person in favor of a "gene in a machine." What I have elsewhere called "reproductive utilitarianism" associates good and bad outcomes exclusively with reproductive success or failure, with no higher or inherent teleology.[9] Is such naturalism compatible with either ethics or religion? I think not. Consider the image of God.

"Made in the Image of God"

Many of us are familiar with these words from Genesis 1:26–31:

> Then God said, "Let us make humankind in our image, according to our likeness; and let them have dominion over the fish of the sea, and over the birds of the air, and over the

cattle, and over all the wild animals of the earth, and over every creeping thing that creeps upon the earth." So God created humankind in his image, in the image of God he created them; male and female he created them. God blessed them, and God said to them, "Be fruitful and multiply, and fill the earth and subdue it; and have dominion over the fish of the sea and over the birds of the air and over every living thing that moves upon the earth." God said, "See, I have given you every plant yielding seed that is upon the face of all the earth, and every tree with seed in its fruit; you shall have them for food. And to every beast of the earth, and to every bird of the air, and to everything that creeps on the earth, everything that has the breath of life, I have given every green plant for food." And it was so. God saw everything that he had made, and indeed, it was very good. And there was evening and there was morning, the sixth day.

Within the Christian tradition, the image of God has often been identified with human intellect and will—with what Thomas Aquinas, for example, calls "reason" and "rational appetite."[10] Intellect and (free) will, in turn, are frequently held to be both what makes us unique and what makes us valuable, what separates us from the animals and what gives us dignity. Our selves, our identities as distinct persons, are due respect because of our capacities for independent thought and action. Because we can formulate and achieve self-conscious ends, we ourselves are to be treated as ends and not as means only (Kant). The problem with this perspective, however, is that it disqualifies from the *imago Dei* those human beings who are not autonomous agents: fetuses, babes in arms, the mentally handicapped, the sick or injured, the demented, the frail elderly. Because I affirm the equal worth of all human lives, I depart from much of the Western tradition and propose that we disassociate the image of God from a hyper-intellectualism that does an injustice to human dependence and emotion. We ought, instead, to reconnect the image with a particular human need and potential: to give and/or receive agapic love.

Here as elsewhere, I identify agape with three interpersonal features: (1) unconditional willing of the good for the other, (2) equal regard for the well-being of the other, and (3) passionate service open to self-sacrifice for the sake of the other.[11] This move is biblical as well as philosophical. If "God is love [agape]" (1 John 4:8), and if "those who abide in love [agape] abide in God, and God abides in them" (1 John 4:16), then being made in the image of God (Gen. 1) must refer essentially to agapic love. To be made in God's image is to embody an impersonal sanctity that ought to be honored and protected, as well as to have the potential for a personal dignity that ought to be respected and admired. We are made, in short, first to be loved and then to love. This judgment is crucial because it severs our axiological value from our ontological uniqueness. It is not what is unique to us as a species (robust self-consciousness) that gives us value but what is shared with at least some other sentient creatures (the need or ability to give or receive agape). In many circumstances, the need for agapic love constitutes the right to receive it; even as, in many circumstances, the capacity for agapic love constitutes the duty to give it.

A common critique of this "ontological" reading of the *imago*, from a theological perspective, is that it invites us to boast. In equating the image of God with something objective about human nature, the argument runs, we are flirting with hubris or works righteousness. Thus, some theologians (e.g., Karl Barth, Helmut Thielicke, and Karen Lebacqz) embrace a purely "relational" view, in which the *imago* is entirely a function of God's attitude toward or will for us. The problem with this line, however, is that it denies the substantive reality of creation. Genesis 1 depicts God creating humankind "in his image," and God calls the result "very good." If, in contrast, the *imago* is all about God, so to speak, then it is *not I* who have been created and declared good but a mere projection of the Deity: God as narcissist. More-over, if the image of God does not refer essentially to human beings, then when we honor that image, we are not attending to fellow creatures but rather, again, to the Deity alone. Some theologians accept this consequence—that God is the only proper object of agape—but I am not one of them. Such a conclusion ignores the second love command of Matthew 22:36–40 or conflates it with the first. Such a vision flirts with Gnosticism, fleeing from the temporal world.

Interpreting the image of God as the need or ability to give or receive agapic love appears to have two additional problems, *from a Darwinian perspective*. First, the interpreta-tion presupposes that beings capable of giving and/or receiving love emerged because of divine intentionality. Genesis speaks of God's "creating humankind" according to a plan and then calling the result "very good." If Stephen Jay Gould is correct, however, the evolutionary processes that cast up *Homo sapiens* are utterly without purpose or direction. There is no progress over time, and no species or feature of a species is predictable in advance. Gould's metaphor of "replaying life's tape" makes it clear that starting history over from any given point would lead to "sensible results strikingly different from the actual history of life."[12] Such arbitrariness certainly seems incompatible with faith in a Creator who intentionally wills the existence of creatures capable of coming into relation with Her.

Second, to the extent that agape involves disinterested concern for others, including openness to self-sacrifice even for a stranger or enemy, it would seem inevitably to be weeded out by natural selection, understood genetically. Agapists willingly reduce, or risk reducing, their reproductive success for the sake of others. Prudence, perhaps even justice-as-reciprocity, might be sustained as a survival value within a Gouldian universe. But a number of human actions, from extrafamilial and transracial adoption, to building handicapped access ramps, to heroic suffering and death at the expense of procreation, must seem like whopping contradictions to evolutionary naturalists who make genetic continuity the sum-mum bonum.[13] This is especially true if naturalism implies physical determinism.

How might one respond to these two problems?

Gould and Non-overlapping Magisteria

Stephen Jay Gould invites us to dissolve the first problem, that of squaring divine intention-ality with evolutionary arbitrariness, by holding that Genesis is not making truth claims about realities in or beyond the world. For Gould, the creation story, like all theological tales, is concerned not with objective facts but with how we articulate subjective values.[14] There can be no conflict between a Judeo-Christian understanding of the image of God and a "Darwin-ian" description of random mutation and natural selection, because the two fall within "non-overlapping magisteria."[15] Religion is about our *making* meaning, while science is about *finding* what actually exists.

I find Gould's views on this topic highly implausible. To be sure, science and religion are typically characterized by quite different epistemic procedures and ontological foci. Sci-ence relies on reason and the five senses, and it is defined by the experimental method, the quest for repeatable results, openness to empirical falsification, and so on. Religion, on the other hand, appeals to a spiritual sensibility and the various passions, and it often rests on revealed faith claims made in sacred texts. Science usually deals with material objects and the causal forces that act on them; religion seeks to intuit or emulate a supernatural Good that lies behind physical objects and forces. Nonetheless, both science and religion remain realist, in an alethiological sense. Both aim, that is, at truth as correspondence to reality—at "saying of what is, that it is" (Aristotle), *adequatio intellectus et res* (Aquinas), semantically linking up words and world (Tarski), and so on. Moreover, at certain levels of generality, science and religion can obviously conflict. If X says that life emerged in part because of intelligent design, for instance, and Y claims that life is the upshot of random and undirected forces, both cannot be right.

The Question of Teleology

If Judaism and Christianity teach that the appearance of beings capable of giving and/or receiving charity was part of a divine plan, while evolutionary biology claims that no purpose (divine or otherwise) was operative, then we clearly have a contradiction. This may be so much the worse for religious faith, of course. It is certainly conceivable that biblical theism is false. But let us not be misleadingly irenic about what is at issue. Reference to divine purpose does not require embracing an interventionist God who directly causes beneficial mutations or independently creates each species with a fixed essence. Such "creationism" was powerfully rebutted by Darwin in *Origin*, and contemporary advocates of "Intelligent Design" are not necessarily committed to such occasionalism.[16] What *is* required by affirmation of Genesis 1:26–31, however, is at least that God created the laws of physics and chemistry that undergird biological evolution and that the evolutionary process has an inherent directionality or conatus that makes the emergence of life and love highly probable, if not inevitable. If all is mere randomness (or hard determinism), the Abrahamic tradition is just wrong.

Admittedly, some neo-Darwinians are inconsistent on this score, arguing simultaneously (1) that teleology or purpose is not a scientific notion and thus that religious exponents of divine design (at any level) are unscientific and (2) that random variation and natural selection disprove or otherwise disallow all purpose in or of nature.[17] You can't have it both ways, however. If science can gainsay divine purpose, then it cannot be unscientific to affirm it. (One might be *mistaken* in affirming design, but that is another matter.) If, on the other hand, teleology is beyond science's ken altogether, then, by definition, science cannot be either for or against divine design as such.

When Jacques Monod declares that "the mechanism of Darwinism is at last securely founded," thus "man has to understand that he is a mere accident,"[18] he is manifestly rejecting Judaism and Christianity. For Monod, Richard Dawkins, Daniel Dennett, and other naturalists, it is *not* the case that God intentionally established the laws of physics, chemistry, and biology and then set the cosmic ecosystem loose to generate results on its own. This denial is different from the rejection of what Darwin called "creationism," in that in the first case even a Deistic or meta-operative God is rejected. Several of Darwin's contemporaries—Harvard botanist Asa Gray, for example—readily accepted evolution as the mechanism for the production of species but continued to see God as the intelligent designer of the laws of evolution itself. Even Darwin conceded at times that nature and its laws were designed. What divided Gray and Darwin was the question whether any *specific* result of evolution is planned. Darwin held that the specific results of evolution were unplanned/undesigned, thus his denial of creationism, while Gray argued that evolution was guided in and through channels preordained by God.[19]

Contra Monod and others, one might hold that the concrete results of the evolutionary process involve an element of chance but that the process was antecedently structured and coherent and pointed toward a particular end—rather like Abner Doubleday inventing the rules of baseball and defining victory but leaving the outcomes of actual games open-ended. Some Victorian Christians even found it more majestic, more suggestive of omnipotence, that God should "make creatures make themselves" than that the Deity should have to tinker ad hoc.[20] Again, however, such teleology-at-one-remove is rejected by Dawkins, Dennett, and at times, Gould. Such a rejection is actually at odds with Darwin's own view, a middle way between Gray and the three "neo-Darwinians."

Conway Morris and Convergence

But what, more positively, could make one think that the messiness of evolution *is* in fact compatible with divine purpose and historical progress? Here the work of the Cambridge paleontologist Simon Conway Morris is helpful. In *Life's Solution*, he provides a cogent reply to Gould's argument concerning "the awesome improbability of human evolution."[21] Conway Morris's specialty is documenting and analyzing the many cases of "convergence" in natural history—for example, the fact that the camera eye has evolved multiple times in genetically unrelated species (e.g., cephalopods and primates). He does not flinch from the conclusion that there are morphological and behavioral niches into which the tree of life will (almost) "inevitably" branch over time. He has even called himself a kind of Platonist.[22]

Gould famously suggested that had the Cretaceous mass extinction not taken place— that is, had the Chicxulub meteor impact not, by chance, helped kill off the dinosaurs sixty-five million years ago, thus allowing mammals (and eventually us) to emerge—intelligent life would simply not have evolved.[23] To this, Conway Morris says, in effect, "Not a bit of it . . . had the dinosaurs not died off, there would ultimately have been intelligent dinos, or their descendants." We still have comparatively little idea of how inanimate chemicals become living organisms, but once there is life, intelligence will eventually emerge. To quote Conway Morris, "The constraints of evolution and the ubiquity of convergence make the emergence of something like ourselves a near-inevitability. Contrary to received wisdom and the prevailing ethos of despair, the contingencies of biological history will make no long-term difference to the outcome. Yet the existence of life itself on the Earth appears to be surrounded with improbabilities. . . . Life may be a universal principle, but we can still be alone."[24]

Conway Morris is both a scientist and a Christian, and he does not hesitate to bring the two disciplines into conversation:

> In essence, we can ask ourselves what salient facts of evolution are congruent with a Creation. In my judgment, they are as follows:
> (1) its underlying simplicity, relying on a handful of building blocks;
> (2) the existence of an immense universe of possibilities, but a way of navigating to that minutest of fractions which actually work;
> (3) the sensitivity of the process and the product, whereby nearly all alternatives are disastrously maladaptive;
> (4) the inherency of life whereby complexity emerges as much by the rearrangement and co-option of pre-existing building blocks as against relying on novelties *per se*;
> (5) the exuberance of biological diversity, but the ubiquity of evolutionary convergence;
> (6) the inevitability of the emergence of sentience, and the likelihood that among animals it is far more prevalent than we are willing to admit.[25]

These lines strongly support the proposition that natural selection is the often harsh, but law-governed, mechanism by which God "creates" complex beings in time—or, if you prefer, by which God allows creatures to create themselves. There is genuine contingency here, but if there is not also some Conway Morris–like teleology to the process,[26] then it makes no sense to talk of a loving Deity forming humanity "in His own image." To say the very least, the facts of convergence make talk of "progress" in evolution perfectly plausible. These facts may not yet amount to a *sufficient* condition for attributing the laws of nature to the designing mind of God, but they are a *necessary* condition for such an attribution. Faith is still required, since the violence and predation associated with natural selection will always raise theodicy questions. But if there is no purpose in and through evolution, Judaism and Christianity are false. Gould notwithstanding, there is that much overlap between science and religion.

Explaining Agape or Explaining It Away?

Now I return to the second problem that evolution potentially poses for my interpretation of the image of God (noted previously): the self-giving nature of agape. There are two related issues here: (a) How could natural selection have first generated and then preserved an altruistic impulse, given its seeming reproductive disadvantages? and (b) If natural selection is behind altruism after all, can or should we continue to practice or applaud it once we know its evolutionary explanation? These two questions, in turn, can be answered only when we understand the relation between genetic and memetic evolution. Take the example of Christianity's founder. Jesus is willing in love to go to the Cross childless and thus must seem, in purely genetic terms, a paradigmatic loser who foolishly surrenders the greatest human good. In cultural terms, in contrast, he is one of the most prolific "breeders" in history: his teachings have spread around the world, influencing countless persons and institutions.[27] Does the Messiah's historic impact represent what might be called "a teleological suspension of the genetic," revealing a higher value than physical progeny? If so, critics of evolution ask, how can blind chance cast up such a purposeful, dignified being who can prefer death to dishonor, cultural redemption to biological reproduction? The question has become perennial. Evolutionary biologists and game theorists have claimed to make important strides in solving this long-standing puzzle, of course. Sophisticated discussions of "the Ultimatum Game" and "the Prisoner's Dilemma"—with titles like "Chaos and the Evolution of Cooperation," "The Arithmetics of Mutual Help," "The Economics of Fair Play," and "Empathy Leads to Fairness"— often claim to explain how naturalistic evolution and traditional virtue are compatible, even mutually implying. The common refrain, however, is that what looks like selflessness actually pays dividends, if only indirectly, either to oneself or one's close biological relatives (so-called kin altruism). In effect, the biologists and game theorists tend to use the assumed reality of (Darwinian) evolution to explain away agape, I fear, even as pious believers use the assumed reality of (biblical) agape to explain away evolution, both sometimes using terms imprecisely.

Now what is someone like myself to do, someone who affirms *both* the reality of robust altruism *and* the fact of biological evolution? How can we reconcile cultural and genetic imperatives? If ideas are analogous to genes, with "survival of the fittest" being applicable to moral traditions as well as physical bodies, what are the mechanisms of and standards for such fitness? The brilliance of many of the game theoretic models is beyond question, but there is often a creeping conflation of mutual advantage or prudence with agapic love or compassion. In addition, causal explanations of impersonal processes (efficient causes) are at times confused with or insufficiently related to the moral motivations of personal agents (final causes). When attempting to reconcile naturalistic accounts of evolution with the existence of altruism, it does not matter whether we talk about "general utility" or "rational cooperation" or "indirect reciprocity." For it is one thing to endorse fairness because it pays or because you fear that you or your relatives will otherwise get the short end of the evolutionary stick; it is something else to affirm another's well-being even though you and yours need never fear injustice or barrenness yourselves—indeed, even though it involves your voluntarily surrendering properly accessible values (like progeny or good reputation).[28] Agape cannot be redescribed as prudence.

Let me state succinctly my main problem with game theoretic and other naturalistic accounts of "altruism," which I treat for present purposes as synonymous with what Christians call "agape" or "love of neighbor." If agape unconditionally wills the good for the other, for the other's and/or God's sake, and if agape is open to a self-sacrifice that outstrips reciprocity (much less personal advantage), then talk of "tit-for-tat," "win-stay/lose-shift," "kin altruism," "indirect reciprocity," and the like is largely beside the point. Such phrases may capture aspects of social *cooperation*, understood as action coordinated for mutual benefit. They may even expand the normal bounds of our concern in some respects, but they still basically reduce love of neighbor to a form of personal prudence. It may be that apparently or reputedly altruistic behavior is, in reality, motivated by fundamentally self-regarding agendas. But then it is better simply to concede that Nietzsche and Freud were right: agapic love of neighbor is unnatural and self-deceived. It can't really be done, at least by the vast majority of individuals, and even to try is likely to leave one frustrated in the end. It is to fail to understand one's own mind and heart as inherited from the Paleolithic past.

Importantly, the judgment that evolutionary theorists often reduce altruism to rational self-interest holds for both biological and cultural evolution. Both genes and memes are selfish, it seems, with universal love being an ideal cultural construct that makes up for genetic reproductive failure. Agape is but a false consolation for the agony of agamy—a kind of evolutionary sour grapes.

The problem with such reductive naturalism is that in "explaining" human behavior in terms of reproductive fitness, it explains away specifically virtuous behavior, and yet such behavior persists. Even reciprocal justice, let alone altruism, at times sounds like a game one plays only so long as defection might be discovered and punished. One feigns fairness or even empathy to get others to cooperate, and to feign these really well, one must make others, and finally oneself, believe that there is real mutuality present. In fact, however, there neither is nor could be such a binding commitment, claim the naturalists. Millions of years of Malthusian scarcity and Darwinian selection have made the human animal irredeemably exploitative and amoral, so there is only temporary expediency, bolstered perhaps by a thoroughgoing delusion. Hence the soliloquy of the selfish gene: "I'll get my person to help others, if they will help him back, and I'll move him to cultivate a personal reputation for reliability to help ensure such a return from others, but I'll also move my person to cheat with impunity if he can, though I won't permit him to know this consciously, lest he give me away." If the person is merely the gene's way of making more genes like itself, a "survival machine" in Richard Dawkins's phrase,[29] then ethics becomes a kind of placebo to keep the patient distracted without really affecting the underlying system.

Let me drive home my point by drawing a contrast between two types of explanation: *explanation-as-translation* and *explanation-as-elimination*. If I say, for instance, "A table is a cloud of molecules, and molecules, in turn, are composed of atoms," I am offering a translation of physical-object-talk into atomic-physics-talk. I might even go further and refer to "protons," "neutrons," and "electrons" or even to subatomic particles like "quarks." In all of these cases, nonetheless, we do not feel that physical-object-talk is somehow invalidated. We continue to speak of "tables," "chairs," and so on without thinking that this is ontologically naive or otherwise inappropriate. It's a matter of context and convenience which idiom we use.

If I say, on the other hand, "A witch is nothing but a neurotic woman and a warlock is nothing but a neurotic man," I am offering an eliminative explanation.[30] In this case, we *do* judge the original object-language to have been invalidated. The *explanans* has not merely explained but has actually explained *away* the *explanandum*. Once one accepts the psychological explanation in terms of neurosis, one stops talking about "witches" and "warlocks." They are seen not to exist, rather like phlogiston's disappearing after the discovery of mean kinetic energy.

I am arguing that naturalistic accounts of altruism are more like explanation-as-elimination than like explanation-as-translation, though this is often not acknowledged.

The Naturalistic Evasion

Strikingly, naturalists frequently have no problem suggesting that *religion* is falsified by naturalistic interpretations of evolutionary biology—see, for example, the recent works of Dan Dennett[31]—but they are often unwilling to see that such interpretations also undermine *ethics*, and for the same basic reasons. I have just discussed the case of religion. Consider further that of ethics. In the classic "naturalistic fallacy," identified by David Hume and named by G. E. Moore, moralists seek to argue from an "is" to an "ought" but can give no grounds for making such a logical connection. Some contemporary philosophers have argued that such grounds can in fact (in value?) be given, that the naturalistic fallacy is not actually fallacious.[32] But what interests me is the other side of the coin, so to speak. In what I call "the naturalistic *evasion*," reductivists often seek to *avoid* moving from the "is" of natural selection to the "ought" of heartless social competition but can give no grounds for *not* making such a logical connection. (The proper tack for Christians, need I add, is not to begin with naturalism in the first place.) Darwin himself writes notoriously, "It may be difficult, but we ought to admire the savage instinctive hatred of the queen bee, which urges her instantly to destroy the young queens her daughters as soon as born, or to perish herself in the combat; for undoubtedly this is for the good of the community; and maternal love or maternal hatred, though the latter fortunately is most rare, is all the same to the inexorable principle of natural selection."[33]

What is the force of the "ought" in this quotation? It sure *sounds* like reproductive consequentialism, however "savage," is to be judged morally good, if not inevitable. Human beings are not bees, but natural selection is thought to bear on *all* living species. How do we escape an obligation to admire *human* hatred and destructiveness when they contribute to "the good of the community"? Nietzsche eschews such an escape, recommending instead a frank will to power that contributes to the evolution of the *Übermensch*, but other naturalists are often not so forthright.

After having told us emphatically that we are "machines created by our genes" to help them replicate themselves and that "universal love and the welfare of the species as a whole are concepts that simply do not make evolutionary sense," Richard Dawkins turns around and declares that "we, alone on earth, can rebel against the tyranny of the selfish replicators."[34] Our genes can't just push us around, so to speak; we are free agents who can and should forge our own humane ends. These comments are sincere, but are they persuasive or even coherent? If, according to Dawkins, the replicator is "the prime mover of all life,"[35] what could rebellion look like? After having said that "the moral sentiments are used [by natural selection] with brutal flexibility, switched on and off in keeping with self-interest" and that "emotions are just evolution's executioners," Robert Wright informs us that "natural selection's indifference to the suffering of the weak is not something we need emulate."[36] He offers the common consolation that to call something "natural" is not to deem it either good or unchangeable,[37] even sounding rather Gnostic in associating evolution with a kind of malevolent Creator. "Just because natural selection created us," he writes, "doesn't mean we have to slavishly follow its peculiar agenda."[38] But then why say that "we're all puppets [to genetic control]" and that love's "very purpose . . . is to attract [a woman] to men who will be good for her progeny"?[39] Despite Wright's protests to the contrary, it often sounds like the gene's interest in self-replication determines what is true and good and beautiful, as well as what we may possibly accomplish. "The gene's-eye view implies that parents are . . . dishonestly manipulative. They want—or, at least, their genes 'want' them—to extract from the child more kin-directed altruism and sacrifice, and thus to instill in the child more love, than is in the child's genetic interest."[40] Teaching altruism equals parental dishonesty! Why not come clean and grant that the biological "is" in fact determines the moral "ought"?

It will be protested that Wright's words, like Dawkins's, leave us free, in theory, to reject the gene's point of view, to refuse to allow selfish genetic drives to be the measure of human veracity and virtue. But Wright, again like Dawkins, gives us only emotive effusion against natural selection's nastiness, even while telling us that the emotions are themselves vehicles of the genes. Theologians who embrace evolution must also explain how moral emotions like sympathy and compassion are not simply in peonage to natural selection—and I take up this challenge later—but for naturalists, emotional objections to natural selection can't be anything more than the gene's allowing its reproduction machine to "have a good cry," all the while winking knowingly at such futility.

Is understanding love in neo-Darwinian terms compatible with living it? Some of our best minds, to repeat, are hopelessly ambivalent. George C. Williams is admirably blunt in describing natural selection as an "evil" process giving rise to "agonistic behavior," but he too does not explain how it can be normatively required (or psychosocially possible) to rewrite nature's gruesome script.[41] The highly imaginative and literate Matt Ridley writes, "Montagues and Capulets, French and English, Whig and Tory, Airbus and Boeing, Pepsi and Coke, Serb and Muslim, Christian and Saracen—we are irredeemably tribal creatures. The neighbouring or rival group, however defined, is automatically an enemy."[42] Yet only two pages later he announces, "My aim is to convince you to try to step out of your human skin and look back at our species with all its foibles. Then we notice that our politics need not be the way it is, for we need not be tribal at all."[43] What? Did I miss something? The irredeemable and automatic is actually the redeemable and voluntary? "Nationalism, borders, in-groups and out-groups, warfare" are all "the consequences of tribal thinking, which itself is the consequence of our evolutionary heritage as coalition-building, troop-living apes,"[44] but if so, how do we escape a belligerent consequential*ism* in ethics? Perhaps the ultimate irony is the thoroughgoing utilitarian Peter Singer's denying the sanctity of human life, even at one point licensing early elective infanticide in the name of general utility, yet wishing to champion "a Darwinian left" in which social justice for the weak prevails.[45] No culture can survive such doublethink for long.

I am not saying that Darwin, Dawkins, Wright, Williams, Ridley, or Singer is himself actively immoral or is self-consciously recommending immorality to others. Again, Ridley is typical in asserting, "That natural selection is cruel says nothing about whether cruelty is moral."[46] I *am* saying, however, that a purely naturalistic theory must elaborate how it allows for morality; it must say *something* about why cruelty is *immoral*. I am not claiming to demonstrate an unavoidable slippery slope from Darwin to Hitler, to borrow the title of a 2004 book, but rather registering a serious challenge that is frequently taken far too lightly. Precisely why, to use Wright's word, is Social Darwinism a "misuse" to be avoided?[47] How, more specifically, can we reconcile the neglect of motive and the denial of purposeful design in nature, on the one hand, with the affirmation that we natural beings are capable of purposeful design in resisting our genes, on the other? If religious believers take refuge in a "God of the gaps," are not many naturalists taking refuge in a "conscience of the gaps"?

It is all too easy to flinch at the crucial moment and relegate science and ethics to Gould's "non-overlapping magisteria." If this divide is the fact of the matter, however, then why is evolutionary psychology supposed to be so revolutionary for morality and faith? If the "is" of evolutionary biology leaves logically untouched the "ought" of altruistic ethics, then why use titles like *The Origins of Virtue* and *Breaking the Spell*? If natural selection is the "origin" of virtue, then that origin isn't you, me, or God. And if a naturalistic account of religion "breaks a spell," a phrase loaded with normative implications, then facts do indeed bear on values. It is as though the canvas were able to protest or even dictate the artist's design, as though the *Mona Lisa* (the work of art, not the living model) were able to resist Leonardo's palate. In reality, however, the *Mona Lisa* simply *is* an expression of the master's genius, and when naturalists tell us that the person and society are an expression of the genome's genius, they are actually leaving us no room to maneuver. A painting has a certain physical quiddity, to be sure, and the specifics of the canvas and oils do set certain limits of size, shape, color, and texture, even as bodies and environments set limits on biological evolution. But the materials in both cases are essentially plastic and incapable of independent action on a naturalistic view.

The rub is that once human beings and their moral minds are judged, in effect, to be epiphenomenal to genes and their reproductive success, there is no higher value than such success—indeed, there are no purposeful personal agents anymore, only biological imperatives operating under the guise of ethical imperatives. With this, we have landed in the vetust and vexing question of how to square human freedom and responsibility with a naturalistic and material account of causal laws. I suggest below this squaring has never been done.

Freedom and Responsibility

Evolutionary psychologists have offered two main responses to the worries about freedom I have articulated. First, they have suggested that our genetic makeup, including the drive to seek reproductive advantage, leaves us free to pursue altruistic ends even as our hardwiring to learn a language does not determine which particular language we speak.[48] Basic dispositions are set by biology, but concrete cultural practices are a matter of both nature and nurture. The brain's chemistry does not explain (or explain away) William Shakespeare and his plays or Mother Teresa and her charity. I find this analogy instructive, but I am concerned that altruism is more like a grammar or syntax than a diction or semantics and that many naturalistic accounts of evolution imply that the grammar of altruism is humanly impossible, no matter what cultural wording we are schooled in. We are not wired for charity, according to many evolutionary psychologists.

Second, some evolutionists object that their analysis of human competition and cooperation is concerned with cultural, rather than biological, evolution. In this case, norms are somewhat analogous to genes, but there is room for the freedom and moral responsibility of persons. Here a genetic legacy is not necessarily the highest good, and no causal laws fully explain human attitudes and social behaviors. This raises the related question of the *scale* of evolution. What, if anything, is the basic unit of natural selection—the gene, the individual, the kin group, the wider community, the species, the clade, or even the entire cosmos—and how does the basic unit relate to higher levels of aggregated complexity, including complex ideas?[49] Darwin wrote briefly of "family" selection in *On the Origin of Species*, and he explicitly discusses group selection, "the welfare of the tribe," in *The Descent of Man*.[50] He generally thought that the unit of selection was the individual organism, however.[51] Some neo-Darwinians think the basic unit is the gene, in contrast, and still others think it is all of the above.[52] Perhaps the most sophisticated view is that cultural evolution is amenable to group selection but that biological evolution is driven by the genes.[53] On this account, self-sacrifice is possible for the sake of the common good, and such virtue might be selected for, culturally, even if this leads to individual reproductive loss or failure in genetic terms.

The sophisticated view represents a nuanced attempt at synthesis; nonetheless, there are three major difficulties with it: (1) It seems to put cultural evolution and biological evolution hopelessly at odds, with the group fostering intentional benevolence and the gene dictating instinctive selfishness. One wants to know how, if at all, conflicts between the cultural and the biological levels can be resolved. (2) Even if cultural evolution can select for intra-group sympathy, this has little to do with genuine agape: group egotism is still egotism, especially if the reason that individuals "cooperate," against their self-interest, with other human beings is social conformism or chauvinistic tribalism. (3) It is hard to see how *any* naturalistic vantage point can allow for individual agents freely maximizing values other than reproductive success and still remain naturalistic. It is difficult to explain, that is, how the personal freedom and intentionality assumed by cultural evolution could have evolved by way of random mutation and natural selection if traditional naturalism is true.[54] I note later that one might in theory appeal to exaptation, the functional shifting of a trait or behavior for a new purpose, to account for agape. But a reductive naturalist cannot provide a motive for why this shift would take place across time. Dawkins, for instance, is ambivalent on the point but typically rejects the possibility of a trait or behavior enduring if it does not redound to reproductive success at the gene level. These three difficulties make a naturalistically reductive account of agape highly implausible.

Even if a purposeful God did not design the universe, purposeful human agents must design their lives if they are to be moral (or immoral). The most striking form of moral design—call it "radical goodness"—is freely to assist unrelated others at cost to oneself and without expectation of return. The most striking form of immoral design—call it "radical evil"—is freely to injure related others with no benefit to oneself and with expectation of retaliation. (The former is true altruism, the latter true perversity.[55]) Some evolutionary thinkers have tried to explain how "moralistic aggression" might have evolved, noting that groups that were better able to "sanction deviants" who transgress social rules would prove better at reproducing themselves. "Social control makes groups adaptive," Christopher Boehm writes, adding that "a band that is disrupted by uncontrolled deviance will reproduce poorly compared to a band that cooperates smoothly."[56] Yet, as Boehm warns, this theory of how punitive justice can sustain community cohesion frequently focuses too exclusively on the restraint of evil and thereby neglects the production of goodness. More specifically, I would note, it can leave unaddressed how a forgiving mercy could appear in the midst of public retributivism, rather like dwelling on the *Pax Romana* to the exclusion of the *Pax Christi*.

And again, how do we reconcile causal biological explanations with purposeful design of *any* kind? Unless that can be done, cultural evolution seems in thrall to, not merely to supervene on, biological evolution—even as the person appears a mere tool of her genes. The thoroughgoing naturalist Michael Ruse, for one, has maintained that morality is "an invention of the genes rather than humans." Indeed, he concludes that "morality is a collective illusion foisted on us by our genes."[57]

Functional Shifts and Spandrels

There are three major alternative etiologies of agape/altruism: (1) it emerged as an evolutionary adaptation—that is, as a trait with selective advantages—and it is still to be explained in terms of its promoting (inclusive) genetic fitness; (2) it emerged as an evolutionary adaptation—for example, as storge, a capacity for selfless care of family—but it has undergone a functional shift that makes it more unconditional and more applicable to unrelated groups; and (3) it is a spandrel—an echo of the divine act of creation, aka the big bang—and as such, it shapes and limits rather than expresses natural selection.[58] To escape Ruse's conclusion that ethics is an illusion, I believe that we must reject (1) and in the process break with pan-adaptationism. We must recognize that not all morphological features and behavioral traits—including the need or ability to give or receive agapic love—can be accounted for by random mutation and natural selection alone. Furthermore, competition for reproductive advantage is not the only game in town. As Peter A. Corning remarks, "Competition and cooperation are not mutually exclusive explanations for human evolution; each played an important role in shaping our evolution."[59]

Alternative (1) explains away the traditional virtue of charity. I have maintained, quite generally, that naturalism in biology, coupled with certain game theoretic models, tends to a reductivism that is incompatible with Christian faith and morals. In effect, it de-radicalizes both the Old and the New Testaments by making God and cruciform goodness disappear. Christianity may be mistaken, of course, but its affirmation of a kenotic and creative God, together with creatures that are called to emulate the Creator with agapic love, is incompatible with any entirely naturalistic, anti-teleological account of evolution based on reproductive advantage alone. These observations do not settle the dispute, but I have tried to show that it is a real dispute. To borrow a phrase from William James, the debate over altruism "feels like a real fight" rather than "a game of private theatricals."

The "fight" in question—I'm aware of the irony of fighting over altruism—is between a naturalism that sees reproductive selfishness (whether of genes or ideas) as responsible for our being and doing and a supernaturalism that sees a divine agape (love for all beings) as our beginning and end. This is, *au fond*, a contest between genetic parochialism and religious universalism. "Religion teaches its adherents that they are a chosen race and their nearest rivals are benighted fools or even subhumans,"[60] Matt Ridley avers, and he has a lot of history to back him up. But this is surely not religion at its best—neither Judaism, Christianity, and Islam nor Buddhism and Hinduism. "Christianity, it is true, teaches love to all people, not just fellow Christians," Ridley concedes, but he is much more impressed by the fact that "the practice, rather than the preaching, of Christianity has been less inclusive."[61]

Then let the criterion be Peircean and pragmatic. If evolution is itself evolving, then the test of supernaturalism may well be a function of beings freely practicing charity and thereby transcending genetic self-interest. The triumph of a culture of charity is the best possible disproof of the tyranny of the selfish gene. Naturalistic evolution is often congratulated for revealing the biological proximity of humanity to the rest of the animal kingdom, this revelation then being credited with inclining us to be more sympathetic to the beasts and globally greener. But this is a non sequitur. If my concern for the whales, say, or over ecological disaster in the Gulf is sparked by that concern's conducing to my eventual reproductive advantage, then it is neither sympathetic nor global. It is, rather, prudential and local. If reproductive advantage is the sole sociobiological game, that is, and if my genotype (or, at most, my species' gene pool) is the unit of selection, then I can only use other individuals and clades and other lands and seas for their genetic utility.[62] There can be no point to preserving an endangered species, or the planet, for its own sake, or God's; one can only employ (if not exploit) nonhuman animals and nonlocal venues as these contribute to my own kind's prudential aims. Indeed, if group selection is ruled out in favor of the gene as the selective unit, then even non-related humans are rivals to be orchestrated for personal advantage rather than fellow creatures to be loved for themselves and their maker.

As Gould and Lewontin have argued, we are not limited, biologically or culturally, to what can be accounted for by functional adaptation; some attributes are structural spandrels. In architecture, a spandrel is the space between arches in the design of a building; in biology, a spandrel is an internal feature of an organism's basic form. The space between arches might subsequently be decorated, but it is not initially planned for its aesthetic worth. Similarly, a phenotypic or behavioral feature of an animal might come along with physical and/or biological constraints, the "laws of nature" and/or "nature's God," rather than selective advantage.[63] To call a trait like altruism a "spandrel" is to affirm the trait's reality but concede that it cannot be explained as arising because of adaptive value. I myself am inclined to construe the human potential for agape to be a function of being made in the image of God, a feature that is a limit on, rather than a consequence of, natural selection. If God is agapic love (1 John 4:8), then to bear the image of God is to have the need or ability to give or receive such love. As a spandrel, agape would be "a positive director and channeler of evolutionary change," to quote Gould's general description of such organizational features.[64]

Alternatively, one might judge altruism to be an "exaptation." If an adaptation is a character trait that arises directly for its current utility, an exaptation, in contrast, involves "the cooptation of a preexisting character for an altered current utility."[65] A spandrel, to repeat, exists for no adaptive reason but as part of an organism's internal engineering; an exaptation, on the other hand, is an adaptation functionally shifted from its original use. In the latter case, the biochemical and social-psychological raw materials for agape would have evolved over time and then been put to a different purpose by a self-conscious agent. Parental affection (storge), for instance, might well be exapted for more general employment by the will of human agents or the grace of the Holy Spirit. But, again, this is not to say that agape itself can be directly caused or explained by reproductive success. Reductionist contentions to the contrary are usually the result of an implausible drive to make morality "scientific" or "naturalized."

If agapism is persuasive, it has two main implications. First, to the extent that "lower" animals need agape, they too are made in God's image (they just don't know it). Second, the need or ability to give or receive agapic love cannot be an adaptive trait generated by random mutation and natural selection. It is, rather, either a functional shift or a nonadaptive spandrel that accompanies these evolutionary mechanisms or makes them possible. In the first case, agape becomes a moral action instead of being a material event; in the second case, it is a sensibility that makes moral action intelligible instead of being a delusion that makes it unintelligible. I know of no knockdown argument to settle this either-or, but establishing that it is one, that these are the only viable alternatives, is a central point of this paper. A "scientific" account of the world that eliminates all teleology from its causal explanations can make no sense of "actions" of any kind—for it, there are only mindless "atoms" and "events." For the believer, in contrast, the universe—including us as moral agents—cannot be adequately explained without reference to purposeful mind.[66] In fact, evolution itself is an evolving gift of a Divine Mind's sacrificial love. (For evolution to be, God had to cease to be all-in-all.) To "Why love?," the theologian can only reply, "Because this is God's will for creatures made in His image, an image designed to converge on sympathy." Human virtue and vice require self-aware motives, but such "inwardness" is not the highest good. That good is God's steadfast holiness, which beckons us to faith and growth at the beginning, middle, and end of the evolutionary process. The beginning is the ordered creation of the world, the middle the Incarnation of Christ, the end the return of time and space to God—like children who have been born, matured, declined, and died.[67]

A Major Objection Rebutted and Put in Context

A major objection might be leveled against my claim that pan-selectionism reduces altruism to prudence. It might be argued that we should distinguish between the causal etiology or effect of a behavior and its conscious motivation. A selfless action done out of love of neighbor and not out of prudential self-interest might nonetheless be of survival value for one's genes. Just because the genes that support altruistic motives were selected for because they contributed to the genes' own survival, it does not follow that the motives themselves are prudential or are aimed at survival. A neo-Darwinian could say that our ability to do mathematics, for instance, is a result of natural selection, but it does not follow that when I reason that the square root of thirty-six is six, the motive I have for saying it is six is prudential. Similarly, many researchers have maintained that giving to others in an altruistic way is positively correlated with happiness. In turn, if being happy has survival value, then the genes for altruistic motives could be selected for without making the motives themselves non-altruistic.[68]

There are several problems with this objection. First, it assumes the very thing that most reductive neo-Darwinians rule out: that conscious agents, that is, minds, have causal powers that transcend mere atoms and events. For such neo-Darwinians, persons and their minds are epiphenomenal to genes and their blind interactions, thus motives for a behavior are inseparable from the biological genesis of that behavior. Genes have no motives, and we are the product of our genes. We may *think* we are being altruistic and that our intentions to help others disinterestedly are causally efficacious, but again to quote Michael Ruse, this is itself "a collective illusion foisted on us by our genes."[69] As Richard Joyce contends, following J. L. Mackie, on the pan-selectionist view, ethics is an "error theory": to understand moral motivation is incompatible with practicing it.[70] All behavior is actually causally governed by its survival value, such that, to repeat, motive is either inseparable from or reducible to reproductive success. To put it another way, Dawkins's "selfish gene" will neither produce nor tolerate a motive that is genuinely prejudicial to reproductive success, since any such altruism must be selected against over time. In spite of our conscious thoughts, this take on modern science allows only one form of causation and so makes us puppets to our genes in much the same way that ancient theology often made us puppets to God's grace.

Second, likening being motivated by altruism to affirming a mathematical conclusion fails to see that the challenge of altruism is that it is self-sacrificial in genetic terms. I do not injure my reproductive fitness by saying that the square root of thirty-six is six, but I do damage it by dying for someone unrelated to me. The motive for my claiming that six is the square root of thirty-six may be that it is the correct mathematical answer, but this leaves intact the neo-Darwinian prime directive—"Do Nothing Altruistic" (DNA)—and so is uncontroversial. One can see how the ability to do math might well have had survival value, and any given mathematical conclusion (at least a correct one) is not at odds with that value. Agape's motivation as genuine surrender of kin selection is a different story, however. Agape equals *miscounting*, on this scenario—how can *that* be advantageous? Even assuming that altruistic behavior makes one happy, which is debatable—was Jesus happy on the Cross?— and that being happy contributes to reproductive success, one must still ask what would move one to be altruistic. If the motive is eudaimonistic, that is, aimed at my own flourishing as the sine qua non, then it ceases to be truly altruistic; but if the motive is really other-regarding, it becomes at best opaque in neo-Darwinian terms. If the gene is the sole unit of selection, then altruism cannot be adaptive; if group selection is allowed, then, as I have argued previously, at most tribalism might be cast up.

All that said, let me put this discussion in a wider context. Not all evolutionary theorists embrace the idea that biological evolution undermines traditional ethics (or religion). Indeed, as I survey the field, there are five major camps regarding nature, ethics (including moral motivation), and the way they interrelate:

1. Nature is red in tooth and claw, full of remorseless competition for survival, and without genuine altruism; thus, we might want to turn *from* it for moral guidance, but we *cannot* so turn because human freedom and willpower are *illusions*. Freedom is an illusion *because* random mutation and natural selection are the only engines of evolution but are blind and mindless. Borrowing a phrase from Jean Paul Sartre, call this "No Exit Absurdism"; exemplars include J. L. Mackie, Michael Ruse, Richard Joyce, and Richard Dawkins at times.

2. Nature is red in tooth and claw, full of remorseless competition for survival, and without genuine altruism; thus, we should turn *from* it for moral guidance, and we *can* so turn because of the *reality* of human freedom or willpower. Freedom is real *in spite of* random mutation and natural selection being the only engines of evolution, because blind matter *can* cast up purposeful mind. Borrowing a phrase from Woody Allen, call this "Being at Two with Nature"; exemplars include Thomas Henry Huxley, Karl Marx, and Richard Dawkins at other times.

3. Nature is red in tooth and claw, full of remorseless competition for survival and without genuine altruism; thus, we should turn *to* it for moral guidance, and we *can* so turn because of the *reality* of human freedom or willpower. Again, freedom is real in spite of pan-selectionism; we should just celebrate dominance and predation, rather than run from them. Borrowing a phrase from Richard Hofstadter, I call this "Social Darwinism"; exemplars include Herbert Spencer, Friedrich Nietzsche, Adolf Hitler, and Ernest Hemingway.[71]

4. Nature is *not simply* red in tooth and claw, containing *both* competition *and* cooperation, *even forms of genuine altruism*; thus, we should turn *to* it for moral guidance,

and we *can* so turn because of the *reality* of human freedom or willpower. For the first time, members of this camp break with the thesis that the only engines of evolution are random mutation and natural selection. Human freedom and willpower are *real*, but they *cannot* be explained on the basis of pan-selectionism alone. Borrowing a phrase from Stuart Kauffman, call this "Being at Home in the Universe"; exemplars include Prince Kropotkin, Stephen Jay Gould, Stuart Kauffman, Dian Fossey, Frans de Waal, and Jane Goodall at times.

5. Nature is *not simply* red in tooth and claw, containing *both* competition *and* cooperation, *even forms of genuine altruism*; thus, we should be *ambivalent* about nature and *turn finally to the supernatural* for moral guidance, and we *can* so turn because of human freedom *and divine grace*. Once more, freedom and willpower are *real*, but not only can they not be accounted for by pan-selectionism, *no purely naturalistic explanation is feasible.* Borrowing a classical phrase, call this "Teleological Theism"; exemplars include Søren Kierkegaard, Charles Sanders Peirce, Vladimir Solovyov, Simon Conway Morris, and Jane Goodall at other times.[72]

Three additional points are crucial. First, *I am identifying a key variety of reductive neo-Darwinism with pan-selectionism*, with the claim that the *only* mechanisms at work in biological evolution are random mutation and natural selection. To reiterate, one version of this view, position 1 in the previous list, finds it impossible to explain the emergence of human freedom as a genuine source of causation. All that exists are atoms and events. A second version, position 2 in the list, affirms freedom but in a way that seems paradoxical. Even as Thomas Aquinas held that God is the sufficient reason for everything that happens but that human agency and responsibility are real, so subscribers to the "At Two with Nature" school hold that random mutation and natural selection can generate voluntary choices and meaningful motives. Both visions claim, in effect, that a free act can be necessitated—in Aquinas's case, by God (*ST* I.22–23); in evolution's case, by genes. In contrast, I am convinced by the work of Roger Penrose and Thomas Nagel that moral motives cannot be generated by buffeted matter alone.[73] The third version of neo-Darwinism, position 3, is out of fashion today for its normative stand, but it rests on the same descriptive premises as position 2.

In fact, we do not know how material contingency or natural necessity could cast up life, much less intelligent agency. Neither random mutation nor natural selection can be appealed to in order to explain the origin of specified "animate" information in self-replicating cells, for instance. Random mutation, by definition, assumes genetic information that is mutable—whether in RNA, DNA, or proteins—and natural selection does not function in an abiotic or prebiotic context. Until there is a self-replicating cell, there is nothing to select for, there is no variable genetic information that might translate into a reproductive advantage (aka differential fitness). In short, both random mutation and natural selection *presuppose* specified information; they do not create it. Thus, we must look elsewhere for an explanation of *the origin of life.*[74]

Second, concerning *the evolution of life to include conscious agents*, some theorists seek to augment random mutation and natural selection as the engines of descent with variation but to remain within a materialistic and chance universe. They point to spandrels and the laws of physics, self-organizing or autocatalytic sets, the multiverse, and so on. The question of the origin of functionally specified information, not mere Shannon information, in biology is analogous to the question of the origin of focused altruism, not mere competitive reciprocity, in ethics. In ethics, the main issue is how genuine self-sacrifice originates and whether random mutation and natural selection can operate to bring about such a behavioral trait independent of or prior to a conscious choice by a rational agent. My thesis has been that neither random mutation nor natural selection can be appealed to in order to explain the origin of focused "moral" other regard.

Consider again natural selection. If the unit of selection is thought to be the gene or the individual, it is especially hard to imagine how self-sacrifice, insofar as it entails reproductive disadvantage or even failure (i.e., death), could be advantageous. Even if the unit of selection is a group or a population, however, the most that natural selection might generate is a tribalism in which the individual is willing to go under for a limited community. This is not the universal charity extolled by Judaism and Christianity. As noted previously, for random mutation, the ethical equivalent is functional shift in which a behavior that evolved so as to serve one purpose is employed for a new and different purpose. For instance, the capacity for empathy that helped bond parents and offspring and thus enhanced survivability of familial genes might be extended in sympathy to non–family members. Again, the problem is that this simply displaces the issue to "Why the shift, why love the unrelated neighbor at the expense of one's own genetic fitness?"

Third, noting that random mutation and natural selection cannot account for specified information or genuine altruism leaves open what *does* explain them. (I am assuming that both information and altruism are real, though some—for example, Michael Ruse—would dispute the latter.) Again as noted, most biologists and philosophers of science continue to seek a materialist or naturalistic explanation, with some defending self-organization theories (e.g., Stuart Kauffman), some citing spandrels and the laws of physics (Stephen Jay Gould and Richard Lewontin), and still others postulating a multiverse in which quantum mechanics casts up every possible object, action, and event (e.g., Stephen Hawking, Leonard Mlodinow, and Max Tegmark). All of these alternatives I am including in position 4 in the previous list. In contrast, some biologists (e.g., Dean Kenyon, Michael Denton, Michael Behe, and Jonathan Wells), some philosophers of science (William Dembski and Stephen Meyer), and many if not most theologians (e.g., Thomas Aquinas, Arthur Peacocke, and Alvin Plantinga) propose some form of intelligent design (ID) as the best explanation. This school, position 5, maintains that ID is necessary, or at least plausible, to account for both the origin and the evolution of creaturely life. This is not a crude importation of myth into science or a mere "God of the gaps," for the contention is that ID is pressed on us by empirical inquiry and scientific rationality themselves. Carefully formulated, ID is itself a scientific hypothesis designed to address the evidence of the orderliness of reality.[75] Of course, if one holds that science, *by definition*, is materialistic and deterministic, ruling out appeals to consciousness and judging agency unreal, then any form of ID will be disqualified ab initio. But then, as Polanyi, Dembski, Meyer, Kauffman, Rosenblum, Kuttner, Penrose, Nagel, and many others effectively point out, both quantum mechanics and social science must be deemed illusions, for these affirm reality as nondeterministic and minds as causal.

Given my own reading, reflection, and experience, I side here with the broad position 5, though I would emphasize that the failure of naturalism does not itself prove supernaturalism. Equally importantly, I seek to augment option 5 by speculating on what is needed to account for both the origin and the evolution of creaturely ethics. The divine mind or something very like it is a defensible inference, I believe, to explain both the origin of human consciousness and the evolution of charity as the highest virtue. Position 3, Social Darwinism, departs from agape, of course, not because voluntary agape is impossible but because it is judged ignoble or even immoral. To the extent that positions 4 and 5 go beyond pan-selectionism, they depart from reductive neo-Darwinism as I define it. The key to position 5 is that it sees nature itself as created and so looks to the source and end of nature (including biological evolution) for moral guidance. That source and end theists call "God." Nature and its laws are not constant—see inflation and the big bang—and evolution itself is evolving, so to avoid mistaking means for ends, we must look beyond the sensible universe for the point of existence.

Conclusion

The mistake of overweening naturalists takes one of two forms: to think that one of the means of evolution (natural selection) is the sole end or to think that there is no end or purpose at all, only accident or necessity. An unavoidable question for both scientist and theologian is whether biological evolution is a self-sufficient and closed material system or, being finite and temporal, requires a first cause and can culminate in a final end. If the system is self-sufficient and closed, governed only by blind physical and chemical processes, how does it first generate the specified information necessary for self-replicating life? How, once life has emerged, are intelligence and altruism cast up out of random mutation and natural selection alone? Once again the teleological evolutionist judges, on scientific grounds, that a closed naturalistic system could not produce life or intelligence and altruism as we know them. Or, more cautiously, she judges that all purely materialistic attempts to explain the origin of life and morality have failed. Given that failure, it is not unreasonable to assume that there must have been purpose or direction built into the scheme and its laws to begin with. The Christian theologian elaborates this point by identifying the first cause and final end of biological evolution with the God who is agapic love.

Robust belief in a loving God may be neither scientifically provable nor scientifically disprovable. To conclude that matter and motion alone cannot generate life as we know it is not, as such, to affirm biblical theism and the *imago Dei*. But such a conclusion removes a major stumbling block to faith, and it represents a major challenge to too easy naturalisms. Christian agapists, in any case, believe that human altruism is an echo of God's original creative act, still audible in creation and still assisted by a supernatural grace. (Compare the cosmic background radiation still detectable from the big bang.) Even as a matter of faith, however, religious belief and ethical conviction must be compatible with true science. Faith and morals may be *above* reason, but they cannot be *against* reason and be intelligible, much less admirable. Thus, we must continue to contemplate both Darwin's finches and Harper Lee's Finch. After all, they have a common "ancestor" in God's agape. But such contemplation can and should be informed by a Christlike love that comprehends and transforms the reciprocity games of nature. Such games are a means to the end of moral community, to the eliciting of self-aware other regard,[76] not the end itself. Graciousness, in the form of agape, undergirds and checks natural selection rather than being its tool.

"Look at the birds of the air; they neither sow nor reap nor gather into barns, and yet our heavenly Father feeds them" (Matt. 6:26). It is indeed a sin to kill a mockingbird . . . but also the Finch who would love it.

Epigraph

William James, "Is Life Worth Living?," in *The Will to Believe and Other Essays in Popular Philosophy* (New York: Dover Publications, 1956), 61. As I make clear, where James here says "adapted," I would say "created."

Notes

An earlier version of this essay was delivered at a conference on "The Pursuit of Happiness," sponsored by the Center for the Study of Law and Religion at Emory. The project was supported by a grant from the John Templeton Foundation. I am grateful to both of these organizations for their generous assistance as well as to the colleagues who commented on my work, especially my respondents, Julia Annas and Michael Broyde.

1. Charles Darwin, *On the Origin of Species* (1859; Cambridge, MA: Harvard University Press, 1964), 89.

2. Some experts may insist that the beauty of a bird's song falls under sexual selection rather than natural selection, but the former is actually a subset of the latter.

3. Harper Lee, *To Kill a Mockingbird* (New York: HarperPerennial, 1960), 103.

4. The terms derive from *arete* (virtue or excellence) and *deon* (duty), respectively.

5. Darwin, *The Voyage of the Beagle* (1839; Cambridge, MA: Harvard Classics, 1909), 29; Darwin, *On the Origin of Species*, 169. See also Charles Darwin, *The Descent of Man, and Selection in Relation to Sex* (1871; London: Penguin Books, 2004), 134.

6. Stuart Kauffman has been arguing a similar point for years; see his *Reinventing the Sacred: A New View of Science, Reason and Religion* (New York: Basic Books, 2008).

7. See the classic film *My Man Godfrey*, with William Powell and Carole Lombard.

8. *Oxford English Dictionary*, compact ed., s.v. "altruism."

9. Timothy P. Jackson, "The Christian Love Ethic and Evolutionary 'Cooperation': The Lessons and Limits of Eudaimonism and Game Theory," in *Evolution, Games, and God*, ed. Martin Nowak and Sarah Coakley (Cambridge, MA: Harvard University Press, 2013), 312.

10. According to Aquinas, "Man is said to be the image of God by reason of his intellectual nature," and properly speaking, "this image of God is not found even in the rational creature except in the mind." See *Summa Theologica*, trans. Fathers of the English Dominican Province (Westminster, MD: Christian Classics, 1981), I.93.4, 6.

11. Timothy P. Jackson, *The Priority of Love* (Princeton, NJ: Princeton University Press, 2003), 10.

12. Stephen Jay Gould, *Wonderful Life: The Burgess Shale and the Nature of History* (New York: Norton, 1989), 48.

13. See Timothy P. Jackson, ed., *The Morality of Adoption: Social-Psychological, Theological, and Legal Perspectives* (Grand Rapids, MI: Eerdmans, 2005), esp. Browning's "Adoption and the Moral Significance of Kin Altruism."

14. Stephen Jay Gould, *Rocks of Ages: Science and Religion in the Fullness of Life* (New York: Ballantine Books, 1999), 54–60.

15. Ibid., 9–10; see also Stephen Jay Gould, *The Hedgehog, the Fox, and the Magister's Pox* (New York: Harmony Books, 2003), 87.

16. See William A. Dembski, "What Every Theologian Should Know about Creation, Evolution, and Design," *Princeton Theological Review*, April 1, 1996, 15–21.

17. See, for instance, Kenneth R. Miller, "The Flaw in the Mousetrap: Intelligent Design Fails the Biochemistry Test," in "Intelligent Design?," special issue, *Natural History*, April 2002, 5.

18. Monod, quoted in Horace Freeland Judson's *The Eighth Day of Creation* (New York: Simon & Schuster, 1979), 217.

19. Darwin explicitly rejected Gray's argument at the end of his 1868 work, *Variation of Animals and Plants under Domestication*. Like Gray, Paul Davies has concluded that "we are truly meant to be here." Davies, *The Mind of God: The Scientific Basis for a Rational World* (New York: Simon & Schuster, 1992), 232.

20. John Hedley Brooke, "Darwin and Victorian Christianity," in *The Cambridge Companion to Darwin*, ed. Jonathan Hodge and Gregory Radick (Cambridge: Cambridge University Press, 2003), 206.

21. Gould, *Wonderful Life*, 24. Gould wants to articulate a third alternative beyond determinism and randomness, what he calls "contingency" (pp. 50–52), but it is hard to see how this differs from arbitrariness. Evolution is not senseless, but it is so unpredictable and without direction as to be utterly non-teleological. Evolution's path is like that of a "drunkard's walk" staggering down the street; see Stephen Jay Gould, *The Structure of Evolutionary Theory* (Cambridge, MA: Belknap Press of Harvard University Press, 2002), 900–901.

22. In conversation.

23. Gould, *Wonderful Life*, 54.

24. Conway Morris, *Life's Solution: Inevitable Humans in a Lonely Universe* (Cambridge: Cambridge University Press, 2003), 328.

25. Ibid., 329.

26. Conway Morris speaks explicitly of "trends" and "progress" in evolution (ibid., 301). Indeed, he writes, "This book aims, if nothing else, to refute the notion of the 'dominance of contingency'" (ibid., 297).

27. I owe this observation to Martin Nowak, in conversation.

28. See Timothy P. Jackson, "To Bedlam and Part Way Back: John Rawls and Christian Justice," in *Faith and Philosophy* 8, no. 4 (October 1991): 423–47; and Timothy P. Jackson, "The Return of the Prodigal? Liberal Theory and Religious Pluralism," in *Religion and Contemporary Liberalism*, ed. Paul Weithman (Notre Dame, IN: University of Notre Dame Press, 1997).

29. Richard Dawkins, *The Selfish Gene* (Oxford: Oxford University Press, 1989), 19. Genes do not typically act alone or determine major traits in isolation; I use the singular term "gene," nevertheless, for convenience sake and because Dawkins has popularized the phrase "the selfish gene."

30. I borrow this example from Richard Rorty, "Mind-Body Identity, Privacy, and Categories," *Review of Metaphysics* 19, no. 1 (September 1965): 24–54.

31. Daniel C. Dennett, *Darwin's Dangerous Idea: Evolution and the Meaning of Life* (New York: Simon & Schuster, 1995); and Daniel C. Dennett, *Breaking the Spell: Religion as a Natural Phenomenon* (New York: Viking, 2006).

32. See, for example, Alasdair MacIntyre, *After Virtue: A Study in Moral Theory* (Notre Dame, IN: University of Notre Dame Press, 1984).

33. Darwin, *On the Origin of Species*, 202–3.

34. Dawkins, *Selfish Gene*, 2, 201.

35. Ibid., 264.

36. Robert Wright, *The Moral Animal: Why We Are the Way We Are* (New York: Vintage Books, 1994), 13, 88, 102.

37. Ibid., 31.

38. Ibid., 37.

39. Ibid., 37, 94.

40. Ibid., 168.

41. George C. Williams, *Adaptation and Natural Selection: A Critique of Some Current Evolutionary Thought* (Princeton, NJ: Princeton University Press, 1966), 193–94. In *Genes in Conflict: The Biology of Selfish Genetic Elements* (Cambridge, MA: Belknap Press of Harvard University Presss, 2006), coauthored with Austin Burt, Robert Trivers locates a fundamental antagonism in all life at the molecular level.

42. Matt Ridley, *The Origins of Virtue: Human Instincts and the Evolution of Cooperation* (New York: Penguin Books, 1996), 166.

43. Ibid., 168.

44. Ibid., 168–69.

45. Peter Singer, *A Darwinian Left: Politics, Evolution, and Cooperation* (New Haven, CT: Yale University Press, 1999).

46. Ridley, *Origins of Virtue*, 155.

47. Wright, *Moral Animal*, 7.

48. Martin Nowak has made this case, in conversation.

49. See F. A. C. C. Chalub, F. C. Santos, and J. M. Pacheco, "The Evolution of Norms," *Journal of Theoretical Biology* 241, no. 2 (2006): 233–40.

50. Darwin, *On the Origin of Species*, 237; and *Descent of Man*, 143.

51. In *On the Origin of Species*, p. 84, for example, Darwin declares that "natural selection can act only through and for the good of each being."

52. Christopher Boehm, Elliott Sober, and David Sloan Wilson are among the growing number of evolutionary biologists who are open to group selection as at least a partial explanation of altruistic behavior. See Boehm, "Explaining the Prosocial Side of Moral Communities," in *Evolution and Ethics: Human Morality in Biological and Religious Perspective*, ed. Philip Clayton and Jeffrey Schloss (Grand Rapids, MI: Eerdmans, 2004); and Sober and Wilson, *Unto Others: The Evolution and Psychology of Unselfish Behavior* (Cambridge,

MA: Harvard University Press, 1998). Richard Dawkins, Robert Wright, and Matt Ridley are among a long-lived majority in rejecting it. Ridley maintains, for instance, that "biologists have thoroughly undermined the whole logic of group selection." See Ridley, *Origins of Virtue*, 175.

53. Cf. Peter J. Richerson and Robert Boyd, "Darwinian Evolutionary Ethics," in Clayton and Schloss, *Evolution and Ethics*. Boehm affirms both "genetic group selection" and "cultural group selection" ("Explaining the Prosocial Side," 95), whereas Richerson and Boyd evidently see group selection as limited to the cultural variety.

54. I say "traditional naturalism," meaning any view that would reduce reality to matter in motion according to deterministic laws. Stuart Kauffman refers to himself as a "naturalist," but his is a "new view of science, reason and religion" that is non-reductive. He gives up, that is, on Newtonian materialism and mechanism, seeing both the biosphere and the econosphere as indeterminate but not random processes. Responsible free will is actual in human beings and not to be explained away "naturalistically," as I would put it. See Kauffman, "Answering Descartes: Beyond Turing," in *The Once and Future Turing: Computing the World*, ed. S. Barry Cooper and Andrew Hodges (Cambridge: Cambridge University Press, 2012).

55. On "spite" in nature, see Kevin R. Foster, Tom Wenseleers, and Francis L. W. Ratnieks, "Spite: Hamilton's Unproven Theory," *Annales Zoologici Fennici* 38 (2001): 229–38. Spiteful action—as, for instance, in green-beard queen killing in the fire ant—is here given a neo-Darwinian explanation as contributing to the inclusive, rather than direct, fitness of an individual. Even though it does not help the individual reproduce, that is, have more progeny, spite makes genetic sense because "it reduces the frequency of competing alleles in the gene pool" (p. 229) and thus benefits already existing kin.

56. Boehm, "Explaining the Prosocial Side," 84–86.

57. Ruse, *Taking Darwin Seriously* (Oxford: Blackwell, 1986), 253.

58. See Stephen Jay Gould and Richard C. Lewontin, "The Spandrels of San Marco and the Panglossian Paradigm: A Critique of the Adaptationist Programme," *Proceedings of the Royal Society of London*, Series B, vol. 205, no. 1161 (1979): 581–98.

59. Peter A. Corning, *Holistic Darwinism: Synergy, Cybernetics, and the Bioeconomics of Evolution* (Chicago: University of Chicago Press, 2005), 42. Corning is no theist, but he goes on to note, "Holistic Darwinism de-emphasizes (without denying) the role of genetic mutations, recombinations, transpositions, etc. as sources of creativity in evolution and emphasizes purposeful innovations which may occur at the behavioral, cognitive, even social levels (inclusive of symbiogenesis)" (p. 44).

60. Ridley, *Origins of Virtue*, 191.

61. Ibid., 192.

62. To say that reproductive advantage is the sole sociobiological game is to say that genetic success determines all human behavior, at least indirectly. For example, in *The Selfish Gene*, Dawkins resolves "to treat the individual as a selfish machine, programmed to do whatever is best for its genes as a whole" (p. 66).

63. Gould, *Structure of Evolutionary Theory*, 43–49. Stuart Kauffman makes a related point: "Darwin's answer to the sources of the order we see around us is overwhelmingly an appeal to a single singular force: natural selection. It is this single-force view which I believe to be inadequate, for it fails to notice, fails to stress, fails to incorporate the possibility that simple and complex systems exhibit order spontaneously." See Kaufmann, *The Origins of Order: Self-Organization and Selection in Evolution* (Oxford: Oxford University Press, 1993), xiii.

64. Gould, *Structure of Evolutionary Theory*, 47. I focus here on spandrels at the organismal level, but in light of population genetics, there is no theoretical reason that equivalent features could not also apply to groups.

65. Ibid., 671.

66. Purposeful mind, in turn, seems to require genuine contingency—even causal indeterminacy—at least at the microcosmic level. See, for instance, the discussion of quantum mechanics and free will in Bruce Rosenblum and Fred Kuttner, *Quantum Enigma: Physics Encounters Consciousness* (Oxford: Oxford University Press, 2006).

67. Cf. Jozef Zycinski's description of God as a "Divine Attractor" in *God and Evolution: Fundamental Questions of Christian Evolutionism* (Washington, DC: Catholic University of America Press, 2006), 6–7.

68. I owe this basic formulation of the objection to an anonymous colleague.

69. Ruse, *Taking Darwin Seriously*, 253.

70. Richard Joyce, *The Evolution of Morality* (Cambridge, MA: MIT Press, 2006), 222–23.

71. In places, Nietzsche denies free will in favor of eternal recurrence and *amor fati*—see, for example, "Thus Spoke Zarathustra" and "The Antichrist"—but elsewhere, he equates "freedom" with the fact "that one has the will to assume responsibility for oneself." See "Twilight of the Idols," in *The Portable Nietzsche*, ed. and trans. Walter Kaufmann (New York: Penguin Books, 1976), 38, 542.

72. If pressed, I would place Darwin himself primarily in position 2, but sometimes 1 or 3 seems more appropriate. His praise of the queen bee, discussed previously, smacks of position 3.

73. See Roger Penrose, *The Emperor's New Mind* (Oxford: Oxford University Press, 1999); and Thomas Nagel, *Mind and Cosmos: Why the Materialist Neo-Darwinian Conception of Nature Is Almost Certainly False* (Oxford: Oxford University Press, 2012).

74. See Stephen Meyer, *Signature in the Cell: DNA and the Evidence for Intelligent Design* (New York: HarperCollins, 2009), including his discussion of "the RNA world" in chapter 14. Michael Polanyi notoriously wrote in 1958, "The rise of man can be accounted for only by other principles than those known today to physics and chemistry." See Polanyi, *Personal Knowledge: Towards a Post-Critical Philosophy*, corrected ed. (London: Routledge & Kegan Paul, 1962), 412. Meyer summarizes the relevant literature over fifty years later and arrives at the same basic conclusion (see *Signature in the Cell*, 332–33).

75. As William Dembski and Stephen Meyer argue at length; see Dembski, *The Design Inference: Eliminating Chance through Small Probabilities* (Cambridge: Cambridge University Press, 1998); and Meyer, *Signature in the Cell* and *Darwin's Doubt: The Explosive Origin of Animal Life and the Case for Intelligent Design* (New York: HarperCollins, 2013).

76. On other-regard, see Gene Outka's classic work *Agape: An Ethical Analysis* (New Haven, CT: Yale University Press, 1972). I am delighted to dedicate my essay to Professor Outka.

Part III

SOCIETY

14

Love, Justice, and Law

The Strange Case of *Watts v. Watts*

M. CATHLEEN KAVENY

WE ALL KNOW the parable of the Good Samaritan.[1] A man was beaten by robbers and left for dead on his way to Jericho. Two passers-by, a priest and a Levite, crossed to the other side of the road rather than help him. But a Samaritan man who saw him was moved to pity. After bandaging the injured man's wounds, the Samaritan contributed his own funds to pay an innkeeper to nurse the man back to health.

As Robert Wuthnow has shown, despite its social and cultural familiarity, many Americans are fuzzy not only about the details of the parable, but also about its framing narrative.[2] Rereading that narrative again in the Gospel of Luke, it reminded me of the contest of wits and wills between teachers and students familiar to anyone who has spent time in law school. The parable, we are told, is elicited by the question of a *lawyer*, who "stood up to test Jesus." He strikes me as young, earnest, and ambitious—someone whom those of us who teach first-year law students might call a "gunner."

"Teacher," he says, "what must I do to inherit eternal life?" Jesus, evidently a natural expert in the Socratic method, immediately throws the question back to the lawyer. "He said to him, 'What is written in the law? What do you read there?'" The lawyer answers, "You shall love the Lord your God with all your heart, and with all your soul, and with all your strength, and with all your mind; and your neighbor as yourself." After acknowledging the answer to be correct, Jesus tries to exit the conversation and move on: he responds, "You have given the right answer; do this, and you will live." But the lawyer is not ready to let the matter go. "Wanting to justify himself," we are told, and evidently wanting to impress Jesus, he asks a follow-up question: "And who is my neighbor?" It is in response to that second question that Jesus gives us the parable of the Good Samaritan.

Three observations come to mind. First, Jesus reframes the question in responding to it: After finishing the parable, Jesus asks the lawyer which of the three passers-by "was a neighbor to the man who fell into the hands of the robbers." As indicated by his acceptance of the lawyer's response, "the one who showed him mercy," the question Jesus actually addressed in the parable is "What does being a neighbor require of us?"

A version of this essay, which was originally commissioned for this book, also appears in Cathleen Kaveny's *Ethics at the Edges of Law: Christian Moralists and American Legal Thought* (New York: Oxford University Press, 2017). Reprinted by permission.

Second, the lawyer's actual question—"Who is my neighbor?"—is never directly answered by Jesus. Nor, for that matter, are more advanced conundrums flowing from that question, such as "What should I do if there is a conflict between myself and a neighbor?" or "How do I handle a dispute between two or more neighbors?"

Third, it is difficult to avoid the suspicion that Jesus—the consummate law teacher or rabbi—saved these harder questions for the test—the life decisions made by those who claim to be his followers. These questions become even more difficult if they are asked not only with reference to individual selves and neighbors, but also with reference to the communities that shape and are shaped by selves and neighbors. These communities, of course, are also shaped by law, which is one of the most important social tools for regulating relations between self and neighbors. Thus the concept of neighbor love is not irrelevant to law. Nor, for that matter, is the idea of conflict among neighbors. It is through our legal system that many of the most serious disputes between and among our neighbors, and between and among our neighbors and ourselves, are articulated, addressed, and resolved.

In my view, therefore, the potential for interdisciplinary work between law and religious ethics is enormous, particularly on matters pertaining to the relationship of love and justice. For example, the extensive normative reflections of religious ethics on the overarching nature and purpose of human society can provide vantage points from which to critique the quotidian decisions of legislatures and courts. Conversely, the manner in which the legal system settles specific cases offers rich material with which to test and to hone more abstract theological and philosophical reflections about personal and social obligations. The fields of law and religious ethics are mutually illuminating in a number of ways. In this essay I would like to further the cause of interdisciplinary work on neighbor love and justice by bringing two seemingly very different perspectives into conversation: that of the distinguished Protestant ethicist Gene Outka and that of the contemporary American common law tradition, as crystallized in the strange Wisconsin case of *Watts v. Watts*.[3]

No contemporary religious ethicist has thought more deeply about Christian love than has Gene Outka, first in his book, *Agape*,[4] and more recently in his extended essay, "Universal Love and Impartiality."[5] In this essay, which is really a small book, Outka makes a theocentric case for love of neighbor: he argues that "Love for God—as the most basic and comprehensive human love of all—includes fidelity to God in loving whom God loves."[6] In addition, he emphasizes the correspondence between the scope of divine love and the range of our own duty to love: "[A]ll people are created, sustained, and redeemed by God. Thus our love should correspond as far as possible to this universal scope."[7] He then goes on to analyze the extent to which the Christian call to universal love accurately can be understood as a call to impartiality. Outka devotes the bulk of his attention to examining whether universal love can be construed as impartiality between our regard for ourselves, on the one hand, and our regard for our neighbor, on the other. Yet he also addresses the question of what it would mean for universal love to be impartial vis-à-vis the conflicting claims of two or more neighbors.

In my view, the common law would be a fruitful conversation partner for Outka because it employs many of the same presuppositions in order to grapple with some of the same issues. For example, a Christian ethicist can find in the common law many echoes of key Christian commitments with respect to moral anthropology, such as the fundamental equality of all human beings. Moreover, the common law is regularly forced to grapple with the question of what protecting the equal dignity of human beings means in concrete and difficult circumstances. One reason these circumstances are difficult, of course, has to do with what Christian ethicists call sin. The realm of contracts, for instance, is the realm of promise-making. People do not always keep their promises. They betray and disappoint one another. In these cases, the legal system frequently has the responsibility to pick up the pieces—and to decide who gets which piece. Contract law forces us not only to deal with conflicts between two or more neighbors but also to grapple with the fact that many conflicts occur between neighbors who cannot each be assigned a halo or a pitchfork, but who are all a mixture of good and bad.

Finally, while Outka does not explicitly address the broader relationship between love and justice, the issue permeates his essay "Universal Love and Impartiality." That relationship, of course, has received a great deal of attention from Christian ethicists on other occasions, including Outka himself. The precise way in which an ethicist relates love and justice depends, of course, on his or her definition of the terms. For example, an ethicist who endorses Anders Nygren's view of Christian love (agape) as selfless *kenosis* will likely want to stress that it operates in a very different sphere from that of justice, which operates to give each person his or her due.[8] Even an advocate of such a view of agape, however, may find it helpful to pay some attention to the requirements of justice, if only because it provides the baseline from which the self-emptying acts of agape are assessed. Other theological accounts of the relationship between love and justice are more positive. Paul Ramsey accepted Nygren's account that agape requires self-sacrificial behavior in the case of a Christian confronted with the demands of a single neighbor. Following Augustine, however, he argued that an articulation of the demands of justice was the response of love to a conflict between two or more neighbors. Justice, on this view, is the form that love takes in social contexts and social controversies.[9]

Outka's own analytical framework offers the possibility of a richly textured relationship between love and justice. Like Ramsey, he is sympathetic to the claim that Christian love demands the pursuit of social justice in the steadfast determination to overcome patterns of injustice that have oppressed both near and distant neighbors. Moreover, Outka's definition of love as universal regard for all those whom God loves provides additional possibilities for considering the relationship of love and justice. In the essay at hand, for example, he considers the ways in which impartiality reflects the demands of universal love of neighbor. Impartiality, of course, is an aspect of justice as well as love. One might extend Outka's questions, probing the issue of what love requires in the context of administering justice. How do the requirements of universal love shape the way that we understand the demands of impartiality in specific cases?

In my view, the common law can help us illuminate these questions, not least because general rules are developed in the context of the actual disputes of particular neighbors, whose particular names and situations remain forever tied to the rule. In order to focus upon these questions as sharply as I can, I will sacrifice breadth for depth, concentrating my discussion on one case, *Watts v. Watts*.[10] Decided by the Wisconsin Supreme Court in 1987, it is commonly included in many first-year textbooks in contract law. It is, however, equally relevant to courses on family law and statutory interpretation, since the case requires the court to determine what sort of private agreements between unmarried heterosexual couples are consistent with the legislative commitment to legal marriage as socially beneficial to the common good.[11]

Sue Ann and James Watts met in 1967, as the cultural and social revolution of the Sixties moved from the coasts to the heartland. She was nineteen years old, living with her parents and working full-time as a nurse's aide. Shortly after they met, James persuaded her to give up her job and her dream of becoming a nurse one day and to move into an apartment that he rented. According to the court, he "indicated" that he would provide for her. Early in 1969, the couple began living together in a "marriage-like" relationship. They held themselves out to the public as husband and wife. Sue Ann took James's last name. They filed joint income tax returns and maintained joint bank accounts as husband and wife. James listed Sue Ann as his wife on medical and life insurance policies. They purchased property and took out loans as husband and wife. Moreover, they had two children together, both of whom were given James's last name.

For over a decade, Sue Ann was a good "wife" to James. She took care of the children, cleaned, cooked, washed the laundry, did the shopping, ran errands, and even maintained the lawn. She acted as his hostess at both social and business-related events. Sue Ann's commitment to his projects, it seems, was both energetic and generous. She fed and cleaned up after James and his employees while his landscaping business built a golf course. Moreover, Sue Ann did office work at his place of business, and even started an enterprise of her own with James's sister-in-law. All this, however, was not enough to cement their loyalty to one another. By 1981, their relationship had broken down irretrievably. Sue Ann claimed that James had made the situation so intolerable for her that she was forced to move from her home. In addition, she asserted that he also barred her from her own place of business.

After a relationship breaks down, the sad matter of dividing the property comes up. Sue Ann claimed that since James and she had functioned like a married couple while they were together, they should function like a divorcing couple now that they were permanently separating. Because Wisconsin is a community property state, she wanted James to transfer to her half the assets they had accumulated in the course of their twelve-year relationship, including the assets of his landscaping business.

The difficulty, of course, is that they never actually *were* legally married. They did not comply with the conditions necessary to achieve legal marriage specified under Wisconsin law. What about common law marriage? Unfortunately for Sue Ann, Wisconsin had abolished common law marriage many years prior to her controversy with James. According to applicable law, marriages contracted in violation of the specified legal requirements were void.

What about James's position? The man who had enticed nineteen-year-old Sue Ann to leave her parents' home and move in with him without so much as a dime store promise ring on her finger suddenly became a charter member of the "Family Values Club." He argued that their relationship undermined Wisconsin public policy stressing the importance of the marital relationship; consequently, the court should not only refuse to divide the property according to the provisions for divorce in the Wisconsin Family Act, it should also refuse to involve itself in such a sordid and immoral situation at all. Instead, the court should leave the money where it was—as it just so happened, entirely with him.

Where do these facts come from? Whose perspective controls their presentation? Who determines the narrative? The answers to these important questions are determined in large part by the procedure of the case: Sue Ann Watts is the plaintiff in *Watts v. Watts*; James is the defendant. Sue Ann filed a complaint setting forth these facts and seeking relief upon a number of legal theories in the trial court. The judge dismissed the complaint for failure to state a claim upon which relief could be granted. Sue Ann then appealed the dismissal of her case to the Wisconsin Supreme Court. For purposes of considering her appeal, the higher court relied upon the version of the facts set forth in her complaint, and asked whether they constitute a valid claim for relief under any legitimate legal theory.

So the facts presented in the opinion reflect Sue Ann's account of the situation. The narrative, however, is the Supreme Court's—the controlling majority selects, orders, and emphasizes certain facts in the course of developing the analysis of the case. We do not, therefore, have access to the essences of Sue Ann or James Watts. In the case of Sue Ann, what we do have is a third-hand account. Sue Ann told her story to her lawyer, who shaped it for presentation to the court. The court, in turn, reshaped it for presentation to the general public who would read the opinion, mainly if not exclusively the legal community. James, alas, appears to us through a lens that is even more distant and distorted. We see his character and actions entirely through Sue Ann's eyes. In essence, his lawyer's argument is that even if he had acted in precisely the beastly manner she said he did, Sue Ann would not be entitled to a penny.

Confronted with the battling couple, we can ask, how do the requirements of the command to universal love, as understood by Outka, bear upon the decision-making of the common law, as crystallized in the case of *Watts v. Watts*? This question, too, is very general. I think, however, we can begin to tackle it by addressing three more specific issues, each of which engages a different aspect of Outka's essay on impartiality.

1. *The Focus of Neighbor Love*: Upon what aspect of the neighbor does universal love focus its regard—aspects that are unique to him or her, or aspects that are held in common with other human beings?
2. *Persons, Rules, and Circumstances*: In addressing conflicts between neighbors, to what degree should we rely upon rules, and to what degree should we take into account distinguishing facts and circumstances of particular cases and people?
3. *An Asymmetry of Agency*: What can agents do for their neighbors that third parties cannot make them do?

Outka touches upon all three issues in his long essay, albeit in varying degrees of detail. The common law, as crystallized in *Watts,* furthers our consideration of them. It also engenders questions of its own, questions that further our understanding of universal love and impartiality. Before going any further, however, it is necessary for me to say something about the stance or vantage point that will organize my consideration of the *Watts* case. In probing the requirements of love, justice, and impartiality, my perspective will largely be that of a judge in the case. It is the judge, after all, who is confronted with the conflicting demands of two or more neighbors: Sue Ann and James Watts. It is the judge who needs to decide their case, taking into account not only unique aspects of their situation, but aspects which they share in common with other similarly situated men and women. It is the judge who must formulate a rule that will affect not only the litigants before him, but other persons in roughly the same circumstances. Finally, it is the judge who must recognize the limits of the judicial ability to remedy situations of human sin, failure, and brokenness.

The Focus of Neighbor Love

According to Outka, all human beings possess "a common status as distinctive creatures of God" and "a common plight as creatures who sin against God" and who are redeemed by Jesus Christ. They also manifest a common dignity as creatures whose value is not earned, but conferred upon each of us by God.[12] In Outka's view, the task of love is to promote the dignity of each and every human being.

Outka does not go into detail about what promoting human dignity entails. Clearly, however, it includes promoting respect for the autonomy of each human being. At the same time, he strongly warns against the "tacit equation of dignity and autonomy." As he recognizes, "autonomy is integral to the neighbor's dignity but not exhaustive of it."[13] Earlier in the essay, in fact, he talks more broadly of promoting the neighbor's well-being, which clearly encompasses other elements of human flourishing. He also approvingly quotes Basil Mitchell: "The love of others, which the Christian ethic demands, involves an active concern for their well-being, and that in turn implies a clear conception of what is best for them, which must, in consistency, be also in essentials what is best for ourselves."[14] Respect for a neighbor's dignity, therefore, means respect for their autonomous self-determination; at the same time, it also requires concern for other aspects of their well-being, whose value is not purely subjective.

Outka does not, however, address two key questions that I want to consider here: What does it mean to respect an agent's autonomy? What is the relationship between respect for autonomy and respect for other aspects of well-being, both with regard to a single agent, and with respect to multiple agents? These questions, alas, are the bread and butter of contract law.

Contract law's basic premise is that the widespread practice of making and keeping promises of exchange allows all involved to bring into being a future that they conceive to be better for themselves and those with whom they are associated.[15] Individual autonomy is honored within the framework of contract law. It is not, however, honored in isolation. Rather, one agent's autonomy is always situated within a broader context that includes the autonomous decision-making of other agents, particularly that individual's contracting partner. Furthermore, autonomy is seen not as an abstract value. Even a cursory examination of the case law reveals its status as a crucial instrument of pursuing individual and social well-being. The law of contracts is practical; it presupposes that the point of autonomy is to exercise it in order to bring about a better future, not to save it in pristine form as a pure capacity.

Moreover, contract law is based upon the public recognition of private promises. This society has decided that the exchange of reliable promises by private persons is so important to the well-being of the whole that the government, in the form of its judicial branch, regularly devotes public resources to managing private disputes. Not only will courts decide if a legally enforceable agreement exists, they will also interpret its terms, determine if it was breached, and provide a remedy (usually monetary damages) ideally designed to put the non-breaching party into the position he or she would have been in had the breach not occurred.

In this setting, then, what does it mean to respect autonomy? The case law reveals that respecting autonomy is a multifaceted task. First, we need to recognize autonomy as a capacity—a capacity, as the legal philosopher Joseph Raz writes, to be "part author" of one's own life.[16] Generally speaking, classical contract law *presumes* that an adult individual is autonomous—and therefore has the capacity to contract. Respect for autonomy—and for equal dignity—comes in that rough-and-ready presumption that another adult is capable of making a legally effective promise. So Sue Ann Watts is presumed to have the capacity to make autonomous choices. It does not matter that she is young, provided she is over the age of majority. While the court presents her as naive—and, dare I say, ditzy—that does not prevent her from making decisions about how to live her life that will be taken seriously by others, and given binding effect by the representatives of society.

Second, we need to think about the external conditions that allow the capacity for autonomy to be exercised. Traditionally, the common law has allowed contracts to be avoided on account of improper pressure exerted by one of the parties at the time the contract was made. The qualifying conditions, however, have been interpreted fairly narrowly. To avoid a contract for duress, for example, requires a party to prove that the other party made an improper (illegal or immoral) threat; it is not enough to show that the other party took advantage of circumstances to charge an outrageous price. More recently, defenses such as undue influence (improper pressure placed upon a susceptible party) and unconscionability ("iffy" bargaining conditions conjoined with an "iffy" substantive deal) have given parties more options to avoid the promises they made under difficult circumstances. Even these categories, however, are interpreted fairly narrowly by the courts.

Third, respecting someone's autonomy in the context of contract law frequently means holding that person to the promise that he or she made at the "magic moment" in which a contract came into being, in which the promise was exchanged for a corresponding promise, or for some other form of consideration. As I noted above, the system creates a heavy presumption in favor of every adult's effective exercise of autonomy. Consequently, respecting autonomy very often means holding agents accountable to a decision to limit their autonomy in order to further another aspect of their well-being, perhaps even to facilitate the exercise of autonomy at a later point in time. For example, if I promise to landscape your yard on Saturday in exchange for your promise to pay me $500, I am no longer free to do what I want on Saturday from that moment forward. But I may take the money to pay my rent, buy my food, or commit to purchase something else that I desire more than my freedom on one Saturday.

What, then, is the relationship between autonomy and well-being? As the foregoing example shows, that relationship is complicated. We need to distinguish between the situation of the *promisor*—the one who autonomously made a commitment to do something in exchange for something else in return—and the *promisee*—the one who received that commitment.

In some cases, a *promisor* will seek legally to avoid a promise made in somewhat compromised circumstances, perhaps by arguing that the stress or financial pressure or lack of options fatally wounded their autonomous capacity to promise. A good example is the phenomenon of rent-to-own contracts, which offer televisions and furniture to people with bad financial histories at exorbitant rates, and sometimes with distasteful penalty clauses.[17] It is understandable that someone might try to avoid such a contract on the grounds of duress or unconscionability. But such an attempt always comes at a price. If the promises I make are not enforceable, no one will do business with me. If no one will do business with me, my options inevitably diminish. My options in this less-than-perfect world, alas, do not include a loan at the prime interest rate or a free television. My options are two: either no television at all or a very expensive television whose price to me exceeds its actual value in most markets by a considerable amount.[18] If the contract is not enforced, the rent-to-own company may take its business elsewhere. It would be nice if it did not do so. But it can and it will. And if it does, both the range of my exercise of autonomy and my well-being may be limited.

Relatedly, it can be tempting to allow some persons or group of persons to avoid disadvantageous contracts by deeming them incapable of forming a valid contract. As feminist legal scholars and critical race theorists have shown, however,[19] the well-being of a person or a socially defined class of people is connected to the power to have one's promises taken as seriously as anyone else's promises—and taking them seriously means enforcing them if necessary. At this point, these scholars' insights converge with Gene Outka's. Although he ultimately rejects impartiality as a full articulation of universal love, he does recognize that it creates a default presumption that we extend the same rights, privileges, and duties to all adult human beings.

More generally, to say of someone that they are unable to contract—to promise and to be relied upon in promising—is to cut them out of a major human activity: exchanging one's own strengths for those of another. I do not mean for a moment to deny the importance of questions concerning the capacity of demonstrably physically or mentally impaired persons to make legally effective autonomous choices. At the same time, I think we need to recognize that it threatens our commitment to the equal dignity of all human beings to be too quick to deprive even vulnerable members of the community of the legal power to exercise their autonomy.

What about the *promisee*? In deciding whether and how to enforce a promise, it is important to remember that both parties to a contract exercise their autonomy to pursue their own conceptions of well-being. Very often, each party pursues that conception by *relying* on the other party's promise in making further autonomous decisions, including decisions to make more promises to other people. You rely on my promise to landscape your yard on Saturday, because you plan to host a career-enhancing corporate picnic on Sunday. You hire caterers and book entertainment. You make other promises and exact other commitments, weaving them together with my promise in order to build your future, in order to promote the cause of your well-being.

The concept of *reliance* is crucial in contract law; it is, I think, underutilized in theological ethics. A richer understanding of the relationship of autonomy and reliance in contract law may help us move beyond a truncated view of autonomy as exclusively associated with and contributing to a radical individualism.

In the American legal system, the general rule is that from the moment the parties exchange promises, those promises are enforceable. This rule goes beyond reliance in two senses. First, one party does not need to rely upon the other party's promise before it becomes enforceable. Second, enforcing a promise characteristically means giving the non-breaching party its full value—not merely compensating for out-of-pocket expenses incurred by the time of the breach. Ordinarily, the courts attempt to give what is called expectation damages—they attempt to put non-breaching parties in the position they would have been in had the promises to them been fulfilled, not merely to put them back in the position they were in before they relied upon the broken promise. An example may help: If you and I agree on a cold day in February that I will rent you my fabulous waterfront beach house on Cape Cod for $1,000 for the entire summer, my promise is enforceable as soon as it is made—even *before* you rely on it by purchasing your plane tickets in March. And if I change my mind in April, you are entitled to the full value of that summer rental for $1,000, not merely compensation for the cost of your tickets.

As this example shows, contract law generally protects the promisee's expectation interest, not merely the reliance interest. Why? While this question is disputed among legal theorists, in my view, the most persuasive answer recognizes not only the role of the *promisor's* autonomy in making the promise, but also the relationship of *promisee's* autonomy and reliance in accepting it. More specifically, we want to encourage promisees to rely upon the promises they receive, to build on them, to count on them in pursuing, confidently, their own notion of well-being. As Lon Fuller said, "to encourage reliance, we must dispense with its proof."[20]

Reliance is the relational counterpart of a promisor's autonomous commitment; it is incorporated as one plank of the promisee's practical reasoning about the future. As Gene

Outka repeatedly cautions, human beings are not isolated monads, but are social beings. That means, of course, that their autonomy is not the exercise of will of an autonomous monad. Outka recognizes the fact that sociality can result in undue pressure on the individual exercising autonomy.[21] As I noted earlier, contract law does as well. But what he might want to explore, in my view, is how in the best of cases, one individual's autonomy and well-being rely upon the autonomous commitments of others. Our autonomous choices are not of interest merely to ourselves, but also to our neighbors. They not only predict them from afar, they attempt to secure them by folding them into binding agreements. And they do so because they want to build upon them in the course of exercising their own autonomy and pursuing their own well-being.

Where could there be or should there be a point of contact between Outka's conception of neighbor love and contract law's account of reliance? I myself think that drawing in an element from Paul Ramsey's account of love might be helpful. Modeling Christian obligations on God's covenant fidelity to humanity, Ramsey defines agape as steadfast love—one might say *reliable* love.[22] A covenant in many cases is another word for a contract.[23] It accounts, in his view, for the capacity of love to bind itself in service to the neighbor, and for the neighbor to rely upon that expression of being bound, even in difficult circumstances.

Reliance, in the context of universal love, can be seen as a response of human sociality, finitude, and contingency to the loving exercise of autonomy. Human beings need to trust and to depend upon one another in order to address problems of finitude and contingency. There is a resultant vulnerability that comes from dependency created by trust. Given human finitude, and sin, there is the possibility of that vulnerability and dependency being betrayed. It is no accident that Ramsey's account of steadfast love did the most work in his groundbreaking book on medical ethics, *The Patient as Person*. Ramsey attempts to enfold the most vulnerable members of the population with a secure promise to care for them. I have already noted Outka's claim that "Love for God—as the most basic and comprehensive human love of all—includes fidelity to God in loving whom God loves."[24] I will suggest that Outka's notion of fidelity or steadfastness applies not only to *whom* God loves, but *how* God loves them, in the manner specified by Ramsey.

Now how does the foregoing analysis of promise-making further our insight into our neighbors, the battling Wattses? The fundamental problem that the court is grappling with in *Watts v. Watts* is that there is clearly reliance, but possibly no promise. More precisely, there is no legally sanctioned promise, made in the context of the exchange of wedding vows. To put it another way, there is reliance, but no solemn covenant upon which to rely.

Can we infer private promises to treat each other as spouses back from the parties' mutual reliance: the tax returns, the kids, the business entertaining? It seems to me that this is not difficult. Contract law frequently infers promises from the activities of the parties, holding that their reality and legal effectiveness are no less real because they are tacit rather than explicit. One could certainly infer that by holding themselves out to third parties as married, the Wattses held themselves out to each other to be married.[25]

What kind of a contract does being married involve? It is, in my view, at the far end of a spectrum of complexity and commitment. At the near end, we can envisage a one-time exchange in which each party's duties are clear: I hire a person to walk my dog. In the middle, we can imagine an ongoing exchange in which one party's duties are subject to a great deal of self-definition: Suppose a college hires a new president, who will have a great deal of discretion in defining the actual content of his or her day-to-day duties. At the far end, we can contemplate an ongoing exchange in which each party's contributions build upon the contributions of the other party: a partnership, in which each shares equally in the costs, risks, benefits, and rewards of the enterprise. The success or failure of one party depends not only on his efforts, but also upon hers. It is at this far end that the contract of marriage belongs.

Marriage, after all, is the quintessential open-ended partnership. Autonomy, reliance, and well-being are intertwined as closely as they could be in this kind of contractual relationship. It seems clear from the facts set forth in the opinion that Sue Ann and James repeatedly made possibly explicit and clearly tacit promises to each other to engage in the kind of open-ended partnership that is marriage. It is also clear that Sue Ann relied upon these promises in numerous ways. We can see the positive reliance in all the things she did, in all her efforts expended on behalf of the landscaping business.

At the same time, and crucially, we can also see it in what she failed to do, so-called "negative reliance." She did not retain her birth name, make an independent life for herself, or even obtain the training she needed to be financially secure, since she counted upon her relationship with James to provide her with material goods. Moreover, she did not formalize their relationship by pressing to marry him in accordance with Wisconsin law.

Why not make the relationship legal? We could look at this question in two ways, in terms of larger social context and in terms of personal incentives. Viewed in terms of broader cultural currents, it is understandable that the Wattses didn't get married right away—it was, after all, the late Sixties when they became involved with one another. But they soon moved into the middle class, tax-paying respectability that was and continues to be so intimately connected with legal marriage.[26]

The situation with respect to individual incentives, however, is a bit more complicated—one might even say paradoxical. If a couple is living together peaceably, there may be no perceived need for the piece of paper that formalizes their relationship. Moreover, as time goes on, legalizing the situation could be embarrassing, particularly for the Wattses, since they had held themselves out as legally married for so long. What would they tell the children? Finally, regularizing their situation could be financially costly and even legally dangerous, since doing so would likely reveal that they had lied to the IRS and other public and private bodies about their marital status. If, on the other hand, the relationship is under threat of dissolving, there is no incentive (especially on his part) to cement the partnership.

In short, for the Wattses, as for many couples, there was a "magic moment," a time at which social forces and personal incentives aligned to encourage them to formalize their relationship and the patterns of reliance that relationship engendered. But they missed that moment. Crucially, however, their life together proceeded in virtually every respect as if they had captured it—until it didn't.

Persons, Rules, and Circumstances

While he does not belabor the point, Outka assumes that universal love may appropriately develop rules of general applicability. He emphasizes, for instance that "moral principles not only tell agents what they may and should do or not do, but also what they may and should resist, object to, and demand."[27] I want to suggest that the common law will force us to face head-on a question which Outka acknowledges but does not fully grapple with in his extended essay: the relationship between universal love and the use of normative rules.

The debate in the 1960s between Paul Ramsey and Joseph Fletcher revealed the complicated nature of the relationship between rules and love.[28] While a full analysis is beyond my scope here, I note that one aspect of their debate is not about whether universal love can be applied in and through rules, but *which* rules should govern: an overarching utilitarian rule that invites us to maximize good consequences across persons, or other rules that place other limits on action that are not consequence-based.

I would like to focus on a different, and perhaps prior, issue: In thinking about what it means to respect or regard the dignity of our fellow human beings, how do we balance regard for their uniqueness as a child of God, and the unique course that their lives take, with regard for the characteristics, needs, and temptations that they have in common with other human beings? This question, it seems to me, is inevitably involved in rule-making.

A good legal or moral rule picks out certain features of a situation as decisive for analysis and places others in the shadows. The substantive justice of a rule depends upon the wisdom and validity of the features selected to count and those dismissed as irrelevant to moral and legal analysis. A substantively unjust rule, say, "All people over six feet tall get a $2,000 income tax credit," can be applied in a procedurally fair way. Its fair procedural application does not obviate its substantive injustice.

In my judgment, the Anglo-American common law tradition acutely raises the question about the relationship of unique persons and situations and general rules in a way worthy of reflection by theological and philosophical ethicists. In fact, the distinguishing feature of that tradition is that judges articulate legal rules and principles not in the abstract, but rather in the course of deciding a specific case or controversy. John Noonan captures the situation in his classic book, *Persons and Masks of the Law*:

> No person itself, the law lives in persons. Rules of law are formed by human beings to shape the attitude and conduct of human beings and applied by human beings to human beings. The human beings are persons. The rules are communications uttered, comprehended, and responded to by persons. They affect attitude and conduct as communications from persons to persons. They exist as rules—not as words on paper—in the mind of persons.[29]

As Noonan's book shows, the common law is made around the hopes, disappointments, and controversies of specific persons, whose names are in the head notes. It is *their* case or controversy which the judge and jury are charged with deciding. That case is irreducibly particular, because it involves the background, training, and social roles, as well as the character strengths and flaws, of the parties to the case. It is set in a particular time and place, which shapes the decision-making process of the plaintiff, defendant, and other agents involved. From God's point of view, the list of facts and circumstances potentially relevant to a full moral analysis of the actions of the parties, and their responsibility for those actions, could well be enormous.

At the same time, the judge is called to decide the case by articulating a general rule, which can be applied in other similar cases. That general rule necessarily picks out certain features of the case as relevant and plays down others. In making these selections, the judge is both forging and expressing the values of the community and determining the fate of the particular litigants before her.

This aspect of the law-making process, I think, should be of interest to Outka for two reasons. The first is that it forces us to grapple with some important questions: In deciding a controversy such as that between the Wattses, in what respect do judges—who are persons—regard the litigants—who are persons—as their neighbors? Do they regard the litigants in their concrete uniqueness, in the midst of the particular circumstances which cause them distress, or do they regard them in the aspects of their situation which are shared in common with others, or at least with a significant segment of the community?

Noonan argues, rightly, I think, that a legal system needs to attend to both general rules and specific persons in order to function well. Paying exclusive attention to particular persons—and our response to them—strangles justice with either favoritism or hatred. There is a reason that a just judge is said to be "no respecter of persons"; justice cannot be done if our friends are always right and strangers and enemies always wrong. At the same time, rules can become hardened and can be applied mechanically, in a way that turns them into masks that hide the humanity of the person before the bench. They can blind us to the true nature of the moral situation. Noonan's classic example, of course, is the way in which African-Americans were classified as property before the civil war.[30] But there are other, less extreme examples. Noonan argues, for example, that the practice of headnotes in commercial case reporters and student study guides to strip all facts out of a case, even the names of the parties, verges on submerging the particular person in the impersonal rule.[31]

Consider the statement of the facts in the Westlaw version of *Watts v. Watts:* "Unmarried cohabitant brought action for accounting and share of accumulated property under theory of express or implied-in-fact contract, and theory of constructive trust based upon unjust enrichment." Does the label "unmarried cohabitants" fully capture the status of the Wattses vis-à-vis each other? Twelve years, two children, many joint tax returns? All those dinners cooked by Sue Ann for all those sweaty workers in James's start-up landscape business? Technically, of course, the term "unmarried" applies to the Wattses. But the other facts left out as irrelevant are, in fact, relevant both to justice and to the ultimate disposition of the case.

It seems to me that in affirming a theocentric account of universal love, Outka will need to affirm the importance of both particularity and generalizability in the course of attending to the neighbor and her situation. We are all unique, yet we are all human beings commonly made in the image and likeness of God. As Noonan's work demonstrates, a commitment to universal love does require appellate judges to recognize the specific persons whose cases are before them as unique individuals. It also requires them to be alert to the ways in which the legal categories they inherit can function to dehumanize those persons, and thereby prove themselves to be in need of rejection or reform. At the same time, however, by virtue of their role-related obligation, in deciding these specific cases, judges need to mark out a general path of action for others in the community to follow.

But how do we or should we account for both aspects of our neighbors in our decision-making? I think the common law does a reasonably good job of accounting for both. In deciding a case like *Watts v. Watts*, the court must articulate a rule, which requires it to pick out some circumstances of the parties as relevant, and to discount others in ways that render them irrelevant. That rule, which will take on a life that is detached to some degree from the case, will go on to be applied to future cases. It is important to note, however, that the discounting and the detachment are always provisional, at least in principle. The rule is articulated in the context of the narrative of the case, which officially does continue to bear the name of and point to the stories of the parties who litigated it. It is more accurate to say that the rule is, so to speak, semi-detached from the case that prompted its formulation.

The case, as precedent, does not disappear. It is not consumed by the rule. It is preserved as the context that makes the rule intelligible. The rule is always subject to the possibility of being qualified or modified with reference to the circumstances of a later case, if the judges deciding it choose to distinguish the original case on the basis of differing facts now found to be salient. Human beings and their stories are unique, but they have some capacities, needs, and temptations in common. We may not be able fully to sort out the relationship between the particularities of individuals and common human nature, but we can ensure that our rules, and the persons whose situation prompted their development, go forward together.

Near and Distant Neighbors

As Outka recognizes, the classical Christian text for love of neighbor, the parable of the Good Samaritan, does not require us to think about how universal love applies in a case of conflict between two neighbors. He asks, "When two or more persons are affected by one's action, does the claim [of the dignity of the human person] furnish any guidance? What especially of situations where the well-being of various persons conflict and choice is unavoidable?"[32]

In considering the matter of conflict between neighbors, the Christian tradition, from Augustine to Paul Ramsey, has focused on questions pertaining to the use of violence to defend one neighbor wrongly attacked by another. The parable is altered to ask what the Good Samaritan would have done if he had come upon the scene a little earlier, as the robbers went about their "fell work."[33] While Outka recognizes the importance of these questions, he also urges us to move beyond those questions to consider situations of conflict between neighbors that do not involve violence.[34]

In my view, one way to grasp the nonviolent conflicts between neighbors is to look at them through the prism of the judicial task. The question of whether love focuses upon regard for the neighbor in her unique particularity, or in the more universalizable aspects of her situation picked out by rules, is intimately entwined with the question of how love requires us to address conflicts among neighbors. In deciding a controversy between neighbors, are judges to do justice to the specific parties before them, in all their particularity, or to formulate a rule that will best serve the community, in particular to guide the behavior of similarly but not identically situated neighbors? The appropriate solution to some particular cases may also best serve the common good. But that is not necessarily so. In other situations, there might be tension between the two goals.

To illustrate and analyze this tension in neighbor love, let us return to the case at hand.

Recall that the judges of the Wisconsin Supreme Court are charged to decide the claims of the Wattses—and those claims are constituted in the midst of their specific situation. But the rule the court announces will bind other people in Wisconsin, shaping the way they live their lives and make their decisions. These people include not only the class of men and women who might or might not get married, but also all the other citizens of Wisconsin. These citizens, through their legislature, adopted the relevant legal framework on marriage and family law. They also pay the taxes that support the judicial resolution of disputes.

The Wisconsin Supreme Court was not deciding this case in a legal vacuum; it was making its decision in view of the normative framework that it discerned in the context of the Wisconsin Family Code. According to the court, the state legislature emphasized the importance of *legal marriage* in formulating and revising that Code. More specifically, the court found that the legislative purpose animating the Code was "to promote the stability and best interests of marriage and the family. . . . Marriage is the institution that is the foundation of family and society. Its stability is basic to morality and civilization, and of vital interest to society and the state."[35] The Court further interpreted the state's abolition of common law marriage, along with its denial of legal status to marriages that do not conform to the statute, as proof of the legislature's judgment that legal marriage is crucial to the well-being of society.

Thus the Wisconsin legislature came to the conclusion that legal marriage is the best foundation for the well-being of most of the population. In light of that conclusion, and its duty of deference to the legislature in interpreting the statute, the Wisconsin Supreme Court judged that it had a fundamental obligation to decide the case in a way that teaches that legal marriage is preferable to less formal arrangements, and to encourage people in the Wattses' general situation toward formalizing their relationships. At the same time, the court noted that fornication and cohabitation are not against the law in Wisconsin. Although the living arrangements of the Wattses were not favored by the law, they did not violate it either. Somewhat surprisingly, the court did not mention, much less belabor, the fact that the Wattses had lied about their status on certain official documents, such as their state and federal tax returns. Nor did it observe that such lies were almost certainly financially beneficial to them.

In cases such as this, then, the faces of those whose situation calls for a remedy are vividly before the judge, while the faces of those whose lives will be affected by the new rule are at best indistinct and hazy. In my view, the insights of theological ethics can help advance our understanding of the legal situation, by framing it in terms of the claims of near and distant neighbors.[36] What do the demands of impartiality, shaped by the insights of universal love, require in such a context? As Outka notes, the requisite impartiality will be concerned with "substantive fairness," not merely with rigid adherence to procedure.[37]

What, then, does substantive fairness require of the *Watts* court? What substantive interests need to be protected? To whom do they belong? Reframing the question in this way allows us to see that the conflict is not merely between two sets of people, near and distant neighbors, each with discrete and possibly opposing interests. Rather, the conflict is also and even primarily between different functions of the law: on the one hand, the remedial function (cleaning up the shards of the Wattses' broken relationship) and on the other hand, the pedagogical and channeling functions (teaching and incentivizing other people not to put themselves in the same position as the Wattses did).

All three functions are substantive, in that they all further substantive interests of society's members. All members of society, furthermore, have an interest in each of the functions being exercised in a vigorous and judicious manner by the courts. To put it another way, the Wattses are not the only ones who have an interest in their particular dispute being settled fairly; we all have that interest, because the remedial function of the law is important to the entire community.

By framing the potential conflict not simply as one between near and distant neighbors, but also as between the remedial and the pedagogical functions of the law, we may, I believe, make substantial progress toward ameliorating it. Let us begin by looking at the broken relationship of the Wattses. How ought it to be remedied, with the very imperfect tools available to the court system? First, it seems clear that Sue Ann and James intended to live together *as if* they were participants in the social institution of marriage. Given that this is the case, it seems as if both ought to have expected that they would separate *as if* they were leaving that institution.[38]

The keywords, of course, are "as if." They never went through with the procedure specified by Wisconsin law as necessary to enter into the state of matrimony. Who is responsible? As tempting as the narrative makes it to absolve Sue Ann from responsibility, we cannot do that without infantilizing her. Nonetheless, we can certainly insist that James is just as responsible for the situation as is Sue Ann.

If we look only at their relationship, what does substantive fairness require? As the court itself noted, letting him keep all the money when both parties are equally guilty of flouting the technical requirements of legal marriage is substantively unfair. James would get a windfall at Sue Ann's expense. He would be rewarded for their mutual walk on the windy side of the law, while she would be punished.

What about the pedagogical function of the law? Does denying Sue Ann recovery teach others about the foundational value of legal marriage, and channel them into that institution? Initially, that might seem to be the case. We can envision the cautionary tale: "Make it legal, or end up alone and penniless like Sue Ann!"

But thinking a bit more deeply, in my view, suggests that denying Sue Ann recovery is not likely to have the desired pedagogical effect, for two reasons. First, the case is about what happens when two people break up—not what happens when they get together. How many people, especially young people, are likely to decide whether or not to get married legally by considering what happens if they eventually fail at their common life together?[39] Some people, of course, may think that far ahead. But how many? The incidence of prenuptial agreements might give us a rough idea of the numbers of people who consider the potential breakup of their future union before entering into it. As of March 2010, only three percent of individuals with a spouse or fiancée had a prenuptial agreement. That number, while up significantly from the one percent reported in a similar study in April 2002, is not a sign that most people are thinking ahead to divorce when planning a marital or quasi-marital partnership.[40] Second, and more crucially, the incentives associated in a rule that would deny recovery to those in Sue Ann's place actually cut both ways. If such a rule were adopted, a woman in Sue Ann's situation might be inclined to insist on a legal marriage before entering into a marriage-like relationship. But a man in James's position would be equally inclined to avoid formalizing the arrangement.

The incentives that count most, it seems to me, are the negative and positive incentives *to marry*, not those that pertain to what happens after a separation whose possibility both parties are likely to discount heavily when moving in together. In days past, many incentives to marry were negative in nature. For example, fornication was not only subject to moral disapprobation, but also illegal.[41] Laws such as these have disappeared from the statute books over time, as the *Watts* court notes. There are still, however, many positive incentives for couples to marry legally. For example, both state and federal law grants tax benefits to married parties, and banks consider the income of both parties in establishing credit ratings and deciding whether to loan money. It would not be difficult to encourage legal marriage—and discourage quasi-marriages such as the Wattses'—by requiring couples seeking financial and other benefits associated with marriage to provide a copy of their marriage certificate. It seems likely that James and Sue Ann would have regularized their situation in order to obtain the tax benefits had they not been able to obtain them simply by lying about their marital status.

An Asymmetry of Agency

The bulk of Gene Outka's essay on "Universal Love and Impartiality" is an attempt to identify the similarities and differences between self-love and love of neighbor for purposes of applying the command to love universally. It would seem, at first glance, that this effort is not relevant to my analysis of what judges should do when confronted with the claims of two battling neighbors, even as they take into account the interests of many neighbors who are more distant from the case. Nonetheless, I think his analysis is deeply relevant because it helps explain the limits of what law can do to remedy situations marred by disappointment and sin. While constraints of space prevent me from fully examining this point, I think it would be useful to outline its kernel. The analysis points, I think, to an additional way in which the insights of theological and philosophical ethics may shed light upon the decisions made by courts.

Briefly, Outka argues that there are several asymmetries between what I can do for my neighbor and what I can do for myself, some of which center around the phenomenon of human agency. I am responsible for my own acts and, ultimately, for my own response to God's call. I am also responsible for carrying out my unique life plan, in the form of pursuing my own vocation. There are corresponding limits, as Outka argues, based in both principled and practical considerations, to what I can do for my neighbor.

Outka observes, for instance, that I can commend love of God to my neighbor, but I cannot love God on my neighbor's behalf. Building upon Outka's observation, it also seems evident that I cannot force a neighbor to simulate the attitude or acts of love toward either God or a fellow human being. Of their nature, such acts must be performed freely. I can urge my neighbors to love each other, but I cannot force them to do so. Furthermore, I can take full responsibility for executing my life plan, but I cannot assume the same level of control over my neighbors' life plans. I can facilitate their vocations, but I cannot fulfill them.

How do the limits of what one agent can do for another affect our understandings of the limits of law in addressing human conflicts? In my view, they explain the degree to which the law is hampered in providing a remedy in the face of human sin and the actions that flow from it. Consider, again, the situation of the Wattses. The ideal resolution of this situation, of course, would be for Sue Ann and James to have a conversion of heart, and to recommit themselves to their love, to their children, and to their joint life plan. It is only that sort of conversion that would meet their mutual expectations, based on mutual promises to live as if they were married to one another.

But it is beyond the power of the law to produce the ideal resolution of this situation. Generally speaking, courts do not order specific performance with respect to personal services. In fact, they are notoriously leery to do so, in part because of the theoretical worry that doing so comes too close to ordering a de facto arrangement of slavery, and in part because of the practical worry that persons who are forced to perform particular functions rarely do so in a way that will meet the needs of the one exacting those functions from them. What, then, are the tools at its disposal? In some cases, it might issue a negative injunction, preventing a breaching party from assuming other obligations that are inconsistent with its contractual obligations. In other cases, it might order the breaching party to transfer property or money to the non-breaching party. But the command to transfer money is not and can never be the equivalent of a command to transfer the loyalties and love of one's heart. That command is beyond the purview of the legal system.

Resolution of the Case

In appealing the dismissal of her case to the Wisconsin Supreme Court, Sue Ann Watts claimed that any one of the following legal theories would justify giving her relief on the facts she averred.

1. She claimed that she was entitled to straightforward division of the assets under the applicable provisions pertaining to divorce under the Wisconsin Family Code.

2. She put forth a novel theory of "marriage by estoppel" in order to receive the same division of assets indirectly. In essence, she claimed that although they were never legally married, justice required that James be "estopped" from denying the fact of their marriage in the context of Sue Ann's claim to an equal share of his assets.
3. She argued that she was entitled to recovery under a theory of an express or implied-in-fact contract between her and James, in which they agreed to distribute their assets equally in the event of a separation.
4. She argued that he was unjustly enriched, and that she was entitled to restitution based on the reasonable value of her services to him and his projects over the years.
5. Finally, she argued that she and James had engaged in a joint venture, and that she was entitled to partition of the assets of that joint venture.

What were the respective views of the parties toward the five theories? Sue Ann wanted recovery under the first or second theory, since either would give her half the assets. The third theory would be acceptable, provided that she could prove that the terms of the contract included a provision for equal division of assets. The fourth theory would be suboptimal, although better than nothing. It treats her as a wage laborer rather than as a full partner. Moreover, the reasonable value of services characteristically provided by women is very low. The fifth and final theory would provide an acceptable recovery to Sue Ann.

James, of course, resisted the applicability of any theory. He argued that both the first and second theories would erode the legislative policy privileging marriage. The third, fourth, and fifth theories, in his view, should also be rejected by the court on the grounds of public policy. In addition to arguing that these theories would also undercut the preferred status of marriage, James strongly implied that it would enlist the court in the unwise and distasteful enforcement of a "meretricious" contract, in which one of the items of consideration was sexual relations. The Latin word "meretrix" means prostitute. By arguing that Sue Ann and he were involved in a "meretricious" contract, he was associating his life partner of twelve years and the mother of his two children with a woman who provides access to her body for money, not love. Doubtless the legal strategy was his lawyer's idea, not James's own. Nonetheless, it would be interesting to know whether he approved of it.

What did the court do? In essence, it split the difference. It did not allow the first or second theories to go to trial, agreeing with James that to do so would undercut legislative policy favoring legal marriage. It did, however, allow Sue Ann's claims to go forward under the third, fourth, and fifth theories, for four reasons.

First, the court noted changing mores on premarital cohabitation, concluding that their arrangement did not violate the common morality. Second, it also observed that numerous courts have distinguished between contracts that are "explicitly and inseparably founded on sexual services and those that are not." A bargain "is not illegal merely because there is an illicit relationship between the two so long as the bargain is independent of the illicit relationship . . ."[42] Third, the court recognized that the result of the judicial system's wholesale refusal to intervene in disputes between unmarried cohabitants would be unfair and harsh. One party would inevitably get an undeserved windfall. The other party, no more guilty than the first, would inevitably be correspondingly penalized. Even granting that the Wattses behaved irresponsibly by holding themselves out as married without in fact being actually married, they were both equally irresponsible. Fourth, and finally, the court observed that this situation could "encourage a partner with greater income potential to avoid marriage in order to retain all accumulated assets, leaving the other party with nothing."[43]

What was the result? The Wisconsin Supreme Court remanded to the trial court, allowing the case to go forward on the contract, unjust enrichment, and partition claims. After a trial, the jury found that Sue Ann and James did in fact have a contract, but awarded her no damages based on that contract. Instead, they gave her recovery on the theory of unjust enrichment, in effect requiring James to compensate her for the reasonable value of the services she rendered.[44] Sue Ann received an award of $113,090.08. According to Sue Ann's expert witness, James's net worth had increased by $1,113,900.88 during their time together.[45] In the end, she was treated as a wage laborer, rather than as an equity partner in the life they created together. What was the difference? In addition to the insult, about a half a million dollars.

I understand the court's reasoning. At the same time, I think the court too quickly rejected the second argument, based on "marriage by estoppel." To say that James should be "stopped" from denying Sue Ann's claim that they were married is not, in my view, to undermine the institution of marriage. It is simply to give appropriate weight to the fact that both parties held themselves out for so long as a married couple to government agencies, financial institutions, their family, friends, and fundamentally, to each other. Third parties harmed by the deception about their status ought to be free to challenge the "marriage" (e.g., the Internal Revenue Service ought to be able to collect back taxes on the grounds that they falsely obtained deductions only available to married people). Yet vis-à-vis each other, neither party ought to be able to deny their marriage-like status. To say that James is "estopped" from denying their marriage is *not* to say that they were *actually* married in the eyes of the law. It is simply to say that *he*, of all people, is not in a position to deny that they were married with respect to Sue Ann's claims against him. That seems about right to me.

Conclusion

Examining the case of *Watts v. Watts* through the dual lenses of theological ethics and legal studies demonstrates that these disciplines bear a rich potential for mutual conceptual illumination, as well as material criticism and enrichment. Several of Outka's claims about the normative content of universal love provide a vantage point for criticism of the reasoning and outcome in *Watts v. Watts*. Outka contends that universal love requires steadfastness and fidelity to both near and distant neighbors; he also insists that such love necessitates substantive, and not simply procedural, fairness in our treatment of these neighbors. As such, laws and legal decisions that strain to articulate viably generalizable rules (for "distant neighbors") at the expense of substantive fidelity to the individual persons involved in a case ("near neighbors") seem to fall short of the demands of universal love. Likewise, Outka's ethical analysis of asymmetries in human relationships of all sorts—between our relationships to ourselves and our neighbors, as well as between our relationships to near and distant neighbors—can help to underscore problems that the law must face, and limits in its ability to remedy them. Indeed, in this case the differences between what we can do for ourselves and what we can do for our neighbors clarifies an analogous difference in the law—between human responses the law cannot require in matters of love and those it should nonetheless require as a matter of law.

Notes

I presented earlier drafts of this paper in colloquia at the University of Virginia's Institute of Advanced Studies in Culture, the Religion Department at Princeton University, and the University of Notre Dame Law School. I am very grateful for the helpful comments received in all these settings.

1. Luke 10:25–37, Mt. 22:34–40, Mk. 12:28–34 (NRSV).

2. Robert Wuthnow, *Acts of Compassion: Caring for Others and Helping Ourselves* (Princeton, N.J.: Princeton University Press, 1991).

3. *Watts v. Watts*, 137 Wis.2d 506, 405 N.W.2d 305 (1987).

4. Gene Outka, *Agape: An Ethical Analysis* (New Haven: Yale University Press, 1972).

5. Gene Outka, "Universal Love and Impartiality," in *The Love Commandments: Essays in Christian Ethics and Moral Philosophy*, ed. Edmund N. Santurri and William Werpehowski, (Washington, D.C.: Georgetown University Press, 1992).

6. Ibid., 2.

7. Ibid., 2–3.

8. Anders Nygren, *Agape and Eros*, trans. P. Watson (Chicago: University of Chicago Press, 1982).

9. See Paul Ramsey, *War and the Christian Conscience* (Durham, N.C.: Duke University Press, 1961), chap. 3.

10. *Watts v. Watts*, 137 Wis.2d 506, 405 N.W.2d 303 (1987). Other jurisdictions have considered these general issues. See, e.g., *Hewitt v. Hewitt*, 77 Ill.2d 49, 394 N.E.2d 1204 (1979), *Kozlowski v. Kozlowski*, 80 N.J. 378 (1979). See also *Marvin v. Marvin*, 18 Cal.3d 660, 557 P.2d 106 (1976).

11. A full consideration of the underlying issues would require accounting for ways in which the law has recognized and protected the rights of women in stable heterosexual relationships that were nonetheless not *marital* relationships. For example, in the eighteenth and nineteenth centuries, the state of Louisiana recognized contracts of plaçage between white men and free women of color. The relationships were sometimes called "mariages de la main gauche," or left-handed marriages. See, e.g., Gwendolyn Midlo Hall, *Africans in Colonial Louisiana: The Development of Afro-Creole Culture in the Eighteenth Century* (Baton Rouge: Louisiana State University Press, 1995).

12. Outka, "Universal Love and Impartiality," 9.

13. Ibid., 71.

14. Ibid., 30, citing Basil Mitchell, *Morality: Religious and Secular* (Oxford: Clarendon Press, 1980), 144.

15. For an introduction to the case law, see E. Allen Farnsworth, *Contracts*, 4th ed. (New York: Aspen Publishers, 2004).

16. Joseph Raz, *The Morality of Freedom* (Oxford: Clarendon Press, 1988), 204.

17. See, e.g., *Williams v. Walker Thomas Furniture*, 350 F.2d 445 (D.C. Cir. 1965). Rent-to-own arrangements have seen a resurgence in the recent recession. See, e.g., Jennifer Latson, "Many Buying into Rent-to-Own Idea during Recession," *Houston Chronicle*, 13 July 2009, www.chron.com/business/article/Many-buying-into-rent-to-own-idea-during-recession-1550537.php.

18. This is not to say that the law ought not to address the disparity in power between merchants and customers. Some scholars have suggested that the appropriate vehicle is consumer protection legislation rather than the common law. See, e.g., Stewart Macaulay, "Bambi Meets Godzilla: Reflections on Contracts Scholarship and Teaching vs. State Unfair and Deceptive Trade Practices and Consumer Protection Statutes," *Houston Law Review* 26 (1989): 575–601.

19. For good introductions to these areas of inquiry, see D. Kelly Weisberg, ed., *Feminist Legal Theory: Foundations* (Philadelphia: Temple University Press, 1993), and Richard Delgado and Jean Stefancic, *Critical Race Theory: An Introduction* (New York: New York University Press, 2001). For close analysis of the leading rent-to-own case using critical race and gender analysis, see Muriel Morisey Spence, "Teaching Williams v. Walker-Thomas Furniture Co.," *Temple Political and Civil Rights Law Review* 3 (1993/1994): 89–105. For a different perspective, see Russell Korobkin, "A 'Traditional' and 'Behavioral' Law-and-Economics Analysis of Williams v. Walker-Thomas Furniture Company," *University of Hawaii Law Review* 26 (2004): 441–67.

20. Lon L. Fuller & William R. Perdue, Jr., "The Reliance Interest in Contract Damages: 1," *Yale Law Journal* 46 (1936): 62.

21. Outka writes: "Often too, both my initiatives and responses are constrained and otherwise affected by interactions with others. In fact our lives are suffused with impure cases: unwanted decisions such as acceding to 'coercive offers' in corporate business transactions, firing incompetent employees in need, giving money under threat to drug addicts, plotting to bring down tyrannical governments, etc. Neither my situation as a recipient nor the complexity of these cases receive their due when we focus single-mindedly on autonomous initiatives." Outka, "Universal Love and Impartiality," 70.

22. See, e.g., Paul Ramsey, *The Patient as Person*, 2nd ed. (New Haven: Yale University Press, 2002), xlv-xlvi.

23. The first meaning of "covenant" offered in the *Oxford English Dictionary* is: "A mutual agreement between two or more persons to do or refrain from doing certain acts; a compact, contract, bargain; sometimes, the undertaking, pledge, or promise of one of the parties. Phrases, to make or enter into a c.; to hold, keep, break c. (No longer in ordinary use, exc. when coloured by legal or theological associations.)." In the legal realm, the term "covenant" connotes a formal agreement, often an agreement under seal.

24. Outka, "Universal Love and Impartiality," 2.

25. Contract law does require a promise to be explicitly made in order to be enforceable. The courts will ask whether one party's conduct would lead a reasonable person in the other party's shoes to infer that a promise had been made.

26. Some scholars are exploring the relationship between legal marriage and economic status. See Christina M. Gibson-Davis, Kathryn Edin, and Sara McLanahan, "High Hopes but Even Higher Expectations: The Retreat from Marriage Among Low-Income Couples," *Journal of Marriage and Family* 67 (2005): 1301–12.

27. Outka, "Universal Love and Impartiality," 70.

28. Outka addresses this debate elsewhere, e.g., in Chapter 4 of *Agape*.

29. John T. Noonan, Jr., *Persons and Masks of the Law*, 2nd ed. (Berkeley: University of California Press, 2002), 4. For my analysis of Noonan's work in a broader theological and philosophical context, see M. Cathleen Kaveny, "Listening for the Future in the voices of the Past: John T. Noonan, Jr. on Love and Power in Human History," *Journal of Law and Religion* 11:1 (1994–1995): 203–227.

30. Noonan, *Persons and Masks*, chap. 2.

31. Ibid., 6–8.

32. Outka, "Universal Love and Impartiality," 7.

33. Paul Ramsey, *The Just War* (New York: Scribner, 1968), 143.

34. "Too often we focus on those cases of human interaction where actual or threatened physical violence looms as a definite possibility, to be either affirmed or rejected. We attend too little to the far more extensive number of cases where no one meaningfully envisages physical violence, not the agent, the recipient, or affected third parties, but where resistance in a wider sense looms as a definite possibility. To attend to the latter encourages us to interpret the law of love comprehensively, in accordance with the claim noted earlier that moral principles do more than tell agents what they may or may not do; they also tell victims what sort of treatment they may and may not object to, resist, or demand." Outka, "Universal Love and Impartiality," 39.

35. *Watts*, 405 N.W.2d at 308 (emphasis omitted). While not uncontroversial, this claim is supported by recent research in family law. See, e.g., Margaret F. Brinig and Steven L. Nock, "Marry Me, Bill: Should Cohabitation be the (Legal) Default Option?," *Louisiana Law Review* 64 (2004): 403–42 and Margaret Brinig, *Law, Family, and Community* (Chicago: University of Chicago Press, 2010), chap. 1.

36. See, e.g., William Werpehowski, "'Agape' and Special Relations," in *The Love Commandments: Essays in Christian Ethics and Moral Philosophy*, ed. Santurri and Werpehowski (Washington, D.C.: Georgetown University Press, 1992), 138–56.

37. Outka, "Universal Love and Impartiality," 12.

38. One might object that this need not be the case; perhaps they saw themselves as deliberately misleading outsiders into thinking they were married, while preserving their own strong sense that they were merely living together. In my view, this objection fails to account for the fact that they held themselves as married to a wide variety of audiences, both public and private—apparently including their own children. Moreover, and more narrowly, the fact that the Wattses held themselves out to the federal and state governments as married for some purposes ought to have led them to expect that those governments would treat them as married for other purposes as well.

39. The American Law Institute has advocated treating cohabiting couples who break up analogously to divorcing couples for purposes of property settlement. See *Principles of the Law of Family Dissolution: Analysis and Recommendations* (Philadelphia: ALI, 2002). That position has been critiqued by a number of family law scholars. See Robin Fretwell Wilson, ed., *Reconceiving the Family: Critique on the ALI Principles of the Law of Family Dissolution* (New York: Cambridge University Press, 2006).

40. Laura Pettreca, "Prenuptial Agreements: Unromantic but Important," *USA Today*, 11 March 2010, www.usatoday.com/money/perfi/basics/2010-03-08-prenups08_CV_N.htm.

41. Wisconsin repealed its criminal prohibition of fornication in 1983.

42. *Watts*, 448 N.W.2d at 311, citing *In Matter of Estate of Steffes*, 95 Wis.2d 490, 514, 290 N.W.2d 697, 709 (1980).

43. *Watts*, 448 N.W.2d at 312.

44. See *Watts v. Watts*, 152 Wis.2d 370, 448 N.W.2d 292 (1992). Why no award on the contract claim? On this second appeal, the Supreme Court found that neither party had the opportunity to argue that the contract had been breached, and remanded to the lower court for a new trial on this issue. After this point, however, the Wattses disappear from the official case reports.

45. James's expert, naturally, set this amount more cautiously; he estimated that James's net worth increased by $851,306.53 during the relevant time period.

15

Global Health Justice

Love as Transformative Political Action

LISA SOWLE CAHILL

GLOBAL HEALTH CARE is a subset of the problems of global justice and global poverty as well as of gender justice worldwide. Problems of global justice, including health-care access, demand a practical and political response from all Christians. This requires that Christians develop the significance of Christian love beyond personal virtue and beneficence and beyond the cultivation of a distinctive communal way of life. These meanings of love are biblically attested, have been central in Christian tradition, and remain vital to Christian ethics today. Yet Christian social ethics for a global era must also show why a personal and ecclesial ethic of love of God and neighbor demands moral responsibility for society and social structures and why that responsibility expands beyond any one culture to an intercultural and interreligious environment. Love must also meet standards of justice, including the empowerment of past victims of injustice. Moreover, a contemporary Christian ethics of love must display the grounds of its hope that change is possible (1 Pet. 3:15).

At least until recently, Catholic social teaching has been stronger than most Protestant social ethics in giving grounds for commitment to global justice, for the belief that structural change can be accomplished, and for the expectation that Christians will find cooperative global partners in this endeavor. Calls for global movement toward the "universal common good" have been prominent in the encyclicals of John XXIII, Paul VI, John Paul II, Benedict XVI, and Francis (Laudato Si, 2015). However, Catholicism has in the past given more limited attention to the biblical and theological bases of Christian identity and Christian ethics as well as to the liturgical and communal formation of Christian virtues that support social action. Protestantism, on the other side, is much more internally diverse than Catholicism (though global Catholicism is hardly unitary). In general, though, many heirs of the sixteenth-century Reformers have been more "Augustinian" in their skepticism about transformation of the social and political order and about the convergence of Christian social ideals and those of other traditions.

Although Augustine expects Christians to engage in politics, he is not optimistic about this-worldly transformation. Peace of a sort can be had as "the well-ordered concord" of civic obedience and rule, but the civic order does not participate in the virtue or peace that comes from charity. "The heavenly city . . . makes use of this peace only because it must," not because earthly peace is a foretaste of redemption (Augustine, *CD* 19.17).

As a result, the theological grounds of a transformationist global social ethic in an Augustinian vein are not highly developed, even though Protestant voices often do call at the practical level for commitment to addressing global problems such as violent conflict, climate change, and the AIDS pandemic.[1] A relative strength of Protestantism traditionally, however, has been the elaboration of a biblically based worldview in which participants engage in character-forming practices and distinctive ways of life. The salient and highly influential American voice in this regard is Stanley Hauerwas.[2] Many Protestant theologians and social ethicists also do bridge over to broader and more pluralistic social and political analysis by invoking philosophically established principles such as justice, equity, respect for persons, and human rights.

Another issue within Christianity's social agenda—one that has become increasingly important in recent decades, especially with the rise of global Christianity—is the need to go beyond simply serving the poor and the excluded by empowering them to identify goals, make demands, and take action. Liberation theologies, Catholic and Protestant, attest to new appreciation of this objective. As movements of decolonization, emancipation, and demo-cratic participation gather force, and as eloquent and socially engaged theologies emerge from Latin America, Africa, and Asia, Christians worldwide recognize that social responsi-bility must take the form of respect for the insights, aspirations, and agency of different communities. Global health-care ethics is an excellent illustration of this challenging trend. The imbalance of global health resources, the cultural and practical limitations of many donor programs, the differences among views of health and health care worldwide, and the need for sustainable health-care structures in the "two-thirds" world all call for innovative and culturally appropriate ways to translate Christian love into more just global patterns of health-care access.

Christian Love and Its Ethical Content

The first problem in moving toward a Christian perspective on global health care is to estab-lish what the basic concept and virtue of Christian love implies for the dispositions and actions of the agent. Much of the twentieth-century discussion of this topic was governed by the proposal of Anders Nygren that love as agape is a form of self-sacrificial concern for the immediate neighbor in need. This proposal must now be brought up against the call for Christians to take active responsibility for structural sin and its reversal. Moreover, if devel-oping the agency of the poor is a proper Christian social goal, love must also be understood at times to involve efforts to change one's own circumstances and those of one's social peers. According to Nygren, however, agape excludes self-interest and the preferential treatment of individuals toward whom one is more closely connected. Agape is disinterested in reci-procity and reward, agape is strictly differentiated from justice, and agape cannot be the basis of a general social ethic because it focuses on the concrete need of the concrete neigh-bor, because it entails the sacrifice of personal welfare, and because it depends on Christian conformity to the example of Christ. Nygren embraces what he interprets to be Martin Luther's position, that the Christian is a channel of God's spontaneous, groundless, self-giving love, one who by grace and faith "allows the divine love to stream out over the world."[3] But Nygren does not connect agape to a specific social agenda or the social and political infrastructures that would be required to embody the effects of love in a society beyond the church.

Neither Luther nor Nygren interpret Christian love streaming into the world as a force for social change that is either defensible in philosophical terms or culturally transformative. Although it is true that for Luther, people of faith are "Christs to one another" and, as "Christians-in-relation," expand the effects of Christian love into their social networks,[4] Luther did not see Christian love as having a significant impact on sinful social structures in "the temporal kingdom." This trajectory has a powerful hold on Christian identity and imagination because of the undeniable grip of sin on the world, the biblical and theological centrality of redemption through the cross, and the importance of encouraging and witnessing to Christian courage and fidelity in hostile environments. This essay will argue, however, that these themes should not be permitted to override the equally authoritative biblical and theological themes of incarnation, resurrection, renewal in the Spirit, and the practical and temporal experience of God's inbreaking reign.

The nineteenth- and early twentieth-century Social Gospel movement and papal social encyclicals already challenged the premise that the effects of love would be limited primarily to the sphere of the church. After the Second World War, in view of an emerging international language of human rights and democracy, Christian churches and theologians began to explore more intensively the possible connections between Christian love and more universal moral themes, values, and principles. The encyclicals of John XXIII (*Pacem in Terrris*, 1963) and Paul VI (*Populorum Progressio*, 1968) spoke of topics like human rights, international development and peace, and the universal common good. From the Protestant side, Gene Outka has been a major force behind a trajectory of convergence between agape as impartial neighbor love and Kantian "respect for persons."[5] The rapprochement between specifically Christian language and concepts and those of Western philosophy and politics has facilitated a Christian move from personal ethics and community ethics to Christian social and political ethics in Western democracies and to a global ethics in which Christians from various regions make common cause with members of other religions and traditions. But as I hope will become clear in the course of this discussion, Christians still need to develop the *theological* reasons why they can trust that their efforts will actually bring results and why they can count on non-Christians to share common goals.

Contemporary Protestant Social Ethics

Toward the latter half of the twentieth century, Christian churches and spokespersons became increasingly visible advocates for social changes such as civil rights, an end to the Vietnam War, and respect for the voices and rights of patients in biomedical decision making. Many theologians were involved in the emergence of the new field of public "medical ethics," which addressed issues such as protection of human research subjects, the use of new technologies with limited availability, the movement in favor of physician-assisted suicide, abortion, and genetic research.[6] All of these had social and policy implications, leading theologians to ponder the meaning and role of their theological convictions in light of broader discussions.

Taking Nygren's treatise on agape as his basis, Gene Outka draws a connection between the universal, generous, and undiscriminating character of agape and the modern conviction of the equal worth of each human being. Following Kant's proposal that moral reason requires "equal regard" for every human individual,[7] Outka concludes that the religious recognition of all as equally creatures of God finds a parallel in the philosophical and humanistic recognition that all persons have irreducible value.[8] Outka further contends that agape entails "active concern for the neighbor's well-being,"[9] understood to include a relation to God;

"psycho-physical" needs such as food, drink, shelter, clothing, affection, and self-respect; subjective identity and integrity; and freedom as initiative and action.[10] In response to the love of God, and granting the limits of finitude,[11] Outka concludes that the agent is morally obligated to seek these goods for others and to do so in *social* as well as personal relations, including cooperation with and for the well-being of those whom the agent will never meet directly.[12] "Pressures" in these directions are included in the biblical expansion of love toward the stranger and enemy.[13]

According to Outka, the outpouring of agape must be limited by justice, insofar as justice requires fair treatment of multiple possible recipients of our beneficence.[14] Given our finite resources, Outka finds agapeistic ethics compatible with a definition of justice as "to each according to his needs," with the needs of all considered equally.[15] Practically, then, those with the greatest need would receive priority in access to resources, a conclusion not unlike the preferential option for the poor found in liberation theology and Catholic social teaching.[16] If not all needs can be met, as is often the case given the scarcity of health-care resources, Outka proposes that similar cases should at least be treated similarly.[17] More than justice, agape refers to deep, basic dispositions and loyalties of the agent.[18] In particular, Outka takes agape to extend beyond justice and foster an imaginative identification with the other and the other's situation as well as a commitment to promote other people's interests actively, attentively, and even at personal cost.[19]

Neither special concern for those to whom we have a special relation ("friends") nor concern for our own welfare is ruled out in Outka's interpretation, as long as all others are regarded for their own sake, not only for our positive relation to them, and as long as self-interest is reined in by the spontaneous generosity of agape.[20] In fact, far from being excluded, reciprocity and communion are "the ideal fruition of agape" by Outka's accounting.[21]

Agape of course presupposes the grace of divine love and communion with God as context and source of personal and social action. Envisioning the possibility of legal and administrative policies that might reform institutional structures in the direction of equal regard and preference for those in greatest need, Outka sounds an Augustinian note:

> Our fear of illness and of dying may be so pronounced and immediate that we will seize the nearly automatic connections between privilege, wealth, and power if we can. . . . And our capacity for taking in rival points of view may be too limited. . . . Those who believe that justice is the pre-eminent virtue of institutions and that a case can be convincingly made on behalf of justice for equal access to health care would do well to ponder such conflicts and perplexities. . . . They would reflect a greater awareness of what we have to confront.[22]

In his 2002 presidential address to the Society of Christian Ethics (SCE), Outka provides additional Augustinian theological resources to begin to address these "recalcitrant" facts of human existence in ways that may advance Christian advocacy for improvements to global health.[23] From the standpoint of particular Christian identity, community, and belief, there is a value to God of creaturely goods that no historical conflict can erase. The already-existing order of things in relation to God is the source of hope, not only for the eschatological reconciliation of conflict but also for the temporal possibility of integrating human loves and human responsibilities to God, neighbor, and self. Even a world "gone wrong" is essentially good and "retains the memory of what it ought to have been."[24] It is possible, therefore, despite sin, to look for "the common good, tranquility, peaceableness, truthfulness, friendliness, justice and the other's advantage."[25] There is a "basic intelligibility of appeals to justice."[26] Those beyond the church—like Muslims—are not in a "kingdom of evil," presumably because of their memory of the good.[27]

This memory of good that enables earthly justice is similar to the idea common to both Aquinas and the Reformers—and perhaps to a lesser degree, Augustine—that human nature and reason are not destroyed by sin. Humans retain the capacity to seek and realize the good in temporal terms, even if human virtues and accomplishments are not salvific. Thomas Aquinas is different from Augustine and the Reformers not because Aquinas sees nature as totally intact or because he sees saving grace as universal but because he sees nature as less corrupted and allows that even purely human virtue is authentic virtue, albeit imperfect (Aquinas, *ST* I-II.65.2). Outka is similar to Aquinas (*ST* I-II.94.2) when he sets out the practical requirements of justice in terms of human well-being or flourishing, emphasizing such goods as truth telling, physical well-being, restraint from domination of others, protection of innocent life, and conservation of the natural environment.[28]

Outka gestures beyond natural justice to the possibility of grace also active in social relations when he claims that "God's love may instruct, empower and transform how we interact with others," especially when we relate to others out of communion with God.[29] In making this point, Outka cites Aquinas's metaphor of the Christian life as "friendship with God."[30] He does not appropriate explicitly Aquinas's view that charity, as a sharing in the divine nature, is the condition of this friendship (*ST* I-II.62.1), and he leaves for another day the status of Muslims in relation to saving grace. This suggests two further tasks for global Christian ethics: to validate the historical and practical sanctification of Christians so concrete social relations are transformed and to extend theologically that process to others so a larger social process is possible. Memory of the good, specified in terms of specific human goods, forms one basis of a common social ethics. Beyond this, the vision of grace as active socially through Christian action gives a special warrant for Christians' investment in the world.

In addition to the theological grounding of a Christian commitment to the world, a robust Christian social ethics will also require theological reasons to hope for actual directions and spheres of transformation in practices, politics, and institutions. These are places in which Christians and others participate and together constitute a common social world. The theological question is whether, beyond the remnants of natural justice, Christ through the Holy Spirit is at work to create these spheres anew. Finally, if Christ's transforming Spirit is in fact present in human social relationships, Christian social ethics demands consideration of the specific means by which or through which this occurs. Such means include corporate action, both local and global, as well as individual conversion and commitment.

The remainder of this essay will take up these challenges. First, it will argue theologically for the security of sanctification as a dimension of saving grace by mining the resources of new interpretations of Luther's view of justification, now proposed to entail participation in Christ. Outka's 2002 SCE address, in which he appeals to the existing order of all things in God as the basis for social action and hope, effectively extends this development. Second, the present essay will offer Christological and Augustinian reasons for Christian commitment to the common good. Third, it will suggest why Augustinian Christians may hope in a "new creation," whose historical beginning enlivens justice in many faiths and cultures. This hope is a premise of any Christian expectation that, despite continuing sin and evil, sanctification can bear fruit in society as well as in the church. Finally, turning to the problem of global justice in access to health resources, I will investigate how the action of Christian churches, local communities, and networks of global cooperation can function together as means of social transformation.

Grace and Sanctification

Although strong doctrines of sanctification are more typically associated with Aquinas and Catholic theology, Augustine and several forms of Protestant theology affirm them as well. Indeed, a new strand of Luther interpretation suggests that a strong doctrine of sanctification may be possible in even this branch of Augustinian Christianity. Since the 1970s, ecumenical discussions between the Orthodox and Lutheran churches, originally in Finland and then internationally, have instigated theological reflection on the Eastern concept of "divinization" (*theosis*) and on whether an analogue can be found in Luther. In the background, obviously, is the increasingly evident phenomenon of globalization and the fact of military and economic exploitation by the more powerful nations, even as overt colonization declines. Looking beyond their own national borders, churches in the so-called developed regions have become increasingly cognizant of global responsibilities. A new Christian commitment to global social justice is captured not only in papal social encyclicals but also in statements and programs of the World Council of Churches and of members churches, such as the Lutheran World Federation.

The theological leader of the new Finnish interpretation of Luther is Tuomo Mannermaa, whose 1980 proposal became available in English almost two decades later.[31] Mannermaa holds that the theology of Luther himself was distorted by later Lutheranism, which followed the theology of Melancthon and the *Formula of Concord* of 1577. The target of the latter was the doctrine of Osiander, and not, as might be assumed, objectionable "Catholic" doctrines of sanctification premised on an essential change in human nature. Osiander agreed with Luther that God dwells in the believer (rather than changing human nature in itself), but he separated the divine and human natures of Christ and emphasized the indwelling of the divine nature alone. In its response, the *Formula of Concord* asserts that the fullness of God dwells in the believer but adds that this indwelling "follows the antecedent justification by faith," to the effect that God is not yet present in the believer when he or she is declared "righteous through faith for Christ's sake." As a consequence, in later Lutheran theology, "grace and gift are separated and emphasis has been laid on the forensic aspect."[32]

According to the Finnish school, however, both grace and gift are given in Christian righteousness, through the indwelling and real presence of Christ. Righteousness is never just forensic but is always effective in the lives of those on whom it is bestowed. "Christ himself, both his person and his work, is the Christian righteousness, that is, the 'righteousness of faith.' Christ—and therefore also his entire person and work—is really and truly present in the faith itself."[33] Faith means precisely "participation in the person of Christ,"[34] and even participation in the divine being, essence or nature.[35] "In other words," according to Luther himself, "God becomes man so that man may become God."[36] In his *Lectures on Galatians*, Luther announces God's promise that "we are to become participants of the divine nature and be exalted so high in nobility that we are not only to become loved by God through Christ, and have His favor and grace as the highest and most precious shrine, but also to have him, the Lord Himself, dwelling in us in His fullness."[37]

The characteristics of God that are present in Christ—albeit not without the continuing struggle with sin[38]—are "righteousness, wisdom, power, holiness, joy, peace, eternal life—and especially love."[39] Hence, the Christian, whose true agent is Christ, is capable of and will do good works.[40] Veli-Matti Kärkkäinen notes that "Luther's understanding of love is completely dominated by his faith in the incarnation," the union of humanity and divinity in Christ and of our humanity with God in Christ.[41] The Christian becomes a "Christ" to the neighbor, identifying with his or her suffering, loving without considerations of worthiness, and willingly taking up Christ's cross.[42]

New Versions of Augustinian Politics

The new appreciation of the unity of justification and sanctification in Luther's own theology furnishes a theological basis on which to affirm that with God's help, the Christian life inaugurates a different historical reality in which the hold of exploitative self-interest and Augustine's *libido dominandi* is loosened. Consequently, the Christian loves the neighbor for Christ's sake . . . but does the Christian love the world and its citizens for themselves? The apparent theological barrier to an affirmative answer is Augustine's proviso that only God is worthy to be loved as an end: other people are loved for God's sake, and all creatures have an instrumental value in relation to love of God. Nevertheless, some revisionist interpretations of Augustine by a new generation of Christian social ethicists are challenging the inference that other persons cannot properly be loved for their own sakes if God is the *summum bonum*. These ethicists seek to build a more engaged, constructive Augustinian politics that can begin to remedy injustices in the globalization era.[43]

Contrary to stereotypes, argues Eric Gregory, Augustine's Christology does not demand a mere grudging acceptance of the earthly city with its worldly "virtues," structures, and systems of order. Gregory is clear-eyed about the "schizophrenic political morality" that can result and has resulted in the past from too strong a distinction of Augustine's "two cities." At one pole is "an otherworldly or sectarian" politics, competing with another that is "zealously persecutorial," and both can encourage Christians to adopt an attitude toward political life of "indifference and ascetic inwardness," disguised as love of God.[44] Innovatively carrying Augustinian theology toward love of creaturely realities in themselves and for the sake of their well-being and fulfillment, Gregory envisions a new compact between Christianity and the meliorist politics of modern liberal democracy.[45] The Christian churches need not wage war against liberalism and all its spawn after all, nor concede that the prospects for historical justice are bleak. Gregory enjoins Christians to join with other citizens in political practices that move toward "an actual society that is more just, more egalitarian, and more charitable."[46]

Gregory agrees with Augustine that human beings are "bundles of loves,"[47] which makes the key religious and moral question the rightful target of those loves. But he takes issue with the idea that, from an Augustinian perspective, the inherently disordered loves of most people and peoples make them ill-suited to be political partners with Christians. Instead, he argues, human beings are capable of feelings of solidarity in response to mutual vulnerability and dependence; this makes possible something like a political ethics of care, restated by Gregory as an Augustinian civic virtue of love.[48] Granting that he stretches Augustine's own worldview, Gregory urges readers to appreciate that Augustine's theology of the incarnation undermines his apparent insistence that no creature is to be loved for its own sake (Augustine, *On Christian Doctrine* 1.22.20). (Here Gregory responds to Hannah Arendt's critique of Christian politics.[49])

Gregory's basic insight is that through the Incarnation, the Word inheres in every creature. "Augustine's God is a worldly God."[50] A key text is Book 10 of *The City of God*. Each and every person is God's temple, "since He deigns to dwell both in the whole harmonious body and in each of us singly (*CD* 10.3)."[51] Therefore, created beings, as loved by God, may also be loved by human beings. As Augustine himself sermonizes, "The love which loves the neighbor is no other than that which loves God. It is not therefore a matter of two loves. With the same love we give the neighbor, we love God too."[52] To so love is to imitate and share in God's own humility. This love also takes us into the realms of citizenship and political responsibility:[53]

> The ontology of Augustinian eudaimonism remains important, but it is radically transformed by a Christology which resists the competitive tournament of loves that critics imagine is inspired by a Platonic theory of the *summum bonum*. If God is in solidarity with humanity through the Incarnation, then creatures can enjoy the gifts of God even as they are perennially tempted to enjoy them in the wrong way. There is, then, an ethical and ontological relation between God and the world.[54]

In a similar proposal, Charles Mathewes sees Augustine as "world-affirming," and even as conducive to a view of the "sacramentality of created reality as a whole."[55] Again taking Augustine's theology of love as his keynote, Mathewes depicts the nature of reality as essentially harmonious rather than agonistic or conflictual.[56] Political conflict is a symptom of disordered loves, but the aim, horizon, and norm of politics is "harmonious community."[57] Thus, political action, while not ultimate, can still be "sacramental," insofar as it mediates proleptically the eschatological community of the kingdom of God.[58] Politics can be part of a eucharistic way of life that transfigures or "transubstantiates" the world.[59] Thus, the churches should be involved directly in civic life; Mathewes offers examples of success from work against poverty and unemployment, the US civil rights movement, and struggles against colonial rule, apartheid, the dictatorship of Pinochet, and Eastern European communism.[60] For Mathewes, "public engagement is inescapably an attempt to participate in the divine work of exultation and glorification—and for us, deification."[61]

An additional implication of both Gregory's incarnational Augustinianism and Mathewes's construal of politics as sacramental and sanctifying is that the grace of Christ is at work not only in the political worlds of Christians but in every person, culture, and religion. In other words, it not only is incumbent on Christians to be committed to the political societies in which they participate; there is also a theological rationale for expecting resonance globally with Christian work for justice and for anticipating that justice will in fact be served through political engagement.

A qualification to be made to the new Augustinian politics of love (here going back to Aquinas and Outka) is that love cannot violate justice, and justice and love require taking the standpoint of the poor. A valid modern insight is that justice requires basic equal regard of all persons, entailing compensatory action toward those most left out of social systems. Although Augustine did not suggest that love must be accountable to justice as basic equality, the idea is latent in Jesus's inclusive kingdom ministry and inclusive table fellowship and in the parables of the widow's mite, the Samaritan woman at the well, and the healing that restores those who are possessed by demons or afflicted by "unclean" illnesses to their social place. Love as equal regard requires empowering the capacity for agency that all individuals and groups value in and for themselves. As Outka concludes, then, love as equal regard cannot exclude an appropriate place for self-interest. Most clearly, action or advocacy on one's own behalf is morally valid in the struggle for equitable political and social participation and for access to basic goods.

Love and Global Health Care

Work for more just global access to the goods of health and health care is a stellar example of the case that Christian love can and should be expressed in the sphere of political and social justice. Christians are obliged and empowered to join efforts with others toward that end, and progress is a warranted hope. Multiple examples could be given of the concrete truth of such claims, particularly in the growing international commitment to alleviate the "diseases of the poor," efforts that have been slowed but not derailed by the global economic crisis.[62]

Contrary to the prevalent misconception that diseases of the poor, like AIDS and malaria, are ignored by the wealthy, global health analyst Laurie Garrett argues that appeals to compassion and altruism have worked incredibly well in drawing world resources to problems of global health.[63] Over the last few decades, the HIV/AIDS pandemic has led to a "surge in funding" for several diseases of the poor, especially AIDS, tuberculosis, and malaria. Moreover, drug companies reduced prices drastically between 1996 and 1999, and donations for health programs increased tenfold. As of August 2006, in the first six years of its existence, the Bill and Melinda Gates Foundation had donated $6.6 billion to global health. Partly at the urging of evangelical Christian supporters, the Bush administration increased its overseas development assistance, especially for health, from $11.4 billion in 2001 to $27.5 billion in 2005, an increase of 250 percent. The President's Emergency Plan for AIDS Relief (PEPFAR) is the US initiative to combat the global HIV/AIDS epidemic. The year 2010 was the first that funding for this program did not increase, owing to unprecedented budget constraints.[64] The World Bank has also impressively increased its attention to AIDS and other diseases in recent years, which is particularly noteworthy since it did not even put health on its official development agenda until 1993. Poor nations themselves also are dedicating a larger percentage of their budgets to health.[65]

Unfortunately, however, not all these programs are proving as effective as they might in curbing AIDS and other diseases. According to Garrett, this is due to many factors, all of which serve as useful reminders of the truth in Augustinian pessimism about human nature. First, funds get siphoned off because of corruption, for example, in the form of padded prices for transport and warehousing and theft of drugs for the black market. Second, funding is undermined by lack of cooperation, coordination, and efficiency among the multiple donor efforts involved in these projects. Third, the effective use of funds is reduced when donors target high-profile diseases rather than more significant killers like maternal death around childbirth or infant death from respiratory and intestinal infections. For example, partly because of the stigma associated with AIDS, most HIV/AIDS-related funding is dedicated to "stand-alone programs" such as education, testing, drug distribution, hospices, and orphanages. Given these programs' isolation from the rest of the health-care system, resources devoted to HIV/AIDS do not benefit the system as a whole.

Fourth, existing infrastructures are inadequate to distribute and administer donated health funds and goods. Of critical importance is the shortage of personnel. Nurses, doctors, and other health workers are attracted to higher-paying jobs in the developed world or in special-target, donor-funded projects in their home countries. As Garrett concludes, "Donors and those working on the ground must figure out how to build not only effective local health infrastructures but also local industries, franchises, and other profit centers that can sustain and thrive from increased health-related spending. For the day will come in every country when the charity eases off and programs collapse, and unless workable local institutions have already been established, little will remain to show for all of the current frenzied activity."[66]

Paul Farmer, lauded for his work among the poor in Haiti and other locales, has learned to "horizontalize" funding so that it affects the broader infrastructure, since most patients suffer from more than one disease.[67] An example is the training of local health workers to "accompany" those receiving home-based therapy. And nurses and doctors are being attracted back to rural health facilities that are on the way to being more than last stops for the dying.[68] At the same time, however, Farmer does agree that very often, if not always, the "stovepiping" of isolated programs can have the pernicious effects on public health infrastructure that Garrett describes.[69]

At least part of the solution may lie in the development of local market participation to empower those who currently do not have access to adequate health care and to help build health-delivery systems. Most theologians and religious bodies interested in alleviating global poverty are highly suspicious of markets, partly because of the Christian ethic of love's long-standing hostility to self-interest and partly because of the actual deleterious effects of global capitalism. Nevertheless, to combat maldistribution of health resources, Garrett advises international leaders and organizations to "draw from the business world."[70] They must be more creative in imagining a way to integrate community health workers into multi-million-dollar budgets and into a local-to-global system of "volume purchasing and distribution, data retrieval, training, and management."[71] Local enterprise could be assisted by aid in a way that might generate a sustainable lift in both the local health-care economy and the health-care infrastructure.

To counter skepticism about the role of the market in fighting poverty, recall the Grameen Bank. In 2006 the Grameen Bank and its founder, Muhammad Yunus of Bangladesh, won the Nobel Peace Prize for improving rural development and reducing world poverty by means of microcredit. Yunus defied both conventional lending policies and cultural taboos by giving money to the poorest of the poor, Muslim women in Bangladeshi villages. These women, often borrowing cooperatively, use tiny loans to enter the local economy, making crafts, raising animals, or selling produce. Even street beggars may open a line of credit of about nine US dollars to sell small items to supplement their incomes. By the time Yunus had received the Nobel, the bank had over eight million borrowers and claimed a 98 percent repayment rate. In its citation, the Nobel Prize committee said, "Micro-credit has proved to be an important liberating force in societies where women in particular have to struggle against repressive social and economic conditions."[72] Sustainable local health-care infrastructures are a necessary part of global health-care justice, and they must be attractive and profitable to local communities, both socially and economically.

One example—not a panacea, to be sure—is a system of local clinics in Kenya seeded by funding from a nonprofit organization started for charitable purposes. Perhaps we can see the organization's founder, Scott Hillstrom, as a North American evangelical Christian analogue of Muhammad Yunus. Hillstrom is a wealthy businessman with wide experience in health care, law, technology, and real estate. After a serious car accident in 1995, he decided to return from early retirement and find something more worthwhile to do with his life and his assets. Inspired by an article he read about children's health in the developing world, as well as by the McDonald's french fry, Hillstrom traveled to Kenya. Hillstrom's idea was to start a chain of local health-care franchises that could reach rural areas with reliable, quality medicines at prices that the people could afford yet were profitable enough to support modest investments and hence to be sustainable within the local economy. In Kenya he met and eventually formed a partnership with Eva Ombaka, a pharmaceutical adviser to the World Council of Churches and an expert on the problem of access to essential drugs.[73]

In 1997 Hillstrom and Ombaka founded the HealthStore Foundation, a federation of clinics owned by nurses who provide essential medicines and basic primary care through a chain of Kenyan community health-care workers. By 2006 the CFW network included sixty-five franchises, serving more than 400,000 patients.[74] Since its inception, the HealthStore Foundation has served over two million patients, mostly lower- and middle-income women and children, and is now headed by a Kenyan director, Liza Kimbo.[75]

According to a report of the World Resources Institute, US Agency for International Development (USAID), and Columbia University Business School, HealthStore works by "harnessing the profit motive to deliver public health in Kenya."[76] Yet that is only part of the picture. HealthStore also harnesses foreign aid to pay for the sustainability of health-care infrastructures. Local investors may be motivated by profits, but the transnational system on which they depend is a nonprofit organization supported by international donors. The HealthStore clinics follow a hybrid public-private micro-franchise model, receiving money for some community outreach programs from the Kenyan government. Additional funders are the Rockefeller Foundation, the Bill and Melinda Gates Foundation, and USAID.[77] Procter and Gamble has distributed a new water purification product through HealthStore clinics,[78] and the franchise chain is participating in anti-malaria medicine research with a grant from ExxonMobil, the cooperation of the Kenyan Ministry of Health, and the World Health Organization.[79]

Starting costs for nurse-owned clinics are approximately US$1,700. HealthStore will provide financing for up to $1,500 ($1,000 at no interest and $500 at below-market interest), though many owners raise the money through family and friends. This indicates a complementary role for additional donor organizations, which could help micro-finance start-up costs for clinic franchises. These complementary donor activities could give people at a lower economic level the chance to become business owners, perhaps via collective ownership. In fact, start-up costs for one of the shops profiled in the World Resources Institute report were funded in part by the Christian charity World Vision.[80]

A main advantage of the franchise model is low-cost sourcing of high-quality drugs, central management of regulatory requirements and quality standards, and membership in a wide network with an aggregate reputation for quality, reliability, and transparency. Fees charged are approximately fifty cents per treatment. Most network clinics are self-sustaining, and the donor funding required for central operations is less than US$1 million annually.[81] "Owning a HealthStore clinic is an attractive career option for Kenya's educated nurses and health workers, counterbalancing the strong economic incentive for immigration to OECD [Organisation for Economic Co-operation and Development] countries. . . . HealthStore clinics offer nurses the potential to earn a safe, comfortable salary while serving their communities, helping to reverse the trend of 'brain drain' plaguing Africa."[82] One of the HealthStore clinics operates in the largest slum in Africa, Kibera in Nairobi. In the Kibera case, a nurse with an existing clinic chose to convert to the HealthStore franchise because of the benefits the organization could offer.[83]

From an ethical and social standpoint, the advantages of this model are obvious: greater distribution of health-care resources and more empowerment of those formerly disenfranchised (no pun intended) from the health-care system and from supporting socioeconomic systems. Quite simply, the resources of well-intentioned donors are being harnessed to opportunities for self-determination and community control over health.

Yet one can also detect potential downsides. The first is that like McDonald's, Health-Stores could displace local business and individual entrepreneurs, further sabotaging the local economy and displacing unique or culturally particular ways of meeting health needs. The whole point of a global franchise system is to maintain standards that are not set locally, while providing goods that are not dependent on local conditions alone. This offers a competitive edge in comparison with other types of independent pharmacies and stores. Although some of these independent stores may be serving patients well, they do not have access to the same products at the same prices as the HealthStore clinics.[84]

Nevertheless, it seems clear that the HealthStore clinics have successfully filled a need that was not being met. Rather than undermining a vibrant economy, they apparently stimulated economic growth in a formerly stagnant or even deteriorating situation. Could HealthStore clinics eventually coexist with additional quality health services options rather than squeezing them all out of the market? Competition is an unavoidable fact of market behavior, and both profits and competition stimulate economic development. Thus, the market can play a positive role in enlarging the presence of sustainable health resources in the developing world. However, the emergence of a thriving market in Kenya or elsewhere will also bring the moral challenges of fair access to the market and appropriate limitation of its scope and effects. In the case of HealthStore specifically, it is important that the US partner is not a for-profit corporation but a nonprofit donor. HealthStore is not, after all, McDonald's.

The HealthStore model of transnational cooperation between donors, governments, and local business is obviously only one way to envision the building of health infrastructures in the developing world. One must also consider other measures that would involve national and global governments, and even corporations. These could include required or voluntary humanitarian licensing of patented drugs for local research or development;[85] innovative approaches to target diseases of the poor that emerge from networks in the developing countries themselves;[86] and the possible use of donor funds to underwrite pharmaceutical development and manufacturing. Internationally, academic institutions can also help regional research institutes and pharmaceutical consortiums to build local scientific and clinical capacity and to boost the economic basis of the health-care access system. Research institutes operating on analogy to HealthStore clinics might develop, patent, and market or distribute pharmaceuticals and other health goods in their own countries or regions, using reasonable profits, along with donor aid, to support their efforts. Research expenditures might be controlled by developing and patenting products that are similar to those already under patent in the first world or by taking advantage of humanitarian licensing provisions.

An example of initiatives that begin at the local level (rather than with international donors) to meet local health needs is a business in Ghana, DanAdams. In 2004 a Ghanaian pharmacist, Yaw Adu Gyamfi, founded a generic drug company with three workers; as of 2007, it had grown to 185 employees who were estimated to be contributing to the support of around 400 other people in the community.[87] DanAdams specializes in antiretroviral, antimalarial, and antituberculosis drugs and drugs to treat opportunistic infections in HIV/AIDS patients. Gyamfi is producing AIDS drugs at US$150 per year, rather than the standard US$350–450. There are twelve thousand HIV patients in Ghana and thirty-five pharmaceutical companies in the country, with an additional seven in West Africa; Gyamfi's company is the only one making generics. The company also networks with local churches to educate people about HIV and affirm the need for testing and treatment.

Bristol-Myers was the only patent-holding company to respond positively to a request from Gyamfi for a license; several others did not reply at all. Therefore, the government of Ghana issued compulsory licenses and, according to Gyamfi, he was subsequently pressured by a visit from the chief executive officer of GlaxoSmithKline. DanAdams did not have on-site capacity to complete the testing required for certification as a drug manufacturer approved by the World Health Organization, certification necessary for receipt of Global Fund money. Consequently, DanAdams sent its samples to South Africa for a testing price of $25,000—a considerable sum for a small company. Gyamfi suggests that a good use of donor funds or of humanitarian action by established pharmaceutical companies would be to cover such testing for generics manufacturers.

Practical strategies that are workable and proven need to be combined with love and a preferential option for the poor to produce more inclusive and more sustainable global access to health-care resources. Christians whose politics are motivated by love must also meet the tests of justice: basic equal respect, empowerment of agency and participation, and development and support of practices and institutions, both local and global, to serve the long-term common good. Even if Christian political activists and donors are motivated by altruistic concern, their efforts will go nowhere or even be deleterious if charity is not expressed as empowerment, participation, and structural justice.

As argued with regard to new interpretations of Luther and Augustine, Christians have theological reasons to be confident in the possibility of moral conversion, to be committed to transformative global politics, to work with multiple cultures and religions to further love and justice, and to expect tangible results. All those concerned need to look at what is concretely necessary for full social participation in different social contexts, while people living in those contexts should and must assume leadership roles. Although excesses of the market and the commercialization of basic human needs and goods are to be condemned, sustainable local health-care equity requires improved economic and social participation. Christian love that seeks justice demands intercultural and interreligious cooperation to devise global health-care systems that best represent and serve the persons and communities whom they directly affect.

Notes

1. Evangelical Christians, for example, were vocal advocates for these causes during the 2008 US presidential election campaign.

2. In an extensive corpus, see, for example, Hauerwas's 2000–2001 Gifford Lectures, *With the Grain of the Universe: The Church's Witness and Natural Theology* (Grand Rapids, MI: Brazos Press, 2001).

3. Anders Nygren, *Agape and Eros*, trans. Philip S. Watson (New York: Harper & Row, 1953), 741.

4. Martin Luther, *On Christian Liberty*, trans. W. A. Lambert, ed. Harold J. Grimm (Philadelphia: Fortress Press, 1957), 31; Luther, *Commentary on the Sermon on the Mount*, in *Luther's Works*, ed. Jaroslave Pelikan (St. Louis: Concordia Publishing House, 1956), 21:109.

5. Gene Outka, *Agape: An Ethical Analysis* (New Haven, CT: Yale University Press, 1972); Gene Outka, "Universal Love and Impartiality," in *The Love Commandments: Essays in Christian Ethics and Moral Philosophy*, ed. Edmund N. Santurri and William Werpehowski (Washington, DC: Georgetown University Press, 1992), 1–103; Gene Outka, "Agapeistic Ethics," in *A Companion to the Philosophy of Religion*, ed. Philip L. Quinn and Charles Taliaferro (Cambridge MA: Blackwell, 1997), 481–88.

6. Lisa Sowle Cahill, "Religion and Theology," in *Methods in Medical Ethics*, 2nd ed., ed. Jeremy Sugarman and Daniel Sulmasy (Washington, DC: Georgetown University Press, 2010), 73–90.

7. Outka, *Agape*, 201. For an overview and comparison with other theories of love, see Stephen J. Pope, "Love in Contemporary Christian Ethics," *Journal of Religious Ethics* 23, no. 1 (1995): 167–97. For Outka's rejoinder and Pope's reply, see "Comments," *Journal of Religious Ethics* 26, no. 2 (1998): 435–44.

8. Outka, *Agape*, 206.

9. Ibid., 260.

10. Ibid., 263–65, 267.

11. Ibid., 270.

12. Ibid., 284–85.

13. Outka, "Comment," 436.

14. Outka, *Agape*, 301.

15. Ibid., 91–92.

16. John Paul II, *Sollicitudo rei socialis* (1987), no. 42.

17. Gene Outka, "Social Justice and Equal Access to Health Care," in *Love and Society: Essays in the Ethics of Paul Ramsey*, ed. James Johnson and David Smith, JRE Studies in Religious Ethics, I (Missoula, MT: Scholars Press and American Academy of Religion, 1974), 200.

18. Outka, *Agape*, 310–11.

19. Ibid., 293.

20. Ibid., 281–81, 285–86, 289. These complications are developed further in Outka, "Universal Love and Impartiality."

21. Outka, "Agapeistic Ethics," 487.

22. Outka, "Social Justice and Equal Access," 204. See also "Universal Love and Impartiality," in which Outka names as "recalcitrant data" "the naïve, the sanguine, and the complacent in our practical thought," as well as "the sin located in our endemic partiality to ourselves" (47).

23. Gene Outka, "Theocentric Love and the Augustinian Legacy," *Journal of the Society of Christian Ethics* 22 (2002): 97–114.

24. Ibid., 104, alluding to Augustine's declaration in *The Confessions*, "Whatever is, is good" (VII).

25. Ibid., 102.

26. Ibid., 105.

27. Ibid., 112. Religious differences, according to Outka, should not be "absolutized."

28. Ibid., 105–11.

29. Ibid., 108, 110. Outka evidently refers here to Christians ("we").

30. Ibid., 110, citing Aquinas, *ST* I-II.65.5.

31. See Tuomo Mannermaa, *Christ Present in Faith: Luther's View of Justification*, ed. Kirsi Stjerma (Minneapolis: Fortress Press, 1998); for history of publication, see "Editor's Foreword," vii. See also Carl E. Braaten and Robert W. Jenson, eds., *Union with Christ: The New Finnish Interpretation of Luther* (Grand Rapids, MI: Eerdmans, 1998), which contains a chapter by Mannermaa, "Why Is Luther So Fascinating? Modern Finnish Luther Interpretation"; and Veli-Matti Kärkkäinen, *One with God: Salvation as Deification and Justification* (Collegeville, MN: Liturgical Press, 2004).

32. Kärkkäinen, *One with God*, 56; see Mannermaa, *Christ Present*, 3–6.

33. Mannermaa, *Christ Present*, 5.

34. Ibid., 8.

35. Tuomo Mannermaa, "Justification and *Theosis* in Lutheran-Orthodox Perspective," in Braaten and Jenson, *Union with Christ*, 33.

36. Ibid., citing an early Christmas sermon, WA1, 28, 25–32.

37. Ibid., 34, citing "*Crucigers Sommerpostille* (1544), WA 21, 458:11–22."

38. Ibid., 20, 63ff., citing for example *Lectures on Galatians*, LW 26:134; 27:72–73.

39. Mannermaa, "Justification and *Theosis*," 35.

40. Ibid., 50.

41. Kärkkäinen, *One with God*, 60.

42. Ibid., 58–61.

43. For a critical overview of some of these authors, see Peter Iver Kaufman, "Christian Realism and Augustinian (?) Liberalism," *Journal of Religious Ethics* 38, no. 4 (2010): 690–724. I agree with Kaufman that, not only was Augustine no liberal progressivist, but once his views on coercion of religious dissidents, torture, and means in war are taken into account, "his tough love no longer looks much like love" (712). However, the worth of these new interpretations does not stand or fall with their strict adherence to Augustine. Rather, as is often done with the "greats" of theological tradition, some revisionist Augustinians are playing on tensions among Augustine's views to arrive at innovative possibilities for the development of his thought.

44. Eric Gregory, *Politics and the Order of Love: An Augustinian Ethic of Democratic Citizenship* (Chicago: University of Chicago, 2008), 21.

45. See ibid., 8 9, for an opening statement of Gregory's thesis.

46. Ibid., 8.

47. Ibid., 21.

48. Ibid., 24, 80.

49. Ibid., 25, referencing Arendt's 1929 Heidelberg dissertation on love and Augustine's *On Christian Doctrine* 1.22.20.

50. Ibid., 323.

51. Ibid., 286.

52. Ibid., 345, citing Augustine, *Sermon* 265.8.9.

53. Ibid., 379–84.

54. Ibid., 323.

55. Charles Mathewes, *A Theology of Public Life* (Cambridge: Cambridge University Press, 2007), 87, 100.

56. Ibid., 276.

57. Ibid., 277.

58. Ibid., 285, 305.

59. Ibid., 294, 315.

60. Ibid., 203, 217, 299.

61. Ibid., 293.

62. See, for example, Sanvee Kokoe Josephine, Akolatse Yao Agapit, and Tatagan-Agbi Komla, *Churches and the HIV/AIDS Pandemic* (Geneva: World Council of Churches / World Alliance of YMCAs, March 2001), www.wcc-coe.org/wcc/what/mission/aids-study-e.pdf, accessed June 21, 2010; Sue Parry, *Responses of the Faith-Based Organizations to HIV/AIDS in Sub Saharan Africa*, www.wcc-coe.org/wcc/what/mission/fba-hiv-aids.pdf, accessed June 21, 2010; Donald Messer, *Breaking the Conspiracy of Silence: Christian Churches and the Global Aids Crisis* (Minneapolis: Fortress Press, 2004); John Paul II, "Address to Promote Health Development Based on Equity, Solidarity, and Charity" (speech, Church and Health in the World: Expectations and Hopes on the Threshold of the Year 2000, November 8, 1997), http://w2.vatican.va/content/john-paul-ii/en/speeches/1997/november/documents/hf_jp-ii_spe_19971108_pastorale-salute.html; and Isabel Phiri and Sarojinii Nadar, eds., *African Women, Religion and Health* (Maryknoll, NY: Orbis, 2006).

63. Laurie Garrett, "The Challenge of Global Health," *Foreign Affairs*, January/February 2007, 14–38.

64. The Henry J. Kaiser Foundation reports, "While appropriations for PEPFAR have fluctuated in recent years, funding has remained essentially flat since 2010" (*The U.S. President's Emergency Plan for AIDS Relief (PEPFAR)*, November 5, 2015, http://kff.org/global-health-policy/fact-sheet/the-u-s-presidents-emergency-plan-for/.

65. Ibid., 17–21.

66. Ibid., 38. Garrett's view that the strengthening of human resources for health is the key to global health equity is confirmed in a report of the Joint Learning Initiative, *Human Resources for Health: Overcoming the Crisis* (2004), www.who.int/hrh/documents/JLi_hrh_report.pdf. The Joint Learning Initiative is a network of global health leaders sponsored by the Rockefeller Foundation and Harvard College and supported by several international donors.

67. Paul Farmer, "From 'Marvelous Momentum' to Health Care for All," *Foreign Affairs*, March/April 2007, 158.

68. Ibid., 156.

69. Ibid., 157.

70. Laurie Garrett, "Midway in the Journey," Global Health: A Foreign Affairs Roundtable, January 24, 2007, www.foreignaffairs.org/special/global_health/garrett, accessed February 5, 2007. This roundtable was conducted online by Foreign Affairs and is no longer available at the site. In it, Paul Farmer, Jeffrey Sachs, Alex de Waal, Roger Bate, Kathryn Boateng, and Laurie Garrett discussed Garrett's essay "The Challenge of Global Health" (see note 63 above).

71. Ibid.

72. Molly Moore, "Micro-Credit Pioneer Wins Peace Prize," *Washington Post*, October 14, 2006, www.washingtonpost.com/wp-dyn/content/article/2006/10/13/AR2006101300211.html, accessed March 17, 2007.

73. Andy Steiner, "A Man with a Mission," *William Mitchell Magazine*, Fall 2004, 10–13.

74. Alyssa Danigelis, "10_HealthStore: In Kenya, a Bare-Bones Health Provider," *Fast Company*, December 20, 2007, www.fastcompany.com/3019113/most-innovative-companies-2007/10healthstore.

75. See the HealthStore Foundation website, www.cfwshops.org/, accessed August 23, 2007.

76. Michelle Fertig and Herc Tzaras, *What Works: HealthStore's Franchise Approach to Healthcare* (Washington, DC: World Resources Institute, November 2005), www.setoolbelt.org/resources/193. The World Resources Institute promotes environmental conservation but is also obviously pro-business. However, the HealthStore Foundation also gets a positive review from the Bellagio Forum for Sustainable Development, an international network of grant-providing institutions committed to "social progress." See Wayne Farmer and Gina Malloy, "The HealthStore Foundation," *The Forum: Magazine of the Bellagio Forum* 14 (March 2006): 12–15, www.cfwshops.org/download/Bellagio_2006.pdf.

77. Fertig and Tzaras, *What Works*, 7.

78. HealthStore Foundation, "Proctor & Gamble," 2006, www.cfwshops.org/news_procter_gamble.html, accessed March 8, 2007.

79. HealthStore Foundation, "ExxonMobil Foundation Anti-Malaria Project," 2006, www.cfwshops.org/news_exxon_mobil_foundation.html, accessed March 8, 2007.

80. Fertig and Tzaras, *What Works*, 32.

81. Ibid., 6.

82. Ibid., 4.

83. Ibid., 34.

84. The case studies of competitors provided by Fertig and Tzaras do include some that appear to be trusted and effective service providers. See *What Works*, 40–42.

85. See Amanda L. Brewster, Audrey R. Chapman, and Stephen Hansen, "Facilitating Humanitarian Access to Pharmaceutical and Agricultural Innovation," *Innovation Strategy Today* 1, no. 3 (2005): 203–16, www.issuelab.org/resource/facilitating_humanitarian_access_to_pharmaceutical_and_agricultural_innovation.

86. Richard T. Mahoney and Carlos M. Morel, "A Global Health Innovation System (GHIS)," *Innovation Strategy Today* 2, no. 1 (2006): 1–12, www.biodevelopments.org/innovation/index.htm, accessed March 17, 2007. As of 2016, this was no longer available at the site.

87. I met Dr. Gyamfi on a panel at the Dorothy Day Center for Faith and Justice, Xavier University, in Cincinnati in April 2007 and obtained most of this information from his presentation and conversation with him. See also the DanAdams website, www.danadamsgh.com/?root=about; and Richard Harris, "Global AIDS Fund Boosts Health, Economy in Ghana," *All Things Considered*, National Public Radio, October 31, 2005, www.npr.org/templates/story/story.php?storyId=4983182, accessed June 22, 2010.

16

Love in the Vocation of Christian Sexual Ethics

A Theologico-Political Meditation

MARK D. JORDAN

ACCORDING TO FAMILIAR PASTORAL ADVICE, human sexual relations must express only a deep and abiding love. Pastors have failed often enough to apply the advice to sexual ethics itself. Even now, when many churches profess to affirm rightly ordered sex, their ethics for it is rarely a work of love.

Instead, Christian sexual ethics has been conducted as controversy. It is one branch of Christian ethics that regularly figures in campaign debates and political reporting. Candidates and network journalists may not care much for Gospel exhortations to selfless humility or courageous pacifism, but they seek out what churches say about contraception or desire between persons of the same genital configuration. Churches are often flattered by this interest. Many court it. They have shown themselves eager to collaborate with all sorts of governments and networks of communication in regulating sex. They have inscribed their views about sex into civil and criminal codes and then enlisted the police as enforcers. Even now, as some Christians back away from legislating religious rules, others boast of wanting to impose them by government decree.

Christian teachings about sex have often preferred to speak a language of power. Sometimes, church and government have joined to fuse Christian precepts with local, national, or imperial strategies. At other times, churches have defied states but then enforced sexual ethics internally through the administration of sacraments, pastoral supervision, and compulsory education. In rearing their young, Christian families mix churchly lessons with prejudices about honor and shame, discipline and indulgence, thrift and waste. So it has hardly ever been possible for Christians to reflect on sex without feeling some combination of legal, political, social, and familial coercions. It cannot be surprising then that love figures belatedly in their reflections. It often appears late and in language hastily borrowed from elsewhere—as an afterthought, an obligatory addition. *Of course* Christian sex should be about love. The *of course* shows the problem. Where is love in the vocation of Christian speech about sex when so many coercions constrain it, outside churches and inside them?

In what follows, I attempt to describe a loving vocation for Christian sexual ethics in the historical present that many of us inhabit. It is a present dominated by a regime of scientific sexuality that Christianity once produced but now seems unable to master.[1] I describe the vocation of Christian ethics under this regime by addressing three questions: What about sex should Christian ethics study? What knowledge of that sex should ethics seek? And what should distinguish a sexual ethics as Christian? I conclude by asking what Christians are supposed to do in the urgent moment while Christian ethics finds its vocation. Each of these sections tries to find a place for love.

What about Sex Should Christian Ethics Study?

Though it is often neglected, the first question to ask about the present vocation of Christian sexual ethics is why Christians need an ethics *for sex* at all. There is no special Christian ethics for blondes or citizens of Missouri because those attributes aren't considered to be ethically significant. When someone asks for an ethics of sex, then, the response should be to pose counterquestions: Why can't you approach sexual situations as you would other situations in your life, following what you have already learned from Christ's new "law" of love? What is it about sex that requires special ethical consideration?

These counterquestions point to a more basic confusion: What do people mean by "sex" when they ask for an ethics to guide or govern it? Or what *should* Christians mean by "sex"? The quantity of both specialized and ordinary speech about "sex" may trick us into thinking that the word's meaning is obvious. It is not. Ambiguities lurk in the simplest English phrases. "To have sex" can mean to engage in certain bodily acts—though we can't agree on what they are or even whether they require bodily contact. More confusingly, "to have (a) sex" means to have a gender—though we can't agree on what goes into gender or how many genders there are. So, for example, it is unclear whether a *sexual* ethic should consider all the aspects or intervals of an erotic encounter or whether a *sexual* ethic needs to ponder drag. More significant, many Christians now seem to be uncertain about whether an ethics of gender should be a part of an ethics of sex or the other way around.

The confusions increase when an ethicist tries to juxtapose our present languages, technical or common, with the inherited library of Christian speech. Earlier Christian communities assumed other scientific and medical theories. They suffered the ambiguities of their own common sense. They had their prejudices and taboos, not to say their erotic tastes. These historical differences hardly disappear when an ethicist turns to the most authoritative inheritance, the Christian scriptures. There are problems of translation but even more of correlation. Many Christians have hoped that their Bible would interpret itself, especially with regard to sex (on one definition or another). It never has. However much they differ in other respects, the authors of the canonical books of the Christian Bible share a reticence to speak about sexual acts in detail. They do not know or else avoid general terms that might be translated as "sex" or "the sexual." Finding a scriptural basis for a sexual ethic requires first of all deciding where the scriptures speak about it. Christians counted as orthodox have resorted to very different passages.[2] They have found in them different meanings for sex and so different tasks for sexual ethics.

(1) For some Christian writers, the task of sexual ethics is to describe the proper use of certain bodily parts—namely, the reproductive organs. The enumeration of these organs has varied with anatomical knowledge, and it has always been conceded that many of them have multiple functions. Still, one kind of Christian ethics wants to focus on their proper functioning in reproduction.

Let me note just two of the problems with this ethical preoccupation. The first is that majority Christianity—the Christianity of the victors—has never considered reproduction by itself to be sufficient ethical justification for sexual activity. Most Christians have approved sex within marriage for the sake of reproduction, citing God's command to the first humans: "Be fruitful, multiply" (Gen. 1:28). Still, the qualification "within marriage" was decisive. Churches held negative views about children born to unmarried partners, and they stigmatized both unwed parents and "bastard" children. So Christian ethicists have exerted themselves to argue that ethically permissible childbearing and child-rearing require a permanent and sexually exclusive relationship of one man and one woman (e.g., Aquinas, *Summa contra Gentiles* 3.122). They try to deduce what responsible reproduction requires. That deduction often makes little mention of love, since experience shows quickly enough that love is not required to conceive children and that they can survive (though rarely flourish) without much of it between their parents.

Traditional arguments about organ function and the requirements of child-rearing presume a sort of timelessness. If it is presumptuous to think that an ethicist can read off God's intentions by quick inspection of an organ's shape, it is particularly presumptuous to think this of organs so evidently tied to the stages of human life. The function of these organs changes over a lifetime, so any account of their teleology must be given a tense or time marker.

The presumption of timelessness becomes even odder when Christians add that the ethics of reproduction changes with history. Beginning with the New Testament, Christian texts have suspended the divine command to multiply in the face of impending eschatological judgment. The most influential scriptural passage is 1 Corinthians 7, in which Paul urges his readers to imitate his own celibacy in expectation of the arduous end-times.[3] The argument hardly stops with him. It recurs in Christian traditions, long after first Christian generations had died without seeing the return of the Lord. Augustine, for example, counters the objection that banning marriage would mean the end of the world by welcoming that end (*De bono conjugali* 10.10). From early on, Christian communities have institutionalized the eschatological refusal of procreation in practices of consecrated singleness for both men and women.

It is not enough to say that Paul or other early Christians were wrong about the timing of the Lord's return. Evidently, they were—and, just as evidently, their eschatological suspension of reproduction outlasted the error. One reason is that the suspension of reproduction is reinforced by a judgment on a second meaning attached to sex.

(2) During much of Christian history, an urgent ethical task was to distance the use of certain organs in responsible reproduction as far as possible from their use in producing pleasure. Sex understood as pleasure has posed a recurring challenge to Christian ethics, especially because pleasure has too often been conceived as the antithesis of love. While love can be understood as the selfless service described in 1 Corinthians 13, pleasure is mere selfishness, the goal and succor of the greedy self. Views like this give Christian ethics the task of stigmatizing pleasure—when pursued for itself, of course, but even when excused by reproduction. Here too Christians have reinterpreted Israelite marriage legislation for the different ethical epoch in which they understood themselves to live. If God once permitted polygamy or concubinage to the Israelite patriarchs, those indulgences are now forbidden to Christians. Even within monogamous Christian marriage, sexual intercourse should be as sober and restrained

as possible, and it should preferably cease altogether once children have been conceived. Augustine, in his influential defense of marriage, makes just this argument by explicit contrast to what was allowed to Israel (*De bono conjugali* 17.19).

Christian authors have stigmatized sexual pleasure in so many ways that it is difficult to survey their reasons. Still, we might distinguish three common grounds for complaint. Sexual pleasure is judged sinful because it is antirational or bestial, because it is intrinsically transgressive or disorderly, and because it is impure or contaminating.

Pleasure as antirational and bestial: Writing about sex (and many other topics), early Christian writers were quick to borrow arguments or conclusions from the more ascetical schools of late ancient philosophy. Following Platonists and Stoics, for example, Christian texts argue that pleasure ties the immortal soul to the perishable body, that it undoes the properly human operation of the soul by overpowering reason, or that it reduces the human to the level of the animal. These arguments are not fully consistent with other Christian doctrines, especially about bodily resurrection. More generally, the view of the body as intrinsically degrading to reason makes God's creation of human beings seem capricious or punitive.

Pleasure as disordered and transgressive: Late ancient philosophical authors, especially if Stoic, held that sexual pleasure could become unnatural when it overran natural limits. Paul borrows their language in Romans 1, perhaps through rabbinic sources, when he describes certain desires as "beyond nature" or "against nature" (Rom. 1:26; but compare God's unnatural action in 11:24). This language resonates with scriptural depictions of sin as a violation of divine ordinance but also with more specific passages about sexual sin. So, for example, Eve's violation of the divine prohibition in the Garden of Eden is interpreted as a transgressive desire (Gen. 3:16). The condemnation of adultery in the Ten Commandments is taken as a rebuke to all unbounded desire (Exod. 20:14; Deut. 5:18). Since the Hebrew scriptures also use adultery as a metaphor for idolatry, excessive desire is quickly enough associated with fundamental rejection of God (e.g., Isa. 50:1–3; Hosea 2:4–9).

Pleasure as impure: It is a short step from the notion that pleasure transgresses the law of God to the view that pleasure is an impurity. While Pauline language for sex is vague about acts, it is vivid about filthiness (Rom. 1:29–32; 1 Cor. 6:9; 1 Tim. 1:9–10). Paul's lists of sins frequently group sexual offenses with others under the expansive stigma of uncleanness. The language of impurity may operate more sweepingly in Christianity just because the New Testament elaborates no code for purity. Absent detailed legislation or ritual prescription, the language of impurity spreads out to cover more and more of bodily life.

Christian ethicists or pastoral writers have often combined condemnation of pleasure with the reproductive imperative to construct a scale of sexual sins. The best sex leads to responsible reproduction with a minimum of pleasure. All other sexual pleasure is seriously sinful, but the worst sin is excessive pleasure generated by genital acts that cannot possibly lead to impregnation. In sum, good sex is modest, fertile intercourse between a man and a woman in a position meant to enhance conception. Bad sex ranges from immodest or deliberately infertile married intercourse, through unmarried male-female intercourse, to the darkest realms of sterile sex (masturbation, same-sex copulation). Seeking scriptural support for such scales of judgment, Christian ethicists have incorporated pieces of the Levitical purity codes, reinterpreted other scriptural stories (such as that of Onan), and filled in the ambiguous terms in the Pauline lists of sins with increasingly detailed acts of imagination.

These scales of sexual sins are hardly consistent across Christian history. Many sexual activities now permitted to Christian married couples in some cultures would have been considered seriously sinful even a hundred years ago—and are still condemned in other cultures. Even more stubborn difficulties in ranking sexual sins come from the very effort to combine teleological arguments about created bodies with the eschatological suspension of reproduction and the overarching stigmatization of pleasure.

The teleological view of organ function holds that God created human genitals for procreation. To use them otherwise is to violate the divine plan. Of course, our genitals in fact function far beyond the limits set by traditional rules for procreative intercourse. Moreover, some "sexual" activities don't involve the genitals directly, and other activities may lead unexpectedly to orgasm. A principle of reproductive function evidently fails to describe our actual physiology.

So why not modify the principle by reasoning backward from how our organs actually do function? Two other principles are invoked to prevent this. First, our physiology of pleasure is put under suspicion by a narrative of original sin. Because of sin, the narrative explains, our genital function is now deeply disordered. It cannot be trusted as a reliable guide to the created order. If we could somehow correct for the distortions of sin, we would still have to confront, second, the eschatological suspension of the divine command to reproduce. Christian rankings of sins want to combine arguments from original design with a claim that the purposes of the original design have been suspended. If Christian asceticism suspends reproduction, then Christian ethics itself overrules the original divine purpose because of later revelation. It replaces an ethic of original purpose with an ethic of radical renewal—but then it wants to constrain any claims for renewal by invoking a narrative of original sin. This is a tensed or historicized ethic, but one in which the plot is tragic constriction. The original teleology of sexual pleasure has been superseded, but no new teleology has been supplied. Sexual pleasure has no future.

Other Christian accounts suspect that sexualized pleasures lurk everywhere in the present. The suspicion of unbounded pleasure leads to an endless search for all of its manifestations and hiding places. The search is not without scriptural warrant. Jesus is reported to have said that a man who looks at a woman with lust in his heart has already committed adultery (Matt. 5:27–28). He may be trying to teach the importance of intention—or the indefensibility of hypocrisy. Many readers have taken him as saying that inward motions of lust should be counted as sexual sins without qualification. So they have concentrated on practices of physical denial and mental surveillance. Suspended from its original teleology in reproduction, animated by sin, sexual pleasure becomes the scattered poison of revolt against God.

(3) Combinations of a qualified imperative to responsible reproduction with the stigmatization of pleasure explain much of the history of Christian sexual ethics. But there have been other ethical meanings of sex—and other scriptural warrants for them. Indeed, sometimes the same scriptural passages get read in another direction. For example, in the first account of human creation (Gen. 1:26–31), God creates human beings as male and female (1:27) before commanding them to be fruitful and multiply in order to take dominion over the earth. Here the sequence of the text suggests that sexual differentiation is for the sake of an increase in numbers that will enable conquest. The divine motive for creating two sexes is reproduction, and the motive for reproduction is earthly dominion. An ethics of sex is fundamentally about the relation of male to female. Its task is to draw out the many consequences

of the original difference in humankind, with regard to reproduction, but also to dominion. For some Christians, the ethics of sex becomes an ethics of original differentiation and then an ethics of divinely instituted hierarchy.[4]

(4) Yet another meaning of sex has been found in the second account of human creation (Gen. 2:5–25). Here sexual differentiation is a sort of divine afterthought. God creates woman because man cannot find a suitable companion among the other animals. Adam recognizes Eve as his equal and so his companion: "bone from my bones, and flesh from my flesh" (2:23). The new companionship is linked, of course, to reproductive copulation or marriage: "This is why a man leaves his father and mother and joins himself to his wife [*or* woman], and they become one body [*or* flesh]" (2:24). Still there is a suggestion here that the task of an ethics of sex would be to explain human interdependence and human community in relation to this oneness.[5]

This reading of Genesis on human difference as companionship helps to reinterpret sexual intercourse as fundamental intimacy, but there are still difficulties. The verse from Genesis describes the union of man and woman in a metaphor of material union. A reader may infer that "becoming one flesh" implies attraction or affection, but the scriptural verse doesn't name them. It does *not* say, "This is why a man joins himself to his wife after falling madly in love with her." Another difficulty is just with the image of a man joining himself to his wife. Leaving aside the emphasis on male prerogative, the material metaphor implies that intimacy happens by means of a single action. It doesn't encourage reflection on the time needed to elicit intimacy, on its waxing and waning. The scriptural verse does *not* say, "A man joins himself to his wife so that they can begin a long journey of mutual discovery."

(5) A final meaning of sex in the inherited Christian texts is the one that many contemporary readers would want to put first: sex as the erotic play of romantic love. Christian tradition has found this meaning in the Song of Songs (or Song of Solomon). The book's origin is obscure and its inclusion in the canon surprising. For the Christian tradition, at least, this frankly erotic text has required considerable reinterpretation. It has been read most often allegorically, as illustrating the soul's union with God or with Christ, considered as spouse. Once the text is allegorized, it becomes all the more remarkable that Christian tradition regularly uses its erotic language to describe moments of highest union with the divine. In this sense, an ethics of sex—or at least an ethics of erotic relation—becomes an ethics of human fulfillment in loving union with God.

Allegorical reading is encouraged by the book's lack of context. The abstraction of its love talk allows it to circulate among very different kinds of lovers, across some differences of culture, age, and gender. The (false?) universality also truncates time. The encounters in the Song of Songs happen outside ordinary time but also in compressed time—in the breathless rush from infatuation to consummation. These lovers burn up time. They mean for it to end in achieved ecstasy—on the wedding night.

Many Christians testify to individual fulfillment in moments of conversion or "mystical" encounter. They expect greater fulfillment after their deaths. Still, they also profess that the whole of humanity is fulfilled by love at the end of history. If nuptial and erotic imagery has been applied to that historical consummation, the scriptural warrants are complicated. Evading a trick question about remarriage, Jesus says that there is in heaven neither marriage nor giving in marriage (Matt. 22:29–31). Some construe this as teaching that there will be no sexual relations in the afterlife. Equally orthodox theologians have also been willing to argue that resurrected bodies would have genitals for beauty's sake. The argument is no odd fancy. It discloses a persistent ambivalence about marriage and the bodies that perform it. Scripture itself includes one eschatological vision of the city of God that depicts it as a wedding (Rev. 19:7–9, 21:2, 21:9, 22:17, after Isa.). The erotic or nuptial imagery that is so famously a part of Christian mystical tradition carries forward into thoughts of resurrected life with God.

These different understandings of the topic of Christian sexual ethics recall different scriptural or theological sources. They also impose different meanings on sex. Sex is understood as a physical act, a desire or disposition, an anatomical difference, an instrument of hierarchical union, and a site of divine union or transformation. Each meaning of sex is correlated with an ethical preoccupation, and each preoccupation establishes a different relation to the language of love. Some authors insist on the direct relation: (married) love is the fulfillment and transformation of sexual capacities. Many others see only an indirect or negative relation: love is always put at risk by the bodily desire of sex. Both relations reduce the complexity of sex but also of love. It is easiest to see this by adding three other meanings of sex emphasized by recent writers.

Our experiences of sex are an obscure and bodily archive of our upbringings, our oldest loves. Our shames and our specific desires, our wounds and joys are configured by episodes and imperatives that preceded our mastery of language. So much of sex was passed down to us by those we loved before we had words for anything. Even now, sex can bring us to our vulnerability as speechless infants. We were taught about sex before we were treated as ethical agents—or allowed to have a sex of our own. We pretend that children don't have sex, when in fact adult sex is so often the repetition of childhood's burdens. Sex life is a memorial of the self's formation.

Again, sexual desire and sexual anatomy offer raw material for systems of political or social power. For example, the impulses and roles that we lump together as "gender" typically claim to be natural. They are supposed to correspond to a duality of genital configurations and of desires for them. Of course, they do not. What nature will not do, human ideologies of nature will: some infants are violently assigned to one or another of the two approved genital types, and many more adolescents are punished for not desiring the prescribed "other sex." A divinely created difference of the sexes and genders then becomes a socially acceptable excuse for enforcing hierarchies of many kinds—which means, for violence of many kinds. Sex is the language of power—or power's favorite channel.

Finally, sexual acts and sexual pleasures are appropriated by prevailing economic systems. If pleasure is desirable, it is valuable—and so it can be sold or used for selling, held out as reward or inducement. These are not the most serious economic appropriations of sex. When an economic system asserts that all human activity should be rationalized for maximum productivity, sexual activity too must be managed as resource. So begins the interest of the modern state or corporation in human sex. The interest extends from the production and maintenance of populations to pleasure itself, which must be measured and hoarded, regulated, rerouted for the sake of larger plans. Sex is currency.

The five traditional meanings have become eight. Sex is an act, a desire or disposition, an anatomical difference, an instrument of hierarchical union, and a site of divine union, but it is also an involuntary memorial of formation, a language of power, and a currency. Other meanings can be attached to sex, but my point may be clear enough: as the meanings multiply, an "ethics of sex" will point to competing tasks. Indeed, we learn something important about the function of the category "sex" in this multiplication. Once we admit a legitimate plurality of meanings, we must expect a plurality of ethical preoccupations. No one ethical formula—no single rule—can be the sufficient basis for a Christian ethics of sex. This conclusion applies as well to formulations about love. We might wish for a simpler world in which sexual dispositions or actions could be determined by strict deduction from a handful of axioms about agape. That is not the world we inhabit—or that God created.

What Knowledge of Sex Should Christian Ethics Presuppose or Put on Offer?

Christian ethics has often been characterized as an ethics of love. If it knows anything, it knows about love. So Christianity would seem especially prepared to apply its knowledge about love to an ethics of sex. Many Christian writers have tried in recent years to do just that. They have encountered some difficulties.

One difficulty is the alleged opposition between Christian agape and "secular" notions of romantic love that are associated with erotic attraction. If the opposition is allowed to stand, then the love that Christianity knows is not erotic love—and may be (if one follows Anders Nygren) the opposite of erotic love.[6] Another difficulty has been the deconstruction of erotic love from all sides—from strong theories as different as psychoanalysis and dialectical materialism. Still, the greatest difficulty theologically has been to understand *when* the question of love should be raised in ethics. Love can't be introduced only at the moment of asking whether love permits this or that sexual action. It must appear long before, in the basic attitude that ethics adopts toward sex. Love doesn't appear in Christian sexual ethics to answer the question, How far can I go? It appears with the question, What really do I know about sex—about its past, present, or future?

Too much Christian "knowledge" about sex has started out from the suspicion that the root of our sexual desires is sinful. So long as this suspicion remains unchallenged, theology's relationship to sex is adversarial. It treats sex as demonic wiles, cascading forms of temptation. Far from encouraging a closer acquaintance with sex, this unloving epistemology counsels the distance of a punitive "objectivity." No sexual experimentation can be allowed; the consequences are too grave. Any counterclaim that sex might offer unexpected means of sanctification is treated as itself an effect of sexual sin. Indeed, it is an old lesson that one of the first consequences of unchastity is mental blindness about the evils of lust. This is a hermeneutic of suspicion in the strongest sense.

I would argue against it that Christian ethics must actually seek loving knowledge of sex before it can speak convincingly—or prophetically. Loving knowledge trusts both that sex is a created good to be loved and that knowing it will require patient attention. Theologians often say that accurate knowledge of God's purposes in creation or providence requires a slow transformation open to correction. What if we applied that counsel to theological knowledge of sex? Imagine a pastor saying, "Give yourself over to God's leading in your erotic life and then report what you learn at church next Sunday." If that seems laughable, it must be because we refuse to apply theological counsels about creaturely learning to the theological knowledge of sex.

The languages used most often by Christian sexual ethics do not encourage patient attention to what God discloses. They mix a few positive platitudes with much longer patches of denigration, mockery, and disgust. They rarely call up affects of admiring attention or delight; they seek instead to produce fear, shame, and prophylactic revulsion. These rhetorical effects follow from deeper compositional choices, including the choice of genre. The dominant genres for Christian sexual ethics have long been medical or legal. For centuries, Christian ethicists have turned either to the physician or to the criminal judge for help in knowing sex. If they have sought particular facts or theories, they have wanted above all to find patterns for authoritative knowledge and its speech. The dependence on the clinic and the court are particularly notable during the last century, but they can be found as far back as the early Middle Ages. The results can be seen at every level of ethical discourse—in the preference for certain terms or analogies, certain causal models and forms of argument, but above all in the habit of ready judgment—in the fluent delivery of diagnosis and prescription, of verdict and punishment. As a result of this long recourse to medical and legal authorities, Christian ethics lacks examples of speech that would enact loving knowledge of sex.

The response to this lack is certainly not to rush out in search of better experts in the newer versions of these fields—in psychology and psychiatry, in sexology, in sociology, in behavioral management or addiction counseling. What Christian sexual ethics needs instead is a different range of genres for speaking about sex. It might begin by looking beyond the ethical canon to other kinds of Christian writing. I have already recalled "mystical" writing that applies erotic imagery to encounters with God. But there are much larger archives of devotional writing: hagiography or spiritual autobiography, moral exhortation, religious lyric, and (of course) prayer and hymnody. All of these offer formal resources for speaking about sex without suspicious judgment. So too do self-narration and testimony, once they are freed from penitential or pseudo-clinical contexts. How many candid accounts of the actual sexual lives of Christians do we have that are not confessions of sin? What do they show about the failures of the dominant Christian genres for sex? Ethicists might attend especially to the narratives of Christians who have been stigmatized for sex: sexual minorities that have been judged queer (in one sense or another), racial or national groups that have been pronounced "oversexed," or other groups that have been labeled "notorious" sexual sinners.

Mysticism, devotional writing, testimony—these are obvious examples of Christian speech from which ethics might begin to develop a range of genres beyond the medical and legal. They point to a vast library of other sources—I mean the texts we call "literature," without ever knowing quite what we mean. I continue to be astonished that contemporary Christian ethicists resist learning from the extraordinary range of formal experiments in modern (indeed, modernist) novels and poems. The failure is particularly notable with regard to sex since so much of literary modernism (loosely construed) has been concerned precisely to find words for it. Christian ethicists—along with criminal lawyers—have spent much of the last century rushing to learn one laboratory language after another. Few of these could be described as languages of loving knowledge. Ethicists would have found better languages—terms, tropes, logics, genres—if they had spent more time learning from novelists and poets.

My insistence that Christian sexual ethics needs to find a new language supposes that it wants to form subjects capable of speaking about sex in new ways. Our ethical inquiries need in some way to reeducate us as speakers. This is not so simple as ruling out certain forms of hate speech—though I would certainly be grateful for a truce governing the most violent language about sexual sinners. The work of linguistic reeducation requires something more difficult: opening a space of experimentation in theological language and then coaching us to adopt the best of those experiments as a new mother tongue.

What kind of knowledge should a Christian sexual ethics offer? The knowledge that there is something misleading in asking for sexual diagnoses or verdicts without asking for a lot of other knowledge first and last. Without finding a language capable of representing sex lovingly. Indeed, more important, without forming subjects capable of speaking sex in love.

What Should Distinguish a Sexual Ethics as Christian?

If the great "law" taught by Jesus Christ is love, then Christian sexual ethics must be distinguished by its teaching about love in sex. Where exactly can that distinction be noticed?

The content of Christianity's sexual prohibitions has never been particularly distinctive. Compared with its rivals in the ancient philosophic schools or other Mediterranean cults, the new religion took up a middle position. Other religious groups were more extravagant in their sexual mythologies, while the philosophical schools had more coherent arguments for fidelity and self-restraint.

Many Christians would say that the Gospel's ethical distinction comes from the claims about its source. Christian ethics is indeed distinctive because of the narrative that authorizes and explains it. But we must then repeat how little grounding there is in the New Testament for such an ethics. For example, the canonical Gospels record very few instructions about sex. Jesus is remembered to have said one unsettling thing about remarriage but much more by way of critique of the biological family.[7] The Pauline letters include sexual terms in lists of sins without specifying their meanings. Paul concedes that marriage is better than unrequited lust, then offers his own unmarried state as the better choice. This lack of specific instruction in the New Testament explains why so much of the scriptural evidence for Christian ethics has been produced by selective reading of "Old Testament" sources. Christians have needed to retain some Israelite sexual legislation as universally binding moral law, while dismissing other parts as superseded ceremony or surpassed concession to "carnal Israel."

If the distinctiveness of Christian sexual ethics must somehow be located in its scriptural sources, then part of that distinctiveness is an *absence* of detailed prescription. This silence has been taken in two different directions. It can be combined with critiques of biological family and stigmatizations of sexual sin to produce an ethic of ascetic denial, in which the only serious Christian life is a life beyond sex. On this view, Jesus said nothing about sex because he called us to leave sex behind. In contrast, the silence might also be taken as an implicit command to discern divine will for sex without recourse to a comprehensive code. Jesus said nothing about sex because he meant us to learn something about ethics while discerning how we are to live it.

In recent years, a number of Christian ethicists have taken up the scriptural silences and critiques of family as an invitation rather than a condemnation. They construct sexual ethics both by appealing to philosophical or scientific discoveries and by turning to other scriptural principles or narratives. Though their conclusions are untraditional, their method is really no different than that of much previous ethical construction. Every Christian sexual ethic has had to borrow material from non-Christian sources in order to proceed. While earlier ethics have focused on the call to renunciation or the symbolism of the marriage covenant, some recent ethicists have looked to other scriptural passages and other sources outside scripture.

Let me give a few examples from a much larger field. Traditionally, Jesus has been the most authoritative example of sexual renunciation. His purity has been so emphasized that it has helped to motivate doctrines about the perpetual virginity and immaculate conception of his mother, Mary. Recent ethicists have pointed instead to the many ways that Jesus deliberately violated expectations about purity. He was known for associating with sexual sinners, and the canonical Gospels show him having prohibited contacts with various stigmatized bodies, not least to heal them. For some ethicists, this implies that Jesus overturns sexual purity codes.[8] Others have argued that while Jesus says rather little about sex, he says a great deal about service to the poor and the abandoned. To judge from the Gospels, his ethical teaching was preoccupied with communal justice. So any ethics of sex that wants to follow the teaching of Jesus would have to begin from a commitment to justice.[9] Still other ethicists point to the ways in which Jesus's commitment to justice overturns existing structures—political, social, and familial. They would argue that a Christian sexual ethics must be equally concerned to resist the encroachments of existing structures of power.[10] A fourth group has responded to Jesus's example as healer to argue that his sexual ethic must be an ethics of wholeness—of personal integration and growth into loving maturity.[11]

I agree with a number of these authors in taking Jesus's silence about sex as a caution against elaborating systems for regulating it or segregating it. In his disregard of the injunction to marry, his transgression of rules about bodily contact, his keeping company with notorious sinners, Jesus refuses to burden sex with symbolic importance. He does not treat bodily purity as equivalent to moral uprightness. Some of his sharpest sayings oppose bodily purity and moral uprightness (Matt. 23:25–28). He shows himself much more ready than those around him to forgive sexual sin. In the most familiar incident (John 8:1–11), Jesus refuses to join the crowd that wants to stone a woman taken in adultery. He thus refuses to carry out a scriptural punishment (Lev. 20:10; Deut. 22:22–24). When his silence shames the crowd into disbanding, Jesus says to the woman, "I do not condemn you." This means, I will not execute you, but it also means, most literally, I will not pronounce on your sin. When Jesus adds, "Go and sin no more," it is not clear that he refers to adultery—much less that he makes his forgiveness conditional on her future perfection. The story shows from beginning to end Jesus's refusal to share in a scriptural judgment on sexual sin. He undoes scriptural codes for sex before the reader's eyes.

Jesus's refusal to participate in the violent extravagance of sexual shame suggests that he means to challenge our cultural and individual exaggeration of sexual sin. The ethical deception in sex is not that it dazzles us into more sins of the flesh but that it tricks us into regarding them as the only sins. Sexual sins are not as a class the worst sins. They are burdened with so much symbolic weight because they are surrounded by old affects of shame. They are tied to our psychological structures, the secrets of our families, and our obsessions with keeping or becoming clean. Churches have spent centuries fulminating against sexual sins as the most prominent and most fatal rejections of God. In this, they have contradicted Jesus's example. They have succumbed to an all-too-human desire to make sex the central ethical matter. If Christian sexual ethics wants to be faithful to the silence of its scriptures, then it too must resist any exaggeration of sex. The teacher of Christian ethics must imitate an incarnate god who refused to deliver a code for sex or to enshrine it as the singular topic of concern.

Believers profess that the story of Jesus is not yet finished. He has not said all that he will say. He has not ended his time with us. Many Christians recite every Sunday the promise that he will return "to judge the living and the dead" in a "kingdom that will have no end." Some scriptural stories about that kingdom, and some mystical visions of it, hint that he might then deliver a fuller account of sex. He would be speaking to glorified bodies, to human bodies in their full maturity, at the end of their development. He would be speaking beyond the symbolic scapegoating written into human cultures. At present, we are, on the scale of salvation history, still not adults—not as individuals, not as cultures. Even our bodies have not yet reached their final maturity. Unless we believe that genitals will disappear from resurrected bodies, we must suppose that they will have some function in that kingdom. Presumably, it will not be reproduction. What then will it be? And what ethical teaching will those glorified genitals elicit from the Lord?

A sexual ethics for the present epoch of salvation history is provisional. It is provisional because God has not finished speaking (or judging), but even more because we are not in our final state—not spiritually, not physically. Rather than trying to predict the final ethics of sex, Christian reflection would do better to dwell on the question whether sex itself is only a provisional feature of human experience. If there is no eschatological future for sex, then Paul is surely right to argue that it is a temporary arrangement for this age as it passes away—or perhaps, like polygamy, a relic of an earlier stage in God's ordinances for humankind. On the other hand, if something like sexual intimacy will remain in resurrected bodies, if sex does have a future in human fulfillment, then the task of ethics is not to inhibit it until it disappears so much as to lead it toward its fulfillment in fuller love, which is future love. Love is the eschatological future of sex—and sexual love will be clearly visible only in the future.

What Are the Obligations of Ethics in the Meantime?

The vocation of Christian ethics at present is to find genres for speech adequate to a loving knowledge of sex while being responsible to Jesus's refusal to participate in violent allegations of sexual sin. Its ways of talking must be marked as provisional because they occur in a pre-eschatological moment before the fullness of human embodiment is revealed. Any ethics that Christians speak now is spoken in a moment suspended before apocalypse—before the disclosure, the uncovering, in which we see our bodies as they are meant to be.

How can a suspended ethics provide pastoral care to the present? What can it say when people come looking for answers? I hardly want to urge pastors—or ethicists—to stop responding while ethics begins to find another way forward. At the same time, I believe that present responses should concede, gladly, a lack of credible rules in order to suggest that rules about sex are not what is needed. Many Christians suffer over their sexuality, feeling that it is an area of special sinfulness. They suffer unnecessarily because of what churches have said. So pastors should relieve that suffering by speaking more responsibly. Believers also suffer unnecessarily because of how they have been raised, because of gender hierarchies, because of commercial promises of sexual bliss. Pastors should help with these by opening a door beyond which sex is not charged with endless shame or exploited as an inducement to perfect fulfillment in the present.

The vocation of Christian ethics is to teach loving knowledge of sex in ways that lead Christian believers toward what God intends to accomplish in sexed bodies. This teaching takes many forms, from catechesis through exhortation or spiritual direction to sacrament and liturgy. It traces out a pedagogy for forming sexual subjects that is markedly different from a number of other pedagogies on offer in contemporary cultures. It differs most of all in its motive, which must be love on the way to an unrevealed fulfillment.

Some Christian ethicists pride themselves on being "countercultural" when they repeat traditional prohibitions in a loud voice. Talking about sex with complete assurance does not oppose our dominant culture. It is exactly what our culture craves. Christian ethics must speak otherwise. It must offer moral teaching that is animated by an irreducible variety of preoccupations, that is pursued as loving knowledge, and that refuses to codify sex out of respect for the example of its Teacher, who has not yet finished teaching—or acting.

Notes

1. This brief sentence gestures toward a long argument by Michel Foucault. For his summaries, see Foucault, *Histoire de la sexualité*, vol. 2, *L'usage des plaisirs* (Paris: Gallimard, 1984), 273–78, and *HS*, vol. 3, *Le souci de soi* (Paris: Gallimard, 1984), 269–74.

2. A historical meditation on Christian ethics has to set boundaries around what will count as Christian. This is always controversial but especially so when the ethical topic is sex. Groups or individuals that dissented from majority views about sex were pronounced heretical, and heretics were typically accused of sexual irregularity. In what follows, I retell views that fit within some ample notion of orthodoxy, while admitting that orthodoxy is always an imposition ex post facto.

3. Here and elsewhere, I follow traditional notions about scriptural authorship. By "Paul," I mean only the author traditionally assigned to a group of New Testament texts.

4. Recall the opening sentence of Thielicke's influential treatise: "Reference to the sexual differentiation in man is one of the axioms repeatedly stressed in biblical anthropology." See Helmut Thielicke, *The Ethics of Sex*, trans. John W. Doberstein (New York: Harper & Row, 1964), 3. Here and in what follows, I don't pretend to offer anything like a complete bibliography. I will often cite only a single example to illustrate a more general point.

5. Augustine's influential discussion of *sacramentum* in marriage (*De bono conjugali*, 7.6) makes this connection. He means by "sacrament" not a recognized liturgical rite so much as the compact or covenant between the partners. The analogy is to the oath of military service, which binds a soldier to the corps. Augustine may also have in mind ancient texts that liken married intercourse to the renewal of a covenant.

6. Anders Nygren, *Agape and Eros*, trans. Philip S. Watson (Philadelphia: Westminster Press, 1953).

7. For a survey of these, see Dale B. Martin, *Sex and the Single Savior: Gender and Sexuality in Biblical Interpretation* (Louisville, KY: Westminster John Knox Press, 2006), 103–24.

8. For example, William Countryman, *Dirt, Greed, and Sex: Sexual Ethics in the New Testament and Their Implications for Today*, rev. ed. (Minneapolis: Fortress Press, 2007).

9. This is one salient feature of the complex analysis in Margaret Farley, *Just Love: A Framework for Christian Sexual Ethics* (New York: Continuum, 2008). The argument from justice appears in a different way in ethical writing indebted to liberation theology.

10. To take some obvious examples: Carter Heyward, *Touching Our Strength: The Erotic as Power and the Love of God* (San Francisco: HarperSanFrancisco, 1989); Marcella Althaus-Reid, *Indecent Theology* (London: Routledge, 2000), perhaps especially 47–86.

11. For example, W. Norman Pittenger, *Making Sexuality Human* (Philadelphia: Pilgrim Press, 1970); John McNeill, *Sex as God Intended* (Maple Shade, NJ: Lethe Press, 2008), recapitulating his arguments from the 1970s.

17

Meditations on Love and Violence

EMILIE M. TOWNES

I WAS INITIALLY SOMEWHAT AMUSED at the invitation to participate in this volume because the key ethical and moral category I deal with in my work and teaching is justice, not love. However, when I hit the global "find" button on the computer to see how I reflect on love, I discovered that it is always twined with justice. This is not surprising given that love and justice are extremely natural if not necessary dance partners. They inform each other and enrich our ethical reflection as moral, believing animals in a vast creation.[1] Justice is the corporate or communal expression of love, our concrete acts to create and broaden spaces in society for human flourishing and creation mending. The invitation to participate in this volume affords me the opportunity to take a step back to explore what it means for me to invoke the category of love in my work and to do so in the format of five meditations on the nature of love—its demands as well as its gifts.

Love is seen as the most crucial and central concept in Christian theology and ethics. However, it is also one of the most theologically, ethically, psychologically, and culturally ambiguous concepts we encounter. Love is considered one of the three primary theological virtues along with faith and hope. In the biblical world, there were at least five words used to designate forms of love: "eros," the search for an object in aesthetic, passionate, or spiritual love; "philia," the preferential bond of affection, friendship, and social solidarity; "storge," the caregiving love of compassion; "agape," the non-preferential, self-giving love of equal respect; and "koinonia," which is love in the mutuality of community, in the sharing of the common life in covenant and commitment. Koinonia is more than a search for an object (eros) or altruistic self-giving (agape). It is an expression of mutuality in which giving and receiving are united, and it is formative for building healthy and just communities.

Koinonia reminds us that life and faith should be lived relationally and not completely autonomously. We are challenged to live our lives faithfully in each breathing moment and to structure our communities and our societies with a sense of dynamic and rich caring for others. More so for all those issues that flow from "quiet" violence, such as the lack of accessible and affordable health care and childcare or the lack of federal and rural development policies, and that are systemic rather than episodic.

If love is to have any enduring meaning, it requires an ethical community. Ethical practice does not occur in human isolation or in individual decision alone. It also arises within community and directly by the commitments of the person. It is in a particular community

303

that the practice of love takes form, receives content, finds direction, achieves fulfillment. In exploring the implications of this robust understanding of love, I begin the following set of meditations by focusing on a small Ohio community.

One: In This Place

In recent years, one piece of literature on love that has been influential for me has been the novel *Beloved* by the African American woman writer, Toni Morrison. Morrison's larger body of work has been an imaginative play-partner and theo-ethical muse in my work. With *Beloved*, Morrison tells the story of US slavery and its violent and brutalizing effects on the body and soul. Reviewers and literary critics often characterize the novel as historical fiction, gothic horror story, or bildungsroman. Others describe her work as more appropriately placed within the literary genre of the fantastic.[2] However one characterizes her work, Morrison crafts *Beloved* from an actual Cincinnati murder case in which a black slave woman killed her children to keep them away from the slave catchers who had come to reclaim them and her for the master from whom she had fled in Kentucky.

Beloved is a horrific ghost story about slavery and its impact on the human soul. The character Beloved, the murdered ghost of the child of the novel's main character, Sethe, appears years after her death as a feral teenager (the age she would have been if she had lived) and begins to suck the remaining life out of Sethe's home and Sethe herself with parasitic vengeance. Through a series of flashbacks, the reader learns about the unspeakable atrocities Sethe and other slaves endured. It is only through the actions of Sethe's younger daughter, Denver, who appeals to the community for help, that the living are saved from the dead. A group of thirty women led by Ella, a former agent for the Underground Railroad, come to Sethe's house at 124 in the rural area close to Cincinnati and exorcize Beloved's ghost before Sethe's spirit and sanity are completely broken by the violent specter's influence.

> Among those not on their knees, who stood holding 124 in a fixed glare, was Ella, trying to see through the walls, behind the door, to what was really in there. Was it true the dead daughter come back? Or a pretend? Was it whipping Sethe? Ella had been beaten every way but down. She remembered the bottom teeth she had lost to the brake and the scars from the bell were thick as rope around her waist. She had delivered but would not nurse, a hairy white thing, fathered by "the lowest yet." It lived five days never making sound. The idea of that pup coming back to whip her too set her jaw working, and then Ella hollered.[3]

In one particularly moving passage earlier in the novel that echoes throughout the book, the ex-slave Baby Suggs preaches a sermon in a clearing in the woods to other ex-slaves just barely living beyond the dehumanizing walls of slavery. Baby Suggs is both mother figure and stabilizing force for Sethe and Denver after their flight from slavery. A self-proclaimed preacher, Baby Suggs, holy, draws on nature to help the other ex-slaves recognize their value and worth. Although Baby Suggs retreats into her own madness after the black community betrays her and fails to warn her or Sethe about the approach of the schoolteacher (the only character of pure evil in the novel and the overseer of the Sweet Home plantation where Sethe had been enslaved), after her death her presence lingers as a source of strength and comfort for the living in counterpoint to Beloved's haunting, destructive presence.

Baby Suggs tells them in the clearing:

"Here," she said, "in this here place, we flesh; flesh that weeps, laughs; flesh that dances on bare feet in grass. Love it. Love it hard. Yonder they do not love your flesh. They despise it. . . . Love your hands! Love them. Raise them up and kiss them. Touch others with them, pat them together, stroke them on your face 'cause they don't love that either. You got to love it, you. . . . This is flesh I'm talking about here. Flesh that needs to be loved. Feet that need to rest and to dance; backs that need support; shoulders that need arms, strong arms I'm telling you. . . . So love your neck; put a hand on it, grace it, stroke it and hold it up. And all your inside parts that they'd just as soon slop for hogs, you got to love them. The dark, dark liver—love it, love it, and the beat and beating heart, love that too. More than eyes or feet.

More than lungs that have yet to draw free air. More than your life-holding womb and your life-giving private parts, hear me now, love your heart. For this is the prize."[4]

This is a concrete material kind of love. It is love of body, love of self. It gives a sense of location and community. This admonishment/sermon to love one's heart is an individual and a communal call to question any radical devaluation of the self and the community in the context of omnipresent structural violence. This line of questioning can and should take a multitude of directions because it addresses the nature of *systemic* violence, not individual sin(s). What does it mean, then, for us to think and live loving our "beat and beating heart"?

Two: Biblical Markers

One resource for the quest for this beating heart is the biblical tradition of lament. As biblical scholar Claus Westermann notes, the rite of lament is the best-known worship observance of ancient Israel for us today.[5] Whether communal or individual, lament is a powerful cry of distress, a rending of the heart in which we name the realities of our situations with as much accuracy and precision as we can. In the Hebrew Bible, communal lament is used by or on behalf of a community to express complaint, sorrow, and grief over impending doom that could be physical or cultural. It could also be a tragedy or a series of calamities that had already happened. This rending of the heart, as Westermann goes on to note, belongs to the events of deliverance.[6]

As Hebrew Bible scholar Walter Brueggeman notes, laments are formful in that they help us see that what is before us can be managed if not transformed.[7] As Joel shows so well, we must do this communally and seek faith-filled ways to work to engage the challenges and, yes, the many forms of violence in our lives and in the lives of others. Communal lament can help us best get at these complex issues. Lament enables us and even requires us to acknowledge and to experience our suffering. We allow the beat and beating heart to guide us in these laments.

For example, in the book of Joel, lament pours forth in potent language that is unequivocal in its anguish. It marks the outlines of the devastation and ruin that have befallen the nation. This is a communal lament of affliction that, with full hearts and genuine worship, evokes an oracle of salvation from God. By putting their suffering into the form of lament, the people of Judah had to first acknowledge the crisis in their midst. Ultimately, by putting words to their suffering, the community could move to a pain or pains that could be named and then addressed.

Lament also means listening to those who are the victims of violence in our world because it may be possible that in listening to their voices, we can find the biblical sustenance to overcome violence and allow love to guide us into the new heavens and new earth today. Matthew 2:18, and Jeremiah 31:15 before it, expresses unbounded grief as the children are slain at Herod's command (Matthew) and sculpts the promise of salvation as the exiles will return to their land (Jeremiah): "A voice was heard in Ramah, wailing and loud lamentation, Rachel weeping for her children; she refused to be consoled, because they are no more."[8] This is a passage of hope as well as lament and can be a way to begin to develop a strategic love by hearing the silence of the victims who can and do protest. These protests reach a place where they can complicate the many forms of violence we experience and the juggernaut of evil that accompanies them. These voices of lament become signs of the spirit.

However, there are those who have no voice or who are not heard, those who cannot see alternatives and work toward them, those whose daily fare is exclusion, denial, death, or annihilation. Isaiah 53:7 speaks of the innocent victim who "was oppressed, and afflicted, yet did not open [his] mouth; like a lamb that is led to the slaughter, and like a sheep that before its hearers is dumb, so [he] did not open [his] mouth." Such victims are silent with no voice, no volition, no vote, and we often choose not to hear or see them or acknowledge the inhumanities piling up in their lives like loose change in the fountain. They are the children of Matthew 2, and will we be Rachel for this day? Will our lives and actions serve as powerful backdrops to the work of Jesus, who comes to save us from our sins, who helps us overcome the violence in our lives, who overturns a misbegotten order in which the Pharaohs and Herods of the world offer up so many of us as surrogates for *their* sacrifice?

Will these surrogates be the foreigner, the masses of colored peoples and cultures, those striving for education in schools that serve only as gigantic holding pens for the mind and the intellect? Will they be the spouse or partner or child who suffers raining blows or debasing language or physical or emotional violation of their bodies? Will the surrogates be the internecine battles in our churches that maim and cripple the Gospel while proclaiming victory and righteousness, economic systems that are more focused on production and the bottom line than human cost and health, or the constant belching of pollution into our air, lungs, very being? Will it be all these and more in a spectral dance of violence and violation? Will it be us?

What godforsakenness we endure in such whirlpools of violence. Turning to legal structures alone is inadequate if we are to effectively oppose this violence, for even legal structures can be built on prettified notions of vengeance or retribution such as the death penalty or war. These are neither substitutes for nor on par with love, community, and holy justice. Our work must involve listening and looking for the lament of the victim in today's world. In doing so, we have a model in Holy Scripture to turn to who is the "perfect" victim. His silence is deliberate (if not strategic), for the silence of the Suffering Servant, Jesus, is calculated. In this silence, Jesus lays bare the nature of violence when someone has been given up and delivered to the executioner's hand by a friend. It is important to acknowledge that the silence, misery, and godforsakenness of the victim have already been revealed through Jesus's witness. If we are to overcome violence, we must pay attention to the ways in which the silence of Jesus is found among the silent and silenced victims of our day.

In this vein, parables can be helpful because their meanings are inexhaustible. Although we cannot confine a parable to an ultimate or final meaning, we are invited to explore and

mine the possibilities for our day in it. Hence, there is no neat set of answers, only possibilities to explore. The only certainty in a parable is that we are invited to see ourselves in all the
characters. Consider Luke's retelling of the conclusion of Jesus's dialogue with the lawyer in
the parable of the Samaritan: "'Which of these three, do you think, was a neighbor of the man
who fell into the hands of the robbers?' The lawyer said 'The one who showed him mercy.'
Jesus said to him, 'Go and do likewise.'" The emphasis is on imitating the Samaritan: go and
do likewise.

The Samaritan story in Luke prompts us to ask, Are we the robbers who have come into
a country and its cultures and extracted its wealth, its resources, and left it half dead or
worse—dependent on our future benevolence or long-term, low-interest loans? Are we the
priests or Levites who have a position of authority and are given accolades and honors?
Although we actually do work hard, we may be tempted to believe that our hard work and the
accolades we may garner from it are the marks of goodness. If so, it may seem to us a righteous act to pass by on the other side of the victim because a sin-sick culture has told us that
we are good without *living* a life of love and justice. Are we the victims who, robbed of our
gifts, denied our humanity, beaten physically, mentally, spiritually, economically, culturally,
and religiously, are trying desperately to limp to Zion even as our life's essence drains from
us? Are we Samaritans going out into a world filled with violence, moving out with a gospel
that is given life and breath in our lives, who bind the wounds of the victims but as hearers of
the parable also know that we cannot stop at binding? Rather, we must go to the roots of
violence to untangle the myriad injustices that give violence its power. Our collective task is
to do all that we believe we can do and also those things we think we cannot do to banish
violence from our lives and the lives of others. Ultimately, with all these possibilities and
more, we have been and will be all the characters of Jesus's parable at some point and sometimes most likely more than one at the same time.

In crafting ways to overcome violence, it may be best to begin with confession, which is
an integral part of lament—that we have done those things that we ought not to have done.
With genuine confession, one built on love and justice, we can begin to hear the truth from
those who have suffered and are suffering the deadly debris of violence in this world. We
listen to those who speak the truth of their realities and act with precision for those who cry
out for justice as well as those held mute or unheard as they yearn for a better tomorrow. To
engage in this radical listening and witnessing requires that we live with humility, acknowledge our complicity, and pray for a way to overcome it.

It is from this place of deep reckoning that is found in lament that we must also spurn
the temptation of seeking martyrdom—for ourselves and for others. In this case, martyrdom
only tips our lives into flurries of self-righteousness and romanticizes and ultimately trivializes the pain and anguish of others. To end violence, we must hear and listen to the silence
and the cries of the victims of violence rather than to the echoes of our egos gone amok in a
haze of self-righteous and ill-considered indignation.

Three: Hearing and Listening

Engaging violence with love can conjure up the ghosts and the terrors in our lives that come
as dancing specters, haunting goblins, or moaning trolls providing the lullabies for the executioners in our society. Mournful laments emerge from the silence and the cries of the victims
of violence. One such lament is sung and lived by the thousands displaced and the lives lost in
the violent aftermath of Hurricane Katrina. There are many points at which the discipline of

ethics and those who practice it have entered in thinking through the ongoing atrocity of the aftermath of this hurricane. We are challenged to consider a question that is framed by the kind of love (and justice) I have been arguing for in this series of meditations: What does it mean when a culture is washed away? This form of violence carries with it the razor-sharp edge of extinction. Therefore, this question comes from my work in the theo-ethical world-views of black religion that necessitate studying culture and history. As any ethicist, I often ask questions like: "Why? How? Who?" These questions do not come from a disinterested, dispassionate place but with the recognition that religion does not sit all by itself glorying in being mystical or mysterious or magical or relevant.

The cultural matrix of New Orleans, in large measure a black creolized culture, was not annihilated, exterminated, or fenced out. It was *washed* away as the levees broke and millions of people fled for their lives (some did not make it) and now have no homes to return to, taking with them their dress, their values, their religion, their language games and schemes—their isness.

New Orleans is the home of jazz, dating from near the beginning of the twentieth century. It comes from Congo Square, where black slaves performed music and chants from their African roots. It comes from Storyville, where prostitutes entertained their clients and musicians provided beat and melody to the movement of bodies. Each area performs this musical form that blends Africa and Europe; the blues, hymns, spirituals; old French and Spanish music—a creolized music form that comes from a people who know what mixing means for the body and blood. Jazz comes straight out of New Orleans black life to make the distinctive sound rolling out of Buddy Bolden's or Freddie Keppard's or Louis Armstrong's cornet, Jelly Roll Morton's piano, Jimmie Noone's clarinet, and George Lewis's trombone. There were Sweet Emma Barrett, Lizzie Miles, and Ann Cook belting out the songs so that when Cook sang "Mama Cookie Blues" or "Sweetest Black Man in Town" hard and strong, she actually stopped traffic on Rampart Street, the historic avenue that is home to Congo Square, Iroquois Theater, and the Eagle Saloon and Oddfellows Hall.[9] Unlike the jazz from Kansas City or New York, New Orleans jazz is meant for dancing rather than for listening. It has a swinging, stomping, syncopated beat one hears in brass bands. This is the culture that has been washed away, and it cannot be fully recaptured in the places where those who created it in New Orleans have now landed in this modern diaspora, for culture and place are deeply linked.

Like jazz, New Orleans gospel music has its own unique sound. From the early three- and four-person quartets and choirs heard in storefront chapels or Spirit-filled churches—it was all a cappella. Other places in the South used tambourine, drums, trumpet, and saxophone. However, folks warmed to musical instruments slowly in New Orleans. The black Baptists and the African Methodist Episcopal religionists would declare that too many instruments were the devil's music. This was despite the fact that these were the same folk who would do a holy dance and shake with spirit on Sunday mornings. It is not surprising then that jazz musicians started playing in church, and when they did, in the 1920s and 1930s, they brought richer musical arrangements that paved the way for the larger choirs of thirty to forty singers accompanied by horns, drums, pianos, organs, and guitars.

However, a cappella and minimal instruments held on through the sounds of the Zion Harmonizers, who are still going strong after more than sixty years and returned to the stage in October after the big storm. Jai Reed, Miss Emma, the Moses Hogan Sisters, the Joyful Gospel Singers, and the Mighty Chariots of Fire continued the New Orleans gospel music sound and message. Aretha Franklin may be the Queen of Soul, but New Orleans's

Mahalia Jackson remains the Empress of Gospel Music, although she has been gone for over thirty years.

One of the tasks of koinonia and the love it evokes is to work for the day that New Orleans and the rest of the devastated areas can return to their vitality. Music is about where you are and where you have come from. This shapes music and the people who make it and experience it in special ways. There are forms of gospel and jazz that come *from* New Orleans, a discrete physical location that teems with a cultural history that shapes its people and the rest of us. When a culture is washed away, the task of a love that acts is to find the strategies to bring, if not coax, that culture and the people who make it and respond to it back. Perhaps it will not be the same, but this is not a tragedy because all cultures that are living must change and grow. This means that both memory and history will be a part of building and rebuilding that culture. It will take the expansive demands of love that can bring them together as glue and cement. This is the concrete response to Baby Suggs's admonition—love your hands, necks, the dark liver, the heart.[10]

How can loving in the face of such a violent and obscene washing away help folk find the will and the fortitude they will need? How can love be a resource in the midst of the various betrayals that built a devastatingly inept and dangerous levee system and the continuing horror that is now largely off our screens as people still cannot go home unless they have access to a fair amount of wealth, power, and influence? An active love, justice, in this context means working with the wealthy and the poor, those who are rebuilding, those who are still in diaspora, those who are responsible for bringing back some version of New Orleans that will hopefully be a panoply of colors and incomes rather than a monotone of wealth and privilege.

Love invites us to explore what has been and to see what can and must be if we are to truly live the great varieties of witnesses we have. In short, we should not practice a malformed love that is nothing more than an over-churchified, solipsistic Matterhorn.[11] There is so much more for us to experience, know, and grow with genuine deep-acting love. When we embrace strength, fear, doubt, certainty, and all those emotions that mark us as humans who seek God as a part of our daily lives, then love becomes a blessing and the forerunner to change that is shaped by those seeking a new heaven and earth.

Love, then, ushers in more than personal reformation. It signals rebuilding and revitalization rather than massaging a few new pieces or people into a bankrupt but seductive societal puzzle. Love demands that the puzzle itself be rethought. We must allow this love that is extremely threatening to the status quo to find its natural home in people's lives and walk with them even as they their dig heels in, shudder, shake, refuse, argue, and turn to the familiars of fear and obstinacy to maintain a social order that ensures that far too many of us are pushed to the margins of our societies structurally and forced to remain there with few resources to dismantle this injustice. Therefore, we seek to find ways to usher that which has been washed away back and help it rebuild anew.

Four: Beginning Again and Again

No, love does not always let things come so easily at times, because love often means we have opened our eyes, hearts, minds, souls, and very spirits and we now see, feel, touch, and smell the joy and the agony living in the brokenness of creation.[12] This is one of the ironies of love. In our yearning for love, we often walk far away from it as we try to come home to it. We often live into the small and narrow spaces of life that stunt our growth and demand far too little of us because far too little is expected from us—or far too little is comfortable. It just may be, then, that love is not a force outside us showering us with its agapic nobility or campy romanticism or hopeless sentimentality.

Love is one more piece to the fabric of the universe, one more way to signal this restless journey we are on, one more sign that the Emmaus Road is not the end of the journey but its beginning. To love, to see a vision, a purpose, a reality offers so much for us that is good and right and just. This can be so profound that it may be that we do not believe we can reach or attain it or are good enough for it. We can resist this "less than" mentality when we realize that love is not the end product on the assembly line of our lives. It is a vital part of our journeys.

One of the many ways in which we come to know God's way in our lives with a richness that ripens, a richness that often disquiets us, is when we see devastating pictures of absolute neglect in the aftermath of Hurricane Katrina, the haunting faces of women and girls who are survivors of war and the rape that comes in almost any war that has been / is / will be fought, the pictures and cries from Honduras, the Uighur in western China's Xinjiang province, the inner cities and rural areas of the United States, the devastation in sub-Saharan Africa due to HIV and AIDS. And there are more images emerging each day because we have not yet found ways to put love into action thoroughly and systematically through justice making. To accomplish this, we must allow ourselves to completely succumb to love as a natural mark of our humanity and not categorize it as a sign of moral rectitude that is too high for us to attain or pursue.

We must learn the lessons we can find if we accept the fullness of our humanity in that moment of loving, that moment when we realize that we cannot do this life alone, and that we are thoroughly caught in the web of creation. This magnificent web is woven with the tensile threads of creation unfolding into creation as we breathe in and out as a testament to God's grace and love alive in our living. What brilliant places we can go if we see our love as a mark of grace as it welcomes us into a soul-deep relationship with ourselves and a God who abides with us with the steady beat of eternity.

Five: Is This the Prize?

As we seek love, to be guided by love and ultimately to love, it is important to do so with the awareness that we must stop drawing ideological and methodological lines between social issues and theological issues.[13] If a genuine love ethic provides us with no greater challenge, it is to realize that the violence of maintaining such lines diminishes our scholarship, weakens our lived witness, and can turn people into social projects rather than human beings.

One way to begin to accept this challenge is to start with the deceptively simple notion that *all* of life is sacred.[14] This runs counter to the Cartesian dualism we often practice that separates body and spirit, female and male, good and evil, and so forth. However, to know, believe, and live an integrated life is to yoke one's whole self in God's spirit, to God's unfolding and ongoing revelation, and to believe in the reality of and the transformative power of God's ongoing revelation as we breathe in and out. It emerges as we walk down the street, speak to others or not, sigh deeply in ecstasy or sorrow, speak out, act up, network, sleep, dream, and wake. All this—and more—is sacred, as we stand rooted firmly in love and justice.

A deeply active love ethic rooted in koinonia is one way to accept Baby Suggs's call to love the heart (for this is the prize), and it encourages all of us to relate to God through and in our humanness. This is *all* of what it is that makes us who we are—mind, body, and spirit—

and so such love must eschew the kind of theological apartheid that often holds us captive in split bodies rather than in broken ones. To live in our *brokenness* is to practice our faith; to live in *split lives* is to create fractured whirlpools of disaster that we think are markers of holiness. When our theo-ethical musings reify such segregation, we no longer practice methodological rigor in our work. Genuine intellectual engagement begins with the concreteness of our humanity rather than in esoteric concepts abstracted from life that teach us or lure us into believing that it is better to live in an unrelenting ontological suicide watch rather than a celebration of the richness and responsibilities of what it means to be created in the image of God.

A deeply active love ethic is a concrete way to live this out. It is that marvelous moment when head and heart and body get on the same page in creation and we begin to engage in deep walking with the Spirit. In doing so, we help folk dare to be transformed. In the dawning of this transformation, we see the vital integration of faith, hope, love, and justice in life where we begin by realizing we *are* created in God's image, God's presence in our lives is in the fabric of our existence, God's love for us is unconditional, and this love moves us to grow in compassion, understanding, and acceptance of each other.

As we learn how to love the heart of others and ourselves, we also practice the formation of a divine/human community based on love and pointed toward justice where we develop concrete strategies to address the many forms of violence—the subtle and the spectacular—that people endure and find ways to survive. Elsewhere, I have described this as rim-bone walking.[15] Here, I call this love.

Notes

1. See Christian Smith, *Moral, Believing Animals: Human Personhood and Culture* (New York: Oxford University Press, 2009). Smith explores what kind of animals we are by probing how our visions of being human shape our actions and the institutions we create.

2. See Toni Morrison, "The Site of Memory," in *Inventing the Truth: The Art and Craft of Memoir*, rev. and exp. ed., ed. William Zinsser (Boston: Houghton Mifflin, 1998), 193–94. Morrison is uncomfortable with this label because she believes her responsibility "is not to lie." She then makes an important distinction between truth and fiction: "It [truth] may be excessive, it may be more interesting, but the important thing is that it's random—and fiction is not random." Then she explains,

> the crucial distinction for me is not the difference between fact and fiction, but the distinction between fact and truth. Because fact can exist without human intelligence, but truth cannot. So if I'm looking to find and expose a truth about the interior life of people who didn't write it . . . then the approach that is most productive and most trustworthy for me is the recollection that moves from the image to the text. Not from the text to the image.

3. Morrison, *Beloved* (New York: Alfred A. Knopf, 1987), 258–59.

4. Ibid., 88–89.

5. Claus Westermann, *The Psalms: Structure, Content and Message*, trans. Ralph D. Gehrke (Minneapolis: Augsburg Publishing House, 1980), 32.

6. Westermann, "The Role of Lament in the Theology of the Old Testament," *Interpretation: A Journal of Bible and Theology* 28, no. 1 (January 1974): 20–21. See also Paul Wayne Ferris Jr., *The Genre of the Communal Lament in the Bible and the Ancient Near East* (Atlanta: Scholars Press, 1992), 10.

7. Walter Brueggeman, "The Formfulness of Grief," *Interpretation: A Journal of Bible and Theology* 31, no. 3 (July 1977): 265.

8. In Jeremiah, Rachel, mother of Joseph and Benjamin, laments the northern tribe's exile to Ramah. Matthew depicts unmitigated grief, but Jeremiah introduces the promise of restoration.

9. The Iroquois Theater was an African American cinema and vaudeville house managed by Clarence Williams in the early twentieth century. Williams was an early to mid-twentieth century jazz pianist, composer, promoter, vocalist, theatrical producer, and publisher. The Eagle Saloon and Oddfellows Hall is a nineteenth-century lodge that is often viewed as the most important surviving building from the early days of jazz. This was the home of the famous "Eagle Band" and was where Buddy Bolden, Freddie Keppard, Buddie Petit, Louis Armstrong, and many other early jazz greats played.

10. While the focus of this essay is the rebuilding of New Orleans, it is important to acknowledge that those who cannot return or choose not to return are faced with the challenges of creating a new cultural matrix in their new places of residence. Like any migrant population, the old is blended with the new to create a new culture in the new location.

11. A phrase used by poet Elizabeth Alexander in an e-mail to the author on July 13, 2009, that was describing another set of circumstances.

12. For me, the brokenness of creation is not negative. Rather, it is descriptive of the ways in which we are challenged to be a part of what feminist theologian Letty Russell calls the mending of creation. It is through our brokenness that we are able to take the various threads of our lives and weave masterpieces of faithfulness. See Letty Russell, *Just Hospitality: God's Welcome in a World of Difference*, ed. J. Shannon Clarkson and Kate M. Ott (Philadelphia: Westminster John Knox Press, 2009), for a fuller discussion of the mending of creation.

13. This final meditation is prompted by an observation by Jennifer Leath that ethicists and theologians (as well as scholars in other theological disciplines) often relegate issues like race (gender, class, age, [dis] ability) to the category of social problems rather than theo-ethical issues and concepts. Theologian James H. Cone, along with other black, womanist, feminist, mujerista, and Minjung theologians, has made this observation. Sadly, standard theological discourse continues to maintain this divide.

14. The definition of sacred I am appealing to is that which is made or declared or believed to be holy, where the holy is that which is derived from or associated with or belongs to a divine power. In this case, the divine power is the Christian God.

15. Emilie M. Townes, "Walking on the Rim Bones of Nothingness: Scholarship and Activism," *Journal of the American Academy of Religion* 77, no. 1 (March 2009): 1–15.

18

Loving Nature

Christian Environmental Ethics

HOLMES ROLSTON III

LOVE IS SO CENTRAL to life that the single English word "love" opens up to become an umbrella. Love is not some distinct behavior with clearly recognized content and boundaries but a varied collection of many kinds of emotions that have in common only some relationship with a quite positive quality. Loves may be self-regarding, mate- and kin-regarding, other-regarding, genetically based, instinctive or acquired during a lifetime, conscious or subconscious, deliberated or spontaneous, proximate or ultimate, intrinsic or instrumental. They may be in-group or out-group, local or global, trans-generational, transformed by experience of the natural world or by cultural and historical ideals, in principle and in practice. These rationales must be mixed and weighted, blended and traded off with consistency and inconsistency. The result may be wandering search and muddling through. The further result can be complex caring amid an embarrassment of riches.

Love brings immediately to mind human interpersonal relationships, but even these are widely diverse and multi-factored. If one asks whether there are trans-human loves, the saints will reply that "God is love"; scientists may doubt that "love" is an appropriate category for describing animal behavior, and certainly, it should not be used for plant behavior. The saints may continue that the two great commandments are to love God and neighbor, but if we ask scientists whether we can or ought to love animals and plants, they may start to say yes and then hesitate in confusion as to whether scientists can speak on "ought" questions. Perhaps a dialogue about whether we ought to love nonhuman others will be illuminating even if this takes some wandering in this wilderness of rationales.

A recurring contemporary theme is that ethics should be "inclusive." Ethicists often have doubts whether ethics can be universal or even transcultural; they wonder whether ethical laws might be no more than socially constructed mores embedded in particular cultures. Ethics is never absolute—so we are told. Postmodernists know that nobody has a "grand narrative." Our ethics will have to be piecemeal, just as our loves are smorgasbord. But these same ethicists seem rather sure that we ought to widen the scope of moral concern to include those earlier outside the pale. Just how inclusive? Is there place for a grand narrative of love from self to family to community, tribe, nation, humanity, life, land, planet, God?

Love Gone Wild: Misplaced?

Love of the wild? A first concern is that there is no love in the wild. We might be foisting an inappropriate emotion onto a loveless nature. The central Christian virtue is love, agape, and this seems nowhere to be found or even remotely approached in wild nature, which is rather a nature "red in tooth and claw." So can Christians love a nature that is mostly tragic struggle? A central biblical commandment is not to kill, but in the wild, predators are condemned to killing. A divinely forbidden moral evil among humans is the vital essence of predatory life. So it may seem that were humans to love such a nature, love would have "gone wild," off the deep end.

Christian love is expressed through kindness, mercy, generosity, compassion, justice, patience, forgiveness. Those virtues do not seem either present in nature or relevant to deciding how to behave when encountering wild nature. The Bible encourages reconciliation, community, harmony, reciprocity, shalom. If such virtues are relevant when encountering nature, they will have to be much recast. Most of the sensibilities we struggle to nourish in civilized beings, much less in Christian believers, are not there in the wild. There is nothing kind, fair, or decent there. We may notice that humans too are predators (heterotrophs that must eat something else). Still, although humans biologically must eat and sacrifice other lives, humans morally ought not to act like beasts. To go wild is to lapse from civilization.

Any loving of wild nature is a loving of amoral creatures. The element of loving regardless of merit (often thought to be especially pivotal in agape) is not relevant here. A Christian may be called to love others who are sinners, devoid of merit, broken. But even where predators eat prey, these killer beasts are not sinning. Love as it reckons with moral failure is distinctive to interpersonal relations. In nature, one is not loving prodigal sons. There is no repaying of evil with good. Nor are we loving the worthless; to the contrary we are finding—well what? Nature red in tooth and claw? Or goodness in creation?

If we set aside sin and redemption, perhaps we could still use the familiar ethical concepts of justice and benevolence, which are also elements of loving others for their own sakes. Justice is, classically, "to each his due," with reference to persons; perhaps animals also have something due, differently from what is due persons but due according to their kind. "A righteous man has regard for the life of his beast" (Prov. 12:10). Oxen are to be rested on the Sabbath (Deut. 5:14; Exod. 20:10); the ox in the pit requires rescue, even at breach of the Sabbath (Luke 14:5). The ox that treads out the grain is not to be muzzled (Deut. 25:4) nor are ox and donkey to be yoked together (Deut. 22:10). Such concerns urge compassionate treatment of domestic animals but tell us nothing about wild nature.

There are biodiverse natural kinds; each may be worthy of respect, but we do not consider each of equal regard—whether microbes or elephants. Justice is often allied with a concept of rights. There are no "rights" in wild nature. Perhaps "rights" appear when humans interact with nature; that has some plausibility with the higher animals, more so with domestic animals in human care—the ox in the ditch. But ascribing rights to insects or forests seems implausible. Even if it were, we may recognize rights in those we do not love. Predatory killers? Good creatures? With rights? To whom justice is owed? Toward whom we ought to be kind? The better category might be intrinsic values found to be present in creation, to which we are drawn in respect and care.

Theologians such as Christopher Southgate have argued that Christians ought to become redeemers or healers of the evils in nature, moderating the suffering there.[1] Southgate hopes for a "pelican heaven," that is, God resurrecting the myriads of animal lives sacrificed in the evolutionary process.[2] But if so, is there a frog heaven? A beetle heaven? Heaven for rattlesnakes?

Compassionate concern for redeeming the myriads of lives across evolutionary history, most of them cut short in early death, soon becomes incredible. If these lives are worthwhile, that must be through some kind of contribution to the ongoing process of life on Earth—not in some heaven to come. Pointless suffering in culture is a bad thing and ought to be removed where possible, but pain in wild nature is not entirely analogous to pain in an industrial, agricultural, and medically skilled culture. Pain in nature remains in the context of natural selection; it is pain instrumental to survival and to the integrity of species.

If there seems no space for agape, perhaps there is place for philia, friendship, the companionship of mutual togetherness. But again, this is not evidently relevant in wild nature. Perhaps some animals, notably dogs and horses, have been socialized enough that they do enjoy companionship with a human master. A dog is man's best friend. Aristotle suggests that animals can express philia (*NE* 1155a). Saint Francis of Assisi calls the creatures great and small his brothers and sisters. Still, it does not seem that one has friendship with the wild animals, bears or wolves, much less those frogs or rattlesnakes.

If there seems no space for agape and little for philia, perhaps there is place for eros—a love that desires to possess, that needs others in self-fulfillment. Here much will depend on the meaning of "possess." If it means that the self is incomplete without the other and reaches out to achieve this completeness, then humans could well be incomplete without loving wild nature and ought to reach out to embrace such nature—an embrace that may involve "letting be," leaving the creatures wild. Wild animals do not need our beneficence, they need us to leave space and let them alone. A common injunction in environmental ethics is that if, enjoying nature, the observer is so close that it affects the animal's behavior, that is too close. Back off.

Much Christian love of nature is of the This Is My Father's World vintage, a sentimental praise of what is lovely in nature: mountain grandeur, spring woodlands, wildflowers, clouds, colorful birds. What of the ugly in nature—predator ripping open prey, deer starving in winter? What of the violent—earthquakes, storms? The Psalmist celebrates the stormy wind fulfilling God's command (discussed later), but Jesus does once rebuke the sea and quiet the wind (Mark 4:39). Christian love toward other persons, of course, is nowhere restricted to the lovely or attractive. It is unbounded, indiscriminate. Jesus bids his disciples "love your enemies," and you will be "sons of the Most High; for God is kind to the ungrateful and selfish" (Luke 6:35). But such love seems also directed to reforming the selfish, the ungrateful. Nonscenic nature, however, is not loved in order to be redeemed.

Is there any sense of "love gone wild" that might seem plausible?

Promised Land, Garden Earth

Loving the wild might be out of bounds, but loving the land is a central theme of the Hebrew Bible. Biblical faith is from the start a landed faith. Israel is given their "promised land—a good and broad land, a land flowing with milk and honey" (Exod. 3:8; Deut. 27:3). The land is watched over by God's care: "The land which you are going over to possess is a land of hills and valleys, which drinks water by the rain from heaven, a land which the Lord your God cares for; the eyes of the Lord your God are always upon it, from the beginning of the year to the end of the year" (Deut. 11:11–12). The Lord owns the land—"The land is mine"—and bestows tenure and usufruct on Israel, their "promised land" (Lev. 25:23).

Walter Brueggemann takes "land as a prism for Biblical faith." "Land is a central, if not the central theme of biblical faith."[3] "The land" is both geographical and symbolic. Yearning for a sense of place is a perennial human longing, of belonging to a community emplaced on landscape, and Israel's sense of living on a land given by God, of human placement on the earth, can yet speak to the landlessness, and lostness, of modern persons. All peoples need a sense of "my country," of their social communities in place on a sustaining landscape they possess in care and in love.

Land is *adamah*, the arable land on which plants can grow and animals can graze. Land is *'eretz*, the terrestrial earth, brought forth on the third day of creation. Israel's promised land is their corner of a larger garden Earth on which humankind (symbolized in Adam and Eve) was placed in primordial time. "The Lord God took the man and put him in the garden of Eden to till and keep it" (Gen. 2:15). By this account, humans are "Earth-gardeners." Humans domesticate earth. Earth is the scene of creative wildness, but such wildness also needs to be tamed, made into a garden, park, cultivated. Although paternalism is today rather suspect, the original context of "dominion" (in medieval Europe) was closely related to "dominus," the Latin for father. Humans are Earth Fathers.

A favored model is that of stewardship, applicable to Israel and primordially applicable to humans on the whole Eden earth. Perhaps the concept of Earth-gardener needs also to be interpreted as Earth-trustee. A steward manages for the benefit of an owner; a trustee cares for that under his or her care. The Hebrews had three different kinds of rulers: prophets, priests, and kings—roles unavailable to nonhumans. Humans should speak for God in natural history, should reverence the sacred on Earth, and should rule creation in freedom and in love. Human "responsibility" on Earth is as good a word as human "dominion" over Earth, indeed a better one, for it captures what dominion originally meant in the famous Genesis charge to Adam and Eve, or what it ought to mean, a stewardship over something entrusted into one's care—the prolific Earth with its hordes of creatures brought forth and found to be very good (Gen. 1:31).

There is concern about proper cares from the first chapter of Genesis. God says to the couple: "Be fruitful and multiply, and fill the earth and subdue it; and have dominion" (Gen. 1:27–28). This seems to teach that the role of humans on Earth is to conquer it. That is what humans should care about: ruling over Earth. Famously, historian Lynn White laid much of the blame for the ecological crisis on the Christian belief that humans had dominion over nature, an attack published in *Science*.[4] God's command for humans to "have dominion" flowered in medieval Europe, licensed the exploitation of nature, and produced science and technology to satisfy human cares, and this has resulted in an ecological crisis. So the Bible launches an arrogantly misplaced care on Earth.

Theologians have replied that appropriate dominion requires stewardship and care.[5] True, there is a sense of dominion that means "Earth-tyrant," humans subduing nature in a repressive sense, as a conqueror does his enemy. But there are more positive senses of dominion. Even within the military metaphor, a general has command over his own soldiers, about whom presumably he cares. Such an "Earth-commander" finds the interests of the commander and the commanded inseparably entwined. There is a salutary view of the just king, to be contrasted with its opposite, the king who rules "with force and harshness" (Ps. 72; Ezek. 34:4).

Yes, Israel was a landed faith, some Christian respondents will concede. But that was Old Testament, not New Testament. Christianity is not a landed faith. Indeed, Christianity is not a worldly faith. Does not Jesus say, "My kingship is not of this world" (John 18:36)? Perhaps there is no pelican heaven, but Jesus did teach that he is taking his disciples to heaven—his father's house with many mansions. Jesus was taken up into heaven, and at death, we leave Earth and go there to be with him.

Jesus did say, "My kingship is not of this world." But understanding context is essential. Teaching as he did in the Imperial Roman world, his reference in "this" is to the fallen world of the culture he came to redeem, to false trust in politics and economics, in armies and kings. In the landscape surrounding him, Jesus found ample evidence of the presence of God. The birds of the air neither sow nor reap yet are fed by the heavenly Father, who notices the sparrows that fall. Not even Solomon is arrayed with the glory of the lilies, though the grass of the field, today alive, perishes tomorrow (Matt. 6). There is in every seed and root a promise. Sowers sow, the seed grows secretly, and sowers return to reap their harvests. God sends rain on the just and unjust. Jesus teaches that the power organically manifest in the wildflowers of the field is continuous with the power spiritually manifest in the kingdom he announces. There is an ontological bond between nature and spirit. This also seems to be connecting the good land, the rural landscape, with deeper natural powers, present also in wild nature.

Creation: Let There Be . . . Swarms!

If we are trying to find our bearings toward wild nature and also get the most inclusive perspective, perhaps the best place to start is to go back to the biblical beginning: to the Genesis creation, now asking not simply if this creation was a garden Earth for human dominion but wondering what to make of its wildness. Was this garden Earth wild? Is it only there for humans to tame and domesticate?

Right at the beginning of the Bible, right at the creation, God is interested in sun, moon, stars, birds, fish, animals—before humans are even on Earth. "In the beginning when God created the heavens and the earth, the earth was a formless void and darkness covered the face of the deep, while a wind from God swept over the face of the waters" (Gen. 1:1 [NRSV]). This wind of God inspires the animated Earth, and "the earth produces of itself" (Mark 4:28).[6] The days of creation are a series of divine imperatives, not so much fiats as commissions: "Let the earth put forth vegetation. . . . Let the earth bring forth living things according to their kinds" (Gen. 1:11, 24). Biblical faith has the conviction that species originate in God's wish. God ordered earth to "bring forth swarms of living creatures" (Gen. 1:20). "Swarms" is the Hebrew word for biodiversity! Adam's first job was, we might say, a taxonomy project, naming the animals. Let the earth bring forth biodiversity.

Yes, the apex of the creation is man and woman, made of mud, made in the image of God, incarnate and set on their garden Earth. Humans prove to be the great challenge to God, the contentious creature, but the world is habitat not only for humans but for the myriads of creatures—from "great sea monsters" to "birds," "beasts," and "creeping things"—which, repeatedly, God finds "good" and bids to "be fruitful and multiply and fill" the waters, the earth, the skies (Gen. 1:20–22). God enjoys the biodiversity. That includes the creepy things, and here we might recall the biologist J. B. S. Haldane's famous remark, when asked by theologians what he had learned about the Creator from studying creation in biology, that God had "an inordinate fondness for beetles."[7]

The fauna is included within the Hebrew covenant. The covenant renewed in the days of Noah—after a natural disaster with divine provision for saving the wild creatures—is quite specific about this:

"Behold I establish my covenant with you and your descendants after you, and with every living creature that is with you, the birds, the cattle, and every beast of the earth with you." . . .

God said, "This is the sign of the covenant which I make between me and you and every living creature that is with you, for all future generations: I set my bow in the cloud and it shall be a sign of the covenant between me and the earth." (Gen. 9:5, 12–13)

"Keep them alive with you" (Gen. 6:19). That certainly sounds like God loves wild nature. To use modern terms, the covenant was both ecumenical and ecological. In theocratic Israel, animals belonged to God, as indeed did all property. "For every beast of the forest is mine, the cattle on a thousand hills. I know all the birds of the air, and all that moves in the field is mine" (Ps. 50:10–11). That includes quite a menagerie. In wilderness desert are "fiery serpents and scorpions" (Deut. 8:15; Num. 21:6); "jackals," "hyenas," "owls," "kites," "ravens," "porcupines," "ostriches," "wild goats (satyrs)," "wild beasts" (Isa. 34). Nor does God forget the flora: "The trees of the Lord are watered abundantly; the cedars of Lebanon which he planted" (Ps. 104:16).

Absent humans, God is there, positively blessing such lands:

Who has cleft a channel for the torrents of rain, and a way for the thunderbolt, to bring rain on a land where no man is, on the desert in which there is no man; to satisfy the waste and desolate land, and to make the ground put forth grass? (Job 38:25–27)

Praise the Lord from the earth you sea monsters and all deeps, fire and hail, snow and frost, stormy wind fulfilling his command! Mountains and all hills, fruit trees and all cedars! Beasts and all cattle, creeping things and flying birds! (Ps. 148:8–9)

Thou crownest the year with thy bounty; the tracks of thy chariot drip with fatness. The pastures of the wilderness drip, the hills gird themselves with joy, the meadows clothe themselves with flocks, the valleys deck themselves with grain, they shout and sing for joy. (Ps. 65:11–13)

God not only blesses humans; God blesses the desolate wastes. These fierce landscapes, sometimes supposed to be ungodly places, are godly after all. God does not want all these places subdued and cultivated; rather, God delights in places with no people.

Although wilderness is a locale of human wandering, searching, self-discovery, encounter with divine presence (to which we return later), taken for what it is in itself before using it to symbolize human hopes and disappointments, wildness in the Bible is never a bad thing. For example, under God, wild asses, eagles, goats, lions, badgers (conies) are born free.

Who has let the wild ass go free? Who has loosed the bonds of the swift ass, to whom I have given the steppe for his home, and the salt land for his dwelling place? He scorns the tumult of the city; he hears not the shouts of the driver. He ranges the mountain as his pasture, and he searches after every green thing. (Job 39:5–8)

Is it by your wisdom that the hawk soars, and spreads his wings toward the south? Is it at your command that the eagle mounts up and makes his nest on high? On the rock he dwells and makes his home in the fastness of the rocky crag. Thence he spies out the prey;

his eyes behold it afar. His young ones suck up blood; and where the slain are, there is he.
. . . Shall a faultfinder contend with the Almighty? He who argues with God, let him
answer it. (Job 39:26–40.2)

> The high mountains are for the wild goats; the rocks are a refuge for the badgers. . . .
> The young lions roar for their prey, seeking their food from God. . . . O Lord, how mani-
> fold are thy works! In wisdom hast thou made them all; the earth is full of thy creatures.
> (Ps. 104:18–24)

This celebrates an ecology, not simply a promised land.

Those roaring lions and blood-soaked eagles are made in divine wisdom. They kill
seeking food from God. The nonhuman creation is wild, outside the hand of man, outside
culture. But it is not outside both divine and biological order. The Creator's love for these
creatures does not conform to human purposes. That God is personal as revealed in interhuman cultural relations does not mean that the natural relationship of God to lions and eagles
is personal, nor should humans treat wild animals as persons. They are to be treated with
appropriate respect for their wildness. The creatures are the proper object for divine love, and
accordingly for human love, caring about them (saving the lions and eagles). And they have
to be cared about according to their kinds, which exemplify a spectrum of wild cares (lions
caring for their cubs and killing zebras to feed them, eagles caring for their eaglets and killing
ground squirrels to feed them). Each form of life has its proper integrity, defended by its
successful caring (its adapted fit), and we humans come to respect, to love that creaturely
integrity. The meaning of the words "good" and "divine" is not the same in nature and in
culture. Nor is the character of the appropriate "love."

Wilderness

Concern for wilderness preservation is sometimes taken as love gone quite wild, new age
spirituality that is naive about real nature red in tooth and claw. Postmodernists may claim
that the whole idea of "wilderness" is a recent social construction, mostly by upscale urban-
ites who wish to recreate there. But both the idea of wilderness and love for it have a venera-
ble history, including ancient biblical history.

Words translated as "wilderness" occur nearly three hundred times in the Bible. A formative Hebrew memory is the years of "wandering in the wilderness," mixing experience of
wild landscape, of searching for a promised land, and of encounter with God. The Pentateuch
wandering is in the *midbar*, uninhabited land where humans are nomads. This common
Hebrew word refers often to a wild field, where domestic animals may be grazed and wild
animals live, in contrast to cultivated land, hence, sometimes "the pastures of the wilderness"
(Joel 1:19–20). Another word is *arabah*, steppe, also translated as desert (Gen. 36:24). "The
land that was desolate [*midbar*] and impassable shall be glad, and the wilderness [*arabah*]
shall rejoice" (Isa. 35:1). Land that lies waste is *chorbah*; land without water is *yeshimon*.

Whether the desert dry valleys or the more moist steppe, wilderness is a locale for
intense experiences—of stark need for food and water (manna and quails), of isolation (Elijah and the still small voice), of danger and divine deliverance (Hagar and Ishmael), of
renewal, of encounter with God (Moses, the burning bush, the revelation of the divine name,
Mount Sinai). There is a psychology as well as a geography of wilderness. There is a theology
gained in the wilderness.[8]

Linguists here will make the point that the Hebrews did not have an exact equivalent of the contemporary English word "wilderness." Those concerned about indeterminacy of translation really ought never ask whether freighted terms from a modern mind-set have exact parallels in ancient languages ("rights," "love," "freedom," "heavens," "hell," "resurrection," "body," "spirit," "soul," "nature"). Ecologists may add that the ancient Hebrews did not know the planetary diversity of wilderness ecosystems—for example, jungles, montane forests, tundra. Such misgivings aside, the Hebrews evidently knew the experience of confronting the wild, perhaps as well as or better than any contemporary linguist or ecologist, farmer or wilderness backpacker.

The kind of wilderness the Hebrews did know often seems to have a negative character, especially contrasted with a promised land flowing with milk and honey. But God can be found there, and the fierce character of the wild landscape also seems to intensify the divine encounter. In the wilderness, the people are tempted to be contentious, murmuring, unruly, and ignorant of the promises and power of God. They wander there until they have learned the lessons of the hardships of the wilderness (Deut. 8:3). The New Testament word most often translated as wilderness is *eremos* (or *eremia*), an isolated place. (This is also the Greek word most often used in the Septuagint to translate the Hebrew words we examined earlier.) The wilderness figures at critical junctures in the life of Jesus.[9] At the opening of Mark's Gospel, John the Baptist, "the voice of one crying in the wilderness," appears, with echoes of Israel's formative exodus encounters and Moses's crying for God in the Sinai wilderness (Mark 1:3; cf. Isa. 40:3). Jesus is baptized by John and then is driven by the Spirit into the wilderness for forty days. The Devil is there, but so is the Spirit. Jesus is tempted to be the wrong kind of messiah, and the Spirit prevails. Jesus is at once with the beasts and ministered to by angels (Mark 1:12). In his experience is found again a spiritual struggle for self-discovery in an environment of wild forces, threat and grace, which, seen in its depths, is encounter with the divine presence.

Jesus is soon found returning to the wilderness (indeed again in Mark's opening chapter): "A great while before day, he rose and went out to a lonely place, and there he prayed" (Mark 1:35; cf. Mark 6:31–32). This records a search for solitude, but the natural environment is the needed ambiance. Peter, James, and John see Jesus transfigured "upon a high mountain apart by themselves" (Mark 9:2).

So wilderness is both a place for persons to encounter God and for persons to encounter a God larger than themselves, larger than human concerns. There is a discovering of God for us complementary with experience of God for wilderness. Just as Job was pointed out of his human troubles toward the wild Palestinian landscape, it is a useful, saving corrective to a simplistic "Jesus loves me this I know," "God is on my side" theology to discover vast ranges of creation that have nothing to do with satisfying our personal desires. What the wildlands do "for us," if we must phrase it that way, is teach that God is not "for us" humans alone. There, man is not the measure of things. God is "for" these wild creatures too. To be self-actualizing under God is a good thing for humans, and it is a good thing, mutatis mutandis, for coyotes and columbines. That is the blessing of divinity in them.

That the fair land of Palestine, with its cities and fields, should again become desert and wilderness is a frequent prophetic threat. The collapse of cultural life in the promised land is indeed a tragedy, and in that sense, a relapse to the wild is sometimes used in the Bible as a symbol for judgment on an aborted, once-promising culture. Jackals roam the land, destroyed in punishment for sin (Isa. 34). Such wildness is a tragedy only in foil to failed culture. There are frequent passages in which natural events—rain, drought, storm, flourishing harvests—are interpreted as means for divine blessing or judgment.[10]

Certain biblical passages suggest that the natural world is implicated in the fall, resulting from human sin (Gen. 3:18, 6:7, 11–13). But these passages are not to be taken to suggest that existing wildlands are fallen, nor that wild nature needs to be redeemed. A peaceable natural kingdom, where the lion lies down with the lamb, is sometimes used as the symbol of fulfillment in the promised land. This too is a cultural metaphor and cannot be interpreted in censure of natural history.

The Genesis of Caring

We have worried that Christian love might stand in stark opposition to anything found in loveless wild nature. Evolutionary history is driven, rather, by self-interest. The framework one expects in contemporary biology might be termed the evolution of "selfishness."[11] That could be a half-truth that goes wrong if taken for the whole. If we are searching for a more comprehensive picture, a complementary way to think of evolutionary natural history is to view it as the generation of "caring"—elaborating, diversifying, conserving, enriching these capacities.

An immediate objection is that the word "caring" is too anthropopathic. Selfishness is, of course, one form of the more inclusive concept "caring" and hardly less anthropopathic. Whatever the vocabulary, for all living beings some things "make a difference"; they do not survive unless they attend to these. There is caring wherever there is "agency," wherever there is "motivation," where there is "locomotion," perhaps even where there are "motors." In more philosophical vocabulary, there is caring wherever values are at stake.

At least after sentience arises, neural organisms evidently "care." Animals hunt and howl, find shelter, seek out their habitats and mates, feed their young, flee from threats, grow hungry, thirsty, hot, tired, excited, sleepy. They suffer injury and lick their wounds. Call these "interests" or "preferences" or whatever. If "caring" is too loaded a term, then call these animal "concerns." Staying alive requires "self-defense," perhaps a more accurately descriptive word for nonmoral animal and plants than the morally laden "selfish." "Fear" too is a form of caring. Living things have "needs." The biological processes must be "pro-life." If you dislike the connotations of "caring," there are dozens of good biological terms that spiral around it.

When humans arrive, "caring" is present by any conceivable standard. So once there was no caring; now "caring" in various forms is dominant in earthen biology. Asking what humans and nonhumans do care about, and how they got to be that way, invites the question, for any who have choices, What ought they to care about? We might discover that among our rich cares, we ought to care about conserving these processes of our genesis on Earth.

An animal is a "going concern." "Skin" is a sign of caring. Looking at "bark" on trees, we might say only that life has to be "protected." But throughout natural history there has emerged a somatic self, with know-how to protect it. If this isn't yet "caring," it is on the threshold edge of it. Caring gets complicated since selves are implicated with other selves. They depend on each other—on mates or what they eat. Organisms make a living in a niche; they get networked and fitted into trophic pyramids, into feed loops and feedback loops. Caring is an organism-in-environment dialectic.

Self-defense requires adapted fit; living things are webbed together in ecosystems and hence their cares. There will be "relations"—in today's fashionable term, "networking." Caring is only self-contained up to a point; after that, it is caring "about" these contacts and processes with which one is networked. The individual is forced to "adapted fit." This requires caring about others, for better or worse, if only a predator caring to catch and eat prey, the prey caring to escape, both caring for their young. Caring will be matrixed and require differential concerns.

In this larger horizon of caring, living things must reproduce. In fact, by Darwinian accounts, that is their priority care, else they go extinct. The Genesis God commands the same thing, as we earlier noticed: "Let the earth bring forth living things according to their kinds" (Gen. 1:24). "Be fruitful and multiply" (Gen. 1:20–22). So behaviors are selected that attend proportionately to the whole family, what biologists call "kin selection." Biologists may still insist that the individual acts "selfishly" in his or her own interests, but "selfish" is now being stretched to cover benefits gained by "caring about" the extended lines of kin and kind, lines that fan out eventually to all conspecifics (half of which are also potential mates, which sometimes also need to be cared about).

So it turns out that any individual immediate life is not exclusively individually owned but is scattered about in the family and that the individual competently defends its so-called self wherever and to the extent that this is manifested in the whole gene pool. This means that values the organism cares about can be held individually only as they are more inclusively distributed. Animals can care about others of their kind (as well as about mates, prey, and offspring). Animals are often social; elk form herds, birds of a feather flock together. This can be for their self-interest; each is safer in the company of others. But there may be more.

Frans de Waal complains that biologists regularly ascribe negative descriptions to primates; they are aggressive, or have enemies, or are selfish; they even cheat and are greedy. Such terms appear in scientific papers as acceptable terminology. But there is among scientists, de Waal complains, a simultaneous refusal to ascribe various positive traits to them, to say that they cooperate, or have friends or companions, much less that they share, or care for each other, or show sympathy. Any such language is unscientific and will be edited out of the journals. Biologists go to great lengths to argue away all evidence of animal altruism, interpreting it as disguised selfishness, or kin selection, or nepotism, and so on.

But de Waal, in his studies of primate behavior, finds that they display an enormous spectrum of emotions in different kinds of relationships. Scientists ought to reflect this fact in a broad array of terms. If, for example, animals can have enemies, they can have friends. If they can hurt, they can help. The problem, he suspects, is that the scientists' socially constructed filter, ultra-Darwinism, prevents their seeing and properly interpreting behavior that is counterevidence to their theory.[12]

Reproduction is typically assumed to be a need of individuals, but since any particular individual can flourish somatically without reproducing at all, indeed may be put through duress and risk or spend much energy reproducing, by another logic we can interpret reproduction as the species keeping up its own kind by reenacting itself again and again. In this sense, a female grizzly bear does not bear cubs to be healthy herself, any more than a woman needs children to be healthy. Rather, her cubs are *Ursus arctos*, threatened by nonbeing, recreating the species by continuous performance. A female animal does not have mammary glands nor a male animal testicles because the function of these is to preserve the animal's own life; these organs are defending the line of life bigger than the somatic individual. The individuals are genetically impelled to sacrifice themselves in the interests of reproducing their kind. What they "care about" is something dynamic to the specific form of life; they are selected to attend to the appropriate survival unit.

Though selection operates on individuals, since it is always an individual that copes, selection is for the kind of coping that succeeds in reproducing the kind, distributing the information coded in the gene more widely. The organism contributes to the next generation all that it has to contribute, what it has achieved that is of value about how to live its form of life well. *Survival is of the better sender of whatever is of genetic value in self into others.* Genes get "spread" around or "distributed" by organisms not simply for their "selves" but to spread what they know to other selves. Genes are selected for what they can contribute to the next generation. To use a metaphor deliberately provocative and contrary to the usual "selfish genes," genes get "shared." If doubters wonder whether this is yet to be called "caring," no doubt it is moving in that direction.

With the evolution of humans, there emerges the most complex caring on Earth. That arises, in part, from the complicated concerns that humans have and their genius for devising ways for pursuing these concerns. Humans care about family, tribe, nation, careers, and ideational causes such as biological science, French literature, or the Christian faith. At basic levels, this is still self-interest, though elaborately networked. But humans do reach some sense of shared common good, of community. Such wider vision requires even more complexity, a complex brain that can evaluate others not only in terms of helps and hurts but also with concern for their health and integrity. This includes knowing a human community, in which mutual reciprocity is possible and treasured, and knowing an ecological community, in which humans can realize and treasure the life-supporting web work. Humans alone on the planet can take a transcending overview of the whole—and care for life on Earth. To that more inclusive caring we next turn.

Person to Planet: Expanding Human Loves

(1) Self-love and Pleistocene appetites. By some biologists' accounts, human capacities for caring are residual from the geological epoch during which we became human. Our appetites are driven by Pleistocene genes. One might first think that since humans presumably evolved as good adapted fits, humans will by nature love the environments in which they evolved. Biologists may call this "biophilia," an innate, genetically based disposition to love animals, plants, landscapes with trees, open spaces, running water.[13] Such biophilia might be a positive Pleistocene relic, but other genetic legacies are problematic.

Any residual biophilia is weak before our much more powerful desires for self-satisfaction and security. People prefer culturally modified environments. The really natural thing for humans to do (our genetic disposition) is to build a culture differentiating (alienating) ourselves from nature. Human agriculture, business, industry, development consumes most of our lives, and the search for pleasant experiences in natural surroundings is only avocational recreation. True, people love a house with a view, with a garden, but they do like a house, a big one, and lots of money (milk and honey) in the bank.

Further—the biologists continue—our evolutionary past did not give us many biological controls on our desires for goods that were then in short supply. We love sweets and fats, of which, in Pleistocene times, humans could seldom get enough. But now we overeat and grow fat. There are few biological controls on our desires to amass goods, to consume; for most people, it has always been a struggle to get enough (indeed for most it still is). When we can consume, we love it and overconsume. Consumer capitalism transmutes a once-healthy pattern of desires into avarice. With escalating opportunities for consumption, driven by markets in search of profits, we need more self-discipline than comes naturally.

Our self-interested tendencies overshoot; we love ourselves (egoism) and our families (kin altruism) and find it difficult to know when and how to say enough.

What we love to do is to increase our security, fencing ourselves off from threatening nature. The Israelites longed to get out of the wilderness into a promised land that could drip milk and honey into their mouths—more and more milk and honey. For all of human history, humans have been pushing back limits. Humans have more genius at this than any other species. Especially in the West, we have lived with a deep-seated belief that life will get better, that one should hope for abundance and work toward obtaining it. Economists call such behavior "rational"; humans will maximize their capacity to exploit their resources. Moral persons will also maximize human satisfactions, at least those that support the good life, which must include not only food, clothing, and shelter but an abundance, more and more goods and services that people want. Such growth is always desirable. That "caring" is of first priority.

Perhaps humans will come to desire sustainable growth, for themselves and their children, extended to tribe and nation. But this Pleistocene legacy leaves humans poorly equipped to deal with the sorts of global-level problems we now face. The classical institutions—family, village, tribe, nation, agriculture, industry, law, medicine, even school and church—have shorter horizons. Far-off descendants and distant races do not have much "biological hold" on us. Across the era of human evolution, little in our behavior affected those remote from us in time or in space, and natural selection shaped only our conduct toward those closer. Global threats require us to act in massive concert of which we are incapable. If so, humans may bear within themselves the seeds of their own destruction. More bluntly, more scientifically put: our genes promote levels and kinds of preferences, human loves, that once enabled our adaptive fit but will in the next millennium prove maladaptive and destroy us.

(2) Communitarian loves: my tribe, my country. Human love can expand to communities in which the self participates. Humans are attracted to appeals to a better life, to quality of life, and they want this not only for themselves but for kindred, not only immediate kin but for future generations. We can use an appeal to still more enlightened self-interest, or perhaps better, to a more inclusive and comprehensive concept of human welfare. Humans have long loved their communities and their countrysides: "America the Beautiful." That expands the ambience of love from self past family to one's people, one's tradition, one's place. That will support sustainable development, an environmental ethic.

This is quite congenial to a bioregional ecology. "That land is a community is the basic concept of ecology, but that land is to be loved and respected is an extension of ethics."[14] Abraham and Lot, and later Jacob and Esau, were already caring for their lands, dispersing their flocks and herds, because "the land could not support both of them dwelling together" (Gen. 13:2–13, 36:6–8). They surveyed the pastures "from the Negeb as far as Bethel" and on to where Abraham's tent was pitched "between Bethel and Ai," on which these nomads realized they were trying to keep too many sheep and goats (Gen. 13.3). The Hebrews worried about livestock trampling and polluting riparian zones (Gen. 29:1–8; Ezek. 34:17–19). They knew to let land lie fallow, on Sabbath. Residents on landscapes live immersed in their native range ecology. They grow to love and respect their landscapes, their promised lands.

Communitarian love is quite congenial not only to ecology but also to evolutionary biology. Well-adapted genetic drives are labile, flexible, especially in vertebrates with well-developed brains. Group selection has been returning to the biological scene. Loyalty to tribe conveys survival value on all, on average, so that it is in any individual's probable advantage to cooperate, even though he or she has some risk of losing (being killed in battle, for instance). So natural selection has favored those genes that caused the early humans to be altruistic toward members of their own tribe. Humans still have those Pleistocene genes innate today.

That makes patriots who love their country, both tribe and lands that the tribe possesses. So the Israelites loving their promised land makes excellent sense from a Darwinian point of view. Elliott Sober and David S. Wilson find both self-interest and altruism as we do "unto others." Within the community, there are the patriots who love their country, the Rotarians building their public spirit, even the Presbyterians loving both self and neighbors. Wilson particularly studied the Calvinists in Geneva.[15]

But as before, such love, admirable as a half-truth, becomes dangerous if taken for the whole. Equally, Sober and Wilson insist there is no "universal benevolence": "Group selection does provide a setting in which helping behavior directed at members of one's own group can evolve; however, it equally provides a context in which hurting individuals in other groups can be selectively advantageous. Group selection favors within-group niceness and between-group nastiness. Group selection does not abandon the idea of competition that forms the core of the theory of natural selection."[16] Darwinian accounts of any behavior need differential survival advantage—a behavior leaving more of one's genes in the next generation than competitors leave. If that vanishes, Darwin is out of business. So we might get human loves expanded to my tribe and my country, agreeably to both biology and Hebrew monotheism. But can human love expand further?

(3) Communitarian loves: cosmopolitan and global. In religious faith, ideas become widely shared. The transmission process is neural, not genetic. One has to be indoctrinated into a religion. Biologically speaking, the problem now is that the new adherents soon cease to have any genetic relationship to the proselytizers. There are more Christians in Europe or North America than in the Middle East, and more Christians in Asia, or Latin America, or Africa than in Europe. Yes, the Calvinist tribe in Geneva prospered, but today there are more Presbyterians in Korea than in any other nation in the world, and those Korean Presbyterians have themselves sent out forty thousand missionaries to over a hundred countries.

Disciples are moved to act not just by their genetic programming. Ideas shared become ideals shared. Disciples teach kindness by word and example and preach about the Good Samaritan and the God of love. When such a religion has been universally shared, it generates concern for other humans near and far, relating to them with justice, love, and respect. The commitment that one has to make transcends one's genetics. Any account of in-group altruism to achieve out-group competitive success is powerless to explain the universalism in the major world faiths. But the major world faiths have escaped tribalism, not only in ideal but also in the real proportionately to their success. The widely shared faith no longer provides any differential survival advantage because it is equally advantageous to all.

This is somewhat like the discovery of fire. That discovery provides survival advantage to those who discover it—for the first winter. By the second or third winter, the competing tribes, who have been peeping through the bushes, know how to build fire too. Maybe the Jews first learned about the benefits of being a Good Samaritan. But today it is a global ideal—at least for disciples in the several faiths who practice it. "You have heard that it was said, 'You shall love your neighbor and hate your enemy.' But I say to you, Love your enemies" (Matt. 5:43). Monotheism is capable of a wider vision. "Go therefore and make disciples of all nations" (Matt. 28:19).

From evolutionary theory, also more inclusively, one can get some reciprocity even with the otherwise competing out-groups. This kind of reciprocity forms the basis of world trade, both cooperative and competitive. Christianity is not adverse to being a good neighbor or being fair and reciprocating in international business. But in the end, when the question is asked, "Who is my neighbor?" the answer comes in terms of who is in need that I can help, with my time, or money, or religion, not who is likely to reciprocate with net gain to my genetic line. There is no longer any differential survival benefit, because all these out-group converts are also winners. There is no longer that competitive edge that Sober and Wilson required at the core of natural selection.

Universal and cosmopolitan convictions crisscross races, nations, and centuries and involve some logic of the mind that is tracking what is trans-genetically right, what is more inclusively loving. Genetic success is necessary but not sufficient to explain this universalism. It makes more sense to say that such religions were discovering what is trans-tribally, trans-culturally valuable. Something has emerged for which biology is not giving us a convincing account. If some missionaries say that "God commands this altruism," that this kind of suffering love is divine, there seems no reason yet forthcoming from the biologists to think otherwise. "Do to others as you would have them do to you" helps us to cope because here is insight not just for the tribe, not just for the nation, but for the world.

(4) Inclusive environmental altruism. The most inclusive of human loves can become cosmopolitan, global, trans-genetic—especially if such expansion is funded by religious conviction. But that might not yet be inclusive enough if it remains devoted to one species. True, *Homo sapiens* is the aristocratic species on Earth. Ethics to date has struggled with impressive, if also halting, success in an effort to evolve altruism in fit proportion to egoism. That has yielded a sense of ethical priority, often ethical exclusivism, toward humans. Humans are on top; only humans count. Love your (human) neighbors, as you do yourself.

From a narrow, organismic perspective that can seem right, since in the prehuman world, everything is making a resource of everything else, so far as it can. Culture is impossible except as built on value captured from nature, assimilating and transforming biotic resources such as energy, nutrients, and structural materials that were formed by other organisms for their own needs. Every other living natural kind defends only its own kind; humans behave that way too, maximizing their own kind—and justifying (defending) their position by claiming to be the central species with and of moral concern. Always prefer humans.

From a wider, ecosystem perspective, such a rationale is oblivious to the way that the system has hitherto contained myriads of species in interdependent tension and harmony, with nothing maximizing itself except by optimizing a situated environmental fitness. From this more comprehensive perspective, persons operating with the prevailing humanistic focus are blind to most of their neighbors. All the rest of the products of the evolutionary ecosystem (or, if you prefer, of God's creation) are counted as resources.

Look at how this plays out with World Health Organization policy: "Priority given to human health raises an ethical dilemma if 'health for all' conflicts with protecting the environment. . . . Priority to ensuring human survival is taken as a first-order principle. Respect for nature and control of environmental degradation is a second-order principle, which must be observed unless it conflicts with the first-order principle of meeting survival needs."[17] That seems quite humane. But "second-order" will typically cash out as "never." In India, this policy certainly means no tigers. In Africa, it means no rhinos. Both will only remain in Western zoos. To preserve, even to conserve, is going to mean to reserve. If there are biodiversity reserves, with humans on-site or nearby, humans must limit their activities. Else there will always be some hungry persons who would exploit these reserves. The continued existence in the wild of most of Earth's charismatic endangered species—the felines, canines, rhinos, elephants, primates—depends on some six hundred major reserves for wildlife in some eighty countries.[18] If these reserves are not policed, they will not be there. And they will not be policed unless some persons in power think that at times saving nature is more important than using the land to feed people directly. Will this include Christians in India and Africa?

Human (humane) ethicists who argue that humans are always first-order only halfway emerge from their environment. They are right about the human excellences. But they defend only their own kind, and in this respect, even when they become cosmopolitan, they do not emerge, they just merge and play by the rules of natural selection; they become moral agents in encounter with other humans, but they do not become moral agents in encounter with nature. Trying to defend the high human value, they act like beasts—looking out for themselves and their kind. In this aggressive attempt, these humane ethicists, Christian or secular, stunt humanity because they do not know genuine human transcendence—an overview caring for the others.

Plainly, humans have expanded their territories all over the globe. But what is an appropriate lifestyle for residing in this globally occupied territory? Always to put themselves first? Nothing more? Rather than using mind and morals, hand and brain, as survival tools for defending the human form of life, the better answer is when mind forms an intelligible view of the whole and defends ideals of life in all their forms. Humans are cognate with the humus, made of dust (as Genesis 2:7 teaches, *adam* from *adamah*), yet unique and excellent in their aristocratic capacity to view the world they inhabit. They rise up from the earth and look over their world (Greek: *anthropos*, to rise up, look up). Persons have their excellences, and one way they excel is in this capacity for overview. They are made "in the image of God" (as Genesis also teaches).

The novelty in the human emergence is class altruism emerging to coexist with class self-interest, sentiments directed not simply at one's own species but at other species fitted into biological communities. Humans ought to think from an ecological analogue of what ethicists have called the original position, a global position that sees Earth as an evolutionary ecosystem. In occupying this position, humans play roles in the storied achievements on Earth. Interhuman ethics, often inspired by Christian compassion, has spent the last two millennia waking up to human dignity. As we expand ethics in this new millennium, a Christian environmental ethics invites awakening to the greater story of which humans are a consummate part.

This is what human dominion potentially meant in Genesis, or should have meant. This is what living in a God-given land of promise offers for a land ethic. This takes humans past *resource* use to *residence* and constrains their policy, economics, science, technology. Being a "resident" is something more than maximum exploitation of one's environment, though it requires resourceful use. Being a "resident" is more than being a "citizen." Such residing takes us past management questions to moral questions. Humans can get "let in on" more value than any other kind of life. They can share the values of others and in this way be altruists. Humans are of capstone value because they are capstone evaluators.

Seen this way, in earlier eras, humans needed an exodus out of nature into culture, but now they want to be liberated out of egoism, out of humanism, into a transcending overview that sees Earth as a blessed land, exuberant with life, a land filled with integrity, beauty, dynamic achievement, and storied history. This is exodus within a promised land.

Without denying that there is value superiority within humans, a Christian environmental ethics says more. It is not just our capacity to say "I," to actualize a self, but our capacity to see others, to oversee a world, that distinguishes humans. Environmental ethics calls for seeing nonhumans, for seeing the biosphere, the Earth, ecosystem communities, fauna, flora, natural kinds that cannot say "I" but in which there is formed integrity, objective value independent of subjective value. Environmental ethics advances beyond humanistic ethics in that it can treat as ends others besides humans. Environmental ethicists see further morally. They can see *without* as well as *within*. They really see the neighbors Jesus commanded us to love, the sparrows that God notices fall, the lilies of the field so splendidly arrayed. In this sense, the capacity for thoughtful residence, for experiencing community with nonhuman others, is as requisite for ethics as any capacity for human self-actualizing. That very self-actualizing in this ethic seeks human self-transcending.

It is commendable to be altruists humanistically speaking. But a really exciting difference between humans and nonhumans is that while animals and plants can count (defend) only their own lives, with their offspring and kind, humans can count (defend) life and even nonlife with vision of greater scope. Humans can be genuine altruists; this begins when they recognize the claims of other humans, whether or not such claims are compatible with their own self-interest. But the evolution of altruism is not complete until humans can recognize the claims of nonhumans—ecosystems, species, landscapes. In that sense, environmental ethics is the most altruistic form of ethics. It really loves others. It transforms residual egos into resident altruists. This ultimate altruism is, or ought to be, the human genius. In this sense, the last becomes the first; this late-coming species with a latter-day ethics is the first to see the story that is taking place. This late species takes a leading role. If this is not *agape*, it is *altruism*.

(5) Promised land, planet with promise. Both Judaism and Christianity, emerging from Judaism, became more universalist and less land-based. In the Diaspora, the Jews were a people without a country, and though this was widely regarded as tragic, Judaism remains a faith that transcends residence in Palestine. Christianity has often been regarded as more spiritual and less material, more universal and less provincial than its parental Judaism. Both these movements out of a geographically particular promised land, which are sometimes thought to make the land irrelevant to faith, can as well make every people residents of a divinely given landscape. In that sense, these faiths may have been mistaken when they became uprooted from encounters with the land. Rather, Christians and Jews ought to have re-rooted in whatever the landscapes of their residence. In this sense, the Jewish vision of a promised land is inclusive, not exclusive.

The American landscape with its purple mountain majesties, fruited plains, fauna and flora from sea to shining sea is divinely created, no less than Canaan from the Negev to Mount Hermon. John Muir, recalling the psalmist, sings, "The forests of America, however slighted by man, must have been a great delight to God; for they were the best he ever planted."[19] And landscapes around the globe, east and west, north and south, on six continents (though not the seventh), have proved homelands that peoples can come to cherish and on which they can flourish.

Anciently, Palestine was a promised land. Today and for the century hence, the call is to see Earth as a planet with promise, destined for abundant life. When Earth's most complex product, *Homo sapiens*, becomes intelligent enough to reflect over this earthy wonderland, nobody has much doubt that this is a precious place. Even Edward O. Wilson, a secular humanist, ever insistent that he can find no divinity in, with, or under nature, still exclaims, "The biospheric membrane that covers the Earth, and you and me, . . . is the miracle we have been given."[20]

Viewing Earthrise from the moon, the astronaut Edgar Mitchell, was entranced: "Suddenly from behind the rim of the moon, in long, slow-motion moments of immense majesty, there emerges a sparkling blue and white jewel, a light, delicate sky-blue sphere laced with slowly swirling veils of white, rising gradually like a small pearl in a thick sea of black mystery. It takes more than a moment to fully realize this is Earth . . . home." Mitchell continued, "My view of our planet was a glimpse of divinity."[21] The astronaut Michael Collins recalled being earth-struck: "Earth is to be treasured and nurtured, something precious that must endure."[22]

When this biospheric miracle is seen as divine gift, grace, that vision of a planet with promise makes all the more alarming our current discovery that this is also a planet in peril. "A generation goes, and a generation comes, but the earth remains forever" (Eccles. 1:4). That ancient certainty needs now to become an urgent future hope.

Love Gone Wild: Good Earth, Cruciform Creation

Christian and Darwinian encounters with wild nature, whatever their differences, both find that life is perpetually renewed in the midst of its perpetual perishing. Life is ever "conserved," as biologists might say; life is ever "redeemed," as theologians might say. In this generating of new life, the good Earth is also cruciform. Such processes, set in their ecological settings, perennially transform disvalues in nature into prolific values, generating the global richness of evolutionary natural history and its exuberance of life.

Christians today, as did ancient Hebrews and New Testament Christians before them, often encounter nature with ambivalence, a seeming mix of some goods and some bads. Looking more deeply into such encounter, we realize the creative character of conflict and resolution. Superficially, so far as nature is antagonistic and discomforting, it has disvalue. With deeper insight, we do not always count environmental conductance as good and environmental resistance as bad, but the currents of life flow in their interplay or, to be more philosophical about it, in their dialectic. An environment that was entirely hostile would slay life; life could never have appeared within it. An environment that was entirely irenic would stagnate life; without struggle, neither biodiversity nor biocomplexity would have evolved. Most of the beauty of life comes out of such conflict and resolution.

Human life too fits into such an ambivalent nature. Without such challenge, human life would never have appeared on Earth. The human hand, with opposable thumb, the human mind, the most complex object in the known universe, came out of such challenging encounter. None of life's heroic quality is possible without this dialectical stress. Evolution and ecology have taught us that every kind of life is what it is environmentally, in its surroundings, not autonomously. Humans too are environmental reciprocals, indebted to our environment for what we have become in ways that are as complementary as they are oppositional. Humans can respect the alien in nature not only in its autonomous otherness but even in its stimulus, provocation, and opposition. This is ethics comprehensively extended once again: Love nature, the gift of grace. Love nature, even when nature confronts us as enemy. Such gift with challenge is a more sophisticated form of creative beauty.

When we confront death, we also think of birth, for the two are inseparable, alike in evolutionary biology and in religious faith. The root idea in the word "nature" is "birthing," as of a woman in labor (Greek: *natans*, giving birth). Birth is a transformative experience in which suffering is the prelude to, the principle of, creation. The world is not a paradise of hedonistic ease but a theater where life is learned and earned by labor. Mothers suffer and regenerate the human community. Death in vivo is death ultimately; death *in communitatis* is death penultimately but life regenerated ultimately: life, death, and regeneration. "Travail," "birthing," is a key to understanding these evils. Paul writes, "The whole creation has been groaning in travail together until now" (Rom. 8:22). That maternal labor is archaic in the antique sense and equally archaic in the foundational sense: perpetual perishing, perpetual regeneration.

Nature is *cruciform*. Every life is chastened and christened, straitened and baptized in struggle. Everywhere there is vicarious suffering, one creature dying that another may live on. Experiences of the power of survival, of new life regenerated out of the old, of creative resilience in the ongoing life struggle—these are Darwinian themes, but they resonate too with the religious conviction that there is something divine about the power to suffer through to something higher. The global Earth is a land of promise, and yet one that has to be died for. The story is a passion play long before it reaches the Christ. Since the beginning, the myriad creatures have been giving up their lives as a ransom for many. In that sense, Jesus is not the exception to the natural order but a chief exemplification of it.

Redemptive suffering is a model that makes sense of nature and history. Darwinians see this truth: there is a struggle for survival. But so far from making the world absurd, such struggle is a key to the whole, as a transformative principle, transvalued into its opposite. The capacity to suffer through to joy is a supreme emergent and an essence of Christianity. Yet the whole evolutionary upslope is a lesser calling of this kind, in which renewed life comes by blasting the old. Life is gathered up in the midst of its throes, a blessed tragedy, lived in grace through a besetting storm.

The care of a shepherd for his sheep is used as a model of divine care. Recall that, as in the metaphors of Psalm 23, the environment of such care is the wilderness, in which there are green pastures beside still waters and also valleys of deep darkness. Sheep need water and forage, and life is like that. Lift this up into an archetype for human life. Pastoral peoples need pasture, but they have also to be led in "paths of righteousness for his name's sake." Divinely given, earthen nature is the original act of grace, but this can be received only by a people disciplined as "thy rod and thy staff, they comfort me." Then, "surely goodness and mercy shall follow me all the days of my life, and I shall dwell in the house of the Lord for ever." There are valleys of deep darkness, but there is a vast earthen and spiritual providence that supports the righteous life. This is the Hebrew "land ethic," continued and enriched when the Good Shepherd searches for the lost sheep (Matt. 18:12).

On Earth, we are shepherded through order and chaos, trials and hardships, rewards and blessings, in both nature and culture. There is continuing grace in a challenging environ-ment. What we get is manna in the wilderness—one day's supply at a time, our daily bread, precariously, and yet day after day after day—all the days of life (Deut. 8:3). It could not be any other way and have authentic lives with their own integrity. Maybe such somber beauty is the gift of an agape love.

Notes

The author thanks William P. Brown, Columbia Theological Seminary, for critical commentary.

    1. Christopher Southgate, *The Groaning of Creation: God, Evolution, and the Problem of Evil* (Louisville, KY: Westminster John Knox Press, 2008).

2. The phrase comes from the luckless backup pelican chick wondered about in Holmes Rolston III, *Science and Religion: A Critical Survey*, new ed. (Philadelphia: Templeton Foundation Press, 2006), 137–40; Jay B. McDaniel, *God and Pelicans: A Theology of Reverence for Life* (Louisville, KY: Westminster John Knox Press, 1989).

3. Walter Brueggemann, *The Land* (Philadelphia: Fortress Press, 1977), 3; Norman C. Habel, *The Land Is Mine: Six Biblical Land Ideologies* (Minneapolis: Fortress Press, 1995); Ellen F. Davis, *Scripture, Culture, and Agriculture: An Agrarian Reading of the Bible* (Cambridge: Cambridge University Press, 2008).

4. Lynn White Jr., "The Historical Roots of Our Ecological Crisis," *Science* 155 (1967): 1203–7.

5. C. Birch, W. Eakin, and J. McDaniel, eds., *Liberating Life: Contemporary Approaches to Ecological Theology* (Maryknoll, NY: Orbis Books, 1990); John B. Cobb Jr., *Is It Too Late: A Theology of Ecology* (Beverly Hills, CA: Bruce, 1972); James W. Skillen and Luis E. Lugo, eds., *Caring for Creation: Responsible Stewardship of God's Handiwork* (Grand Rapids, MI: Baker Books, 1998); James A. Nash, *Loving Nature: Ecological Integrity and Christian Responsibility* (Nashville: Abingdon Cokesbury, 1991).

6. Greek: "automatically."

7. Recalled in G. Evelyn Hutchinson, "Homage to Santa Rosalia, or Why Are There So Many Kinds of Animals," *American Naturalist* 93 (1959): 145–59.

8. Terry L. Burden, *The Kerygma of the Wilderness Traditions in the Hebrew Bible* (New York: Peter Lang, 1994).

9. Ulrich Mauser, *Christ in the Wilderness* (Napierville, IL: Alec R. Allenson, 1963).

10. Jeanne Kay, "Concepts of Nature in the Hebrew Bible," *Environmental Ethics* 10 (1988): 309–27.

11. Richard Dawkins, *The Selfish Gene*, new ed. (New York: Oxford University Press, 1989).

12. Frans de Waal, *Good Natured: The Origins of Right and Wrong in Humans and Other Animals* (Cambridge, MA: Harvard University Press, 1996).

13. Edward O. Wilson, *Biophilia* (Cambridge, MA: Harvard University Press, 1984).

14. Aldo Leopold, *A Sand County Almanac* (New York: Oxford University Press, 1969), viii–ix.

15. David Sloan Wilson, *Darwin's Cathedral: Evolution, Religion, and the Nature of Society* (Chicago: University of Chicago Press, 2002).

16. Elliott Sober and David Sloan Wilson, *Unto Others: The Evolution and Psychology of Unselfish Behavior* (Cambridge, MA: Harvard University Press, 1998), 9.

17. World Health Organization, Commission on Health and Environment, *Our Planet, Our Health: Report of the WHO Commission on Health and Environment* (Geneva, 1992), 4.

18. Laura Riley and William Riley, *Nature's Strongholds: The World's Great Wildlife Reserves* (Princeton, NJ: Princeton University Press, 2005).

19. John Muir, *Our National Parks* (Boston: Houghton Mifflin, 1901), 331; Ps. 104:16.

20. Edward O. Wilson, *The Future of Life* (New York: Alfred A. Knopf, 2002), 21.

21. Mitchell, quoted in Kevin W. Kelley, ed., *The Home Planet* (Reading, MA: Addison-Wesley, 1988), at photographs 42–45.

22. Michael Collins, "Foreword," in Roy A. Gallant, *Our Universe* (Washington, DC: National Geographic Society, 1980), 6.

19 •:•

The Double Love Command and the Ethics of Religious Pluralism

ERIC GREGORY

> The significant things are the distinctive patterns of story, belief, ritual, and behavior that give "love" and "God" their specific and sometimes contradictory meanings.
>
> —George Lindbeck, *The Nature of Doctrine*

IT WOULD BE IMPOSSIBLE to tell the history of modern Christian ethics without paying attention to the ways in which the realities of diversity have shaped its concerns. In a theological register, responses to these realities have run the gamut from lamenting an existential threat to celebrating a providential gift. Biblical narratives, from Babel to Pentecost, are marshaled for each approach (cf., e.g., Gen. 11; Rom. 12; 1 Cor. 12; Rev. 7). What cannot be denied is the extent to which recognition of diversity has sponsored and determined much of the intellectual agenda of the discipline known as "Christian ethics." For example, increased attention to diversity has energized discussions of *moral* pluralism (in terms of seemingly incommensurable values or even the plural nature of the good itself) and *political* pluralism (in terms of social practices and institutional arrangements that accommodate difference).[1] Resurgent debates in Christian ethics about natural law, human rights, or the common good—and related ones about "public reason" or "multiculturalism"—display this concentration on plurality in relation to rival approaches to morality and politics.[2]

Language of equality, alterity, and respect pervade these discussions. Virtues such as fidelity, tolerance, and humility figure prominently. The vigor of these debates, of course, is predicated on different uses and applications of these terms. Some suggest pluralism is a peculiar problem of modernity, a post-Enlightenment anxiety about difference bound up with massive cultural and intellectual change. These changes and the anxieties they promote, we are told, only accelerate with globalization, technological advances, and mass migration.

Strictly speaking, pluralism is but one normative response to facts of plurality. Like the category of religion this side of Luther's reading of Paul, it may be a decidedly modern way of thinking about and living with diversity. Indeed, genealogists frequently point out that "religion" and "pluralism" arose in tandem in the discursive practices of modernity. They bear the marks not simply of philosophical inquiry or crises of faith but of politics and history as well.

Historically distant cultures and thinkers recognized diversity. But they did not construct or experience its challenge as moderns do. Even if we resist efforts to identify a single essence of religion or modernity, it is clear that many previous generations did not operate with notions of "religious pluralism" as an analytic framework. Others admit this distance, but they argue valuable resources within the historic Christian tradition might be reconstructed in light of our contemporary social experience.[3] So assessments of diversity and pluralism are themselves plural, and often contradictory.[4]

Many academic disciplines and religious communities share these animating dynamics. But they have found particular expression in Christian ethics through ongoing debates about the distinctiveness of Christian ethics and the relation of Christianity to liberal democracy. No doubt issues raised by *religious* pluralism overlap with concerns about *moral* and *political* diversity. They find parallels in the negotiations of intra-religious difference that characterize the diversity of Christian ethics itself, not to mention fraught ecclesial discourse within Christian denominations. Indeed, they are profoundly interrelated. In Christian ethics, for example, appeals to plural traditions and plural narratives abound. Translation and charitable interpretation of conceptual schemes are heralded as ways to deepen theological and ethical commitments. Rational reconstruction of historical figures, texts, and cultures is increasingly the norm in both Protestant and Roman Catholic moral theology. This work—whether it compares Augustine and Kant or Aquinas and Barth—shows how the varieties of Christian ethics *already* reflect difference in Western thought. Moreover, broader approaches in comparative ethics within and across traditions remain high on the agenda.[5] There is a new generation of scholars conversant in both "Christian ethics" and "comparative religious ethics." As a whole, however, engagement with non-Christian religions has been less prominent in Christian ethics than engagement with secular philosophy, the social sciences, and Protestant–Roman Catholic ecumenical dialogue.

Analyses of moral and political pluralism do admit analogies to religious pluralism. They tap into disputes over basic assumptions about human nature, truth, and the very category of "religion."[6] Christian ethicists regularly examine forms of skepticism and relativism in moral and political arenas. Burdened by a history of Christian conquest, they consider multiple expressions of Christian witness with respect to morality and politics. They lift up lives thought to embody paradigmatic Christian virtue in relation to non-Christian neighbors (often ones that did not benefit from balancing openness with commitment). Relational pairings of universal-particular, insider-outsider, and nearness-distance are dominant themes. At the same time, much of contemporary interreligious dialogue focuses on global ethical issues that touch on concerns with liberation and healing transformation. Ironically, however, explicit focus on religious pluralism as such has not been a dominant subject in Christian ethics. By my lights, inquiry into the implications of the depth and integrity of religious diversity for Christian ethics remains relatively undeveloped. This neglect stands in sharp contrast to analytic philosophy of religion, systematic theology, and religious ethics more generally. Despite important developments in the church and the wider world, Christian ethics has yet to bring its many resources to bear on religious pluralism.

Of course, this claim assumes those resources matter. To frame the approach in these terms risks seduction and conceit, implicating Christian ethics in yet another form of oppositional hegemony, identity politics, and static universalism. It turns religious pluralism into a problem to be solved *by* Christian ethics rather than a shared reality to be engaged *within* Christian ethics. Moreover, why privilege the contribution of Christian ethics, especially if untutored in the necessary linguistic, anthropological, and historical knowledge? Perhaps religious pluralism is a topic best left to philosophers, theologians, and "religious ethicists"? No doubt Christian ethicists have much to learn from these increasingly sophisticated literatures (as well as their weaknesses). They typically raise the hermeneutical challenge of comparison and tax the analogical imagination in light of religious pluralism more acutely. But it is not uncommon for Christian ethicists to feel stretched by multiple sources between the doctrinal, the historical, the ethnographic, and the practical. In addition to their urgency in a global age that suffers the consequences of mapping "believers" against "unbelievers," many of the issues raised by religious pluralism are so native to the established concerns of Christian ethics that their neglect seems increasingly odd. At the very least, the resemblances between intra-Christian ethical pluralism and religious pluralism themselves invite comparison.[7]

The present essay does not claim to correct this neglect in any comprehensive way, let alone provide a theology of religious pluralism, a method for comparative theology, or an ethics of discipleship for a multi-faith world. The issues raised by religious diversity within the lived religion of Christian communities have varied pastoral and theoretical dimensions. They also press us in deeply personal ways. Perhaps more than moral or political pluralism, they raise explicitly missiological and soteriological issues absent in most Christian ethics. This absence is instructive, but I here bracket whether it is necessary. Rather, I aim to elevate ways in which one familiar topic—often taken in complicated ways to be a hallmark of Christian ethics—bears on the subject.

The centrality of love in divine revelation is itself notable for approaching religious pluralism from within Christian ethics. It invites welcome comparison of diverse treatments of love (and its analogues) in Christian and non-Christian figures and traditions. Comparison might reveal differences in degree as well as differences in kind, dislocating the familiar analyses of agape, eros, caritas, and philia. Such an approach would expand our conceptual repertoire even as it sheds light on existing terms and ways of living a worthwhile life. Christian beliefs and practices could only be enriched by apt comparison. The *methodological* issues raised by comparison with non-Christian traditions strike me as not qualitatively different than existing efforts to compare visions of love within Christian traditions.

But related questions remain internal to Christian ethics. Should love assume priority relative to other virtues in discussions of religious pluralism? How does Christian discourse of love relate to religious diversity? How should Christians love non-Christians with respect to their religious convictions? Do Christians properly love their neighbor by calling them to relationship with the God of the Christian faith? The issues raised by these questions are frustratingly complex and resist easy judgments. There seem no responses that are not misleading or risk sentimentalism. They also trade on neuralgic issues in the history of theology, especially theodicy and election.

My ambition is limited. It is decidedly confessional rather than apologetic, taking my cue from those in the Christian tradition who confess no God *above* the Trinity. I want to signal how some aspects of Christian love relate to religious pluralism in light of an insistence on the priority of divine transcendence of the One who sends and vindicates Jesus. This signaling is an invitation to attend to the relatively unexamined resemblances between issues within Christian ethics and discussions of religious pluralism. The goal is to stimulate both theological and ethical reflection by framing the familiar in a novel context. Making these connections explicit is one way to subject discussions of both Christian love and religious pluralism to critical scrutiny.

Gene Outka is justifiably regarded as the keenest interpreter of Christian agape in modern Christian ethics. I take his theocentric interpretation of Christian love as my guide by identifying two persistent themes from his corpus: equal regard of persons and the interrelatedness of the love commands. Outka's interpretations have a decidedly Protestant lineage and emphasis on God's prevenient grace. They rely on a creedal tradition emerging from the biblical narrative "always respectfully, holding that one should, as far as possible, not only give a faithful account of it but take it with governing seriousness when one assimilates new insights."[8] But they are far from idiosyncratic. They are shaped by engagement with many Christian traditions, especially informed by the ethical and theological legacies of Augustine, Søren Kierkegaard, and Karl Barth. No doubt they merit further development. Not every Christian account would assent to them. Nevertheless, Outka's identification of normative links among love of God, self, and neighbor reflects essential commitments for the formation of Christian identity. Loves signal what we most care about. They invite specification for a Christian ethics of religious pluralism. With Outka, then, my inquiry seeks to avoid "vapid amiability where one is wholly content to be part of a directionless exchange of viewpoints."[9]

A Modest Proposal

In contrast to Christian ethics, religious pluralism is a major topic in contemporary philosophy and theology. Philosophical treatments typically focus on the rationality of belief, the nature of truth claims, and epistemic consequences of disagreement. Christian philosophers play a notable role in these debates.[10] Theological treatments typically focus on what might be learned about God from non-Christian religions and the salvific prospects of their adherents. Competing theological judgments often depend on different philosophical orientations.[11]

Most of these discussions trade on the well-worn and pedagogically accessible categories of exclusivism, inclusivism, and pluralism. They display the influence of John Hick, despite various efforts to enrich or challenge their heuristic value.[12] Some Christian ethicists have regarded this paradigm a parochial feature of secular liberalism. Stanley Hauerwas, for example, characteristically worries that "even the attempt to develop such typologies betrays ideological presumptions."[13] John Milbank argues they retain "covert Christianizations."[14] Still, despite suspicions, these categories have proved resilient.

Briefly, pluralism names an approach that finds salvific truth in all religions. There is no one true religion. None have an epistemic advantage. Many religions promote moral and spiritual transformations that are worthy of admiration. Divergence about sacred value appears so historically and culturally conditioned that adherence to one or another religion seems arbitrary. An effort to locate something common or essential to all religions typically underlies this project.

Exclusivism elevates difference as a form of steadfast faithfulness and responsibility to truthfulness, not arrogance. Idolatry is its central concern and ultimate sin. Some unique features of a religion (such as revelation or grace) warrant an epistemic confidence that characterizes other religions in terms of error and rejection. On these terms, what some describe as "multiple religious belonging" would be considered an oxymoron. For example, exclusivism would hold that the relationship between Christian faith in a triune God and other religious confessions is primarily one of discontinuity, not fulfillment or mutual appreciation. God's revelation in Christ is determinative; grace is not mediated through non-Christian religions. The salvation of non-Christians is typically denied. Affirming and denying beliefs is simply our existential condition that gives rise to plurality itself.

Inclusivism affirms the presence of God in multiple religious practices. But it maintains one revelation as authoritative, even when denied or unacknowledged. Christian inclusivists, for example, might maintain a high Christology (*Christus solus*) with the hope of an open soteriology. They express confidence in God's reconciling work in Christ for the world (2 Cor. 5:19). But they emphasize humility in view of our provisional capacity to know God or the fate of others in the same way that God knows. In passages like Matthew 25, they find biblical witness that honors the religious meaning of lives that do not explicitly confess the lordship of Jesus (often by defining the first love commandment by its fulfillment of the second). This approach finds many supporters in academic theology across the ecumenical spectrum. Yet critics argue this position inherits the problems of both exclusivism and pluralism.

The pluralist approach can seem attractive today given widespread concerns about intolerance and religious violence. A tolerant society, on this view, demands a tolerant theology—where that in turn means regarding each tradition equally right about matters religious. Pluralism is politically salutary and socially necessary. Yet the status of pluralism as a powerful ideal has been subject to increased criticism in both religious studies and theology.[15] Ironically, many find it does not recognize deep differences in religious traditions and thereby perpetuates its own disrespect of diverse religious cultures. It produces an illusion that religions are primarily manageable sets of (inadequate) freestanding propositions rather than comprehensively self-involving forms of life. It domesticates religion by making it a matter of private belief.

However one evaluates the constraints of this typology, each position invokes intellectual and moral virtues worthy of attention. They direct us to important issues. There is virtue in the economy of the paradigm itself. While no position fully persuades, no alternative vocabulary or conceptual innovation has succeeded in overcoming its generativity. But classification is a tricky business. It is always value-laden. Classifiers and their critics often do not make explicit their own normative commitments. I agree with those who find this particular system of classification limiting. It is reductive in too many ways, especially for the purposes of theological or ethical analysis.

To be sure, disciplinary boundaries are porous. Ethics saturates these discussions of religious pluralism. Philosophers dispute the justice and charity of the exclusivist's God. They question the moral compass of those who would worship such a God. Inclusivists work to reconcile the finality of God's self-revelation in Christ, the goods of church membership, and the evident piety of other traditions. Moreover, though in different ways, the influential proposals by John Hick, Karl Rahner, and Paul Knitter found in this literature all make other-regarding love basic to their approach to religious pluralism.[16] These discussions can rehearse a familiar trajectory found especially in the liberal Protestant tradition of "ethicizing" Christian doctrine, particularly through a language of love that subordinates theology to the rational purity of ethical universals available to human experience. The particulars of religious commitments, on these terms, are celebrated as a symbolic vehicle for something else. This is not the route I propose to pursue.

Karl Barth's dialectical approach to "religion" as a creature of grace remains salient.[17] Following Barth, I do not wish to pit dogmatics against ethics. Following Augustine, I do not wish to oppose confession and virtue. Both are interdependent. The coordination of the two love commandments is always "theological" and "ethical."[18] What I want to do is explore ethical dimensions that emerge from two explicitly Christian theological commitments about otherness. My account is necessarily concise and highly selective. It borrows heavily from Outka's insights regarding love's symmetries and asymmetries. But their application to religious diversity is my own.

Equal Regard: Love's Symmetry

Gene Outka's *Agape: An Ethical Analysis* did not propose a theory of love. The formal purpose of that work was to contribute "to our understanding of what love has been taken ethically to be, rather than what it must be."[19] Outka details the basic features of the agapist literature since Anders Nygren's own influential paradigms.[20] Like Nygren's text, however, Outka's work resists a clear distinction between the descriptive and the normative. Outka's comparisons, like all acts of comparison, are interpretive. In submitting various strands in the literature to analysis, Outka's framing of the normative content of neighbor love has been profoundly influential. Consider, for example, his opening summary statement: "Agape is a regard for the neighbor which in crucial respects is independent and unalterable. To these features there is a corollary: the regard is for every person qua human existent, to be distinguished from those special traits, actions, etc., which distinguish particular personalities from each other."[21] The centrality and permanence Outka assigns to "equal regard" is not explicitly developed in relation to religious diversity. Most critical discussions have focused on its relation to Kantian "respect for persons" and subsequent debates about individualism, special relationships, self-sacrifice, and the role of emotions in the moral life.[22] But I take Outka's term of art to be a fertile route into love's relation to religious diversity.

The focus here is anthropology. Most fundamentally, the priority of equal regard elevates the priority of persons. Persons are made in the image of God. That is to say, all human persons have irreducible value independent of assessment of their beliefs or actions. Their "worth and dignity" is always enjoined; it is "independent and unalterable."[23] All attempts at domination are ruled out. Religious liberty is defended. Neighbors, like God, are honored in their definite otherness.

This commitment to a person "qua human existent" risks sterile description and abstract platitude. Fears of theological redundancy emerge. But for Outka, positing the essential equality of persons before God is foundational.[24] To conceive of human dignity strictly in relation to God poses familiar difficulties, both metaphysical and political. But it is also phenomenologically rich and morally demanding.

The intrinsic value of all persons does not arise from their own merit, let alone utility for one's own well-being. It is not something to be proven or justified. On Christian terms, value is secured from eternity by God's own identification with humanity. It belongs to those inside and outside the visible church. Refusals of equal regard betray a possessiveness and inordinate self-love that Augustinians term sin. The great damage of sin is manifest in disordered loves. A characteristic form of disordered loving is grasping at the good rather than being in relation to it with others. The darkness of sin is birthed in the radical freedom of love itself: the *mala voluntas* closed to others and to God. In a fallen world, Augustine observes, the perversity of pride inclines us to hate "a fellowship of equality under God" (Augustine, *CD* 19.12). The lustful goal of self-mastery issues a consuming mastery of others that also distorts the self. This is what Kierkegaard diagnoses as the "I intoxicated in the other-I."[25] Love's inward curvature denies a shared origin and even the possibility of a shared destiny. As such, human value is bound to a complex theological scheme that identifies agape as the practical corollary of grace: the bestowal of divine love, which Outka reckons, is "surely universal."[26] Any person, including the self and the religious "other," is rendered as a subject embraced by this divine love.

Equal regard is an analogue of this divine love. It is the love revealed in the compassion of Christ and the compassion of the Good Samaritan. To love God is, at least in part, to love what God loves. This requires the cultivation of virtue and the enabling power of grace. But as Outka notes, neighbor love is "more than a mere means through which we love God."[27] The neighbor is a discrete recipient of love. Love of neighbor is not a mere repetition of love for God.

Christians, therefore, encounter any person with gratitude, care, and arresting attention that acknowledges their status as a creature beloved of God. Such an outlook is "both attitudinal and intentional in nature, i.e., it includes both a judgment and an undertaking."[28] As Outka makes clear, this guarantee of equality does not require identical treatment. Equal regard also does not deny particularity or individuality: "one may reject atomistic individualism but not thereby shrug off as historically passé the claim that the individual has irreducible significance."[29] This significance implies concern for the particularity of individual lives before God. The Christian hope is that God may be enjoyed communally. Its orienting vision is a shared life of the people of God as the body of Christ. But God addresses the self and the other in their concrete singularity. Faithful responses to God arise in our sociality. But they remain distinctly *our* response. To borrow from David Kelsey, personal identities in relation to God are "unsubstitutable."[30]

Agapic love as "equal regard" resists generalizing abstractions that threaten discussions of religious identity. As Kathryn Tanner puts it, "God's creative concern for a person finds that person as the particular person he or she is and not simply as a member of some universal society of creatures."[31] In Outka's idiom, each person has a "noninterchangeable pilgrimage" on his or her journey to God.[32] It is a journey known only to God in its fullness. Thus, there are limits to the harms and benefits we can do for others.[33] Faith and repentance may be mysterious, but they are not transferable.

Such agency partially resembles—and ultimate derives from participation in—the creative agency of God. God's own radical and eternal self-giving (*pro nobis*) is not a giving up or loss of divinity (*in se*). This serves as a parable of the human condition. Identity is constituted in relation to others, not an original solitude. Grace comes to us from without. Yet the self is never merely a passive stream. The human person is neither an object of pure reception nor a mere channel of other-regard. Outka affirms a constitutive interdependence in our historical identities, but the self is not "a kind of reed on the intersubjective field."[34] Divine affirmation of distinctive persons and vocations warrants concern for the self and the other.[35]

Valuing *particular* persons through mutual recognition is honoring to God. Agape, for example, "enjoins one to identify with the neighbor's point of view, to try imaginatively to see what it is for him to live the life he does, to occupy the position he holds."[36] This description means the neighbor's "point of view" also has worth. The neighbor is a fellow creature able to track meaning and value. If Augustine is right, we are all restless until we rest in God. Neighbor love remains open to competing interpretations of divine action. Given the dynamics of sin and evil, disagreement is expected.[37] Conflicts are not merely apparent or verbal. Given serious difficulty with our desires and our intellect, some may be simply endured with forbearance. Some must be opposed without usurping divine judgment. Even the most ecumenical theology can be pushed to the limit of enmity if it is indexed to justice.

But the complexities of religious traditions, unlike individual propositions, resist wholesale rejection. They usually defy general characterization in any meaningful sense. It takes a lot of work to avoid trivial generalization and get to the point of achieving disagreement. It is hard to imagine the development of Christian theology without sustained engagement with, and education by, various philosophical and religious traditions and their spiritual practitioners. These historical precedents, admittedly partial and imperfect, show that interreligious dialogue is not simply an occasion for greater understanding and tolerance. These goods should not be underestimated. But most of these developments have been understood in terms of relations of similarity and difference rather than raw assertion of identity. They have been catalysts for a deepening of the faith that seeks understanding through spiritual transformation.

Faith in the action of God means that Christian identity is never fixed by exclusion.[38] Improvisation, argument, and discovery are endemic to the confession of grace and ongoing recognition of the Spirit. Virtues like love are always in motion, participating in a divine love that experienced death and resurrection. Given epistemic fallibility and the inadequacy of language about God, attention persists even when the other's point of view is taken to be erroneous or misguided. In fact, religious "others" can be considered justified in their beliefs even if they are thought to hold false beliefs. One might even regret that certain forms of religious life that we find enchanting are unavailable given human finitude as well as the diminishments wrought by sin.[39] These attitudes can be distinguished from self-doubt, counter-assertion, or minimalist notions of toleration.

Agreement and reconciliation are welcomed when possible. Self-critical apologetics remain necessary for acts of judgment. But agape demands a Christian approach to religious pluralism that is without fear or defensiveness. There is neither epistemic nor affective closure in the search for wisdom. Christian confession of the goodness of the world invites joy and wonder in relation to its diversity. These are the critical labors of non-possessive love that register a Christian desire for truth *and* relationship in a world marked by stubborn violence and ignorance. The Christian does not live by differentiation from the non-Christian, hunting down idolatry and occupying the territory of true faith.

To be sure, religious diversity can be construed theologically as an artifact of human rebellion. Naming idolatry is not the exclusive province of religious exclusivists. Consider, for example, the many contemporary Christian ethicists critical of those who "worship manna." All reality rests in the gracious love of God. But for the Augustinian at least, corrupt knowledge corresponds to a corrupt refusal of this love. Unlike the historicism about religion that opens this essay, this claim about human nature is perennialism on stilts. Such is our lot in this interim of the time between the times. All religions, including Christianity, stand under the judgment of God. Christian humility does not preclude testifying to this prophetic judgment. But the God who justifies the ungodly in their unbelief does not *belong* to Christianity or the church. Diversity has been made a gift to the church through divine providence. In any case, love is for the *actual neighbor* rather than an imagined conception of the good. Just as "sin remains parasitic on a good creation," the fundamental value of persons posited by a divine love is deeper than any human distortion.[40]

As should be clear, my appropriation of Outka's discussion of the justifying reasons of such agape traverses familiar theological controversies. Outka highlights Kierkegaard's religious commitment to equality and Barth's attention to neighbor love partaking in the seriousness of a divine command. These distinguish the *content* of agape in relation to nontheological grounds for equality, including "the intrinsic goodness of communion with God and the correlative treatment of witness."[41] They bear directly on beliefs and practices regarding religious diversity. To these I now turn.

Following at a Distance: Love's Asymmetry

A persistent feature of Outka's work is the claim that God is the subject of unique veneration. The love of God is "the first and greatest commandment" (Matt. 22:38). God, not social cohesion or civilizational progress, is the highest good. God is not to be measured against other goods. There is nothing beyond the triune God. God is the source of all that is true, good, and beautiful. This wild and complex God knows us better than we know ourselves. Another corollary follows that is prominent in the Augustinian tradition: "fellowship with God is the greatest of all goods, the only source of inexhaustible happiness, the herald of our final destiny."[42] Turning away from this fellowship is Adam's mysterious sin, the primal disruption of friendship with God and others.

Augustine's obsession with the safety of his immutable God funds many critics, especially *within* the Christian tradition. They find the concrete neighbor lost in the intensity of his strenuous mood, not to mention his doctrine of eternal alienation. Authentic encounter with religious others is never risked in his passion for deliverance from the wounds of nature. Disembodied souls remain only as steps in the ascent to the eternal perfection of a God that he cannot lose. All other loves are unstable, swallowed up into (his) God. All forms of secular life must be directly sanctified or abandoned. In fact, given the pervasiveness of sin and self-deception, Augustine often leaves the impression that God is the only good we might safely wish for our neighbor because it is what he most desires. It is the only good without qualification. It is the only good that exists for its own sake.

Alternative stories can be told about Augustine's anxiety.[43] Like Kierkegaard's account of God as the "middle term," to love the neighbor "in God" is meant to protect the neighbor from the self's thieving and possessing tendencies.[44] It is not accidental that Augustine's famous vision at Ostia followed shared conversation. Yet we have serious difficulty in desiring this good in the right way. Dialogical self-awareness is prone to view others merely as potential coreligionists in *our* imagined new life of grace. Even willing others to love God can be an entirely self-enclosed monologue. Augustine practically invents the idea that confession harbors defensive vanity and prideful domination. Our own piety must be subject to relentless criticism as we progressively reshape our existence and redirect our desires in response to grace. For Augustine, ultimately, we must defer genuine happiness (and holiness) to the hope of afterlife. All piety in time is veiled as a work in progress for the *viator*.

This does not mean all love is a semblance, but it is one way to affirm the truth in Luther's dictum that we live *simul justus et peccator*, simultaneously justified and sinner. There is no closure this side of the eschaton. Critics of Christian efforts to love their non-Christian neighbor in this world might prefer a dose of otherworldly hyper-Platonism. Augustine was that rare church father who lived a good part of his life as a non-Christian. Despite his many religious conversions and beautiful rhetoric, however, his own example of interreligious dialogue was not a model of charitable engagement or transfigured generosity.

Outka's God-centered ethic does not travel in an excessively monistic direction. Human flourishing consists in the love of God *and* love of neighbor. Temporal goods and virtues have their integrity and intelligibility, albeit in relation to God. This relation is neither inscrutable nor obsessive. We are accountable to various finite goods. They buoy us in the sufferings of creaturely life. The transcendent God revealed in creation, the covenant with Israel, and the incarnation of Jesus Christ are not jealous of *any* temporal love. Fellowship with *this* God need not crowd out recognition of other loves or other goods. Religious cultures, therefore, are not divided into the kingdoms of good and evil. By my lights, Augustine's own intoxication with God admits as much. Proximate ends are not always only means to an ultimate end. If God's power is fully expressed in an eternal act of self-pouring love, then the highest good is always a common good.

But, alongside latter-day Augustinians like Kierkegaard and Luther, Outka helpfully emphasizes the sui generis character of a relation to God. There is a "difference between loving God oneself and commending love for God to others."[45] Divine love always exceeds our reciprocity: "even if you have thrust in as far as possible, the source is always a bit further in."[46] In itself, humanity cannot establish this fellowship. God alone desires this relationship and creates the desire for it within us. God alone is the agent of conversion. The original movement is unilateral. From our side, "to love and glorify God should be equated with nothing else."[47] As the Westminster Catechism famously opens, to "glorify God and to enjoy him forever" is our "chief end." Despite analogies of grace, love for God is finally intelligible when it is radically distinguished from all other loves. This supreme and passionate devotion cannot be transferred to "our neighbors or ourselves on pain of idolatry."[48] The neighbor is not God. Creatures are to be loved as creatures. God is to be loved as God.

Yet love to God is allied inexorably to love for neighbor. They do not exist without each other. Both are *commanded*. The second is *like* the first. In Outka's terminology, they are governed by "mutual irreducibility and mutual inherence."[49] The difficult logic of these loves assumes neither subordination nor (necessary) competition. This nuanced yet definite account of the relationships between love commandments is an important contribution to Christian ethics. What implications follow for religious diversity?

The unity in diversity of the love commands suggests another route into love's relation to religious diversity, particularly in terms of the goodness of the God relation and the character of the church's witness *for* the world. To love what God loves, Outka counsels, "differs from insisting that we are to love others *as* God loves them."[50] We can never substitute for God. This means we can never presume to play God. We can never command belief.

In a fruitful reading of Hans Frei, Outka helpfully focuses on normative questions about the identity of Jesus and its relevance for interactions with others. These "ethical extrapolations" fall under what Outka describes as a motif of the Protestant Reformers: "that of following after rather than imitating."[51] We are not second Christ figures. God may love others into freedom, but we must not. The influence of Barth is notable. To "follow after"— *after* revelation, *after* grace, *after* cross and resurrection—again sets a limit on our activities. They especially limit pretensions of salvific love from the human side. The church, for example, "can only follow Jesus and not reproduce his work."[52] The person and work of Jesus remains unique and distinct. It is the mysterious particularity that guarantees universality. This is the joy, the promise, and the scandal of the Gospel.

To identify Jesus as savior and mediator does not deny he also is a model for Christian ethics. Who God reveals Jesus to be is held in concert with who Jesus reveals God to be. The Christian community finds warrant for a "normative universalism" in the inclusive activity of Jesus, who includes all humanity in his humanity. In faith, it points to the evangelical mission of God in Word and Sacrament. Such testimony is both belated and anticipatory. Looking backward and forward, it involves witness, service, and hope for everyone. Messianic witness includes exhortation and proclamation through the Spirit to God in Christ. But it does not place the religious "other" under the law of our self-interpretations or ontological imaginations. Nourished by the practices of the church as a pilgrim community called by God, such activity is not a program or achievement. It is a fitting expression of neighbor love taken up by the life of the church as a whole. The church lives by faith that God will make use of the obedience of sinners. It looks to the obedience of the One who was a sacrifice for the "sins of the whole world" (1 John 2:2) and "made our wisdom, our righteousness and sanctification and redemption" (1 Cor. 1:30). That we belong to this God is our "only comfort in life and death," as the Heidelberg Catechism puts it. Life in the visible church externally reminds us of this comfort.

Christians, however, are not the guardians of divine grace. Outka elegantly describes this account of Christology and ethics in these terms: "when we release our works from the weight of a final seriousness they cannot bear, we may be able to display a certain lightness in the way we comport ourselves, a lightness that resembles only superficially the frivolous or the complacent."[53] That is to say, the confident faith of those beloved of God sets them free to love others in freedom. For Barth, the triune God gathers and sends the Christian community to witness to this freedom on a corporate and cosmic scale. This affirmation of the missional nature and purpose of the church is central to any Christian ethics and to any Christian who seeks to follow this triune missionary God.

The neighbor, however, is not simply the patient of Christian love. Love is not a prudential strategy for effective evangelism, however problematically that term has been understood. They too have a mission to the Christian community. In a remarkable exegesis of the parable of the Good Samaritan, Karl Barth renders any neighbor as the "representative of the divine compassion."[54] In Barth's hands, this most famous story is not moralized by appeal to boundary-breaking universalism or the reduction of love to God to neighbor love. It does not celebrate an "anonymous Christian" imitating a predetermined notion of Christian virtue. But it also does not imagine the Christian in the role of the Good Samaritan to the world, a self-serving temptation in situations of cultural privilege. Rather, the event of mutual encounter is itself a transfiguring sacrament of grace.

The neighbor is *actually* the bearer of the mercy of God in the drama of salvation. In and through wounded humanity, we are opened to the goodness of God in the sacred presence of the neighbor. Here Barth records the many strangers in redemptive history narrated in the canon, outsiders who come from surprising places into the circle of divine election. For Barth, such neighbors are "a visible sign of invisible grace, a proof that I, too, am not left alone in this world, but am borne and directed by God."[55] Any response to Jesus Christ—revealed as the divine neighbor with humanity—involves a response to God and neighbor. Loving and being loved, in the vulnerable solidarity of this grace, is a proleptic enactment of the kingdom. The church bears witness to the fragile beauty of this reality in its social practices of giving and receiving.

Conclusion

Religious diversity shapes much of contemporary Christian experience and self-understanding. For many, it is a regrettable feature of life. There is a palpable sense of loss and tragic distortion. This can fund resentment or resignation. Others evaluate it positively as enriching possibilities for transforming their relationship with God, who loves in freedom. Diversity reflects the radical plurality of the divine life itself. A plurality of crowded religious options is part of the joy of creaturely existence. Still others find the life of the Christian pilgrim exists between some mixture of these passions. They express the eschatological tension of living between the "already" and the "not yet." Whatever perspective is taken, exploration of *ethical* commitments that follow from Christian confession in relation to this reality of religious diversity is inescapable. It is already changing the landscape of the discipline of Christian ethics. Caught today between so many religious and secular fundamentalisms, Christian ethicists should not allow their attention to other pluralisms to marginalize greater attention to the distinctiveness of this most human form of otherness.

Notes

1. For a helpful survey of these themes, see John Kelsay, "Plurality, Pluralism, and Comparative Ethics: A Review Essay," *Journal of Religious Ethics* 24, no. 2 (Fall 1996): 403–28; Ian Markham, *Plurality and Christian Ethics* (Cambridge: Cambridge University Press, 1994); and Michael Kessler, ed., *Political Theology for a Plural Age* (Oxford: Oxford University Press, 2013).

2. I borrow the language of rivalry from a philosophical work that has exercised significant influence on Christian ethics: Alasdair MacIntyre, *Three Rival Versions of Moral Inquiry* (Notre Dame, IN: University of Notre Dame Press, 1991). For theological criticism of MacIntyre's notion of rivalry, see Luke Bretherton, *Hospitality as Holiness: Christian Witness amid Moral Diversity* (Burlington, VT: Ashgate, 2006).

3. See Oliver O'Donovan, "Reflections on Pluralism," in *The Kuyper Center Review: Politics, Religion, and Sphere Sovereignty*, ed. Gordon Graham (Grand Rapids, MI: Eerdmans, 2010), 1–13; and David Decosimo, *Ethics as a Work of Charity: Thomas Aquinas and Pagan Virtue* (Stanford, CA: Stanford University Press, 2014).

4. See Susan Parsons, *Feminism and Christian Ethics* (Cambridge: Cambridge University Press, 1996), especially 1–13.

5. See, for example, William Schweiker, *Theological Ethics and Global Dynamics: In the Time of Many Worlds* (Oxford: Blackwell, 2004); Aaron Stalnaker, *Overcoming Our Evil: Human Nature and Spiritual Exercises in Xunzi and Augustine* (Washington, DC: Georgetown University Press, 2009); David Clairmont, *Moral Struggle and Religious Ethics: On the Person as Classic in Comparative Theological Contexts* (Oxford: Wiley-Blackwell, 2011); Elizabeth M. Bucar, *Creative Conformity: The Feminist Politics of U.S. Catholic Women and Iranian Shi'i Women* (Washington, DC: Georgetown University Press, 2011); Elizabeth M. Bucar and Aaron Stalnaker, eds., *Religious Ethics in a Time of Globalism: Shaping a Third Wave of Comparative Analysis* (New York: Palgrave Macmillan, 2012); and G. Scott Davis, *Believing and Acting: The Pragmatic Turn in Comparative Religion and Ethics* (Oxford: Oxford University Press, 2012).

6. For an instructive account, see Paul J. Griffiths, *Problems of Religious Diversity* (Oxford: Blackwell, 2001).

7. On resemblance and the tasks of comparison, see David Decosimo, "Comparison and the Ubiquity of Resemblance," *Journal of the American Academy of Religion* 78, no. 1 (March 2010): 226–58. Decosimo's essay helpfully shows ways comparison "is as powerful in what it tends to hide as in what it reveals" (236).

8. Gene Outka, "The Particularist Turn in Theological and Philosophical Ethics," in *Christian Ethics: Problem and Prospects*, ed. Lisa Sowle Cahill and James F. Childress (Cleveland, OH: Pilgrim Press, 1996), 107. For Outka, "God is neither governed nor circumscribed by the tradition. . . . But those in the tradition rely on what we see as God's self-disclosure in this particular history" (108). For a revealing contrast to this approach to the Christian tradition, see Gene Outka, "Remarks on a Theological Program Instructed by Science," *The Thomist* 47, no. 4 (October 1983): 572–91.

9. Gene Outka, "Theocentric Love and the Augustinian Legacy: Honoring Differences and Likenesses between God and Ourselves," *Journal of the Society of Christian Ethics* 22 (2002): 98–99.

10. See, for example, Alvin Plantinga, *Warranted Christian Belief* (Oxford: Oxford University Press, 2000), especially 422–57; and Linda Zagzebski, "Self-Trust and the Diversity of Religions," *Philosophic Exchange* 36, no. 1 (2006): 63–75.

11. For two different accounts, see George Lindbeck, *The Nature of Doctrine* (Philadelphia: Westminster Press, 1984); and Kevin Hector, *Theology without Metaphysics: God, Language, and the Spirit of Recognition* (Cambridge: Cambridge University Press, 2011).

12. On the origins, value, and limitations of the paradigm, see Michael Barnes, *Theology and the Dialogue of Religions* (Cambridge: Cambridge University Press, 2002); and Gavin D'Costa, *Christianity and*

World Religions: Disputed Questions in the Theology of Religions (Oxford: Wiley-Blackwell, 2009). Barnes argues that these categories "remain all too easily at the level of 'isms'" and "tends to serve the interests of the pluralist agenda only" (8). D'Costa also argues Hick's pluralism can be read as "a new form of triumphalism and imperialism, albeit of an agnostic type" (10).

13. Stanley Hauerwas, *The State of the University: Academic Knowledges and the Knowledge of God* (Oxford: Blackwell, 2007), 65. Kathryn Tanner also argues that "pluralist theories of religion are implicated, despite their best intentions, in colonialist forms of discourse," in "Respect for Other Religions: A Christian Antidote to Colonialist Discourse," *Modern Theology* 9, no. 1 (January 1993): 1–18. For a critical engagement with the politics of Tanner's theology in light of religious pluralism, see Hugh Nicholson, *Comparative Theology and the Problem of Religious Rivalry* (Oxford: Oxford University Press, 2011).

14. John Milbank, "The End of Dialogue," in *The Future of Love: Essays in Political Theology* (Eugene, OR: Cascade Books, 2009), 282. Milbank also points out that these approaches give little attention to the "idea that religions can be considered as social projects as well as worldviews" (285).

15. See Tomoko Masuzawa, *The Invention of World Religions: Or, How European Universalism Was Preserved in the Language of Pluralism* (Chicago: University of Chicago Press, 2005); and Courtney Bender and Pamela E. Klassen, eds., *After Pluralism: Reimagining Religious Engagement* (New York: Columbia University Press, 2010).

16. See Karl Rahner, *The Love of Jesus and the Love of Neighbor* (New York: Crossroad Publishers, 1983); John Hick, *An Interpretation of Religion: Human Responses to the Transcendent* (New Haven, CT: Yale University Press, 1989); and Paul F. Knitter, *Jesus and Other Names* (Maryknoll, NY: Orbis, 1996).

17. For an excellent overview of Barth's discussion of religion, see Garret Green, "Introduction: Barth as Theorist of Religion," in Karl Barth, *On Religion* (London: Bloomsbury, 2013), 1–35. Green shows that Barth does more than attack "religion" as a Christian heresy.

18. On this relationship, see also Edward Vacek, *Love, Human and Divine: The Heart of Christian Ethics* (Washington, DC: Georgetown University Press, 1994). Vacek's account of love explicitly unites moral theology, dogmatics, and spirituality.

19. Gene Outka, *Agape: An Ethical Analysis* (New Haven, CT: Yale University Press, 1972), 4.

20. Anders Nygren, *Agape and Eros*, trans. Philip Watson (Philadelphia: Westminster Press, 1953). It is noteworthy in this context that Nygren's classic text, and its generative method of "motif research," was intended as a contribution to the history of religions and comparative philosophy of religion. I do not here address the fraught history of religious comparison through the lens of love's relation to justice, especially in terms of Jewish-Christian dialogue. For a recent treatment, see Leora Batnitzky, "Love and Law: Some Thoughts on Judaism and Calvinism," in *Kuyper Center Review: Revelation and Common Grace*, ed. John Bowlin (Grand Rapids, MI: Eerdmans, 2011), 157–72. Batnitzky helpfully avoids Nygren's distorting contrasts even as she identifies relevant theological and anthropological ones.

21. Outka, *Agape*, 9.

22. See Stephen Pope, "Love in Contemporary Christian Ethics, *Journal of Religious Ethics* 23, no. 1 (Spring 1995): 167–97.

23. Outka, *Agape*, 13.

24. Outka cites from Søren Kierkegaard's *Works of Love*: "Your neighbor is every man, for on the basis of distinctions he is not your neighbor, nor on the basis of likeness to you as being different from other men. He is your neighbor on the basis of equality with you before God: but this equality absolutely every man has, and he has it absolutely" (*Agape*, 159).

25. Søren Kierkegaard, *Works of Love*, trans. Howard Hong and Edna Hong (New York: Harper & Row, 1962), 68.

26. Outka, *Agape*, 212. Many find that only a doctrine of universal salvation can meet the demands of theodicy. See, for example, Marilyn Adams, *Horrendous Evils and the Goodness of God* (Ithaca, NY: Cornell University Press, 1999). Outka argues that "all human beings are included in the range of Jesus' redemptive activity," in "Universal Love and Impartiality," in *The Love Commandments: Essays in Christian Ethics and Moral Philosophy*, ed. Edmund S. Santurri and William Werpehowski (Washington, DC: Georgetown University Press, 1992), 8. Outka's formulation is ambiguous, and he typically expresses an eschatological reserve about God's ultimate judgment. Of course, the scope of divine love and human freedom with respect to

redemption remain disputed in Christian theology in ways that admit multiple interpretations (i.e., reprobation, purgatory, annihilationism, or universalism). I simply note that Outka's vision of last things appears closer to Barth than to Augustine. For a critical reading of Augustine's effort to hold together his account of grace with human kinship in creation, see John Bowlin, "Hell and the Dilemmas of Intractable Alienation," in *Augustine's City of God: A Critical Guide*, ed. James Wetzel (Cambridge: Cambridge University Press, 2012), 186–204. From different angles, see Keith A. Johnson, *Rethinking the Trinity and Religious Pluralism: An Augustinian Assessment* (Downers Grove, IL: InterVarsity Press, 2011); and Brian Brown, John Doody, and Kim Paffenroth, eds., *Augustine and World Religions* (Lanham, MD: Lexington Books, 2008).

27. Outka, "Universal Love and Impartiality," 73.

28. Outka, *Agape*, 131.

29. Gene Outka, review of *Religion and the Individual: A Jewish Perspective*, by Louis Jacobs, *Shofar* (Summer 1994): 109.

30. See David Kelsey, *Eccentric Existence: A Theological Anthropology* (Louisville, KY: Westminster John Knox Press, 2009), 357–401.

31. Tanner, "Respect for Other Religions," 14.

32. Outka, "Universal Love and Impartiality," 64.

33. See Gene Outka, "On Harming Others," *Interpretation* 34 (1980): 381–92.

34. Gene Outka, review of *Character, Vision and Narrative*, by Stanley Hauerwas, *Religious Studies Review* 6, no. 2 (April 1980): 112.

35. See, for example, Outka's discussion of Barth on "obedient willing" and "personal providence" in "Universal Love and Impartiality," 50–53.

36. Outka, *Agape*, 311.

37. In an otherwise critical review of *Prospects for a Common Morality*, Alasdair MacIntyre commended Outka's Augustinian account as a singular effort to explain "some aspects of moral and philosophical disagreement." See Alasdair MacIntyre, "Prospects for a Common Morality," *Philosophy and Phenomenological Research* 55, no. 2 (June 1995): 487.

38. On Christianity and relational identity, see Kathryn Tanner, *Theories of Culture: A New Agenda for Theology* (Minneapolis: Fortress Press, 1997).

39. On the reality and danger of "spiritual" regret, see Lee Yearley, "Conflicts among Ideals of Human Flourishing," in *Prospects for a Common Morality*, ed. Gene Outka and John P. Reeder (Princeton: Princeton University Press, 1993), 233–53. Such recognition is an important part of Charles Taylor's account of modern secularity in which religious faith is taken to be "one human possibility among others." See Charles Taylor, *A Secular Age* (Cambridge, MA: Belknap Press, 2007), 3.

40. Gene Outka, "Augustinianism and Common Morality," in *Prospects for a Common Morality*, 142.

41. Outka, *Agape*, 206.

42. Outka, "Augustinianism and Common Morality," 126.

43. See Eric Gregory, *Politics and the Order of Love: An Augustinian Ethic of Democratic Citizenship* (Chicago: University of Chicago Press, 2008); and Charles Mathewes, *A Theology of Public Life* (Cambridge: Cambridge University Press, 2007).

44. For Kierkegaard, "the love-relationship is a triangular relationship of the lover, the beloved, love—but love is God. Therefore to love another person means to help him to love God and to be loved means to be helped" (*Works of Love*, 124; see also 70 and 87).

45. Outka, "Universal Love and Impartiality," 65.

46. Kierkegaard, *Works of Love*, 26.

47. Outka, "Theocentric Love and the Augustinian Legacy," 99–100.

48. Ibid., 101.

49. Outka, "Self and Other in a Theological Framework," in *A Just and True Love: Feminism at the Frontiers of Theological Ethics*, ed. Maura A. Ryan and Brian F. Linnane (Notre Dame: University of Notre Dame Press, 2007), 141.

50. Outka, "Theocentric Love and the Augustinian Legacy," 102.

51. Gene Outka, "Following at a Distance: Ethics and Identity in Jesus," in *Scriptural Authority and Narrative Interpretation*, ed. Garrett Green (Minneapolis: Augsburg Fortress Press, 1987), 150.

52. Ibid.

53. Ibid., 155.

54. Karl Barth, *Church Dogmatics*, ed. G. W. Bromiley and T. F. Torrance (London: T&T Clark, 2009), 1.2, 416.

55. Ibid., 436.

20

Neighbor Love in the Jewish Tradition

RONALD M. GREEN

Do not seek revenge or bear a grudge against one of your people, but love your neighbor as yourself. I am the LORD.

—Leviticus 19:18

THE APPEARANCE OF THE LOVE commandment in the book of Leviticus startles us. Leviticus, with its long lists of cultic ordinances and dietary and sexual restrictions, is not the place that one expects to find what many regard as the epitome of biblical ethics. And yet here the commandment is, immediately before prohibitions on the mating of different animal species or the wearing of clothing woven of two kinds of material.

In fact, the love commandment is not out of place. As a part of the "Holiness Code" detailed in Leviticus, it belongs to the effort to create a holy people. As Israel's God is holy, so his covenanted people must exhibit the highest levels of ritual, spiritual, and moral purity. The love commandment is a moral expression of this demand for holiness.

Nevertheless, the embedding of the love commandment in the ritual context of Leviticus has tended to diminish its salience in the biblical tradition. When the love commandment is mentioned, what usually comes to mind are its expressions in the New Testament, especially the Gospel texts of Mark 12:31, Matthew 22:39, and Luke 10:27. Christianity is the religion of love, whereas Hebrew faith and the rabbinic Judaism it gave rise to are the religions of ritual and law. The Levitical commandment itself, when it is not overlooked, becomes a casualty of this superficial contrast. At best, it is regarded as a subordinate concern in Judaism or a feeble anticipation of the great emphasis on love in the Christian tradition.

In what follows, I want to examine in some depth the Hebraic and later Jewish understandings of the love commandment. I will explore several questions. What is the meaning of the commandment in its biblical context? How was it interpreted in the later rabbinic tradition? And how do its interpretations and applications compare with those found in the New Testament? As we will see, these questions yield complex answers and significant disagreements, but the disagreements within each tradition, Judaism and Christianity, are greater than the disagreements between them. In all respects, the love commandment of Leviticus 19:18 lays the foundation for a shared Jewish and Christian ethic of love.

"You Shall Love"

As stated in Leviticus, the love commandment has three principal elements: the command itself, "you shall love," *veahavta* (וְאָהַבְתָּ); "the neighbor," *lere'akha* (לְרֵעֲךָ); and "as yourself," *kamokha* (כָּמוֹךָ). Each element has variations of meaning in the biblical texts and Jewish tradition. Of these three, the command to love, while by no means transparent in its meaning, raises the fewest questions and has stirred the least debate. In general, the word "love" as used here, with the root *ahav* or *ahev*, appears to carry the same range of meanings in the Hebrew Bible and later Judaic texts as it does in English. Like the English word "love," it is used to signify passion, desire, satisfaction, contentment, friendliness, intimacy, attachment, or esteem. It is frequently used to denote a father or mother's love for a child (Gen. 22:2, 25:28, 37:3, 44:20) or a husband's love for his wife. Isaac's love for his wife, Rebekah (Gen. 24:67), is expressed with this word, as is a husband's love for one special wife among others (Deut. 21:15; 1 Sam. 1:5). The same root is used for Jonathan's affection for his friend David (1 Sam. 18:1, 3; 20:17; 2 Sam. 1:26) and Saul's love for David (1 Sam. 16:21). On a less lofty plane, Isaac is said to "love" game as Rebekah prepared it (Gen. 27:4, 9, 14). Here and elsewhere, the verb *ahev* seems to express preference, as in several texts (Gen. 25:28, 37:3, 4; Deut. 21:15; 1 Sam. 1:5).[1]

Almost everywhere that it is used to express affection between people, ranging from marital love to friendship, the Septuagint translates the root *ahev* with the Greek word *agape*. This is the same Greek word used in the New Testament in all expressions of the love commandment. Hence, we can conclude that there is significant continuity in the meaning of the word "love" itself across the Bible. As in the Gospels, the word "love" in Leviticus 19:18 has the sense of strong attachment, affection, and concern. If there is any difference in the precise nature of or extent of love as it is commanded in Leviticus and later expressions, it cannot be found by focusing on the word "love" alone.

Shubert Spero observes that the rabbis tended to develop the behavioral rather than the emotional implications of the love commandment, perhaps because they perceived the difficulty in commanding a feeling.[2] Thus, Maimonides, the authoritative twelfth-century commentator and codifier of Jewish law (*halachah*), in his discussion of the love commandment emphasizes acts of kindness and respect that express it. To love the neighbor, says Maimonides, requires one to speak positively of him and "have compassion upon his possessions."[3] Maimonides also itemizes the many personal acts of benevolence that rabbis preceding him had interpreted as expressing neighbor love, such as visiting the sick, consoling the bereaved, burying the dead, dowering the bride, and rejoicing for the bride and groom. All things that you want others to do for you, said Maimonides, "do them for your brother."[4] As Spero observes, while deeds were foremost, this emphasis on loving acts presumes a "positive attitude and feeling to the other."[5]

"The Neighbor"

This element of the Levitical love commandment has probably occasioned more intense debate between the Jewish and Christian traditions and within each tradition than any other. In 1888 the noted German Jewish philosopher Hermann Cohen was asked to submit an opinion in a criminal case brought by the community of Marburg against an elementary school teacher who was charged with insulting the city's Jewish community. Two years earlier, the teacher had delivered a public address in which he asserted that the Levitical commandment was valid only among Jews and had no reference to non-Jews, whom, the teacher said, the Talmud permits Jews to rob and cheat. The court sought two expert opinions. Paul Lagarde, a polymath biblical scholar and violent anti-Semite, defended the teacher's statements and subsequently published his opinion in an anti-Semitic journal. In response, Cohen published his expert opinion in the case as a treatise, "Neighbor-Love in the Talmud," the first of several essays on this topic that marked Cohen's transformation from a Kantian philosopher to a philosophical scholar of Jewish ethics. Both the Jewish community of Marburg and Cohen won a victory when the accused was sentenced to fourteen days' imprisonment and required to pay for costs. But the victory was short-lived. In the decades ahead, Lagarde's views, not Cohen's, were to dominate German culture and help lay the foundations of the Holocaust.

The contending positions in the Marburg trial reflect differences in interpretation reaching back into the biblical text itself. Even within Leviticus 19, two competing interpretations can been found. One holds that the neighbor (*re'a*) must be regarded as only the fellow Israelite. It bases this conclusion on an apparent parallelism between the first and second half of verse 18. Since the first half prohibits bearing a grudge "against one of your people" (*bne amekha*), the second half must also be limited only to other Israelites (or Jews). Pointing to verse 34 sometimes reinforces this reading: "The alien living with you must be treated as one of your native-born. Love him as yourself, for you were aliens in Egypt. I am the LORD your God."[6] Here, the love commandment is explicitly applied to the resident alien (*ger*), though not to all human beings. This extension of the commandment would not be needed, it is argued, if 19:18 applied universally and not just to the fellow Israelite. In addition, in later rabbinic teaching and the Talmud, the *ger* is sometimes taken to be a proselyte, one who either has converted or is about to convert to Israelite faith.

Both these readings can be contested. The second half of verse 18 might as easily be read to expand the first half as repeat it, and verse 34 must also be considered in its entirety. The closing phrase "for you were aliens in Egypt" is a leitmotif of biblical teaching, repeated in the Pentateuch several times in conjunction with key passages of ethical instruction (Exod. 22:21, 23:9; Deut. 10:19). But if the alien in one's midst is likened to the Israelites in Egypt, then the commandment to love the alien would have universal intent and merely repeat in other terms the neighbor love of Leviticus 19:18. As Hermann Cohen points out, the Israelites were not about to convert to Isis worship, so the *ger* here cannot be merely a proselyte.[7] As aliens to every feature of Egyptian culture, the Israelites represent the universal other. Hence, the command to love the alien as oneself must be taken as another call to universal human regard.

These contesting readings of the neighbor as either the fellow Israelite or any other person that one might encounter appear elsewhere in the Bible. For example, in Exodus 2:13, Moses witnesses a fight between two Hebrews and asks, "Why do you strike your fellow [*re'akha*]?" suggesting that the term *re'a* may apply only between Jews. But in Exodus 11:2, God instructs Moses to command the Israelites who are about to leave Egypt to "ask, every man of his neighbor [*re'ehu*] and every woman of her neighbor [*re'utha*], for silver and gold jewelry." Here neighbor can refer only to the Egyptian. This same ambiguity of meaning, evidenced in many other texts, leads Ernst Simon, in a masterful review of the issue, to conclude, "The scriptural evidence . . . is insufficient to tell us with certainty who is my neighbor, whom I am commanded to love as myself." Reviewing this evidence, Simon continues:

The term *re'a* appears to be used in a variety of ways with no single meaning as its controlling center. It serves as the designation for diverse relationships between and among a variety of persons. There is no fixed usage that makes it possible for us to determine unambiguously what is the essence of a *re'a*, or what is the essential nature of the relationship to a *re'a*. . . . The one reliable conclusion is that *re'a* is consistently a person who is near to you, and one with whom you may maintain diverse relationships. These relationships . . . cover a range from intimate friendship to active enmity.[8]

When we turn from the biblical texts to later writers of the Jewish tradition, the picture changes considerably. Simon reports that "with few exceptions," rabbinic writers of the Talmudic period interpret the neighbor to be the fellow Jew and "seem consistently to have construed our moral duties restrictively, giving special status and claims to other Jews, rather than to men in general."[9] One graphic illustration is found in the Mishnah to the Talmud tractate Baba Kama (37b). At issue is the biblical commandment in Exodus 21:35 requiring the owner of an ox that has gored and killed his "neighbor's" ox to sell the live ox and divide both the price of it and the carcass of the dead ox with the neighbor. The Mishnah states,

> In the case of the private owner's cattle goring the ox consecrated to the temple, or consecrated cattle goring a private ox, there is no liability, for it is stated: the ox of his neighbor, not [that is to say] an ox consecrated to the temple. Where an ox belonging to an Israelite has gored an ox belonging to a Canaanite, there is no liability, whereas where an ox belonging to a Canaanite gores an ox belonging to an Israelite . . . the compensation is to be made in full. (Baba Kama 37b)[10]

In this passage, the term "neighbor" is used restrictively. It excludes cattle that are the property of the temple, since this institution is not literally "the neighbor." And it also excludes the Canaanite dwelling nearby, since this non-Jew too does not qualify as a "neighbor." Throughout the Talmud, similar interpretations of biblical commandments to respect the neighbor are often interpreted in such a way as to limit the meaning of the person at issue to include only the fellow Jew. Thus, further on in Baba Kama, we read that the biblical command requiring return of the brother's lost property (Deut. 22:1–3) applies only when the brother is a Jew (Baba Kama 113b). Tractate Sanhedrin, which deals with weighty matters concerning capital offenses, records the opinion that someone who intended to kill an animal but killed a human being or intended to kill a Canaanite but mistakenly killed an Israelite is not punished with death, because capital punishment requires the intent to kill a human being and "the neighbor" (Sanhedrin 78b). But since the heathen is not a "neighbor," the perpetrator is not liable for a capital offense. (The text informs us, however, that God will punish the killing of a Canaanite.)

These and similar passages have fueled the kinds of anti-Semitic charges raised before and after the Marburg trial.[11] Responding adequately to them requires a treatise in its own right. Part of the problem, as Hermann Cohen noted in his own expert opinion on the subject, is the "unclassical style and restless dialectic" of Talmudic commentary (*gemara*). As Cohen observes, "Thoughts were not sketched and developed through the setting of a problem, but produced in an exegetical manner. . . . Therefore, the discussion does not always proceed in an objectively logical way, but rather in a highly formal manner."[12] For example, the seemingly callous text that appears to liken the Canaanite to an animal and that frees one who intended to murder a gentile from capital liability must be understood within the full context of Talmudic discussion of capital offenses. In general, with the growth of ethical sensitivities, the rabbis were loath to impose the harsh punishments prescribed by scripture. One Talmudic text declares that a Sanhedrin (Jewish court) that imposes the death penalty even once in seventy years is to be called "a destructive (or bloody) tribunal" (Makkoth 7a). Thus, the rabbis consistently sought ways to avoid imposing the death penalty. The principle was that "when there is a doubt in a capital charge, a lenient attitude must be taken" (Sanhedrin 79a). Since the penalty required the presence of the intent to kill a human being, someone killing a human being but intending to kill an animal is spared the punishment. Similarly, by invoking the narrowest possible reading of the biblical term "neighbor," the rabbis were able to spare from death the individual who unintentionally killed an Israelite while intending to kill a Canaanite. (The parallelism here between the Canaanite and the animal is an unfortunate accident of the Talmudic dialectic.) Thus, a deeply humanistic effort here provides grist for an indictment of rabbinic exclusivism.

It is true, of course, that the success of this argument rests, in part, on the existence of rabbinic opinions identifying the neighbor as only the fellow Jew. And while this was by no means the only viewpoint present among rabbinic authorities, such opinions can be found. However, they too usually reflect complex considerations. Many pertain to harsh biblical discussions of the idolatrous nations surrounding Israel that lead to legal (*halachik*) rulings in the Talmud that assume the impossibility of establishing moral relationships with "heathens." Thus, we read that an Israelite woman "should not suckle a child of a heathen, because she rears a child for idolatry; nor should a heathen woman [be allowed to] suckle a child of an Israelite woman, because she is liable to murder it" (Avodah Zarah 26a). Always faithful to the biblical text, the rabbis could not simply avoid these exclusionary attitudes.

Other rulings involve non-Jewish gentiles generally but are based on the difficulty or impossibility of reciprocity when gentile laws are not in harmony with the humanitarian laws of the Jews. An example is provided by the requirement that a gentile pay full damages if his ox gores a Jew's and his exclusion from the requirement that the remaining assets be shared. The background of this ruling is the presumption that Israelites are required to exercise special care with regard to dangerous animals, something not done by or required of the non-Jew. (However, the same reasoning also excludes nomadic Israelite herders from the protections of this rule [Sanhedrin 57a].) Commenting on the Talmud's penalty of full damages for the heathen, Maimonides describes this as "a fine imposed upon heathen because, being heedless of the scriptural commandments, they do not remove sources of damage. Accordingly, should they not be held liable for damage caused by their animals, they would not take care of them and thus would inflict loss on other people's property."[13]

One could go on, ruling by ruling, examining the logic of gentile exclusions in the Talmud and related rabbinic teachings. Many respond to the biblical assumption of a threatening and dangerous world of ancient Israel's idolatrous enemies; others seek to integrate the requirements of different, autonomous legal systems. And some reflect the ongoing tensions between Jews and non-Jews in the course of centuries of Diaspora existence. For example, the biblical requirement that one return a neighbor's lost property was qualified for the gentile whose differing legal traditions might lead him to accuse of theft a law-abiding Jew seeking to return property.[14]

Overall, one cannot ignore the fact that the lofty ethic of neighbor love first enunciated in Leviticus was often interpreted in ways that confined its most demanding implications to the fellow Jew and excluded gentiles. This remains true to this day in some quarters of the ultraorthodox Hasidic community. For example, Rabbi Schneur Zalman of Liadi (1745–1812), founder of the Habad (Lubavitch) community, writes in his *Liqqutei Amarim* that "all Israelites are called real brothers by virtue of the source of their souls in the one God," but he does not extend this brotherhood to non-Jews.[15] In our day, this attitude may contribute to a perceived tendency on the part of some Lubavitchers and other Hasidim to assign a lesser moral status to gentiles, which has led to episodes of bitter conflict.[16] Thus, we can say that the persecution and exclusion of Jews by the gentile world has sometimes generated a vicious cycle of mutual exclusion and mistrust.

From at least the Enlightenment forward, but with anticipations in the developing international culture of the high Middle Ages,[17] rabbis and progressive Jewish thinkers sought to reexamine those elements in the Talmud that appeared to exclude the non-Jew from the protections of the love commandment. Drawing on more generous teachings of the Talmudic tradition, they sought to reestablish the Bible's own suggestions of the meaning of the commandment as requiring universal ethical regard. In the modern period, Hermann Cohen's Marburg opinion is a leading example of such an effort. For Cohen, the essential concept of monotheism, the oneness of God, requires a corresponding unity of mankind and a universality of moral respect. The understanding of God as the parent of humankind requires us to treat each fellow human being as a brother or sister. "The concept of the father," says Cohen, "leads to the fundamental concepts of equality and community."[18]

"As Yourself"

This third element of the Levitical formula occasioned considerable debate among the rabbis. Two major problems were discussed. One concerned how much one should extend oneself on the neighbor's behalf. Does the love commandment require one to make efforts for the neighbor as great as you might make for yourself or beloved family members? Does it perhaps require you to risk your life? A second problem concerned the adequacy of the reciprocity implicit within the requirement as a standard for moral judgment. Do one's own needs and inclinations serve as an appropriate guide in exercising regard for the other, or can this lead to a hopeless subjectivism in moral judgment and possible harm to the neighbor?

The first of these questions, concerning the extent of the obligation to aid the neighbor, is the subject of a famous Talmudic debate about two travelers far from civilization on a remote desert road. One of them has a pitcher of water. "If both drink, they will both die, but if one only drinks, he can reach civilisation." Must the owner of the water share it with his neighbor? The Talmud at this point records two opinions. "The Son of Patura taught: It is better that both should drink and die, rather than that one should behold his companion's death. Until R. Akiba came and taught: 'that thy brother may live with thee:' thy life takes precedence over his life" (Baba Mezia 62b).

Akiba's teaching here expresses the fundamental rabbinic conviction that precisely because of the sanctity of a human life, each person has a moral obligation to preserve his own life and moral agency. Within the rabbinic corpus, this supports the teaching that almost any ritual commandment, such as observance of the Sabbath, must be broken if needed to save one's own or another's life. While one cannot kill another human being to save one's life (apart from the immediate need of self-defense), neither is one required to place oneself in extreme danger on another's behalf.[19] The rabbis even imposed limits on self-sacrifice where charity was concerned. At a rabbinical synod at Usha in the second century, it was instituted that to prevent one from becoming a burden on others, it was forbidden to give more than a fifth of one's possessions to charity (Kethuboth 50a). None of these limitations ruled out altruistic acts as permissible and even, in some cases, as required. For example, the biblical prohibition "Do not stand idly by when your neighbor's life is threatened" (Lev. 19:16) was understood to require active efforts to help save another's life, even at some personal risk. Thus, one is morally bound to rescue a drowning person even if it entails risk since the other is sure to drown unless saved, while the danger to oneself is uncertain.[20] Furthermore, as Louis Jacobs points out, in the hypothetical case discussed by the Son of Patura and Akiba, the consequence of sharing is death for both, which clearly violates the duty of self-preservation. It remains unclear from the text, however, whether one is permitted to sacrifice his life for the neighbor, by giving the flask to the other. Jacobs argues that Jewish teaching and Jewish history did not lack such "Fools of God."[21] Nevertheless, because of the Jewish tradition's strong emphasis on the duty of self-preservation, the precise extent of allowable self-sacrifice may be one area in which Christian and Jewish interpretations of the love commandment part ways.[22]

The second problem of whether one's own interests can form an adequate basis for moral judgment has long been noted by moral philosophers who have discussed the love commandment (or its closely related biblical counterpart, the Golden Rule). Thus, Immanuel Kant, in the course of introducing his own concept of morality's supreme principle, describes as "banal" a negative version of the Golden Rule ("What you would not wish done to yourself, do not to another"), which he says cannot furnish the basis of obligatory duties to another because "the criminal would argue on this ground against the judge who sentences him."[23] Kant's point seems to be that if one's own subjective preferences and aversions are made the basis of moral judgment, one could easily be lead to favor intuitively unacceptable rules of conduct. A judge heeding his own subjective distaste for imprisonment would fail to administer justice. To avoid such conclusions, Kant insisted on guiding judgment by the categorical imperative, which requires measuring individual volitions in terms of their suitability for becoming universal standards of conduct.

The rabbis seem to have been aware of the issue raised by Kant. A rabbinic commentary on Genesis (Midrash Rabbah) records a debate between Rabbi Akiba and Ben Azzai. At issue was the question of which text contains the Torah's most important principle. Akiba declares it to be Leviticus 19:18, but Ben Azzai says that it is Genesis 5:1 "This is the book of the generations of Adam. In the day that God created man, in the likeness of God made he him." Ben Azzai explains why the Genesis account is superior: "You must not say, 'Since I have been humiliated, let my fellow man also be humiliated; since I have been cursed, let my neighbor also be cursed.' For, as R. Tanhuma pointed out, if you act thus, realize who it is that you are willing to have humiliated—'him whom God made in His likeness.'"[24] A modern commentator, Rabbi David Horwitz, explains Ben Azzai's position by pointing to the limits of using one's own interests as the basis for moral judgment: "What if someone lacks elementary self-respect? What if he does not care if he is cursed and reviled, etc.? Such a person could conceivably claim, 'I indeed fulfill the requirements of Love your neighbor as yourself. But my conception of loving myself entails not minding if I am cursed, reviled, etc. Hence, I am morally consistent if I act this way towards others.'" One way of remedying this problem, says Horwitz, is by affirming that there are "objective standards of human dignity that no man may transgress or trespass."[25] This is what Ben Azzai does in affirming the centrality of the teaching that each human being is created in the image of God.

The Akiba–Ben Azzai dispute reminds us that the love commandment in Leviticus and subsequent rabbinic interpretations has always been connected to our shared descent from Adam as well as the universal fatherhood of God.[26] Indeed, according to some interpretations, this universalizing conception is to be found in the very meaning of the phrase "as yourself" (*kamokha*) in the Levitical commandment. Thus, the great enlightenment philosopher Moses Mendelssohn and Naphtali Herz Wessely argue in their treatment of the verse in the *Be'ur*, a 1783 translation and commentary of the Bible,[27] that the commandment in Leviticus 19:18 cannot mean to love someone else as one loves oneself, because such a degree of love for another is impossible. *Kamokha*, they maintain, does not mean "as yourself" but "that which resembles you." Thus, the commandment should be read, "love your fellow, for he is like you, equal to you and resembling you, for he was also created in the image of God; he is human, like you." This includes all human beings, since all of them were created in the divine image.[28] Writing later, Hermann Cohen applauds the Wessely-Mendelssohn translation and offers Leviticus 19:18 as "Love your neighbor; he is like you."[29] According to these traditions of thought from Ben Azzai forward, it is our divinely endowed and shared human nature that provides the most basic rationale for love and that guides its application in practice.

Christian Comparisons

Against the background of these continuities and differences in Jewish approaches to the love commandment, we are better positioned to understand Christianity's debt to the Hebrew and Jewish traditions as well as Christianity's innovations and departures.

The Two Commandments—Jesus's explicit citations of the love commandment (Mark 12:31; Matt. 19:19, 22:39; Luke 10:27) arise within a context of challenge and polemic.[30] In Mark 12, for example, its mention occurs after a series of challenges by the Sadducees intended to snare Jesus into saying something regarded as hostile to either his coreligionists or the Romans. "One of the teachers [or "experts"] of the law" then joins the discussion and asks, "Of all the commandments, which is the most important?" Jesus replies first with a recitation of the Shema, the proclamation from Deuteronomy 6:4 that is the centerpiece of the morning and evening Jewish prayer services: "Hear, O Israel: the Lord our God, the Lord is one." He adds the next Deuteronomic verse—"Love the Lord your God with all your heart and with all your soul and with all your mind and with all your strength"—and then states the love commandment, concluding with the remark "there is no commandment greater than these."

Some commentators have seen this pairing of the Shema, with its vertical link to God, and the love commandment, with its horizontal directionality to the neighbor, as unique to Jesus and a distinctive feature of Christian understanding.[31] But we have seen that the stress on God's sovereignty and unity are intimately associated in both Hebrew and Jewish thought with the love commandment. That Jesus's teaching here is fully continuous with the Hebrew-Jewish traditions is signaled by what Johannes Nissen describes as the "irenic tone" of the Gospel text.[32] In the Markan account, when Jesus has replied to him, the expert on the law comments, "Well said, teacher," and he then adds his own summary of prophetic teaching as a restatement: "To love him with all your heart, with all your understanding and with all your strength, and to love your neighbor as yourself is more important than all burnt offerings and sacrifices." The narrative concludes, "When Jesus saw that he had answered wisely, he said to him, 'You are not far from the kingdom of God'" (Mark 12:32–33).[33]

The Golden Rule—In addition to its expressions of the love commandment, the New Testament also offers two statements of the Golden Rule (Matt. 7:12; Luke 6:31). The Golden Rule is conceptually linked to the love commandment since both formulations offer principles of conduct that take one's own concerns as a guide to how one should treat the neighbor.

Like the love commandment, the Golden Rule is presented as epitomizing the Torah's ethical and religious teachings. In Matthew, Jesus describes the Golden Rule as summing up "the law and prophets."

The Golden Rule, of course, is not confined to Christianity. It appears in many other world religious traditions, including Hinduism and Confucianism.[34] In Judaism, its most famous expression appears in a passage of the Talmud where we read that "a certain heathen" came before the sage Shammai and said to him, "Make me a proselyte, on condition that you teach me the whole Torah while I stand on one foot." Shammai is said to have driven the heathen off with a stick. The heathen then went to Hillel, who apparently received him graciously and answered, "What is hateful to you, do not to your neighbour: that is the whole Torah, while the rest is the commentary thereof; go and learn it" (Shabbath 30b–31a).

There is a long history of discussions comparing this negative version of the Golden Rule with its positive expression in the Gospels. Some Christian commentators have seen it as lacking the sense of overflowing love for the neighbor of the Christian versions, while Jewish commentators have defended it as a more realistic, rights-oriented guide to conduct and less prone to requiring acts of extreme altruism.[35] Philosophical analysis reveals that since the wishes underlying any proposed act of conduct can be stated both negatively and positively (e.g., "wanting something to happen" is the same as "not wanting something not to happen"), the negative and positive expressions of the rule are therefore at least potentially equivalent.[36] This is even true when extreme acts of altruism or benevolence are concerned. If another person is in need, the negative version requires assistance, since if we were in need ourselves, we would not want others to deprive us of aid.[37] In any case, since the Golden Rule is also given positive expression elsewhere in the Talmud in a statement attributed to Hillel (Aboth, Mishnah 12), it is hard to establish a significant difference on this matter between the Christian and Jewish teachings. It appears that Jesus's teachings were largely consonant with those of first-century Judaism.

The Hillel passage does, however, have one other implication for our understanding of Jewish teachings about the love commandment during this period. The text itself immediately follows several others contrasting Hillel's "gentleness" with Shammai's "impatience." In the preceding passages, Shammai is presented as gruffly driving off questioners, some of whom had previously placed bets concerning which sage would be more welcoming. The heathen who comes before Shammai and Hillel as a potential proselyte belongs to this narrative context. His request that the sage make him a proselyte on the condition that the sage recite the whole Torah while standing on one foot can be seen as a deliberate and provocative challenge, rendering Shammai's hostile response understandable. Hillel, however, passes the test in terms of both the graciousness and wisdom of his response. This suggests his teaching was one that could be understood and appreciated even by an antagonistic heathen interrogator. Surely, this would not be true if the meaning of the rule Hillel offered was confined only to one's Jewish coreligionist, as opposed to being a norm epitomizing the best of gentile and Jewish wisdom and applicable all human beings. Hillel's statement of the Golden Rule in this context, therefore, provides further evidence for the universalizing understanding of the love commandment during these crucial formative years of rabbinic Judaism.

Love of Enemies—In Matthew 5, following the beatitudes, Jesus offers a series of contrasts between the old law of the Torah and his teaching. In 5:43 and following nos., he offers the contrast, "You have heard that it was said, 'Love your neighbor and hate your enemy. But I tell you: Love your enemies and pray for those who persecute you." In Luke 6:27–31, this teaching is repeated and connected with the Golden Rule. In relation to Hebrew and Jewish teaching, however, the contrast offered in Matthew is odd. Popular sentiments may have reflected this attitude, perhaps drawing it from harsh biblical texts directed against Israel's foes (such as the many imprecations against enemies in the Psalms). But there is only one rabbinic teaching to this effect, and in full awareness of the Levitical text that explicitly prohibits revenge or the bearing of grudges, it interprets the "enemy" as the Israelite neighbor who is actively engaged in sin (Pesachim 113b). Elsewhere in the Talmud, attitudes of hatred and revenge are condemned. "Our Rabbis taught: Thou shalt not hate thy brother in thy heart. One might have believed one may only not smite him, slap him, curse him, therefore the text states: 'In thy heart'" (Arakin 16b). Another text seeks to illustrate the degree of dispositional purity required here:

> What is revenge and what is bearing a grudge? If one said to his fellow: "Lend me your sickle", and he replied "No", and to-morrow the second comes [to the first] and says: "Lend me your axe"! and he replies: "I will not lend it to you, just as you would not lend me your sickle"—that is revenge. And what is bearing a grudge? If one says to his fellow: "Lend me your axe", he replies "No", and on the morrow the second asks: "Lend me your garment", and he answers: "Here it is. I am not like you who would not lend me [what I asked for]"— that is bearing a grudge.

The passage continues by identifying those who truly love God: "Has it not been taught: Concerning those who are insulted but do not insult others [in revenge], who hear themselves reproached without replying, who [perform good] work out of love of the Lord and rejoice in their sufferings" (Yoma 23a).

While the similarities to Christian teaching here are obvious, it is also true that the figure of Christ in the Gospel narratives introduces a new element. The events of Christ's life and death, especially his refusal to defend himself, and his words on the Cross—"Father, forgive them, for they do not know what they are doing"—become exemplary of a love of one's enemy that is a hallmark of the Christian ethic. As Johannes Nissen puts it, Christ "is a living parable of non-resistance to evil and love of enemies."[38]

The element of radical commitment to one's neighbor's welfare is illustrated by the treatment of the love commandment in Luke 10 and the parable of the Good Samaritan that one finds there. Here, once again, we encounter the "expert in the law" who questions Jesus, asking, "What must I do to inherit eternal life?" Jesus asks in turn, "What is written in the law?" Now it is the teacher of the law who replies by citing the twin commandments of love of God and love of neighbor. When Jesus says that he has answered correctly and encourages him to follow this teaching, the expert, wanting "to justify himself" presses further: "And who is my neighbor?" he asks. This leads Jesus to recount the parable, which he concludes with the question, "Which of these three [the priest or Levite who abandoned the wounded victim or the Samaritan who succored him] do you think was a neighbor to the man?" When the expert replies, "The one who had mercy on him," Jesus concludes by saying to him, "Go and do likewise."

What distinguishes this treatment of the love commandment is its emphasis on active service to the neighbor, even one that might be an enemy. Jesus transmutes the question, "Who is my neighbor?" into the question, "which of these men was a neighbor?" moving the emphasis from abstract question to the lived exemplification of neighbor love. While the teacher answers the questions intellectually, Jesus counsels him to *act* accordingly. The parable also makes clear that neighbor love extends beyond our accustomed communities of friends or coreligionists. In the world of first-century Judaism, the Samaritans, as Spero observes, were primarily political enemies of the Jewish people. To urge Jews in first-century Judea that the real key to eternal life is to broaden the application of "Love thy neighbor" to include the Samaritans and the Romans, or possibly to start with the Samaritans and the Romans, is comparable to urging Israelis today that their primary moral problem is to begin to learn to love the Arabs.[39]

We have seen that there is support in rabbinic texts for similar regard for the stranger and even the foe. But in the sacrificial life and death of Jesus, this aspect of the love commandment was certainly intensified and moved to the center of Christian ethics, with profound implications for all domains of the ethical life, including the conduct of warfare, sexual relations, and bioethics.[40] Now, vulnerability to the other and radical self-sacrifice become hallmarks of neighbor love in ways that Judaism, with its moral emphasis on preserving one's life and agency, would not allow. The Johannine teaching, "Greater love has no one than this, that he lay down his life for his friends" (John 15:13), although not alien to rabbinic teaching when specific circumstances dictated it,[41] nevertheless has comparatively lesser resonance in Jewish ethics. Kenneth Reinhard is correct, therefore, when he observes, "Whereas in Christianity, the Scriptural exempla of neighbor-love begin with the good Samaritan's gifts of food, clothing, and shelter (Luke 10:25–37) and culminate in Jesus' sublime self-sacrifice on the Cross, in the rabbinic tradition the list of deeds which fulfill the Levitical injunction expands downwards from the upper limit drawn by death, multiplying in the direction of increasingly minuscule, and often negative, acts of everyday courtesy and concern."[42]

But if Christianity intensifies the demands of the love commandment, it also almost simultaneously limits them. Perhaps passionate and self-emptying love for the neighbor thrives less well in the context of a large national community than it does within an intense community of mutual love. It is not surprising, therefore, that while the Gospel of John intensifies the love commandment, it also narrows it. Thus, immediately preceding John 15:13, Jesus is reported as saying, "My command is this: Love each other as I have loved you." While scholars disagree about just how narrow the focus is here, the teaching of this Gospel seems directed at the circle of Jesus's most devoted followers.[43] Perhaps reflecting the circumstances of the early Christian community at the time of writing of this late Gospel witness, the followers appear as an embattled community whom the world hates and persecutes (John 15:18–25). As Nissen observes, "The injunction to love one another reflects the condition of the Johannine community drawn together into communal solidarity in the face of the hostility of the . . . world."[44]

Of course, in some rabbinic writings recorded in the Talmud and elsewhere, we see this same tendency to narrow and intensify the focus of the love commandment. Persecution, it seems, may enhance identification with the fellow members of one's group, but it does not usually lead to universalism. Only deeper reflection on our shared humanity, and perhaps a pause in persecution, can do that.

Conclusion

Alan T. Davies remarks, "Judaism and Christianity, although discrete religions, are really variations on a theme."[45] This insight applies well to the Jewish and Christian appreciations of the love commandment, which are remarkably continuous with one another. Both traditions develop the moral and spiritual heights of this teaching and explore the challenges they pose. The Christian tradition, drawing on the witness of Christ, sometimes takes the love commandment in its most intensely self-sacrificial direction, privileging the life and well-being of the neighbor even at great cost or risk to oneself. Because of its stress on the sanctity of each human life, including one's own, Judaism rarely goes this far. Both traditions relate the love commandment to the oneness of God and the brotherhood and sisterhood of all human beings. Both draw on experiences of bitter oppression and suffering to develop the commandment's theme of universal human regard and compassion. And both, in the face of persecution, sometimes close in on themselves, reserving love, in its most demanding sense, for the brother or sister in faith. The tensions between these interpretive possibilities are the legacy of the Jewish and Christian traditions' shared indebtedness to Leviticus's great commandment.

Epigraph

The epigraph is a translation from the New International Version (1984).

Notes

1. Edward Lipinski, "Love in the Bible," *Encyclopaedia Judaica*, 2nd ed. (Farmington Hills, MI: Gale, Macmillan Reference USA, 2007), 13:227–29.

2. Shubert Spero, "The Self and the Other," in *Morality, Halakha and the Jewish Tradition* (New York: Ktav, 1983), 201.

3. Rambam, Hilkhot De'ot 6:3, www.chabad.org/library/article_cdo/aid/910346/jewish/Deot-Chapter -Six.htm.

4. Rambam, Hilkhot Aveil 14:1, www.chabad.org/library/article_cdo/aid/1181895/jewish/Avel-Chapter -14.htm.

5. Spero, "Self and the Other," 201.

6. Translation, New International Version, 1984.

7. Hermann Cohen, "Die Liebe in den Begriffen Gott und Mensch" (1900), in *Der Nächste: Vier Abhandlungen über das Verhalten von Mench zu Mensch nach der Lehrer des Judentums* (Berlin: Schocken Verlag, 1935), 61. All translations from this volume are my own.

8. Ernst Simon, "The Neighbor (*Re'a*) Whom We Shall Love," in *Modern Jewish Ethics*, ed. Marvin Fox (Columbus: Ohio State University Press, 1975), 31.

9. Ibid., 34.

10. I. Epstein, ed., *Babylonian Talmud* (London: Soncino Press, 1935).

11. For a more recent use of selected Talmudic passages to paint a picture of Jewish exclusivism, see Elizabeth Dilling, *The Jewish Religion: Its Influence Today*, 4th ed. (Chicago: Elizabeth Dilling Foundation, 1964), www.come-and-hear.com/dilling/dcontents.html.

12. Cohen, "Die Nächstenliebe im Talmud," in *Der Nächste*, 41.

13. Maimonides, *The Code of Maimonides*, bk. 11, *The Book of Torts*, trans. Hyman Klein (New Haven, CT: Yale University Press, 1954), 8.5.29.

14. "Gentile," *Jewish Encyclopedia* (New York and London: Funk & Wagnalls, 1907), 5:619.

15. Simon, "Neighbor (*Re'a*) Whom We Shall Love," 44.

16. For a very critical account of Lubavitcher attitudes as contributing to overt discrimination against non-Jews, see Stephen G. Bloom, *Postville: A Clash of Cultures in Heartland America* (San Diego: Harcourt, 2001).

17. See, for example, Simon's discussion of love in the writings of Rabbi Menahem Ha-Meiri (1249–1306), who rose to eminence in Provence during the late thirteenth and early fourteenth centuries: "Neighbor (*Re'a*) Whom We Shall Love," 47–48.

18. Cohen, "Die Liebe in den Begriffen Gott und Mensch" (1900), 61.

19. For discussions of the limits of the obligation of self-sacrifice, see C. W. Reines, "The Self and the Other in Rabbinic Ethics," in *Contemporary Jewish Ethics*, ed. Menachem Marc Kellner (New York: Sanhedrin Press, 1978), 162–74.

20. Ibid., 170.

21. Louis Jacobs, "Greater Love Hath No Man: The Jewish Point of View of Self-Sacrifice," *Judaism* 6, no. 1 (1957). Reprinted in Kellner, *Contemporary Jewish Ethics*, 182.

22. Nachmanides denied that "as yourself" required or permitted extreme self-sacrifice on the grounds that such a commandment would be psychologically unrealistic. He also read it as inconsistent with the teaching of Rabbi Akiba—"thy life comes first." See Spero, "Self and the Other," 202.

23. Immanuel Kant, *Groundwork of the Metaphysics of Morals*, In *Immanuel Kant: Practical Philosophy*, trans. and ed. by Mary J. Gregor (Cambridge: Cambridge University Press, 1996), 80n.

24. The original, shorter version of this debate appears in the Palestinian Talmud, Tractate Nedarim 9:4; *Midrash Rabbah: Genesis* (London, 1977), chap. 24, 6–7, p. 204.

25. David Horwitz, "The Fundamental Principle of the Torah," *YU* [Yeshiva University] *Torah Online*, Sivan 5769, 29, www.yutorah.org/sidebar/lecture.cfm/734849/rabbi-david-horwitz/the-fundamental-principle -of-the-torah.

26. Louis Finkelstein interprets the basis of Azzai's disagreement with his teacher and father-in-law as stemming from the fact that the phrase "thy neighbor" does not necessarily include all of God's creatures. See his "The Underlying Concepts of Conservative Judaism," *Conservative Judaism* 26, no. 4 (1971): 8.

27. *Be'ur* to Lev. 19:18; the commentary to Leviticus was prepared by H. Wessely and was supervised and edited with bracketed additions by Mendelssohn

28. Eugene B. Borowitz, Raphael Jospe, and Hannah Kasher, "Love: Post-Biblical," *Encyclopaedia Judaica*, 2nd ed., 13:231. Also, Spero, "Self and the Other," 204.

29. Hermann Cohen, "Über Wurzel und Ursprung des Gebots der Nächstenliebe," in *Der Nächste*, 15.

30. Outside the Gospels, the love commandment is also offered in Rom. 13:9; Gal. 5:14; and James 2:8.

31. Johannes Nissen, "The Distinctive Character of the New Testament Love Command in Relation to Hellenistic Judaism: Historical and Hermeneutical Reflections," *New Testament and Hellenistic Judaism* 1 (1995): 127–29.

32. Ibid., 129.

33. The Matthean text (22:34–40) omits the agreement of the teacher of the law, perhaps because of its tendency to contrast Jesus and the Jewish interpreters of the law.

34. Jacob Neusner and Bruce Chilton, eds., *The Golden Rule: The Ethics of Reciprocity in World Religions* (New York: Continuum, 2008).

35. Andrew H. Plaks, "The Golden Rule," *Encyclopedia of Religion* (Farmington Hills, MI: Gale, Macmillan Reference USA, 2005), 3631.

36. Marcus G. Singer, "Golden Rule (1967)," *Encyclopedia of Philosophy*, 2nd ed., ed. Donald M. Borchert (Detroit: Macmillan Reference USA, 2006), 4:144–47.

37. This point is made by Spero, "Self and the Other," 208.

38. Nissen, "Distinctive Character of the New Testament," 141.

39. Spero, "Self and the Other," 216.

40. See Ronald M. Green, "Christian Ethics: A Jewish Perspective," in *The Cambridge Companion to Christian Ethics*, 2nd ed., ed. Robin Gill (Cambridge: Cambridge University Press, 2011), 145–61.

41. See Reines, "Self and the Other in Rabbinic Ethics"; Spero, "Self and the Other," 222–26; and Jacobs, "Greater Love Hath No Man."

42. Kenneth Reinhard, "The Ethics of the Neighbor: Universalism, Particularism, Exceptionalism," *Journal of the Society for Textual Reasoning* 4, no. 1 (November 2005), http://jtr.lib.virginia.edu/volume-4-number-1/the-ethics-of-the-neighbor-universalism-particularism-exceptionalism/.

43. "The object of Christian love for John is only what belongs to the community under the Word, or what is elected to belong to it, that is the brotherhood of Jesus." Ernst Käsemann, *The Testament of Jesus: A Study of John in Light of Chapter 17*, trans. G. Krodel (Philadelphia: Fortress Press, 1968), 19; J. Knox, *The Ethic of Jesus in the Teaching of the Church: Its Authority and Relevance* (Nashville: Abingdon, 1961), 95–96.

44. Nissen, "Distinctive Character of the New Testament," 143.

45. Alan T. Davies, "Love and Law in Judaism and Christianity," *Anglican Theological Review* 64, no. 4 (1982): 454.

21 ⁝•

Neighbor Love in Muslim Discourse

JOHN KELSAY

DISCOURSES ON LOVE abound in Muslim poetry and prose. As Paul Heck argues, it is possible to understand Sufi texts in particular as holding for an ideal of universal love: as each and all are loved by God, so each and all should love in God; the Sufi is one who exhibits universal compassion.[1] In Heck's account, such notions provide the makings of a cosmopolitan ethic by which contemporary Muslims may construct a mode of social-political discourse focused on tolerance and inclusion.

Perhaps Heck is correct about Sufism; certainly an understanding of Sufi discourse on these matters is important, not least because of its massive influence in Muslim societies during the late medieval and early modern periods. From the fourteenth through the late eighteenth or early nineteenth centuries, it seems that most every Muslim male (and not a few females) had acquaintance with one or more form of Sufi practice. Some of the orders or organizations had local or regional provenance, while others were truly international. And while the discourse of more contemporary political and religious thought is often critical of Sufism, the phenomenon is still part of Muslim societies. In more remote settings, but also among certain urban elites, the ideal of the saint whose behavior is typified by universal love is revered.

Nevertheless, I am going to take a different tack. The modern critique of Sufi practice rests to a great extent on the judgment that the spirituality—and the ethical stance—of the great masters constituted a departure from normative tradition. The Qur'an, the reports (*ahadith*) of Muhammad's example, and the consensus of recognized scholars (i.e., members of the *ulama*, or learned class) all suggest a different understanding of neighbor love than the one traced by Heck. This is at least the line of those critical of Sufism; I shall follow their lead, though with greater attention to historical context. Thus, I shall argue that there is reason to say that Muslim discourse regarding neighbor love correlates with a notion of ordered relationships, in which the duties associated with love are distinguished—for example, one loves other Muslims in a certain way, non-Muslims in another. In some sense, these differences correlate with a judgment about the relative closeness (or distance) of persons to God. Indeed, some texts suggest that the test of a Muslim's character has to do with whether he or she loves as (or what) God loves and also hates as (or what) God hates. This notion of differentiated loves correlates with the sort of social-political order envisioned in the discourse of *fiqh* or

Shari'a reasoning as it developed during the Abbasid period (roughly, 750–1258 CE). My primary example in this regard will be the norms governing the use of military force.

I begin by presenting a few of the salient texts. I then take up the ways these relate to judgments about political order and military force during the Abbasid period. I conclude with some discussion of the ways the notion of differentiated love relates to contemporary Muslim argument and in turn to certain accounts of love in Christian ethics.

No one truly has faith until he provides his neighbor with security from injuries.[2]

We can begin a survey of relevant texts with this saying attributed to the Prophet. The meaning seems obvious enough. One test of faith—here in the sense of the kind of conviction that is heartfelt and thus not "merely" a matter of verbal testimony—is one that provides neighbors with security. The word "neighbor" (*jar*) is a matter of proximity; thus, true faith involves a kind of care for those who live "in one's neighborhood."[3] Security from "injuries" (*bawa'iq*) points to concerns related to bodily integrity, economic security, freedom from coercion in matters related to religion, and the like.

The matter is more complicated than it seems, however. This saying is a part of a longer report in which we are told that Muhammad said, "God has distributed character traits even as God distributed provisions. Almighty God gives the goods of worldly existence [*al-dunya*] to one whom He loves and also to one whom He does not love, but God does not give religion [*al-din*] except to the one whom He loves."[4] Then, too, we read in another report that the Prophet said, "There are three classes of neighbors. There is a neighbor with a single right; a neighbor with double rights; and a neighbor with triple rights."[5] As this report continues, we learn that the third is a neighbor who is a Muslim "with relation" (a family member or one bound by kinship or marriage). The neighbor with double rights is a Muslim, so a member of the community of faith, but not of one's family. And the neighbor with a single right is one who is *al-mushrik*, one who is guilty of identifying (and revering) creatures with the Creator.

The import of these sayings is thus that proper care for neighbors involves making distinctions. One is supposed to provide neighbors with security. One can say that all those within one's sphere of influence impose a claim in this regard. But the claim is stronger, and thus one's response may be different, depending on the class to which the neighbor belongs. Further, the differentiated response suggested with regard to the ways Muslims ought to practice neighbor love reflects God's distribution of goods. One might say that true believers are those who treat their neighbors in a manner consistent with the policy or practice of the Almighty. To love one's neighbor rightly is thus to respond to him or her in ways befitting a particular neighbor's relation to God.

Such an understanding receives further support in a number of other sayings attributed to the Prophet. The goal of submission or of bringing one's life and one's world into a pattern of behavior consistent with God's guidance involves assigning priority to some relations over others. Thus, Muhammad, as the ideal practitioner of faith, can say, "No one truly believes until I become dearer to him than his parents, his children, and all humanity."[6] Believers are friends to one another; their friendships with non-Muslims are subject to review with respect to the way these affect the cause of God. When non-Muslim neighbors show enmity through behaviors that put them at odds with the divine policy, they should be given opportunity to repent; if they persist, then one should consider the report in which Muhammad says,

When God loves a person, He calls Gabriel and says: I love so and so, so you should love that person. Gabriel then loves the person, and announces in heaven: God loves so and so, so you should love that person. Then those dwelling in heaven love the person, and the person enjoys favorable relations on earth. But when God does not like someone, He calls Gabriel and says: I hate so and so, so you should hate him. Gabriel then hates the person, and announces to those dwelling in heaven: God hates so and so, so you should hate that person. All then hate the person, and hatred for such a one is established in the earth.[7]

One ought to love neighbors in a manner consistent with God's love. One also ought to hate as God hates. Thus, when companions of the Prophet answer the question "Do you know which acts are most dear to God?" by citing prayer, almsgiving, and the exertion of effort in God's way, Muhammad corrects them: "The act most dear to God is love for God's sake and hate for God's sake."[8]

The notion of God's loves and hates seems crucial for an understanding of neighbor love in Islam. It is worth noting the various ways in which verses of the Qur'an reflect the idea. With respect to God's loves, we read that

> God loves those who turn to Him, and who keep themselves clean. (Qur'an 2:223)

> God loves those who fight "in solid lines for His cause, like a well-compacted wall." (Qur'an 61:5)

> God loves judges who are fair. (Qur'an 5:42)

> God loves those who do good. (Qur'an 5:93)

> God loves those who are mindful of Him. (Qur'an 9:4)

> God loves those who seek to purify themselves. (Qur'an 9:108)

Correspondingly, God hates—actually the typical locution in the Qur'an is that God "does not love"—the arrogant (4:36, 31:8), those who are traitors or ingrates (2:278, 3:32, 22:38), those who transgress (2:191, 7:55), those who commit excess (5:87), those who spread news about scandal (4:148), those who are stingy (4:37) or who give in order to be seen (4:38), and those who spread corruption in the land (2:208).

What is the social meaning of such claims? Here it is useful to recall the narrative of God's dealings with humanity suggested by the Qur'an and outlined in a variety of texts familiar to Muslims. God's creation of the world is purposeful (e.g., at Qur'an 21:16–17: "We did not make it for sport"). In particular, human beings are given life so that "we might test you, to see which of you will be foremost in doing good" (Qur'an 11:7). Provided with the capacity to recognize their obligation to serve the Creator, human beings nevertheless prove to be "tyrannical" and "foolish." They "forget" their condition as creatures and fail to live within the "limits set by God." In doing so, they "harm themselves" and deserve God's judgment. (See Qur'an 33:72, 2:190–94, 2:54, among others.)

God is merciful, however, and thus, God sends prophets to "remind" human beings of their duty. The number of prophets corresponds to that of the "peoples" or "communities" of human beings. But the greatest of prophets are those who bring a text, thereby enabling the establishment and maintenance of communities with an ongoing mission to humanity. Moses brings the Torah to the people of Israel. Jesus brings the Gospel to a portion of the people of Israel; these constitute a new community. Finally, Muhammad brings the Qur'an to those who speak Arabic.

For our purposes, the point of the narrative is the notion of God's quest for human beings who will accept the role of vice regency, in the sense of serving as stewards of the creation. In that vein, the establishment of the aforementioned communities constitutes a particularly important development. The gathered believers are to exhort and support one another, spending their time, money, and lives in the task of bringing themselves and the world around them into conformity with divine guidance. Thus far (i.e., to the point in the narrative when Muhammad enters), the divine purpose is at best only partially achieved. The succeeding generations of Israel and of the followers of Jesus failed to adhere to the original message. They added to and took away from the prophetic teaching, creating the peculiar admixture of truth and error characteristic of the religions we know as Judaism and Christianity. Now, then—that is, in these latter days—Muhammad brings the Qur'an, calling the tribes of the Arabian Peninsula—and through them, all humanity—to the practice of *al-islam*, "the submission" in the sense of effort to adhere to the guidance of God.

The *umma* or community of faith is distinguished by its love. God joins the members together in love; they are to love one another, in accord with the norm: Love others in a manner appropriate to their relation to God. So we read at Qur'an 3:102–10:

> You who believe, be mindful of God, as is His due, and make sure you devote yourselves to Him, to your dying moment. Hold fast to God's rope all together; do not split into factions. Remember God's favor to you; you were enemies and then He brought your hearts together and you became brothers by His grace; you were about to fall into a pit of Fire and He saved you from it—in this way God makes His revelations clear to you so that you may be rightly guided. Be a community that calls for what is good, urges what is right, and forbids what is wrong: those who do this are the successful ones. Do not be like those who, after they have been given clear revelation, split into factions and fall into disputes: a terrible punishment awaits such people. On the Day when some faces brighten and others darken, it will be said to those with darkened faces, 'How could you reject your faith after believing? Taste the torment for doing so,' but those with brightened faces will be in God's grace, there to remain. These are God's revelations: We recite them to you with the Truth. God does not will injustice for His creatures. Everything in the heavens and the earth belongs to God; it is to Him that all things return. You are the best community singled out for human beings; you order what is right, forbid what is wrong, and you believe in God.[9]

This text can serve as the charter for an account of the Muslim community as one characterized by the love of its members for one another. To be precise, we should speak of this love as a kind of solidarity. Members are loyal to one another. They trust one another, in the context of a shared commitment to the divine cause. In this, they do not automatically hate those outside the divinely created fellowship. They call others to join, understanding this in terms of offering God's gift of true guidance to humanity. Such outreach is fraught with danger for believers, however. Thus, only a few verses after the charter of Qur'an 3:102–10, believers are warned, "Do not take for your intimates such outsiders as spare no effort to ruin you and want to see you suffer. . . . Here you are, you love them, but they do not love you." (3:118–19).[10] The solidarity of the *umma* establishes a rank ordering of loves by which the believers' duties to one another may be said to have priority or be more extended than their duties to those outside the circle of fellowship. To cite one final report: the Messenger of God said, "A Muslim is brother to a Muslim. He does not injure him, he does not disgrace him, he does not hate him. Piety is here. . . . Every Muslim's blood, property and honor are sacred to another Muslim."[11]

I do not claim that this list of texts provides a complete account of Muslim discourse regarding neighbor love. I do claim that the material suggests a way of thinking that runs contrary to the Sufi discourse mentioned at the outset of this essay. And I also claim that the notion of differentiated loves correlates with some of the most prominent features of Muslim political and military discourse as represented in the work of jurists during the Abbasid period.

Why focus on this period? The Abbasid caliphate held sway over large portions of the historically Muslim regions for five centuries. While its dominance was never total, and the excellence of its policies a matter of considerable debate, Abbasid rule nonetheless set precedents to which Muslims in succeeding generations recurred and that continue to influence contemporary believers. When older historians characterized the period as "formative" or "classical," they perhaps claimed too much. At the same time, if the idea is to locate precedents that occupy an important space in ongoing conversations about the duties of Muslims, the years between 750 and 1258 are clearly important.

Indeed, during this period, the great collections of prophetic sayings on which I have been drawing came together. One can find reports of Muhammad's words and deeds in texts that are—or at least purport to be—dated before 750. But the works of Bukhari, Abu Dawud, and others were first circulated during the Abbasid years. And while there is to date no strong scholarly consensus challenging the traditional Muslim account by which a standard edition of the Qur'an is attributed to the time of the caliph 'Uthman (d. 656 CE), John Wansbrough and others have made a good case that a number of features of the established text actually comport well with a longer period of development in which the give-and-take of Muslim and non-Muslim intellectuals encouraged elaborations of a largely oral scripture up to sometime in the ninth century.[12]

We need not resolve such text-critical questions to make the point I have in mind. The necessary point is made by way of discussion of materials that clearly have an Abbasid provenance. It is uncontroversial that the great schools of Shari'a reasoning took shape during this period. For the works attributed to al-Shaybani (d. 804), al-Shafi'i (d. 820), and Ahmad ibn Hanbal (d. 855), Abbasid policies formed the background for responses to questions about the proprieties of Muslim practice. And even though the *Muwatta* attributed to Malik ibn 'Anas (d. 775) derives its special authority from the idea that it exemplifies the consensus of scholars in Mecca and Medina in the earliest (and thus, pre-Abbasid) periods, the extant versions of the text are actually from the ninth century; they are clearly the work of editors who want to lay claim to the mantle of antiquity as they participate in the discourse of their day.[13]

All of these works presuppose the legitimacy of certain social and political arrangements. The authors disagree on a number of particular judgments, of course. That is why the notion of "schools" or trajectories of interpretation within the discourse of Shari'a reasoning makes sense and why someone like the great al-Tabari (d. 923) could write a book with the title "The Differences of Opinion among the Scholars Regarding Armed Struggle and the Taxation of Conquered Peoples."[14] On the following matters, however, the scholars agree.[15] Thus, a legitimate social order is one in which institutions are arranged in ways that reflect the priority of adherence to divine guidance. Islam is thus the established religion of state.

Other modes of practice (Judaism and Christianity, for example) find their place under the umbrella or "protection" of Islam.

In accord with the establishment of Islam, the ruler should be a Muslim. He should make himself familiar with the Qur'an, reports of the Prophet's words and deeds, and other sources by which believers strive to comprehend divine guidance. But he should not regard himself as self-sufficient in these matters. In some sense, the ruler's legitimacy depends on participation in a process of consultation with other Muslims. The leader should thus foster arrangements by which members of the learned class feel free to offer informed responses to questions of state. If some of these are critical of particular policies, the ruler does well to listen and to engage in further consultation so as to make an informed judgment about the dissenter's claims. He must balance this respect for difference of opinion with the duty to maintain order, of course. In this sense, the process of consultation is not wide open. Those whose criticisms foment rebellion should be warned and, if necessary, disciplined. I shall return to this point. For now, it is enough to note that a process of consultation among believers is an important aspect of the kind of social arrangement identified as "Islamic."

I have already noted that non-Muslim modes of religious practice find their place in relation to the Islamic establishment. The order envisioned by al-Shaybani and others focuses on the need to establish, maintain, and defend a geopolitical entity devoted to the implementation of God's standard. This is the political meaning of the phrase *dar al-islam*, which may be translated as the "house," "abode," or "territory" in which Islam is established. In a way consistent with the verses of Qur'an 3:102–10 (see previous citation), the mission of the Muslim community is to call others to Islam. Should non-Muslim rulers and their communities deem this invitation persuasive and pronounce themselves Muslims, they become part of the Islamic state. If they do not, then they may acknowledge the authority of that state by entering into a tributary relation. This at least suggests that a particular group of non-Muslims is not likely to threaten the security of *dar al-islam*; it may also leave open the possibility that some tributaries will perceive the excellence of Muslim practice and over time establish stronger ties.

In the event tributary relations are not established, then war may be required. It is important here to note the intentionality of the standard texts. The point is the establishment, maintenance, and defense of a legitimate political order. Some of the texts suggest that fighting to bring a resistant non-Muslim community to heel is in the interest of the security of the *dar al-islam*. Others suggest it is a duty with respect to opening the possibility for non-Muslims to live under the protection of a legitimate order or to providing individuals with freedom to hear and acknowledge the call of Islam, in which case one might understand war as a means by which the gift of good governance is brought to non-Muslims. In any case, the resulting order establishes a set of relations by which non-Muslims are brought under the protection of Islam. And their place in the *dar al-islam* is set in a manner consistent with the differentiated loves outlined earlier in this essay.

The juridical discussion of armed force in relation to apostasy provides a good example of this, as does the argument regarding fighting with rebels.[16] In the former case, we are to envision a situation in which an entire group—say, the population of a region within the territory of Islam—announces that it no longer considers itself Muslim, preferring another marker of identity (Christian, Jewish, polytheist, or some other). The public demonstration of this change includes an attempt to throw off the yoke of Muslim government. Fighting ensues, and eventually the Muslim forces are victorious. What happens to the defeated apostates? According to al-Shaybani, they are treated as captives, but with a special proviso. The adults are ordered to return to Islam. If they comply, their status as Muslims is reconfirmed, and they are free members of the community. If they do not, then the men are executed, according to the standard punishment for apostasy. Women who refuse are not to be killed, but they are also not restored to their former position. Indeed, they cannot even be regarded as slaves. They are in a kind of limbo, along with their children, who are identified according to the religion of their parents.

Interestingly, al-Shaybani's discussion of fighting against apostates includes a section on dhimmis, those "protected" and, in some sense, tolerated because they agree to pay tribute to the Muslim establishment. Suppose, al-Shaybani's interlocutor asks, that a group of dhimmis "violated their covenant and fought the Muslims, do you think that their status would be equivalent to that of the apostates who go over to the dar al-harb?"[17] Al-Shaybani's reply is affirmative. The ensuing discussion focuses on the treatment of these people, once fighting ends. Women and children are taken as captives; unlike the apostates, however, the men are not killed—they become captives. If the defeated dhimmis accept a return to the status quo ante, they are not liable for damage caused during the fighting. If they do not, then they should be enslaved.

For our purposes, the important feature is the way religious standing correlates with differential treatment. In the first case, apostasy is associated with treason. Those who "turn" violate agreements with God and the Muslim state. In the second, the breach of contract by rebellious dhimmis has to do with the state only. So long as they agree, their prior standing is restored.

Similarly, the set of judgments pertaining to rebellion reflects the importance of religious standing. The term "rebel" (*baghi*) provides a juridical designation for a group of people (i.e., not a single individual or two) who present an organized front of armed protest against the established government and who appeal to Muslim sources as providing reasons for their actions.[18] The presence of these factors sets them apart from other troublemakers, for example, highway robbers or "adventurers." Jurists like al-Shaybani held that fighting against rebel groups was justified and that so long as an uprising persisted, loyalist forces should prosecute matters aggressively. They are not to violate the Prophet's various orders prohibiting the direct, intentional targeting of noncombatants, of course. But state forces may and should use force in the degree necessary to bring the rebels to heel. Once that goal is accomplished, the rebels are restored as members of the community. Indeed, that is the goal of fighting, in accord with Qur'an 49:9–10:

> If two parties of believers fall to fighting, then make peace between them. And if one party of them does wrong to the other, fight the one that does wrong until it returns to the way of God; then, if it returns, make peace between them with justice, and act equitably. Lo! God loves those who act equitably. The believers are brothers: so make peace between your brothers and observe your duty to God, that you may receive mercy.

Along these lines, al-Shaybani indicates that rebels ought not be penalized or held liable for damage caused during the fighting.

As with the case of apostates, the discussion of rebellion includes a section on dhimmis:

> If the rebels sought the assistance of a group of dhimmis, who took part in the fighting with them, do you think that [the dhimmis' participation in the fighting] would be regarded as a violation of their agreement [with the Muslims]?

> [al-Shaybani] replied: No.
> I asked: Why?
> He replied: Because they were in the company of a group of Muslims.[19]

The text continues with al-Shaybani indicating that the dhimmis, like the rebels, should not be considered liable for injuries inflicted or destruction of property so long as these took place during the course of fighting. Unlike the case in which dhimmis who rise up are considered by way of analogy with apostates, those who fight with rebels never actually altered their status. Their participation is understood as a continuation of their protected status. It is simply a question of which group of Muslims receives their tribute.

In either set of cases, differences in treatment accord with judgments about religious status. As noted earlier, submission to God involves loving as God loves and hating as God hates. More prosaically, those who engage the Muslim state in fighting receive differential treatment in accordance with their standing vis-à-vis the faith.

Such differential treatment is standard in Abbasid-period juridical works. And these set precedents that remained throughout the period of Muslim empires. While precise details can vary, the notion that "regular" Muslims (i.e., those whose mode of practice is recognized as valid by state institutions) owe something to one another rather distinct from what they owe to the protected communities or to apostates (not to mention heretics) seems to be a consistent pattern. In this, of course, Muslim policies do not seem much different from those in which other forms of religious-moral practice are identified with state institutions.

But what happens when the patterns associated with this form of political order fall into disrepair or even out of use? Beginning in the eighteenth century, European incursions into areas a scholar like al-Shaybani would have considered the territory of Islam led to significant changes. By the early nineteenth century, for example, British domination led a jurist like Shah 'Abd al-'Aziz, scion of an important family of *ulama* with connections in Delhi, to issue a ruling that India should no longer be considered Muslim territory. One aspect of British policy in the background of this ruling involved favoring Shi'i over Sunni Muslims—thus, overturning the old order in which Sunni Islam formed a part of the imperial establishment.[20]

The story of imperial decline, in South Asia, Iran, and finally, with respect to Ottoman Turkey, has been told elsewhere, and we need not rehearse it here. Instead, in this context, it is important to appreciate that religious status continues to have major political significance in twentieth- and twenty-first-century Islam. Following the Turkish decision to forgo financial and other support for the Ottoman sultan in 1924, Muslims engaged in a brief argument over the institution of the Caliphate, the question being, What sort of institutions can signal the unity of Muslims throughout the historic territory of Islam, and indeed around the world? By the late 1930s, however, the focus of debate had become the form of an "Islamic" state. Authors like Hasan al-Banna, founder of the Muslim Brothers' movement, and Abu'l a'la Mawdudi, the leading intellectual of the Jama'at-e Islami in Pakistan, made notable contributions in this connection, in effect translating precedents from the old imperial forms into modern territorial states. Mawdudi's contributions to the Pakistani constitutional debate provide a good example. In 1947 Muhammad 'Ali Jinnah spoke as the president to the Constituent Assembly of a state that would soon celebrate its official birth. Building Pakistan, he said, would require each and all to work for the common good. People should leave behind old differences and even learn to separate questions of religion from political life:

If you change your past and work together in a spirit that every one of you, no matter to what community he belongs, no matter what relations he had with you in the past, no matter what his color, caste, or creed, is first, second and last a citizen of this State with equal rights, privileges and obligations, there will be no end to the progress you will make. . . . I cannot emphasize it too much. We should begin to work in that spirit and in course of time all these angularities of the majority and minority communities, the Hindu community and the Muslim community—because even as regards Muslims, you have Pathans, Punjabis, Shias, Sunnis, and so on . . . will vanish. . . . To my mind, this problem of religious differences has been the greatest hindrance in the progress of India. Therefore, we must learn a lesson from this. You are free; you are free to go to your temples, you are free to go to your mosques or to any other places of worship in this State of Pakistan. You may belong to any religion or caste or creed—that has nothing to do with the business of the State. . . . [If Pakistanis adhere to this line of thinking,] you will find that in course of time Hindus would cease to be Hindus and Muslims would cease to be Muslims, not in the religious sense, because that is the personal faith of each individual, but in the political sense as citizens of the state.[21]

Remembering that the establishment of Pakistan occurred partly because of the inability of some Muslim leaders to trust their Hindu counterparts in the struggle to throw off British rule, one of Jinnah's biographers asks, "What was he talking about? Had he simply forgotten where he was?"[22] Well—probably not. It is true, though, that developments in the new state would shortly move in a very different direction, to the point that a Shi'i Muslim like Jinnah or a follower of the Ahmadiyyat movement like Muhammad Zafrullah Khan (Jinnah's foreign minister) would find it difficult to function in the institutions of state. In 1953 and 1954 popular protests aimed at Ahmadis led the government to declare martial law. Mawdudi's writing in support of the protests led to criminal proceedings and even a sentence of death, which was subsequently withdrawn.[23] By the time of the 1956 constitution's approval, it was clear that a significant sector of public opinion favored not only a designation of Pakistan as an Islamic republic, governed by the Qur'an and the example of the Prophet, but also a way of defining the boundaries of Islam so as to delimit participation by Ahmadis. In 1973 a constitutional amendment settled the question, declaring the Ahmadiyyat a non-Muslim sect.

For Mawdudi and those following his lead, the establishment of differential treatment went to the heart of the identification of Pakistan as an Islamic state. As he put it in various writings, adherence to Islam involves one in a revolutionary struggle by which the guidance of God is set against *jahiliyya*—a kind of heedlessness by which human beings seek to find their own way. Liberal democracies and authoritarian or totalitarian orders alike exemplify this departure from God's plan. In diverse ways, all may also be characterized as antihuman, for it is only through living within the limits set by God that human beings may approach their destiny. One must love as God loves and hate as God hates; thus, one relates to human beings in ways appropriate to his or her relation to God. In a discussion of the nature of an Islamic state, Mawdudi indicates that there are two types of citizenship, the one pertaining to Muslims, the other to dhimmis. Speaking of the first, Mawdudi writes,

Upon the shoulders of the Muslim citizens of an Islamic State devolves the main burden of running it in accordance with Islam's best traditions, as they alone are supposed to believe in it implicitly. On them alone it enforces its laws as a whole and enjoins them to carry out all its religious, moral, cultural and political directives. It invests them with all its obligations, and demands from them every sacrifice for the defense of its realm. Concurrent with this, it gives them the right to choose the Head of their State and to be the members of its Parliament. It also entitles them to be appointed to the key posts, so that the basic policy of this ideological state remains in conformity with the fundamentals of Islam.[24]

For dhimmis, by contrast,

> Islam furnishes a guarantee of protection of life and limb, property and culture, faith and honor. It enforces only its law of the land on them and it gives them equal rights with Muslims in all civil matters. They are eligible for all kinds of employment except for key posts: they have an equal share with Muslims in the matter of all civil liberties, and even in economic matters no discrimination is made between a Muslim and a dhimmi. Furthermore, the dhimmis are exempt from the responsibility of the defense of the state, which devolves exclusively and entirely on the Muslim citizens.[25]

In defense of such distinctions, Mawdudi argues that all states are ideological and that in the interests of maintaining the commitments that define proper order, all states must recognize distinctions analogous to his two types of citizens. Perhaps he is right. Nevertheless, Muslim critics of Mawdudi, as of the broader project of defining an "Islamic" state, often note the ways in which the ideal lends itself to policies that stifle dissent, embed discrimination, and encourage intercommunal violence. If forms of political order built around notions of differential loves were ever appropriate, they are so no longer. In a time when Muslims increasingly live in contexts where relations of trust and equity with non-Muslims are required for survival and flourishing, new readings of the Qur'an and the example of the Prophet are both possible and necessary. Thus, an author like Bassam Tibi can argue for a recovery of modes of social and political thought he associates with "Islamic humanism."[26] Here the emphasis is on sources of guidance Muslims share with non-Muslims. In particular, the notion that given proper institutions, groups of human beings are able to reason their way to practices that serve the common good is critical. Jinnah's 1947 address might be seen as one example of the potential political significance of this notion. By contrast, the vision by which Mawdudi and others transform the differential loves developed in correlation with the politics of empire into the setting of modern states consigns humanity to a future of civilizational conflict. Far better for Muslims and others to adhere to the norms of constitutional democracy, in which rights and duties are apportioned without reference to religion or belief. As Tibi has it, the stakes are high:

> In the world of Islam there is a call for a return of history, reviving collective memories about Islamic glory. This glory can be defined in different ways. Is it the glory of Islamic jihad conquests? Or is it the glory of the grammar of Islamic humanism? This is a question of high pertinence for the twenty-first century. Due to inner-Islamic diversity, there are different Islamic options and therefore different answers to these questions. It follows that there are tensions between rival traditions within Islam itself; the grammar of Islamic humanism and shari'a reasoning. . . . I argue for a revival of the humanist tradition in Islam. In our present post-bipolar age of inter-civilizational value conflict, humanism builds bridges. By contrast, claims to remake the world on the basis of shari'a reasoning alienate Muslims from the rest of humanity. The Islamist project of a "shari'a state" also

contributes to polarization within the Islamic umma. In contrast, the revival of the tradition of Islamic humanist rationalism . . . bridges contemporary Islamic civilization with
the non-Muslim other in a context of pluralism.[27]

As noted at the outset of this essay, Muslim discourses about love abound. Some of the
most important correlate with the form of particular social and political arrangements. In
this sense, Muslim notions of neighbor love often reflect arguments about justice: who owes
what, and to whom? The idea that love requires the differential treatment of human beings,
construed in terms of their membership in groups occupying distinctive places in an order
in which Islam is established as the religion of state, is an important part of historic Muslim
tradition. It is not the whole of the tradition, of course; and in a contemporary setting,
where notions of democracy, human rights, and the rule of law have made strong inroads
around the globe, a contest for the definition of Islam is ongoing. That contest is most often
conducted as an argument about justice, particularly in relation to the order appropriate to
an Islamic state. As I have suggested here, however, such debates also reflect notions of
love—of God and of one's neighbors. And this opens the door to comparisons—not only in
terms of various Muslim conceptions of love but with respect to Christian and other forms
of discourse.

In this regard, I wish to make a few observations concerning the particular trajectory of
neighbor love outlined in this essay—that is, the notion that love requires differential treatment of neighbors, which in turn reflects distinctions in those neighbors' relationships to
God. Recall the saying attributed to Muhammad: "The act most dear to God is love for God's
sake and hate for God's sake."[28] Of course, it is clear that "hate" does not involve a denial that
Muslims owe something basic to nonbelievers. But the language is jarring, at least in connection with a certain kind of Christian discourse. In James Gustafson's phrase, an ethic developed largely from Christian sources suggests that human beings "are to conduct life so as to
relate to all things in a manner appropriate to their relations to God."[29] If one substitutes
"neighbors" for "things," one has a sentence that seems to resonate with Muslim discourse.
But does it make use of the language of hate?

If I may speak from experience, it is certainly true that the Presbyterian congregations in
which I grew up—and the one in which I now participate—were very reluctant to speak about
hate in positive terms. Generally passed on by means of social sanctions—that is, a child who
spoke about hating someone would quickly be told that this was inappropriate speech, and
even one who spoke about hating some*thing* was likely to receive a warning about the dangers
of this emotion—the reluctance about hate is in fact well-grounded in the confessions and
catechisms of the Presbyterian Church (USA). Thus, the Heidelberg Catechism provides the
following exposition of the commandment "You shall not kill":

Q. What does God require in the sixth commandment?
A. That I am not to abuse, hate, injure, or kill my neighbor, either with thought, or by
   word or gesture, much less by deed . . .
Q. But does this commandment speak only of killing?
A. In forbidding murder God means to teach us that he abhors the root of murder,
   which is envy, hatred, anger, and desire for revenge, and that he regards all these as
   hidden murder.
Q. Is it enough, then, if we do not kill our neighbor in any of these ways?

A. No; for when God condemns envy, hatred, and anger, he requires us to love our neighbor as ourselves, to show patience, peace, gentleness, mercy, and friendliness toward him, to prevent injury to him as much as we can, and also to do good to our enemies.[30]

The Westminster Shorter Catechism makes a similar connection between the sixth commandment and the prohibition of hatred and points to the directive to petition God on behalf of one's enemies in its exposition of prayer.[31] And the Declaration of 1967 surely provides instruction about the practice of love in its discussion of reconciliation: "The church, in its own life, is called to practice the forgiveness of enemies and to commend to the nations as practical politics the search for cooperation and peace."[32] A bit less formal, and for that reason more deeply embedded in the lives of particular congregations, is the treatment of biblical texts like the Sermon on the Mount (with its exhortation to love enemies), James 2:1–9 (suggesting that neighbor love requires impartiality), and above all for Presbyterians, the parable of the Good Samaritan (Luke 10:25–37). To return to Gustafson's maxim: discourse about love in contemporary Presbyterian communities encourages the consideration that since God loves each and all, relating to all things in a manner appropriate to their relations to God involves universal love, impartial treatment, and beneficent action.

That said, a number of things are missing from this account. For example, what is one to do with the depiction of love in 1 John, where it seems clear that the author's concern is with love for the members of one's community, in connection with the threat posed by "the world" and by those who "went out from us, but they did not belong to us; for if they had belonged to us, they would have remained with us" (2:19)?[33] Such threats make it appropriate to exhort believers, "Do not love the world nor the things of the world." Here, love is loyalty to the believers, and those outside the circle of truth are a source of worry. Or with respect to hate, what is there to say about Psalm 97:10 and other texts that declare, "The Lord loves those who hate evil"? If one moves, as many do, to the notion that "evil" here connotes "evil acts," so that one distinguishes between "the sin and the sinner," there is nevertheless the affirmation of Psalm 139:21–22:

> Do I not hate those who hate you, O Lord?
> And do I not loathe those who rise up against you?
> I hate them with perfect hatred;
> I count them as my enemies.

And indeed, hatred may be ascribed to God, as in Proverbs 6:16–19, a text that intensifies the difficulty of separating evil acts from evildoers:

> There are six things that the Lord hates,
> Seven that are an abomination to him;
> Haughty eyes, a lying tongue, and hands that shed innocent blood,
> A heart that devises wicked plans, feet that hurry to run to evil,
> A lying witness who testifies falsely, and one who sows discord in a family.

Perhaps most significant in a Presbyterian frame is Romans 9:11–13, a classic locus for discussions of the doctrine of election. Commenting on the Genesis 25 story of the birth of

Jacob and Esau and, in particular, on God's declaration that "the elder shall serve the younger," Paul cites Malachi 1:2–3: "As it is written, 'I have loved Jacob, but I have hated Esau.'" Here the point is to illustrate the "hardening" characteristic of a portion of the people of Israel and the correlative opening of membership in the community of the elect to Gentiles. In Malachi, the point is a more nationalistic one by which the defeat and desolation of the descendants of Esau at the hands of Israel is explained.

Now, one way to take these observations would be to say that in any religious-moral tradition, one will find multiple trajectories of discourse in which basic sources are read in ways that involve selection. In the Sufi discourse mentioned at the outset of this essay, texts that emphasize differential loves and assign a positive value to hate are downplayed or ignored. In the discourse of differentiated loves that took shape in the Abbasid period, texts the Sufis emphasized were similarly glossed as marginal or were reinterpreted in ways that correlated with notions of the Muslim duty to superintend Jews, Christians, and others, protecting these groups and all of humanity from the results of religious-moral error. Likewise, the texts of Christian tradition exhibit a certain plasticity, and it is not strange that groups of Presbyterians in the twentieth and twenty-first centuries emphasize some to the exclusion of others.

But this descriptive point seems to ignore the concern raised by Bassam Tibi with respect to the attempt of some contemporary Muslims who read the Qur'an and reports of the exemplary practice of the Prophet in ways that justify a set of relations between Muslims and non-Muslims reminiscent of the social-political institutions of the Abbasid caliphate, albeit in a world that is radically changed. Place the old judgments in the setting of a modern state, Tibi argues, and you have already departed from them. The notion of neighbor love as requiring differential treatment based on religious affiliation was crafted by people who thought it the best "fit" with the social and political needs of their day. One honors their effort by doing something similar in a new setting. For Tibi, that involves a recovery of Islamic humanism in recognition of the fact that globalization makes a certain pluralism inevitable. Equal respect, or equal regard for one's neighbors—regardless of religious affiliation—becomes important in a way it was not in a condition of empire.

Similarly, I judge that Presbyterian congregations—at least, the ones I know well—developed the interpretive strategies described previously in connection with their particular situation in the United States of America. In that context, it was important to find a way to read texts that stressed universal and impartial love. As well, it was important to marginalize the discourse of hate, not least by pointing to a number of examples that might suggest a gloss on the warning of James 1:20: "the anger [and also, the hatred] of human beings does not accomplish the righteousness of God." It seems to me that this remains a good strategy for all, with respect to the practice of neighbor love.

Notes

1. Paul Heck, "Mysticism as Morality," *Journal of Religious Ethics* 34, no. 2 (June 2006): 253–86.

2. Al-Haj Maulana Fazlul Karim, trans., *Al-Hadis: An English Translation of Mishkat al-Masabih*, 3rd ed. (New Delhi: Islamic Book Service, 2001), bk. 1, p. 254, report 43w. N.b.: *Mishkat al-Masabih* is a compendium of reports of the exemplary practice of Muhammad, in which various texts from the six collections counted as canonical by Sunni Muslims are conveniently listed. In this case, the translator has included the Arabic text. While I have consulted his translation, I have altered it to fit my sense of the Arabic. Usually, this involves a more literal rendering than the one provided by the translator.

3. Wehr's dictionary indicates the possible meanings as "to be adjacent" or in another form "to share a border." P. 173, re: *j-w-r. Arabic-English Dictionary: The Hans Wehr Dictionary of Modern Written Arabic*, 4th ed., ed. J. M. Cowan (Urbana, IL: Spoken Language Services, 1993).

4. Karim, *Al-Hadis*.

5. Ibid., bk. 1, p. 255, report 46w.

6. Ibid., p. 97, report 13.

7. Ibid., p. 502, report 265.

8. Ibid., pp. 505–6, report 273.

9. Here I am using the translation by M. A. S. Abdel Haleem. See *The Qur'an* (Oxford: Oxford University Press, 2004).

10. Ibid.

11. Karim, *Al-Hadis*, bk. 1, p. 298, report 74.

12. See John Wansbrough, *Qur'anic Studies: Sources and Methods of Scriptural Interpretation* (Oxford: Oxford University Press, 1977); John Wansbrough, *The Sectarian Milieu: Content and Composition of Islamic Salvation History* (Oxford: Oxford University Press, 1978).

13. On the dating of *al-Muwatta*, see Norman J. Calder, *Studies in Early Muslim Jurisprudence* (Oxford: Oxford University Press, 1993).

14. For a convenient translation of portions of Tabari's work, see Yasir S. Ibrahim, *Al-Tabari's Book of Jihad: A Translation from the Original Arabic, with an Introduction, Commentary, and Notes* (Lewiston, NY: Mellen, 2007).

15. For more detail on the following summary, see John Kelsay, *Arguing the Just War in Islam* (Cambridge, MA: Harvard University Press, 2007), and literature cited there.

16. For what follows, see Majid Khadduri, trans., *The Islamic Law of Nations: Shaybani's Siyar* (Baltimore: Johns Hopkins University Press, 1966), 195–253.

17. Ibid., 218, sec. 1257.

18. It is worth noting that a standard dictionary such as Wehr's (op. cit., p. 83) indicates that the root meaning of b-gh-y suggests transgression. In the juridical context, the term is functionally tied to a law of rebellion.

19. Khadduri, *Islamic Law of Nations*, 235, secs. 1401–4.

20. See the discussion in S. A. A. Rizvi, *Shah 'Abd al-'Aziz: Puritanism, Sectarian Politics, and Jihad* (Canberra: Ma'rifat, 1982).

21. For the entire set of remarks, see Muhammad 'Ali Jinnah, *Speeches and Writings of Mr. Jinnah*, ed. Jamil-ud-Din Ahmad (Lahore: Sh. Muhammad Ashraf, 1964), 2:399–405. I discuss this speech in relation to another set of issues in David Little, John Kelsay, and Abdulaziz Sachedina, *Human Rights and the Conflict of Cultures: Western and Islamic Perspectives on Religious Liberty* (Columbia: University of South Carolina Press, 1988), 43–44.

22. Stanley Wolpert, *Jinnah of Pakistan* (New York: Oxford University Press, 1984), 340.

23. See the discussion in Seyyed Vali Reza Nasr, *Mawdudi and the Making of Islamic Revivalism* (New York: Oxford University Press, 1996).

24. Sayyid Abul A'la Maududi, *First Principles of the Islamic State*, 2nd ed., trans. and ed. Khurshid Ahmad (Lahore: Islamic Publications Limited, 1960), 65.

25. Ibid., 66. More generally, see Nasr, *Mawdudi and the Making*.

26. See Bassam Tibi, "Islamic Humanism vs. Islamism: Cross-Civilizational Building," *Soundings: An Interdisciplinary Journal* 95, no. 3 (2012): 230–54.

27. Ibid., 249–50.

28. Karim, *Al-Hadis*, pp. 505–6, report 273.

29. See James Gustafson, *Ethics from a Theocentric Perspective* (Chicago: University of Chicago Press, 1981), 1:113.

30. *The Constitution of the Presbyterian Church (U.S.A.): Part I, Book of Confessions* (New York: Office of the General Assembly, 1983), 4.105–4.107.

31. Ibid., 7.246 and 7.293.

32. Ibid., 9.45.

33. Here and elsewhere, I am using the translation in the New Revised Standard Version of the Bible.

Afterword

WILLIAM WERPEHOWSKI

Love and Christian Ethics addresses significant authors, texts, and topics dealing with the interlaced meanings of divine love, love for God, neighbor love, and love for oneself. A recurring question is whether and how the Christian moral life amounts to a kind of eudaimonism. The book also offers insights and arguments that develop alternative accounts of the normative content of the command to love the neighbor as oneself. Beyond these concerns, the collection practically reframes an ethic of agape regarding (and this is a partial list) love's motivational effectiveness, sexual life, the moral repair of communities, and interreligious exchange.

Each of these achievements sets productive, overlapping directions for further study. The return to classic figures and discussions prompts us to lean hard against forgetting, burying, or presumptuously moving on from them and others like them for the sake of the next new thing. Eudaimonism's "fit" with Christian ethics, moreover, remains a remarkably contested question to this day. Lively and challenging viewpoints about what neighbor love essentially is challenge us in turn to probe further into relevant theological warrants and appeals. Practical reorientations afford the opportunity to pick up where authors have left us so that we may critically advance their work and, following their example, reimagine agape in still other novel contexts.

In what follows, I take up the achievements and future directions that correspond to them. My comments will be tentative and necessarily brief.

In my judgment, *Love and Christian Ethics* accomplishes and promises more than what I have just summarized and more than what I consider in the following. My selection and analysis undoubtedly reflect concerns and interests of my own, and topics and essays that I do not highlight may well be on balance more pressing than those I do.

Christian Loves and Human Flourishing

In attending to the interconnections between God's love and human love for God, self, and neighbor, a number of authors reconsider not only figures such as Augustine, Thomas Aquinas, Kierkegaard, Kant, and Rahner, but also Anders Nygren's *Agape and Eros*, a founding, flawed, and highly controverted study. To cover Nygren anew is an especially good thing, for it would be a terrible mistake to suppose that this 1930 classic has been not only surpassed but in a sense erased (except for the purpose of straw man critique) by John Burnaby's *Amor Dei* and later criticism. Indeed, Edmund N. Santurri's positive appeals to Nygren and Lisa Cahill's reconsideration of Lutheran ethics in critical response to the latter attest, in different ways, to *Agape and Eros*'s ongoing vitality.[1]

Love and Christian Ethics should persuade students and scholars to turn to other notable works that may not, for whatever reason, be widely read today. Edward Vacek's rich and sweeping piece on "the problematic love of God" might lead readers to Kenneth Kirk's *The*

Vision of God, which addresses the links among worship, ethics, and self-regard in a fashion that remains unique and indispensable.[2] Some may find it surprising that Karl Barth also, with Vacek, rejected the Protestant "Puritanism" that reduces love of God to obedience or service—his rejection is worth a look.[3] Paul Ramsey, following a tradition that included his teacher H. Richard Niebuhr, strongly associates our love of God with faithfulness, as it corresponds to God's loving faithfulness, to God's wayward human creation, and to fidelity to the neighbor's good. This does not dissolve the love of God into something else; rather, it specifies its meaning at its core.[4] As for worries about collapsing our love for God into "obedience," we may think twice after viewing Herbert McCabe's Thomistic claim that the logic of commanding and obeying is that of "*sharing* in another's practical wisdom" and hence of sharing "one mind."[5] This perspective may be surprisingly congenial to Vacek's emphasis on love as "participation." Friendly as well to the idea that loving God is a kind of philia tested and purified in history would be the spiritual writings of Thomas Merton over the course of his life. There we find a combination of resolve and revision and of solitude and solidarity that could enrich our thinking.[6]

Consider another example in the same vein. Terence Irwin draws a useful contrast between "moderate" and "radical" traditions comparing Christian and Greek conceptions of love. The traditions deny and affirm, respectively, a "sharp contrast" between these conceptions. In his *Basic Christian Ethics*, Ramsey at first seems to follow Nygren in defining agape as "disinterested" concern for the neighbor. According to the radical tradition that includes the latter, agape is disinterested in that it is indifferent to value, indifferent to the self's well-being, and strictly nonselective (i.e., universal). Yet Ramsey appears not at all to be about "repudiating" or "replacing" the Greek understanding; rather, he is bent on *transforming, redirecting*, and *relocating* it. His basic conviction is that Christian love above all else places itself "on the side of the neighbor" for her own sake, and not on the side of and for the sake of oneself. With this transformation in place, Ramsey can and does endorse self-love and the love of "superior values" as "secondary but essential" for Christian ethics. As Gene Outka has shown, self-love is "justified derivatively" from neighbor love,[7] and the love of the good is put to use in service of the beloved.[8] Ramsey's chapter on "vocation" in *Basic Christian Ethics* leaves a secondary but essential place for "special relations" too.[9] So if Ramsey is not a "radical," is he then a "moderate"? One may say that as long as one adds that he is a moderate seeking radically to transform Greek versions of ethics to the extent that their eudaimonism gives up on or hedges concerning the placement of disinterested love of neighbor on "the ground floor of Christian ethics."

Jean Porter, John Hare, and Frederick Simmons join Irwin in reflecting on eudaimonism and Christian moral existence. Porter presents a clear and engaging contemporary Thomist defense of the consistency of the view that "the [moral] agent necessarily aims at her own happiness in every act, and that the virtuous will . . . is disposed . . . to aim at something beyond the agent's own good as an individual." Her case is deftly questioned by Hare, who offers a revisionist Kantian rejoinder that in fundamental respects reaches back to Scotus and, before him, Anselm. Following and pondering their disagreements over the ends of human agency and the possibility of genuine conflict between an individual's flourishing and duties to wider communities is at once intense, illuminating, and delightful. Simmons's precise statement of distinguishable interpretations of eudaimonism is a valuable aid. Aquinas holds to the Aristotelian view that the moral life "aims at one's own eudaimonia." Although he is generally not classified as a eudaimonist, Kant nonetheless affirms that the "attainment of eudaimonia corresponds to fulfillment of moral duty." Yet this difference and for that matter the dispute between Porter and Hare ought not lead us to lose sight of *convergence* between

Aquinas and Kant on how personal agency ideally coheres: (1) as Hare writes, "the standard case of action is one that starts from inclination," and (2) "the best kind of human life is one in which inclinations have been trained to fit with moral law."

Simmons thinks about Christian love and moral life in the light of Aristotelian eudaimonism and reaches a penetrating conclusion about *variance* in compatibility; its "adequacy . . . as a framework for Christian morality proves sensitive to the stage of salvation history in which it is assessed." The anguish and suffering that is part and parcel of the disciple's "bearing her cross" may reach to the point of "ceasing to sense God's love" even while she lives with moral integrity. Therefore, "at this stage of salvation history, the Christian moral life may sometimes not . . . be effectively eudaimonist." Christian eschatological faith, however, authorizes the stance that "although the Christian moral life may not be eudaimonist now, in the end it effectively is."

This position can be tested and sharpened by way of concrete theological examples. I mention two. First, Simmons takes up at length Jesus's cry of dereliction from the Cross: "My God, my God, why have you forsaken me?" (Matt. 27:46, Mark 15:34). Karl Barth responds to it, theologically and pastorally, with these words.

> This is comforting. What are our doubts and despairs, disguised or acute, compared with His dereliction, which was also and especially suffered by Him in our place? This means, however, that *in fellowship with Him* we have to reckon seriously with the fact that our cross will take, and may never lose, this character. . . . *Unless we are to evade our sanctification at the decisive point,* we have to bear it, to see it through, in this character. *The only thing is that in so doing we are not forsaken* by the One who raised and answered the question whether he was not forsaken by God. *At this point, then, we find ourselves in the deepest fellowship with Him.* (my italics)[10]

Barth is saying that "the dignity of the cross" borne by disciples includes at its limit forms of doubt and despair that, however horrible and devastating, stand in the shadow of those of the Son of God and just so mark our *sanctification*—shall we say "our *flourishing* in holiness"?— decisively. At this limit, in faith, we find fellowship with Jesus Christ—in which for the sake of our flourishing, shall we say, we have an "interest"?—most deeply. It would be good to see Simmons go to work with this text.

The second example, having to do with eschatology, is a prayer by Therese of Lisieux. We find it in the Catechism of the Roman Catholic Church at the conclusion of a discussion of "merit":

> After earth's exile, I hope to go and enjoy you in the fatherland, but I do not want to lay up merits for heaven. I want to work for your *love alone*. . . . In the evening of this life, I shall appear before you with empty hands, for I do not ask you, Lord, to count my works. All our justice is blemished in your eyes. I wish, then, to be clothed in your *justice* and to receive from your *love* the eternal possession of *yourself*.[11]

Is Therese's "act of offering" eudaimonist? If so, how and why? If not, then what? Simmons's technical categories of "self-transcendence," "self-effacement," and the like could possibly be measured as well as vivified through answers to these questions.[12]

Concluding this section, I observe that the quest for precision *and* its limits is salutary for theological ethics. In the case at hand, Josef Pieper attempts more precisely to identify

Christian "happiness" with "felicity, beatitude, bliss," which should not "be in any way confused with 'eudemonism.'"[13] I simply commend attention to the claim and cannot evaluate it
now. On the other side, and here it appears that Simmons and I agree, it may be that the
history of any individual Christian's moral life will be in itself resistant to eudaimonist interpretations that look past, smooth over, or even deny the reality of severe *discontinuity* in
moral agency. In a splendid review of Jennifer Herdt's splendid study of the historical legacy
of the splendid vices, Gilbert Meilaender questions a

> picture of the Christian life [that] is almost exclusively one of continuity between what we
> have been and are, and what by God's grace we will be. The model is an incarnational one.
> . . . But there is another model, one that emphasizes experienced discontinuity in the Chris-
> tian life, a model of cross and resurrection. If the first model suggests a transformation that
> fulfills and perfects the self, the second model suggests a death to self and fulfillment only
> on the other side of a new creation. . . . The task of Christian ethics is . . . to seek ways to do
> justice to the place of both continuity and discontinuity in the grace-filled life of virtue.
> This is, in the end, a theological necessity.[14]

The flourishing of the fallen human creature in Jesus Christ, the incarnate Son of God, is also
and always dying *to oneself* and living anew in Jesus Christ, crucified and risen.

The Meaning of Neighbor Love

Over the years, Gene Outka has refined, reformulated, and maintained his original statement
of the normative content of agape. Its "most central feature" is "equal regard" or "universal
love," an independent and unalterable regard for the neighbor qua human existent.[15] It is
independent of particularizing differences between human beings and promises permanence
and stability. Agape seeks the good of the neighbor for her own sake and in virtue of God's
equal and unconditional love for her and all.[16] Self-sacrifice, rather than being, as many have
claimed, "the purest and most perfect manifestation of agape,"[17] is better comprehended as
having "only *instrumental* warrant. Self-sacrifice must always be purposive in promoting the
welfare of others and never simply expressive of something resident in the agent. It is simply
one possible exemplification and by-product of devotion to others for their own sakes."[18]
Friendship or "mutuality," an interpersonal bond that manifests philia because it presupposes
a loving response in kind to love extended, stands as agape's "internal ideal fruition."[19] Substantively, philosophically, theologically, and ecumenically, this formulation is enormously
compelling.

One can readily read Dr. Martin Luther King Jr.'s early writings on Christian love along
similar lines. Following Nygren, King distinguishes agape from eros and philia by highlighting defining features of "equal regard." For example, "And when you come to love on this level
you begin to love men not because they are likable, not because they do things that attract us,
but because God loves them and here we love the person who does the evil deed while hating
the deed that the person does."[20] Self-sacrifice in the form of costly nonviolent resistance to
racist injustice is a means to serve the unjust neighbor's good; her heart or conscience may be
stirred through shame and self-criticism so that she sees her error and comes to respect the
adversary she opposed and subordinated.[21] One could even say that nonviolent struggle for
King sounds a note of equal regard for self and other, since he points out that it "first does
something to the hearts and souls of those committed to it. It gives them self-respect; it calls

up resources of strength and courage that they did not know they had."[22] The "ideal internal fruition" of nonviolent agape is "to win the friendship of all the persons who had perpetrated this [unjust] system in the past" and to forge what King called "the beloved community."[23]

But King also depicts agape as "redemptive good will for all" and notably allies it at times with the faith that "unmerited suffering is redemptive."[24] Does the depiction and alliance intimate a more integral connection between neighbor love and self-sacrifice than what Outka proposes? In addition, and as Albert Raboteau argues in a classic study, at the root of King's entire social vision is a sturdy belief in "the interrelatedness of human beings—the hidden wholeness that binds us all together."[25] Raboteau cites King's oft-repeated "eloquent formula": "All life is interrelated. All men are caught in an inescapable network of mutuality, tied in a single garment of destiny."[26] Does this belief hint at a perspective on agape in which a kind of "friendship" is *always already* in play?

Independently of King but attuned to a host of resonant resources, Edmund N. Santurri and Stephen J. Pope pick up these intimations, respectively. Their contributions are astute, thorough, and creative. Santurri defends the "contentious proposal" that constitutive of agape is a theological virtue that incorporates "precisely an agent's disposition to sacrifice the interests of the self for the good of the neighbor," "however else that love must be described." He explicitly rejects the "instrumental warrant" proposal and argues instead that self-sacrifice is "*internal* to the concept of agape." Pope draws from "the tradition flowing from Thomas Aquinas" to show that agape is not a "type" of love separate from and superior to other "types" like eros and friendship.[27] Grounded in the "eternal procession of the Holy Spirit from the radically self-giving and mutual love of the Father and the Son," Christian neighbor love is always a kind of friendship love that "exists when one treats any neighbor (including an offensive one) as a friend 'in God,' and this can take place whether or not there is mutuality or shared religious belief." The two authors, it is important to add, acknowledge an indispensable role for other regard. For Santurri, what is internal to agape strictly speaking is "*self-sacrifice for the neighbor's sake*," that is, "*for the genuine good of the neighbor*" (italics original). For Pope, the grace of "friendship with God makes possible the generous, nonreciprocal love of neighbor."

I have one question for Santurri. Thinking in part and for the moment with Pope, I wonder whether Santurri's internalist view can be improved if the notion of self-giving moves to the forefront. Many if not all of Santurri's "Johannine trajectories" fall right in line with Herbert McCabe's (and, I assume from his essay, Pope's) understanding of the implications of the Nicene doctrine that the only Son of God, true God from true God, is begotten, not made, and consubstantial with the Father. The very being of the Son is eternally constituted by the self-giving love of the Father, and that love is fully communicated in return. With the incarnate Son, "it is into this eternal exchange of love between Jesus and the Father that we are taken up, this exchange of love that we call the Holy Spirit."[28] As McCabe has it, the Son's "equality with God" in this connection *means* to be "loved into existence" by the Father, "to be an equal to whom the Father can give himself in love."[29] Jesus Christ's incarnate suffering and dying for us and for our salvation is but the expression of this love in sinful human history. Giving to self-giving, into which we are "taken up," a metaphysical and ethical priority modifies Santurri's internalist account some, but it would be a modification that seems to me more coherently to depict, align, and bring into closer proximity with self-sacrifice other authentic expressions of agape that are also *but not in that sense* "self-emptying." The relevant virtue of love becomes one that in any case disposes one to *devote oneself, offer oneself, avail oneself, generously make a gift of one's "own" attention, talents, resources, time, interests, and more,* to the neighbor. The beloved may abide in these kinds of love as she may within what we deem the more strictly "self-sacrificial" kind, and the lover may abide as well in just such a merciful and empowering love as it is given by God in Jesus Christ. Note also that my suggestion provides Santurri with what looks like a more effective answer to the criticism ("Criticism 2" in his essay) that love in the community of heaven cannot be defined essentially as self-sacrifice. He claims that there is self-sacrificial love in the Kingdom of God even if there are no self-sacrificial actions, but I'm not convinced by his answer. I do think he can save his point by repairing, directly and distinctively, to the idea of "*eternal self-giving*" (italics original).

I have one question for Pope. Against Nygren and other so-called hyper-Augustinians who identify "friendship as the antithesis of the self-sacrificial love expressed on the cross," Pope writes that "we must note the essential but sometimes misunderstood point that charitable friendship involves a *transformation* of the agent from one who is, in one way or another, marked by a fundamental egoistic self-centeredness to one who is at least on the way to being more capable of self-giving love" (italics original). The word "transformation" has appeared at pivotal points in this essay before. It is a term patient of a range, though not an unlimited range, of meanings. For the sake of argument, I will invoke Pieper's definition since it pertains closely to the specific point that Pope wishes to make—the relation between eros and charity—and applies exactly to the broader theological theme that underwrites his essay—the relation between nature and grace.

> The classical statement of the relationship of grace and nature speaks not only of presupposition and intactness but also of the perfecting of what man by nature is and has. . . . "Perfection" in *caritas* . . . may very well mean that eros, in order to keep its original impulse and remain really love, above all in order to attain the "foreverness" that it naturally desires, must transform itself altogether, and that this transformation perhaps resembles passing through something akin to dying. . . . *Caritas*, in renewing and rejuvenating us, also brings us death in a certain sense.[30]

One could say, as a matter of "theological necessity," that the continuity of nature and grace goes hand in hand, somehow, with the discontinuity of death and resurrection to new life. Thus, thinking in part and for the moment with Santurri, I ask Pope whether, on this side of the cross, his stress on friendship love rooted in God's self-giving should be critically and dialectically tempered by building internally into Christian neighbor love a disposition to self-sacrifice. Doing so may not only take seriously the costliness of agape in a death-dealing world; it may also count honestly how it is that new life in Christ regularly presupposes death to the loving self's still-stubborn incurved desiring.[31]

Love and Society

Part 3 of this volume tackles a number of moral and religious subjects by practically reframing an agape ethic. Here in short order are four illustrations.

Lisa Cahill brings Christian love to the issue of global health care not only by insisting that "love must be structured by justice, and justice and love require taking the standpoint of the poor"; she also directs us to love's motivational effectiveness and to the revisions to Augustinian ethics that such effectiveness demands. As she writes, "Christians still need to develop the *theological* reasons why they can trust that their efforts will actually bring results and why they can count on non-Christians to share common goals." As I read Cahill, Christian love must be reframed through new attention to its unity in difference with the theological virtue of hope and hope's object, the universal promise of God's royal victory over sin and death for the world and its well-being.

Following a provocative historical survey of Christian sexual ethics, Mark Jordan situates its present inquiries *vocationally*. He calls for a research program that discovers "genres for speech adequate to a loving knowledge of sex while being responsible to Jesus's refusal to participate in violent allegations of sexual sin. Its ways of talking must be provisional because they occur in a pre-eschatological moment before the fullness of human embodiment is revealed." Jordan also gets me imagining parallel vocations to discover and communicate "loving knowledge" of, say, political or business life that calls forth and calls into question fitting and unfitting applications of Christian love to race, policing, warfare, profit making, financial investments, and the like.

Margaret Farley and Emilie Townes contribute to social ethics through their attention to moral repair in response to violence in its many forms. Farley's category of "anticipatory forgiveness" in the midst of manifest human violation and resistance to it locates the disposition to love—to unconditional, forgiving love—within circumstances that lead others solely to displace it in the name of justice. Her ideas suggest a comparison with King. Townes's "meditations" address the moral conditions of *cultural* repair, in particular to the shattered communities of post-Katrina New Orleans. The conditions include (1) nesting agape within koinonia, for "it is in a particular community that the practice of love takes form, receives content, finds direction, achieves fulfillment"; (2) "materializing" love in a "love of body, love of self" that generates critique and opposition to structurally violent devaluations of self and community; (3) engaging the biblical tradition and lived reality of *lament* both in acts that listen and look for the voices of victims silenced by structural violence and in acts of confession for complicity. Prepared thereby to "see, feel, touch, and smell the joy and the agony living in the brokenness of creation," we may be ready "to put love into action thoroughly and systematically through justice making." Where Cahill pursues agape's motivational effectiveness, Townes accounts for its availability for discernment; moreover, in demanding we "stop drawing ideological and methodological lines between social issues and theological issues," the latter generally complements Jordan's recognition that the vocation of Christian ethics is itself a vocation concretely to love.

Eric Gregory's application of Outka's ethic of equal regard to the rudiments and details of interreligious conversation and disagreement strikes me as being stunningly on point. His work cuts through difficulties engendered by John Hick's inclusivist/exclusivist/pluralist typology and launches a distinctive agenda for not only interreligious dialogue but also a viable theology of religions.

One does well in all these instances to urge and to welcome forward movement along the paths our authors have charted and taken.

Notes

Love and Christian Ethics is dedicated to Gene Outka. The reasons for the honor, given his remarkable contribution and influence to his field, are legion. I also have personal reasons to honor him. At Princeton, Gene Outka signed me into my first religion course, a course in ethics taught by Paul Ramsey. I took courses with him in Religion and Morality, Religious Language, and most memorably, Nineteenth-Century Religious Thought. He advised my senior thesis, and he supported my candidacy for doctoral study and agreed to be my mentor at Yale. On more than one occasion, Outka permitted me with many others to be a teaching assistant for his big lecture course on Religious Ethics and Moral Problems. There were graduate courses too, and the doctoral dissertation that he advised after more or less giving me the perfect topic. He worked terribly hard to get us all jobs. Since then, he has been a steadfast friend and senior colleague. Through all these years, Outka inspired me with his moving commitment to and modeling of what Spinoza called the "intellectual love of God." There's more, too much more to mention. Thank you, Gene.

1. See William Werpehowski, "Anders Nygren's *Agape and Eros*," in *The Oxford Handbook of Theological Ethics*, ed. Gilbert Meilaender and William Werpehowski (Oxford: Oxford University Press, 2005), 433–48.

2. Kenneth Kirk, *The Vision of God* (London: Longmans, Green, 1931). Note Frederick V. Simmons's use of Kirk in his essay in this volume.

3. Karl Barth, *Church Dogmatics* (Edinburgh: T&T. Clark, 1958), IV/2:793–99.

4. Paul Ramsey, *Basic Christian Ethics* (Louisville, KY: Westminster John Knox Press, 1993), 2–24.

5. Herbert McCabe, *God Matters* (London: Continuum, 1987), 228–29.

6. For one relatively early example, see Thomas Merton, *No Man Is an Island* (New York: Barnes and Noble Books, 2003).

7. Gene Outka, *Agape: An Ethical Analysis* (New Haven, CT: Yale University Press, 1972), 68–70.

8. Ramsey, *Basic Christian Ethics*, 92–116.

9. Ibid., 153–90.

10. Barth, *Church Dogmatics*, IV/2:612–13.

11. *Catechism of the Roman Catholic Church* (New York: Doubleday, 1995), par. 2011.

12. I thank Fred Simmons and Jeffrey Stout for conversations that helped my thinking about eudaimonism and ethics.

13. Josef Pieper, *Faith, Hope, Love* (San Francisco: Ignatius Press, 1997), 278.

14. Gilbert Meilaender, review of *Putting on Virtue: The Legacy of the Splendid Vices* by Jennifer A. Herdt, *Studies in Christian Ethics* 23 (February 2010): 102.

15. Outka, *Agape*, 285.

16. Ibid., 9–24.

17. Ibid., 278.

18. Ibid., 279.

19. Gene Outka, "Universal Love and Impartiality," in *The Love Commandments*, ed. Edmund N. Santurri and William Werpehowski (Washington, DC: Georgetown University Press, 1992), 89.

20. Martin Luther King Jr., *I Have a Dream* (New York: HarperCollins, 1992), 32.

21. Ibid., 12, 60.

22. Ibid., 60.

23. Ibid., 30.

24. Ibid., 31–32, 69, 134.

25. Albert J. Raboteau, "A Hidden Wholeness: Thomas Merton and Martin Luther King, Jr.," *Spirituality Today* 40, no. 4 (Winter 1988), http://opcentral.org/resources/2015/01/19/albert-j-raboteau-a-hidden-wholeness-thomas-merton-and-martin-luther-king-jr/.

26. Ibid. For but one of many original sources of the "eloquent formula," see Martin Luther King Jr., *A Testament of Hope* (New York: Harper One, 2003), 210.

27. For my rather different, ecumenical try in the same spirit, see William Werpehowski, *Karl Barth and Christian Ethics: Living in Truth* (Burlington, VT: Ashgate, 2014), 151–67.

28. McCabe, *God Matters*, 20.

29. Ibid., 18.

30. Pieper, *Faith, Hope, Love*, 280–81.

31. I reflect on the continuity and discontinuity of Christian moral agency in *Karl Barth and Christian Ethics*, 135–50.

Contributors

Lisa Cahill is the J. Donald Monan Professor in the Theology Department at Boston College, where she has taught since 1976. She has also been a visiting professor at Georgetown and Yale Universities. Her major publications include *Love Your Enemies: Discipleship, Pacifism and Just War Theory* (Fortress, 1994), *Sex, Gender, and Christian Ethics* (Cambridge University Press, 1996), *Family: A Christian Social Perspective* (Fortress, 2000), *Bioethics and the Common Good* (Marquette, 2004), *Theological Bioethics: Participation, Justice, and Change* (Georgetown University Press, 2005), *Genetics, Theology, Ethics: An Interdisciplinary Conversation* (Crossroad, 2005), and *Global Justice, Christology, and Christian Ethics* (Cambridge University Press, 2013). A fellow of the American Academy of Arts and Sciences, Cahill is past president of the Society of Christian Ethics and the Catholic Theological Society of America.

Margaret A. Farley is Gilbert L. Stark Professor Emerita of Christian Ethics at Yale Divinity School. She is the author or coeditor of seven books, including *Personal Commitments: Beginning, Keeping, Changing* (Harper, 1986), *Compassionate Respect* (Paulist, 1996), and *Just Love: A Framework for Christian Sexual Ethics* (Continuum, 2008). Professor Farley is the recipient of eleven honorary degrees and a variety of fellowships and awards, including the 1992 John Courtney Murray Award for Excellence in Theology, the 2008 Grawemeyer Award in Religion, and the 2016 Society of Christian Ethics' Lifetime Achievement Award. She was a founding member of Yale–New Haven Hospital's Bioethics Committee, and she served for eight years as codirector of the Yale University Interdisciplinary Bioethics Center. She is currently codirector of the All-Africa Conference: Sister to Sister, which facilitates responses by women religious to HIV/AIDS in sub-Saharan Africa. She is past president of both the Society of Christian Ethics and the Catholic Theological Society of America.

M. Jamie Ferreira is Carolyn B. Barbour Professor Emerita of Religious Studies at the University of Virginia. Her major publications include *Doubt and Religious Commitment: The Role of the Will in Newman's Thought* (Oxford University Press, 1980), *Scepticism and Reasonable Doubt: The British Naturalist Tradition in Wilkins, Hume, Reid, and Newman* (Oxford University Press, 1986), *Transforming Vision: Imagination and Will in Kierkegaardian Faith* (Oxford University Press, 1991), *Love's Grateful Striving: A Commentary on Kierkegaard's Works of Love* (Oxford University Press, 2001), and *Kierkegaard* (Wiley-Blackwell, 2009).

Ronald M. Green is Eunice and Julian Cohen Professor Emeritus for the Study of Ethics and Human Values and Professor of Religion, Emeritus, at Dartmouth College, where he has been a member of Dartmouth's Department of Religion since 1969. Professor Green was the founding director of the Office of Genome Ethics at the National Human Genome Research

Institute of the National Institutes of Health and also served as director of Dartmouth's Institute for the Study of Applied and Professional Ethics. His most recent books are *Babies by Design: The Ethics of Genetic Choice* (Yale University Press, 2007) and *Kant and Kierkegaard on Time and Eternity* (Mercer University Press, 2011). He has been a Guggenheim Foundation Fellow, secretary of the American Academy of Religion, and president of the Society of Christian Ethics.

Eric Gregory is professor of religion at Princeton University. The author of *Politics and the Order of Love: An Augustinian Ethic of Democratic Citizenship* (Chicago University Press, 2008), Gregory has received fellowships from the Erasmus Institute, the Safra Foundation Center for Ethics, the National Endowment for the Humanities, and the Tikvah Center for Law and Jewish Civilization.

John Hare is Noah Porter Professor of Philosophical Theology at Yale Divinity School. His best-known book, *The Moral Gap* (Oxford University Press, 1996), develops an account of the need for God's assistance in meeting the moral demand of which God is the source. Hare is also the author of *God's Call* (Eerdmans, 2001), *Why Bother Being Good?* (InterVarsity Press, 2002), *God and Morality: A Philosophical History* (Blackwell, 2007), and *God's Command* (Oxford, 2015). He has written a commentary on Plato's *Euthyhphro* in the Bryn Mawr series and *Ethics and International Affairs*, with Carey B. Joynt. He has given both Gifford and Wilde lectures.

Terence Irwin is professor of ancient philosophy, Keble College, University of Oxford, and previously served on the faculties of Cornell and Harvard Universities. He is the author of a three-volume survey of the history of ethics, *The Development of Ethics: A Historical and Critical Study* (Oxford University Press, 2007–09), and has also published books on Plato's *Ethics* (Oxford University Press, 1995) and Aristotle's *Nicomachean Ethics* (2nd edition, Hackett, 1999). He is a fellow of the British Academy.

Timothy P. Jackson is professor of Christian ethics at Emory University. He previously held teaching positions at Rhodes College, Yale University, Stanford University, and the University of Notre Dame, and he has been a fellow at the Center of Theological Inquiry, the Whitney Humanities Center at Yale University, the Center for the Study of Religion at Princeton University, and the Program for Evolutionary Dynamics at Harvard University. His major publications include *Love Disconsoled: Meditations on Christian Charity* (Cambridge University Press, 1999), *The Priority of Love: Christian Charity and Social Justice* (Princeton University Press, 2003), and *Political Agape: Christian Love and Liberal Democracy* (Eerdmans, 2015).

Mark D. Jordan is Andrew W. Mellon Professor of Christian Thought in the Divinity School and professor of studies of women, gender, and sexuality in the Faculty of Arts and Sciences at Harvard University. He taught previously at the University of Notre Dame, Emory University, and Washington University and has held Guggenheim, Fulbright-Hays, and Luce fellowships. His books include *The Invention of Sodomy in Christian Theology* (University of Chicago Press, 1997), winner of the 1999 John Boswell Prize for lesbian and gay history; *The Ethics of Sex* (Wiley-Blackwell, 2002); *Telling Truths in Church: Scandal, Flesh, and Christian Speech* (Beacon, 2004); *Rewritten Theology: Aquinas after His Readers* (Wiley-Blackwell, 2005); *Blessing Same-Sex Unions: The Perils of Queer Romance and the Confusions of Christian Mar-*

riage (University of Chicago Press, 2005); *Recruiting Young Love: How Christians Talk about Homosexuality* (Chicago, 2011); and *Convulsing Bodies: Religion and Resistance in Foucault* (Stanford University Press, 2015).

M. Cathleen Kaveny is the Darald and Juliet Libby Professor at Boston College, a position that includes appointments in the Theology Department and the Law School. After she had clerked for the Honorable John T. Noonan Jr. on the US Court of Appeals for the Ninth Circuit, she spent three years practicing health-care law in Boston before she entered academia. She has published widely at the intersection of law, religion, and ethics, most recently *Law's Virtues: Fostering Autonomy and Solidarity in American Society* (Georgetown University Press, 2012), *A Culture of Engagement: Law, Religion, and Morality* (Georgetown University Press, 2016), and *Prophecy without Contempt: Religious Discourse in the Public Square* (Harvard University Press, 2016). She is a past president of the Society of Christian Ethics.

John Kelsay is associate dean in the College of Arts and Sciences, Distinguished Research Professor, Richard L. Rubenstein Professor of Religion, and Bristol Distinguished Professor of Ethics at Florida State University. He serves as editor of *Soundings: An Interdisciplinary Journal*, director of FSU's Center for Humanities and Society, and was coeditor of the *Journal of Religious Ethics*. He has received fellowships from the Princeton University Center for Human Values, the John Simon Guggenheim Foundation, and the Institute for International Integration Studies at Trinity University in Dublin, Ireland. His major books include *Human Rights and the Conflict of Cultures* (coauthored; University of South Carolina Press, 1988), *Just War and Jihad* (coedited; Greenwood Press, 1991), *Islam and War: A Study in Comparative Ethics* (Westminster John Knox, 1993), and *Arguing the Just War in Islam* (Harvard University Press, 2007).

Oliver O'Donovan was professor of Christian ethics and practical theology at the University of Edinburgh from 2006 to 2013, before which he was Regius Professor of Moral and Pastoral Theology and Canon of Christ Church at the University of Oxford from 1982. He is a past president of the Society for the Study of Christian Ethics and is a fellow of the British Academy and the Royal Society of Edinburgh. He was also a member of the Second Anglican-Roman Catholic International Commission. His publications include *The Problem of Self-Love in Saint Augustine* (Yale University Press, 1980, 2006), *Begotten or Made?* (Oxford University Press, 1984), *Principles in the Public Realm: The Dilemma of Christian Moral Witness* (Clarendon, 1984), *Resurrection and Moral Order: An Outline for an Evangelical Ethics* (Eerdmans, 1986), *On the Thirty-Nine Articles: A Conversation with Tudor Christianity* (Paternoster, 1986, 1993, SCM, 2011), *Peace and Certainty: A Theological Essay on Deterrence* (Eerdmans, 1989), *The Desire of the Nations: Rediscovering the Roots of Political Theology* (Cambridge University Press, 1996), *From Irenaeus to Grotius: A Sourcebook in Christian Political Thought, 100-1625* (with Joan Lockwood O'Donovan, Eerdmans, 1999), *Common Objects of Love: Moral Reflection and the Shaping of Community* (Eerdmans, 2002), *The Just War Revisited* (Cambridge University Press, 2003), *Bonds of Imperfection: Christian Politics, Past and Present* (with Joan Lockwood O'Donovan, Eerdmans, 2004), *The Ways of Judgment* (Eerdmans, 2005), *A Conversation Waiting to Begin* (SCM, 2009), *The Word in Small Boats: Sermons from Oxford* (Eerdmans, 2010), *Self, World, and Time: An Introduction* (Eerdmans, 2013), and *Finding and Seeking* (Eerdmans, 2014).

Thomas W. Ogletree is the Frederick Marquand Professor Emeritus of Ethics and Religious Studies at Yale Divinity School and the Yale University Department of Religious Studies. He has also served as dean of Yale Divinity School and the Theological School at Drew University. He is the author of *Christian Faith and History: A Critical Comparison of Ernst Troeltsh and Karl Barth* (1965), *The Death of God Controversy* (1966), *The Use of the Bible in Christian Ethics: A Constructive Essay* (1983), *Hospitality to the Stranger: Dimensions of Moral Understanding* (1985), and *The World Calling: The Church's Witness in Politics and Society* (2004), all of which are available from Westminster John Knox Press. He was a president of the Society of Christian Ethics, an editor of *Soundings*, the founding editor of the *Annual of the Society of Christian Ethics*, and an officer on the editorial board of the *Journal of Religious Ethics*.

Stephen J. Pope is professor of theology at Boston College. Among many publications, he has written *The Evolution of Altruism and the Ordering of Love* (Georgetown University Press, 1994), *Human Evolution and Christian Ethics* (Cambridge University Press, 2007), and *A Step Along the Way: Models of Christian Service* (Orbis, 2015); he has also edited *The Ethics of Aquinas* (Georgetown University Press, 2001), *Common Calling: The Laity and the Governance of the Church* (Georgetown University Press, 2004), and *Solidarity and Hope: Jon Sobrino's Challenge to Christian Theology* (Orbis, 2008).

Jean Porter is John A. O'Brien Professor of Theology at the University of Notre Dame. Her books include *The Recovery of Virtue: The Relevance of Aquinas for Christian Ethics* (Westminster John Knox, 1990), *Moral Action and Christian Ethics* (Cambridge University Press, 1995), *Natural and Divine Law: Reclaiming the Tradition for Christian Ethics* (Eerdmans, 1999), *Nature as Reason: A Thomistic Theory of the Natural Law* (Eerdmans, 2005), and *Ministers of the Law: A Natural Law Theory of Legal Authority* (Eerdmans, 2010). She has served on the editorial boards of the *Journal of Religious Ethics*, the *Annual of the Society of Christian Ethics*, *Theological Studies*, *Studies in Christian Ethics*, *Theology Today*, and the *Journal of the American Academy of Religion*, and she is a past president of the Society of Christian Ethics.

John P. Reeder Jr. is Professor Emeritus of Religious Studies at Brown University. He was also the Henry Luce Professor of Comparative Ethics at Amherst College in 1984–85 and has been a visiting professor at Yale University, Princeton University, and Harvard Divinity School. His major publications include *Source, Sanction, and Salvation: Religion and Morality in Judaic and Christian Traditions* (Prentice Hall, 1988) and *Killing and Saving: Abortion, Hunger, and War* (Pennsylvania State University Press, 1996). With Gene Outka, he has coedited *Religion and Morality* (Doubleday, 1973) and *Prospects for a Common Morality* (Princeton University Press, 1993).

Holmes Rolston III is University Distinguished Professor and Professor of Philosophy Emeritus at Colorado State University. He has written nine books, most recently, *A New Environmental Ethics: The Next Millennium for Life on Earth* (Routledge, 2012), *Three Big Bangs: Matter-Energy, Life, Mind* (Columbia University Press, 2010), *Genes, Genesis and God: Values and Their Origins in Natural and Human History* (Cambridge University Press, 1999), *Conserving Natural Value* (Columbia University Press, 1994), *Philosophy Gone Wild: Environmental Ethics* (Prometheus, 1989), *Environmental Ethics: Duties to and Values in the Nat-*

ural World (Temple University Press, 1989), and *Science and Religion: A Critical Survey* (new edition, Templeton, 2006). Rolston is past and founding president of the International Society for Environmental Ethics, a founding editor of the journal *Environmental Ethics*, and a founding member of the International Society for Science and Religion. He has been a Gifford Lecturer, won the Templeton Prize in Religion, and received the Mendel Medal.

Edmund N. Santurri is professor of religion and philosophy and past director of both the Ethical Issues and Normative Perspectives and the Great Conversation programs at St. Olaf College. He is the author of *Perplexity in the Moral Life: Philosophical and Theological Considerations* (University of Virginia Press, 1987) and coeditor of *The Love Commandments: Essays in Christian Ethics and Moral Philosophy* (with William Werpehowski, Georgetown University Press, 1992).

Frederick V. Simmons is the Houston Witherspoon Fellow in Theology and the Natural Sciences at the Center of Theological Inquiry. Previously an assistant professor of ethics at Yale Divinity School, he has also taught at Amherst College, La Pontifícia Universidad Católica del Ecuador, and La Universidad Politécnica Salesiana.

Emilie M. Townes is dean of Vanderbilt Divinity School and E. Rhodes and Leona B. Carpenter Professor of Womanist Ethics and Society, formerly having served as the Andrew W. Mellon Professor of African American Religion and Theology at Yale Divinity School and as the Carolyn Williams Beaird Professor of Christian Ethics at Union Theological Seminary. She was the first African American woman elected to the presidential line of the American Academy of Religion and became president of the academy in 2008. She has authored *Womanist Justice, Womanist Hope* (Scholars Press, 1993), *In a Blaze of Glory: Womanist Spirituality as Social Witness* (Abingdon, 1995), *Breaking the Fine Rain of Death: African American Health Issues and a Womanist Ethic of Care* (Continuum, 1998), and *Womanist Ethics and the Cultural Production of Evil* (Palgrave Macmillan, 2006). She has edited two collections of essays: *A Troubling in My Soul: Womanist Perspectives on Evil and Suffering* (Orbis, 1993) and *Embracing the Spirit: Womanist Perspectives on Hope, Salvation, and Transformation* (Orbis, 1997). She is also coeditor with Stephanie Y. Mitchem of *Faith, Health, and Healing in African American Life* (Praeger, 2008) and a coeditor with Katie Geneva Cannon and Angela Sims of *Womanist Theological Ethics: A Reader* (Westminster John Knox, 2011). Townes is a fellow of the American Academy of Arts and Sciences.

Edward Collins Vacek holds the Stephen Duffy Chair in Systematic Theology at Loyola University and is a member of the Society of Jesus. He has also taught at Weston Jesuit School of Theology and Boston College. Vacek is the author of *Love, Human and Divine: The Heart of Christian Ethics* (Georgetown University Press, 1996).

William Werpehowski is the Robert L. McDevitt, KSG, KCHS and Catherine H. McDevitt, LCHS Professor in Catholic Theology at Georgetown University. Before his appointment at Georgetown, Werpehowski taught at Villanova University for several decades and directed its Center for Peace and Justice Education. He is the author of *American Protestant Ethics and the Legacy of H. Richard Niebuhr* (Georgetown University Press, 2002) and *Karl Barth and Christian Ethics: Living in Truth* (Routledge, 2014) and the coeditor of *The Love*

Commandments: Christian Ethics and Moral Philosophy (with Edmund Santurri, Georgetown University Press, 1992), *The Essential Paul Ramsey* (with Stephen Crocco, Yale University Press, 1994), and *The Oxford Handbook of Theological Ethics* (with Gilbert Meilaender, Oxford University Press, 2005). He is a past president of the Society of Christian Ethics.

Index

Basic Christian Ethics (Ramsey), 14n8, 376
beatitudes, 24
beggars, response to, 28, 29. *See also* poverty
Beloved (Morrison), 304–5
beloved, valuable property present in, 37, 39–40
beneficence: agape and, 277; animals and, 10, 315; charity and, 219; duty to love and, 96, 101; enemies and, 180; gratitude and, 106n16; in Kant, 96–99, 100, 101, 103–4, 105; love command and, 95; mercy and, 220; neighbor love and, 93–94
Bible: Christian tradition, role in, 3–4; forgiveness in, 155–56; lament in, 305; land in, 315, 316; neighbor in, 349; reading of, love of God and, 120; sexuality and, 291; wildness in, 318–19
biblical love commandments, 4, 19. *See also* love commands
Biggar, Nigel, 198
Bill and Melinda Gates Foundation, 282, 284
biodiversity, 10
biology, naturalism and, 8
birds, 226–27, 245
"blank check" problem, 134
blessedness, 7, 24, 200–202
boasting, exclusion of, 45
Boehm, Christopher, 238–39
Bossuet, Jacques-Bénigne, 37
Boulding, Maria, 53
Brady, Bernard, 111, 125n9, 129n112
Bright, Pamela, 52
Brink, David, 205n25
Broadie, Sarah, 207nn43–44, 208n48
Brueggeman, Walter, 305, 316
Brümmer, Vincent, 119
Brunner, Emil, 1
Buddhism, 151n97
Burnaby, John, 1, 3, 54, 375
Burridge, Richard A., 186n14
business, vocational treatment of, 12, 381
Butler, Joseph, 142n2, 204n6

Cahill, Lisa, 9, 12, 31, 35n20, 375, 380–81
Cain, 38
Calvin, John, 86, 192, 325
capitalism, 283
caring, 321–23
caritas, 1, 113, 190, 213, 334, 380. *See also* charity
caritas-synthesis, 215, 224n31
Cartesian dualism, 228
Cassian, John, 218
Cates, Diana, 6, 132–33, 138, 144n19, 150n86
Catholicism and Catholic theology: Catechism, 12, 377; justice in, 274; moral, 1, 2; possibilities associated with, 9; reason emphasized in, 3
centrality of love: belief in, 1, 13; need for questioned, 3, 15n24
Chadwick, Henry, 53

charity: in Aquinas, 213–15; defined, 13, 15n29; effects of, 219–20; as friendship, 213–15, 217–18; guilt and, 219; heretics and, 219; justice and, 220; love, other, relation with, 8; order of, 47, 48; paternalism and, 220
cheek, striking/turning other, 28, 29
children of God, 138–39
choice: desire and, 64–69; in Kant, 65–66; will and, 71
Christian love: Aristotle and, 36, 206n31, 206n33; development of, 4; as egalitarian, 181–82; egoism and, 40–41, 46–47; ethics and, 1–3, 8–10, 13, 51, 55, 112, 194–99, 210–15, 219–22, 275–76, 297, 299, 328, 334, 341, 357, 376; eudaimonism and, 12, 46–47, 195–203, 377; forgiveness and, 160–64; good and, 47, 49n15, 50n25; health care and, 275–76; identity and, 13; mutual love and, 184–85; and selectivity, 47, 48; self-sacrifice and, 72; self-transcendence and, 195, 200–201; voluntarism and, 39–40, 44–45. *See also* agape
Christian tradition: criticism of, 1; Greek philosophy influence on, 4; love prominence in, 2; moderate *vs.* radical, 37–38; overview of, 3–5
Chrysostom, John, 218
church community, forgiveness in, 167–68
City of God: earthly city, contrast with, 41; as theme, 52
City of God (Augustine), 49n18, 51, 55, 203n1, 206n35, 274, 280–81, 337
civic friendship, 220–22
Cohen, Hermann, 348, 350
commands. *See* love commands
communication, self-, 121
communion, 8, 122, 123, 127n69, 129, 184, 213, 217, 228, 277, 339
communitarian love, 324–25
community: church, forgiveness in, 167–68; ethics and, 303–4; in Islam, 363–64; nature and, 324–25
compassion: "blank check" problem and, 134; in Cates, 6, 132–33, 138, 144n19; "children of God" concept and, 138–39; cost of, 134–35; empathy *vs.*, 6, 138; friendship and, 132–33, 151n103; justice and, 134; in Kierkegaard, 6, 135–36, 138, 148n73; in nature, 314–15; neighbor love and, 135–36, 141–42; normative identifications and, 137–38; origin of, 6; Other and, 132–33, 133–35; parental love and, 139–40, 152nn116–17, 152n108; reason and, 133–34; responsibility and, 133–34; in Schopenhauer, 131, 138; self-love and, 6, 132–33; self-sacrifice and, 135–36, 148n74, 149n78; suffering and, 131, 137–38; in Wyschogrod, 6, 134–35, 138
concern (defined), 36
concupiscent love, 211–12
Cone, James H., 312n13
confession, 10, 307

eros: agape contrasted with, 1, 2, 37; love, other, relation with, 8; love for God as, 6, 122–23; sexual ethics and, 295–96, 297; term usage, 37
eschatology, 184, 191, 198, 202–3, 292, 294, 344n26, 377, 381
eschaton, 10, 135, 340
eternal life, well-being, seeking through, 4, 46
ethical significance of love: assessments of, 4; theories concerning, 6–8
ethics: Christian love and, 275–76; community and, 303–4; defined, 55; environmental, 326–27; eudaimonism and, 193, 206n27; evolution and, 242–45; friendship and, 210, 216; good and, 2; health care and, 275–76; inclusivity in, 313; justice and, 277; in Kant *vs.* Aquinas, 5; koinonia in, 310–11; law and, 254–55; love and, 12, 13; love-justice relationship in, 8–9; love neglected in, 1, 2, 3; pluralism and, 333–34; Protestantism and, 274–75, 276–79; theological, and common law, 8–9. *See also* morality; sexual ethics
Eucharist, 115, 119; Eucharistic way of life, 281
eudaimonia: in Aristotle, 203n1, 207n44; in Augustine, 191–92; Christ and, 201–2; and Christian love, 12; Christian love and, 195–203; crucifixion and, 201–2; eudaimonism and, 192–95; friendship and, 39; in Kant, 205n23; morality and, 190–91, 202–3, 208n51; self-transcendence and, 196–97; theoretical aspects of, 7; translation of, 190
eudaimonism: in Aristotle, 193; Christian love and, 12, 46–47, 195–203, 377; defined, 190; ethics and, 193, 206n27; eudaimonia and, 192–95; flourishing and, 194–95; friendship and, 215–19; in Greek theory, 41, 42, 46; in Luther, 192; morality and, 7, 190–91, 193–94, 205n21, 208n51, 375; neighbor love and, 190–91, 376; psychological, 204n3; in Scotus, 205n21; self-effacement and, 197–98; and self-sacrifice, 46; theoretical aspects of, 7
Everyman, 52, 56
evolution: agape and, 8, 230, 240–41; altruism and, 233–35, 242–43, 247n52; creation and, 231–32, 232–33; ethics and, 242–45; freedom and, 237–39; intelligence and, 232; interpretation of, 8; responsibility and, 237–39; self-sacrifice and, 230; teleology and, 231–32. *See also* naturalism
experiences, spiritual, 118–19
Ezekiel: activities of, 21; God's promise proclaimed by, 20; on heart and spirit, 24

faith: conflict and, 25; eudaimonism and, 193, 198; forgiveness and, 165; grace and, 279; in Islam, 363, 367; koinonia and, 303; land and, 316; love for God and, 111; in Luther, 192, 279; morality and, 176; neighbor love and, 361; reason and, 245
falsehood: constraint against, 28; in prophecy, 22, 31; in swearing, 28; in witness, 22

family of God, building more inclusive, 25, 26
fanatic, attitude of, 42, 43
Farley, Margaret, 6–7, 12, 381
Farmer, Paul, 283
fasting, 24, 31
fatherless children, needs of, addressing, 23
Fear and Trembling (Kierkegaard), 91
Fee, Gordon, 187n24
Fénelon, François, 37, 49n24
Ferreira, M. Jamie, 5, 135–36, 144n30, 146n53, 146n63, 148n76
festival: of booths, 23; of weeks, 23
fiction, 311n2; exclusion and, 339
fidelity in marriage, challenges of, 25
Finnish school, 9, 279
fiqh (Shari'a reasoning), 11, 360–61
Fletcher, Joseph, 2, 262–63
Flood, 43
flourishing, 194–95, 375–78
forgiveness: as active, 164; anticipatory, 167–68, 381; in Arendt, 157–58; atrocities and, 157, 169n6, 169n8; in Bible, 158; challenges to, 157–59; Christ and, 161–62; Christian love and, 160–64; in church community, 167–68; conflict and, 156–57; continued injury and, 166–67; creative love and, 160; of debt, 23; in Derrida, 158–59; in Dickinson, 165–66; as divine attribute, 44; globalization and, 157; God and, 44, 161–62, 165–66; in Islam, 156; in Judaism, 155–56; judgment and, 163; justice and, 166–67; "letting go" and, 164–65; love commands and, 160; love's role in, 12; meanings of, 164–67; missioned, 161–64; pain and, 156–57; reflections on, 6–7; sin and, 161–62; unconditional, 159
Formula of Concord, 279
friends: laying down life for, 38, 41–42, 47, 171, 173–75, 179, 191, 208n55; love's embrace of multiple, 6; self-giving of, 6
friendship: agape and, 151n103, 208n50; anti-eudaimonism and, 215–19; in Aquinas, 211–13, 217–19, 220, 223n14; in Aristotle, 39, 46, 47, 84–85, 191, 212, 215, 217, 218, 223n14; attributes of, 39; benevolence and, 217; in Cates, 132–33; charity as, 213–15, 217–18; civic, 220–22; compassion and, 132–33, 151n103; egoism and, 210; ethics and, 210, 216; eudaimonism and, 39; extent of, 47; with God, 213; grace and, 213–15, 217; interpretation of, 8; in Kierkegaard, 143n12; love, charity as, 8; in nature, 315; neighbor love as, 12; self-love in, 6, 37; self-sacrifice in, 46, 380
Furnish, Victor Paul, 30, 34n17, 187n16

game theory, 233–34
Gandhi, Mahatma, 30
Garrett, Laurie, 282, 288n70
gender, 291, 294–95

HIV/AIDS, 282, 285
Hoffman, Martin, 150n89, 151n93
Holocaust, 157, 158
homosexuality: contemporary discussions of, 27; in Deuteronomy, 22
hope, 188n38, 203, 278, 303, 338, 381
human and divine love compared, 38, 39–40, 45, 140–41, 337–39, 341
human beings: caring and, 323; kinship of all, 11; as "made in the image of God," 228–30, 246n10; value of, 43–44, 45
Hume, David, 235
Hurricane Katrina, 10, 307–9
Hursthouse, Rosalind, 207n47

idolatry: death penalty for, 22; examples of, 20; material greed amounting to, 31; self-sacrifice and, 176
imaginative empathy, 137
incarnation, 9, 54, 175–78, 187n23, 188n35, 241, 280–81, 340
incest, 22, 26
inclination: agency and, 70, 77; in Kant, 78–80, 83, 88n10, 91, 96–97, 105; in Kierkegaard, 92; love commands and, 95
inclusivism: eudaimonia and, 193; pluralism and, 336
inclusivity: in ethics, 313; pluralism and, 336
Institutes of the Christian Religion (Calvin), 192
integrity, 167, 377
intelligence, 232
intentionality, 227–28
interreligious dialogue, 12, 333, 339, 340, 381
Iroquois Theater, 308, 312n9
Irwin, Terence, 4, 12, 207n43
Isaiah: activities of, 21; message delivered by, 20, 33n2
Islam: apostasy in, 365–66; community in, 363–64; forgiveness in, 156; hate in, 362; humanism and, 12, 369, 372; neighbor love in, 11–12, 360–72; prophets in, 362–63; rebellion in, 366–67; state and, 364–65; Sufism and, 360; Sunni, 372n2. *See also* Abrahamic faiths; Muslims
Israel, people of: disobedience of, 20, 21; God's love for, 32; narrative of, 19–20

Jackson, Timothy, 2–3, 8, 186n2, 210, 212, 215, 224n31
James, William, 226, 245
Jankélévitch, Vladimir, 158, 166, 169n8, 169n10
jazz, 308
Jesus: crucifixion of, 201–2, 208n55, 377; death of, 30, 34n18, 38, 54; as empowering love, 177; forgiveness and, 161–62; good in teachings of, 30; gospel, God's kingdom in, 2; on law and prophets, 24–25, 27; love commandments of, 6, 24,

173, 174, 179–80, 336, 340, 347, 356–57; love for Peter of, 174–75; love initiative taken by, 38; message, responses to, 24, 32; prophetic calling described by, 26; resurrection of, 54, 202; sermons by (*see* Sermon on the Mount); sexual code lacking from, 9, 299–300; in wilderness, 320
Jinnah, Muhammad 'Ali, 367–68
Johann, Robert, 1
Johannine doctrine: of divine and human love, 38–39; self-sacrifice in, 172–75, 191
John: on brotherly love, 47; crucifixion in, 208n55; forgiveness in, 163; love commands in, 42, 171; love for God and, 114. *See also* Johannine doctrine
John XXIII, Pope, 276
Jordan, Mark, 8–9, 12, 381
joy, 200; charity and, 219–20; forgiveness and, 165; morality and, 211; self-sacrifice and, 208n55; suffering and, 330; sympathetic, 151n97
Joyce, Richard, 241
Judaism: forgiveness in, 155–56; Golden Rule in, 355; love command in, 348; neighbor love in, 11, 347–58. *See also* Abrahamic faiths
Judeo-Christian tradition, environmental ethics within, 10
judges, authority and responsibilities of, 22–23
judgment: forgiveness and, 163; of self-sacrifice, by world, 181–82
justice: American Protestant promotion of, 2; calls for, 19; in Catholic social teaching, 274; charity and, 220; compassion and, 134; conceptions of, 12; in Deuteronomy, 20, 23; in encyclicals, 274; ethics and, 277; forgiveness and, 166–67; good and, 73n12; in Levinas, 145n46; love's relationship to, 8–9, 12; moral responsibility for, 9; in nature, 314; practicing, 38; Protestantism and, 274–75; in religious traditions, importance of, 9; self-love and, 145n46; social, 236, 255, 282; and temptation of mind, 55. *See also* law
justification: doctrine of, 40, 160, 278, 280
just peacemaking, 31

Kant, Immanuel: affect in, 77–79, 89n28; agency in, 80–81, 83, 376–77; ambition in, 79; apathy in, 79; Aquinas as precursor to, 5; choice in, 65–66; deliberation in, 80–82; duty in, 76, 78–79; duty to love in, 5, 88n10, 96–104; emotion in, 76–77; eudaimonia in, 205n23; fear in, 79; "friend of man" in, 79–80; God in, 86–87; happiness in, 84, 87, 100–101; Kierkegaard vs., 91–92; love commands in, 75, 96–104; neighbor love in, 96–97, 99–100; obligation in, 101–2; passion in, 77–79; perfection in, 87; practical love in, 75, 76–77, 82, 88n9; reason in, 76–77; respect in, 77, 81–82, 100, 102–3; Spinoza in, 86; views of, 12; virtue in, 97–99; will in, 83
Kärkkäinen, Veli-Matti, 280